GLOBAL CIVIL SOCIETY 2001

Helmut Anheier, Marlies Glasius, and Mary Kaldor, Editors

OXFORD

UNIVERSITY PRESS

OXFORD
UNIVERSITY PRESS

Great Clarendon Street, Oxford OX2 6DP

Oxford University Press is a department of the University of Oxford.
It furthers the University's objective of excellence in research, scholarship,
and education by publishing worldwide in

Oxford New York

Athens Auckland Bangkok Bogotá Buenos Aires Cape Town
Chennai Dar es Salaam Delhi Florence Hong Kong Istanbul Karachi
Kolkata Kuala Lumpur Madrid Melbourne Mexico City Mumbai Nairobi
Paris São Paulo Shanghai Singapore Taipei Tokyo Toronto Warsaw

with associated companies in Berlin Ibadan

Oxford is a registered trade mark of Oxford University Press
in the UK and in certain other countries

Published in the United States
By Oxford University Press Inc., New York

First published 2001

British Library Cataloguing in Publication Data

Data available

Library of Congress Cataloging in Publication Data

Anheier, Helmut, Marlies Glasius and Mary Kaldor, eds.
Includes index

ISBN 0-19-924643-2
ISBN 0-19-924644-0 (pbk.)

Design in Rotis
by Hardlines, Charlbury, Oxford
Page lay-out by Ben Cracknell Studios
Printed in Great Britain
on acid-free paper
by The Bath Press Ltd, Bath, Avon

Foreword

The emergence of a *global civil society* is perhaps one of the most momentous developments taking place in the world today, and its exploration one of the major challenges for the social sciences in the years to come. The editors and various authors of the Global Civil Society Yearbook are among the first to take on this demanding and highly complex topic with an ongoing perspective in mind. Their contributions make clear how much conventional social science thinking is called into question by this new concept, called 'fuzzy and contested' by the editors. At a fundamental level, the difficulties the social sciences have in dealing with a term like 'global civil society' demonstrate how they still have to overcome the legacy of their foundation in the nineteenth-century nation state. In this respect, the Yearbook and the wider effort it stands for represent an important element of the modernisation of the social sciences themselves.

The intellectual history of the term 'civil society' is closely intertwined with that of the nation state. It relates to the notion of citizenship, the limits of state power, and the foundation as well as the regulation of market economies. The prevailing modern view sees civil society as a sphere located between state and market: a buffer zone strong enough to keep both state and market in check, thereby preventing each from becoming too powerful and dominating. Of course, the global system cannot today be described or analysed just on the level of nation states. Around the world, nation states see their claims to sovereignty radically reshaped. The global marketplace, the proliferation of transnational corporations, and new communications technology exert powerful influences on governments and citizens alike.

If civil society, rather than the state, supplies the 'grounding of citizenship' and is therefore crucial to sustaining an open public sphere, how can this be achieved outside the realm of the nation-state? If civil society is fundamental to constraining the power of both markets and government, and if neither a market economy nor a democratic state can function effectively without the civilising influence of civic association, how can this 'balancing act' be achieved at a global level? Can the concept of a global civil society provide an answer?

The further development of democracy within states could be greatly enhanced by transnational forms of democracy. Taking globalisation seriously means emphasising that democratisation cannot be confined to the level of the nation-state. A global public sphere outside the state and the market is needed: an arena for public life created by citizens. The continued process of modernisation increases individual autonomy and requires individuals to define and redefine their identity—as citizens of particular locales, countries, regions, and, increasingly, the world. Globalisation is also about individual autonomy, responsibility, and participation.

As the Yearbook demonstrates, there is a groundswell of 'globalisation from below' involving many millions of ordinary people as well as organised groups of all kinds. In the globalisation era of the early twenty-first century, states, like transnational corporations, cannot escape the surveillance of the wider global community. As the number of democratic countries in the world grows, local groups subject to discrimination or oppression have access to international audiences to whom to air their grievances. We can make progress towards a world in which even the largest states conform to emerging codes of international law.

At the same time, in the global age it is no longer possible for companies to hide away what they do in any one part of the world from the gaze of interested groups and associations elsewhere. Consumer groups, moreover, have the capacity to hit corporations where it hurts by directly affecting company profits. Rogue corporations exist, as do rogue states, and both are increasingly under the scrutiny of global civil society.

This Yearbook is the first major product of a truly collaborative research process. It brings together two units of the London School of Economics and Political Science (LSE): the Centre for the Study of Global Governance, which originated the idea, and the Centre for Civil Society. The synergies between these two centres are exemplary for the interdisciplinary and comparative perspective the LSE wishes to encourage. In particular, the Yearbook accommodates an emphasis on concepts and the history of ideas rooted in the European social science tradition, and at the same time brings in more empirical approaches characteristic of American sociology and political science. As such, the Yearbook, like the LSE itself, is at the crossroads of major intellectual traditions.

In line with the LSE tradition, it also looks beyond the academy to engage with activists and practitioners in global civil society, national and international policy-makers, and corporate executives. While the publication of the Yearbook is one of the main focuses of the Global Civil Society Programme, it comprises much more than just the production of a book. By generating a number of small and large events around the Yearbook, the Centres try to provide a forum for increased communication and mutual understanding between, on the one hand, policy-makers, international civil servants, and global business executives and, on the other hand, citizens and civic activists operating across borders.

This began nearly two years ago when an international group of 40 leading scholars, practitioners, and policy-makers on civil society was invited to LSE to discuss the aims and contents of this ambitious publication. The discussion was centred around three basic themes: concepts of global civil society, what issues should be addressed, and how one might measure global civil society. Subsequently, the two Centres organised a smaller consultation meeting specifically for activists and practitioners in global civil society, most of them representing international NGOs in the fields of conflict resolution, development, the environment, fair trade, human rights, gender, and peace and disarmament.

A number of expert meetings were convened in relation to the topics of the chapters. The first of these was a seminar on the relation between global civil society and new information technology, followed by a seminar on how to democratise the international biotechnology agenda, a conference on global governance and financial crises, and a debate on the role of global civil society in relation to humanitarian intervention. In addition, the two Centres organised public lecture series and lunch-time seminars on a wide range of topics related to global civil society.

Thus, even before the publication of the first Yearbook, hundreds of people from all regions of the world have been involved in the project by participating in the brainstorm meetings, seminars, and conferences, by becoming a part of a network of volunteer 'civil society correspondents', and by writing chapters or by doing quantitative research. This approach can be time-consuming, but it is commensurate with the vision of the editors that the Yearbook project itself should be an ever-deliberative exercise in global civil society.

Anthony Giddens

Director, London School of Economics and Political Science

25 May 2001

Acknowledgements

We are grateful for the valuable support and contributions from many individuals and organisations, without whom this Yearbook would not have been possible. The final product remains, of course, the sole responsibility of the editors.

Editorial Committee

Helmut Anheier, Marlies Glasius (managing editor), Mary Kaldor, Diane Osgood, Frances Pinter, Yahia Said.

Advisory Board

Attendants, Brainstorm Conference, 4–5 February 2000
Sergio Andreis, Andrew Arato, Daniele Archibugi, John Boli, Chris Brown, Nicholas Deakin, Alex De Waal, Meghnad Desai, Pavlos Eleftheriadis, Anthony Giddens, Mark Hoffman, Jason Hunter, Anthony Judge, John Keane, Azfar Khan, Radha Kumar, David Lewis, Sarah Lister, Ferenc Miszlivetz, Robin Murray, Kumi Naidoo, Andrew Passey, Jenny Pearce, Mario Pianta, Margo Picken, Adam Roberts, Andrew Rogerson, Saskia Sassen, Mukul Sharma, Philippe Schmitter, Robin Sharp, Salma Shawa, Hazel Smith, Nuno Themudo, Ivan Vejvoda.

Attendants, Activist and Practitioner Round Table, 24 May 2000
Paul Anderson, Anthony Barnett, Rosemary Betchler, Jeannette Buiski, Simon Burall, Mark Curtis, Harriet Fletcher, Caroline Harper, Colin Hines, Kumari Jayawardene, Manuela Leonhardt, Ian Linden, Miles Litvinoff, Ursula Owen, Anne Pettifor, Liz Philipson, Shona Pollock, Babu Rahman, Brita Schmidt, Urmi Shah, Fran Van Dijk, Hilary Wainwright.

Other Members
Abdullahi An-Na'im, Peter Baehr, Mient Jan Faber, Richard Falk, Ann Florini, David Held, Jeremy Kendall, Riva Krut, Susannah Morris, Andres Penate, Hakan Seckinelgin.

Consultations

Virtual Civic Space, Seminar, 21 June 2000: Input on Chapter 6
Sergio Andreis, Peter Armstrong, Garegin Chookaszian, Jerry Everard, Donald Maynard, Joseph Migga Kizza, Simon Moores, John Naughton, Ursula Owen, Daniel Pare, Andy Pratt, James Slevin, Anuradha Vittachi, Jim Walch, Keith Yeomans.

Financial Crises and Global Governance, Conference, 13–14 October 2000: Input on Chapter 3
Michel Aglietta, Sudipto Bhattacharya, Michele Boldrin, Alistair Breach, Stefan Collignon, Giancarlo Corsetti, John Eatwell, Roger Farmer, Douglas Gale, Andrew Gamble, Anthony Giddens, Andrew Glyn, Charles Goodhart, Ilene Grabel, Joanne Hay, K. S. Jomo, Anupam Khanna, Timothy Lane, Richard Layard, Karin Lissakers, Robin Murray, Gabriel Palma, Ann Pettifor, James Putzel, John Reed, Geneviève Schméder, Hyun Song Shin, Tran Jimmy Van Hoa, Oleg Vyugin, Robert Wade, David Webb.

Global Civil Society and the International Agro-Biotech Agenda, Seminar, 24 October 2000: Input on Chapter 4
Philipp Aerni, Biljana Amman, Klaus Amman, Sophie Amman, Sheena Boughens, Ann Foster, Anil Gupta, Philip James, Penny Janeaway, Carol King, Muffy Koch, Tell Muenzing, Fernando Ortiz Monasterio, Harry Post, Peter Pringle, Nikolaus Schultze, Lloyd Timberlake, Kitty Warnock.

A Decade of Humanitarian Intervention, Seminar, 29 November 2000: Input on Chapter 5
Ulrich Albrecht, Ghanim Al-Najjar, Chris Brown, Susan Carruthers, Jerzy Celichowski, Christine Chinkin, Kevin Clements, Patrick Cullen, Alex De Waal, Andrew Duncan, Mient Jan Faber, Matthew Foley, Sabine Freizer, Paola Grenier, Vladimir Grigorov, Fred Halliday, Marit Haug, Radha Kumar, Margot Light, Sarah Lister, Susan Moeller, Tasneem Mowjee, Dimitrina Petrova, Frances Pinter, Hakan Seckinelgin, Martin Shaw, Jonathan Steele, David Styan, Jan Urban, Susan Woodward, Martin Woollacott.

Other Input
Correspondents: Input on chronologies
Andres Falconer, Zafarullah Khan, Svitlana Kuts, Ahmad Lutfi, Alejandro Natal, Yahia Said, Shameem Siddiqi, Sunna Trott, Barbara Wisniewska.

Input from Oxford University Press
Dominic Byatt, Jacqueline Sells, Amanda Watkins.

Input from representatives of intergovernmental organisations
Raouf Abdel-Kader (UN), Tarek Abou Chabake (UNHCR) Vittoria Cavicchioni (UNESCO), Renu Corea (UNDP), Adele De Gentile Woods (OECD), Liviu Enasoae (UN), Henny Helmich (OECD), Bela Hovy (UNHCR), Rose Khin-Wai-Thi (UNESCO), Denise Lievesley (UNESCO), David Stewart (UNDP), Mignon van der Liet (UNHCR).

Others who provided input or support
Eileen Barker, Chaloka Beyani, Mary Blair, Fanny Calder, Marina Calloni, Lisa Carlson, Nancy Cartwright, Deborah Cass, Christine Chinkin, John Clark, Stan Cohen, Tim Forsyth, Richard Fries, Fred Halliday, Fiona Hodgson, Loek Holman, Ronald Inglehart, Ramin Kaweh, Jenny Kuper, Regina List, Robin Luckham, Nadia McLaren, Robin Mansell, Paula Marshall, Maxine Molyneux, Tasneem Mowjee, Michael Oliver, Anne Phillips, Simone Remijnse, Jean Richardson, Lester Salamon, Lynne Segal, Sharon Shalev, Gerry Simpson, Wojtech Sokolowski, Isambard Thomas, Douglas van den Berghe, Rob van Tulder, Karen Wright.

Research assistants
Amar Bokhari, Jerzy Celichowski, Patrick Cullen, Panagiotis Flessas, Ljiljana Grubovic, Sigrun Hardardottir, Zafarullah Khan, Jai Motwane, Martyn Oliver, Andy Roberts, Federico Silva, Gayathri Sriskanthan, Nidhi Trehan.

Administrative support
Elizabeth Bacon, Barbara Baum, Joanne Hay, Helen Reilly, Sue Roebuck, Jane Schiemann.

Design & production
Michael James (copy editor), Mitch Januszki (indexer), Stefan Hamilton (proof-reader), Hardlines (design), Ben Cracknell Studios, Norwich (page make-up) , Michael Rowe, Wren & Rowe (front cover design).

Financial Support
We gratefully acknowledge the financial support of the following organisations:
The Atlantic Philanthropies
Ford Foundation
John D. and Catherine T. MacArthur Foundation
Olof Palme Memorial Fund
Rockefeller Brothers Fund
Rockefeller Foundation

Finally, a special thanks is due to the Managing Editor, Marlies Glasius, who carried the burden of organising the Yearbook, including commissioning chapters, arranging workshops, supervising data collection, compiling the chronology, commenting on everything, and supervising production. She succeeded in doing this with intellectual flair, administrative efficiency, calm, and good humour.

Contents

Chronologies

Tables

Tables in Table Programme

Figures in Table Programme

Contributors

Dr Helmut K. Anheier is Director of the Centre for Civil Society at the London School of Economics and Political Science (LSE) and Reader in the Department of Social Policy. Prior to this he was a Senior Associate at Johns Hopkins University, Associate Professor of Sociology at Rutgers University, and a Social Affairs Officer at the United Nations. His work has focused on civil society, the non-profit sector, organisational studies and policy analysis, and comparative methodology. He is a founding editor of *Voluntas* and author of over 200 publications in several languages. His present research examines the emergence of new organisational forms in global civil society, and will also explore methodological aspects of social science research on globalisation.

Professor Meghnad Desai is Professor of Economics and Director of the Centre for the Study of Global Governance at the LSE. He was Director of the LSE's Development Studies Institute from 1990 to 1995 and has been at the LSE for over 30 years. In 1991, he was created Lord Desai of St Clement Danes. His latest book, to be published by Verso in 2001, is *Marx's Revenge: The Resurgence of Capitalism and the Death of Statist Socialism.*

Dr Marlies Glasius has been a Research Officer at the Centre for Civil Society, LSE, and managing editor of this Yearbook since 2000. She studied international law as well as English literature at the University of Amsterdam, and holds a PhD with distinction in Human Rights from the University of Utrecht. In 1999 she published *Foreign Policy on Human Rights: Its Influence on Indonesia under Soeharto.* Before joining the Centre, she was most recently engaged in consultancy work for Novib, the Dutch partner in Oxfam International, and in the NGO coalition 'Free and Safe Referendum in East Timor'. Her present research concerns the influence of NGOs on international treaty-making processes.

Professor Mary Kaldor joined the LSE in 1999 as Director of the Programme on Global Civil Society at the Centre for the Study of Global Governance. Previously, she taught and conducted research at the University of Sussex for 30 years. She was a founder member of END, and was Co-Chair of the Helsinki Citizens' Assembly. She is currently a member of the International Independent Commission to investigate the Kosovo Crisis, established by the Swedish Prime Minister and chaired by Richard Goldstone, which published the *Kosovo Report* in autumn 2000. Her most recent work, *New and Old Wars: Organised Violence in a Global Era* (1999), has been translated into seven languages. She is currently writing a book on global civil society.

Professor John Keane founded the London-based Centre for the Study of Democracy in 1989. He is currently Professor of Politics at the University of Westminster and a Fellow of the Royal Society of Arts. He was born in Australia and educated at the universities of Adelaide, Toronto, and Cambridge. Among his many books are *Democracy and Civil Society* (1988); *The Media and Democracy* (1991); the prize-winning biography *Tom Paine: A Political Life* (1995); *Reflections on Violence* (1996); *Civil Society: Old Images, New Visions* (1998); and a biography of power, *Václav Havel: A Political Tragedy in Six Acts* (1999). He is currently writing a full-scale history of democracy. During 2001/2002, he will hold the Karl Deutsch Distinguished Professorship at the Wissenschaftszentrum, Berlin.

Mr John Naughton is a Senior Lecturer in Systems at the Open University and leader of the Faculty of Technology's Going Digital project. One of his current research interests is Open Source Teaching. He is also a Fellow of Wolfson College, Cambridge where he runs the College's Press Fellowship Programme and coordinates Cambridge's contribution to the Internet Political Economy Forum. He has been a weekly columnist in the *Observer* since 1987 and is now the paper's Internet columnist. *A Brief History of the Future* (1999), his book on the development and significance of the Internet, is published in the UK by Phoenix and in the US by Overlook Press.

Dr Diane Osgood is an environmental economist specialising in the development of appropriate and sustainable market products and technologies in developing countries. She holds a PhD in environmental economics from the LSE. Since 1992 she has worked as an independent consultant on issues such as corporate responsibility, sustainable development, and agricultural development. In the early 1990s she worked on biodiversity issues for UNEP, the World Bank, and international NGOs. Since 1997 she has worked on the social aspects and public concerns surrounding agricultural biotechnology.

Professor Mario Pianta is Professor of Economic Policy at the University of Urbino and is an associate researcher at ISRDS, an institute of the National Research Council in Rome. He holds a PhD from the LSE (1984), has been Visiting Scholar at the Institute for Policy Studies in Washington DC (1986) and Research Fellow at Columbia University, New York (1986–87). He is Vice-President of Lunaria, a civil society organisation in Rome, and has been involved in several international campaigns on economic and peace issues. He works on global civil society, international economic policy, technological change, and employment.

Dr Frances Pinter has been a Visiting Fellow at the Centre for Civil Society, LSE, since 2000. She is the founder of Pinter Publishers, and in the mid-1990s she established the Centre for Publishing Development for the Open Society Institute/Soros Foundations Network, which assists the development of the independent publishing sector in the former communist bloc. Frances Pinter was educated in the United States, Switzerland, and the United Kingdom and holds a PhD in International Relations from University College London. She is currently pursuing her interest in using ICT to foster the strengthening of civil society.

Mr Yahia Said is a Research Officer at the Centre for the Study of Global Governance at the LSE. His experience combines academic research with private sector work and activism. Prior to joining the LSE he worked as a corporate finance consultant with Ernst & Young in Russia. He also worked as a project coordinator with the Helsinki Citizens' Assembly in Prague. Yahia Said specialises in issues of economic transition and security in post-communist societies. His publications include 'Restructuring the Military Sector in Slovakia' in *The End of Military Fordism,*. Mary Kaldor (ed) (1998) and 'Oil and Human Rights in Azerbaijan', co-authored with Mary Kaldor in *Human Rights and the Oil Industry*, Asbjorn Eide (ed) (2000).

Part I: Concepts of Global Civil Society

CHAPTER 1

INTRODUCING GLOBAL CIVIL SOCIETY

Helmut Anheier, Marlies Glasius, and Mary Kaldor

The words 'global' and 'civil society' have become commonplace during the last decade. Yet what they mean and how they come together are subject to widely differing interpretations. For some, global civil society refers to the protestors in Seattle and Prague or Greenpeace's actions against trans-national corporations: in other words, a counter-weight to global capitalism. For others, the words have something to do with the infrastructure that is needed for the spread of democracy and develop-ment: the growth of professional associations, consumer organisations, and interests groups that span many countries. Yet others identify the phenomenon with the efforts of groups like Save the Children or Médécins sans Frontières to provide humanitarian assistance: global solidarity with the poor or oppressed. Or perhaps the term just refers to the growing connectedness of citizens: Internet chatrooms, networks of peace, environmental or human rights activists, student exchanges, or global media.

It is no wonder that, apart from a few political activists and policy experts, most people, including many social scientists, have little understanding of what global civil society means and implies. It has not yet become what sociologist Zerubavel (1991) calls an 'island of meaning' in the conceptual landscape of modern social science and policy-making. The 'market', the 'state', and, in recent years, even 'civil society' have to varying degrees become such 'conceptual islands' that we use in everyday language as well as for policy purposes and in social science analysis. While we associate certain distinct qualities and characteristics with terms like the 'market' and the 'state', and have at least some notion of the quantitative dimensions involved, no such con-ventional understanding exists for 'global civil society'.

While the 'unfamiliar words', as John Keane puts it in Chapter 2, may have little intuitive meaning, they suggest at the same time, something unconventional, even dramatic. The term takes the perhaps most important social science (re)discovery of the 1990s — civil society —and places it in a framework that ultimately transcends conventional social science categories. The concept posits the existence of a social sphere, a global civil society, above and beyond national, regional, or local societies.

Our aim in producing a Yearbook was to try to establish an 'island of meaning'. We set out to analyse and describe, to map both conceptually and empiric-ally, what we mean when we talk about 'global civil society'. We hoped to be able to draw conclusions that would be relevant and useful to the various actors who participate in global civil society. But in producing the first edition of the Yearbook what we think we have learned is where to begin our investigation. Whether we are talking about the debates about the meaning of the concept or the problems of data collection, our end-point turns out to be our starting point. We have learned, at least to some extent, where we need to look to find out more about global civil society and with whom we need to engage to develop the conceptual underpinning of the project. So we are not informing our readers as we imagined, although we hope there is a lot to be gleaned from this first Yearbook; rather we are, in effect, asking our readers to participate in a journey of discovery. As we see it, the Yearbook is itself a part of global civil society: a terrain for developing ideas, investigating issues, and gathering information that does not readily fit existing categories and cannot be found in conventional sources. We invite your reactions, comments, and feedback.

In introducing the Yearbook, we focus on four themes that emerge out of our first efforts. First, we set out three propositions about global civil society that are both initial conclusions and hypotheses for future research. Second, we provide a thumbnail sketch of the evolution of the concept and the competing definitions. Third, we discuss the problem of data collection and the challenge of 'methodo-logical nationalism' (Beck 2000; Shaw 2000; Scholte 1999). In the last section, we summarise the key conclusions for both activists and policy-makers that can be drawn from the studies undertaken for the individual chapters.

Three Propositions about Global Civil Society

Proposition 1: Global civil society as a reality

The first proposition is that the *spread of the term 'global civil society' reflects an underlying social reality.* What we can observe in the 1990s is the emergence of a supranational sphere of social and political participation in which citizens groups, social movements, and individuals engage in dialogue, debate, confrontation, and negotiation with each other and with various governmental actors—international, national, and local—as well as the business world. Of course, there have historically existed elements of a supranational non-governmental sphere. The Catholic Church or Islam have long had 'global' aspirations and maintained far-reaching operations for centuries; colonial empires have come and gone; political entities like the Commonwealth, the UN, and the European Union emerged; international non-governmental organisations like the Red Cross and Red Crescent Societies have operated above the national level for many years, as have political organisations like the Socialist International and the peace and environmental movements. What seems new, however, is the sheer scale and scope that international and supranational institutions and organisations of many kinds have achieved in recent years. The number of organisations and individuals that are part of global civil society has probably never been bigger, and the range and type of fields in which they operate never been wider: from UN conferences about social welfare or the environment to conflict situations in Kosovo, from globalised resistance to the Mutual Agreement on Investments to local human rights activism in Mexico, Burma, or Timor, and from media corporations spanning the globe to indigenous peoples' campaigns over the Internet.

This conclusion is supported by four types of information that have been used in producing the Yearbook: data on international non-governmental organisations (INGOs) (see Tables 1.1–1.3 and Part IV of this Yearbook) and on parallel summits (see Chapter 7), our chronology, and the qualitative information contained in the issue chapters.

INGOs are autonomous organisations that are non-governmental, that is, they are not instrument-alities of government; and non-profit, that is not distributing revenue as income to owners; and formal, legal entities (see Salamon and Anheier 1997). Many INGOs employ staff and are professional organisations. They can include campaigning groups like Amnesty International or Greenpeace, the famous 'brand names' of global civil society; professional societies like international employers federations or trades unions; charities like Christian Aid or CARE; think tanks and international commissions.

INGOs are not new. They date back to the nineteenth century, but the term itself is of more recent origins, coined during the League of Nations period. The earliest INGO is generally said to be the anti-slavery society, formed as the British and Foreign Anti-Slavery Society in 1839, although there was a transnational social movement against slavery much earlier. The International Committee of the Red Cross (ICRC) was founded by Henri Dunant in 1864 after his experiences in the Battle of Solferino. By 1874, there were 32 registered INGOs and this number had increased to 1,083 by 1914 (Chatfield 1997). INGOs grew steadily after World War II but our figures show an acceleration in the 1990s. Around one quarter of the 13,000 INGOs in existence today were created after 1990 (see Table R19 in Part IV). Moreover, membership by individuals or national bodies of INGOs has increased even faster; well over a third of the membership of INGOs joined after 1990. These figures include only NGOs narrowly defined as 'international'; they do not include national NGOs with an international orientation.

What our figures also show is that during the 1990s, INGOs became much more interconnected both to each other and to international institutions like the United Nations or the World Bank (see also Table R21). Thus, not only has the global range of INGO presence grown during the last decade, but the networks linking these organisations are becoming denser as well. In Held's terms (Held *et al.* 1999), our data suggest that global civil society is becoming 'thicker'.

INGOs are, however, only one component of global civil society. Individuals, grass-roots groups, loose coalitions, and networks all play a part in a global public debate. Moreover, since most INGOs are organisationally based in the northern hemisphere near international institutions and donors, the data on INGOs exaggerates the role of northern groups. Another lens through which to view the growth of global civil society is through parallel summits. These are gatherings of INGOs, other groups, and individuals that generally but not always take place in parallel to important inter-governmental meetings.

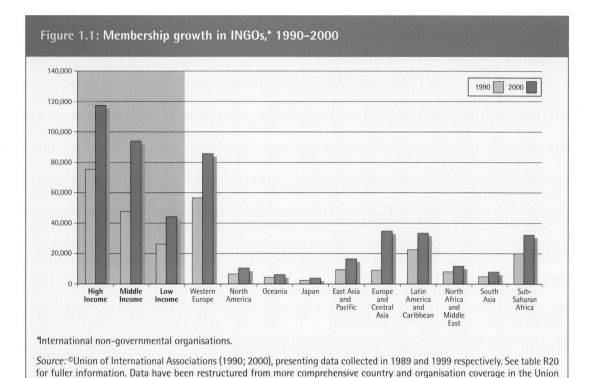

Figure 1.1: Membership growth in INGOs,* 1990–2000

*International non-governmental organisations.

Source: ©Union of International Associations (1990; 2000), presenting data collected in 1989 and 1999 respectively. See table R20 for fuller information. Data have been restructured from more comprehensive country and organisation coverage in the Union of International Associations' *Yearbook of International Organizations.*

Like INGOs, parallel summits have a long history. At the Hague Peace Conference in 1899, non-governmental groups organised a parallel salon for diplomats to meet with concerned citizens, various

Table 1.1: Links between INGOs and IGOs*

	Type	1990	2000	% growth
Total orgs. cited as having links with others**	INGOs	8,690	11,693	35
	IGOs	1,769	1,732	–2
	Total	10,459	13,425	28
Total citations	INGOs	35,020	69,922	100
	IGOs	23,191	36,383	57
	Total	58,211	106,305	83
Average citations per org.	INGOs	4	6	48
	IGOs	13	21	60
	Total	5.6	7.9	42

* International governmental organisations

** See Table R21 for further information.

Source: ©Union of International Associations (1990; 2000), presenting data collected in 1989 and 1999 respectively. Data have been restructured from more comprehensive country and organisation coverage in the Union of International Associations' *Yearbook of International Organizations.*

petitions with numerous signatures were submitted to the official conference, and an independent activist produced a daily conference newspaper (Charnovitz 1997: 196–7). Likewise, there were international congresses of citizens on issues like peace or labour solidarity throughout the nineteenth century. But even in the 1970s and 1980s these were exceptional events. It is only in the 1990s that both international governmental summits and parallel summits gathered pace as a normal way of doing politics. Pianta shows in Chapter 7 that parallel summits increased from around two a year in the period 1988–91 to over 30 a year in the period 2000–1. Participation in these events also increased. Around a third involved more than 10,000 people and several involved tens of thousands, especially in 2000 and 2001. INGOs play an important role in the coordination of parallel summits but, as Pianta shows, there are many different types of groups and individuals also involved.

Our chronology of global civil society events covers the decade 1990–9 and we have a more detailed chronology for the year 2000 which we will bring up to date every year. Covering the past from the point of view of global civil society is difficult because global civil society events are much less well reported than global governance or global corporations; we have relied on individual correspondents but the network of correspondents we are building is still patchy. Nevertheless, the chronology shows what the figures both on INGOs and on parallel summits fail to cover: the range of protests relating to global issues, against the activities of governments or multinational corporations on environmental issues, dam- building, social issues, indigenous people's rights, democracy and human rights, or peace. Moreover, it is evident that these take place predominantly outside Europe and North America.

The growth of global civil society has been facilitated by the growth of resources available to civil society. These resources are of two kinds: technology and money. Increases in Internet usage and both mobile phones and land lines has greatly facilitated the construction of networks and has allowed greater access for groups outside the main centres of international power (Chapter 6). Thus, even taking just membership of INGOs, we can see in Table 1.2 that membership of low- and middle-income regions (70 per cent and 98 per cent respectively) has increased

faster than membership in high-income regions (56 per cent). The biggest increases have been for eastern Europe and Asia, although this is not reflected in the membership densities because of rapid population growth. Likewise, there has been a big increase in the economic importance of NGOs during the last decade. Specifically, governments and international institutions have greatly increased the amounts of development funds channelled through NGOs (OECD 1997). In addition, private giving has also increased from both foundations and corporations. In Chapter 8, it is estimated that global civil society receives approximately $7 billion in development funds and $2 billion in funds from US foundations. Figures collected by the Johns Hopkins Comparative Nonprofit Sector Project (Salamon *et al.* 1999) show that the number of full-time equivalent employment in INGOs for France, Germany, Japan, the Netherlands, Spain, and the United Kingdom alone amounts to over 100,000 and that volunteers in INGOs represent an additional 1.2 million full-time jobs in these countries (Table R24). Even without precise and comprehensive figures, available data

Table 1.2: Membership of INGOs, 1990–2000

	1990			2000			Growth 1990–2000	
	Member-ship of INGOs	Member-ship density*	Share of total %	Member-ship of INGOs	Member-ship density*	Share of total %	Member-ship % of INGOs	Member-ship density*
High Income	75,016	93		117,377	135		56	46
Middle Income	47,547	45		94,089	62		98	40
Low Income	25,938	8		43,967	12		70	41
Western Europe	6,547	150	38	85,518	221	33	52	47
North America	6,533	24	4	10,257	33	4	57	41
Oceania	4,042	197	3	6,382	280	2	58	42
Japan	2,347	19	2	3,569	28	1	52	48
East Asia and Pacific	9,255	6	6	16,393	9	6	77	55
Europe and Central Asia	8,940	46	5	35,235	74	14	335	62
Latin America & Caribbean	22,697	52	15	33,565	65	13	48	25
North Africa & Middle East	8,242	35	6	11,964	39	5	45	13
South Asia	5,121	5	3	8,136	6	3	59	30
Sub-Saharan Africa	20,076	39	14	32,763	51	13	63	30
World	148,501	30	100	255,432	43	100	72	42

* Per million of population

Source: ©Union of International Associations (1990; 2000), presenting data collected in 1989 and 1999 respectively. Data have been restructured from more comprehensive country and organisation coverage in the Union of International Associations' *Yearbook of International Organizations*. See table R20 for fuller information.

suggest the significant economic scale of INGO activities.

Finally, the three chapters that deal with global issues on bio-technology, global finance, and humanitarian intervention all show in dramatic ways how citizens' groups of various types and persuasion have come to play a crucial role during the last decade in raising public consciousness, taking action, and even influencing public policy.

Proposition 2: Global civil society and globalisation

The second proposition is that *global civil society both feeds on and reacts to globalisation.* Like global civil society, 'globalisation' is also a new concept with different meanings. In every day usage it tends to refer to the spread of global capitalism. In the social science literature it is usually defined as growing interconnectedness in political, social, and cultural spheres as well as the economy, something which has been greatly facilitated by travel and communication (see Held *et al.* 1999). It is also sometimes used to refer to growing global consciousness, the sense of a common community of mankind (Shaw 2000; Robertson 1990).

The above proposition applies to all three senses. On the one hand, globalisation provides the bedrock for global civil society, the supply side of the phenomenon that pushes it on. There does seem to be a strong and positive correlation between what one might describe as 'clusters of globalisation' or areas of what Held *et al.* (1999: 21–5) call 'thick globalisation' and clusters of global civil society. In particular, *one of the most striking findings of the Yearbook is that global civil society is heavily concentrated in north-western Europe,* especially in Scandinavia, the Benelux countries, Austria, Switzerland, and the United Kingdom. Thus, for example, 60 per cent of the secretariats of INGOs are based in the European Union (Table R19 in Part IV) and one third of their membership is in western Europe (Table 1.2). In addition, over half of all parallel summits have also been organised in Europe. This area is also the most densely globalised, whether we mean the concentration of global capitalism as measured by the presence of transnational corporations and the importance of trade and foreign investment; or growing interconnectedness as measured in terms of Internet usage or outward tourism; or the growth of global consciousness as

evidenced by the absence of human rights violations, the values of tolerance and solidarity, or—more concretely—the ratification of treaties.

On the other hand global civil society is also a reaction to globalisation, particularly to the consequences of the spread of global capitalism and interconnectedness. Globalisation is an uneven process which has brought benefits to many but which has also excluded many. It is those who are denied access to the benefits of global capitalism and who remain outside the charmed circle of information and communication technology who are the victims of the process and who organise in reaction: the demand pull of global civil society. They are now also linking up with those in the North who form a new kind of solidarity movement. The old solidarity movement supported Southern aspirations for national liberation; members of this new movement seek to revitalise Southern and Northern self-determination by joining the struggle against the disempowerment and social injustice brought about by unbridled global capitalism.

This new form of activism takes place against the background of the 'development industry' and the spread of INGOs in the South for service delivery and development assistance. Together, activism and developmentalism may explain why, after Europe, the figures on INGOs show the greatest membership densities not for other advanced industrial countries but for countries in Latin America and sub-Saharan Africa (see Table 1.2). The relatively low membership densities in East Asia, South Asia, and North America are to be explained, in the case of East Asia, by the relatively low degree of INGO organisation in general and, in the case of South Asia (particularly India) and the United States, by the relative lack of interest of local NGOs in global issues.

But is not only the range and density of INGO networks that matter in relationship to globalisation. Our studies of specific global issues show *that global civil society is best categorised not in terms of types of actors but in terms of positions in relation to globalisation.* All three of the issue chapters in the Yearbook adopt a similar categorisation of global civil society actors, as shown in the Table 1.4.

The first position is that of the *supporters:* those groups and individuals who are enthusiastic about globalisation, whether we are talking about the spread of global capitalism and interconnectedness or the spread of a global rule of law as well as global consciousness. They include the allies of transnational

Table 1.3: Focal points of globalisation, rule of law, and global civil society

GLOBALISATION

Top TNC host countries		Top Internet using countries		Top outbound tourism countries	
Country	Top TNC HQs per million population	Country	Internet use as % of population	Country	Outbound tourism per capita
Sweden	0.45	Sweden	56.4	Switzerland	1.72
Netherlands	0.32	United States	55.8	Austria	1.64
France	0.22	Norway	52.6	Sweden	1.29
Finland	0.19	Iceland	52.1	Poland	1.28
United Kingdom	0.19	Denmark	48.4	Hungary	1.22
Australia	0.16	Netherlands	45.8	Singapore	1.18
Germany	0.15	Singapore	44.6	Malaysia	1.16
Japan	0.13	Australia	43.9	Estonia	1.14
Canada	0.10	Finland	43.9	Germany	1.01
United States	0.10	Canada	42.8	Denmark	0.94
Italy	0.07	New Zealand	39.0	Finland	0.92
Venezuela	0.04	Austria	36.9	Lithuania	0.88
Spain	0.03	Belgium	36.3	United Kingdom	0.86
		Korea, Rep.	34.6	Ireland	0.82
		United Kingdom	33.6	Netherlands	0.82
		Switzerland	33.1	Latvia	0.80
		Japan	30.5	Belgium	0.76
		Ireland	27.5	Norway	0.70
		Germany	24.3	Canada	0.58
		Italy	23.3	Lebanon	0.39

INTERNATIONAL RULE OF LAW

Top treaty ratifying countries		Top human rights respecting countries		Top transparent (non-corrupt) countries	
Country	Ratifications 22 major treaties	Country	Mention in 3 major HR reports	Country	Corruption Perception Index 2000
Australia	22	Canada	0	Finland	10.0
Austria	22	Costa Rica	0	Denmark	9.8
Belgium	22	Denmark	0	New Zealand	9.4
Bulgaria	22	Iceland	0	Sweden	9.4
Costa Rica	22	Luxembourg	0	Canada	9.2
Croatia	22	Mali	0	Iceland	9.1
Cyprus	22	Malta	0	Norway	9.1
Ecuador	22	Netherlands	0	Singapore	9.1
Germany	22	Samoa	0	Netherlands	8.9
Greece	22	São Tomé & Principe	0	United Kingdom	8.7
Italy	22	Slovenia	0	Luxembourg	8.6
Luxembourg	22	Sweden	0	Switzerland	8.6
Netherlands	22			Australia	8.3
Norway	22			United States	7.8
Panama	22			Austria	7.7
Portugal	22			Hong Kong	7.7
Romania	22			Germany	7.6
Slovak Republic	22			Chile	7.4
Slovenia	22			Ireland	7.2
Spain	22			Spain	7.0
Sweden	22				

GLOBAL CIVIL SOCIETY

Top INGO host countries		Top INGO & IGO leaders suppliers		Top tolerant countries	
Country	INGO density per million of population	Country of nationality of leaders	Leaders per million of population	Country	% citizens object to immigrant neighbours
Belgium	163.3	Barbados	29.6	**Sweden**	2.8
Luxembourg	141.5	Belgium	18.6	**Iceland**	3.0
Barbados	100.0	**Luxembourg**	18.6	Brazil	3.5
Switzerland	85.1	**Iceland**	14.2	Australia	4.6
Iceland	49.8	Malta	10.3	**Netherlands**	5.3
Denmark	46.6	Belize	10.0	Argentina	5.7
St. Lucia	44.9	**Switzerland**	9.2	Colombia	6.9
Fiji	41.6	**Denmark**	8.5	Uruguay	7.1
Netherlands	38.5	**Netherlands**	7.0	**Luxembourg**	8.4
Trinidad and Tobago	35.4	**Finland**	5.6	**Germany**	8.6
Malta	33.4	**Norway**	5.1	Spain	9.3
Norway	30.0	**Sweden**	5.1	Latvia	9.8
Sweden	28.7	**United Kingdom**	4.6	**Switzerland**	10.0
Samoa	27.8	Fiji	3.7	United States	10.1
Austria	24.6	New Zealand	3.6	Peru	10.3
Finland	24.6	**Austria**	3.5	Albania	10.6
United Kingdom	23.1	France	3.5	**Denmark**	10.6
Bahrain	22.7	Guyana	3.5	Georgia	10.8
Cyprus	20.4	Ireland	3.5	Russian Federation	11.0
France	20.1	Singapore	3.3	**Norway**	11.2

Countries occurring in six or more of the categories are shown in bold.

For more detailed information and sources, see Tables R3, R6, R10, R11, R12, R13, R19, R22 and R26 in Part IV of this Yearbook.

business, the proponents of 'just wars for human rights', and the enthusiasts for all new technological developments. These are members of civil society, often, but not necessarily, close to governments and business, who think that globalisation in its present form is 'a jolly good thing' and that those who object just fail to understand the benefits.

The second position is that of the *rejectionists:* those who want to reverse globalisation and return to a world of nation-states. They include proponents of the new right, who may favour global capitalism but oppose open borders and the spread of a global rule of law. They also include leftists who oppose global capitalism but do not object to the spread of a global rule of law. Nationalists and religious fundamentalists as well as traditional leftist anti-colonial movements or communists who oppose interference in sovereignty are also included in this group. They think all or most manifestations of globalisation are harmful, and they oppose it with all their might. One might also think of this group as fundamentalists, but we rejected this term as being

judgemental. Cohen and Rai's (2000: 2) term 'transformative' was also rejected because what distinguishes these groups is that they tend to want to go backwards to an idealised version of the past rather than transform into something new.

The third position is that of the *reformists,* in which a large part of global civil society resides. These are people who accept the spread of global capitalism and global interconnectedness as potentially beneficial to mankind but see the need to 'civilise' the process. These are the people who favour reform of international economic institutions and want greater social justice and rigorous, fair, and participatory procedures for determining the direction of new technologies, and who strongly favour a global rule of law and press for enforcement. Reformists are a large category, which includes those who want to make specific and incremental change as well as radicals who aim at bigger and more transformative change. (Pianta believes a further distinction should be made between *reformists* and *radicals;* see Chapter 7.)

Table 1.4: Global civil society positions on globalisation

	Types of actors	Position on globalisation	Position on plant biotechnology	Position on global finance	Position on humanitarian intervention
Supporters	Transnational business and their allies	Favour global capitalism and the spread of a global rule of law	Favour plant biotechnology developed by corporations, no restrictions necessary	Favour de-regulation, free trade and free capital flows	Favour 'just wars' for human rights
Rejectionists	Anti-capitalist social movements; authoritarian states; nationalist and fundamentalist movements	Left oppose global capitalism; right and left want to preserve national sovereignty	Believe plant biotechnology is 'wrong' and 'dangerous' and should be abolished	Favour national protection of markets and control of capital flows. Radical rejectionists want overthrow of capitalism	Oppose all forms of armed intervention in other states Intervention is imperialism or 'not our business'
Reformists	Most INGOs; many in international institutions; many social movements and networks	Aim to 'civilise' globalisation	Do not oppose technology as such, but call for labelling information and public participation in risk assessment; sharing of benefits	Want more social justice and stability Favour reform of international economic institutions as well as specific proposals like debt relief or Tobin tax	Favour civil society intervention and international policing to enforce human rights
Alternatives	Grass roots groups, social movements and submerged networks	Want to opt out of globalisation	Want to live own lifestyle rejecting conventional agriculture and seeking isolation from GM food crops	Pursue an anti-corporate life-style, facilitate colourful protest, try to establish local alternative economies	Favour civil society intervention in conflicts but oppose use of military force

The final group we have called the *alternatives:* these are people and groups who neither necessarily oppose nor support the process of globalisation but who wish to opt out, to take their own course of action independently of government, international institutions, and transnational corporations. Their primary concern is to develop their own way of life, create their own space, without interference. This manifests itself in the case of biotechnology in growing and eating organic food, with global capitalism in local money schemes, opposition to brand names, and attempts to reclaim public space, and in the case of humanitarian intervention in making non-military 'civil society interventions' in conflicts.

In other words, one way of defining or understanding global civil society is as a *debate about the future direction of globalisation and perhaps humankind itself.*

Proposition 3: **Global civil society as a fuzzy and contested concept**

Thus, we can conclude that something new and important is happening and that it has a close and multifaceted relation with globalisation, but we are still not able to map its contours satisfactorily and, even more importantly, we are still not able to find an agreed meaning for what it is that is happening. Our third proposition is that *global civil society is a fuzzy and a contested concept.*

Both the fuzziness and the contested character of the concept can be attributed to its newness. It is fuzzy because the boundaries of the concept are not clearly defined. Even where there is an agreed core of meaning, it is not always clear what is to be included and what is to be excluded. In part, the problem arises because the term has both normative and descriptive content and it is not always possible to find an exact correspondence between the two. But the fuzziness also arises because the concept steps over or outside many familiar social science categories that are frequently caught up with nineteenth-century notions of the nation state that have entered into common parlance. 'Social participation' is taken to mean participation in the context of a national or local society, as are political action and engagement in most social movements. By contrast, we find it difficult to think of social participation in global networks, political action in relation to global events, and movements that take on global rather than national issues. The international relations literature speaks of transnational civil society, yet at the same time there is doubt about the very existence of such a society without the presence of an effective state (Brown 2000). Sociologists identify the emergence of a world society, but many see it as little more than a thinly disguised form of US cultural dominance (Meyer, Boli, and Ramirez 1997). Economists point to the emergence of global markets and institutions for labour, finance, production, information, or e-commerce, yet critics are eager to emphasise the predominance of large corporations and the concentration of decision-making power in a handful of metropolitan areas such as New York, London, Frankfurt, and Tokyo (Hirst and Thompson 1999). Political scientists analysing the spread of democracy around the world proudly anticipate the age of global democracy, only to find that democratic participation is eroding in many countries of the West and that democracy is frequently made subject to national interests in dealings with countries like China, Indonesia, or Russia (Forsythe 2000).

Global civil society is also a contested concept because it is new and therefore can be interpreted by both practitioners and social scientists as they choose. Or, to put it another way, the term is used differently according to political predilections and inherited understandings. Among policy-makers, especially in the West, there is a tendency to conceive of global civil society as the spread of what already exists in the West, especially in the United States, as a 'metaphor for Western liberalism' (Seckinelgin 2001). The movements that demanded civil society in Latin America and eastern Europe in the 1980s are understood as having wanted to build democracy on a western model. Support for civil society is seen as a kind of political *laissez-faire,* the political equivalent of neo-liberalism. Civil society is seen as a way of minimising the role of the state in society, both a mechanism for restraining state power and as a substitute for many of the functions of the state. Transposed to the global arena, it is viewed as the political or social counterpart of the process of economic globalisation, that is to say, liberalisation, privatisation, deregulation, and the growing mobility of capital and goods. In the absence of a global state, an army of NGOs performs the functions necessary to smooth the path of economic globalisation. Humanitarian NGOs provide the safety net to deal with the casualties of liberalisation and privatisation strategies in the economic field. Funding for democracy-building and human rights NGOs is supposed to help establish a rule of law and respect for human rights without taking account of the primary responsibility of the state in these areas.

Among activists, however, civil society has a different meaning. It is not about minimising the state but about increasing the responsiveness of political institutions. It is about the radicalisation of democracy and the redistribution of political power. For activists in eastern Europe or Latin America, civil society refers to active citizenship, to growing self-organisation outside formal political circles, and expanded space in which individual citizens can influence the conditions in which they live both directly through self-organisation and through pressure on the state. Transposed to a global level, this definition encompasses the need to influence and put pressure on global institutions in order to reclaim control over local political space.

The fact that these same words are understood in very different ways paradoxically creates a shared terrain on which individuals and representatives of organisations, institutions, and companies can communicate with each other, can engage in a common dialogue. Precisely because of these different understandings, the proponents and opponents of global capitalism can come together within what appears to be a shared discursive framework. The Yearbook is one expression of this shared terrain.

Evolution of the Concept of Global Civil Society

Both the term 'civil society' and the term 'global' have a long history stretching back to antiquity. One of the reasons it is so easy to contest contemporary meanings is that it is possible to select different classic understandings of a concept to suit current political and theoretical presuppositions. This is why it is useful to know a little more about the history of the concept, even though our version of history is selective as well.

From Greece to Scotland: civil society vs barbarians

The term 'civil society' has a direct equivalent in Latin *(societas civilis)*, and a close equivalent in ancient Greek *(politike koinona)*. What the Romans and Greeks meant by it was something like a 'political society', with active citizens shaping its institutions and policies. It was a law-governed society in which the law was seen as the expression of public virtue, the Aristotelian 'good life'. Civilisation was thus linked to a particular form of political power in which rulers put the public good before private interest. This also very clearly implied that, both in time and in place, there were people excluded, non-citizens, barbarians, who did not have a civil society.

The term is used throughout European history, but it gained more prominence when philosophers began to contemplate the foundations of the emerging nation state in the seventeenth and eighteenth centuries. A key assumption for the concept of civil society was the Christian notion of human equality. At that time, it was linked to the idea of a rights-based society in which rulers and the ruled are subject to the law, based on a social contract. Thus, civil society was contrasted with the state of nature, although conceptions of the state of nature varied. For Thomas Hobbes, one of the earliest writers on civil society, the state of nature was a 'warre . . . of every man against every man' (1990: 88) and the main benefit of living in a civil society was physical security. For Locke, on the other hand, the state of nature was more prone to war than was civil society but its main characteristic was the absence of a rule of law. Locke was concerned about restraints on arbitrary power; thus the rights enjoyed in civil society also included the right to liberty and to private property.

The Scottish Enlightenment thinkers of the eighteenth century were the first to emphasise the importance of capitalism as a basis for the new individualism and a rights-based society. One of the most extensive treatments of civil society is by Adam Ferguson, in *An Essay on the History of Civil Society* (Ferguson 1995), first published in 1767. In this book, he tried to resurrect the Roman ideal of civic virtue in a society where capitalism was taking the place of feudalism. In order to have a civil society, men — not women, of course, in that age — need to take an active interest in the government of their polity instead of just getting rich and diverting themselves. That still has some resonance in the present use of the term. But, as for the seventeenth century writers, the dividing line for Ferguson and his contemporaries was still between civil society on the one hand and despotism or 'savage' living on the other. A problem with the modern use of 'civil society' is that we might want to preserve the connotation of non-violent interaction based on equal rights while we disavow the Euro-centric assumption of savages vs civilised people, but the two are historically connected (see for instance Comaroff and Comaroff 1999 on this line of criticism).

Hegel and de Tocqueville: civil society vs the state

Ferguson was widely translated, and made more of an impression in Germany than in Britain (Oz-Salzberger 1995: xxv). Kant and Hegel were among the readers (see Keane in Chapter 2 for a brief description of Kant's thinking on civil society). Hegel had a great deal to say about civil society, not all of which is easily understandable, but one of the most important points for the further development of the concept is that he saw civil society as something separate from, although symbiotic with, the state (Hegel 1991). Civil society for him consisted of men trading and interacting socially, but it was separate from government and purely public activity. This also explains why Karl Marx, strongly influenced by Hegel, had an extremely negative view of civil society (Marx 1975). Hegel thought the pursuit of self-interest by individuals in civil society was balanced by a consciousness of interdependence and also by the role of the state as mediator. But Marx equated civil society, in its German translation 'Bürgerliche Gesellschaft', with bourgeois society, and narrowed it to only economic life in which everyone pursued his own selfish interests and became alienated from his own human potential and his fellow people. If that had remained the prevailing idea about what civil society is, we would probably not be taking such an interest in the concept today.

The other important nineteenth century thinker was Alexis de Tocqueville. In his study of democracy as practised in America, de Tocqueville argued that the guarantee of individual liberties was to be found in what he called 'democratic expedients'; these included local self-government, the separation of church and state, a free press, indirect elections, an independent judiciary, and, above all 'associational life'. In America, he was greatly impressed by the extent of associations in civil life and put forward the argument that active associations were a condition for freedom and equality. As the state took over more and more functions of daily life, as the division of labour became more complex and as demands for the redistribution of wealth increased, an active voluntary sector was necessary to provide a check on state power.

> As soon as several inhabitants of the United States have taken up an opinion or a feeling they wish to promote in the world, they look for mutual assistance; and as soon as they have found one another out, they combine. From that moment they are no longer isolated men, but a power seen from afar, whose actions serve for example and whose language is listened to . . . Among the laws that rule human societies, there is one which seems to be more precise and clear than all the others. If men are to remain civilised or to become so, the art of associating together must grow and improve in the same ratio as the equality of conditions is increased. (de Tocqueville 1945:117–18)

While de Tocqueville did not use the term 'civil society', his argument about the virtues of associational life continues to inform modern-day thinking about it, particularly in the United States (Putnam 2000).

From Gramsci onwards: civil society between the state and the market

The concept of civil society was rescued for modern use by Antonio Gramsci. Gramsci was a member of the Italian parliament and general secretary of the underground Italian Communist Party when he was arrested by Mussolini in 1926 at the age of 35. He spent the next ten years in prison, writing. In his *Prison Notebooks,* he also discusses civil society (Gramsci 1971). In his interpretation, he goes back from Marx to Hegel, who saw civil society as all kinds of social interaction, not just economic ones. Gramsci then goes a step further, and divorces the notion of civil society from economic interactions. He views civil society as consisting of cultural institutions, notably the church (in Italy the omnipresent church rather obviously got in the way of a purely economic, Marxist view of society), but also schools, associations, trade unions, and other cultural institutions. Gramsci is ambiguous about this civil society of his. On the one hand, it is through this cultural 'superstructure' that the bourgeois class imposes its hegemony, using it to keep the working class in its place. On the other hand, it is a kind of wedge between the state and the class-structured economy, which has the revolutionary potential of dislodging the bourgeoisie. Unlike in Russia in 1917, the revolution would not come suddenly but through a prolonged war of position, and civil society represented the trenches in which and over which this war was fought. So here one has the first germs of the idea that most people now have of civil society as 'between the state and the market'. It is important to keep in mind, however, that Gramsci intended this idea of civil society, as the non-state *and* non-economic area of social interaction, to be only temporary and strategic, a tool in the revolutionary struggle.

The rediscovery of civil society

None of this is stated very clearly in Gramsci. It is stated confusingly, self-contradictorily, and certainly not as one of his central theses. Nevertheless, Gramsci's idea of civil society as the non-state *and* non-economic area of social interaction, which he himself seems to contradict a few pages later in the *Prison Notebooks* (see for instance Gramsci 1971: 263), has become the dominant one, perhaps also because of the growing importance attached by sociologists and political thinkers to intermediate associations (Durkheim 1984). There are a few related explanations for the dominance of the Gramscian meaning. The term 'civil society' very nearly died out in west European and American political thought (see Cohen and Arato 1992: 159–74). There were some followers of Gramsci especially in the Italian and Spanish Communist parties but there was little debate or interest. When the term really resurfaces, it is with dissidents against the authoritarian state both in Latin America and in central Europe for whom the idea of civil society as something separate from the state was strategically useful (see Cohen and Arato 1992: 29–82).

In Latin America, the situation of left-wing intellectuals of the 1970s and 1980s was very similar to Gramsci's, fighting fascist dictatorships in which capitalists were by and large colluding with the state but in which, in the words of Fernando Cardoso (1979: 48), 'authoritarianism is still underdeveloped: it [the state] may kill and torture, but it does not exercise complete control over everyday life'. In such states there was some room for civil society and, as Alfred Stepan (1988: 5) put it: '"Civil society" became the political celebrity of the abertura', the political opening that evolved gradually in Brazil between 1974 and 1985. Latin American thinkers, first of all in Brazil, appear to have been attracted to the idea of civil society because it was a term that could unify entrepreneurs, church groups, and labour movements in their opposition to the regime and because as a force in society it could be distinguished from political parties, which many felt had been discredited, as well as from the kind of mass mobilisation by skilful populists that had been endemic in various Latin American countries (see Stepan 1988: 3–7; O'Donnell and Schmitter 1986: 49–52; Weffort 1989).

With the central Europeans it was somewhat different. Intellectuals in Czechoslovakia, Hungary, and Poland, such as Jan Tesar (1981), Vaclav Havel (1985), Gyorgi Konrad (1984) and Adam Michnik (1985) revived the term to mean autonomous spaces independent of the state; their understanding was closer to de Tocqueville's than to Gramsci's. They wanted to emphasise self-organisation, individual responsibility, the power of conscience. Thus, terms like 'anti-politics', '*parallel polis*', 'living in truth', or

the 'power of the powerless' were alternative expressions of their concept of civil society (see also Cohen and Arato 1992; Keane 1988; Kaldor 1999 on the importance of these figures).

Gramsci wrote (1971: 265) that

A totalitarian policy is aimed precisely:
1. at ensuring that the members of a particular party find in that party all the satisfactions that they formerly found in a multiplicity of organisations, i.e. at breaking all the threads that bind these members to extraneous cultural organisms;
2. at destroying all other organisations or at incorporating them into a system of which the party is the sole regulator.

For intellectuals behind the Iron Curtain, it was precisely the total control over all aspects of every day life that was the target of their efforts (see Arendt 1968; Lefort 1986). While state terrorism was more spectacular in Latin America, with military regimes 'disappearing' thousands of people in each country in a matter of months, civil society in the Gramscian sense was snuffed out more successfully by the longer rule and more totalitarian aspirations of communism in eastern Europe and the USSR. In a totalitarian state, where the distinction between the interests of the people and the interests of the state is categorically denied – hence 'people's republics' – central European dissidents began to believe that conceiving of 'civil society' as association between people away from the tentacles of the state was the way to begin resisting the state.

The central European and the Latin American thinkers had several things in common. The way in which they conceived of civil society, it was not just a means to achieve the overthrow of the regime they lived in. They were more interested in 'reclaiming' space that the authoritarian state had encroached upon than in taking over the reigns of power (see especially Havel 1985; Weffort 1989; ironically, Vaclav Havel became President of Czechoslovakia and Francisco Weffort became Brazil's Minister of Culture under Cardoso's Presidency). This space had to be kept open and alive as a necessary complement to a healthy democracy, an antidote to narrow party politics, and a bulwark against future threats to democracy.

Thinkers and activists from both regions were also strongly influenced by the idea of human rights, which had gained international prominence with the adoption of US congressional legislation, the signing of the Helsinki Accords, and the entry into force of the two main UN human rights conventions, all in the mid-1970s. In their thinking, individual human rights and civil society together were the complements and guarantors for effective democracy.

Finally, while very much focused on curing their national societies, opposition figures from both regions also learned the value of international solidarity. It was strategically necessary for them to link up with others across borders, with those who could speak up for them in international forums, who could criticise the policy of their own governments towards these dictatorships, and, last but not least, who could fund them (see Keck and Sikkink 1998: 79–120 for the Latin-American networks, and Kaldor 1999 for the European ones).

After Latin America and central Europe, the civil society idea has been spreading like wildfire. On the one hand, it has increasingly occupied the emancipatory space left by the demise of socialism and national liberation. Particularly in dictatorships or countries emerging from dictatorship, people have apparently felt the relevance of the concept: in the Philippines and South Korea, in South Africa, and in the Arab world. It has become equally popular, however, in places that have not recently experienced dictatorship, in western Europe and North America but also in India, for instance. In western Europe and North America this has something to do with concern over the erosion of democracy through the apathy and disillusionment of the electorate. The idea of civil society is seen as a way of revitalising democracy. In recent decades, fewer and fewer people have been joining political parties, and more have joined environmental, peace, and human rights groups like Greenpeace and Friends of the Earth, Amnesty International, and the anti-nuclear movement. The name increasingly given to this phenomenon is 'civil society'. Both the leftist great hopes of the all-powerful, all-providing state and the rightist belief that leaving everything to the market delivers benefits to all have lost appeal. While politicians have invented the 'Third Way', many people now seem to be placing their hopes for society in this 'third force'.

On the other hand, the concept has also been taken up by Western governments and international institutions who understand civil society as 'catching up' with the west and who find the concept useful for implementing programmes of economic and political reform. After the end of the cold war, ideological objections to cooperation with citizens groups dissolved and it became more difficult to ally with authoritarian governments—something which had earlier been possible under the cold war umbrella. Cooperation with civil society was seen as way to legitimise programmes of economic reform and to stabilise market societies. This also provides a rather more cynical explanation for the spread of 'civil society' in the developing world: since donors have adopted the dogma that strengthening civil society is good for development, using the language of civil society is good for funding applications.

Descriptive and normative conceptions

One thing that helps to explain the present universal popularity of 'civil society' is its very fuzziness: it can be all things to all people. In particular, there is a conflation of an empirical category, which is often referred to as NGOs or the non-profit or voluntary sector, with a political project. In the first meaning, it is simply a label for something that is out there, a category, that is both non-profit and non-governmental. On the other hand, in the way the central Europeans and Latin Americans were using it, it is more a political project, a sphere through which to resist, pressure, or influence the state and increasingly also the market. This ideal type can have various characteristics, all of which are hotly debated.

First, it is argued that the fact that people are getting together regularly for a variety of purposes, from playing cards to saving the environment, generates trust between people in a society. This is also referred to as 'social capital' (Putnam, 2000; Fukuyama 1995). More politically minded proponents usually insist (like Adam Ferguson) that civil society consists of active citizens who take an interest in public affairs. Also based partly on the classical, eighteenth century notion, civil society can be seen as essentially non-violent and resisting violence, for instance through Gandhian forms of civil disobedience. Finally—and this is a more modern component of the ideal—being part of civil society is sometimes seen as a commitment to common human values that go beyond ethnic, religious, or national boundaries.

The problem with a purely normative definition of civil society is, however, that defending civil society as a 'good thing' threatens to become tautological: civil society is a good thing because it espouses the values we hold. Anyone who fails to hold these values is not part of civil society. And whose values are these? The desirability of absolute non-violence, for instance, is not something everyone agrees about. And are nationalist and fundamentalist movements part of civil society? Where and how do we draw boundaries?

Emergence of global civil society

Until recently, civil society was primarily thought of as a national concept (yet another consequence perhaps, of the methodological nationalism of the social sciences referred to below). In reality, of course, self-organised non-profit associations and social movements have been networking across borders for nearly two centuries, even if this has dramatically accelerated in recent decades. But an important point about the way in which central European and Latin American intellectuals began to talk of civil society is that they made this transnationality a central element in it. This goes quite against Ferguson and his contemporaries, for whom defining civil society was part of building the concept of the nation state. It also differs from the line starting with Hegel, in which an abstract civil society-state dialectic is paramount and the idea of cross-links with other civil societies and other states is not considered. But for those dissidents in the 1980s it was strategically necessary to link up with others across borders. Keck and Sikkink (1998: 13) have described this as the 'boomerang pattern.' When it comes to human rights, the problem is very much national, but the solution lies partly in finding allies beyond one's own dictatorial state. In both Latin America and Central Europe the cold war was understood as a key component of authoritarianism, a way in which repression was legitimised. The Latin American dictators made an ideology of their national security doctrines, while the east Europeans were crushed in the name of the struggle against Western imperialism. Hence, crossing borders to oppose the cold war, especially in Europe, was an important element of the citizens' struggle against dictatorship; this is why in Europe the term 'pan-European civil society' preceded 'global civil society'.

Environmental groups have always stressed the transnational nature of their activism, for a slightly different reason. For them, the problems are global. One Chernobyl, or one state's misbehaviour on CO_2 emissions, affects us all. It is perhaps with them that the talk of 'one world' and 'global solutions'

originated (Lipschutz 1996; Wapner 1996). The newer anti-capitalist movement has taken the same tack. In fact, one of its slogans is 'Globalise the resistance'. In the 1990s, that deliberate transnationality also takes on more than a strategic meaning, however, it becomes a moral-political statement against ethnic nationalism and religious fundamentalism.

Transnational vs global

Many authors are referring to the new phenomenon we discuss in this Yearbook as 'transnational civil society' (Florini 2000; Keck and Sikkink 1998; Smith *et al.* 1997). They say that 'global civil society' sounds too grandiose; in the sense of something that really brings together people from every part of the globe, it just isn't there, and it is not inevitably going to be there either. In the empirical sense, they have a point. Some parts of the world are much more linked up than others. There are few links with Equatorial Guinea or Mongolia. We nevertheless prefer to speak of a 'global civil society', for three reasons.

First, while 'global civil society' may overstate what is really out there, 'transnational civil society' understates it. All one needs to be transnational is a single border-crossing. In that sense, as we outlined above, civil society has been transnational for at least 200 years. 'Transnational' does nothing to capture the revolution in travel and communications but also the opening up of many formerly closed societies that has really made civil society much more global in the last ten years than it has ever been before.

Second, only 'global civil society' can be posed as a counterweight to 'globalisation'. Both are just processes. If formal democracy remains confined to the level of the state, while various economic, political, and cultural activities are indeed going global, then only a global civil society can call them to account. While we believe that globalisation has both good and bad sides, representation of citizens' interests becomes a problem when the market and other transnational phenomena take over from the state. Corporations are not democratically elected, and while there are now more democratically elected national governments than ever before, citizens have no direct control over what these governments do at the now all-important international level. A world government with a world parliament is one utopia, of course, but like earlier utopias could easily turn into global totalitarianism. Global civil society, on the other hand, may be a more viable way of 'taming', 'humanising', 'calling to account', indeed 'civilising' globalisation.

Third, the term 'global civil society' has a normative aspiration that 'transnational civil society' does not. Just as the term 'human rights' has a universalistic intent that 'civil rights' lacks, global civil society can be seen as an aspiration to reach and include citizens everywhere and to enable them to think and act as global citizens. Some of the literature on globalisation stresses the emergence of a global consciousness, an 'imagined community of mankind' (Shaw 2000; Robertson 1990). In particular, two world wars and the threat of a nuclear war generated this global consciousness; the holocaust and Hiroshima have become global collective memories. In this sense, global civil society is an expression of that consciousness even if the participants cannot travel or even use the telephone.

Definitions

As in the case of national civil societies, part of the attraction of the term 'global civil society' is that different people feel at home with different conceptions of it. This Yearbook reflects that diversity. Rather than providing a definitive definition of global civil society, it has been our intention as editors to offer this and future Yearbooks as a continuing platform for an exchange of ideas about the meaning of 'global civil society'. We have opted for this approach because we believe that debating what global civil society means contributes to the emergence of an animated, open, and self-reflexive global civil society.

For our table programme in Part IV of the Yearbook, 'Records of Global Civil Society', however, we had to operationalise the concept. We have chosen the following, purely descriptive, definition: global civil society is the sphere of ideas, values, institutions, organisations, networks, and individuals located *between* the family, the state, and the market and operating *beyond* the confines of national societies, polities, and economies. While we recognise that global civil society is ultimately a normative concept, we believe that the normative content is too contested to be able to form the basis for an operationalisation of the concept. We do give attention to the normative dimensions of global civil society in our table programme, but it would go against our conception of global civil society as an open, contested, and contestable concept to

fill in this normative content in any definite way (see Anheier in Part IV of this Yearbook).

Other authors in this Yearbook have chosen different interpretations. In Chapter 7, for instance, Mario Pianta appears at first to adopt a similar definition: 'the emerging global civil society has to be conceptualised, with all its ambiguities and blurred images, as the sphere of cross-border relations and collective activities outside the international reach of states and markets' (p. 171). However, he then hones in on a narrow, more political and more normative characterisation:

> '*Despite extreme heterogeneity and fragmentation, much of the activity in the sphere of global civil society consists of what Richard Falk (1999: 130) has termed "globalisation from below", a project whose "normative potential is to conceptualise widely shared world order values: minimising violence, maximising economic well-being, realising social and political justice, and upholding environmental quality"*' (p. 171).

In Chapter 2, on the other hand, John Keane takes a much more holistic approach. He thinks the trend, beginning with Gramsci, to consider commercial life as not part of (global) civil society, has been a mistake. Other authors oscillate between these and other definitions, emphasising different aspects of global civil society such as its struggle against unbridled global capitalism (Desai and Said, Chapter 3), its attempts to understand, resist, or democratise a new science like biotechnology (Osgood, Chapter 4), its responses to the challenge of violent conflicts (Kaldor, Chapter 5), its pioneering of information and communications technology (Naughton, Chapter 6), and the way it gets funded (Pinter, Chapter 8).

Describing Global Civil Society: The Challenge of Methodological Nationalism

The concept global civil society is not only difficult to define and to fit into conventional social science terminology, it is also difficult to measure using standard systems of social and economic accounts. By and large, all these systems tend to be territorially bounded.

To see how national and international statistical offices find it difficult to think about a world that is no longer made up of national societies and domestic economies as major building blocks,[1] let's consider the economic statistics and the System of National Accounts (SNA) (United Nations 1993). This example illustrates both the problem and the potential strategy towards a solution for the purpose of measuring global civil society.

Adding the gross national product of all *national* economies of the world's 180 plus countries would yield the approximate monetary value of global economic activity. Yet this value would not be the same as the size of the *globalised* economy, nor would it be identical to the value of the total *international* economy. The national economy would be conceptualised and measured with the help of the SNA; the international economy would be indicated, on the assumption that the national economy is the unit of analysis, by import-export statistics and the rest-of-the-world accounts in the SNA. Yet the SNA is of little help when it comes to the globalised economy, which involves integrated finance, production, and distribution systems across many countries and spanning different regions and continents. Such globalised elements of the economy emerge from the integrated economic activities of separate or joined-up businesses across countries, and it is these elements that go unnoticed in conventional economic statistics. Thus, the term global economy is outside the SNA's conceptual and empirical space.

What becomes clear in the case of the SNA could be demonstrated with many other statistical systems. It is basically the insight that the sequence 'national → international → global' is not a linear extension of the same data. The sequence contains an important qualitative difference that escapes international statistical systems—a difference that becomes fundamental once the nation state or the national economy is no longer the frame of reference for what is to be measured. Three very different examples might help illustrate the gap in information about the emerging institutional infrastructure and values of global civil society.

1. In recent decades, international NGOs have become an important relay in funding flows from OECD countries to developing countries and the transition economies in central and eastern Europe (Anheier and Salamon 1998; Smillie 1995; Pinter 2001). These funding flows involve bilateral and multilateral aid in addition to private philanthropic and other non-profit contributions as well as corporate finance. Yet no international statistical agency collects systematic information on the full network in financial intermediation of NGOs, including the role of grant-making foundations (Anheier and List 2000). Data focus on either the country origin or the recipient country, leaving the intermediary role of NGOs unspecified (see OECD 1997; also Chapter 8 by Frances Pinter). The state-to-state view of statistical reporting prevails, thus ignoring the fact that an increasing portion of aid flows via private organisations.

2. The rise and continuing expansion of multinational corporations, international organisations, and international NGOs brought with it growing numbers of professionals who increasingly spend large parts of their working lives in organisations, working environments, and cultures that may have little connection with their specific country of origin. While these 'international professional migrants' may be less numerous than the mass of low-income workers moving from the South to the North, their numbers are even less systematically recorded despite their immense economic importance and impact on an emerging global culture.

3. The 'small world' experiments in sociology have shown that a randomly selected number of citizens in OECD countries could with some degree of probability reach any other randomly selected fellow citizen in fewer than five steps by going through a sequence of personal contacts (Kochen 1989; Wasserman and Faust 1994: 53–4). Numerous other studies in social network analysis have demonstrated the importance and implications of 'connectedness' for the functioning of local communities, for getting jobs, for social mobilisation, and for the spread of information and innovations of all kinds (Powell and Smith-Duerr 1994). Increasingly, with greater mobility and migration, and better and cheaper technology, these contacts reach across borders and people's life takes place in networks that span different countries, cultures, and continents (Castells 1996). Yet this global connectedness, crucial for social cohesion, political mobilisation, the flow of information, and, particularly, economic and cultural change, remains uncharted by official statistics and only superficially explored by the social sciences.

---

[1] *There are some parallels between today's situation and the struggle in the late Middle Ages encountered with the concepts and imagery of the emerging modern world of the Renaissance, so aptly described by historians like Huizinga (1954) and Crosby (1997) and sociologists such as Elias (1982).*

Although we could add more, these examples should suffice to show the growing awareness about the emergence of an economic, social, political, and cultural sphere above and beyond the confines of national economies, societies, polities, states, and cultures. At the same time, this awareness is accompanied by some unease and sometimes even defensiveness: many conventional concepts and terminology based on the nation state and national economy and society fall short in their ability to capture global civil society. Given the lack of adequate conceptual development, theories are few and better explanations continue to be frustrated by a paucity of systematic data and empirical information that can be used as evidence. Simply put: existing statistical systems are based on the notion of the nation state—a unit that seems ill-suited for the kinds of data and information needed for mapping and measuring global civil society.

Once fully developed, however, the information included in the Yearbook is to provide the beginnings of a systematic profile of the contours, composition, and developments of global civil society. It is our hope that over time the data presented in the various chapters and the tables and chronology in Part IV, updated annually, will become a central reference point for empirical and theoretical work on global civil society. We also hope that this information will be of use to policy-makers and practitioners.

Chapter Conclusions

Apart from the three general conclusions that have emerged from this book, set out above, some powerful specific conclusions can also be drawn on the basis of the different chapters.

In Chapter 2, John Keane draws attention to the role of global civil society as an antidote to violence and hubris. While global civil society can occasionally be helpless in the face of violence and can be hubristic itself, its strength lies in its ability to call power-holders to account, thus inching the world towards greater parity, openness, and humility.

In Chapter 3, Meghnad Desai and Yahia Said describe how formerly marginal anti-capitalist movements from different regions and with different priorities have come together to form a cacophonous but loud and consistent call of protest. Global capitalism must either learn to seriously engage with these protests and join in the attempt to civilise

globalisation, or prepare for more massive and more violent protests ahead.

In Chapter 4, Diane Osgood points out that, in the debate on plant biotechnology, lack of a common language and hence of agreed priorities has prevented trusted leaders from emerging, and that this problem is likely to be exacerbated as the technology develops. Civil society leaders need to 'speak science' and scientists need to learn to 'speak society'. A more respectful dialogue must take the place of the scaremongering on the one side and contempt on the other, which has characterised too much of the debate so far.

In Chapter 5, Mary Kaldor describes how, largely due to the efforts of global civil society, the notion of humanitarian intervention has taken the place of a state-centred ideology in which sovereignty overruled all humanitarian and human rights considerations in international relations. She goes on to discuss how, as the international community blundered its way through a number of conflicts in the 1990s, global civil society has remained deeply divided over the questions whether, how, and when military force should be used for humanitarian purposes. The most viable form of humanitarian intervention in the future may be a long-term international presence in conflict-prone areas that includes civil society actors, international agencies, and international peace-keeping troops on a much larger scale than has been the case so far, coupled with a readiness to risk the lives of peace-keeping troops to save the lives of others where this is necessary.

In Chapter 6, John Naughton describes how global civil society has taken to the Internet with its libertarian ethos, its decentralised architecture, and its low operating costs like a duck to water over the last decade. However, these characteristics of the Internet are not intrinsic: they are man-made and they can be changed. States are adopting legislation to restrict freedom of expression on the Internet, and corporations are inventing technology to undermine the anonymity of the Internet in the interests of e-commerce. Global civil society needs to wake up to these threats and respond to them in two ways. First, it must begin to consider Internet freedoms as an advocacy issue instead of as an instrument it can take for granted. Second, it must stay one step ahead of governments and corporations in helping to develop and adopt new advances in the technology that can reinforce its subversive, liberating character.

In Chapter 7, Mario Pianta has undertaken a survey of global civil society's parallel summits to official summits. He draws the following broad conclusion: official summits that are only framing issues are most likely to be open to dialogue with global civil society as represented in the parallel summit; summits in charge of rule making or setting policy will be less so; and summits with enforcing power tend to be closed to civil society influence. Global civil society is not going to take such treatment from the second and third categories lying down, however. It will continue to contest unaccountable decision-makers by convening parallel summits, if necessary by defying restrictions imposed by local authorities or by convening them in a different place from the official summit.

In Chapter 8, Frances Pinter attempts to chart the primary sources of funding of global civil society organisations and the ways in which different types of bodies get funded. She notes that there is a growing convergence around a handful of core issues among the major donors which can be interpreted variously as evidence of an emerging cultural cosmopolitan consensus or of a move towards a domesticated, donor-led global civil society that is subservient to the dictates of global capitalism. She also concludes, however, that money alone can't buy you global civil society: human, social, organisational, and informational resources are at least equally essential.

These studies are beginning to give us some insight into what global civil society is concerned about, and how it works. In the second Yearbook, these and other cartographers will be mapping further aspects of the 'conceptual island' that is global civil society. This first Yearbook is just the beginning of a process that we hope will enable us to understand and describe this new phenomenon called 'global civil society'.

References

Anheier, H. K. and List, R. (2000). *Cross-Border Philanthropy: An Exploratory Study of International Giving in the United Kingdom, United States, Germany and Japan.* West Malling, Kent: Charities Aid Foundation, Centre for Civil Society and The Johns Hopkins University.

Anheier, Helmut K. and Salamon, Lester M. (1998). *The Nonprofit Sector in the Developing World.* Manchester: Manchester University Press.

Arendt, Hannah (1968). *The Origins of Totalitarianism.* New York: Harcourt, Brace Jovanovitch.

Beck, Ulrich (2000). 'The Postnational Society and its Enemies'. Public lecture, London School of Economics and Political Science, 24 February.

Brown, Chris (2000). 'Cosmopolitanism, World Citizenship, and Global Civil Society'. *Critical Review of International Social and Political Philosophy,* 3: 7–26.

Cardoso, Fernando Henrique (1979). 'On the Characterization of Authoritarian Regimes in Latin America', in David Collier (ed.), *The New Authoritarianism in Latin America.* Princeton, NJ: Princeton University Press.

Castells, Manuel. (1996). *The Rise of Network Society.* Oxford: Blackwells.

Charnovitz, Steve (1997). 'Two Centuries of Participation: NGOs and International Governance'. *Michigan Journal of International Law,* 18: 183–286.

Chatfield, Charles (1997). 'Intergovernmental and Nongovernmental Associations to 1945', in Jackie Smith *et al.,* *Transnational Social Movements and World Politics: Solidarity Beyond the State.* Syracuse, NY: Syracuse University Press.

Cohen, Jean L. and Arato, Andrew (1992). *Civil Society and Political Theory.* Cambridge, MA: MIT Press.

Cohen, Robin and Rai, Shirin M (eds) (2000). *Global Social Movements.* London: Athlone Press.

Comaroff, John L. and Comaroff, Jean (1999). *Civil Society and the Political Imagination in Africa: Critical Perspectives.* Chicago: University of Chicago Press.

Crosby, Alfred (1997). *A Measure of Reality: Quantification and Western Society 1250–1600.* New York: Cambridge University Press.

Durkheim, Emile (1984). *The Division of Labour in Society* [De la Division du Travail Social] (2nd edn). Basingstoke: Macmillan.

Elias, Norbert (1982). *The Civilising Process* (two vols). New York: Pantheon

Falk, Richard (1999). *Predatory Globalisation: A Critique.* Cambridge: Polity Press.

Ferguson, Adam (1995[1767]). *An Essay on the History of Civil Society* (ed. Fania Oz-Salzberger). Cambridge: Cambridge University Press.

Florini, Ann M. (ed.) (2000). *The Third Force: The Rise of Transnational Civil Society.* Washington, DC: Carnegie Endowment for International Peace.

Forsythe, David (ed.) (2000). *Human Rights and Comparative Foreign Policy.* Tokyo, New York: United Nations University Press.

Fukuyama, Francis (1995). *Trust: The Social Virtues and the Creation of Prosperity.* London: Hamish Hamilton.

Gramsci, Antonio (1971). *Selections from the Prison Notebooks* (ed. and trans. Quintin Hoare and Geoffrey Nowell Smith). London: Lawrence and Wishart.

Havel, Vaclav (1985). *The Power of the Powerless: Citizens Against the State in Central-Eastern Europe.* London: Hutchinson.

Hegel, Georg Wilhelm Friedrich (1991[1820]). *Elements of the Philosophy of Right* (ed. Allen W. Wood, trans. H. B. Nisbet). Cambridge: Cambridge University Press.

Held, David, McGrew, Anthony Goldblatt, David, and Perraton, Jonathan (1999). *Global Transformations.* Cambridge: Polity Press.

Hirst, P. and Thompson, G. (1999). *Globalization in Question: The International Economy and the Possibilities of Governance.* Cambridge: Polity Press.

Hobbes, Thomas (1990[1650]). *Leviathan* (ed. Richard Tuck). Cambridge: Cambridge University Press.

Huizinga, J. (1954). *The Waning of the Middle Ages.* New York: Doubleday.

Kaldor, Mary (1999). *Bringing Peace and Human Rights Together* (Public Lecture No. 9, The Ideas of 1989 Lecture Series). London: Centre for the Study of Global Governance, London School of Economics.

Keane, J. (ed.) (1988), *Civil Society and the State: New European Perspectives.* London: Verso.

— (1998). *Civil Society: Old Images, New Visions.* Cambridge: Polity Press.

Keck, Margaret E. and Sikkink, Kathryn (1998). *Activists beyond Borders: Advocacy Networks in International Politics.* Ithaca, NY: Cornell University Press.

Kochen, Manfred (ed.) (1989). *The Small World.* Norwood, NJ: Ablex Press.

Konrad, Gyorgy (1984). *Anti-Politics.* London: Quartet Books.

Lefort, Claude (1986). *The Political Forms of Modern Society: Bureaucracy, Democracy, Totalitarianism* (ed. and introduced by John Thompson). Cambridge: Polity Press.

Lipschutz, Ronnie D. with Mayer. Judith (1996). *Global Civil Society and Global Environmental Governance: The Politics of Nature from Place to Planet.* New York: SUNY Press.

Marx, Karl (1975). 'On the Jewish Question', *in Karl Marx and Frederick Engels, Marx and Engels 1843-1844* (Collected Works, Vol. 3). London: Lawrence and Wishart.

Meyer, J., Boli, J., Ramirez, F. (1997). 'World Society and the Nation State'. *American Journal of Sociology,* 103: 144–81.

Michnik, Adam (1985). 'The New Evolutionism', in *Letters from Prison and Other Essays.* Berkeley and London: California University Press.

O'Donnell, Guillermo and Schmitter, Philippe (1986). *Transitions from Authoritarian Rule: Tentative Conclusions about Uncertain Democracies.* Baltimore: Johns Hopkins University Press.

OECD (1997). *Geographical Distribution of Financial Aid to Developing Countries.* Paris: OECD.

Oz-Salzberger, Fania (1995). 'Introduction', in Adam Ferguson, *An Essay on the History of Civil Society* (ed. Fania Oz-Salzberger). Cambridge: Cambridge University Press.

Pinter, Frances (2001). 'The Role of Foundations in the Transformation Process in Central and Eastern Europe', in Andreas Schlüter, Volker Then, and Peter Walkenhorst (eds), *Foundations in Europe: Society, Management and Law.* London: Directory of Social Change.

Putnam, Robert D. (2000). *Bowling Alone: The Collapse and Revival of American Community.* New York: Simon and Schuster.

Powell, Walter and Smith-Duerr, Laurel (1994). 'Networks and Economic Life', in Neil J. Smelser and Richard Swedberg (eds), *The Handbook of Economic Sociology.* Princeton, NJ: Princeton University Press.

Robertson, R. (1990). *Globalisation: Social and Cultural Theory.* London: Sage.

Salamon, L. M. and Anheier, H. K. (1997). *Defining the Nonprofit Sector*. Manchester: Manchester University Press.

Salamon, L. M., Anheier, H. K., List, R., Toepler, S., Sokolowski, S. W. and Associates (1999).

Global Civil Society: Dimensions of the Non-profit Sector. Baltimore. MA: Johns Hopkins University, Institute for Policy Studies' Center for Civil Society Studies.

Scholte, Jan (1999). 'Globalisation Prospects for a Paradigm Shift', in M. Shaw (ed.), *Politics and Globalisation*. London: Routledge.

Seckinelgin, Hakan (2001). 'Civil Society as a Metaphor for Liberalism'. Conference paper for the International Studies Association, Hong Kong, July 2001.

Shaw, Martin (2000). *Theory of the Global State: Global Reality as an Unfinished Revolution*. Cambridge: Cambridge University Press.

Smillie, Ian (1995). *The Alms Bazaar: Altruism Under Fire: Non-Profit Organizations and International Development*. London: Intermediate Technology Publications.

Smith, Jackie, Charles Chatfield, and Ron Pagnucco (ed.) (1997). *Transnational Social Movements and World Politics: Solidarity Beyond the State*. Syracuse, NY: Syracuse University Press.

Stepan, Alfred (1988). *Rethinking Military Politics: Brazil and the Southern Cone*. Princeton, NJ: Princeton University Press.

Tesar, Jan (1981). 'Totalitarian Dictatorships as a Phenomenon of the Twentieth Century and the Possibilities for Overcoming Them'. *International Journal of Politics*, 11/1: 85–100.

Tocqueville, Alexis de (1945[1835]). *Democracyin America*. New York: Vintage Books.

UIA (Union of International Associations) (1905–1999/2000). *Yearbook of International Organizations: Guide to civil society networks*. Munich: K. G. Saur.

UN (United Nations) (1993). *System of National Accounts*. New York: United Nations. See also http://www.un.org/Depts/unsd/sna/ sna1-en.htm

Wapner, Paul (1996). *Environmental Activism and World Civic Politics*. New York: SUNY Press.

Wassermann, Stanley and Faust, Katherine (1994). *Social Network Analysis*. Cambridge: Cambridge University Press.

Weffort, Francisco (1989). 'Why Democracy?', in Alfred Stepan (ed.), *Democratizing Brazil: Problems of Transition and Consolidation*. New York: Oxford University Press.

Zerubavel, Eviatar (1991). *The Fine Line: Making Distinctions in Everyday Life*.
New York: Free Press.

CHAPTER 2

GLOBAL CIVIL SOCIETY?

John Keane

A New Cosmology

All human orders, hunting and gathering societies included, have lived off shared images of the cosmos, world-views that served to plant the feet of their members firmly in space and time. Yet very few have fantasised the linking of the five oceans, six continents, and peoples of our little blue planet wrapped in white vapour. Each of these world-views in the strict sense emerged only after the military defeats suffered by Islam, in modern Europe. They included the forceful global acquisition of territory, resources, and subjects in the name of empire; the efforts of Christendom to piggyback on imperial ventures for the purpose of bringing spiritual salvation to the whole world; and the will to unify the world through the totalitarian violence of fascism and Marxism-Leninism. Each of these globalising projects left indelible marks on the lives of the world's peoples, their institutions and ecosystems, but each also failed to accomplish its mission. In our times, against the backdrop of those failures, the image of ourselves as involved in another great human adventure, one carried out on a global scale, is again on the rise. A new world-view, radically different from any that has existed before, has been born and is currently enjoying a growth spurt: it is called 'global civil society'.

These unfamiliar words 'global civil society'—a neologism of the last decade— are fast becoming fashionable. They were born at the confluence of three overlapping streams of concern among publicly minded intellectuals at the end of the 1980s: the revival of the old language of civil society, especially in central-eastern Europe, after the military crushing of the Prague Spring in 1968; the new awareness, stimulated by the peace and ecological movements, of ourselves as members of a fragile and potentially self-destructive world system; and the widespread perception that the implosion of Soviet-type communist systems implied a new global order.[1] Since that time, talk of global civil society has become popular among citizens' campaigners, bankers, diplomats, non-governmental organisations, and politicians—the term even peppered the speeches of former US Secretary of State, Madeleine Albright (2000)—to the point where the words themselves are as fickle as they are fashionable. The phrase 'global civil society' must certainly be used with caution. Like all other vocabularies with a political edge, its meaning is neither self-evident nor unprejudiced. When used carefully as an ideal type, which can in turn be wielded for purposes of descriptive interpretation, or political calculation, or normative judgement,[2] global civil society refers to the contemporary thickening and stretching of networks of socio-economic institutions across borders to all four corners of the earth, such that the peaceful or 'civil' effects of these non- governmental networks are felt everywhere, here and there, far and wide, to and from local areas, through wider regions to the planetary level itself.

Global civil society is a vast, interconnected, and multi-layered social space that comprises many hundreds of thousands of self-directing or non-governmental institutions and ways of life. It can be likened—to draw for a moment upon ecological similes—to a dynamic biosphere. This complex biosphere looks and feels expansive and polyarchic, full of horizontal push and pull, vertical conflict, and compromise, precisely because it comprises a bewildering variety of interacting habitats and species: organisations, civic and business initiatives, coalitions, social movements, linguistic communities, and cultural identities. All of them have at least one thing in common: across vast geographic distances and despite barriers of time, they deliberately

---

[1] *Among the earliest expressions of these concerns is the theory of a 'world civic culture' in Boulding (1988); the idea of 'global civilization' in the working paper by Richard Falk (1990); the theory of the 'internationalisation' of civil society and the terms 'cosmopolitan civil society' and 'global' or 'transnational' civil society in Keane (1989; 1991: 135) and Ougaard (1990). Among the first efforts to draw together this early work is Lipschutz (1992: 389–420).*

[2] *The importance of distinguishing among these different usages is analysed in more detail in my introduction to Keane (1988[1998]; 1998).*

organise themselves and conduct their cross-border social activities, business, and politics outside the boundaries of governmental structures, with a minimum of violence and a maximum of respect for the principle of civilised power-sharing among different ways of life.

To liken global civil society to a vast biosphere that stretches to every corner of the earth is to underscore both its great complexity and, as we shall see, its vulnerability to internal and external interference. Just as nearly every part of the earth, from the highest mountains to the deepest seas, supports life, so too global civil society is now found on virtually every part of the earth's surface. To be sure, everywhere it is tissue-thin, just like the natural biosphere, which resembles a paper wrapping that covers a sphere the size of a football; and its fringes, where ice and permafrost predominate, are virtually uninhabited. In the interior of the Antarctic, only restricted populations of bacteria and insects are to be found; and even on its coasts there are very few living inhabitants. Global civil society is similarly subject to geographic limits: whole zones of the earth—parts of contemporary Afghanistan, Burma, Chechnya, and Sierra Leone, for instance—are no-go

> Global civil society is a vast, interconnected, and multi-layered social space that comprises many hundreds of thousands of self-directing or non-governmental institutions and ways of life.

areas for civil society, which can survive only by going underground. But in those areas of the earth where it does exist, global civil society comprises many biomes: whole areas, like North America and the European Union, characterised by specific animals and plants and climatic conditions. Each biome in turn comprises large numbers of living ecosystems made up of clusters of organisms living within a non-living physical environment of rocks, soil, and climate. These ecosystems of global civil society—cities, business corridors, and regions, for instance—are interconnected. And they are more or less intricately balanced through continuous flows and recycling of efforts among, as it were, populations of individuals of the same species, which thrive within communities,

such as smaller cities, that are themselves embedded within non-living geographic contexts.

Biospheric similes are helpful in picturing the contours of global civil society, but they should not be overextended, if only because global civil society is not simply a naturally occurring phenomenon. Although it is naturally embedded within a terrestrial biosphere, global civil society is an ensemble of more or less tightly interlinked biomes that are in fact *social* processes. The populations, communities, and ecosystems of global civil society comprise flesh and blood, symbol-using individuals, house-holds, profit-seeking businesses, not-for-profit non-governmental organisations, coalitions, social movements, and cultural-religious groups. Its biomes feed upon the work of charities, lobby groups, citizens' protests, small and large corporate firms, independent media, trade unions, and sporting organisations: bodies like Amnesty International, Sony, the Catholic Relief Services, the Federation of International Football Associations, Transparency International, the International Red Cross, the Ford Foundation, News Corporation International, and the Indigenous Peoples Bio-Diversity Network. Such bodies lobby states, bargain with international organisations, pressure and bounce off other non-state bodies, invest in new forms of production, champion different ways of life, and engage in direct action in distant local communities: for instance, through 'capacity-building' programmes that supply jobs, clean running water, sporting facilities, hospitals, and schools. In these various ways, the members of global civil society help to conserve or to alter the power relations embedded in the chains of interaction linking the local, regional, and planetary orders. Their cross-border networks help to define and redefine who gets what, when, and how in the world. Of great importance is the fact that these networks have the power to shape new identities, even to stimulate awareness among the world's inhabitants that mutual understanding of different ways of life is a practical necessity, that we are being drawn into the first genuinely transnational order, a global civil society.

Defined in this way, the ideal-type concept of global civil society invites us to improve our understanding of the emerging planetary order, to think more deeply about it, in the hope that we can strengthen our collective powers of guiding and transforming it. This clearly requires sharpening up our courage to confront the unknown and to imagine different futures.[3] And it most definitely obliges us to abandon some old certainties and prejudices grounded in the past. The words 'global civil society' may be said to resemble signs that fix our thoughts on winding pathways that stretch not only in front of us but also behind us. To utter the words 'global civil society', for instance, is to sup with the dead, with an early modern world in which, among the educated classes of Europe, 'world civil society' meant something quite different than what it means, or ought to mean, today. Just how different our times are can be seen by dwelling for a moment on this older, exhausted meaning of 'world civil society'.

Consider the works of two influential authors of the eighteenth century: Emmerich de Vattel's Le droit des gens (1758) and Immanuel Kant's Idee zu einer allgemeinen Geschichte in weltbürgerlicher Absicht (1784) and Zum ewigen Frieden (1795).[4] These books stand at the end phase of a long cycle of European thinking which understands civil society (societas civilis) as the condition of living within an armed legal order that guarantees its subjects stable peace and good government. 'A State is more or less perfect according as it is more or less adapted to attain the end of civil society', wrote de Vattel, for whom the distinction between state and civil society was literally unthinkable. A civil society is a special form of government. It 'consists in procuring for its citizens the necessities, the comforts, and the pleasures of life, and in general their happiness; and in securing to each the peaceful enjoyment of his property and a sure means of obtaining justice, and finally in defending the whole body against all external violence' (de Vattel 1758: Ch. 1, section 6). Kant joined him in making it clear that civil society in this normative sense was not necessarily synonymous with the modern territorial state and its legal codes (ius civile). Their classically-minded theory of civil society emphasised that war-mongering among states and what Kant called the 'unsocial sociability' of subjects could be cured by subordinating them within a cosmopolitan alliance of states that is overridden and protected by its own legal codes. De Vattel insisted that states are obliged to respect and to protect what he called the universal society of

> These networks have the power to shape new identities, even to stimulate awareness among the world's inhabitants that mutual understanding of different ways of life is a practical necessity

the human race. 'When . . . men unite in civil society and form a separate State or Nation . . . their duties towards the rest of the human race remain unchanged' (1758: Ch. 1, section 11). Kant went further. He envisaged a 'law of world citizenship' (ius cosmopoliticum) which binds citizens and states into a higher republican commonwealth of states. This commonwealth, which resembles not a peace treaty (pactum pacis) but a league of peace (foedus pacificum), would put an end to violence for ever by treating its subjects as citizens of a new law-governed political union. This union he called 'universal civil society' (einer allgemein das Recht verwaltenden bürgerlichen Gesellschaft) (1784: fifth thesis).

The subsequent birth of modern colonial empires, the rise of nationalism from the time of the French Revolution, and the near-triumph of a global system of sovereign territorial states arguably confounded this eighteenth-century vision of global government or a world civil society. Two centuries later, the concept of 'international society', familiar in the work of scholars like Hedley Bull and Martin Wight, tried both to register this historical change and to preserve something of the old-fashioned meaning of societas civilis. The global system of interlocking territorial states was said not to resemble Hobbes' classic description of a lawless state of nature racked by deathly strivings after power over others. Territorial states were rather seen by Bull and others as socialised by the behaviour of other states. They were linked into 'the most comprehensive form of society on earth', an increasingly global framework of mutually recognised, informal customs, and formal rules: diplomatic protocol, embassy functions, multilateral treaties, and laws governing matters as diverse as trade and commerce, war crimes, and the right of non-interference (Bull and Holbraad 1978: 106). These state-enforced customs and rules that limit sovereignty by respecting it came to be called 'international society', a state-centred term that Hedley Bull considered to be a basic precondition of contemporary world order. International society, he

---

[3] A stimulating example of such rethinking that is guided by the idea of a global civil society is Edwards (2000).

[4] The emergence of the distinction between civil society and governmental/state institutions is examined in Keane (1988 [1999]).

wrote, 'exists when a group of states, conscious of certain common interests and common values, form a society in the sense that they conceive themselves to be bound by a common set of rules in their relations with one another, and share in the working of common institutions' (Bull 1995: 13; see also Bull 1990).

Contours

The terms 'world civil society' and 'international society' still have their champions,[5] but from the standpoint of the new concept of global civil society their 'governmentality' or state-centredness are today deeply problematic. Neither the classical term *societas civilis* nor the state-centric concept of 'international society' is capable of grasping the latter-day emergence of a non-governmental sphere that is called 'global civil society'. These words, 'global civil society', may well sound old-fashioned, but today they have an entirely new meaning and political significance. This is why the quest to map and measure the contours of global civil society is essential for clarifying both its possible conceptual meanings, its empirical scope and complexity, and its political potential.

The principle is clear—theories without observations are bland, observations without theories are blind—but the task is difficult. Some sketchy data are available thanks to the path-breaking contributions of bodies like the Union of International Associations, the Index on Civil Society project supported by CIVICUS (World Alliance for Citizen Participation), the Ford Foundation-funded comparative study of civil society in 22 countries, and this Global Civil Society Yearbook. These efforts confirm the widespread impression that, during the past century, the world has witnessed a tectonic—two hundred-fold—increase in the number and variety of civil society organisations operating at the planetary level.[6] Today, in addition to many hundreds of thousands of small, medium, and large firms doing business across borders, there are some 40,000 non-governmental, not-for-profit organisations operating at the global level; these international non-governmental organisations (INGOs) currently disburse more money than the United Nations (excluding the World

> The terms 'world civil society' and 'international society' still have their champions, but their state-centredness is today deeply problematic . . .

Bank and the International Monetary Fund); while more than two-thirds of the European Union's relief aid is currently channelled through them.

The actual contours of global civil society nevertheless remain elusive, for understandable reasons. Histories of the globalisation of civil society—studies of the rise of cross-border business, religion, and sport, for instance—are in short supply.[7] Most data are nation-based and systems of national accounting provide few detailed statistics on the economic contribution of corporations with a global reach (see Chapter 1). Researchers also disagree about which criteria—book translations, diasporas, links among global cities, the spread of the English language, telephone traffic, geographic locations of Web-sites, the mobility patterns of corporate nomads—are the most pertinent for picturing the networked character of the emerging global society. In-depth, qualitative accounts of global summits, forums, and other eye-catching events like the global campaign against landmines and public protests against the G7 powers are also rare. And studies of the intimate details of everyday life, especially research that concentrates on the civilising and socialising effects at the global level of matters like food consumption and television news-watching, are virtually non-existent.

These empirical and technical barriers to mapping and measuring global civil society are compounded by a basic epistemological difficulty. Simply put, its actors are not mute, empirical bits and bytes of data. Linked to territories but not restricted to territory, caught up in a vast variety of overlapping and interlocking institutions, these actors talk, think, interpret, question, negotiate, comply, innovate, resist. Dynamism is a chronic feature of global civil society:

[5] *Examples include Ralf Dahrendorf's stimulating neo-Kantian defence of a universal civil society in Dahrendorf (1988: 189): 'The next step towards a World Civil Society is the recognition of universal rights of all men and women by the creation of a body of international law.' Compare the argument that a 'mature anarchy' among states is a precondition of a strong 'international society' in Buzan (1991: 174–81).*

[6] *See the data covering the period 1909–97 presented in the Union of International Associations (1997-98: Vol. 4, 559); compare Risse-Kappen (1995), Matthews (1997: 50–66); and the misleadingly titled, country-by-country study by Lester M. Salamon et al. (1999).*

[7] *But on these topics see Hobsbawm (1989), Beeching (1979), and Maguire (1999).*

not the dynamism of the restless sea—a naturalistic simile suggested by Victor Pérez-Diaz (1993)[8]—but a form of self-reflexive dynamism marked by innovation, conflict, compromise, consensus, as well as rising awareness of the contingencies and dilemmas of global civil society itself. This civil society enables its participants—athletes, campaigners, musicians, religious believers, managers, aid-workers, medics, scientists, journalists, academics—to see through global civil society by calling it both *our* world and (more impersonally) *this* world. For this reason alone, those who speak of global civil society should not lose sight of its elusive, *idealtypisch* quality. The concept of global civil society has what Wittgenstein called 'blurred edges'. It is an ill-fitting term clumsily in search of an intelligent object that is always a subject on the run, striding unevenly in many different directions.

Sustained and deeper reflection on the subject, and a willingness to puncture old thinking habits, are definitely warranted. An example is the need to question the current tendency to speak of civil societies as 'national' phenomena and, thus, to suppose that global civil society and domestic civil societies are binary opposites. In fact, so-called domestic civil societies and the emerging global civil society are normally linked together in complex, cross-border patterns of looped and re-looped circuitry; or, to switch to similes drawn from the field of physics, the domestic and the global are marked by strong interactions of the kind that hold together the protons and neutrons inside an atomic nucleus. The use of ecological similes earlier in this essay may be questionable, but it serves the basic purpose of identifying the urgent need to develop theoretical imagery for better imagining global civil society, as it is and as it might become.

The rule of thumb, both in the past and in the present, is that the liveliest local civil societies are those enjoying the strongest links with the global civil society. So, in practice, the development of modern civil societies within the framework of European states and empires contained from the outset the seeds of their own transnationalisation. The roots of local civil societies are partly traceable to the revival of towns in Europe during the eleventh century, a revival that marked the beginning of the continent's rise to world eminence—and its laying of the foundations of a global civil society.[9] Although the distribution of these European towns—unusual clumps of people engaged in many different tasks, living in houses close together, often joined wall to wall—was highly uneven, with the weakest patterns of urbanisation in Russia and the strongest in Holland, they were typically linked to each other in networks or archipelagos stretching across vast distances. Wherever these urban archipelagos thrived, they functioned like magnets that attracted strangers fascinated by their well-lit complexity, their real or imagined freedom, or their higher wages. Towns like Bruges, Genoa, Nuremberg, and London resembled electric transformers. They constantly recharged life by adding not only motion but also tension to its elements. Town-dwellers seemed to be perpetually on the move. The constant rumble of wheeled carriages, the weekly or daily markets, and the numerous trades—floor polishers, pedlars, sawyers, chair-carriers—added to the sense of motion across distance. All these occupations rubbed shoulders with members of the better sort: merchants, some of them

> . . . Neither is capable of grasping the latter-day emergence of a non-governmental sphere that is called global civil society.

very rich, masters, mercenaries, engineers, ships' captains, doctors, professors, painters, architects, all of whom knew what it meant to travel through time and space.

The winding, twisting layout of towns added to their appearance of geographic and social dynamism. Medieval Europe was one of only two civilisations—the other was Islam—that fashioned large towns with an irregular maze of streets. What was different about the medieval and early modern European towns was their unparalleled freedom from the political authorities of the emerging territorial states. Local merchants, traders, craft guilds, manufacturers, and bankers formed the backbone of a long-distance money economy endowed with the power to dictate the terms and conditions on which governments ruled. Seen in this way, urban markets were the cuckoo's egg laid in the little nests of the medieval

---

[8] *Compare my remarks on the self-reflexivity of actually existing civil societies in Keane (1998: 49ff.).*

[9] *The section that follows draws upon Braudel (1981: Ch. 8). The urban origins of civil society are explored more fully in my work in preparation,* Global Civil Society?

towns. These nests were woven from various non-governmental institutions, which together with the markets helped to nurture something brand new: unbounded social space within which the absolutist state could be checked, criticised, and generally held at arm's length from citizens.

The birth of civil societies in this sense heralded the dawn of universal history marked by the constant reciprocal interaction between local and far-distant events (Aron 1978: 212–23). So it can be said that the eighteenth-century vision of cosmopolitanism defended by Vattel, Kant, and others was a child of local civil societies; and that cosmopolitanism was the privilege of those whose lives were already anchored in local civil societies. The other-regarding, outward-looking openness of these societies—their glimpse of themselves as part of a wider, complex world—constantly tempted them to engage that enlarged world. True, this worldliness, helped along by the superior naval power, deep-rooted pugnacity, and comparative immunity to disease that had earlier facilitated the rise of the West from around 1500 onwards often triumphed in violent, uncivilised form. Among its landmarks, which now appear barbaric by today's standards of civility, are the ruthless aggression of Almeida and Albuquerque in the Indian Ocean, the destruction of the Amerindian civilisations of Peru and Mexico, and the generalised hostility towards peoples as diverse as Muslim traders in the Mediterranean basin and aboriginal hunters and gatherers in such countries as Australia and Canada (McNeill 1963: Ch. 11). And yet—the birth and maturation of global civil society has been riddled with ironies—the worldliness of early modern civil societies undoubtedly laid the foundations for their later globalisation. An example is the colonising process triggered by the British Empire, which at its height governed nearly one-third of the world's population. Unlike the Spanish colonies, which were the product of absolute monarchy, the British Empire was driven not only by maritime-backed colonial power but also non-state initiatives, either for profit (as in the Virginia Company and the East India Company) or for religious ends, evident in extensive Christian missionary activity and the emigration of

dissenters: Puritans to New England, Quakers to Pennsylvania, Methodists to Australia, and Presbyterians to Canada.

Overdeterminations

The neologism 'global civil society' belatedly names this old tendency of local and regional civil societies to link up and to penetrate regions of the earth that had previously not known the ethics and structures of civil society in the modern European sense. But the neologism points as well to current developments that speed up the growth, and greatly 'thicken', the networks of transnational, non-governmental activities. What drives this globalisation of civil society? Its activist champions and their intellectual supporters sometimes pinpoint the power of autonomous moral choice. Treading in Gramsci's footsteps, usually without knowing it, they define global civil society as the space of social interaction 'located *between* the family, the state and the market and operating *beyond* the confines of national societies, polities, and economies' (Chapter 1, p.17). That leads them to speak, rather romantically, of global civil society as a realm of actual or potential freedom, as a 'third sector' opposed to the impersonal power of government and the greedy profiteering of the market (households typically disappear from the analysis at this point). 'Civil society participates alongside—not replaces—state and market institutions', write Naidoo and Tandon. Global civil society 'is the network of autonomous associations that rights-bearing and responsibility-laden citizens voluntarily create to address common problems, advance shared interests and promote collective aspirations' (1999: 6–7).[10] Such purist images reduce actually existing global civil society to campaign strategies harnessed to the normative ideal of citizens' autonomy at the global level. That in turn creates the unfortunate impression that global civil

---

[10] *The more recent campaign writings of Kumi Naidoo develop less romantic and more sophisticated images of global civil society, which, however, continues to be understood as the space wedged between global market forces and various forms of government (see for example Naidoo 2000: 34–6).*

society is a (potentially) unified subject, a 'third force',[11] something like a world proletariat in civvies, the universal object-subject that can snap its chains and translate the idea of a 'World Alliance for Citizen Participation' (Tandon 1999: 5) into reality, therewith righting the world's wrongs.

Although many things can be said for and against these conceptions, it is worth noting here that their Gramscian bias, which draws a thick line between (bad) business backed by government and (good) voluntary associations, leads them to understate the over-determined character of global civil society. 'Solidarity and compassion for the fate and well-being of others, including unknown, distant others, a sense of personal responsibility and reliance on one's own initiative to do the right thing; the impulse toward altruistic giving and sharing; the refusal of inequality, violence, and oppression' (de Oliveira and Tandon 1994: 2–3)[12] are undoubtedly significant, even indispensable motives in the globalisation of civil society. But one-sided emphasis on the free civic choices of men and women has the effect of obscuring other planetary forces that currently constrain and enable their actions.

Turbo-capitalism

Turbo-capitalism is undoubtedly among the principal energisers of global civil society.[13] To understand why this is so, and what the term 'turbo-capitalism' means, a brief comparison needs to be made with the system of Keynesian welfare state capitalism that predominated in the West after World War II. For some three decades, market capitalist economies like the United States, Sweden, Japan, the Federal Republic of Germany, and Britain moved in the direction of government-controlled capitalism. In terms of the production of goods and services, firms, plants, and whole industries were very much national phenomena; facilitated by international trade of raw materials and foodstuffs, production was primarily organised within territorially-bound national economies or parts of them. Markets were embedded in webs of government (Hobsbawm 1979: 313). In the era of turbo-capitalism, by contrast, markets tend to become disembedded. Turbo-capitalism is a species of private enterprise driven by the desire for emancipation from taxation restrictions, trade union intransigence, government interference, and all other external restrictions upon the free movement of capital in search of profit. Turbo-capitalism has strongly deregulatory effects, and on a global scale. The transnational operations of some 300 pace-setting firms in industries such as banking, accountancy, automobiles, airlines, communications, and armaments—their combined assets make up roughly a quarter of the world's productive assets—no longer function as production and delivery operations for national headquarters (Barnet and Cavanagh 1995: 15). Bursting the bounds of time and space, language and custom, they instead function as complex global flows or integrated networks of staff, money, information, raw materials, components, and products.[14]

Admittedly, the degree to which turbo-capitalist firms operate globally, like border-busting juggernauts, should not be exaggerated. Turbo-capitalism has a marked geographic bias. Its home base frequently lies within the OECD countries, and the capital, technology, and trade flows that it effects tend to be concentrated, for the time being, within rather than among the European, Asian-Pacific, and NAFTA/Latin American regions.[15] Only one of the top 100 transnational corporations has its headquarters outside the OECD, and nearly 60 per cent of world trade is between high income countries (see Tables R3 and R2 in part IV of this Yearbook) Yet, wherever the turbo-capitalist economy gains the upper hand, it has definite globalising effects. It leads to sharp increases in profit-driven joint ventures and co-production, licensing and sub-contracting agreements among local, regional, and global firms. For the first time ever, modern capitalist firms have unlimited grazing rights. Helped along by trade and investment liberalisation and radical improvements in transportation and communication

---

[11] The temptation to see global civil society in this way is evident in the introduction to Florini (2000: 1–15).

[12] Similar views are defended in Korten (1990) and in Habermas (1996: Ch. 8). The chief theoretical limitations of the (neo-) Gramscian approach are analysed in my forthcoming Global Civil Society? and in Keane (1998: 15–19).

[13] The term 'turbo-capitalism' is drawn from Luttwak (1999). It will be seen that my substantive account of the impact of the process differs considerably from that of Luttwak.

[14] By 1997 there were some 53,000 transnational corporations with 450,000 foreign subsidiaries operating worldwide. They spanned the world's principal economic regions in virtually every sector, from finance, raw materials, and agriculture to manufacturing and services. Selling goods and services to the value of some US$9.5 trillion in 1997, these transnational enterprises accounted for 70 per cent of world trade and around 20 per cent of the world's overall production. Some relevant data are usefully summarised in Held and McGrew (2000: 25). (See Table R3 in part IV of this Yearbook)

[15] Compare Hirst and Thompson (1999) and Mittelman (2000: 20–1).

technologies, they can do business anywhere in the world. The exceptions—North Korea, Afghanistan, Sierra Leone—prove the rule, especially since the collapse of the Soviet Empire and the beginning of the Chinese experiment with state-engineered market reforms. Some economists describe this trend in terms of the historic development of global commodity chains: geographically dispersed yet transactionally linked sequences of functions in which each phase adds market value to the overall worldwide process of production of goods or services (Gereffi 1996: 427–39; Gereffi and Korzeniewicz 1994: Ch. 5).

> The Gramscian bias of the activists and their intellectual supporters draws a thick line between (bad) business backed by government and (good) voluntary associations . . .

When Adam Smith famously analysed the 'division of labour' within the emerging civil societies of the Atlantic region, his references to the specialisation of workers within different parts of the production process had no specific geographic connotations. He could suppose that industries and services of all kinds enjoyed a 'natural protection' from foreign competition thanks to the vagaries of geographical distance. That supposition continued to be plausible even during the vigorous growth spurt of international economic integration before World War I and until two decades ago, when shallow integration (Dicken 2000: 5)—arm's length trade in goods and services among independent firms and through international movements of capital—was the norm. The system of turbo-capitalism, by contrast, draws everybody and everything within its wake into processes of deep integration, which extend from visible and invisible trading to the production of goods and services by means of globally connected commodity chains organised by transnational corporations.

These processes of deep integration are highly complex and uneven. Turbo-capitalism has unleashed globalising forces but this has not yet resulted in a fully globalised world economy. Turbo-capitalism does not lead to a 'global marketplace', let alone a 'global village'. Its effects are variable, ranging from very weak or non-existent forms of integration to very strong or full integration. At one end of the continuum stand whole peoples and regions who are routinely ignored by the dynamics of turbo-capitalism. Some parts of sub-Saharan Africa fall into this category; such areas, victims of 'capitalist apartheid'—a term used by the Peruvian economist Hernando de Soto[16]—suffer the consequences of organised neglect by turbo-capitalist investors. Elsewhere, further along the continuum, straightforward exchange across vast distances between wealthy core and poorer peripheral areas—for instance, the exporting of granite mined in Zimbabwe to the kitchens and bathrooms of western Europe—is the norm. Then, at the opposite end of the continuum, there are sectors of economic life, like the highly unstable, twenty-four-hour financial speculation conducted in cities like New York, London, and Tokyo, in which the whole earth is a playground for turbo-capital.

Within the industrial and service sectors of global civil society, turbo-capitalism also slices through territorial and time barriers by bringing about highly complex forms of market integration involving the fragmentation of production processes and their geographical relocation and functional reintegration on a global scale. In accordance with what can be called the Low Cost and Safety Principle, turbo-capitalist firms globalise production by transferring sophisticated state-of-the-art production methods to countries where wages are extremely low. A number of poorer countries, Mexico and China among them, are consequently now equipped with the infrastructural means of housing any service or industrial operation, whether airline ticket and holiday telephone sales or capital-intensive, high-tech production of commodities like computers and automobiles. Such trade and investment within firms also leads to the formation of a global labour pool.[17] When businesses develop globally interconnected chains of investment, resources and finished products and services workers based in richer countries like Germany and France are effectively forced to compete with workers living in places—China, Singapore, Taiwan, South Korea—where wages are

---

[16] *De Soto (2000) argues that some five-sixths of humanity has been denied the economic fruits of globalisation.*

[17] *Estimates are that about a third of world trade is now taken up by trade between one part of a global firm and its other affiliates, and the proportion is growing. Such 'self-trading', oiled by so-called transfer pricing, is strongly evident in the operations of firms like General Electric, which like many other firms operating across the Mexican-US border ships machinery components to its own subsidiary in Nuevo Laredo.*

low and social entitlements of workers are either poorly protected or non-existent.[18]

Market Contradictions

The striking social discrepancies produced by market processes within global civil society have led some observers—Sakamoto Yoshikazu, for instance (2000: 98–116)—to question whether market forces with such destructive consequences properly belong within the category of global civil society. Yoshikazu's query is important, if only because it exemplifies the strong tendency within the existing academic literature on global civil society to draw upon the deeply problematic, originally Gramscian distinction between civil society—the realm of non-profit, non-governmental organisations—and the market— the sphere of profit-making and profit-taking commodity production and exchange. Yoshikazu, treading Gramsci's path, mistakenly conflates the different possible usages— empirical interpretation, strategic calculation, normative judgement—of the concept of global civil society. On that basis, his understandably strong dislike of the socially negative (disruptive or outright destructive) effects of market forces within actually existing civil societies moves him to banish the market altogether from the concept of global civil society. The reasoning secretly draws upon the distinction between 'is' and 'ought' in order to defend the latter against the former. The term global civil society is thereby turned into a normative utopia. Ethically speaking, it becomes a 'pure' concept: an unadulterated 'good', like a sparkling coveted diamond that all would want to prize, especially if offered it on a soft velvet cushion of fine words. Yoshikazu's normative reasoning is tempting—who but curmudgeons, ideologists, and crooks could be ethically opposed to civil society in his sense?—but it should be rejected, for three reasons. Normatively speaking, it implies that global civil society could in future survive without money or monetary exchanges, rather as nineteenth- century and early-twentieth-century communists disastrously imagined that future communist society would be bound together by such attributes as love, hard work, and mutuality. In matters of strategy, the purist concept of global civil society fares no better. If the aim is to create and/or to strengthen global civil society by displacing market forces, then anything related to the market—money, jobs, workers, trade unions— cannot by definition be of much use in struggles to achieve that civilising

goal. Otherwise, the means—the commodification of social relations—would corrupt and potentially overpower the envisaged end: the humanisation of social relations. It seems, unrealistically, that global civil society will be possible only if people behave as good people. Work, trade unions, corporate philanthropy, small businesses, advanced technologies supplied by transnational firms: none of this (it is supposed) could or should play a part in the struggle to expand and thicken the cross-border social networks that comprise global civil society.

Finally, there is a strong empirical objection to the attempt to separate markets from global civil society. The dualism between market and global civil society wielded by Yoshikazu and others is a phantom, a bad abstraction, for in reality markets are always a particular form of socially and politically mediated interaction structured by money, production, exchange, and consumption. Global civil

> . . . this one-sided emphasis on the free civic choices of men and women has the effect of obscuring other planetary forces that currently constrain and enable their actions.

society as we know and experience it today could not survive for a day without the market forces unleashed by turbo-capitalism. The converse rule also applies: the market forces of turbo-capitalism could not last a day without other global civil society institutions, like households, community associations, regions, and linguistically shared social norms like friendship, trust, and non-violent cooperation.

To emphasise that market activity is always socially embedded runs counter to the view of those who warn that 'global capital' is a profits-hungry

[18] *The figures are telling of this new development: in 1975, the top dozen exporters of goods were almost all rich capitalist countries with relatively small wage differentials. The highest average hourly wage was in Sweden (US$7.18); the lowest was in Japan (US$3), a differential of just under two-and-a-half times. By 1996, driven by the forces of Turbo-capitalism, a global labour pool had developed, with a corresponding dramatic widening of wage differences. The highest average hourly wages were found in Germany (US$31.87) and the lowest in China (US$0.31): a pay differential of more than a hundred times. The striking differences are of course compounded by much longer hours of work (sometimes up to 80 hours a week) and poorly protected working conditions in the low-wage sectors of the global economy. See Anderson and Cavanagh (2000: 30).*

juggernaut ruthlessly breaking down political borders and smashing through walls of social restraint embodied in local communities and other institutions. 'Cold-blooded, truly arm's-length and therefore purely contractual relations exemplify the entire spirit of turbo-capitalism', writes Luttwak (1999: 43). Such descriptions of the spread of global business correctly capture something of its swashbuckling, buccaneer, time-and-distance-conquering tendencies. They also point to its amoral profiteering as a consequence of companies' geographic separation of investment decisions and their social consequences. These descriptions pose a normative problem: the need to deal politically with the chronic tendency of

> **Global civil society as we know and experience it could not survive for a day without the market forces unleashed by turbo-capitalism**

commodity production and exchange to pick the locks of global civil society and to roam freely through its rooms, like a thief in the night. 'As long as capitalism remains triumphant', comments Soros, 'the pursuit of money overrides all other social considerations . . . The development of a global economy has not been matched by the development of a global society' (1999: 102).

While these claims are sobering, they arguably exaggerate the degree to which turbo-capitalism has become unhinged or disembedded from the emerging global civil society. No business, global business included, can properly function as business unless it draws upon and nurtures the non-market environment of civil society in which it is more or less embedded. The artificial distinction between 'the market' and 'global civil society' obscures this fundamental point and in so doing obscures a basic dynamic of our times: the tendency of turbo-capitalism to nurture and simultaneously disorder the structures of global civil society within which it operates.

It is important to grasp these positive and negative dynamics. On the positive, society-enhancing side, some sectors of global business greatly 'thicken' the communications networks that enable all organisations and networks to operate at the global level. Under modern conditions, states rather than global businesses have often been the inventors of new technologies of transport and communication. While this rule holds true, say, for the World Wide Web and geostationary satellites, subsequent new investments in these and other communications technologies are typically market-driven: they go where the returns are high. The commercial introduction of these technologies, as well as wide-bodied jet aircraft, fibre optics, super-freighters, and containerisation, have several cumulative—revolutionary—effects. Through leased networks, organisations large and small can now operate over vast geographical distances, thanks to the growth of country-to-country links, regional hub-and-spoke networks, and global telecommunications services (Langdale 1989). There is a sharp reduction of both the operating costs and the time it takes both information and things and people to move from one part of the world to another. The friction of distance is greatly reduced.[19]

Business firms also have socialising effects by virtue of their tendency to cluster geographically in the ecosystems of global civil society, in towns and cities that form part of a wider region. They create regionally-based 'untraded interdependencies' (see Storper 1997; also Amin and Thrift 1994). Examples of such thriving regions include Seoul-Inchon, southern California, the M4 corridor, and the conurbations of Stuttgart, Tokyo, Paris-Sud, and Milan. The recently created Special Economic Zones, open coastal cities, and priority development areas in China also count as striking examples. Like bees to a hive, firms swarm to such places not simply because it is profitable (thanks to reduced transaction costs) but because their own profitability requires the cultivation of densely textured socio-cultural ties ('untraded interdependencies') that come with agglomeration. The regional civil society becomes the hive and propolis of business activity. Firms find that face-to-face interaction with clients, customers,

---

[19] *The growth of market-driven communications within global civil society 'shrinks' the world, even though this time-space contraction is extremely uneven. Shaped like a slim octopus with the globe half in its clutches, influential cities, together with powerful national economies and globe-straddling firms, are drawn together as if they are part of the same body; but while certain places and people become the head and eyes and tentacles of global civil society, whole geographic areas and whole peoples, many millions of them, are left out and left behind in the spaces between the slim tentacles of communication.*

and competitors is easier. They find as well that their chosen patch contains social spaces for gathering business information, monitoring and maintaining patterns of trust, establishing common rules of business behaviour, and socialising with others: in places like clubs, bars, cinemas, theatres, sports venues, and restaurants. And the regional civil society acts as 'technopole' (Castells and Hall 1994) or 'technology district' (Storper 1992). It enables firms to enhance their capacity for technical innovation: they can better develop, test, mimic, and track innovations, find new gaps in the market, and react more quickly to changing patterns of demand.

Turbo-capitalist firms, aided by the local and regional networks of smaller firms with which they do business, also have definite civilising effects on the global civil society in which they are embedded. For a start, the hundreds of thousands of firms that inhabit the markets of global civil society are generally antipathetic to violence. Some of them, in certain contexts, have shameful records of colluding with the violence of political authorities hell-bent on destroying their opponents—as happened in South Africa before the revolution against apartheid, or as now happens in the global small arms industry. There are even global businesses, like the diamond and cocaine trades, that operate through murderous networks of armed guerillas. Yet—the qualification is important—most global businesses share a commonly perceived, long-term interest in the eradication of violence. Their chief executive officers, for instance, do not like working within the deathly shadows of knee-capping, abduction, or murder. In general, the conduct of business, which requires the freedom to calculate risk over time, prudently and without interruption, is made difficult or impossible when violence threatens, which is why investment is chronically low, or non-existent, in zones of uncivil war, like Sierra Leone, southern Sudan, Chechnya, and parts of the former Yugoslavia.

Turbo-capitalist firms also generate—for some people—income, goods and services, and jobs (50 per cent of the world's manufacturing jobs are now located outside the OECD region, a twelve-fold increase in four decades). These firms produce some measure of 'social capital' by training local employees in such skills as self-organisation, punctuality, and forward-looking initiative. Particularly in the field of consumer retailing, through commercial radio and television, firms also engage local cultures for the purpose of constructing convincing worlds of more or less shared symbols, ideas, and values. Consumer retailing by transnational conglomerates demonstrates the obsolescence of the neo-Gramscian distinction between struggles for meaningful authenticity (for instance, in the idioms of food, dress, language, music, and dance) in the realm of 'civil society' as narrowly conceived by Yoshikazu and others, and money-centred conflicts over wealth and income in 'the economy'. To the extent that global civil society becomes media-saturated, with intense pressure to consume, conflicts about the generation of wealth and income within 'the economy' are

> Most global businesses share a commonly perceived, long-term interest in the eradication of violence. Investment is chronically low, or non-existent in zones of uncivil war.

simultaneously disputes about symbolic meanings (see Ong 1999). The development of up-market services—hotels in Dubai boasting seven-star status and featuring exotic menus of breaded Dover sole and char-grilled bison fillets—and the down-market retailing of products like McDonald's, Pepsi, and American television programmes to the villages of south Asia and central America and to cities like Shanghai, Sydney, Johannesburg, and Cairo, if anything, have the effect of accentuating local cultural diversity within global civil society. This is partly because profit-seeking, turbo-capitalist retailers themselves see the need to tailor their products to local conditions and tastes; and also because (as Marshall Sahlins has wittily pointed out[20]) local consumers display vigorous powers of reinterpreting and 'overstanding' these commodities, thus giving them new and different meanings.

---

[20] Sahlins (1999: 34): 'Why are well-meaning Westerners so concerned that the opening of a Colonel Sanders in Beijing means the end of Chinese culture? A fatal Americanization. But we have had Chinese restaurants in America for over a century, and it hasn't made us Chinese. On the contrary, we obliged the Chinese to invent chop suey. What could be more American than that? French fries?'

Market Failures

Caution should certainly be exercised on this last point, for the truth is that global corporations today enter our living rooms aglow in public-image or 'pro-social' advertising. Many firms, backed up by high-flying, well-paid 'ethics officers', present the world with their 'we too are citizens of the world' corporate credo and do their best to distract their (potential) critics from saying that these firms employ eight-year-olds in sweatshops or brazenly trample upon the environment. Corporate advertising is a potential menace when it comes to understanding clearly the dynamics of global civil society. Although turbo-capitalism feeds and fuels the delicate social ecosystems of the emerging global civil society, sadly this is only half the story, essentially because turbo-capitalism also operates as a contradictory force within global civil society. Like a predator, it misuses and depletes its resources, endangers some of its species, even ruining whole habitats, the effects of which ricochet throughout the ecosystems of global civil society. Not surprisingly, the predatory effects of turbo-capitalism meet resistance: global resistance that ranges from micro-experiments with credit unions, maximum wages, and time banks, through petitions (like the Jubilee 2000 campaign, which has collected 25 million signatures worldwide in favour of debt cancellation—see Chapter 3) to militant street protests by individuals and groups, gas masks and megaphones in hand, who are convinced that the cutting edge of anti-capitalist politics is extra-parliamentary.

The sources of this protest against turbo-capitalism are not hard to find. To begin with, the business units of turbo-capitalism chronically exercise what C. B. Macpherson (1973: 42–50; 71–75) once called 'extractive power' over their workers and other dependents, for instance through day-by-day hiring and firing practices and their ability to pay ruinously low, take-it-or-leave-it wages. These businesses also have at their disposal the power to ruin others' lives by deciding to invest here and not there, or instead by moving their investments from here to there. Global civil society is also under great

> Many global corporations today enter our living rooms aglow in public image or 'pro-social' advertising to distract potential critics from saying they employ eight-year-olds or brazenly trample upon the environment

pressure to adopt more or less unaffordable turbo-capitalist living standards, many of them originally American, like automobility, Windows 2000, microscooters, Mastercards, shopping malls, and endless chatter about 'choice'. If during the eighteenth century a cosmopolitan was typically someone who thought *à la française*, who in other words identified Paris with cosmopolis, then three centuries later, thanks to turbo-capitalism, a cosmopolitan might turn out to be someone whose tastes are fixated on New York and Washington, Los Angeles, and Seattle.

Pressured by turbo-capitalism, global civil society, which otherwise displays a strong tendency towards polyarchy, naturally cradles new property relations, with staggering discrepancies in wealth and income distribution. The economies of giant firms like Ford and Philip Morris exceed the gross domestic products of countries like Norway and New Zealand. Meanwhile, a small elite of winners, the 'transnational managerial class' (Cox 1986), less politely the bourgeois cosmocracy—corporate executives, peripatetic lawyers, rock-stars, jet-age nomads living in penthouse apartments in choice locations, like the Upper East Side of Manhattan—monopolises more than its share of wealth and income. The combined wealth of the world's richest 200 billionaires reached an astonishing US$1.1 trillion in 1999, the year in which the combined incomes of 582 million people living in the least developed countries was US$146 billion, or less than a dollar a day. The three richest people in the world own assets that exceed the combined GDP of the world's 48 poorest countries (Hirsh 2000: 79; Mittelman 2000: 246). For the time being, this bourgeois cosmocracy exercises power globally over a mass of survivors or losers of varying affluence or poverty. They do so despite the opposition of market-shy governments and the growth of new forms of transnational protest, like the recent battles for the streets of Seattle, Prague, and Québec City led by groups like Earth First! and the Ruckus Society, and backed up by contingents of farmers, environmentalists, students, aboriginal rights activists, and trade unionists.

Not surprisingly—a final item on the balance sheet— turbo-capitalism strengthens the hand of market domination over the non-profit institutions of civil society, which are twisted and torn into bodies that obey the rules of accumulation and profit-maximisation. Some non-governmental organisations formerly dependent on government funding, like the Seattle-based service agency Pioneer Human Services, opt for self-financing through their own for-profit business enterprises. Market forces produce great inequalities among INGOs: Greenpeace, with a $100 million annual budget, and the World Wildlife Fund, with $170 million, are wealthier than the UN Environment Programme and most other state-level governments they deal with (Shaw 2000: 14). In some sectors, it is as if the emerging global civil society is merely the appendage of the turbo-capitalist economy. Some non-governmental organisations—so-called business NGOs or BINGOs—even explicitly model themselves on business enterprises by developing commercial departments, head-hunters, media sections, and private fund-raising and investment strategies. The neat division between the corporate and NGO worlds consequently becomes blurred.

The New Medievalism

Although turbo-capitalism is arguably the force that most strongly energises the non-governmental sector from within, global civil society is not simply its child. To repeat: global civil society is overdetermined by various forces. It is a 'syndrome' (Mittelman 2000) of processes and activities which have multiple origins and multiple dynamics, some of them—like the recent collapse and discrediting of communism—more conjunctural than deep-seated. Together, these forces ensure that global civil society is not a single, unified domain and that it is not turned into something that is coming to resemble a combined factory, warehouse, and shopping mall retailing consumer products on a global scale—let's say, a version of Disney's 'Its a Small World After All'. Global civil society is not simply reducible to the logic of commodity production and exchange, which helps to explain why the ideal of a global civil society currently appeals to an astonishing variety of conflicting social interests, ranging from groups clustered around the World Bank to broad-minded Muslims defending their faith and radical ecological groups pressing for sustainable development.

If the institutions of global civil society are not merely the products of civic initiative and market forces, then is there a third force at work in nurturing and shaping it? It can be argued that global civil society is also the by-product of state or inter-state action, or inaction. Examples are easy to find. Most obvious is the set of political institutions and agreements that play a vital role in fostering the growth of turbo-capitalism, for instance the 'Final Act' of the Uruguay Round of trade negotiations, a 1994 agreement that had the backing of 145 states and that led to the establishment of the World Trade Organisation and to the extension of the principle of freer trade into such areas as copyrights, patents, and services. Meanwhile, in fields like telecommunications and air, land and sea traffic, political bodies such as the International Postal Union, most of them resting formally on agreements to which states are signatories, exercise formidable regulatory powers that enable many parts of global civil society to keep moving at a quickening pace (see Tables R6 and R10 in part IV of this Yearbook).

Government agencies, much more than corporate philanthropy, also currently play a major, positive-sum role in protecting, funding, and nurturing non-profit organisations in every part of the earth where there is a lively civil society (Salamon 1999, see also Pinter, Chapter 8).[21] Included in this category are civil organisations that operate on the margins of the governmental institutions that license them in the first place. Examples include the International Committee of the Red Cross which, although non-governmental, is mandated under the Geneva Convention and is linked to states through the organisation of the International Federation of Red Cross and Red Crescent Societies; similarly, the International Association of Religious Freedom, a forum for inter-religious dialogue, has accredited NGO status at the UN and UNESCO levels. State-funded systems of mass higher education linked together by shared languages, common teaching and research methods, staff and student exchanges, and compatible hardware also fall into this category of state-enabled civil organisations. Governmental institutions also sometimes operate as important catalysts of activity within global society, for instance by hosting global conferences like the much-publicised 1992 Global Forum and Earth Summit held in Rio de Janeiro, and the follow-up women's and population conferences in Beijing and Cairo (see Pianta, Chapter 7).

---

[21] The comparative findings are cited in Evans (1997); and on the funding of Japanese INGOs by the Ministry of Foreign Affairs and Ministry of Posts and Telecommunications, see Menju and Aoki (1995).

This logic of catalysis is also evident in the proliferation of human rights groups like Charter 77 after the 1975 signing of the Helsinki Accords, one of whose 'baskets' required signatories to guarantee the civil and political rights of their citizens; similar catalytic effects have resulted from the 1993 Vienna Conference on Human Rights, where 171 states reaffirmed their commitment to the principle of the 'universal nature of the rights and freedoms' specified in the International Bill of Human Rights.

These well-known examples illustrate the less familiar rule that global civil society should not be thought of as the natural enemy of political institutions. The vast mosaic of groups, organisations, and initiatives that comprise global civil society are variously related to governmental structures at the local, national, regional, and supranational levels. Some sectors of social activity, the so-called anti-government organisations (AGOs), are openly hostile to the funding and regulatory powers of state institutions. Other sectors, for instance those in which the acronym NGO rather means 'next government official', are openly collaborative, either serving as willing contractors for governments or aiming at dissolving themselves into governmental structures (Tendler 1982). Still others (GONGOs or GRINGOs, like the International Air Transport Association and the World Conservation Union) are the dependent creations of state authorities. In between these two extremes stand those social actors (for example, Médecins sans Frontières, Oxfam, Greenpeace) who slalom between self-reliance and legal and political dependency. They form ad hoc partnerships with governments; lobby donor intergovernmental bodies like the World Bank to change their policies; and work with other non-governmental organisations in rich and poor countries, zones of peace and war alike.

More reflection is definitely needed on the complex, unstable relationship between global civil society and the hotchpotch of political-legal institutions in which it is embedded (see Young 1994; Rosenau and Czempiel 1992). One important generalisation can safely be made, which is that unlike the early modern civil societies, which typically hatched within the well-established containers of empires and territorial states, global civil society has emerged and today flourishes in the absence of a global state or world empire. Practising the art of *divide et impera* from below, well-organised actors within global civil society, turbo-capitalist firms for instance, often manage to transform territorial governments into their submissive courtesans or to evade the regulatory hand of such governments, whose own attempts to guard jealously their own remaining sovereign powers ties the hands of transnational governing bodies like the United Nations.

Those who conclude from these trends that the term 'global civil society' is therefore meaningless—as if the term could only ever be the Siamese twin of the term 'global state' (Brown, 1999)—overlook the novelty of our situation. It is true that there is currently no global state and that it is most improbable that in future one could be developed, assuming that it would be desirable to do so. The current growth spurt of global civil society under 'lawless' conditions outpaces governments of all descriptions, and it contains within it a pressing constitutional agenda: the need to find the appropriate form of global governance so that something like publicly accountable, multi-level government can develop on a global scale.

There is currently no consensus about what form this agenda might take, partly because of the inordinate strength of those forces that champion unregulated, free market turbo-capitalism *über alles* and partly because some of their opponents slam 'globalisation' in the name of stronger and more nationalist territorial states or through vague notions of 'deglobalisation' and the 'deconcentration and decentralisation of institutional power' through 'the re-empowerment of the local and the national' (Bello 2000). It should be obvious that global civil society requires political and legal protection through legal and political bodies that guarantee basic freedoms of association, protect those whose voices are ignored, enforce contracts, preserve property, and rule against violent crimes (Christenson 1997; Falk 1992). Less obvious is which courts, governments, or governing regimes are reliably capable of granting such protection. Some political theorists defend the

> Although turbo-capitalism is arguably the force that most strongly energises the non-governmental sector from within, global civil society is not simply its child...

neo-Kantian principle of a transnational democratic legal order, a community of all democratic communities, something resembling a global *Rechtsstaat* of the kind implied in Art. 28 of the Universal Declaration of Human Rights: 'Everyone is entitled to a social and international order in which the rights and freedoms set forth in the Declaration can be fully realised.' Others anticipate a second-best scenario that owes everything to Emmerich de Vattel: a complex international system of nominally sovereign, democratic states that are the voting members in a variety of international forums. Still others foresee a new compromise between these two options: a cosmopolitan process of democratisation through which citizens gain a voice within their own states and in sites of power among their states (Archibugi and Held 1994).

There are evidently no guarantees that any of these competing views can or will prevail, not least because the form of political-legal institutions that currently frames global civil society has much more in common with the world addressed in Johannes Althusius's *Politica* (1614), a many-sided world of overlapping and potentially conflicting political structures, primordial groups, and differently sized political associations, and federalist strivings for both particularism and universalism, community, and ecumene (see Althusius 1614; von Gierke 1966 [1880]). From a normative point of view, it may be that this Althusian world of political structures will facilitate a new, multi-layered global political settlement defined by a core of institutions designed to rein in the most destructive behaviours and a periphery of governing institutions based on more voluntary and non-coercive regulations (Edwards 2000). This is the undecided future. For now, it is clear that global civil society is today flourishing within a thoroughly modern, strangely 'neo-medieval' mélange of overlapping legal structures and political bodies that come in all shapes and sizes. The emerging patterns of regulation of the Internet are a pertinent example. The healthy mix of self-regulation and no regulation that once characterised the medium is now withering away. So too is the presumption that the Internet abolishes both geographical boundaries

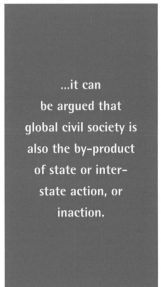

...it can be argued that global civil society is also the by-product of state or inter-state action, or inaction.

and territorially based laws. In fact, a regulatory net is being cast over the Internet by three intersecting types of political institutions. Territorial states like South Korea have outlawed gambling Websites; in Britain, the Regulation of Investigatory Powers Act has granted the police broad powers of access to e-mail and other online communications; and a French court has banned the Internet portal firm Yahoo! from providing French users with images of Nazi memorabilia otherwise posted on its American sites. Meanwhile, supranational institutions are also experimenting with their regulatory powers. A new European Union law drawn from the Brussels Convention entitles consumers to sue EU-based Internet sites in their own countries so long as it can be proved that the site was targeted at their countries; the Hague Convention aims to enforce foreign judgements in matters such as contractual disputes, libel and intellectual property claims; and the Council of Europe has drafted the world's first global treaty on cyber-crime, which aims to harmonise laws against hacking, child pornography, and Internet fraud (see Naughton, Chapter 6). Finally, the 'neo-medieval' pattern of multiple jurisdictions is reinforced by moves by e-commerce firms to claw back regulatory powers through so-called mechanisms of alternative dispute resolution: in effect, they are pushing for a new market-based system of private laws which would enable companies to operate outside of the courts within a minimum framework of 'safe harbour' rules guaranteeing privacy and consumer protection.[22]

This mélange of political and legal structures in the field of the Internet is present in many other policy areas, so much so that the so-called system of 'global governance' hardly deserves the name 'system'. It comprises a clutter of nation states and regional and local governments; intergovernmental agencies and programmes, like United Nations Children's Fund (UNICEF) as well as intergovernmental structures with sectoral responsibilities like the World Trade Organisation and the OECD; and the International Court of Justice and other global institutions seeking

[22] Economist, *13 January 2001*: 25–7.

> **Global civil society has emerged and today flourishes in the absence of a global state or world empire**

to enforce the rule of law. The hotchpotch system of global governance also includes global accords, treaties, and conventions such as the Montreal Protocol covering ozone levels; policy summits and meetings like the Davos World Economic Forum; and new forms of public deliberation and conflict resolution like truth commissions that have a global impact. Summarising the dynamics of these interacting and overlapping neo-medieval structures is not easy, but they are undoubtedly having the effect of slowly eroding both the immunity of sovereign states from suit and the presumption that statutes do not extend to the territory of other states. There are many tendencies in this direction. INGOs are licensed by bodies like the Council of Europe and the United Nations. Non-governmental groups participate in election monitoring and as *amici curiae* in the proceedings of such bodies as the European Court of Justice and the Inter-American Court of Human Rights. War crimes cases are given global publicity thanks to new bodies like the Hague Tribunal; the project of establishing an international criminal court is nearly completed; and local courts show ever greater willingness to prosecute symbolically 'foreign' acts of wrongdoing.[23]

An Earthly Paradise?

Such 'legalisation' of global civil society, the effort to remedy its permanent crisis of representation by giving it legal and political voices and injecting the principle of public accountability into governing institutions, has deeper roots in the post-eighteenth-century opening of state constitutions to international law (Stein 1994). It arguably helps stabilise and perhaps strengthen this society, even though it does not turn it instantly into paradise on earth. Global civil society is certainly rich in freedoms beyond borders, for example, to invest and to accumulate money and wealth; to travel and to reunite with others; to build infrastructures by recovering memories, protecting the vulnerable, and generating new wealth and income; to denounce

and to reduce violence and uncivil war; and, generally, to press the principle that social and political power beyond borders should be subject to greater public accountability. Such freedoms are currently unfolding in a hell-for-leather, Wild West fashion, and are also very unevenly distributed. The freedoms of global civil society are exclusionary and fail to produce equalities; in other words, global civil society is not really global. It is not a *universal society*.

Vast areas of the world, and certainly the large majority of the world's population who live there, are excluded. They are made to feel like victims of a predatory mode of foreign intervention: they are shut out from global civil society, or uprooted by its dynamism, imprisoned within its discriminatory structures and policies, like unpayable debt-service payments, or victimised by scores of uncivil wars (Dallmayr 1999; Falk 1999: Chs 3, 5, 8). Still others—many Muslims say—are made to feel that the enormous potential of global civil society to expand dialogue among civilisations, to 'affirm differences through communication', is being choked to death by the combined forces of global markets and military might, manifested for instance in the violent repression of the Palestinians by the dangerous alliance between the United States and Israel.[24]

Then there are the cruel facts of communication poverty. Three-quarters of the world's population (which now totals 6 billion) are too poor to buy a book; a majority has never made a phone call; and only 1 per cent currently have access to the Internet (Keane 1999). All these points serve to fuel the conclusion that global civil society is currently a string of oases of freedom in a vast desert of localised injustice. Not only that, but the privileges within this oasis cannot be taken for granted, for the plural freedoms of global civil society are threatened constantly by the fact that it is a breeding ground for manipulators who take advantage of its available freedoms. The growth of borderless exchanges encourages winners, global corporations for instance, to cultivate ideologies that slake their thirst for power over others. Free market, IMF ideologies linked with turbo- capitalism—talk of deregulation, structural

---

[23] *From the* Los Angeles Times *(11 August 2000: A11) comes a random example: the order, applied during early August 2000 by a US District Court in Manhattan, requiring Radovan Karadzic to pay $745 million to a group of twelve women who filed a civil suit, accusing him of responsibility for killings, rapes, kidnappings, torture, and other atrocities.*

[24] *Interview with Professor Abou Yaareb al-Marzouki, Hammamet, Tunisia, 18 April 2001.*

adjustment, opportunity, risk-taking, consumer choice—have a strong affinity with these corporate winners.

Borderless exchanges also produce strong political reactions in favour of the local and national, for instance among losers who react to their dis-empowerment resentfully by taking revenge upon others, sometimes cruelly, guided by ideological, uncivil presumptions like xenophobic nationalism. In other words, global civil society is constantly threatened with takeovers in the name of some or other organised ideology. Ideologies like the free market and nationalism take advantage of the growth of global civil society by roaming hungrily through its free social spaces, treating others as competitors or as enemies to be defeated or injured or left to starve to death. Inequalities of power, bullying, and fanatical, violent attempts to de-globalise are chronic features of global civil society. Understood normatively as a transnational system of social networks of non-violent polyarchy, global civil society is a wish that has not yet been granted to the world.

On Violence

Violence is undoubtedly among the greatest enemies of global civil society, whose tendency to non-violence stems partly from the fact that its participants more or less share a cosmopolitan outlook, for instance by displaying a strong dislike of war, a facility for languages, or a commitment to ordinary courtesy and respect for others. Given this tendency towards non-violence, it should come as no surprise that the contemporary revival of interest in civil society and the corresponding invention of the new term 'global civil society' have much to do with such twentieth-century experiences as total war, aerial bombardment, concentration camps, and the threat of nuclear annihilation. World War II was undoubtedly a turning point in the contemporary history of global civil society. That global war certainly encouraged post-colonial and 'liberation' struggles and hence the spread of the modern territorial state system throughout the rest of the world (Badie 1992). But it also triggered exactly the opposite trend: the long-term delegitimisation of state sovereignty because of the total mobilisation and sacrifice of untold millions by both victorious and vanquished states, who stood accused for the first time (in the Nuremberg and Tokyo tribunals) of committing not just war crimes but the 'crime of war' (Habermas

1997: 126; see also the important study by Bass 2000). There followed a nuclear age, in which the chilling fact of nuclear-tipped sovereignty has brought the world together by subjecting it to the permanent threat of mutually assured destruction many times over.

Today, global civil society lives in the shadow of an unresolved problem: the role to be played by nuclear-tipped states in the post-cold war world system. This system is dominated by the United States, the world's single superpower, which can and does act as a 'swing power' backed by nuclear force. As such, it is engaged in several regions without being tied permanently to any of them, but its manoeuvres are complicated by the fact that it is presently forced to coexist and interact peacefully with four great powers, three of whom are nuclear powers: Europe, China, Russia, and Japan (Buzan 2000). The geometry of this arrangement clearly differs from the extended freeze imposed by the cold war, when, according to Raymond Aron's famous formula, most parts of the world lived in accordance with the rule, 'peace impossible, war unlikely'. With the collapse of bipolar confrontation, this rule has changed. There is no evidence of the dawn of a post-nuclear age and the freedom from the fear of nuclear accident or attack that that would bring. Nowadays, as Pierre Hassner (1995) has put it so well, peace has become a little less impossible and war is a little less unlikely, principally because a form of unpredictable anarchy has settled on the whole world.[25] The probability of a nuclear apocalypse, in which the earth and its peoples are blown sky-high, may have been reduced, but major wars remain a possibility, including even the use of nuclear-tipped weapons in conflicts that originate in local wars.

Future historians may well look back on the past half-century and see it as the prelude to a barbarous form of Hobbesian 'mediaevalism' (first envisaged by Guglielmo Ferrero), a global order riddled with violence, suspicion of enemies, and restless struggles that produced universal fear. Perhaps indeed our fate has been so decided. And yet, among the most promising signs within global civil society is the renewal of a civilising politics, that is, networked public campaigns against the archipelagos of incivility

[25] *See the concluding interview in Hassner (1995), especially p. 332: 'In the past, the doctrine of deterrence matched the civil character of our societies: an invisible hand, or abstract mechanism, took charge of our security, and we did not have to bother our heads with it. But today the nuclear issue can no longer be considered in isolation; it is inextricably mixed up with everything else.'*

existing within and beyond its frontiers. These campaigns have a long history (see White 1968; Pei-heng 1981: Ch. 2; Seary 1996). They extend back in time, for instance to movements against slavery and trafficking in women and children; the birth of the International Committee of the Red Cross (first named the International Committee for Relief of Wounded Soldiers) after the 1859 Battle of Solferino; the founding of The Save the Children Fund after World War I; and Médecins Sans Frontières after the Biafran War. Oxfam, established to provide civilian relief to Greece when it was still under Nazi occupation, against the wishes of the British government, counts as another example.

Such civil initiatives against incivility, the attempts to build 'bridgeheads' for expanding the reach of global civil society, are today a feature of all zones of violence. Some efforts, like that of Saferworld, are aimed at publicising and restricting global arms flows. Other organisations like Human Rights Watch actively 'witness' others' suffering in violent areas like Burma, Sierra Leone, Rwanda, and southern Sudan. Or they push for the elimination of landmines or bio-logical weapons, or (like Amnesty International, which has more than one million members in 162 countries) campaign against political repression, especially maltreatment of the body and unfair imprisonment. Still others attempt to negotiate ceasefires or to provide comfort for lives ruined when civilians are turned into refugees. And some groups find themselves targets of global criticism for prolonging or complicating uncivil wars, for instance by sheltering hostages, feeding aggressors, or serving as cover for warring armies.

Social campaigns to civilise global civil society—to democratise or publicly control the means of violence (see Keane 1995a)—are among its vital preconditions. Yet they are hampered by countervailing trends, which are perhaps better described as a single dilemma that the defenders of global civil society need to recognise, to worry about, and practically to address. Put simply, the dilemma confronting global civil society is that while it is vulnerable to violence, whether from within or without, and needs armed protection, its members (by

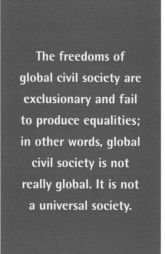

The freedoms of global civil society are exclusionary and fail to produce equalities; in other words, global civil society is not really global. It is not a universal society.

definition) do not have the available means of violence (police and standing armies) to eradicate that violence unless of course they resort to picking up the gun to wield violence—against themselves (see Kaldor, Chapter 5).

This weakness of global civil society is partly traceable to its own plural freedoms: to the extent that global civil society enjoys such freedoms it can easily be taken for a ride by mercenaries, gangs, wired-up hooligans, mafia, arms traffickers, terrorists, private security agents, and psycho-killers, all of whom cavort with the devil of violence by using, misusing, and abusing the peaceful freedoms of that society (see Findlay 1999). Global civil society is further threatened by the fact that the organised violence (potentially) needed to protect its citizens has a nasty habit of getting out of hand: arms breed arrogance, thereby threatening everything that global civil society stands for. As the merchants of the early civil societies of the Italian city-states first recognised,[26] standing armies are as dangerous as they are necessary. The citizens of global civil society thus require limited armed protection.

If that is so, then defenders of global civil society must bite the bullet, quite literally. For among the most difficult political problems yet to be solved is if, how, and when armed intervention can legitimately be used to keep alive, even to extend, the project of global civil society. Many activist supporters of global civil society understandably shy away from talk of violence: like the International Network of Engaged Buddhists, they have a principled commitment to active non-violence or they have simply seen enough of violence and therefore pragmatically prefer pacific means of protecting and nurturing the lives of defenceless citizens. Conventional 'realists', by contrast, doubt that civil society can become the good-natured cavalry of freedom. They point out that might often triumphs over right. They defend the formula that sovereigns are those who actually decide to use force to protect citizens, which begs hard normative questions about who can and who should shield our

[26] See the remarks on the relationship between markets and organised violence by Lasswell (1935: 23).

emerging global civil society from violence, and under what circumstances. The answer provided by the post-Shoah advocates of 'just' or humanitarian war—that the violent enemies of global civil society should be fought wherever they make a move—arguably legitimises eternal war, particularly in a world bristling with incivility.

Or does it? The geo-military scope of non-nuclear humanitarian intervention is arguably constrained by the fact that the United States, despite its ability to act as a 'swing power', is presently forced to coexist and interact peacefully with the four great powers of Europe, Japan, China, and Russia. Not only that, but especially under 'post-Vietnam', conditions, when log-rolling politicians' fear of casualties leads them to rely on the use of computerised, 'risk-free', aerial bombardment as their preferred means of 'humanitarian intervention', war can be waged only by the superpower, it seems, in a very limited number of uncivil contexts: like those of Kosovo, where the marauding forces to be bombed are geographically strategic but without powerful friends, and weak enough to be defeated easily but sufficiently strong to make the sensible calculation to refrain from using further violence (see Luttwak 2000; other limitations of 'post-heroic' aerial bombardment are examined in Ignatieff 2000*a*, *b*). These preconditions of successful military intervention are exacting. They imply that most patches of the earth where global civil society has made little or no headway—Russia, China, Afghanistan, Pakistan, Algeria, Saudi Arabia—are for the moment safe in their outright opposition to its principles and practice.

Hubris

Hubris is also an enemy of global civil society. Its critics, including those who question the very concept because there is 'no common global pool of memories; no common global way of thinking; and no "universal history", in and through which people can unite' (Held 1995: 125; the same point is made in Bozeman 1984), overlook or understate the advantages of the heterogeneity of global civil society. It resembles a bazaar, a covered kaleidoscope of differently sized rooms, twisting alleys, steps leading to obscure places, people and goods in motion. It is marked by increasing differentiation, thickening networks of ever more structures and organisations with different but interdependent *modi operandi*, multiplying encounters among languages and cultures, expanding mobility, growing unpredictability, even (despite growing numbers of full-time moderators and mediators) a certain depersonalisation and abstractness of its social relations. Such complexity is sometimes said to be a threat to democracy (Matthews 1997: 64). That is false, as John Dewey (1978) long ago emphasised, for the struggle against simplified definitions of 'the social good' is a hallmark of a mature civil society. It is nevertheless true that complexity alone does not release global civil society from the laws of hubris. It is not only that the plural freedoms of global civil society are severely threatened by a political underworld of secretive, unelected, publicly unaccountable institutions, symbolised by bodies like the IMF and the WTO. The problem of hubris is internal to global civil society as well: just like the domestic civil societies that form its habitats, global civil society produces concentrations of arrogant power that threaten its own openness and pluralism.

Stronger legal sanctions and armed protection can ameliorate these inequalities, but are there additional ways of ensuring that its social freedoms can be nurtured and redistributed more equally at the world level? The growth since the mid- nineteenth century of a globe-girdling, time-space conquering system of communications, beginning with inventions like overland and underwater telegraphy and the early development of international news agencies like Reuters and culminating in the more recent development of geo-stationary satellites, digitalised media, and the growth of giant media firms like Thorn-EMI, News Corporation International, Sony, and Bertelsmann is arguably of basic importance in this respect (Hugill 1999). It goes without saying that this global communications system is an integral—

> The contemporary revival of interest in civil society has much to do with such twentieth-century experiences as total war, aerial bombardment, concentration camps, and the threat of nuclear annihilation.

supremely aggressive and oligopolistic—sector of today's turbo-capitalism. Ten or so vertically integrated media conglomerates, most of them based in the United States, dominate the world market (Herman and McChesney 1997). They prioritise advertising-driven commercial ventures: music, videos, sports, news, shopping, children's and adults' filmed entertainment. Programme-making codes, in the field of satellite television news for instance, are consequently biased in various ways. They are subject to specific rules of mise-en-scène. And material fed to editors by journalists reporting from or around trouble spots (called 'clusterfucks' in the vernacular) is selected, shortened, simplified, repackaged, and then transmitted in commercial form.

Yet for all these turbo-capitalist biases, global communications media do not simply produce turbo-capitalist audiences who are politically inactive. 'The dictatorship of the single word and the single image, much more devastating than that of the single party', laments Eduardo Galeano, 'imposes a life whose exemplary citizen is a docile consumer and passive spectator built on the assembly line following the North American model of commercial television'.[27] Such laments are overdrawn, partly for reasons (cited above) to do with the marketing process itself: the retailing of products like American movies has had the effect of enhancing local cultural diversity within global civil society, partly because profit-seeking, turbo-capitalist retailers themselves see the need to tailor their products to local conditions and tastes. Local consumers of commercial television reciprocate: they display vigorous powers of investing these commodities with new and different meanings.

The globalisation of media has also had a rich, if wholly ironic, political effect, especially from the time of the protest of youth against the Vietnam War: it has contributed to the growth of a plurality of differently sized public spheres, some of them global, in which many millions of people witness mediated controversies about who gets what, when, and how (see Keane 1995b).[28] Not all global media events—sporting fixtures, blockbuster movies, media awards, for instance—sustain global public spheres. But within the besuited world of diplomacy, global

business, inter-governmental meetings, and NGOs, thanks to wide-bodied jet aircraft, computerised communications, and satellite broadcasting with large footprints, the public practice of non-violently monitoring the exercise of power across borders has taken root. These global public spheres—the term is used here as an ideal type—are sites within global civil society where power struggles are visibly waged and witnessed by means other than violence and war: they are the narrated, imagined non-violent spaces within global civil society in which millions of people witness the powers of governmental and non-governmental organisations being publicly named, monitored, praised, and condemned, despite barriers of time and space.

Although still rather issue-specific and not yet strongly institutionalised, global public spheres, helped along by initiatives like Transparency International and nurtured by channels like CNN and the BBC World Service (which attracts 150 million viewers and listeners each week), have several interesting effects, some of which are 'pre-political'. Global public spheres, for instance, interpolate citizens of the new global order, in effect telling them that, unless they find some means of showing that global civil society is not theirs, then it is. In this way, global public spheres function as temporary resting places beyond familiar horizons; they give an entirely new meaning to the old watchword of Greek colonisation, 'Wherever you go, you will be a *polis*'. Within global public spheres, people rooted in local physical settings increasingly travel to distant places, without ever leaving home, to 'second homes' within which their senses are stretched.

Hailed by media narratives that probe the wider world in tones of (ironic) intimacy, the members of global civil society become a bit less parochial, a bit

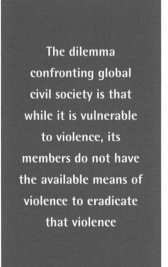

The dilemma confronting global civil society is that while it is vulnerable to violence, its members do not have the available means of violence to eradicate that violence

---

[27] *Eduardo Galeano, cited in the epigraph in Herman and McChesney (1997: vi). More prudent assessments are presented in Ong (1999); Packer (1995); and Schudson (1997).*

[28] *Adam Michnik has suggested that the recent growth of global public opinion can be seen as the rebirth in different form of an earlier parallel trend, evident within nineteenth-century socialist internationalism, that came to an end with World War I (interview, Washington DC, 21 April 2001).*

more cosmopolitan. Global publics are taught lessons in the art of flexible citizenship: they learn that the boundaries between native and foreigner are blurred and that they have become a touch more footloose. They learn to distance themselves from themselves; they discover that there are different temporal rhythms, other places, other problems, other ways to live. They are invited to question their own dogmas, even to extend ordinary standards of civility—courtesy, politeness, respect—to others whom they will never meet (Toulmin 2000). Global public spheres centred on ground-breaking media events like Live-Aid can even be spaces of fun in which millions taste something of the joy of acting publicly with and against others for some defined common purpose. Global publics, like the recent UN-sponsored multimedia event 'A World Freed of Violence Against Women', can also highlight cruelty; and global publics can also be sites of disaster, spaces in which millions taste unjust outcomes, bitter defeat, and the tragedy of ruined lives.

The public spheres housed within global civil society also have more directly political effects. Especially during dramatic media events—like the nuclear meltdown at Chernobyl, the Tiananmen massacre, the 1989 revolutions in central-eastern Europe, the overthrow and arrest of Slobodan Milosevic—public spheres intensify audiences' shared sense of living their lives contingently, on a knife edge, in the subjunctive tense. The witnesses of such events are encouraged to feel that the power relations of global civil society, far from being given, are better understood as 'an arena of struggle, a fragmented and contested area' (Keck and Sikkink 1998), the result of moves and counter-moves, controversy and consent, compromise and resistance, peace and war. Public spheres not only tend to denaturalise the power relations of global civil society. They most definitely increase its self-reflexivity, for instance by publicising conflicting images of civility, civilisation, and civil society. Publicity is given as well to the biased codes of global media coverage and to hostile coverage of global civil society itself, for instance by airing claims that it is a soft term without specific gravity, a Western dogma, a mere smokescreen for turbo-capitalism, that is, a mere vehicle for 'the useful idiots of globalization' (Rieff 1999).

In these various ways, global public spheres heighten the topsy-turvy feel of global civil society. Doubt is heaped upon loose talk that anthropomorphises global civil society as if it were a universal object/subject, the latest and most promising

> The problem of hubris is also internal to global civil society: it produces concentrations of arrogant power that threaten its own openness and pluralism

substitute for the proletariat or for the wretched of the earth. Global public spheres make it clearer that 'global civil society', like its more local counterparts, has no 'collective voice', that it alone does nothing, that only its constituent individuals, group initiatives, organisations, and networks act and interact. Global publics consequently heighten the sense that global civil society is an unfinished, permanently threatened project. They shake up its dogmas and inject it with energy. They enable citizens of the world to shake off bad habits of parochialism, to see that talk of global civil society is not simply Western bourgeois ideology, even to appreciate that the task of painting a much clearer picture of the rules of conduct and dowries of global civil society, a picture that is absent from most of the current literature on globalisation, is today an urgent ethical imperative.

Democracy

The contemporary growth of global publics certainly points to the need to bring greater democracy to global civil society.[29] By throwing light on power exercised by moonlight or in the dark of night, global publics keep alive words like 'freedom' and 'justice' by publicising manipulation, skulduggery, and brutality on or beyond the margins of global civil society. Global publics, of the kind that in recent years have monitored the fate of Aung San Suu Kyi, muck with the messy business of exclusion, racketeering, ostentation, cruelty, and war. They chart cases of intrigue and double-crossing. They help audiences to spot the various figures of top-down power on the world scene: slick and suave managers and professionals who are well-practised at the art of deceiving others through images; kingfishers who first dazzle others then stumble when more is required of them; quislings who willingly change sides

---

[29] *The exclusion of the theme of public spheres from virtually all of the current literature on globalisation is criticised by Slaatta (1998). A similar point is made implicitly by Appadurai (2000).*

under pressure; thugs who love violence; and vulgar rulers, with their taste for usurping crowns, assembling and flattering crowds, or beating and tear-gassing them into submission.

Global public spheres can also probe the powers of key organisations of global civil society itself. Reminders are served to those who read, listen, and watch that its empty spaces have been filled by powerful but unaccountable organisations (like the WTO and the International Olympic Committee) or by profit-seeking corporate bodies that permanently aggravate global civil society by causing environmental damage or swallowing up others by producing just for profit rather than for sustainable social use. Global public spheres can as well help question some of the more dubious practices of some non-profit INGOs: for instance, their bureaucratic inflexibility and context- blindness, their spreading attachment to market values or to clichés of project-speak, or their mistaken belief in the supply-side, trickle-down model of social development. Public spheres can point to the post-colonial presumptuous-ness of some INGOs, their bad habit of acting as their brothers' keepers, like missionaries, in so-called 'partnerships' that are publicly unaccountable. And public spheres can criticise their smartly-dressed, self-circulating, middle-class elites, sometimes dubbed the 'Five Star Brigade', whose privileges and privileged behaviour contradict the principles for which global civil society should otherwise be rightly cherished its diversity of equal organisations, its open toleration of differences, the speed and flexibility with which it forms complex, shifting alliances around a plurality of shared values and interests.[30]

Exactly because of their propensity to monitor the exercise of power from a variety of sites within and outside civil society, global public spheres—when they function properly—can help to ensure that nobody monopolises power at the local and world levels. By exposing corrupt or risky dealings and naming them as such; by wrong- footing decision-makers and forcing their hands; by requiring them to rethink or reverse their decisions, global public spheres help remedy the problem—strongly evident in the volatile field of global financial markets, which turn over US$1.3 trillion a day, 100 times the volume of world trade—that nobody seems to be in charge. And in uneven contests between decision-makers and decision-takers—as the developing controversies within bodies like the International Olympic Committee show—global public spheres can help prevent the powerful from 'owning' power privately. Global publics imply greater parity. They suggest that there are alternatives. They inch our little blue and white planet towards greater openness and humility, potentially to the point where power, whenever and wherever it is exercised across borders, is made to feel more 'biodegradable', a bit more responsive to those whose lives it shapes and reshapes, secures or wrecks.

References

Albright, M. (2000). Focus on the Issues: *Strengthening Civil Society and the Rule of Law. Excerpts of testimony, speeches and remarks by U.S. Secretary of State Madeleine K. Albright.* Washington, DC: United States Government Publication and http://www.secretary.gov

Althusius J. (1614). *Politica Methodicè digesta atque exemplis sacris & profanis illustrata.* Herborn: First Edition.

Amin, A. and Thrift, N. (ed.) (1994). *Globalization, Institutions and Regional Development in Europe.* Oxford: Oxford University Press.

Anderson, S. and Cavanagh, J. (2000). *Field Guide to the Global Economy.* New York: Free Press.

Appadurai, A. (2000). 'Grassroots Globalization and the Research Imagination'. *Public Culture*, 12/1: 1–19.

Archibugi, D. and Held, D. (ed.) (1994). *Cosmopolitan Democracy.* Cambridge: Cambridge University Press.

Aron, R. (1978). 'The Dawn of Universal History', in Miriam Conant (ed.), *Politics and History: Selected Essays by Raymond Aron.* New York and London: Free Press.

Badie, Bertrand (1992). *L'état importé: L'occidentalisation de l'ordre politique.* Paris: Fayard.

Barnet, R. J. and Cavanagh J. (1995). *Global Dreams: Imperial Corporations and the New World Order.* New York and London: Simon and Schuster.

Bass, G. J. (2000). *Stay the Hand of Vengeance: The Politics of War Crimes Tribunals.* Princeton and Oxford: Princeton University Press.

Beeching, J. (1979). *An Open Path: Christian Missionaries 1515–1914.* London: Hutchinson.

---

[30] *Some of these undemocratic tendencies within non-governmental organisations—satirised in the South African joke that those lucky to have an NGO job can 'EN-J-OY' life—are discussed in Ndegwa (1996: esp. Ch. 6); Smith (1990); and Sampson (1996).*

Bello, W. (2000). 'The Struggle for a Deglobalized World'. http://www.igc.org/trac/feature/wto/8-bello.html (September).

Boulding, E. (1988). *Building a Global Civic Culture: Education for an Interdependent World*. New York: Syracuse.

Bozeman, A. B. (1984). 'The International Order in a Multicultural World', in Hedley Bull and Adam Watson (ed.), *The Expansion of International Society*. Oxford: Clarendon.

Braudel, F. (1981). *Civilization and Capitalism: 15th–18th Century*, Vol. 1. London: Collins.

Brown, C. (1999). 'Cosmopolitanism, World Citizenship and Global Civil Society' (unpublished paper). London.

Bull, H. (1990). 'The Importance of Grotius in the Study of International Relations', in Bull *et al.* (ed.), *Hugo Grotius and International Relations*. Oxford: Clarendon.

— (1995). *The Anarchical Society: A Study of Order in World Politics* (2nd edn). New York: Macmillan.

— and Holbraad, C. (ed.) (1978). *Power Politics*. Leicester: Leicester University Press.

Buzan, B. (1991). *People, States and Fear: An Agenda for International Security Studies in the Post-Cold War Era*. New York and London: Wheatsheaf.

— (2000). 'Rethinking Polarity Theory: Reflections on the Meaning of "Great Power"'. London: Centre for the Study of Democracy (March).

Castells, M. and Hall, P. (1994). *Technopoles of the World: The Making of 21st Century Industrial Complexes*. London: Routledge

Christenson, G. A. (1997). 'World Civil Society and the International Rule of Law'. *Human Rights Quarterly*, 19: 724–37.

Cox, R. (1986). 'Social Forces, States, and World Orders: Beyond International Relations Theory', in Robert O. Keohane (ed.), *Neorealism and its Critics*. New York: Columbia University Press.

Dahrendorf, R. (1988). *The Modern Social Conflict: An Essay on the Politics of Liberty*. London: University of California Press.

Dallmayr, F. R. (1999). 'Globalization from Below'. *International Politics*, 36: 321–34.

de Oliveira, M. D. and Tandon, R. (1994). 'An Emerging Global Civil Society', in *Citizens: Strengthening Global Civil Society*, Washington, DC: Civicus.

de Soto, Hernando (2000). *The Mystery of Capital: Why Capitalism Triumphs in the West and Fails Everywhere Else*. London: Bantham.

de Vattel, Emmerich (1758). *Le droit des gens, ou principes de la loi naturelle, appliqués à la conduite et aux affaires des nations et des souverains*. London: First Edition

Dewey, J. (1978). 'Civil Society and the Political State', in Jo Ann Boydston (ed.), *John Dewey: The Middle Works, 1899–1924*. Carbondale and Edwardsville: South Illinois University Press.

Dicken, P. (2000). *Global Shift: Transforming the World Economy* (3rd edn). London: Paul Chapman.

Edwards, M. (2000). *Future Positive: International Co-operation in the 21st Century*. London: New York University Press.

Evans, P. (ed.) (1997). *State-Society Synergy: Government and Social Capital in Development*. Berkeley: University of California at Berkeley Press.

Falk, R. (1990). 'Economic Dimensions of Global Civilization'. Global Civilization Project, Center for International Studies, Princeton University.

— (1992). *Explorations at the Edge of Time: The Prospects for World Order*. Philadelphia: Temple University Press.

— (1999). *Predatory Globalisation: A Critique*. Oxford: Polity Press.

Findlay, M. (1999). *The Globalisation of Crime: Understanding Transitional Relationships in Context*. Cambridge and New York.

Florini, A. M. (ed.) (2000). *The Third Force: The Rise of Transnational Civil Society*. Tokyo and Washington, DC: Japan Centre for International Exchange and Carnegie Endowment for International Peace.

Gereffi, G. (1996). 'Global Commodity Chains: New Forms of Coordination and Control Among Nations and Firms in International Industries'. *Competition and Change*, Vol I: 427–39.

— and Korzeniewicz, M. (eds) (1994). *Commodity Chains and Global Capitalism*. Westport, CT: Praeger.

Habermas, J. (1996). 'Civil Society and the Political Public Sphere', in *Between Facts and Norms*. Cambridge, MA: MIT Press.

— (1997). 'Kant's Idea of Perpetual Peace, with the Benefit of Two Hundred Years' Hindsight', in James Bohman and Matthias Lutz-Bachmann (eds), *Perpetual Peace: Essays on Kant's*

Cosmopolitan Ideal. Cambridge, MA and London: MIT Press.

Hassner, P. (1995). *La violence et la paix: De la bombe atomique au nettoyage ethnique*. Paris: Espirit.

Held, D. (1995). *Democracy and the Global Order: From the Modern State to Cosmopolitan Governance*. Stanford: Stanford University Press.

— and McGrew, A. (eds) (2000). *The Global Transformations Reader*. Oxford: Polity Press.

Herman, E. S. and McChesney, R. W. (1997). *The Global Media: The New Missionaries of Corporate Capitalism*. London and Washington: Cassell.

Hirsh, M. (2001). 'Protesting Plutocracy'. Special Davos edition of *Newsweek* (December 2000–January 2001).

Hirst, P., and Thompson, G. (1999). *Globalization in Question*. Oxford: Oxford University Press

Hobsbawm, E. (1979). 'The Development of the World Economy', *Cambridge Journal of Economics*, 3: 305–18.

— (1989). *The Age of Empire 1875–1914*. London: Weidenfeild and Nicolson.

Hugill, Peter J. (1999). *Global Communications Since 1844: Geopolitics and Technology*. Baltimore and London: The John Hopkins University Press.

Ignatieff, M. (2000a). *Virtual War*. London: Chatto and Windus.

— (2000b). 'The New American Way of War'. *The New York Review of Books* (20 July): 42–6.

Kant, I. (1784). *Idee zu einer allgemeinen Geschichte in weltbürgerlicher Absicht*, first published in the *Berlinische Monatsschrift*. Berlin.

— (1795). *Zum Ewigen Frieden: Ein philosophischer Entwurf*. Königsberg.

Keane, J. (1988[1998]) (ed.). *Civil Society and the State: New European Perspectives*. London: University of Westminster Press.

— (1990). 'The Future of Civil Society', in Tatjana Sikosha (ed.), *The Internationalisation of Civil Society*. The University of Amsterdam Press.

— (1991). *The Media and Democracy*. Cambridge: Polity Press.

— (1995a). *Reflections on Violence*. London: Verso.

— (1995b). 'Structural Transformations of the Public Sphere'. *The Communication Review*, 1/1: 1–22.

— (1998). *Civil Society: Old Images, New Perspectives*. Oxford and Stanford: Polity Press.

— (1999). *On Communicative Abundance*. London: Centre for the Study of Democracy.

Keck, M. E. and Sikkink, K. (1998). *Activists beyond Borders: Advocacy Networks in International Politics*. Ithaca and London: Cornell University Press.

Korten, David (1990). *Getting to the 21st Century: Voluntary Action and the Global Agenda*, West Hartford, Connecticut: Kunarian Press.

Langdale, J. V. (1989). 'The Geography of International Business Telecommunications: The Role of Leased Networks'. *Annals of the Association of American Geographers*, 79: 501–22.

Lasswell, H. D. (1935). *World Politics and Personal Insecurity*. Chicago: McGraw-Hill.

Lipschutz, R. (1992). 'Reconstructing World Politics: The Emergence of Global Civil Society'. *Millennium*, 21: 389–420.

Luttwak, E. (1999). *Turbo-capitalism: Winners and Losers in the Global Economy*. New York: Weidenfeld and Nicolson.

— (2000). 'No-score war'. *Times Literary Supplement*, 14 July: 11.

Macpherson, C. B. (1973). *Democratic Theory. Essays in Retrieval*. Oxford: Clarendon.

Maguire, J. (1999). *Global Sport. Identities, Societies, Civilizations*. Cambridge: Polity.

Matthews, J. T. (1997). 'Power Shift'. *Foreign Affairs*, 76/1: 50–66.

Menju, T. and Aoki, T. (1995). 'The Evolution of Japanese NGOs in the Asia Pacific Context', in Tadashi Yamamoto (ed.), *Emerging Civil Society in the Asia Pacific Community*. Singapore: Institute of South East Asian Studies.

Mittelman, J. H. (2000). *The Globalization Syndrome: Transformation and Resistance*. Princeton, NJ: Princeton University Press.

McNeill, W. H. (1963). *The Rise of the West: A History of the Human Community*. Chicago and London: University of Chicago Press.

Naidoo, K. (2000). 'The New Civic Globalism'. *The Nation*. 8 May: 34–6.

— and Tandon, R. (1999). 'The Promise of Civil Society', in *Civil Society at the Millennium*. West Hartford, Conn: Civicus.

Ndegwa, S. N. (1996). *The Two Faces of Civil Society: NGOs and Politics in Africa*. West Hartford, Conn.: Kumarian.

Ong, A. (1999). *Flexible Citizenship: The Cultural Logics of Transnationality.* Durham, North Carolina: University of North Carolina Press.

Ougaard, M. (1990). 'The Internationalisation of Civil Society'. Copenhagen: Center for Udviklingsforskning (June).

Parker, R. (1995). *Mixed Signals: The Prospects for Global Television News.* New York: Twentieth Century Fund Press

Pérez-Diaz, Victor M. (1993). *The Return of Civil Society: The Emergence of Democratic Spain.* Cambridge, MA and London: Harvard University Press.

Pei-heng, C. (1981). *Non-Governmental Organizations at the United Nations: Identity, Role, and Functions.* New York: Praeger.

Rieff, D. (1999). 'The False Dawn of Civil Society'. *The Nation*, 268, no. 7 (February): 11–16.

Risse-Kappen, T. (ed.) (1995). *Bringing Transnational Relations Back In: Non-State Actors, Domestic Structures and International Institutions.* Cambridge: Cambridge University Press.

Rosenau, J. N. and Czempiel, Ernst-Otto (eds) (1992). *Governance Without Government: Order and Change in World Politics.* Cambridge and New York: Cambridge University Press.

Sahlins, M. (1999). *Waiting for Foucault and Other Aphorisms.* Charlottesville and Cambridge: Prickly Pear Press.

Salamon, L. (1999). 'Government and Nonprofit Relations in Perspective', in Boris, T.E and Steuerle, C.E. (eds.) *Nonprofits and Government: Collaboration and Conflict.* Washington, DC: Urban Institute.

— Anheier, H. K., List, R., Toepler, S., Sokolowski, S. W. and Associates (1999). *Global Civil Society: Dimensions of the Non-profit Sector.* Baltimore, MA: Johns Hopkins University, Institute for Policy Studies' Center for Civil Society Studies.

Sampson, S. (1996). 'The Social Life of Projects', in Chris Han and Elizabeth Dunn (eds), *Civil Society: Challenging Western Models.* London: Routledge.

Seary, B. (1996). 'The Early History: From the Congress of Vienna to the San Francisco Conference', in Peter Willetts (ed.), *'The Conscience of the World': The Influence of Non-Governmental Organisations in the UN System.* Washington, DC: Brookings Institution.

Schudson, M. (1997). 'Is There a Global Cultural Memory?' (unpublished paper). University of California at San Diego.

Shaw, T. (2000). 'Overview—Global/Local: States, Companies and Civil Societies at the End of the Twentieth Century', in K. Stiles (ed.), *Global Institutions and Local Empowerment: Competing Theoretical Perspectives.* New York: Macmillan.

Slaatta, Tore (1998). 'Media and Democracy in the Global Order'. *Media, Culture and Society*, 20: 335–44.

Smith, B. H. (1990). *More than Altruism: The Politics of Private Foreign Aid.* Princeton, NJ: Princeton University Press.

Soros, G. (1998). *The Crisis of Global Capitalism.* London: Little Brown.

Stein, E. (1994). 'International Law in Internal Law: Toward Internationalization of Central Eastern European Constitutions'. *American Journal of International Law*, 88: 427–50.

Storper, M. (1992). 'The Limits to Globalization: Technology Districts and International Trade'. *Economic Geography*, 68: 60–93.

— (1997). *The Regional World: Territorial Development in a Global Economy.* New York: Guilford Press.

Tandon, R. (1999). 'Civil Society Moves Ahead'. *1999 Annual Report,* Washington, DC: Civicus.

Tendler, J. (1982). *Turning Private Voluntary Organizations into Developmental Agencies: Questions for Evaluation* (Program Evaluation Discussion Paper 12), Washington, DC: USAID.

Toulmin, S. (2000). 'The Belligerence of Dogma', in Leroy S. Rounder (ed.), *Civility.* Notre Dame: University of Notre Dame Press.

Union of International Associations (ed.) (1997–98). *Yearbook of International Organizations*, Vol. 4 (34th ed). Munich: Union of International Associations.

von Gierke, O. (1966 [1880]). *The Development of Political Theory.* London: Allen and Unwin.

White, L. C. (1968). *International Non-Governmental Organisations.* New York: Greenwood.

Yoshikazu, S. (2000) 'An Alternative to Global Marketization', in Jan Nederveen Pieterse (ed.), *Global Futures: Shaping Globalization.* London and New York: Institute of Social Studies.

Young, O. (1994). *International Governance: Protecting the Environment in a Stateless Society.* Cornell: Cornell University Press.

Part II: Issues in Global Civil Society

CHAPTER 3

THE NEW ANTI-CAPITALIST MOVEMENT: MONEY AND GLOBAL CIVIL SOCIETY

Meghnad Desai and Yahia Said

Washington DC, Prague, Seattle, Davos, and wherever 'the money men' meet have been the foci of protest which have mobilised a broad coalition of groups, activists, and lay individuals. While they may differ on many things, they agree on one. They consider many of the recent developments in globalisation as harmful, disruptive of their communities, and destructive in the long run. Such protests have taken many by surprise both in their scope and in their intensity, and have contributed to the increased interest in civil society in recent years. The protesters rarely attack globalisation as such, targeting instead corporate globalisation, global capitalism, the neo-liberal order, multinational companies, international financial institutions (IFIs), and trade agreements. Whatever the target, however, these protests are often branded as anti-globalisation. The counter-argument is usually a defence of globalisation as helpful to the world at large in enhancing output growth by expanding trade, helping the developing countries industrialise, and affording an opportunity for the first time in human history to eradicate world poverty.

In a framework where globalisation is understood as a symbiotic relationship between global capitalism and global civil society, this chapter analyses the interactions between the two. These interactions make up what we define as global civil society irrespective of whether or not it includes the market (see Chapter 2 for different definitions of global civil society).

Given the breadth of its subject, this chapter focuses on money and finance as a proxy for global capitalism. This simplification is permissible for three reasons:

1. Finance is the dominant force in global capitalism. Financial flows far exceed trade flows and play an ever-growing role in every market transaction. Any sizeable trade today will almost certainly include bank credits on both sides, hedges against exchange rates and commodity price fluctuations in the form of futures and derivatives, and other forms of insurance. The growth and spread of the financial services industry and the unprecedented liberalisation of financial markets can be explained by the investment needs of the new industrial paradigm. The shift to information and communication technologies requires the mobilisation of vast financial resources, and global finance is the fastest way to achieve that. Similar financial booms occurred during previous technological revolutions (Perez 2000).

2. The financial services industry is among the main promoters of global capitalism, pushing for the opening of new markets and ever deeper liberalisation. The financial services industry is more dependent than any other on the low inflation advocated by the neo-liberal orthodoxy. Currently, the industry is pushing hard for the expansion of the WTO into the area of finance and investment through the General Agreement in Trade on Services (GATS). This will significantly expand the organisation, giving it jurisdiction over two-thirds of world GDP and bringing it into areas that affect every aspect of human life.

3. As we explain below, the financial services industry has traditionally been singled out for moral condemnation. So it is today, when it represents an extreme version of global capitalism. Financial juggernauts several times larger than many countries, fat-cat investment bankers and IMF executives playing God, astronomical profits on both the upside and the downside of the economic cycle, and bizarre financial products seemingly useless for anything other than the enrichment of those who invent them make finance an inevitable and often convenient target for those seeking to confront global capitalism.

Money and Morality

Our analysis deals with the ways in which global civil society has responded to the many activities of the financial sector—domestic and international, private and public—as they have affected the lives of the people. Finance is organised, complicated, and pervasive. It comprises bank loans and debts, bonds and share markets, central bank and IMF regulation, and new innovative services such as futures and derivatives. It operates around the globe for 24 hours a day from places like the City of London and New York's Wall Street.

Financial developments have been at the forefront of globalisation. But even so, the core of financial market activities is age-old: buying and selling, borrowing and lending. The world has been familiar with money, credit, and exchange for millennia. There are deeply ingrained moral attitudes about money, exchange, and credit which shape the response of global civil society to recent developments.

Money has long been regarded as morally questionable. It is thought to be barren, which in turn calls into question the morality of charging interest. Money is often alleged to break up established communities, leaving atomised rootless individualism in its wake. Money is said to devalue relationships by reducing them to a financial calculus; money-using societies are contrasted with 'primitive' or pre-modern societies, which are said to embody more genuine emotional relationships since they are based on barter or gifts rather than monetary exchange. The anti-money critique leads to a utopian vision in which monetary exchange is superseded and relations based on 'real' values are re-established.[1] Against this is the view that money is an enabling, liberating, and helpful device which oils the wheels of commerce and brings prosperity all round.

There have always been religious and philosophical objections to monetary transactions. The ideal is the self-sufficient household, or even the self-sufficient community, based on barter. Aristotle believed that money should be limited to restoring self-sufficiency. 'Interchange of this kind is not contrary to nature and is not a form of moneymaking: it keeps to its original purpose—to re-establish nature's own equilibrium of self-sufficiency.' The objection is thus more to profiting from the use of money than from money in itself. If money is barren, it should not be made to yield a return. This logic is at the heart of the medieval Christian ban on usury as well as the Koranic injunction against charging interest on credit.

It was in the eighteenth century with Bernard Mandeville, David Hume, and Adam Smith that a new understanding of money emerged. Smith reversed the story about the naturalness of self-

sufficiency by asserting that mankind had a 'propensity to truck, barter and exchange'. It was this propensity, motivated by self-interest, that brought happiness. Smith was aggressively modernist and did not concede anything to the earlier moral discourse about the immorality of exchange. He argued that the 'system of natural liberty' guaranteed prosperity not only to some but to all: 'the Kings of primitive tribes could not have gained such wealth' (Smith in Desai 2001 forthcoming).

Against Smith, Marx argued that whereas in previous modes of production the purpose of money was to facilitate the exchange of commodities (C-M-C), under capitalism its purpose was to increase the quantity of capital (M-C-M).

The sociologist George Simmel saw money 'as an instrument of freedom, and a condition for the extension of individual personality and the expansion of the circle of trust; but, at the same time, as a threat to the moral order' (Parry and Bloch 1989: 3). That threat came from the transition that money facilitated from Gemeinschaft (community) to Gesellschaft (association) (Tönnies 1955), encouraging rational calculation and abstract relationships as opposed to the primacy of feelings and emotion in traditional society.

Marcel Mauss, the French anthropologist, argued that money not only dissolves bonds of community but also allows for a separation between persons and things (Mauss 1996) . This is the one aspect of money which has been crucial in globalisation. According to Simmel:

Money permits possession at a distance. Only in the form of money can profits be easily transferred from one place to another, allowing for a spatial separation between the owner and his property which 'enables his property to be managed exclusively according to objective demands while it gives its owner a chance of leading his life independently of his possessions' (quoted in Parry and Bloch 1989: 5).

The change from an Aristotelian to a Smithian view of money was not accidental. For about a thousand years before the Iberian maritime expansion of 1490s which inaugurated the modern world system, Europe was starved of precious metals. It ran an adverse balance of trade with Asia, mainly India and China, and exported gold and silver to pay for imports from Asia. Money, being scarce, was expensive and interest

---

[1] *In some of this discussion we rely on Parry and Bloch (1989). The quotations from Aristotle and Simmel are taken from this source.*

rates were high. But the arrival of bullion from the Iberian colonies of West Africa and South America changed that. It affected social relations, favouring Peruvian merchants at the expense of the old landed wealth. Things began to be bought and sold for money which were previously not subject to exchange. Commerce began to create more wealth than agriculture had done for millennia. Money became the gateway to modernity and capitalism.

That does not, however, mean that traditional societies did not use money or that money coincided with modernity or the frail identification of money and capitalism with the West. The use of money has been found to be very important in many traditional pre-capitalist economies. The reciprocal inter-dependence of non-monetary, caste-based exchange of the Hindu jajmani system—a classic example of village self-sufficiency—is a myth propagated by modern (Western) investigators who wanted to see non-monetary exchange as a feature of 'traditional' society. As Parry and Bloch say:

> What implicitly seems to underlie the misrepresentation is a deeply entrenched notion about the transformative potential of money such that its presence becomes an index of a 'modern' society, with the corollary that in a 'traditional' one it can only be of peripheral significance. (1989: 7; see especially also Fuller 1989)

Thus we can dismiss the notions that traditional societies were based on real relationships unmediated by money, and that money, like the serpent in the Garden of Eden, arrived and corrupted the innocent. Money, and our views of its good or bad effects, are therefore never context-free. Our culture—that is, the modern, post-colonial, post-imperial world as it has come to be shaped by two centuries of industrial capitalism—is shot through and through with money and its higher form, credit. Indeed, it is impossible to imagine our economy without money, though pockets of 'local money' networks survive which use labour time as units of account and even means of payment. (see Box 3.6)

The major concerns we have, however, are not with such local pockets of resistance but with global finance and especially the ways in which global civil society has encountered the massive money flows which have become the distinguishing feature of globalisation. It is here that we encounter the contrasting views of money as barren or liberating, and it is these that we must consider in more detail. These two competing views of money and its usefulness represent the two extremes and the many possible positions between them.

At one extreme there is the libertarian view in which the market and all its works are benevolent and beyond criticism. An allied view is that, benevolent or not, the market is a self-organising process and its regulation self-defeating and counterproductive. There is the moderate view that the market is more or less self-regulating but needs an occasional correction. Then there is the view that the market is prone to failure and the state should be ever-ready to regulate it. This view easily slides into one which sees the market as chronically malfunctioning and hence in need of overarching control. The extreme view would be a rejection of the market and all its works and its replacement by a self-conscious democratic rule of 'Society' (Desai 2001). There is extremism at either end of the spectrum in which one celebrates the market while the other excoriates it. In between are nuanced objections, not to abstractions such as the 'market' or 'money' but to concentrations of economic power (transnational/global corporations) or to excessive income and wealth inequalities; not against 'market failures' in general but environmental degradation or racial or gender discrimination; not to flows of capital as such but to the uses to which they are put and the returns obtained and to inequalities of power in international trade. The theme common to all of these is the economic or the monetary link which unites them.

Given the Manichean division at the extremes and the multiplicity of nuanced attitudes in the middle, it is necessary to distinguish the types of money flows or trading arrangements which attract different degrees of protest. Capital flows are singled out because it is the unregulated, or at least freer, flow of capital in the last 10 to 15 years which, in our view, marks out the new phase of globalisation.

Capital Flows: Types, Impacts, Responses

The shock of globalisation and the flows of capital it sets up are not new phenomena in world history. Trade has taken place between the different continents by sea or land for millennia. Europe and Asia especially have a continuous history of trade and gold flow, which goes back to the

The message is abundantly clear. There is no confusion, dithering, or doubt:

> *The IMF and the World Bank, far from bringing economic stability and reducing poverty, are destroying the environment and impoverishing people. Their calls for dialogue are just a public relations ploy and the announced reforms are cosmetic. The Bretton Woods institutions should be abolished and all Third World debt cancelled. Moreover, the entire political and economic system of global capitalism needs to be overhauled. This is to be achieved by a global movement of solidarity opposed to the neo-liberal model imposed by multinational companies, the rich countries, and their minions at the World Bank and the IMF.*

This was, in short, the message delivered by Katerina Liskova one of the leaders of the Movement Against Economic Globalisation (INPEG), the coalition of NGOs and activists which organised the anti IMF/World Bank protests in Prague in the autumn of 2000. Katerina was speaking at a panel debate organised by Czech President Vaclav Havel at Prague Castle. The 20-year-old activist delivered this defiant message flanked by World Bank President James Wolfenson and IMF Managing Director Horst Kohler. UN Human Rights Commissioner Mary Robinson was moderating this unique forum, which also included international financier and philanthropist George Soros, Jubilee 2000 founder Ann Pettifor, Filipino academic/activist Walden Bello, and South African Minister of Finance Trevor Manuel. Despite the predictability of the protesters' message, the global financial leaders seemed dumbfounded. Wolfenson just reiterated his readiness for dialogue while Kohler insisted that he also had a heart. Indeed, World Bank and IMF representatives always appear hurt andsurprised when attacked by civic activists.[1]

The International Bank for Reconstruction and Development (IBRD), also known as the World Bank, and the International Monetary Fund (IMF) emerged out of the Bretton Woods conference held in the US in 1944. They were designed as components of an international regime of fixed exchange rates which was meant to deliver growth and stability to the post-war world economy. British economist John Maynard Keynes, who believed that public intervention could improve on market outcomes, at least in the short run, was one of the founding fathers of the two institutions.

The organisations were shaped by their origins. First, they are proactive; they are supposed to combat 'market failures' on a global scale: poverty in the case of the World Bank and financial instability in the case of the IMF. Second, they tend to be elitist and undemocratic primarily because they are dominated by their founder and main donor, the United States, and because they are run by 'experts' who don't expect ordinary people to understand complex economic problems. Over time neo-liberal economists came to represent the overwhelming majority of these 'experts', reflecting both trends in the economic profession and political change in the major donor countries. US and Western domination in general meant that political considerations often prevailed over economic ones in determining World Bank and IMF policies, especially when it came to regimes which were deemed pro-Western or at least anti-Communist. This continued even after the end of the cold war, as was the case with billions of IMF and World Bank dollars loaned to Russia with the aim of propping up President Yeltsin and his 'reformers'.

The combination of activism and elitism described above meant that the Bretton Woods institutions were, and continue to be, attacked from both right and left. Extreme neo-liberals who see no point in public intervention, especially at the international level, view the IMF and the World Bank as examples of 'big government'. The Meltzer Report commissioned by the Republican majority in the US Congress exemplifies this approach, albeit with some moderation (IFIAC 2000). The report is critical of the proactive 'mission creep' at the Bretton Woods institutions and stresses the potential for market distortions caused by their interventions, such as the displacement of private investment and moral hazard. Attacks from the right have increased since the two institutions, especially the World Bank, embarked on a number of reforms aimed at increasing transparency and dialogue and taking policies beyond the neo-liberal scriptures. It is because of the constant attacks from the right that IMF and World Bank officials feel hurt when they are attacked form the left.

The leaders of the IMF and the World Bank believe that they have gone out of their way to accommodate activists' concerns and point out that the institutions are constrained by the will of the member states. They blame both developed countries for holding the purse strings too tight and developing country governments for blaming the IMF and the World Bank for their own failures.

Ann Pettifor partially agrees with this opinion but she would not go as far as to blame the developing countries for the debt crisis. At the Prague Castle meeting she invited activists to direct their attention to the 'puppet masters' in the G7 countries instead of the Bretton Woods institutions. This opinion was seconded by George Soros, who believes that things would be a lot better if developed countries adhered to their commitment to allocate 0.7 percent of their GDP to foreign aid.

The World Bank, the IMF, and other international institutions are facing similar problems of content—guiding principles, mission, goals—and form—accountability and participation, checks and balances. Solving these issues in each institution separately seems inefficient if not impossible. There is a need to explore 'global' solutions such as a set of common principles, parameters, guidelines, or common structures such as an Ombudsman or appeals court. International institutions may even share an 'upper/second chamber', like the ones proposed by the Angela Wood of the Brettonwoods Project (Wood 2001), which would better represent poor countries or non-state actors. Speaking at the Prague Castle meeting, Mary Robinson congratulated Katerina on her courage and proceeded to outline such a global solution. She calls it the 'rights-based approach' and it entails cross-referencing trade and global finance rules with human rights principles and environmental norms.

Such 'global' solutions, however, require a political momentum which does not seem available at the moment. Quite the contrary: the new unilateralist US administration is likely to attempt to curtail the Bretton Woods institutions, reducing them to extensions of US foreign policy. While Walden Bello sees no problem in a tactical alliance with the extreme right against the Bretton Woods institutions, other activists would think twice before hopping into bed with the likes of Pat Buchanan. They may also heed the sombre observation raised by the South African Finance Minister Trevor Manuel, at the Prague Castle meeting. He pointed out that, without the IMF and the World Bank, only three countries in sub-Saharan Africa would have access to external financing. Time will show whether activists will be able to keep the heat on the IFIs without playing into the hands of the extreme right.

Phoenicians. The dawn of capitalism in the 1500s introduced a new element of violence in the relationships of trade and gold flow between Europe and Africa and the Americas. Massive gold flows to Europe were forcibly extracted from the older civilisations of those continents. This sorry saga has been well mapped out by Immanuel Wallerstein in his many writings (see, for example, Wallerstein 2000).

With the industrial revolution, capital and commodity flows took very different forms and had a very different impact. Now labour could be harnessed at home and abroad without coercion; surplus could be extracted from labour made more productive by new machines. Capital began to flow outwards to the periphery as much as it flowed back in the form of repatriated profits. The periphery was transformed in the process of colonisation by the flow of industrial capital. Soon the colonies began to crave their emancipation, which to them implied their own industrialisation, and decided upon independence to pursue capital accumulation and industrial self-sufficiency. In this new context after 1945, private flows of capital from the core to the periphery dried up. Much of the capital flowed within the core. The flows from the core to the periphery took the form, for the first time in history, of massive government-to-government transfers and some smaller flows from the multilateral lending institutions set up at the Bretton Woods conference in 1944—the World Bank and the International Monetary Fund (IMF)—to the countries of what in the 1950s came to be called the Third World.

The founders of the Bretton-Woods system believed that they had discovered the magic formula which would harness the creative forces of capitalism while mitigating its negative side effects. A fixed exchange-rate regime backed by the promise of IMF intervention was supposed to help everyone reap the fruits of free trade without worrying about instability. Aid facilitated by the World Bank was meant to help address issues of poverty and inequality.

The 1970s and the petro-dollar debt

This new dispensation persisted until the early 1970s. At that juncture the first of many events occurred which began the transformation of the post-war world by what we now call 'globalisation'. The United States came off the dollar-exchange standard and the Bretton Woods system of fixed exchange rates collapsed. The quadrupling of oil prices generated a massive transfer, of up to about 5 per cent of their GDP, from the OECD countries to the oil-exporting countries. This was the largest flow in the 200 years since the industrial revolution of money from the developed countries to the (oil-exporting) developing countries. This in turn led to the recycling of petrodollars, which brought private bank loans from developed-country banks to the developing countries. This integration of the periphery into the global banking world heralded a new phase of the world economy.

The first crisis of the 1980s

It was when international debt became a problem in the early 1980s that we may say global civil society encountered the financial world. As Marx saw 150 years ago, capitalist power relations are non-coercive in a crude physical sense. The distancing between the owner of capital and its effects on the ground further complicates the agency problem. When debt piles up and interest payments mount, the poor may starve but whose fault is it really? The borrowers—those in power in the developing countries—eagerly shift the blame to the lenders—the IMF or Western banks. The IMF and the banks accuse the borrowers of economic mismanagement. But the real reason for the debt crisis was that the developed world had decided to put its house in order, adopted monetarist policies, and began to borrow rather than print money. This led to the turnaround in the bond markets when interest rates rose from 5 per cent to 15 per cent in nominal terms and from around minus 10 per cent to plus 10 per cent in real terms.

Through the 1980s, as country after country with debt problems had to seek IMF loans and submit to structural adjustment, civil society everywhere began to realise the severe impact such flows could have on daily life. It was as if, until then, people had been insulated from the outside world of global finance whose rules were non-negotiable even to their sovereign governments. Governments tried to bear down on their people in order to repay their debts, however wisely or foolishly the money had been used, and in response to the protests of their people could only plead helplessness in the face of IMF or foreign banks. In the years since independence people had thought that their governments were on their side or could at least be brought round to their side, and had some power to better their lives, as they had been promised. Now there was a cleavage between them and their governments, which pointed a finger at a bigger external power.

It was in devising defensive responses to this new situation that civil societies began to form in many countries. Until then, there had been a unity between the state and the people, which had arisen from twentieth century independence movements in Asia and Africa. Now the people had to articulate their voices against the state, even their own state. People began to build defensive, cross-class alliances to fight against the cutbacks in food subsidies, rises in taxes and prices, unemployment, shutdown of public facilities, pricing of previously freely available goods, and so forth (Cornia et al., 1987).

The resolution of the debt crisis of the 1980s was in one sense surprising and in another quite business-like. It took the intervention of the US government in the form of Brady Bonds (see Box 3.7, Glossary) to allow the banks to do what they normally do with bad debts: write them off. After much misery, much of the debt was written off, converted into equity, swapped for factories in debtor countries, or forgiven in recognition of some environmental good deed. It was painful and messy but once the write-off had been agreed by the developed country governments (which had to bear the tax burden of debt write-offs) the private commercial debt issue was resolved.

The 1990s: the peso and the Asian crises

The events of the 1990s were yet another phase of the movement that had started in the 1970s. Communist economies had by then collapsed and begun their transition to market economies. China had adopted market-oriented policies, albeit without renouncing socialism. Stock markets were springing up all over the emerging market economies. Developed countries had all by then deregulated capital movements. The financial markets and the foreign exchange markets were dealing in $1 trillion per day, helped by the revolution in telecommunications and information technology. The preferred form of capital flow was equity rather than debt. Foreign direct investment (FDI) flows to the Third World were soon outstripping foreign-aid flows by a factor of 4 to 1.

Two further shocks jolted the brave new world of global finance during the 1990s. First was the Mexican peso crisis in December 1994. Having followed an orthodox fiscal and monetary policy, much to the approval of the IMF, Mexico loosened the purse-strings in a pre-election year and made a risky dollar conversion of its debt. The uprising in Chiapas coincided with a transition to a new presidency, and the credibility of the peso collapsed. A massive rescue operation of $18 billion had to be organised by the IMF. A bad deflationary year followed in 1995 with much loss of output, but 1996 saw a recovery and a flow of funds back into Mexico.

The other shock was the Asian crisis of 1997 and 1998. This spread across nations previously hailed as miracle economies. Starting with the Thai bhat, the currency depreciation and stock market collapse moved to Malaysia, then to Indonesia, and finally to South Korea. The Asian crisis was truly the first crisis of globalisation of the late twentieth century. It started on the periphery but spread to the metropolis via Russia. It originated in the financial sector, which is at the forefront of globalisation. Its resolution, partially at least, came when the US Federal Reserve cut interest rates three times in quick succession in recognition of the likely impact of the crisis on US stock markets.

The Asian crisis was special in that it was triggered by bank lending rather than by portfolio investments or FDI. It took place in countries with high growth rates, high savings rates, and generally good macro-economic policies. The IMF misdiagnosed the crisis as one of 1980s-style macroeconomic mismanagement. But it was a private lending crisis, not a public finance one. The policy of pegged exchange rates proved to be inconsistent with unrestricted bank lending from abroad. What seemed like risk-free lending became risky when the bhat could no longer hold on to its peg to the US dollar. Since the bulk of the debt liability was in foreign currency, the domestic central bank could not help by performing its function as lender of last resort.

The Asian crisis was serious in terms of loss of output and currency depreciation. It also meant a substantial adverse impact on living standards of many people who had just recently emerged from poverty (see Box 3.2). In some countries, especially Indonesia but also Thailand and South Korea, the crisis became one of political authority. South Korea succeeded in making a transition to democracy and a peaceful change of regime, and Thailand reformed its constitution. Indonesia also went through a traumatic transition to democracy which remains fragile. The democratic deficit enhanced the need for civil society to organise resistance movements. By its clumsy intervention, the IMF seemed to be as

In East Asia, it was reckless lending by international banks and other financial institutions combined with reckless borrowing by domestic financial institutions—combined with fickle investor expectations—which may have precipitated the crisis; but the costs—in terms of soaring unemployment and plummeting wages—were borne by workers. Workers were asked to listen to sermons about bearing pain just a short while after hearing, from the same preachers, sermons about how globalisation and opening up capital markets would bring them unprecedented growth.

(Stiglitz 2000: 1)

East Asia enjoyed an unprecedented 7 per cent GDP growth per year for the last two decades of the twentieth century. This enabled some countries in the region, namely, Hong Kong, South Korea, Singapore, and Taiwan, to become the only ones to actually make the transition from Third World to First World. Following the 1997 crisis, the region's economies shrank by 4 per cent (United Nations 1999). Inflation and unemployment, hitherto virtually unknown in most of these countries, sky-rocketed. Although most of the region's economies managed to recover by 1999, they remain below their potential level had pre-crisis trends persisted:

GDP deviation from pre-crises growth trend in 1999 (%)	
Indonesia	−16.6
Malaysia	−7.2
Korea	−12.9
Thailand	−14.5
Source: World Bank (2000)	

The crisis left these countries with a heavy public debt burden, forcing the governments to spend a greater proportion of GDP on interest payments.

Increase in debt servicing costs as % of GDP after the crisis	
Indonesia	3.9
Malaysia	2.2
Korea	0.5
Philippines	2.1
Thailand	10.3
Source: World Bank (2000)	

While most of the region's economies are growing again, the social consequences of the crisis persist. In the aftermath of the crisis, the number of people in the region earning less than $1 day increased. by 10 million (18 per cent).

South Korea, which had an unemployment rate of 2 per cent before the crisis, was still reporting a rate of 4 per cent at the end of 2000, despite the fact that the economy grew by 9.5 per cent in the same year. Real unemployment is even higher, as unemployment numbers do not reflect either the percentage of people who are nominally employed but receive no salary or the 117,000 migrant workers who had to leave South Korea after the crisis. South Korea also had no unemployment insurance until the crisis. The scheme since established does not cover most of the unemployed. Real wages declined by 14 per cent in the aftermath of the crises after growing by 7.3 per cent in 1996. This, combined with inflation, led consumer spending to decline by 12 per cent, the steepest drop in South Korean history. The result of all this is a persisting increase in poverty. Before the crisis 7.5 per cent of the urban population were poor. This number jumped to 23 per cent at the height of the crises and was standing at 14 per cent at the end of 1999, despite the recovery.

In Indonesia, unemployment rose from 4.9 per cent to 13.8 per cent after the crisis. Real wages dropped by between 40 per cent and 60 per cent. The percentage of people living in poverty jumped from 11 per cent in 1996 to 20 per cent at the end of 1999, an addition of 20 million people.

In Thailand, unemployment remains at three times the pre-crisis level, despite strong recovery. Combined with a 6 per cent decline in real wages, this translates into an increased incidence of poverty of 15 per cent.

Hong Kong and South Korea are the only East Asian countries who have an unemployment insurance system. In Hong Kong unemployment rose from 2.2 per cent in 1997 to 5 per cent in 1998. At the end of 2000 it stood at 5 per cent despite two consecutive years of growth.

The cost of the Asian crisis, 1996–1999

	1996	1997	1998	1999
GDP growth rates (%) (IMF)				
Total	6.6	5.2	−4.0	
Hong Kong	4.5	5.0	−5.0	2.9
Indonesia	8.0	4.5	−13.0	0.3
Korea	6.8	5.0	−6.7	10.7
Malaysia	10.0	7.3	−7.4	5.7
Philippines	5.8	5.2	−0.6	3.3
Singapore	8.0	8.4	0.4	5.4
Taiwan	5.7	6.8	4.7	5.7
Thailand	5.9	-1.7	−10.0	4.2
Unemployment as a percentage of workforce (ILO)				
Hong Kong	2.8	2.2	4.7	6.3
Indonesia	4.0	4.68	5.46	N/A
Korea	2.0	2.6	6.8	6.3
Malaysia	2.5	2.5	3.2	3.4
Philippines	7.4	7.9	9.6	9.37
Singapore	3.0	2.4	3.2	4.6
Taiwan	N/A	N/A	N/A	N/A
Thailand	1.08	0.87	3.41	3.0

Sources: Stiglitz (2000); United Nations (1999); World Bank (2000).

much part of the problem as of any solution. The insistence of the Malaysian Prime Minister, Dr Mahathir, that controls on capital movements be revived in face of IMF opposition strengthened this impression, as in the event Malaysia did insulate itself against the worst effects of the crisis.

Calls for reform of the international financial institutions, for a new 'global financial architecture', were made in the wake of the Asian crisis during the summer of 1998. But the resolution of the immediate impact on US markets by the Federal Reserve cooled the ardour for any fundamental change among the G7 countries. No lender of last resort has been set up at the global level. The IMF escaped either bolstering of its powers or downsizing, as advocated by the Meltzer Report for the US Congress (IFIAC 2000). There were some changes in terms of greater transparency, greater accountability, and wider consultation with developing countries.[2] But there was no radical reform.

Growth and persistence of foreign direct investment

Through the 1990s, despite the peso and the Asian crises, the movement of FDI to developing countries proved much less volatile than that of portfolio capital or bank lending. This has not excused FDI from criticism and its volume now exceeds that of foreign aid by between three and four times. While the large volume of turnover in the foreign exchange and bond markets—$1 trillion plus daily—attracts much attention, it is FDI which has effects at a local level and has longer-term effects on growth, employment, and the environment than portfolio capital. Its spread is confined to a small number of countries with high savings rates, large pools of semi-skilled labour, good governance, and high levels of literacy. There is, however, no IFI which monitors FDI or polices its accountability. Within the domestic jurisdiction of all OECD countries, there are tough regulations on corporations (for example, the US Justice Department's moves against Microsoft) and regulatory bodies such as the Securities and Exchange Commission in the US and the Financial Services Authority in the UK. There is, however, no move afoot today for a global regulator of FDI. The Multilateral Agreement on Investments (MAI) was an attempt to

2 *For an overview of the Financial Stability Forum and other IMF reforms, see IMF (URL).*

introduce a uniform structure of rules for both domestic and foreign capital, but it did not extend to a uniform and universal regulation regime such as exists in individual OECD countries. The demise of the MAI was due as much to protests by the NGOs as to the reluctance of the US Congress to contemplate symmetric treatment of foreign and domestic capital. (see Box 3.3)

If there has been no global move towards regulation of FDI or any serious move for the reform of the IFIs, there has been a successful single-issue movement—Jubilee 2000—for the reduction of Third World debt.(see Box 3.4) While the petrodollar debt owed to commercial

banks caused serious debt default problems in the 1980s and much misery, it was resolved, as noted above, by some cancellation of debt, some payment in lieu in the form of environmental policy changes, and even some capital sales. Public debt has proved to be a much tougher nut to crack. For one thing, the World Bank, as well as the governments of developing countries who are the lenders, do not believe in writing off bad debt. What is a sound commercial practice is forbidden to public agencies. This is a peculiar example of the inflexibility of government finance.

This Third World debt arises from a small amount of intergovernmental or IFI lending to some very

---

Box 3.3: The demise of the MAI

At the end of 1998, negotiations within the framework of the Organisation for Economic Cooperation and Development (OECD) for a Multilateral Agreement on Investment (MAI) were abandoned. The collapse of the negotiations was precipitated by a number of factors including a broad international campaign coordinated by Friends of the Earth, 50 Years Is Enough, and other international and local groups.

The MAI was intended to promote cross-border investments by providing a unified set of rules governing interactions between governments and investors worldwide. The rules proposed were favourable to investors, prohibiting governments from discriminating among or against them and giving investors the right to prosecute offending governments in international courts. For example, the agreement would have eliminated a government's right to place certain industries or areas of activity out of reach for foreign investors. It would have prohibited the imposition of local content or other performance requirements committing foreign investors to purchase a certain proportion of their outlays from local suppliers or to create local jobs. It would have allowed investors the freedom to move money in and out of countries without restrictions and prohibited any form of expropriation.

The negotiations, which were taking place largely unnoticed since 1995, began to attract unwanted attention after the Asian crisis of 1997. The crisis left both governments and activists with little appetite for further financial-market liberalisation.

Disagreements among G7 countries were also on the rise. The US wanted to maintain the right to persecute companies investing in Cuba or Iran. France wanted to protect its film industry from Hollywood. Hungary wanted to preserve employee and management-centred privatisation schemes. In the end it was France's withdrawal from the process which sealed the MAI's fate.

Activists succeeded in amplifying and leveraging government disagreements up to the point of defeating the MAI.

The critical method employed by anti-MAI campaigners was education and information. They provided in-depth analysis of the proposed agreements and their possible environmental, social, and political implications. They published glossaries explaining obscure legal and trade terms and provided real-time coverage and analysis of the negotiating positions.

This was probably the first time such negotiations were conducted in the spotlight of public attention. It presented a radical break from the tradition of conducting negotiations among technocrats away from public scrutiny, providing only a doctored summary of concluded agreements to the public and parliaments at the ratification stage.

One may agree with the technocrats' contention that the popularised version of the MAI draft agreements and the analysis of their impact by NGOs are not scientifically accurate or that many of those involved in the debates were not qualified to pass judgement on such matters. This is changing poor countries in the late 1980s and early 1990s, including Uganda, Mozambique, and Niger. The original principal has now mushroomed into a much larger sum due to the inability of many of the debtor countries to service it, as unpaid instalments have been added and compounded. The size of the debt now bears little relation to the original amount. Debtor countries have been weakened by the collapse of primary commodity prices since the late 1970s and many local and civil wars. Individual G7 countries have taken some initiatives; the UK has been in the lead since 1990, when John Major was briefly the Chancellor of Exchequer, and has accelerated this lead under Chancellor Gordon Brown; but the World Bank's Highly Indebted Poor Countries (HIPC) initiative has been on the table since the mid-1990s. It has been mired in inaction. The total amounts are smaller than those in the 1980s but the debtor countries are now much poorer. It is also more difficult to persuade countries, especially the G7 which dominate the voting in the IFIs, to agree to any debt forgiveness.

Paradoxically, Third World debt, which Jubilee 2000 focused on, has little to do with globalisation. Indeed, it is the countries which cannot access the private lenders in the form of either debt or equity because

rapidly, however, and many activists today have access to high-quality research on economic issues. The campaign against the MAI was, however, a breakthrough in terms of democratising international trade negotiations by providing the public with an alternative opinion; forcing politicians to scrutinise the proposed agreement; and requiring the technocrats to be more transparent and to defend their positions to a sceptical public.

The MAI negotiations also witnessed increased cooperation/coordination between NGOs and governments trying to alter or stop the agreement altogether. France used NGO arguments against the agreement in both domestic and international deliberations. The government-commissioned Lalumière Report, conducted in the summer of 1998, relied heavily on NGO testimony to justify France's reservations (Friends of the Earth 1998a).

The MAI defeat was a temporary and, some would say, a pyrrhic victory for civil society. Most groups involved in the campaign would have preferred to see an alternative agreement which would regulate foreign investments in ways that protect the environment, labour, human rights, and indigenous cultures. Many wanted to see multinational corporations and financiers brought under national or international jurisdiction. An international agreement on investment is necessary to avoid a race to the bottom among governments in their quest for foreign investments. Faced with the choice between a dangerous treaty and an even more dangerous lack thereof, campaigners, unable to come up with a comprehens-

ive alternative, opted for the latter. They leveraged the nationalism of individual governments to derail the whole process.

Offering suggested changes to the MA is a trickier issue. Whereas it is important to eliminate the MAI's worst features in case the agreement goes forward, but [sic!] eliminating those sections alone would not result in an acceptable agreement. Good rules on investment would include binding language on investors' responsibilities for the environment, workers and human rights. Therefore, signalling any support for the MAI in exchange for textual changes can be dangerous because the agreement as a whole is fundamentally unbalanced in favour of investors. (Friends of the Earth 1998b)

The issues covered under the MAI are back on the table again through the General Agreement on Trade in Services (GATS) in the framework of the WTO. GATS covers a much wider area of activities than investment alone and is already the target of intense opposition from activists worldwide (see for instance the World Development Movement URL). Will they be able to advance an internationalist alternative or will they ally themselves with protectionists to derail the whole process as they did with the MAI?

by Ann Pettifor, Programme Coordinator, Jubilee Plus at the New Economics Foundation, UK, and previously director of Jubilee 2000 UK.

Jubilee 2000 succeeded in many ways, but fell far short of achieving its goal of 'cancelling the unpayable debts of the poorest countries by the year 2000'. But the campaign could be said to have had some success in several respects:

1. It placed the issue of third world debt firmly on the political agenda. The campaign was launched in 1996. In 1998 a MORI poll commissioned by the aid agency CAFOD revealed that 69 per cent of the public wanted the British government to celebrate the millennium by cancelling Third World debt rather than building the Millennium Dome. At the end of the campaign, another MORI opinion poll commissioned by CAFOD found that two-thirds of those with an opinion supported Jubilee 2000. Only one in ten people actually opposed the Jubilee 2000 campaign, indicating that concern about corruption in the Third World did not reduce support for debt cancellation (CAFOD, press release, 7 July 1999). In a poll commissioned by *The Scotsman* during the 2001 British general elections, the issue of Third World debt was considered more important by Scottish voters than the issue of Europe (*The Scotsman*, 15 May 2001).

2. A global social movement was built, united around this one issue. By 2000, after just four years of campaigning, there were Jubilee 2000 campaigns, of varying strengths and character, in 68 countries. The national campaigns were autonomous but shared overall goals, symbols, and information—and a tremendous sense of solidarity. The campaigns were based in countries as diverse as Angola and Japan, Colombia and Sweden, Honduras and Israel, Togo and the United States (Jubilee 2000 URL). The ability to cooperate and coordinate our campaigning was greatly enhanced by use of the Internet.

3. Confidence was built in developing country governments. In their negotiations with the Bretton Woods Institutions and with Paris Club bilateral creditors, the representatives of poor debtor nations were often cowed by the financial power and clout of bureaucracies serving the G7 powers. The growth of a social movement in the North that supported their human rights and called for international financial justice encouraged developing country representatives to strengthen their negotiating stances and to appeal

over the heads of bureaucracies like the IMF to the electorates in Western countries. President Obasanjo of Nigeria used this tactic in the US and in a meeting with the G7 in Japan before the 2000 Okinawa Summit. And at the UN Financing for Development Conference in New York in May 2001, the G77, led by Iran, made strong challenges to the OECD countries on the debt issue.

How did we achieve this? The main reason for our success in fthe UK was that millions of ordinary people supported the campaign. Without them, there would have been no successes. However, Jubilee 2000 did facilitate their involvement. Below we list some of the techniques used by the coordinating group in London and suggest action points for other campaigners:

- First, study the problem very carefully and produce an analysis and long-term strategy which reflects many approaches. We describe this as similar to the challenge facing diamond-cutters: they sometimes study a stone for two years before cutting it; they then cut it in a way which will give maximum reflection of all the facets. Many issues, like trade for developing countries and the role of the IMF and the World Bank are not analysed precisely and accurately, and therefore do not give maximum reflection to all facets of the problem. Part of getting this right is a matter of instinct, based of course on experience and extensive knowledge—rather like sailor Ellen McArthur's success in 'reading the winds' during her historic round the world race.

- Look for a strong and straightforward argument—for example, a moral or social one—which will encourage people to attempt to get to grips with technical or political issues.

- Use the campaign's core issue as a rallying point for diverse groups, individuals, and organisations that wouldn't usually work together. In other words, build a coalition. But don't be choosy about who is in it; welcome anyone on the sole condition that they back the principles underlying your campaign.

- Coalitions are difficult to handle; some are loose, with no leadership and little coherence. Ours was strong, with clear leadership. One of the key responsibilities of the leadership must be to maintain respect and communication with all partners, regardless of their level of knowledge, experience, political or financial influence, and political or religious allegiance or background. Allow a thousand flowers to bloom; be very open and inclusive. Support members of the coalition by providing easily digestible information, which can be adapted to their needs. This is particularly important for those that do not usually work on the issue. Allow others to use the branding to promote their own organisation, to raise funds, and to promote their own particular contribution to the campaign.

- Make the campaign brief (this is less threatening to established coalition members) and set a deadline to achieve the key objective(s); and stick by this 'closing date' This helps to keep a broad front of organisations together.

- Make use of world events which illustrate your case—for example, the floods in Honduras, after which that country paid more in debt service than it received in aid. This means being 'opportunistic' and responding quickly to events.

- Devise easy, specific and non-threatening actions that ordinary people will feel confident and justified in undertaking in order to express the case for the campaign.

- Write a petition and ensure that its wording is carefully devised to unite the widest possible range of people behind the campaign. Don't use it just for counting signatures but apply it as part of a wider process and opportunity for engaging and educating people.

- If you are campaigning for changes in the South, be sure to provide a platform in the North for spokespersons from the South. Make it possible for them to speak for themselves and to speak directly about their experience.

- Keep looking for opportunities to raise expectations beyond those that may be considered normal but which retain a sense of 'just about possible'. This builds excitement, energy, and leadership. We used goals that were beyond reasonable expectations yet were on the edge of practicality, pushing the boundaries.

- Involve different faiths in the campaign: once people of faith are properly involved then the campaign becomes difficult to resist. They and their organisations need to be closely involved both internationally and locally.

- The coordinating group must genuinely have the will and commitment to be very open in communicating information. You must believe that ordinary people will be able to grasp and deal with complex issues. Our supporters astonished officials and politicians with their grasp of complex facts.

- Be prepared to take measured risks. We often did not have more than three months funding in the bank.

- Keep the campaign fashionable and ahead of the game by (a) involving celebrities; and (b) loudly acknowledging and celebrating successes and achievements. But be aware of the risks and limitations of celebrity involvement; and don't waste their time unless you have something that really meshes with their profile and commitment. Ensure that the relationship is a two-way one: that they get something out of it too.

- The core coordination team should be made up of people with a diversity of backgrounds and cultures in order to reflect the full range of interest in the campaign.

- All individuals and organisations taking part in the campaign must keep focused on its overall mission and goals; their own agendas must be subservient to it. Working for campaigns like these should not be considered a safe career move.

These are some of the techniques we used. None of them, however would have worked without the willingness of ordinary people to give precious time, resources, and commitment to the campaign. The credit for the success of Jubilee 2000 belongs overwhelmingly to these millions of people, most of whom will never be recognised for their role but who used their individual strengths to promote the cause of the most indebted nations. They achieved this at a time when 'aid fatigue' was supposedly pervasive and deep cynicism about the motives and altruism of voters was widespread.

they are abysmally poor that are forced into the arms of governmental or multilateral institutional lenders. Their plight is an aspect of the unequal nature of the global power structure as enshrined by the UN constitution, which gives veto power to the permanent members of the security council, and in the decision-making structures of the Bretton Woods institutions. The Asian crisis was a crisis of countries that had become just rich enough to be attractive to private lenders. The public-debt crisis is that of countries that are too poor to be of interest to commercial lenders and too weak to be a threat to the powerful governments which have lent them money.

Anti-capitalism: An Overview

Throughout the 40 or so years following 1945, there was a vibrant anti-capitalist movement, in the form either of orthodox Leninist Communist parties or of democratic socialist parties. Feminist and civil rights movements were added to this worldwide. The focus everywhere was the state because the state was seen as an instrument of control over capital or over the unequal power structure. Political parties of the left were part of this broad protest movement even when they were in office, as were the trade unions which supported these parties. The 1960s saw a big explosion of these movements across Western Europe and in the USA at a time when 'capitalism in one country' was perhaps performing at its best in terms of full employment and growth. The 1970s saw a worsening of economic performance, with stagflation and a deepening of the crisis of the state, but also of resistance against it. But even in the 1970s the various national movements were separate; only the environmental movement forged global interconnections. It was the changes in the 1970s and in the 1980s discussed above which shattered the logic of capitalism or socialism in one country and began to shape the new global economy not as an ecological ideal but as an economic reality.

The anti-capitalist movement of the 1960s and 1970s was wounded if not defeated by the structural changes which capitalism underwent in the 1980s in the developing countries. The collapse of the Soviet Union demoralised the Leninist left and shut down many Communist parties. There was instead a growth of NGOs, many of them concerned with development or ecological issues. Other movements, like the women's movement and human rights campaigns,

survived the neo-liberal onslaught of the 1980s. They have now emerged as the opposition to globalisation in the 1990s and beyond. Their numbers are larger, both individually and in their memberships. They are more globally networked. They are also less connected with political parties. In the following sections these movements are analysed in terms of their stances on the financial effects of globalisation.

The last ten years have witnessed historic changes in the world system. The state socialist countries of Europe have transformed themselves into fledgling democracies and fragile market economies. Across OECD countries, social democratic parties in office or out of it have rethought their old philosophies and abandoned any desire for state ownership or control of capital. A system of countries each pursuing 'capitalism in one country' with weak articulation through trade has changed into one with strong articulation through international capital flows, inter-country, inter-corporate competition, flexible exchange rates, and converging long-term interest rates through global bond markets. Governments have suffered a narrowing of their scope for fiscal discretion. Stock markets have grown in size and numbers across the world. The logic of globalisation is one of unregulated global flows and a single bond market, although that logic is as yet far from realised.

Civil Society and Global Finance: Four Responses

Interactions between civil society and global capitalism take place at two friction points. At one point, society is reacting to market encroachment on both personal and public spaces: consumerism, atomisation, the erosion of public services, and nation state models of democracy. At the other, society is reacting to socio-economic consequences of capitalism such as poverty, inequality, and instability.

At these friction points the anti-capitalist movement raises two corresponding sets of questions:

1. What are the boundaries of the market? How are they determined and enforced?
2. Can the market be trusted to produce just and stable outcomes or does it require external intervention? How would such intervention be carried out?

These questions, although as old as capitalism itself, have gained in relevance over the past 20 years, providing an impetus to the anti-capitalist movement. The reasons for this renewed attention are set out below.

First, there is a perception that liberal democracy is lagging behind neo-liberal economics or even being threatened by it (Mittelman 2000). The neo-liberal reforms rammed through during the 1980s by right-of-centre governments in the West and by the IMF in the East and the South, the inexorable encroachment of the market into the public sphere, the unchecked reign of multinational corporations, and the apparent inability of national leaders to challenge any of the above has given the anti-capitalist movement a new angle of attack.

Second, the abandonment of nation state-based answers to the contradictions of capitalism, be they the welfare state in the North or state-sponsored development or superpower patronage in the South, is generating pockets of extreme poverty in both rich and poor countries. While overall levels of prosperity are increasing, the situation at the bottom of the socio-economic ladder has actually been deteriorating. The widening gap between rich and poor, both within and between countries, is increasingly difficult to conceal, justify, or sustain.

The anti-capitalist movement has changed in tandem with its target. In the era of state capitalism the focus was on the state. Some wanted to capture it, others to reform it, and yet others just wanted it out of the way. Today, attention is shifting to the corporation as the main target of the anti-capitalist movement. Some strands of the movement against corporate globalisation would even call for protecting and strengthening the territorial state while others demand solutions that require the creation of a global welfare state. To be sure, the state, especially in the G7 countries, remains an important target for many movements. There is a growing awareness, however, of the limitations of state power under globalisation.

The movement against global capitalism falls into four groups: isolationists, supporters, reformists, and alternatives. As with all such classifications, no movement, campaign, or event can be allocated solely to any one of the categories. Many shift from one to the other depending on the issue, event, or time frame in question.

Isolationists

In addition to remnants of Communist and Stalinist groups, isolationists include some environmental groups such as Friends of the Earth, who tend to be more radical in their economic than in their ecological agenda; think tanks and groups promoting national solutions to Third World development issues, such as Focus on the Global South; anti-globalisation groups such as the International Forum on Globalisation, Global Exchange, and 50 Years Is Enough; local social movements such as the Landless Peasants Movement in Brazil (MST); individuals such as Walden Bello and Noam Chomsky; and media outlets such as Le Monde Diplomatique.

The isolationists represent the only global civil society response to global capitalism which openly claims to be anti-globalisation. The isolationists call directly or indirectly for the abolition of the existing global economic order. Walden Bello says:

> *Indeed, I would contend that the focus of our efforts these days is not to try to reform the multilateral agencies but to deepen the crisis of legitimacy of the whole. I am talking about disabling not just the WTO, the IMF, and the World Bank but the transnational corporation itself. And I am not talking about a process of 're-regulating' the TNCs but of eventually disabling or dismantling them as fundamental hazards to people, society, the environment, to everything we hold dear. (Bello 2000)*

Other isolationists are less categorical. Many call for 'economic diversity' (Friends of the Earth 2000), presumably allowing for certain elements of global capitalism to continue in some areas. The demands they advance, however, can hardly be compatible with a functioning market economy, particularly given their objection to such concepts as economic growth or comparative advantage.

Isolationists treat globalisation and global capitalism as synonyms. They oppose globalisation in most of its manifestations, promoting instead deglobalization (Bello 2000) or localization (Hines 2000) which entails:

- economic subsidiarity: trade should be minimised, goods should be produced as closely as possible to the site of consumption;
- *political subsidiarity:* states and local communities should be re-empowered at the expense of transnational corporations and international organisations, decisions should be

taken as closely as possible to where they take effect; and

- *self-sufficiency:* resources for investment should be mobilised locally, reliance on foreign investment should be minimised.

In their blanket opposition to the IMF and the World Bank, left-wing isolationists find strange bed-fellows among their right-wing rivals and supporters of global capitalism. To quote Bello on this subject:

The motivation of the incoming Republicans in criticising the IMF and World Bank lies in their belief in free-market solutions to development and growth. This may not coincide with that of progressives, who see the IMF and World Bank as a tool of US hegemony. But the two sides can unite behind one agenda at this point: the radical downsizing, if not dismantling, of the Bretton Woods twins. (Bello 2001)

On the specific issues of global finance, the isolationists hold the following positions.

Public debt. Third World debt is a direct consequence and responsibility of Western powers, banks, and international lending institutions. Loans were knowingly made to corrupt and/or incompetent Third World leaders for political reasons, for example to ensure loyalty during the cold war or to perpetuate a relationship of dependence. Lending was also used as a beachhead to secure access for transnational corporations. Hence, all Third World debts should be written off. Moreover, given the real transfers[3] from the Third World to the rich countries caused by unfavourable terms of trade and interest payments and outright looting in colonial days, the debt relationship should be reversed. In the future, Third World countries should avoid borrowing altogether and rely on their own resources for investments.

Short-term capital flows. Equity investments, derivatives, and foreign exchange transactions are all part of a global casino. On the upside, they only enrich Western speculators; on the downside, they cause widespread suffering to working people both in the North and in the South. Speculators often get bailed out by the IMF and other rescue programmes. They may even benefit from crises, as did George

Soros, attacking the European Union's exchange rate mechanism and the Thai bhat.

Short-term capital flows are inherently volatile and destabilising. The responsibility for financial crises such as those in 1997–8 lies squarely on the shoulders of Western speculators and their private-sector counterparts in the afflicted countries. It also lies with the IMF, which forced the emerging economies to liberalise their capital markets in the first place. Post-crisis IMF interventions bail out speculators while aggravating the effects on working people. Countries should have the option to introduce currency and exchange controls and opt out of the global capital market altogether.

Long-term foreign direct investments. Foreign investments benefit only the multinational corporations that make them. They serve to perpetuate the exploitation of the poor and destroy the environment. Consequently, structural adjustment programmes and other liberal reforms aimed at encouraging foreign investments are part of the same conspiracy:

DEBT → DEBT CRISIS → STRUCTURAL ADJUSTMENT → OPENING TO TRANSNATIONAL CORPORATIONS

Self-reliance and self-sufficiency are the only way forward. This is the unifying slogan which brings together the isolationists in the Third World with protectionists in the North by shielding national favourites, such as state-sponsored manufacturing industries, in the developing countries and sunset industries, such as the car industry, in developed ones.

Supporters

Civil society responses to global finance in the 'supporters' category include no movements and very few NGOs. They consist mainly of organisations, groups, media outlets, think tanks and individuals lobbying on behalf of business, be it an individual company, an industry, or private enterprise in general. Examples of supporters include the Centre for Civil Society in India, the Chamber of British Industry in the UK, the American Enterprise Institute in the US, The Economist, The Wall Street Journal, the Meltzer Commission, and Thomas Friedman.

Although attention is usually devoted to instances when the interests of civil society collide with those of global capitalism, the interactions between the two are not always negative. Civil society may benefit

---

[3] *Adverse terms of trade meant that Third World countries over many years sold relatively cheap raw materials to industrialised countries in exchange for relatively expensive manufactured goods.*

when market expansion takes place at the expense of authoritarian regimes, fundamentalism, or autarky. Capitalism can also be more just and efficient than such alternatives as feudalism or central planning. This is the main rationale behind civil society responses which are unequivocally supportive of global capitalism in its current form. Supporters are indeed, the most influential of the civil society responses to global capitalism.

Since they occupy the two extreme ends of the spectrum, it should come as no surprise that supportive responses to global capitalism often coincide with isolationist positions. For diametrically different reasons both are dismissive of reforms and global governance proposals aimed at mitigating the negative consequences of global capitalism. The most important point of agreement among them is the equation of globalisation and global capitalism. As Thomas Friedman says:

> The driving idea behind globalization is free-market capitalism—the more you let market forces rule and the more you open your economy to free trade and competition, the more efficient and flourishing your economy will be. Globalization means the spread of free-market capitalism to virtually every country in the world. Globalization also has its own set of economic rules—rules that revolve around opening, deregulating and privatising your economy. (Friedman 2000)

Global capitalism, according to its supporters, is not only the best way to prosperity: it is the only way. 'There Is No Alternative' (TINA) is an often-repeated argument to this end. TINA does not only mean that anyone who refuses to open up to global capitalism will be left behind; it also points to the perils of rolling back global capitalism. Supporters claim that if governments and international organisations succumb to anti-capitalist sentiments and try to rein in global capitalism, then globalisation as a whole will be rolled back, leading inevitably to results similar to those encountered when the previous era of globalisation came to an end early in the twentieth century, namely, war, fascism, and communism.

Supporters not only bristle at all forms of anti-capitalism but also reject most reform proposals. According to the supporters, all the injustices and inefficiencies attributed to global capitalism are not a result of too much market but of too little.

Government interference of all kinds, including protectionism, welfare provisions, corruption, and incompetence is, according to them, responsible for the plight of the poor. The *Economist* (2000) states:

> Governments are apologising for globalisation and promising to civilise it. Instead if they had any regard for the plight of the poor, they would be accelerating it, celebrating it, exalting it . . .

Supporters attack the World Bank and the IMF for even listening to NGOs, let alone engaging them in any serious deliberations. Many of them are actually opposed to these and other international institutions as examples of interventionist big government. On the specific issues of global finance, the supporters hold the following positions.

Public debt. Most of the burden of Third World debt is the responsibility of corrupt and incompetent governments. Cancelling it will not help these countries but may actually hurt them if it is seen as rewarding bad government. Government lending in the future should be kept to a minimum and used mostly as an instrument of foreign policy. Even international lending institutions should try to stay out of the debt market. The Meltzer Report (IFIAC 2000), for example, recommends that the World Bank use grants rather than loans, but these should be disbursed through private service providers instead of being handed to governments.

Short-term flows. Short-term flows, be they loans, portfolio investments, foreign-exchange transactions, derivatives, or other exotic instruments are all part of the proper functioning of market mechanisms. Derivatives, for example, help distribute risk in a way that best reflects market realities and the preferences of individual market participants. Crises attributed to short-term flows, such as the Asian crisis, always have their roots in government interference, in this case Asian crony capitalism and subsequent IMF intervention. The answer is, therefore, always more liberalisation.

Long-term foreign direct investment. FDI is the best way to match savings and investments worldwide. It allocates financial resources to their most productive use, promotes the best technologies, and produces the most-needed products and services. Moreover, FDI is the best way to transfer know-how and technology, business prowess, and even democratic culture. FDI is the only way for the Third World to catch up.

Not only is it self-defeating for countries to place any restrictions on foreign investment; they should do their utmost to attract it. This is done through neo-liberal reforms including deregulation, privatisation, small government, balanced budgets, and tight money. The pain and dislocation caused by these policies are all justified by the expected benefits.

Reformists

The majority of movements, organisations, and campaigns active in the area of global finance are reformist. They include the bulk of the labour movement and associated think tanks such as the Institute for Policy Studies; development organisations such as Oxfam and WorldVision; watchdogs such as the World Development Movement and the Bretton Woods Project; issue-specific campaigns such as Jubilee 2000 and Action pour une Taxe Tobin d'Aide aux Citoyens (ATTAC); and individuals such as George Soros and Ann Pettifor. Even James Wolfenson, the head of the World Bank, could be included in this category.

Reformists comprise a broad category ranging form NGOs dedicated to monitoring the IMF to those IMF employees who are serious about reform. The reformists aim 'at partial change to try to offset current injustices and inequalities' (Cohen and Rai 2000: 2). Unlike the isolationists, movements demanding cancellation of Third World debt or IMF reforms are not pursuing a radical new social order.

The reformists pursue variations on the 'social democratic' agenda for the global era. Their aim is to maintain the advantages of the capitalist model while mitigating its excesses through re-regulation and redistribution. As the largest US trades union states:

We need a global New Deal that establishes new rules to temper the excesses of the market; promote sustainable egalitarian growth; and assure the rights of working people everywhere are respected.
(AFL-CIO 1998)

The reformists view themselves as the only true defenders of globalisation. They believe that both isolationist calls to reverse the process and supporters' insistence on 'ultra-liberal' forms of global capitalism are bound to derail globalisation, with tragic consequences. According to reformists, globalisation can succeed only if it is civilised and made more democratic, equitable, and stable.

Reformists propose a variety of global governance solutions to address this task. These proposals are usually built around reforming or augmenting existing international institutions or establishing new ones.

The reformists advance a set of global governance initiatives such as the Tobin tax (explained below) or regulations for multinational corporations, which may actually require a global state to implement. John Cavanagh says:

Some scholars such as Walden Bello, argue that developing countries would be better-off with no international financial institution rather than the IMF because this would allow local and national governments and citizens groups more autonomy in pursuing alternative development strategies. However, in an era of global capital, we would ideally have international financial institutions that could help reduce volatility and contagion in ways that can not be accomplished through nation states. An International Bankruptcy Authority has already been discussed. In addition, a number of scholars have proposed the creation of a new Global Financial Authority or a Global Central Bank. (Anderson and Cavanagh 2000)

On the specific global finance issues the reformists hold the following positions, although given the wide range of groups in this category the positions listed here are not all encompassing:

Public debt. Both developed and developing countries share the responsibility for the debt overhang and should share the burden of its resolution. For example, countries should be compensated for failed structural adjustment programmes or World Bank projects, which would offset some of their outstanding obligations. Debt should be cancelled for the poorest countries. The burden for the rest should be reduced to a level where it does not jeopardise their ability to provide basic human services. An International Bankruptcy Mechanism should be established to deal with debt cancellation and restructuring in situations when countries are no longer capable of meeting their debt obligations (Anderson and Cavanagh 2000).

Both lenders and borrowers should ensure that lending proceeds through an open and transparent process to avoid misuse through corruption or incompetence. Civil society should be involved in all stages of the process.

Short-term flows. The position of the reformists on short-term flows is close to that of the isolationists. Instead of dismissing these flows out of hand, however, the reformists seek solutions which would reorient them from speculation to long-term investment. Countries should have the option to impose 'speed bumps' and other defensive measures based on internationally agreed criteria. The IMF should not pursue the opening up of the capital account in member countries but should leave that to the discretion of governments. In case of crises, rescue packages should be aimed at minimising the negative impact on the real economy as opposed to bailing out reckless investors.

At the global level, proposals to tame short-term flows range from strengthening existing regulations to the establishment of a global lender of last resort/central bank and a Tobin tax. Named after the Nobel Prize-winning economist James Tobin of Yale University, such a tax of anything between 0.05 and 0.25 per cent levied on all foreign-exchange transactions would act as a deterrent to speculative transactions. The ATTAC platform claims that:

Even fixed at a particularly low rate of 0.05%, the Tobin tax would gather close to 100 billion dollars a year. Collected, primarily, by industrialised countries, where the largest financial centres are located, the sum could be redirected to international organisations for activities aimed at fighting inequality, promoting education and public health in poor countries and food security and sustainable development. This kind of mechanism would put sand in the gears of speculation. It would feed the logic of resistance, give citizens and nations back some room to manoeuvre and in particular it would show that politics can be restored to its proper place.
(Platform ATTAC 1998)

Long-term foreign direct investment. Few reformists would deny the benefits of foreign investment. Like the supporters, the reformists believe that foreign investment is the best way to allocate capital to its most productive uses. It is also the only way for poor countries to catch up with the rich given the difference in savings rates.

As discussed above, the reformists promote solutions which would redirect short-term flows to longer-term investments. The reformists, however, reject the link between neo-liberal structural adjustment policies and the flow of investments. Indeed, they reject neo-liberal structural adjustment policies because of the pain they cause to the poorest in society, their 'one-size-fits-all' approach, and the fact that they have not even been proved to promote growth or investment.

The reformists also emphasise the need to augment private investments by public funds to achieve development goals. According to the ICFTU (2000), for example, public investments by both national governments and IFIs should be targeted at social protection, primary education, health care, and employment.

Alternatives

The anti-capitalist protests in Seattle 1999, Washington 2000, and Prague 2000 were driven by the alternatives. Alternatives exist both as organisations—for example, the Zapatistas, Adbusters, and Reclaim the Streets—and as 'submerged networks' which come to the fore only around certain campaigns or exercise resistance through a particular lifestyle, such as INPEG (see Box 3.1), which existed only for the purpose of organising the Prague protests, or alternative money (LETS) groups (see Box 3.1). Alternatives are wary of leaders but there are alternative spokespeople like Naomi Klein and Subcomandante Marcos. (see Box 3.5)

Instead of aiming to transform or reform global capitalism, the alternatives are concerned with reclaiming 'things' from the encroaching market and creating space for alternatives. They are concerned with the political and cultural consequences of capitalism as much as they are with its economic and environmental costs. They perceive the encroachment of the market into the public space as a threat to democracy, which takes the form of 'corporate censorship' in the North and human rights abuses in the South (Klein 1999).

The fact that the alternatives comprise broad coalitions means that it is difficult to pin down their agenda or even what they stand for. But instead of being a weakness, the lack of a 'little red book' is

The story of the Zapatistas' uprising is a textbook example of the relation between the local and the global in civil society today. The Zapatista Army for National Liberation burst on to the international stage when it seized several towns and villages in Mexico's poorest state of Chiapas on 1 January 1994. The insurgency coincided with the launch of the North American Free Trade Agreement and made a mockery of Mexico's planned celebration of joining the First World. The armed stage of the uprising lasted for only twelve days but it succeeded in drawing international attention to the plight of Mexico's indigenous population and forced the government to give serious consideration to their demands.

The desperate insurgency had every chance of being drowned in blood or joining the long list of forgotten ethnic conflicts. Instead the Zapatistas succeeded in tapping a vast transnational network of civic activists who provided it with visibility, protection, legitimacy, and support. Naomi Klein says:

> The Zapatista uprising was a new way to protect land and culture: rather than locking out the world, the Zapatistas flung open the doors and invited the world inside.
> (Klein 2001)

The Zapatistas brought networking to a new level. Their ideas, which spread initially through word of mouth, dominate the Internet. According to Naomi Klein, there are at least 4,500 Zapatista websites based in 26 countries. There is a Zapatista cottage industry selling 40 kinds of T-shirts, baseball caps, posters, and Mayan dolls. Zapatista gatherings—Encontros—both in Mexico and elsewhere are attended by thousands of activists from all over the world. Their latest event, the Zapatour, in which the movement's masked leaders toured the country promoting their cause, culminated with a 150,000-strong rally in Mexico City.

One of the secrets behind the Zapatistas' success is their ideas as formulated by the movement's eloquent non-leader Subcomandante Marcos. These ideas go far beyond the immediate demands of the Mayan communities to articulate an alternative global vision. Marcos is inviting the millions 'stood-up' by globalisation to unite behind the Chiapas Indians by defining the 'savage capitalism of the end of the 20th century' as the common enemy. Anyone who feels disenfranchised by global capitalism can join the Zapatistas by doing whatever they can wherever they are.

The Zapatistas are sceptical both of cosmetic reforms and of 'fascist' nationalist solutions. Indeed they are sceptical of any ready-made alternatives, promoting instead a 'revolution which makes the revolution possible'. Their main goal is to create the democratic space in which alternative social proposals can compete and coexist with each other as long as they are just. Marcos says, describing the revolution:

> It will be, primarily, a revolution which is the result of the struggle on different social fronts, with many methods, within different social forms, with different degrees of commitment and participation. And its results will be, not a party, organisation or alliance of victorious organisations with its specific social proposal, but a chance for a democratic space in order to resolve the confrontation among diverse political proposals. This democratic space for resolution will have three fundamental premises which are inseparable historically: democracy, in order to decide upon the dominant social proposal, liberty in order to subscribe to one or the other proposal and justice in which all proposals should be enclosed. (Don Durito 1995)

This ambiguity combined with the movement's aversion to hierarchy and classical concepts of leadership make it ideal for the alternatives. Indeed, these ideas are the closest thing to a 'manifesto' for the alternative stream of the anti-capitalist movement. Klein says:

I may never have made the pilgrimage to Chiapas, but I have watched the Zapatistas' ideas spread through activist circles, passed along second- and third-hand: a phrase, a way to run a meeting, a metaphor that twists your brain around. Unlike classic revolutionaries, who preach through bullhorns and from pulpits, Marcos has spread the Zapatista word through riddles. Revolutionaries who don't want power. People who must hide their faces to be seen. A world with many worlds in it. A movement of one 'no' and many 'yesses'. (Klein 2001)

Many of those who made the 'pilgrimage' to Chiapas went on to play a critical role in the major anti-capitalist protests in Seattle, Prague, and Davos. Zapatista slogans, ideas, non-hierarchical methods of organisation, irreverence, humour, and romanticism are omnipresent in alternative anti-capitalist events. Indeed it is hard to say today who needs the other more, the Zapatistas or the alternatives.

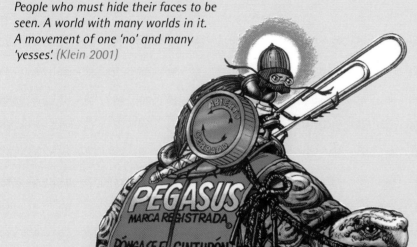

Don Durito

Beetle Nebuchadnezzar, aka Don Durito, Errant Knight and his mount Turtle Pegasus who gets vertigo when cruising at speeds in excess of 50 cm per hour. Durito is the true author of most of Subcommandante Marcos' communiqués or at least those of them that are more serious. His main concern is whether and when the Zapatistas are going to defeat neo-liberalism. Durito also has the answers to both questions, which are 'yes' and 'after a long time' respectively.

Civil society responses to global capitalism extend beyond protests and lobbying to 'practical' alternatives. In the area of money and finance such alternatives include LETS schemes and other money alternatives, micro-lending and Grameen banking, and socially responsible investment. These alternatives can be isolationist, reformist, supporter, or alternative in nature depending on their compatibility with global capitalism. They also vary in spread and success.

According to Project LETS (URL) there are around 500 LETS schemes and networks in 36 countries. The average size of these schemes is 50–60 participants although larger ones can have thousands of participants.

A typical example of LETS schemes is Ithaca Hours, based in the small university town of Ithaca, New York. One Hour is equivalent to $10 or one hour of work. The core of the system is a bi-monthly tabloid in which people and businesses that accept Ithaca Hours advertise their products and services. Each advertiser receives Four Hours so that s/he can purchase other peoples' products. The currency is limited to a 20-mile radius and payments can be made in both dollars and hours. The scheme involves about 2,000 participants (Lietaer 2001). Since LETS currencies are usually based on the exchange of labour hours, most LETS schemes are community-based, although this is changing with the advent of the Internet. Formalised LETS schemes are usually political rather than practical in nature. Environmental sustainability, anti-consumerism,

and efforts to promote community cohesion and culture are among their main motivations. Formalised LETS schemes are trying to carve out space away from the market and as such could be designated as alternative.

The most prevalent forms of alternative money, however, are neither political nor formalised. Money shortages due to state failure or neo-liberal reforms may force millions in developing and transition countries to seek alternatives to money. In the former Soviet Union people augmented barter arrangements originally developed to deal with the shortage economy to handle the tight money of shock therapy. Such arrangements involve the exchange of both goods and services, including labour hours. Rather than being an alternative to market relations such arrangements are part of the new market economy in these countries.

The Grameen Bank extends loans as small as $50 to the poorest people in rural Bangladesh. The loans are given without collateral. The main clients are women whom the bank deems more likely to spend the money wisely and to repay it on schedule. The bank relies on community and peer pressure to ensure repayment. As such it uses social capital in the form of community relations and gender as a substitute for collateral and as a way to reduce lending costs. Grameen banking and similar forms of micro-lending have been extremely successful, reaching 14 million people in December 1999, a growth of 82 per cent in two years (Empowering Women with Microcredit 2000). The success of Grameen banking has prompted aid agencies, international lending institutions, and commercial banks to emulate it in other countries. Originally, Grameen banks were all NGOs. Micro-lenders today are divided between NGOs, who have predominantly a social/environmental agenda, and banks. Grameen banking and other forms of micro-lending are firmly anchored within market structures. They could be designated as reformist since they correct a market failure by extending lending to the poorest people who are usually shunned by commercial banks.

Socially responsible investing (SRI) is the most successful of the practical alternatives. Indeed, it is becoming so commonplace for pension funds—the largest portfolio investors—to demand SRI from their fund managers that it is gradually becoming the norm rather than the alternative. In 1999 over $2US trillion were invested in socially responsible ways, accounting for 13 per cent of assets under management in the United States. This represented a growth of 45 per cent over the 9 per cent figure for 1997 (Social Investment Forum 1999). The numbers are expected to grow especially since SRI funds are proving to be as profitable as, if not more so than, traditional ones. SRI is also spreading into Europe, albeit at a slower pace. The introduction of regulation in the UK requiring pension funds to disclose SRI policies has provided a needed boost.

British SRIs are estimated to have £45 billion under management. There are several varieties of SRI, from passive screening ofcompanies according to certain criteria to the active use of corporate governance mechanisms to inject environmental sustainability and labour and human rights standards into corporate policies. SRI could be described as supportive because it takes place within the framework of global capitalism, using its existing tools and mechanisms. One could say that SRI proves that market mechanisms such as corporate governance are the most efficient way to produce desired public goods without government intervention.

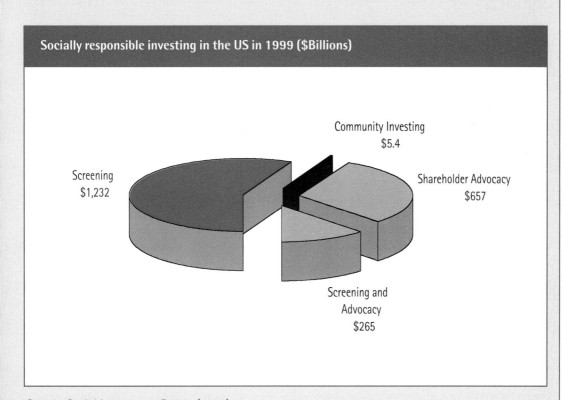

Socially responsible investing in the US in 1999 ($Billions)

Community Investing
$5.4

Screening
$1,232

Shareholder Advocacy
$657

Screening and
Advocacy
$265

Source: Social Investment Forum (1999).

Table 3.1: Civil society responses to global finance	ORGANISATION					ACTIVITY					POSITION			
	INDIVIDUAL	NGO/GROUP	MOVEMENT/NETWORK	THINKTANK/ACADEMIA	MEDIA/WEBSITE	INFORM/EDUCATE	LOBBY	MOBILISE	SERVE	RIOT/CELEBRATE	REJECTIONIST	SUPPORTIVE	REFORMATIVE	ALTERNATIVE
ATTAC			◉	●		●		◉					●	
Bank Information Center		●				●	○	●			●		◉	
Bankwatch		●				○	◉	●			●		◉	
Bello, Waldon	●					●		◉			●			
Brettonwoods Project		◉		●		●	◉						●	
Centre for Civil Society				●		●		●				●		
Corporate Watch		●				○		●			◉		●	
Don Durito (Subcomandante Marcos)	●							●	●		○			●
Economist					●	●	◉					●	◉	
Fifty Years is Enough		●						●			●			
Financial Times					●	●	◉					◉	●	
Focus on Global South				●		●		◉			●			
Friedman, Thomas	●					●	◉					●	◉	
Friends of the Earth		◉	●				◉	●			●		◉	
Global Exchange		●	◉			○		●			●			
Grameen Bank		●				○			●				●	
INPEG			●					◉		●				●
Institute for Policy Studies				●		●	●	○			◉		●	
International Forum on Globalization		◉	●			●		◉			●			
Ithaca Hours			●					◉	●		●			◉
Jubilee 2000			●			○	◉	●					●	
Klein, Naomi	●					●		◉						●
Landless Peasants Movement (MST)			●					●	○	●	●			●
Le Monde Diplomatique					●	●		◉			●			◉
Meltzer Commission				●		●	◉					●		
Nader, Ralph	●							●			●			
OneWorld.net					●	●			◉		◉		●	○
Oxfam		●				○	◉	●					●	
Reclaim the Streets			●					●		●	●			●
Ruckus Society		●							●	●				●
Social Investment Forum		●				◉	○	●				●	◉	
Stiglitz, Joseph	●					●	◉						●	
Wall Street Journal					●	●	●					●		
Wolfenson, James	●					○	◉		●			◉	●	
World Development Movement		●	◉			●	○	●					●	
Zapatistas (EZLN)			●					●	○	●	●			●

● PREDOMINANT   ◉ SIGNIFICANT   ○ TO SOME EXTENT

translated into an advantage, ensuring mass appeal, especially among the young.

> *It's not the last gasp of the old left, or the resurgence of the new right. It's not protectionism, or even anarchism. It's something entirely different; something fresh being pieced together from the shards of old ideas, and glued with new solutions for a new age. (Kingsnorth 2000)*

The alternatives do not necessarily seek to overthrow capitalism and are definitely not interested in gaining power. They seek instead to defend a 'way of life' and thus, place a strong emphasis on cultural issues. It is not surprising that their protests look more like cultural happenings than political action. Indeed, the alternatives' grasp of popular culture is one of their main strengths.

The alternatives have a schizophrenic relationship to globalisation. On the one hand, by espousing many isolationist ideas they appear anti-globalisation; on the other hand they are fiercely global in placing a strong emphasis on solidarity or, as Reclaim the Streets puts it: 'The resistance will be as transnational as capital'. The alternatives are also the most techno-logically savvy of all the resistance movements, which further ties them to globalisation. Similar groups are described as 'anarcho-techies' by John Naughton in Chapter 6.

There are parallels between the alternatives of today and the radicals of the 1960s. For example, the radicals brought together emancipatory and rights politics of the 'old' and the life politics of the 'new' social movements. The alternatives reproduced this link in the form of the Longshoremen providing protection to the anti-sweatshop student demon-strators in Seattle. The radicals and the alternatives are also similar in their emphasis on popular culture and forms in general. But there are also differences between the two: chief among them is that the 'authority' being challenged today is the corporation, not the state.

Alternatives do not have a particular position on global finance issues. Instead they espouse a mixture of isolationist and, to a lesser degree, reformist ideas.

Conclusion: The Total Is More Than the Sum of the Parts

Civic responses to capitalism are as old as the system itself. Reactions to money are even older. Isolationists, supporters, reformists, and alternatives existed previously in various forms. Most of the time, governments and markets confronted or ignored them when they could not co-opt them. Lately, the individual responses have been coming together, creating something larger than the sum of its components. In Seattle and Prague, a myriad of individuals, organisations, movements, ideas, and methods came together to deliver a message so powerful that it took everyone by surprise.

Seattle and Prague, however, are only the most visible expression of global civic responses to capitalism. The various responses are actually working together all the time.

The alternatives lend mass appeal and visibility to what would otherwise be marginal isolationist and reformist movements. They also create the space where the various responses come together. The isolationists with their militancy and radical demands keep the issues alive and sharpen the debate. The ultimate winner from these synergies are the reformists, who eventually fill the gap between the supporters and the isolationists with constructive solutions.

Civic responses to global capitalism are also coming together across regions despite supporters' claims to the contrary. The Zapatistas not only were saved by global solidarity; they are also the inspiration for alternatives worldwide. IMF and World Bank reforms are influenced by demonstrations in Turkey, Nigeria, and Argentina as much as they are by riots in Prague and Washington. The Jubilee 2000 campaign would not have achieved what it did had it not been a truly global movement.

What is it that brings Ann Pettifor, Katerina Liskova, George Soros, and Walden Bello together to dress down the heads of the World Bank and the IMF?[4] Why would the leaders of the Bretton Woods institutions subject themselves to such public

---

[4] *Katerina Liskova is one of the organisers of the Prague World Bank/IMFD protest. Ann Pettifor is the founder of Jubilee 2000 campaign to cancel Third World debt. Walden Bello is a radical Filipino academic and anti-capitalist activist. Gorge Soros is a financier and philanthropist. The four participated in a meeting held at Prague castle together with the heads of the IMF and World Bank hosted by Czech President Vaclav Havel (see Box 3.1).*

upbraiding? After all, activists were championing Third World issues before Katerina was born. Soros made his millions even earlier, totally unaware of Bello and his fellows in the national liberation movement. Twenty years ago most anti-capitalist activists did not even know who the leaders of the Bretton Woods institutions were, and if they did they wouldn't have dreamt of sitting with them at the same table.

It could be that for the first time in decades the bottom rung seems to have dropped from the global social ladder, that along with overall prosperity there are more and more pockets around the world where people seem to have nothing to lose. Regardless of where they are, people are terrified by widening disparities. Many are all too aware that the Zapatista insurrection and Landless Peasant Movement land occupations are comparatively benign outbursts by those left behind, that unless something is done we can expect more violent eruptions with unpredictable consequences.

It could be that even those enjoying the fruits of prosperity are feeling less and less in control of their lives. It is, after all, frustrating to get virtually identical economic policies no matter whom you vote for and to watch your elected representatives facilitate or at best stand by helplessly as markets devour precious public space.

Maybe the whole thing is just a successful public relations stunt by the alternatives who are deftly mixing pop culture and information technology to lend a sheen of novelty and broad appeal to tired slogans. The new anti-capitalist movement may just be giving a new form to an old idea. Like its predecessors, it is unlikely to succeed in terms of defeating global capitalism (after all, supporters are the most influential of the civic responses to global capitalism) but it may just transform it.

Given the cacophony of voices behind it, the message from Seattle and Prague may be neither coherent nor constructive. It is more like an alarm, a shout of protest and despair. But it is loud enough that corporations, international organisations, and governments can ignore it only at their peril.

References

AFL-CIO (1998). 'US Workers Addressing the Global Crisis' (Executive Council Statement). Monterey, California (14 October).

Anderson, Sarah and Cavanagh, John (2000). *Bearing the Burden: The Impact of Global Financial Crisis on Workers and Alternative Agendas for the IMF and Other Institutions*. Washington DC: Institute for Policy Studies. http://www.ips.dc.org.

Bello, Walden (2000). Excerpted from a talk delivered at a series of engagements during the demonstrations against the World Economic Forum in Melbourne, Australia, 6–10 September. http://www.focusweb.org.

— (2001). 'Is Bush Bad for the World Bank?' January. http://www.corpwatch.org.

Cohen, Robin and Rai, Shirin (2000). *Global Social Movements*. London: Athlone.

Cornia, Giovanni Andrea, Jolly, Richard, and Stewart, Frances (1987). *Adjustment with a Human Face*. Oxford: Clarendon Press.

Desai, M (2001). *Marx's Revenge: The Resurgence of Capitalism and the Death of Statist Socialism*. London: Verso.

Don Durito of the Lacandon Errant Knight for whom Sup Marcos is shield-bearer (1995). *Durito IV: Neoliberalism and the Party-State System*. Mexico: Zapatista Army of National Liberation, 11 June. http://www.eco.utexas.edu/faculty/Cleaver/chiapas95.html

Economist (2000). 'The Case for Globalization'. 21 September.

Emerging Markets Companion (1996–9). *Brady Bond Primer*. http://www.emgmkts.com/research/bradydef.htm

Empowering Women with Microcredit (2000). *Microcredit Summit Campaign Report*. http://www.microcreditsummit.org/campaigns/report00.html

Friedman, Thomas (2000). *The Lexus and the Olive Tree; Understanding Globalization*. New York: Anchor. http://www.lexusandtheolivetree.com/globalization.htm

Friends of the Earth (1998a). *MAI Update*, October. http://www.foe.org.

— (2000). *Towards Sustainable Economies: Challenging Neoliberal Economic Globalisation*. 1 December. http://www.foei.org.

— (1998b). *Licence to Loot: The MAI and How to Stop it*, http://www.foe.org/international/loot.html

Fuller, C. J. (1989) 'Misconceiving the Grain Heap: a Critique of the Concept of the Indian Jajmani System', in Jonathan Parry and Bloch, Maurice

Derivatives

Futures, puts, options and other financial instruments which are derived from others, such as commodity prices, shares, and bonds. Derivatives are often used as insurance against unfavourable movements in the underlying instruments. In portfolio investments derivatives are used to achieve a specific risk/return profile.

Futures

Financial instrument constituting a bet on the direction of the price of a certain commodity or exchange rate.

Foreign Direct Investment (FDI)

'Refer to Investment Flows aimed at acquiring a lasting management interest (10% or more of voting stock) in an enterprise operating in an economy other than that of the investor' (World Bank 1998–1999).

Portfolio investment

The purchase of debt, equity and other financial instruments. Equity portfolio investments usually stop short of obtaining management control in a particular enterprise. The goals of portfolio investments vary from growth to income to value preservation against adverse shocks.

Brady Bonds

'Named after US Treasury Secretary Nicholas Brady, who in association with the IMF and World Bank sponsored the effort to permanently restructure outstanding sovereign loans and interest arrears into liquid debt instruments . . . Principal and certain interest is collateralized by U.S. Treasury zero coupon bonds and other high grade instruments. Creditor banks exchanged sovereign loans for Brady bonds incorporating principal and interest guarantees and cash payments. Debtor governments had their principal, interest and interest arrears reduced. Countries involved in the Brady Plan restructuring: Argentina, Brazil, Bulgaria, Costa Rica, Dominican Republic, Ecuador, Mexico, Morocco, Nigeria, Philippines, Poland, Uruguay. Potential future candidates for Brady Plan restructuring: Ex-Soviet Union (Vnesheconobank), Nicaragua, Panama, Peru' (Emerging Markets Companion 1996–9).

(ed.), *Money and the Morality of Exchange*. Cambridge: Cambridge University Press.

Hines, Colin (2000). *Localisation: A Global Manifesto*. London: Earthscan.

ICFTU (International Confederation of Free Trades Unions) (2000). 'Securing the Conditions for Reducing Poverty and Achieving Sustainable Growth'. Statement by the ICFTU, TUAC, and ITS to the Spring 2000 meeting of the IMF and the World Bank in Washington DC.

IFIAC (International Financial Institution Advisory Commission, 'Meltzer Commission') (2000). *Report* (March). http://www.house.gov/jec/imf/ifiac.htm.

IMF (International Monetary Fund). http://www.imf.org

Jubilee 2000. http://www.jubileeplus.org

Kingsnorth, Paul (2000). 'Seeds of the New in the Prague Autumn'. *The Ecologist*, 30/8: 44-5.

Klein, Naomi (1999). *No Logo: Taking Aim at the Brand Bullies*. New York: Picador.

— (2001). 'The Unknown Icon'. *Guardian* (3 March).

Lietaer, Bernard (2001). *The Future of Money*. London. Century.

Mauss, Marcel (1996). *The Gift: Forms and Functions of Exchange in Archaic Society*. London: Cohen and West.

Mittelman, James (2000). *The Globalization Syndrome, Transformation and Resistance*. Princeton: Princeton University Press.

Parry, Jonathan and Bloch, Maurice (1989). 'Introduction: Money and the Morality of Exchange', in Jonathan Parry and Bloch Maurice (ed.), *Money and the Morality of Exchange*. Cambridge: Cambridge University Press.

Perez, Carlota (2000). 'Technological Revolutions and Financial Capital', paper presented at 'The Other Canon Conference', Oslo.

Platform of ATTAC (Action pour une Taxe Tobin d'Aide aux Citoyens), 3 June. http://www.attac.org.

Project LETS. http://lentils.imagineis.com/letslist

Reclaim the Streets. http://www.reclaimthestreets.net

Social Investment Forum (1999). *1999 Report on Socially Responsible Investing Trends in the United States,* November. http://www.socialinvest.org/areas/research/trends/1999-Trends.htm

Stiglitz, Joseph (2000). 'Democratic Development as the Fruits of Labor', Keynote Address, Industrial Relations Research Association, Boston, January. Taken from Anderson and Cavanagh. http://www.ips.org

Tönnies, Ferdinand (1955). *Gemeinschaft und Gesellschaft* (Community and Association) (trans. Charles P. Loomis). London: Routledge and Kegan Paul.

United Nations (1999). *World Economic and Social Survey*. New York: United Nations.

Wallerstein, Immanuel (2000). *The Essential Wallerstein*. New York: New Press.

Wood, Angela (2001). *Structural Adjustment for the IMF Options for Reforming the IMF's Governance Structure*. Brettonwoods Project (January). http://www.brettonwoodsproject.org/briefings/reform/sapimf.html

World Bank (1998–1999). *World Development Report: Knowledge for Development*. New York: Oxford University Press

— (2000). *East Asia: Recovery and Beyond*. Washington, DC: World Bank.

World Development Movement. http://www.wdm.org.uk/campaign/GATS.htm

CHAPTER 4

DIG IT UP: GLOBAL CIVIL SOCIETY'S RESPONSES TO PLANT BIOTECHNOLOGY

Diane Osgood

Introduction

Global civil society's response to the introduction of plant-based biotechnology crops is unprecedented. While there has always been, and most likely always be, resistance to the introduction of new technologies—from steam trains to cars, personal computers, and nuclear weapons—the response of global civil society to biotechnology has been wider and more networked, multi-faceted, and global than to any previous innovation. Reactions to biotechnology have been intertwined with the anti-capitalism and anti-globalization campaigns, creating a heady cocktail of fear of 'Franken-foods', rejection of the globalising economy, and mistrust of both government regulators and corporate public-relations campaigns.

The technologies in question have been developed over the past 30 years. In the US in the early 1970s, research proposals for genetic engineering projects involving micro-organisms sparked fears that a deadly breed of 'supergerms' could be inadvertently created. Some civil society organisations protested loudly, but these protests were not internationally coordinated or sustained. Nonetheless, in 1974 scientists agreed to adopt strict, self-imposed guidelines for laboratory work on DNA. The US government also imposed restrictions, but lifted them in the mid-1980s because it was satisfied that the experiments were safe. The biotechnology race began. Companies started investing millions of dollars in biotechnology for both pharmaceuticals and agriculture. After much corporate lobbying, the Bush Administration in 1992 simplified the approval process for agricultural biotechnology products, dramatically reducing the required testing to the same standard as non-genetically modified foods. Under this legislation, companies are free to undertake additional testing and are not required to label products containing genetically modified (GM) products. This legislation sparked the beginnings of opposition to GM foods. In the US, Jeremy Rifkin initiated the 'pure food campaign' and called for a moratorium on GM foods.

Rifkin was soon backed by a loose alliance of small farmers, consumers, and animal rights groups, first across the US and then internationally. By the mid-1990s, the stream of protests had become fierce, international, somewhat networked, and forceful, with demonstrations, protests, destruction of products and test plots, and consumer boycotts in many countries.

By the late 1990s, the movements had became more coordinated; and international anti-biotechnology leaders of NGO movements emerged: Greenpeace (URL), Vandana Shiva, Jeremy Rifkin. Grass-roots activists who took personal stands against GM but did not lead their own organisations became international heroes: José Bové, Arpad Putsei. Elite *dramatis personae* emerged: the Prince of Wales, Bob Shapiro, Gordon Conway. Despite the variety of players, voices, and views, the 'anti-biotech moment' became a forceful wave. Networks, partnerships, and websites bridged the physical gap between groups and individuals. The floodgates were opened in Europe with consumer boycotts and pressure that led to changes in supermarket and food producer policies. Within two years, the European Union placed a three-year moratorium on commercial plantings of GM crops. In the late 1990s companies were being subjected to the unavoidable attention of the media, most of whose reporting was very negative. Nor could companies conceal their operations in developing countries: what happened in India became instantly known in London, and therefore in Brazil.

Various explanations were advanced for this eruption of protest. Anger was stirred by corporate and government arrogance at trying to pass new 'impure', insufficiently tested foods on to the unsuspecting consumer. Government refusal to mandate labelling bred more distrust, being generally seen as a result of heavy lobbying from the agro-science sector. Meanwhile, ecologists warned the public about the potential of genetically manipulated organisms (GMOs) to displace or corrupt natural organisms, irreversibly harming landscapes and natural biodiversity. Health advocates worried about allergenicity and carcinogenic effects. Nationalists, regionalists, and decentralists of various kinds were concerned about biotechnology as a powerful new weapon in the arsenal of American homogenisation. Professionals in developing countries and their allies in international NGOs were concerned about the possible widening of the already dramatic gaps in wealth and power between North and South. They saw the biotechnology revolution as another chapter in the continued exploitation of the South's resources by the North. Others in the South were more concerned about being bypassed by a powerful technology.

Global civil society's response to plant biotechnology is an example of the development of a truly global reaction: active participation from groups and individuals around the globe creating links across borders and time zones, and forging unlikely partnerships. In addressing this response and its likely development, this chapter first reviews the concept of plant biotechnology and its current status, then covers the key issues of concern to global civil society. It then examines four categories of global civil society groups and their actions. Finally, the chapter reaches the conclusion that biotechnology, in some shape or form, is with us to stay. It also concludes that global civil society's involvement in plant biotechnology will help shape the evolution of the growing application of biotechnology in the food chain and in medicine. The issues involved include ecological and human health safety levels, labelling and disclosure, monitoring and verification of environmental and health impacts, ethical dimensions, and trade.

This chapter addresses plant biotechnology only within the context of agriculture. Plant biotechnology is the first food product using transgenetics to be commercialised, and therefore also the first to provoke public reaction. The main focus is on crops with genetically engineered transgenes for herbicide and insect resistance because these products are currently planted and consumed on a large scale. To keep the discourse focused on the issues that have to date provoked the strongest response from global civil society, other types of non-plant, non-crop biotechnology are not considered. Nonetheless, it is important to take note of the application of biotechnology in other, related fields. Biotechnology has been used in the pharmaceutical industry for many years; for example, much of the insulin produced today is based on biotechnology. At present,

issues of risk perception, choice, and information availability differ greatly as between biotechnology in medicine and in crop production. However, we can expect that as the technology advances and enters new realms of health interventions, such as vaccines genetically engineered into bananas, global civil society will pose new questions and generate fresh debates. Biotechnology is also developing in animal breeding and fisheries; for example, the US Department of Agriculture is funding research on catfish containing DNA from salmon, carp, and zebrafish, which makes them grow up to 60 per cent faster than they would otherwise. However, at the time of writing, no animal GM products had been commercialised.

Definitions and Status of Global Plant Biotechnology

Definitions

Biotechnology is a broad concept embracing an assortment of techniques used in agriculture and medicine to create or modify living organisms for human use. The selective breeding of plants and animals to promote desirable characteristics is as old as agriculture itself worldwide. For plants, traditional breeding has developed new lines and varieties over the centuries by sexual crossings and selection, usually between two varieties but sometimes between related species, in an attempt to introduce a useful characteristic from one to the other. Technically, this is known as 'plant biotechnology'. However, in common parlance, 'biotechnology' has taken on new meanings derived from recent breakthroughs in manipulating DNA. Instructions inserted into their DNA effectively tell plants how to construct themselves.

Modern plant biotechnology takes three forms:

- *tissue culture*, in which new plants are grown from individual cells or clusters of cells, often bypassing traditional cross-fertilisation and seed production;
- *marker-aided selection*, in which DNA segments are used to mark the presence of useful genes which can then be transferred to future generations through traditional plant breeding using the markers to follow inheritance; and
- *genetic engineering* (GE), in which one or more genes are transferred from one organism to

Box 4.1: Timeline of plant biotechnology development

1973: Genetic engineering (GE) invented by Cohen and Boyer. Demonstrations against GE in the United States.

1974: Asilomar conference in California, scientists agree to adopt strict, self-imposed guidelines for laboratory DNA manipulation. Building blocks of understanding DNA (Late Cot and Rot curves) develop. It emerges that plants contain a complex set of nuclear RNAs and that only 25 per cent of this complexity has been previously under-stood. As well, many genes are active in plant cells and are highly regulated in the plant life cycle. In sum, it becomes clear that plant cells resemble animals cells, but it remains unknown how individual genes are regulated or how sets of genes co-express in space and time.

1979: Dr Bedrock and colleagues in UK show plant DNA can be cloned and replicated in bacteria.

Early 1980s: Start of creating libraries of plant genomes.

1983: Group of scientists from Ghent (Belgium), St Louis (Missouri), and Washington/Cambridge (Massachusetts) show independently that antibiotic resistance markers work. Dr Hall transfers one gene from French bean into sunflower cells, 'Sunbean' plant created. Cover of *New York Times* and *Time* Magazine.

Early 1990s: Dr Feldman and colleagues discover for the first time a relatively simple way to clone plant genes associated with interesting mutant phenotypes. This greatly speeds up the technology process.

1992: US regulation simplifies approval process for biotechnology products and confirms that no labels are required on products.

1994: First crop released and planted in small quantities in Canada.

1996: First significant commercial plantings in the US. Plantings also in China, Argentina, and Canada.

1998: Consumer boycotts in Europe gather speed; test plots destroyed in Europe and India.

1999: First significant anti-biotechnology demonstrations in US (Boston); first commercial plantings in Europe; farmers gather in India and try to burn down Monsanto headquarters.

2000: First plant genome sequenced, the Arabidopsis. Three-year moratorium in Europe for commercial plantings; biotechnology industries launch 'Biotech Council' information campaign in the US.

2001: The genome of rice sequenced; Japan, Australia, New Zealand, and many other countries regulate labelling; demonstrations in the Philippines against planting of GM crops.

Compiled from Goldberg (2001) and EC (2000).

---

another without sexual crossing. This may include transgenes—the moving of one gene from one species into another or the rearranging of one species' own genes (commonly referred to as 'genomics').

In the debate, these three forms are often confounded. This chapter focuses on the second and third. The terms 'genetically engineered' and 'genetically modified' are often interchanged, and are used in references to GE and GM crops and plants. These are all 'genetically modified organisms', a term that refers to any organism, plant or animal, that has been somehow modified at the genetic level.

Development and status of plant biotechnology

Despite the media frenzy in Europe and growing attention in North America, most people do not realise the extent and range of biotechnology and its

Plant's common name	Countries where planting has been authorised	First year authorised for planting (HT / BT / other)	Approved for human consumption?	Approved for animal feed?
Carnation	Australia	Florigene, 1995 (other)	No	No
	EU	Florigene, 1995 (other)	No	No
		Florigene, 1997 (other)	No	No
Chicory	EU	Bejo Zaden BV, 1996 (HT)	No	No
	USA	Bejo Zaden BV, 1996 (HT)*	Yes	No
Cotton	Argentina	Monsanto, 1995 (HT)	No	No
	Australia	Monsanto, 1995 (HT)	No	No
	Canada	Calgene, 1994 (HT)	Yes	Yes
		Monsanto, 1995 (HT)	Yes	Yes
	Japan	Calgene, 1994 (HT)	Yes	Yes
		Monsanto, 1995 (HT)	Yes	Yes
	UK	Monsanto, 1995 (HT)	No	No
	USA	Calgene, 1994 (HT)	Yes	Yes
		Calgene, 1997 (HT + BT)	Yes	No
		Dupont, 1996 (HT)	Yes	No
		Monsanto, 1995 (HT)	Yes	No
Papaya	USA	Cornell University, 1996 (Other)	Yes	No
Potato	Canada	Monsanto, 1995 (BT)	Yes	Yes
		Monsanto, 1996 (BT))	Yes	Yes
	USA	Monsanto, 1995 (BT)	Yes	No
		Monsanto, 1996 (BT)	No	No
		Monsanto, 1998 (Other)	No	No
		Monsanto, 1999 (BT)	No	No
Maize	Canada	AgrEvo, 1995 (HT)	Yes	Yes
		BASF, 1996 (HT)	Yes	Yes
		Ciba-Geigy, 1995 (BT)	Yes	Yes
		DeKalb, 1995 (HT)	Yes	Yes
		DeKalb, 1996 (BT)	Yes	Yes
		Monsanto, 1995 (BT)	Yes	Yes
		Monsanto, 1996 (HT)	No	Yes
		Monsanto, 1996 (HT + BT)	Yes	Yes
		Mycogen, 1995 (BT)	Yes	Yes
		Pioneer Hi-Bred, 1994 (HT)	Yes	Yes
		Pioneer Hi-Bred, 1996 (HT + BT)	Yes	Yes
		Plant Genetic Systems, 1995 (HT)	Yes	Yes
		Zeneca, 1996 (Other)	Yes	Yes
	Argentina	AgrEvo, 1995 (HT)	Yes	Yes
		Ciba-Geigy, 1995 (BT)	Yes	No
		Monsanto, 1995 (BT)	Yes	Yes
		Monsanto, 1996 (HT)	No	No
		Mycogen, 1995 (BT)	Yes	No
	Japan	AgrEvo, 1995 (HT)	Yes	Yes
		Ciba-Geigy, 1995 (BT)	Yes	Yes
		Monsanto, 1995 (BT)	Yes	Yes
		Mycogen, 1995 (BT)	Yes	Yes
		Pioneer Hi-Bred, 1996 (HT + BT)	No	Yes
	EU	AgrEvo, 1995 (HT)	No	No

* Different variety

Plant's common name	Countries where planting has been authorised	First year authorised for planting (HT / BT / other)	Approved for human consumption?	Approved for animal feed?
		Ciba-Geigy, 1995 (BT)	Yes: Denmark, UK, The Netherlands	Yes: The Netherlands
		Monsanto, 1995 (BT)	Yes: UK	Yes: The Netherlands
		Mycogen, 1995 (BT)	Yes: UK, Denmark, the Netherlands	Yes: The Netherlands
	USA	AgrEvo, 1995 (HT)	Yes	No
		AgrEvo, 1998 (HT)	No	Yes
		AgrEvo, 1998 (HT)*	No	No
		Ciba-Geigy, 1995 (BT)	Yes	No
		DeKalb, 1995 (HT)	Yes	No
		DeKalb, 1996 (BT)	Yes	No
		Monsanto, 1995 (BT)	Yes	No
		Monsanto, 1995 (BT)*	No	No
		Monsanto, 1996 (HT + BT)	Yes	No
		Monsanto, 1996 (BT)	Yes	No
		Mycogen, 1995 (BT)	Yes	No
		Pioneer Hi-Bred, 1996 (HT + BT)	Yes	Yes
		Plant Genetic Systems, 1996 (HT)	Yes	No
	South Africa	Monsanto, 1995 (BT)	Yes	Yes
Oilseed rape	Canada	AgrEvo, 1994 (HT)	Yes	Yes
		AgrEvo, 1995 (HT)	Yes	Yes
		AgrEvo, 1996 (HT)	Yes	Yes
		AgrEvo, 1997 (HT)	Yes	Yes
		Calgene, 1994 (Other)	Yes	Yes
		Monsanto, 1995 (HT)	Yes	Yes
		Monsanto, 1996 (HT)	Yes	No
		Monsanto, 1997 (HT)	Yes	Yes
		Pioneer Hi-Bred, 1996 (HT + BT)	Yes	Yes
		Plant Genetic Systems, 1994 (HT)	Yes	Yes
		Plant Genetic Systems, 1995 (HT)	Yes	Yes
		Plant Genetic Systems, 1996 (HT)	Yes	Yes
	Japan	AgrEvo, 1994 (HT)	Yes	Yes
		AgrEvo, 1995 (HT)	Yes	Yes
		AgrEvo, 1995 (HT) *	No	Yes
		AgrEvo, 1996 (HT)	Yes	Yes
		AgrEvo, 1997 (HT)	Yes	Yeed
		Monsanto, 1995	Yes	Yes
		Plant Genetic Systems, 1994 (HT)	Yes	Yes
		Plant Genetic Systems, 1995 (HT)	Yes	Yes
		Plant Genetic Systems, 1996 (HT)	Yes	Yes
		Plant Genetic Systems, 1997 (HT)	Yes	Yes
	EU	AgrEvo, 1994 (HT)	No	No
		AgrEvo, 1995 (HT)	No	Yes: UK
		Plant Genetic Systems, 1994 (HT)	No	No
		Plant Genetic Systems, 1995 (HT)	Yes: UK	Yes: UK
	USA	AgrEvo, 1996 (HT)	No	No

Table 4.1 continued

Plant's common name	Countries where planting has been authorised	First year authorised for planting (HT / BT / other)	Approved for human consumption?	Approved for animal feed?
		AgrEvo, 1997 (HT)	Yes	No
		Calgene, 1994 Other)	Yes	No
		Monsanto, 1999 (HT)	No	No
		Plant Genetic Systems, 1996 (HT)	No	No
Soybean	USA	AgrEvo, 1996 (HT)	Yes	No
		AgrEvo, 1998 (HT)	No	No
		Dupont, 1997 (Other)	Yes	No
		Monsanto, 1994 (HT)	Yes	Yes
	EU	Monsanto, 1994 (HT)	Yes: The Netherlands, Denmark, UK	Yes: UK, The Netherlands,
	Argentina	Monsanto, 1994 (HT)	Yes	Yes
	Canada	Monsanto, 1994 (HT)	Yes	Yes
	Japan	Monsanto, 1994 (HT)	Yes	Yes
	Mexico	Monsanto, 1994 (HT)	Yes	Yes
Sugar Beet	USA	AgrEvo, 1998 (HT)	No	No
Rice	USA	AgrEvo, 1999 (HT)	No	No
Tomato	USA	Agritope, 1996 (Other)	Yes	No
		Calgene, 1992 (Other)	Yes	No
		Calgene (Other)	No	No
		DNA Plant Technology Corporation, 1994 (Other)	Yes	No
		Monsanto, 1995 (Other)	No	No
		Monsanto, 1998 (BT)	Yes	No
		Zeneca, 1996 (HT)	Yes	No
	Japan	Calgene, 1992	Yes	
Flax	Canada	University of Saskatchewan, 1996 (HT)	Yes	Yes
	USA	University of Saskatchewan, 1996 (HT)	Yes	No
Squash	Upjohn, 1994	USA (Other)	Yes	No

Source: OECD*b* (URL).

adoption. The information is publicly available but somewhat difficult to track down. The lack of awareness partially stems from the complexity of agriculture at the global level; few non-experts grasp either the extent of international trade in commodity and other crops or the sophistication of many of the larger-scale commercial farms. It also results from the breadth of applications of this technology: few non-experts would be aware of the genetic work being done on trees, flowers, and humble vegetables. Clearly, the media, despite wide coverage in Europe, have not presented a global view.

This section provides an overview of the most important developments in terms of commercial releases. Tables 4.1 and 4.2 provide a quick global overview of which crops with which gene traits are being planted where, and whether they have been approved for human and/or animal consumption, as at the end of 1999. From carnations to squash, maize to soya and cotton, each commercialised crop is listed with reference to its genetic trait with information on GM research crops in the OECD. Data sources are scattered and often conflicting. The best source of crops data is the International Service for the

The list includes field trials of genetically modified organisms that have taken place in OECD member countries. It also includes data from other countries provided.

Poplar	Carnation
Squash	Pea
Chicory	Fungus
Grape	Apple
Sunflower	Melon / Squash
Creeping bentgrass	Brassica
Turnip rape	Walnut
Flax	Petunia
Virus	Papaya
Canola	Carrot
Sugarcane	Brown mustard
Strawberry	Marigold
Barley	Eggplant
Lettuce	Clover
Cucumber	

Sources: OECDa (URL) and UNIDO (URL).

tobacco and cotton. Europe, on the other hand, started commercial planting only in 1999 and has very few hectares planted.

An informative way to investigate the development and status of GM crops is to look at the traits of the GM crops rather than location. Currently there are four general types of traits used as commercial GM crops, as outlined below. In the next section the health and environmental concerns of global civil society for these technologies are outlined.

1. *Herbicide tolerance* (HT). The insertion of a herbicide tolerant gene into a plant enables farmers to spray over their fields wide-spectrum herbicides, such as Monsanto's Roundup Ready or AgrEvo's Liberty Link, killing all plants except GM crops. The key intended benefit is lower herbicide use, as farmers can spray later in the season and therefore less often. As well, farmers who combine these crops with no-till or low-till technology should experience decreased soil erosion. Alleged disadvantages include the risk of

Acquisition of Agri-biotech Applications (ISAAA) (URL), and the following data has been taken from ISAAA and OECD publications. The aim is to give an overview of the status of GM crops; because of data biases, most of the information concerns OECD countries. To provide as complete a picture as possible, the section provides data on hectares per country, GM trait basis, commodity crop basis, and product basis.

The world area under GM crops is expanding rapidly. The OECD estimates the GM area for 2000 to plateau just above 42 million hectares (Mio ha). This development has occurred in only the last five years. Research on GM crops for uses in agriculture started in the 1980s, but sales of first commodity seeds began only in the mid-1990s. The first significant sowings of GM crops (2.6 Mio ha) took place in 1996, almost exclusively in the US. Since 1996, the areas have increased dramatically to reach 41.5 Mio ha in 1999. Adoption of transgenic crops is progressing at a much faster pace than has been the case for other innovations in hybrids (EC 2000). As shown in Table 4.2, most of the GM crops are grown on the American continent. China alone represents about 3 per cent of the 1999 world GM area, and is currently planting

Table 4.2: Development of GM area by country (Mio ha)

	1996	1997	1998	1999	% of total GM crop (1999)
USA	1.45	7.16	20.83	28.64	69.1
Argentina*	0.05	1.47	3.53	5.81	14.0
Canada	0.11	1.68	2.75	4.01	9.7
China	1.00	1.00	1.10	1.30	3.1
Brazil*	0.00	0.00	0.00	1.18	2.8
Australia	0.00	0.20	0.30	0.30	0.7
South Africa	0.00	0.00	0.06	0.18	0.4
Mexico	0.00	0.00	0.05	0.05	0.12
Europe	0.00	0.00	0.002	0.01	0.03
Spain	0.00	0.00	0.00	0.01	0.02
France	0.00	0.00	0.002	0.00	0.00
Portugal	0.00	0.00	0.00	0.001	0.00
Romania	0.00	0.00	0.00	0.002	0.00
Ukraine	0.00	0.00	0.00	0.001	0.00
Total	2.61	11.510	28.623	41.480	100.00

*Following a court ruling, sowings of GM crops are not allowed in Brazil and public authorities are committed to controlling them. However, certain sources mentioned that at least 10% of the Brazilian soybean area in 1999 is GM. The GM area would be located in the south of the country and the seeds would be fraudulently imported from Argentina. The estimated GM soybean area reported here is based on figures from the Argentina's *Direccion de Economia Agraria* and from the Argentinean seed association.

Source: EC (2000).

DIG IT UP: GLOBAL CIVIL SOCIETY'S RESPONSES TO PLANT BIOTECHNOLOGY Diane Osgood developing herbicide resistance more rapidly than by conventional usage, the related risk of developing 'superweeds', and an increase in herbicide use following the introduction of the technology on a commercial scale, at least in Argentina (Pengue 2000).

2. *Insect resistance* (BT). By inserting genetic material found naturally in soil from Bacillus thuringiensis (BT) into seeds, scientists have modified crops to allow them to produce their own insecticides. BT is the only commercialised insecticide GE crop. The BT gene responsible for producing the toxin is directly inserted into the plant to produce pest-resistant varieties. For example, BT cotton combats bollworms and budworms, whereas BT maize protects against the 'European' maize borer. The intended benefits include a sharp decline in the use of pesticides, many of which are known to be very toxic to farm workers and the environment. Higher yields resulting from more efficient pest management have also been documented in some, but not all, fields. The main concern is the build-up of resistance in target insects. This is a great concern to the organic movement because application of non-GE BT is one of its key pest-management tools. Other concerns include unintended impacts on non-target insects and any tertiary negative environmental impacts.

3. *Virus resistance* (VR). A virus-resistant gene has been introduced in tobacco, the sweet potato, and the tomato. The insertion of another gene protects potatoes from a virus that causes 'leaf roll', a disease which is usually transmitted through aphids. For that reason, a significant decrease in the amount of insecticide used is expected. The introduction of a virus-resistant gene in tobacco may offer similar benefits. Very little field data is available on the impacts and benefits of this technology; the concerns are parallel to those listed above for HT and BT.

4. *Quality traits* (QT). Quality traits are engineered to bring new benefits directly to the end-consumer of the plant. Today, there are very few quality traits-crops in the ground, with less than 50,000 hectares given over to them in Canada and the USA. Current crops include high-oleic soybeans, high-oleic canola/rapeseed, and laurite canola, which all are considered to deliver 'healthier' oils to the consumer. Concerns centre on the effects of cross-breeding with natural relatives, especially rapeseed and canola, and on new health risks. Box 4.3 indicates GM crop area by the above four traits.

Issues and Objections to Plant Biotechnology

The underlying tone of global civil society's concerns about the health and environmental safety effects of GM crops is sceptical. Many of the concerns raised by global civil society are not supported by current research, but this does not allay fears. On the contrary, much of global civil society no longer believes that science is sufficiently knowledgeable about the medium-and long-term effects of these technologies. Groups are calling for studies examining the broader implications for human and animal health and ecosystem functions. The neutrality of government-and industry-supported science is also questioned. Furthermore, trust in governments' abilities to regulate and take decisions in the public interest has continued to decline over the last ten years; this is particularly true in Europe and, to some extent, India, Brazil, and South Africa. The tone of scepticism is often intangible and difficult to document, yet it is a powerful motivator for many groups within global civil society.

A review of the literature, websites, and media clippings over the past three years shows that objections and arguments about plant biotechnology fall into four general categories: human health, environment, right-to-know, and ethics. Most global civil society groups have taken actions—from public

---

Box 4.3: GM crop area by trait: pesticide-like crops dominate

Of the 41.5 Mio hectares sown with transgenic crops in 1999, the distribution of traits in order of importance is as follows:

- Herbicide tolerant (HT) GM crop with 69% of total,
- Insect resistant, GM with 21%, using mostly Bt genes
- GM crops containing both genes (HT + IR) represented 7%
- Virus resistant (VR) GM crop (almost exclusively Chinese tobacco) nearly 3%
- Quality traits (QT) less than 50,000 hectares in 1999 were planted.

Source: EC (2000)

Globally, soybeans and corn are the frontrunners. Of the 41.5 Mio hectares sown on a commercial basis in 1999, 53% were soybeans, 27% corn, 9% cotton, 8% rapeseed, 2% tobacco, and 0.1% potatoes. Commercialised GM soybeans were first sown in 1996 in two countries—the USA and Argentina—and represented respectively 1.6% and 0.8% of their total soybean area. They were largely herbicide tolerant. In 1999, GM soybean area represented nearly one third of the world total soybean area and nearly 47% of the area of countries producing GM soybeans. One result is that the world supply of non-GM soya has dramatically declined, creating a speciality market for some countries.

Development of GM soybean area worldwide (Mio ha)

	1996	1997	1998	1999	2000 (e)	GM % of total crop (1999)
USA	0.40	3.64	10.12	15.00		51
Argentina	0.05	1.40	3.43	5.50		75
Canada		0.001	0.04	0.10		10
Brazil				1.18		10
Romania				0.001		
Total	0.45	5.04	13.59	21.78	22.5	47

For every commercialised GM crop, there are scores being developed in laboratories around the world. It is close to impossible to complete an extensive list of GM crops experiments, but the list in Table 4.2 provides a good window for future developments. This is the list of crops by common name from OECD's database of field trials.

Development of GM corn area worldwide (Mio ha)

	1996	1997	1998	1999	2000 (e)	GM % of total crop (1999)
USA	0.30	2.27	8.66	10.30		36
Argentina		0.07	0.09	0.31		11
Canada	0.001	0.27	0.30	0.50		44
South Africa			0.05	0.16		5
France			0.002	0.000		0.0
Spain				0.01		0.2
Portugal				0.001		0.4
Total	0.30	2.61	9.11	11.28	10.5	28.0

Source: EC (2000)

awareness campaigns to demonstrations, consumer boycotts, and crop destruction—based on one or more of these key concerns. (see Table 4.5)

Within each of the four categories, there are sub-topics. Whereas some global civil society groups employ blanket justifications for their objections—for instance, 'GM foods are unhealthy'—many others focus on specific sub-topics—for example, GM foods may cause allergic reactions in some people. Hardly surprisingly, the latter approach has been more successful in engaging scientists (from both public and private sectors) and policy-makers. Many global civil society groups have no interest in engaging with policy-makers, industry leaders, or scientists. (The differentiating characteristics of the groups are discussed below.)

In addition to the four general categories of concern, the research found a set of specialist topics surrounding the use of plant biotechnology. Few global civil society groups publicly address these issues, however, some of those that do have had notable influence on some policy-makers. Key specialist topics covered here include intellectual property rights, the neutrality of science and ethics of communications, capacity and capacity building, and farmers' rights.

This section outlines the four main themes of human health, environment, right-to-know, and ethics, and provides some details on the sub-topics within each category. Four specialist topics are then briefly discussed. The review is not meant to be an exhaustive examination of all the concerns and issues surrounding biotechnology. Rather, it aims to frame the issues for the purpose of discussion. Readers are directed to websites and publications in the list of references for more in-depth reviews on the topics covered.

Human health

The concern is that genes inserted into GM foods may unwittingly create health problems. GM crops enter the food chain directly, as vegetables (such as tomatoes), processed cereals (such as wheat or maize), and processed ingredients (for example, sugar from sugar beet). Some of the most common sources are derivatives of soy used in process foods. GM foods also enter the human food chain indirectly through livestock and fish that have been fed GM grain (for instance, shrimp fed on GM soy, cattle on GM maize and soy).

Concern about human health was highlighted in the Starlink case, in which GM maize approved solely for animal feed in the US was found in the human food chain in the US and a few other countries. Allergenicity was the primary concern, and the US authorities quickly concluded through an expert commission that the likelihood of allergic responses to the inserted gene was present but small. The consensus of the commission was that while Cry9C, the gene in Starlink maize, 'has a "medium likelihood" to be an allergen, the combination of the expression level of the protein and the amount of corn found to be commingled poses a "low probability" to sensitise individuals to Cry9C' (EPA 2001). A few months after this report was released, 48 cases were filed at the US Food and Drug Administration claiming allergic reactions to unknowingly eaten Starlink. At the time of writing, the cases had not yet been investigated (Kaufman 2001). The main concerns are:

- *Potential risks to human health resulting from the use of viral DNA in plants and anti-biotic markers.* The question is whether the viral or anti-biotic marker genes used in GM plants will be passed directly into the human system when the food is digested. If so, will they cause any harm? Although there is no current evidence that they pose a risk, long-term studies are required, and the public no longer believes that science is sufficiently knowledgeable about its claims (May 1999).

- *Prospective implications for human nutrition.* Some groups, particularly those associated with 'holistic' views of ecology and human health, are concerned about the long-term health implications of humans consuming 'mixes of genes' hitherto unknown in the human diet.

- *Potential problems with allergenicity of GM plants for food use.* If a gene from a brazil nut is inserted into a soy plant, will people allergic to brazil nuts suffer from eating the soy? Known allergens such as nuts and pollens are not used in current research or product development, for obvious reasons. However, scientists are integrating genes previously not in the human diet, and there are new concerns about allergenicity and how to test for it.

- *The fate of DNA in the digestive system.* Will DNA be passed through the body and play havoc with our digestive systems? Is there a risk of DNA from GM foods being passed into sewer systems? This concern intensifies for the potential future use of GM plants to deliver vaccines and other pharmaceuticals. Currently there is no evidence of a potential problem. However, given the low levels of trust and scientific evidence, and the unknowns about the engineering of vaccines into plants, many groups remain very concerned and are unconvinced that sufficient research has been done.

- *The use of substantial equivalence in the risk assessment of GM food.* Currently many risk assessments conclude that a GM food is so similar to a non-GM food that it is 'substantially equivalent' and therefore requires no additional testing and scrutiny. This is the logic that led to the decisions not to label GM foods in the US and (previously) in the EU. However the general public, particularly in Europe, does not trust this scientific judgement or the conclusion that GM food needs no more testing than non-GM food.

Environmental concerns

Understanding the scope and depth of potential environmental effects of GM crops is a complex task. First, the link between cause and effect is poorly understood. Second, potential direct and indirect effects need to be distinguished. Third, the relationship between results of laboratory, semi-

'One day children may get immunized by munching on foods instead of enduring shots' (Langridge 2000).

The second and third generations of GM crops are maturing rapidly in laboratories around the world. A large proportion of the new generations will be 'functional foods': those which deliver a claimed consumer benefit such as taste, nutritional value, or drug delivery system.

A review of current research indicates where some of the research might bring us (Grain 2000):

- 1997: First human clinical trials of an edible vaccine; potatoes genetically engineered against E.coli.
- 1999: research at Cornell University advances use of potatoes and bananas.
- Large Scale Biology Corporation (US) is developing a patient-specific non-Hodgkins lymphoma vaccine in plants to speed up production process
- Scripps Research Institute is working on edible HIV vaccine, currently using cowpeas.
- CSIRO, Australia, has grown measles-fighting tobacco plant.

field—that is, fully enclosed greenhouses—and open-field studies is not clear. Scaling up from farm field tests to impacts of regional and national planting must include the indirect effects of farming practices as well as external environmental influences. This is hard to achieve by modelling or even empirically. In addition, we must ask whether the effects on individual organisms (plants or animals) can provoke impacts on entire communities or populations.

There is, however, another important component of the complexity: the lack of comparative data for non-GM crops. Questions are being asked of GM crops that have never been asked of conventional or organic agricultural practices, making meaningful comparison impossible.

Risk is another difficult issue. How much risk is acceptable? When do the benefits outweigh the risks? How do scientists select insects or plants to study for negative impacts?

The remainder of this sub-section outlines the key areas of potential impacts of the immediate farming and off-farm environment.

Out-crossing and GM crops 'escaping' into the wild. Out-crossing occurs when pollen from GM plants mixes with that of non-GM plants, resulting in a cross-breed. The first 'danger' is that, if the GM plant is herbicide-resistant, the new 'offspring' varieties may inherit tolerance to the herbicide, resulting in a 'super weed' that farmers cannot easily eliminate. Second, if the GM plant has an insecticide gene—BT, for example—the resulting offspring may have a weakened version of the BT gene, speeding up the process of long-term insect resistance to BT. Third, if the GM crop is planted near to wild relatives (such as potatoes in Peru, wheat in Turkey, maize in Mexico), outcrossing to wild relatives can change the genetic make-up of the wild plants. Can GM crops survive in the wild and therefore 'escape' from farmers' fields? If so, they will change the local biodiversity, possibly displacing the stock of wild relatives or other important plant species over time. A recent study indicates that herbicide-resistant GM crops are not able to survive off the field, and therefore do not pose such a threat (Crawley *et al.* 2001). However, this study does not confirm that all GM crops will die out in the wild, nor does it provide comparative data about GM crops as opposed to traditionally bred crops 'escaping'. Wild relatives of crops are invaluable to agriculture as a gene-pool. However, there are many direct and indirect factors influencing the behaviour and ecology of wild relatives and the ecology of farmers' fields.

Non-GM crops also 'outcross' and 'escape' into the wild from farmers' fields. The question is: do GM crops pose a higher risk than traditional varieties of out-crossing and provoking damage?

Impact on non-target organisms. GM crops, especially those with herbicide resistance and integrated pesticide genes, may affect other plants and animals in the immediate environment. For example, the BT genes inserted into maize target a certain type of insect. But what is the impact on non-targeted insects? Will GM crops affect below-ground life forms, such as earthworms, termites, or nematodes? Will changes in herbicide use affect other plants? These types of questions are under review by many scientific institutes, but results to date have been somewhat contradictory and mostly laboratory-based. The differences between natural interactions in a laboratory and in the open field are difficult to quantify, let alone to explain in non-specialised media. The study most covered by the media is the laboratory study that indicated that monarch butterflies are harmed by GM crops with the BT gene, from which it remains unclear what the 'real' impact in farmers' fields will be.

Additional questions need to be asked. What are the comparative effects of conventional farming methods? Certainly conventional applications of pesticides affect non-target organisms. Do GM crops negatively affect non- targets more or less than these methods under various conditions and farming methods?

Loss of on-farm biodiversity. Related to the impact on non-target organisms is the concern about knock-on effects on local ecosystems through biodiversity loss. As individual species may be harmed, will GM crops lead to the loss of biodiversity? There are two types of on-farm biodiversity concerns, one direct, the other indirect. First, crop ecosystems, despite their monoculture character, serve as a habitat for many insect and small 'weed' populations. Will GM crops endanger this biodiversity? Will the technology make the crops so strong that no weeds, wildflowers, insects, or birds will be able to compete with or consume the crops, thus decreasing biodiversity both on and off the field? This is also an issue for human welfare, since in developing countries these 'weeds' are often sources of food and medicine. Furthermore, there is *some* evidence that BT crops may promote the evolution of insect pests by provoking a change in mating behaviour over time when insects are constantly exposed to BT maize (Cerda and Wright 2000). Over time, this could lead to the development of new species. Second, will GM crops displace local varieties of crops, leading to the long-run loss of indigenous species? Again, what is the comparison with non-GM farming methods?

Resistance build-up. Transgenic plants producing environmentally benign *Bacillus thuringiensis* (BT) toxins are increasingly utilised for insect control, but their efficacy will be short-lived if pests adapt quickly. This is of particular concern because BT is the most widely used natural insecticide in agriculture and is used in organic farming. Several insects have developed BT resistance under laboratory selection, although only one—the Diamondback moth—has developed resistance in the field (Heckel 2000). Resistance management and support for farmers is in place in OECD countries, but many are concerned that in developing countries resistance build-up cannot be easily managed.

Effects on soil fertility and other unknown risks. The long-run impact of GM crops on soil fertility is unknown. There are studies that show that BT binds in soils and is present 234 days after harvest. What is it doing, what are its effects? Current studies indicate it is neither active nor affecting the below-ground environment. There is a great need for research in this area (Stotzky 2000).

This category of environmental concern brings to the fore the lack of comparative data, as little is known about the long-term impacts of current agricultural practices on soil fertility. Even less is documented for tropical soils.

Ethical issues

There are two central ethical issues: one about the technology, the other about its commercial use. For many consumers and members of global civil society, manipulation of a plant at the genetic level is simply wrong, immoral, unethical, or against human nature. Recent polls show that European consumers agree with the statement: 'even if GM food has advantages, it is against human nature' (*Eurobarometer* 2000). This opinion is held worldwide. Some critics, such as the Prince of Wales, claim GM crops are 'anti-God', that 'God did not intend us to meddle with nature'. Other critics, many of whom are non-religious, simply state that genetic engineering of plants (and animals) is anti-nature. This 'nature versus technology' debate is an interesting revision of 'rationalist versus romanticist' arguments. These types of arguments tend to rally many global civil society groups while infuriating industry scientists who constantly point out that farmers have been 'tampering' with nature for millennia. On this point alone, the gulf between the pro- and anti-biotech groups seems wide and unmoving. These 'ethical' issues are very deep-rooted, often accompanied by strong emotions, and for many groups they are the linchpin to the entire debate. Hearing scientists, policy-makers, industrialists and others disregard or dismiss their concerns only broadens the gulf and intensifies the anger and mistrust.

The second set of ethical issues focuses on the food industry's behaviour and perceived large profits. Global civil society points out that we risk the independence of our food chain if multinationals' efforts to vertically integrate their businesses and control the value chain from 'plough to plate' are not curtailed. Consumers and consumer-related global civil society groups have mobilised against this risk. For example, there have been boycotts and demonstrations at supermarkets, with groups publicly 'rewarding' supermarket chains that remove GM products from their home brands and chastising those who don't. Farmers, on the other hand, have generally been less organized. Some fear a pending dependency of farmers on products of multinational agribusinesses: once sold a herbicide resistant seed, will farmers lose their right to choose which herbicide to use? Are there boundaries to the controls farmers can develop? These concerns are only fuelled by the arrogance displayed by many captains of industry.

Consumers' rights and labelling

Loud and coordinated voices from global civil society are claiming the 'right to know' if a food product contains a GM product or by-product. This information is desired on a variety of personal, ethical, and environmental grounds, as discussed above. Many feel that industry and government were arrogant, short-sighted, and ill-advised not to enforce labelling from the very beginning. This simply fuels the fury of global civil society groups, which are seeking the mandatory labelling of GM foods worldwide as a single target action. For example, Consumers International (URL), the global federation of consumer organisations, claims: 'The use of genetic engineering is something in which there is almost universal interest amongst consumers. Consumers therefore want labelling of all foods that are derived from gene technology'.

Opponents of labelling argue that it is not straightforward. Many admit that labels may be meaningless due to the complexity of food production and the difficulty of preserving the identity of GM products through the food production chain. Furthermore, when does a food product contain a GMO? In many cases the new genes are not present in the part of the plant which ends up on the supermarket shelf or dining table. For example, refined oil extracted from GM soy does not contain any detectable remnant of the genetically modified

DNA which was codified for its construction (May 1999). Conversely, in lecitihin, which is an additive derived from a mixture of unrefined acids from soya, traces of genetically modified DNA can be found if it comes from GM soya. It's safe to say the average person consumes much more refined soya oil than lecitihin, GM or not. The traceability or otherwise of DNA has serious implications for those lobbying for labelling. Should we label all products that are sourced from GM plants, or only those in which traces of the DNA can be found? The percentage of GM products allowed to go unlabelled in a food item is also hotly contested. (see Box 4.6)

Specialist issues

As mentioned above, in addition to the four general areas of concern, the research has identified four additional topic areas. These are considered specialist areas either because they require specialist knowledge and/or because only a minority of global civil society groups has publicly communicated their concerns in these areas.

Intellectual property rights (IPR). IPR is a broad term used to cover patents, designs, trademarks, plant breeders' rights, copyright, and trade secrets. These are crucial because they determine ownership and therefore who will benefit in the long run from the technology. The hottest subject within the realm of biotechnology is the use of patents. Patents[1] are used to protect the genes and technical processes required to produce a GM plant. In addition, companies have tried, sometimes successfully, to patent plant varieties such as basmati rice.

Who has access to the genes, necessary technological tools, and processes will influence the direction of research and development. This in turn will largely dictate who has access to GM crops, for good or bad, and at what prices. The issues are complex, however, two key implications of IPR and patents in biotechnology are central concerns of global civil society. First, agricultural biotechnology has largely been incubated and promoted by the private sector. Currently about 75 per cent of the

---

[1] *A patent is granted to the owner of the invention for up to 20 years for a monopoly of limited scope. It is effective only in the country that grants the patent. IPR laws vary from country to country, and a successful attempt to harmonise this area takes the form of a GATT Agreement on Trade Related Aspects of Intellectual Property Rights (TRIPS). Patents are used to protect the genes and technical processes required to produce a GM plant.*

One of the problems of labelling GM crops is that there currently no international standard on the minimum content of GM food allowed under labelling programmes. Below are a few examples of current approaches.

European Union	Labelling required for consumer food items that contain more than 1% GM product.
Japan	Nearly 30 biotechnology food items will be subject to labelling if they contain more than 5% GM products.
Australia, New Zealand	Labelling for less than 1% after 2001.
Indonesia, Korea, Saudi Arabia, and Switzerland	In the process of setting labelling standards.

developments in agricultural technology flow from research undertaken by the corporate sector (ISAAA 1999), which is self-reinforced by patents (discussed below). As a result, most current research and development (R&D) in plant biotechnology reflects market- driven interests. Companies focus on meeting the needs of large-scale farms in developed regions where they can expect significant financial returns on their R&D. Products for poor farmers and those in non-lucrative markets will most likely not be developed. Hence, we have seen the development of crops for large-scale farms in developed countries, but very few technologies tailored to the needs of poor and small-scale farms in developing countries.

In addition, there is a related 'double brain drain': many of the best young plant scientists go directly to the private sector, while established public sector scientists rely on corporate funding and thus steer their efforts towards potential commercial applications.

Second, the 'IPR imbalance' is self-reinforcing. The more patents are developed in the private sector, the more difficult it is for the public sector to carry out biotechnology R&D. While experimental use of patented products and processes is not usually an infringement of the rights of the patent owner, patents can prevent a new invention from easily reaching the public domain. Furthermore, public research institutes lack the experience and expertise to untangle the complex web of intellectual property held on parts of products or processes required by their research. One strategy, albeit still fairly

infrequent, has been for multinational corporations to donate intellectual property to public-sector research groups. However, outside the US, it is not a well-rehearsed procedure, and most research institutes in developing countries do not know how to obtain required intellectual property clearance or donation from private sector owners.

Information and communications: 'Waiter, there's a gene in my soup'. In a recent survey, only 11 per cent of respondents in Europe reported that they felt adequately informed on biotechnology (*Eurobarometer* 2000). It is assumed that this figure is loosely representative of most of the OECD, but it would be much lower for developing countries.

There are two related problems. There is an 'asymmetry of knowledge' between scientists and the general public on scientific knowledge and understanding of the technology and its functions. This is compounded by a 'symmetry of ignorance' among scientists, policy-makers, and the public about each other's real aims and concerns. As long as scientists maintain that they will consider only 'objective truths' without any regard for the public's subjective fears, there can be no real communication. This is particularly true of the 'ethical' issues involved. Equally, if the opponents of biotechnology are seen to be 'scare-mongering', communication and understanding likewise falter. Quality information, from all points of views and spectrums, along with a sincere effort to describe the technology in lay terms, is difficult to find. It is particularly scarce in developing countries.

Three types of public information are cited as most required to meet the communications needs of global civil society (Meridian Institute 2000):

- *Media coverage.* In the North, particularly in Europe, there is widespread criticism of the media for their role in framing the current debate as extreme, frightening, and difficult to understand. In developing countries the power of the media is even greater, given the generally limited access to the Internet and dialogue venues. Global civil society groups seem united in the call for more quality media coverage that offers a broader diversity of opinion and expertise about plant biotechnology.

- *Internet-based resources.* Many global civil society organisations rely on the Internet to facilitate global and local information exchange. Biotechnology information list servers, NGO and public research institute websites, and dialogue spaces have all played a critical role in shaping the current debate. The major concern is the reliability of information posted on the web. In addition, for global networking it has become a critical organisational tool as well. However, in developing countries access is often severely limited.

- *Credible scientific review.* There is a tremendous need for credible and transparent processes for answering important scientific questions. Many global civil society groups simply do not accept the neutrality of current science because of the interconnections between research institutes and corporations. As a result, some global civil society groups are not willing to accept 'scientific findings' on the human or environmental effects of GM crops. Most groups recognise the need for more transparent processes to address the difficult issues, and often call for independent panels, academic conferences, and stakeholder dialogues to bring scientists and concerned members of the public together. Some global civil society groups will never accept scientific views. For example, deep ecologists reject the reductionist approach of molecular biology on principle.

Capacity and capacity building. The main capacity-building issue concerns developing countries, which lack a public research base, political processes, and legal infrastructure to 'make up their own minds and regulate' GM technology. A nation that can confidently make decisions about whether to import and/or export GM products, develop new products domestically, or allow field trials of GM crops requires a regulatory infrastructure involving policies, procedures, technical reviews, and research. This concerns all civil society groups. For example, the Green Belt Movement in Kenya expresses concerns about whether African nations have the skill, expertise, and political will to regulate this new industry. Some bilateral and multilateral aid is addressing this issue, but most groups agree there is a tremendous amount of work to be done.

As the debate becomes more sophisticated and complex, some global civil society groups indicate that capacity building is an issue also for developed Northern countries. Biotechnology's cross-cutting reach across issues of health, environment, regulation, agriculture, fisheries, and other areas renders current government structures unable to regulate efficiently or effectively. Government agencies are traditionally 'silos' by structure, and buckle under the demands to share information, reformulate categories of food and pesticides, and so forth. One indication of the challenge is the GM BT potato that was regulated in the US under procedures for a pesticide, not a human food, because the BT gene is a registered and recognized pesticide.

Farmers' rights. 'Farmers' rights' are not a defined set of rights. The expression was coined in the mid-1990s by RAFI (URL), a nimble and creative global civil society group, to create awareness that farmers should be granted certain basic rights. Saving seed is one such right. Traditionally bred varieties produce viable seeds which farmers have saved and used for millennia. Modern agriculture introduced hybrid crops, which are ideally repurchased each year to ensure top performance. While hybrid seeds will not reproduce exactly the same characteristics season after season, farmers can replant them if they wish. GM seeds, however, are currently being sold with an obligation for farmers not to save seeds. The infamous terminator technology was devised to tackle this problem: if the technology is developed, it will render offspring seeds from biotech seeds sterile with the specific 'terminator' gene. The tremendous outcry from global civil society groups provoked at least one multinational biotechnology company, Monsanto (URL), to undertake not to commercialise seed-sterilising technologies.

Framing Global Civil Society Groups and their Positions

How has global civil society reacted to these issues? First, it is important to note that the reaction has indeed been global. It is global in a physical sense; GM crops are rapidly spreading throughout all continents. Transnational corporations and internationally networked NGOs are the key players, and the latter are particularly dependent on inexpensive global communications, that is to say, the Internet and telecommunications.

For this analysis, the following groups were included in the research:

- NGOs, NGO networks, social movements (such as Greenpeace, Friends of the Earth (URL), Confédération Paysanne;

- individuals (for example, Vandana Shiva, Gordon Conway);
- think tanks and commissions (EU-US biotechnology Consultative Forum); and media and specialised websites (websites of NGOs and think tanks as well as publicly accessible specialist list servers).

This research examined over 500 websites and scanned the international printed media for the period of January 1999–Febuary 2001. The analysis employed four general categories of groups to organise the hundreds of NGOs, websites, think tanks, and individuals considered. (See Chapter 1, pp. 7–10). It is difficult to reduce heterogeneous groups that often hold significantly differing outlooks and motivations. This exercise is accompanied by the usual caveats: not one social movement fits exactly

Table 4.3: African perspective on the potential of GM crops for African needs

Crop	Constraints	Status global	Status Africa
Maize	Disease, insect pest and drought and weed	Commercial application	
	European corn borer	Commercial application	South Africa: BT maize
Cotton	Insect pests	Commercial application	South Africa: BT cotton
Cassava	African cassava Mosaic virus	R & D	R & D
Sweet potato	Virus disease Weevil damage Vitamin A	Pipeline Pipeline	Pipeline
Potato	Virus	Commercial application	Field trials (South Africa)
	Potato tuber moth damage	Commercial	Pipeline (Egypt)
Wheat	Diseases	Commercial application	
Banana	Sigatoka leaf spot Weevil damage Nematode damage	Ready field testing R & D Pipeline	
Tomato	Virus disease	Commercial application	Field testing (Egypt)
Tomato and other fruits e.g. banana	Ripening perishability Virus disease	Commercial application delayed ripening	
Papaya		Commercial application	
Maize, cotton, and soyabean	Herbicide weeding	Commercial application	
Maize and cotton	Herbicide tolerance	Commercial application	Pipeline (Mauritius)
Sugarcane	Weeding Sugarcane mosaic virus Insect pests	Field trials Field trials R & D	Field trials (South Africa)

Source: ISAAA (1999).

The Rural Advancement Fund International (RAFI URL), soon to be renamed, is illustrative of the power of the virtual postage-stamp sized NGO. It is smart, highly wired, fast, seemingly intangible yet highly respected for its breadth of knowledge and chutzpah. RAFI works with members of the business community and governments even as it directs campaigns against them.

Headquartered in Winnipeg, Canada, RAFI has seven staff members in three countries. The group is dedicated to the conservation and sustainable improvement of agricultural biodiversity and to the socially responsible development of technologies useful to rural societies. RAFI is concerned about the loss of genetic diversity, especially in agriculture, and about the impact of intellectual property on agriculture and world food security. During its 22-year history it has run a low-cost operation with high-class knowledge management. It reaches enviable standards of efficiency and ability to market ideas.

Battling against 'unfair' intellectual property rights (IPR) on plant varieties is a main item in RAFI's workload which brings it into the centre of the plant biotechnology debates. Recently RAFI forced a private research institute in Australia to drop two patents on cow peas because it had discovered that the germ plasma originated from a public trust gene bank. This work led to the reversal of the patents and the investigation of a subsequent 147 similar patents.

One of RAFI's finest tools is its sharp tongue and a willingness to use it for or against a company. 'We are obnoxious, and that is part of our strategy. It gets us attention', explains Pat Mooney, director of RAFI. Indeed, on its website RAFI describes itself as 'smart assed enough to even tell the Vatican what to do'. Of course, its 'effectiveness' is relative to one's viewpoint. When Pat Mooney coined the term 'Terminator', it did not please members of the life-science industry. However, within weeks it was clear that his quick wit had started a public relations campaign against the seed sterilising technologies, such as that patented by Delta and Pine Land. The development of the technology has not ended, but several companies have publicly stated they will not engage in related research.

---

into a general 'box', social movements and groups change over time, and each group contains diverse elements (Cohen and Rai 1999). In the plant biotechnology arena, the boundaries between many of the groups are blurred on various issues. In fact, it is this blurring that has made the movements so polymorphous, dynamic, and thus fascinating. The four categories are explained below.

Rejectionists: 'GM is the problem, so is the system. We want a GMO free world.'

Members of these groups believe plant biotechnology is 'wrong' and 'dangerous' and should be abolished. They oppose it with all their might, and often refer to themselves as 'protecting the environment and consumer'. Rejectionists are against field trials, publicly funded research into GM crops, and any GM food products entering the food chain. They call for a GMO-free world. They cite a mix of ethical, moral, social, and environmental reasons, and although they may not agree on all of them, they agree on the need for a ban. This creates strong single-focus alliances. The alliances are mostly national and global, and have built active networks of knowledge and ideas for anti-GMO action. They seek 'to cram the gene genie back in the bottle', as one anonymous anti-GMO demonstrator said at the May Day protest in London. Some Rejectionists use civil disobedience and violence. Groups in this category have occasionally destroyed property. For example, activists in many countries have ripped test plots out of the ground and destroyed GE grain. In India, poor farmers were mobilised to burn down the Monsanto Plc headquarters (Shiva 1999). Many other Rejectionist groups abhor any violence or destruction of property and do not condone their peers' actions. The violence thus far experienced has been narrow in scope and more of an aberration than a *modus operandi* for the Rejectionists.

Rejectionist groups do not condone cooperation in the form of participation in stakeholder debates with industry or government. They see their views and wishes as diametrically opposed to those of the life-science industry, and therefore do not support any dialogue with them. Simply put: big business wants to make money from GE crops, Rejectionists want no GE crops at all, and never the twain shall meet.

Representative groups include Greenpeace International, Friends of the Earth, Research Foundation for Science, Technology and Ecology (India) (URL), Dig It Up (URL), Foundation on Economic Trends (US), and the Safe Food Coalition (South Africa) (URL).

Reformists: 'We need new systems'

Reformist groups hold that political and governance systems, not plant biotechnology, are 'the problem'. Although plant biotechnology might be good for humanity in the future, in its present form it is not. They want to reform the institutions and the decision-making process and to improve accountability and civil society participation. In general they seek changes in policy and law at the national and international levels that remove obstacles to dealing with current injustices and inequalities. These groups seek full consumer choice through labelling and information, the power to ban GM product imports at the national level, and public participation in establishing field trials and risk assessments. For reformists, the linchpin issue is sharing the benefits. How can we ensure that the technology actually helps the poor and excluded and not merely the wealthy multinational companies? Furthermore, how can we ensure that the technologies are truly environmentally beneficial and do not just increase the pollution caused by heavier use of chemical pesticides or genetic drift? Ingredients of the answers to these questions include intellectual property rights, patenting of life forms stewarded by indigenous communities, support for public research to counterbalance corporate scientific powers, and capacity building in developing countries in all aspects of technology development and application, including political systems to regulate it. One critical strategy for Reformists is to call for international labelling on all GM food products. The Reformists are characterised by a willingness to participate in public debate, stakeholder dialogue with 'the enemy', and any other process aimed at addressing the 'problems' of GM crop production and products in a constructive way. Representative Reformist groups include the Rockefeller Foundation, Bread for the World, Consumers International (URL), and the Consumers' Association (URL).

Supporters: 'The problem is not the technology, it's the Luddites who don't understand it and are trying to block it using Franken-scare tactics.'

The Supporters are members of civil society who promote the belief that agro-biotechnology is a very powerful tool to help increase the world's food supply while simultaneously decreasing the environmental degradation of agricultural production. They are often, but not necessarily always, close to governments and business. The Supporter groups believe that the public's ignorance and misunderstanding of science are the root cause of an unnecessary backlash against agro-biotechnology. The 'Frankenstein food' and 'superweed' scare tactics appal them. They fight for good science to be heard, understood, and disseminated by the media. These groups tend to feel that the issues are scientific rather than social or civil. However, some groups in this category argue that there are serious political and capacity-building issues in developing countries. This is important because poor capacity at the national governmental level acts as a barrier to the technologies' wider adoption. Capacity here refers to the ability to legislate for GM crops approval and establish biosafety measures. It also refers to the national capacity to fund and train scientists and farmer extension to develop and disseminate relevant GM crop technologies. Supporters are a small group and often affiliated with organisations which are not understood to be part of 'civil society', namely, business, government, and publicly funded research institutes. For example, Africabio is a technically an NGO and therefore a civil society group, yet has much interaction with and support from industry and pro-GMO research institutes.

The NGO key players in this category are the International Service for the Acquisition and Application of Agro-biotechnology (ISAAA) and AfricaBio.

	Reformists e.g. Rockefeller Foundation, Bread for the World, WRI, International Consumers Association, etc.	Rejectionists e.g. Greenpeace (URL), FoE, Rafi, Vandana Shiva	Alternatives e.g. Confédération Paysanne, Soil Association (URL)	Supporters e.g. ISAAA (URL), AfricaBio
Human health	More studies under transparent conditions and broad participation in definition of 'safety'	Halt all consumption, animal and human, until more tests have been undertaken	Insist on strictest labelling to ensure ease of avoiding products containing GMOs	Sufficient studies done to meet national regulations. Update if necessary.
Environmental health	Same as above, with need for extensive field testing	Halt all test plots and commercial planting until more is understood about impacts in complex ecosystems, i.e. Five year moratorium campaign in Europe	Legislate for mandatory large distances (100–200 kilometres) to isolate all GM field trials and commercial planting to avoid any cross breeding/pollution	Need assessments of relative environmental damage/benefits to other forms of agriculture.
Right to know, transparency of process, etc.	Promote more transparency and accountability in the rules and practices governing biotechnology adoption, e.g. citizen's juries, stakeholder dialogue, support for participation in Biosafety Protocol, etc.	Mandate Biosafety Protocol to supersede WTO, thus allowing countries to ban imports of GMOs. Support for regions to become GMO free and for full labelling on all products with GMOs.	Create own food chains via local and international webs of organic and biodynamic farming communities. Do not participate in stakeholder dialogues; avoid 'co-option' by such processes.	WTO rules supported —a country cannot reject GMOs because they are substantially equivalent to non-GMO commodities. Companies will engage in stakeholder dialogue, but market forces prevail.
Ethical issues	No firm consensus on this issue, but the need to work through bioethical consider-ations, especially in non-Western cultures.	Genetic engineering is meddling with nature and against what God intended.	Give us the space and freedom to reject this technology and pursue and alternative lifestyle.	Rationality of science over religious or romantic notions of nature. Science is science, not religion.

Alternatives: 'We want to live in our own spaces, away from GM foods and GE agriculture.'

The primary concern of Alternative groups is to develop their own way of life and to create their own alternative lifestyle and space where they can live without the influence or effects of plant biotechnology. For the most part they reject 'conventional' agricultural development and seek isolation from GM food crops. In some instances these groups combine the anti-GM message with a call for local production and self-sufficiency of food (for example, campaigns for urban gardens, 'eat locally', 'food miles'). Others ignore the providence question and simply want GMO-free food and to live in a GMO-free environment. Not only does this category of groups demand full labelling on all products containing any GMOs, they demand large-scale physical isolation of GM crops to reduce risks of cross pollination or 'genetic pollution'. Members of these groups may or may not actively oppose plant biotechnology *per se*. The Soil Association (URL) and other organic movements are alternative groups that are anti-GM but are specifically fighting for organic food production.

Global civil society cooperation + alliances = strength

As with any set of categories, the lines between the four groups are often blurred on many of the issues. Many alliances have been formed across the groups and continents. Many Reformists want 'GMO-free space' in which to live, as do most Rejectionists. The difference is the focus of the key messages and activities. One example of a cross-group alliance is the Five Year Freeze Campaign (URL), a network of 50 NGOs calling for a five-year freeze on all field testing, planting, and importation of GMOs into Europe. Although all the groups in the coalition agree that the freeze is necessary, their reasons differ. The Rejectionists within the coalition see it as a ploy to get a permanent ban on GE crops. The Reformists cite the precautionary approach and the need for more time to debate the issue in public as justifying a temporary ban and a proposed public process to decide at the end of five years what should happen. A few Alternatives have joined the coalition, mainly to help assure them GM-free zones.

This mix of incentives and underlying goals has apparently not weakened either the message or its delivery to society at large. While internal disagreements and inter-group politics exist, the outward appearance is of a fairly united front on many of the issues. Internationally, the anti-GE campaigns continue to bring together a rich array of groups and individuals, most of whom normally would not interact. For example, in the UK the Soil Association (the UK's largest organic agriculture organisation) and environmental groups such as Friends of the Earth and Greenpeace work with local grass-roots organisations such as women's groups and similar groups in developing countries, such as the Greenbelt Movement in Kenya, consumers' associations, and Indian and Asian farmers' movements.

The unusual mix and blurring of stances on particular issues lends the anti-biotechnology global civil society movement the strength and colours of a woven tapestry. It is unpredictable, it is polyvocal; but, most importantly, it offers the movement enough representative variety so that most members of society can identify with at least one of the sub-groups. A single mother in a Parisian high-rise apartment block may not identify with an angry youth or eco-warrior working for Greenpeace, but most likely she will listen to the Baby Milk Coalition or the Consumers' Association. Likewise, farmers in France find solidarity with housewives in the UK and activists in Brazil.

Regional differences

The research shows some regional differences in civil society groups' reactions to plant bio-technology. The main difference tends to be 'volume': the extent to which groups are actively engaged in the issue, gaining media coverage, networking with other groups, and aiming to impact government and industry behaviour. Europe has been a hotbed of activity since the mid-1990s, whereas in the US only pockets of activity are evident, even today. The Philippines and India have active and vocal opposition and supporting groups, while most of their neighbours in Asia do not. In Latin America, Brazil is the most internationally networked country. This is in contrast to Mexico, which has some approved GM crops and an important presence of illegal GM maize, yet civil society groups became active only a few years ago.

Why is the epicentre of rejection in Europe, and particularly in the United Kingdom? The answer must include recent food scandals and deep-seated political and cultural attitudes of many civil society groups. Britain and Europe are still reeling from the devastating BSE crisis that struck their cattle industries. Early in the crisis the UK government denied that there was any risk to humans, a claim that sadly turned out to be untrue. BSE in animals and consequently the new variant of CJD in humans arose as an unintended effect of a new agricultural practice—the introduction of scrap animal meat and body parts into cattle feed—without sufficiently wide-ranging consultation about the possible consequences (May 1999). In addition, the UK and European governments' first attempts to halt the spread of the disease did not include public consultation. Although BSE strictly had nothing to do with genetic manipulation, the BSE debacle and government's failures taint all discussions of GM foods in the UK and in Europe more generally. Another part of the story relates to European civil society groups rejecting the 'Americanisation' of European agricultural practices and food habits. Many of the civil society groups link their rejection of the 'evil American empire' with a hatred or fear of globalisation in general. The link to the latter was made potently clear at the spring 2000 demonstrations in the Lozere, France, when protestors demonstrated against both GM agriculture and the World Trade Organisation while smashing the windows of a McDonald's restaurant. These demonstrations brought global civil society together just as they did in Seattle, Prague, and Davos. Northern NGOs supported the presence of Southern civil society groups and leaders such as Martin Khor and Vandana Shiva. The 'star' of the Lozere event was José Bové , a French farmer who was later tried with five other men for damaging the McDonald's restaurant. José Bové became an overnight cause célèbre, who speaks out worldwide against the Americanisation of culture, globalisation in general, and GM crops as a symbol of what is wrong with the world.

A third factor making for Europe's strong anti-GM crop movements is the media. Regular media coverage of issues related to biotechnology began in 1997 in most of Europe. By 1998, stories were appearing weekly. In the UK during the peak of protests in the spring and summer of 1999—when demonstrators were blocking shipments of GM crops in the Netherlands, dumping GM soy in Brussels and Paris, and ripping up test plots in the UK—a story about GM crops or research ran on the front cover of at least one newspaper almost daily. Media coverage never reached such saturation in other parts of the world, least of all in the US.

News from the South also featured in Europe, and some of the most actively networked and global players in the debate are civil society groups from the South. The motivation and focus of Southern groups tends to be very different from those of their European allies. They share concerns about health and safety based on an innate mistrust of government and industry. However, an additional issue arose early in the debate. A review of the foremost concerns of civil society groups in developing countries (Osgood 2000) showed the key issues to be:

- access to, and benefits from, biotechnology;
- issues of choice, control, and regulation;
- impact on poor farmers;
- environmental impacts; and
- ethical and moral dilemmas.

The key difference between Northern and Southern civil society groups can be simply stated. The major focus in Europe is on the potential impact of technology on consumers' health and rights and on the countryside; the farmer's voice is seldom heard, with the potent exception of the Confédération Paysanne led by José Bové. In the South, by contrast, farmers are central to the issues, and efforts are made to include their voices directly in the protests. For example, Rejectionists from the South tend to focus on the political as well as the social aspects of the biotechnology debate. Two classic Rejectionist groups are the Research Foundation for Science Technology and Ecology (URL) in India and the Third World Network (URL) based in Malaysia. The Indian organisation is run by Vandana Shiva and proactively fights GM worldwide. While it opposes agro-biotechnology for all of the reasons given above, its main focus is on the impact of the technology on poor farmers: environmental hazards of chemicals, equity issues of not saving seeds, the loss of indigenous biodiversity, the economic and social implications of buying seeds and other essential inputs from multinational companies, and the ethical or moral problem of 'playing God'. Shiva is well known for her call to end Monsanto's days in India, and she views globalisation and the growth of multinationals as a root cause of the biotechnology problem. The Third World Network, views all genetic engineering as an instrument of recolonisation, and argues that

Box 4.8: Global civil society impacts the food retailing industry

The retailing industry is the linchpin in the food market due to its proximity to consumers. In addition, over the last years, a global concentration process has increased the market power of retailers. They are in a key market position that allows them to amplify consumer preferences and relay them to the food industry. Any restrictive approach on GM food has cascading effects on the upstream side of the food chain, on domestic as well as on foreign markets.

In Europe, consumer mobilisation and negative perception of GM crops has directly affected the strategy of food retailers. Faced with growing popular pressure to phase out GMOs in the late 1990s, combined with the then legal uncertainties on GM food labelling, many retailers framed new policies on GM food. Supermarket chains first took action in the UK, and the movement spread to continental Europe. Retailers did not align on a single non-GM model. Rather, they adopted various types of action. Retailers who took a restrictive stance on GM food mainly focused on own-brands, for which they committed themselves to phase out GM ingredients. Today, where such phasing out is not possible, compulsory labelling applies, in accordance with EU legislation.

European retailers have moved to meet and further shape the demand for non-GM food, in contrast with the wait-and-see approach adopted by the bulk of North American retailers. In the meantime, food processors and grain companies have been hard-pressed to segregate GM from non-GM products and regionalise their production to avoid GM ingredients where possible.

Some retailers formed group initiatives, such as consortia or GM-free working groups. These initiatives enable group members to share the burden of reorganisation of the supply chain and give them additional weight in the food processing industry. On the other hand, individual initiatives are likely to diminish the negotiating power of the chain with regard to food processing.

---

the developing world holds the solutions to its own problems and should be allowed to develop these free from pressure from Northern financial interests. These two organisations often send representatives to key global events, from Seattle to demonstrations in the US and Europe, negotiations of the Biosafety Protocol, and international technical and civil society conferences on biotechnology. They are truly global players, exploiting the Internet and inexpensive air travel to cover the issues from every possible angle. The groups' leaders, Shiva and Khor, have been awarded many international awards for their work.

Reformists are also active in Southern countries. The Institute for Sustainable Development in Ethiopia is a good example. The group is not completely hostile towards GM technologies. It argues that the technology must address farmers' 'real needs', which it currently does not do in Ethiopia because it is being developed by large corporations that neither understand nor care about the reality of small-scale farming in Africa. The Institute demands that the technology be delivered in an environment where it

can be monitored and regulated and where the potential for accidents is minimised. Although the Institute focuses on Africa, and Ethiopia in particular, it is representative of many Reformists from other Southern countries. Despite being highly globally linked, it has no website.

Other Reformist Southern civil society groups focus on national capacity to handle the complex issues of plant biotechnology, and link less frequently than other groups to the international debate. The concern about regulation and national capacity to monitor and verify impacts and ethical trade is crucial. In South Africa, the lack of public consultations before tests and commercial releases of GM crops has goaded South Africa's Safe Food Coalition (URL) into action.

Of the environmental issues, Reformists and Rejectionists alike are generally most concerned about indigenous biodiversity and have come to the GM issue from other civil society concerns. An example of this is *Accion Ecologica* (URL) in Ecuador, which is mainly involved in tropical rain-forest issues and the

A jury at Norwich, UK, Crown Court found 28 Greenpeace UK activists not guilty of theft after GM maize planted by Aventis at Lyng, UK, was destroyed on 26 July 1999. The activists were caught at the scene of the crop destruction, many of them photographed with plants and digging equipment. The jury failed to reach a verdict on a second charge of causing criminal damage. Prosecutors decided not to have a retrial.

Greenpeace UK executive director Lord Melchett was among the activists under trial. As Melchett promised after the trail, the campaigning to end release of GM crops in the UK continues.

The outcome of the trial encourages civil society activists to continue to take direct action and jeopardises the required crop trials which could later lead to commercial releases.

offices at Cornell University in the US. Its sole *raison d'être* is to promote the use of agro-biotechnology by assisting the transfer of biotechnology 'solutions' to developing countries to increase crop productivity and incomes among resource-poor farmers. Current work includes tissue-culture bananas, multi-purpose trees, and a virus-resistant sweet potato in Kenya. In addition, ISAAA works on rice, papaya, and sweet potatoes in Vietnam, Indonesia, Malaysia, the Philippines, and Thailand. Late in 2000, ISAAA joined forces with another African-based Supporter, AfricaBio, whose purpose is to ensure that Africa can decide for Africa which agro-biotechnologies are relevant and that they are used properly.

Civil society groups which display Alternative characteristics are primarily Northern and have no visible representation in Southern countries. Alternatives may exist in countries such as Brazil, China, and South Africa, where there is substantial commercial planting of GM crops. However, their quest for isolation and peace would most likely prevent them from becoming connected to the global movement.

Global civil society actions and methods

Global civil society groups have taken various types of action during their campaigns on plant biotechnology. Demonstrations, direct action, letter writing, lobbying, and citizen's juries have all been undertaken recently on various sub-topics within the general debate. Sometimes the actions are implicitly supported by the government. For example, in the UK, the destruction of GM crop field sites by protestors was not punished (see Box 4.9). On other occasions the actions have had little influence on government or the private sector.

Table 4.5 presents a sample of the actions taken for specific campaigns and the types of groups involved over the last seven years. It is far from exhaustive. It does show that Rejectionists and Reformists often join forces, occasionally together with Alternatives.

rights of indigenous peoples. It sees GM crops as a possible threat to the sensitive tropical forests and indigenous peoples, and therefore calls for strong international regulation of GE products. Similarly, the Pesticide Action Network, based in Senegal, has entered the global debate because it sees GM as an extension of excessive use of pesticides and herbicides. The Pesticide Action Network addresses these issues globally, and has offices and links in many developed countries. Another group, the International Genetic Resources Action Information (URL) in the Philippines and Spain, fights to protect farmers' rights to seeds and the maintenance of indigenous varieties. In the plant biotechnology debate, it is primarily concerned about the potential impact of biotechnology on agricultural biodiversity. Other key groups include The Green Belt Movement in Kenya, which primarily encourages rural women to plant trees. It entered the GM debate mainly to express concern about the impact on Kenyan crops and biodiversity and on African governments' abilities to regulate the technology.

There are also Supporters in the Southern countries. The most developed Supporter group is ISAAA, based in Kenya and the Philippines with

Conclusions

Despite the protests, participation in political and industry processes, consumer boycotts, and direct action in many parts of the world, plant and agro-biotechnology are unlikely to go away. For the Rejectionists, this is a dire forecast. For the Reformists, Alternatives, and Supporters, it means an increased workload because the issues and concerns will not evaporate as the technology spreads. Although in some parts of the world its adoption may be slowed over the next few years, in the long term it is unlikely to be altogether dispensed with. There are three key reasons for this. First, the private sector has invested substantial scientific and financial resources in it, creating a momentum that would be difficult to reverse. Indeed, the current US government explicitly supports corporate investment in biotechnology and life sciences. Second, the public sector has also made significant investments; more importantly, many public research institutes and influential bodies, such as the US National Academy of Science, agree that the technology has an important role to play in meeting world food demands. Third, the next generation of GM products may be less controversial. For example, in the near future, GM products are likely to emerge that, rather than food for human consumption, are an extension of industrial biotechnology using agriculture, such as producing plastics from corn,. These products may require fewer regulatory approvals and be less controversial from a public point of view, and could therefore help to ensure the technology's survival, regardless of public opinion on GM food.

In the next five to ten years, as the technology develops and global civil society continues to engage with the issues, there are four key points to watch and consider:

1. The pace of innovation will quicken.

For example, a few months ago the sequencing of plant genomes was not part of the public's consciousness. The public vaguely knew that scientists were making progress in understanding plant genomics. At the time of writing, two plants have been entirely decoded, including rice, a major food crop for a large part of the world. Today, genomic work is under way on hundreds of plant and animal species, as is transgenetic engineering from viruses, bacteria, and animal genes. The speed of innovation has implications for health and safety and society's capacity to regulate and monitor the risks and impacts. The pace of innovation requires global civil society to consider three wide-ranging sets of questions. What are the broader impacts of the new technologies? What are the alternatives? What expert

and governmental capacity is required for regulating and monitoring the developments?

First, global civil society needs to ensure that, as the technology and its uses advance, we also increase work on, and understanding of, integrating ecosystem and human health complexity with biotechnological developments and applications. This is particularly true for work on tropical ecosystems, in which there is even less understanding of complex ecological dynamics, and for people who are undernourished or in stressed health situations. Comparative studies are required which take into account social influences such as diets, general health and fitness, and the socio-economic realities of the target consumers. This will require broadening our view of environmental and health effects beyond the current narrow approach to encompass the ethical and social issues raised by global civil society.

At the same time, *we must be able to ask what the alternatives are*, and for this we need a better understanding of the complex ecological interactions involved in 'traditional' agriculture and food delivery. *Focusing narrowly on the impacts of GM crops will rob us of a complete understanding of our options.*

Second, the rapid advance of technology also will require accelerated capacity-building in government, societal governance, and policy research in developing countries, particularly in sub-Saharan Africa. Capacity is required for national regulatory processes as well as for international agreements and complex matters such as bio-safety. In the medium term, the private sector is likely to continue to shift its focus from Europe to Africa and other parts of the developing world such as China. This implies that these regions need legal and scientific capacity-building today as well as in preparation for future developments. In addition, the rapid development of the technology, most of which is and will remain in the private sector, means that there will be fewer and fewer experts who can be called on by government and civil society to provide 'neutral' evidence and advice about the developing technologies and their potential impacts. For example, only five expert witnesses were identified in the US to consider the Starlink allergenicity case.

For many reasons, trusted expert capacity is the most critical issue global civil society faces in the next five to ten years. Without reliable expert information, governments and civil society will be handicapped in making recommendations, judgements, and policy to guide the development of biotechnology. The obvious solution—training more scientists—will be effective only in the long term and only if the scientists have sufficient incentives to remain in the public sector. Global civil society must address this issue in a new and creative way for the short and medium term. Otherwise, its efforts will be crippled by a lack of scientific understanding. Reformists need to give top priority to capacity building for the next few years. Rejectionists and Alternatives also need to keep up with the science and the social impacts and to join forces with some Reformists to address the massive information gap about the impacts of conventional food production. Without this information, the debate cannot mature.

2. We lack trusted leadership.

For good or bad, there are no clear leaders who are trusted, respected, and heard by all sides of the debate. Each 'domain' has its key ringleaders, but the other sides do not trust them. At best they are *dramatis personae*, but they are tainted by being viewed as biased experts in the field. More importantly, they are also involved in other work and are not perceived to be totally dedicated to the 'cause' of plant biotechnology. NGOs follow the international call leaders such as Vandana Shiva, Jeremy Rifkin, Pat Mooney, and Peter Melchett, while scientists gather around fellow scientists of international acclaim who remain in the public sector, such as Peter Raven, Norman Borlag, and Swaminathan, a Nobel Laureate and authority on the Green Revolution. *Lack of a common language and hence of agreed priorities prevents a leader from emerging, as there are few civil society leaders who 'speak science' and few scientists who 'speak society'.*

It is unrealistic to seek a figurehead for a polyvocal, often contradictory, amorphous movement. However, global civil society groups should be aware of the need for communication and leadership and foster respectful interactions between experts from all sides. Reformists, Rejectionists, Supporters, and Alternatives alike need to take up the challenge to develop a common language from which stronger leadership should develop.

3. The economics are important.

Three related economic trends will help shape the technology. First, 75 per cent of agricultural developments are currently in private sector laboratories (ISAAA 1999), and intellectual property rights (IPR) protect these investments. This implies that most developments will need to meet the financial requirements of their investors rather than those of poor farmers in developing countries. In addition, it remains unclear whether the IPR held by the private sector will hinder public-sector technology development. Second, we can expect continued investment in plant biotechnology for commodity crops. How will these developments change the *locus* and economics of production for commodities such as sugar, palm oil, and peanuts? How will this affect the poor producers of the world? Third, given the economic realities and patterns of IPR, how will the benefits be shared? The plants and genes originated in the common. Reformists and Supporters need to assume leadership, in partnership with businesses and government, in devising creative solutions that encourage and enable the private sector to re-infuse the commons and to find ways to ensure that benefits are shared as equitably as possible. These sentiments are commonplace in the language of the Convention on Biological Diversity and those who work in this domain. However, global civil society has yet to deliver workable, replicable, efficient programmes for sharing the benefits of plant biotechnology and its products. This is a major and urgent task for the next five years.

An additional noteworthy economic trend is the expectation that genetic engineering and genome work will become less expensive. Assuming IPR barriers are either porous or short, might we see a mushrooming of medium-size participants in developing countries? If this scenario develops, how will small and medium-sized technology companies be regulated in countries with inefficient regulatory practices? Most developing countries will consume their own products, thus avoiding Biosafety Protocol requirements. Global civil society, especially large Reformist organisations and Supporters, need to address *now* national capacity building for regulation and monitoring of technology development. On the other hand, if R&D does not grow in developing countries, will the convergence between research and development on genomics and traditional plant breeding squeeze out those countries that have no genomic capabilities? This is a hard question that most Rejectionists, Reformists, and Alternatives have not begun to ask. However, ignoring future trends in technology development and patterns of technology concentrations is not helpful. Reformists and

Campaign	Activity	Types of groups involved	Examples
Labelling	Direct action mainly in Europe with limited action in the US	Reformists	Dumping GM food in government doorways in Europe, boycotting food products, leafleting food stores
	Lobby UN/Codex for mandatory labelling: letters, visits, etc	Reformists, Alternatives	Letter writing/e-mail campaigns by Women Say No to GMOs (URL), several developing country NGOs, etc.
	Campaigns for regional labelling laws	Reformists, Alternatives	California Right to Know (URL), Australian and NZ NGOs strive for labelling
GM out of food supply and/or consumer boycott	Letter writing and e-mail campaign to governments and food companies	Rejectionists	Greenpeace, True Food, Einkaufsnetz (Germany), Reseau-Info-Conso (France): ban growing GM crops worldwide, pressure on food companies
	No GM foods for relief aid to India	Rejectionists	Vandana Shiva calls for no GM food in relief aid for India
	Online debates	Rejectionist vs Reformists	Prince of Wales Forum, various chat rooms on web
	Lobby governments for Consumer Charter for right to remain GM-Free	Alternatives	'Women Say No to GMOs' campaign to isolate test and crop sites
General public awareness/information	Websites, public gatherings, information handouts on general and specific details of GM; interaction with media	Rejectionists, Reformists, Alternatives	Dedicated websites against GM, 'The Organic Picnic' for 3,000 in London, leafleting supermarkets, press releases
	Consumer guides to avoid GM foods	Alternatives, Rejectionists	Greenpeace's online guide, Soil Association organic food guide, etc.
End field tests and planting GM crops in country/world	Information with no specific call to action	Reformist	GeneWatch UK publishes Internet information on field trials.
	NGOs block seeds despite no law forbidding them for import (Aerni, Anwandar, and Rieder 2000)	Rejectionists	Greenpeace intercepts seed to Philippines
		Rejectionists	

Campaign	Activity	Types of groups involved	Examples
End field tests and planting GM crops in country/world cont.	Destruction of GM field trials, commercial fields, and contaminated crops		'Dig it Up' network with GeneticSNowBall, GeneticX, Indian Farmer's Union, etc. to mobilise public to protest planting
Terminator technology and farmers' rights	Citizens' Jury	Reformists	ActionAid in India held jury of small poor farmers to decide if they want GM crops or not
	Public information	Rejectionists, Reformists	Website material, media campaign
	Lobby US governments	Rejectionists, Reformists	RAFI and others lobby to revoke patent
	Lobby board of directors of company	Reformists	Rockefeller Foundation President speaks to Monsanto's Board of Directors, resulting in promise not to commercialise sterile seeds
Intellectual property rights	Targeted communiqués to experts/NGOs/media	Rejectionists, Reformists	Internet coverage of Indian government's revoking of W.R. Grace's species patent on GM cotton
	Legal challenges and court cases	Rejectionists	RAFI challenge to Monsanto's species patent on GM soy at European patent office.
	Pressure on political leaders	Reformists, Rejectionists	End basmati rice patents: postcards to Prince of Liechtenstein to drop patent owned by company he chairs
More testing and national/international regulation	Call to test GM products as rigorously as drugs	Reformists	Friends of the Earth (URL) and networks
Company-specific activities	Demonstrations against Monsanto	Rejectionists	Demonstrations in India, Brussels, London, Boston, St. Louis, etc.

Supporters need to start bravely debating the economic and social consequences of different models of technology diffusion and development. Only then will they be able to help governments and civil society prepare for mushrooming national development, or the risk of exclusion, or the many possibilities in between the two extremes.

4. Chaos theory still applies.

While is it irresponsible to scaremonger, we need to ask whether an unexpected accident will occur in the next few years. Chaos theory, rather than unilluminated fear, predicts that it will. We know that grains are moved and commingled in processing, seeds for planting get mixed (for example, the accidental planting of unapproved Liberty Link rape seed from Canada in the UK in 2000), and the isolation of crops is not yet always assured. The Starlink case in the US is indicative of the potential and the quality of governmental and societal reaction. The products were quickly taken off the shelves, the company involved apologised and moved rapidly to repair the damage, and consumers were apparently left unscathed. It was a safe dress-rehearsal for the next mishap. But have we really seen the end of such cases? Is it global civil society's role to help the public, grass-roots organisations, local and national government, and industry learn from these accidents and to build effective systems for emergency response? This is easier in countries such as the United States. What would have happened if Starlink had been imported to India or Egypt?

All civil society groups need to blow the whistle when things go wrong. But playing a role in the prevention of accidents is even more critical. Not all groups need to take on the same role. Rejectionists and Alternatives are best suited to remain critical watchdogs. Reformists need to work with communities, industry, and government to develop long-term strategies to ensure that the environmental and social consequences of plant biotechnology are understood, accepted, monitored, and verified. And when something does go wrong, Reformists need to lead the way and collaborate with all other civil society groups to frame swift and sane responses and remedies. Supporters also have a critical role. They need to work directly with industry to help it hear and understand the public's many and changing concerns.

To work effectively, all global civil society groups need to be well versed in the subject matter and focus on solid, fair communications. The lack of a common language and respectful dialogue generates misunderstanding, spreads fear, and widens the gulf between most groups. Society leaders need to 'speak science' and scientists need to learn to 'speak society'.

What global civil society does today and how it reacts to plant biotechnology is not about Round Up-Ready Soya, and BtMaize. It is not about the growing of commercial GM crops in Europe or the diffusion of Golden Rice. It is not even about labelling. It is, however, about the future, and how future technologies will affect our environment and society. How society shapes regulation, focuses R&D, decides on benefits and access, and determines safety standards and monitoring today sets a precedent for the future. As the complexity of the technology rapidly increases, so will the complexity of the issues, economics, and potential risks. The world will require frameworks, case studies, and lessons from the past. This is what global civil society is creating here and now.

I would like to thank Amar Bokhari for his assistance in assembling the data for this chapter.

References

Accion Ecologica. http://www.pt-rs.org.br

Aerni, Philipp, Anwandar, Sybil, and Reider, Peter (2000). 'Acceptance of Modern Biotechnology in Developing Countries: A Case Study of the Philippines'. *International Journal of Biotechnology*, 1-29.

California Right to Know. http://www.calrighttoknow.org

Cerda, H. and Wright, D. (2000). 'Can Resistance to Insecticidal Transgenic Plant Produce a New Species of Insect Pest?: Implications of Development Asynchrony of Resistance Pest to Bacillus Thuringiensis Transgenic Crop'. Paper Delivered to a Conference on the Environmental Implications of Genetically Modified Plants with Insect Resistance Genes, Berne, September.

Cohen, Robin and Rai, Shirin (2000). *Global Social Movements*. London and New Brunswick: The Athlone Press.

Consumer Association, GM food campaign. http://www.which.net/campaigns/gmfood

Consumers International. http://www.consumers
international.org

Crawley, M.J., Brown, S. L., Hails, R. S., Kohn, D. D.
and Rees, M. (2001). 'Transgenic Crops in
Natural Habitats'. *Nature*, 409: 8.

Dig It Up. http://www.dig-it-up.uk.net

Eurobarometer 53 (2000). Directorate-General
Education and Culture, European Commission,
October. http://europa.eu.int/comm/dg10/
epo/eb/eb53/eb53.html

Eichenwald, Kurt (2001). 'For Biotech, a Lost War'.
International Herald Tribune, 26 February.

EPA (Environmental Protection Agency) (2001).
Press Release, posted on http://www.epa.gov/
pesticides/biopesticides/ , 7 March.

EC (European Commission) (2000). *The Agricultural
Situation in the European Union* Luxembourg, EC.

Five Year Freeze Campaign. http://www.glc10.dial.
pipex.com

Friends of the Earth. www.foe.co.uk

Goldberg, Robert (2001). 'From Cot Curves to
Genomics: How Gene Cloning Established New
Concepts in Plant Biology'. *Plant Physiology*,
125: 4–8.

Grain (2000). 'Eat Up your Vaccines'. *Seedling
Newsletter*, December.

Greenpeace. http://www.greenpeace.org

Heckel, David (2000). 'Genetic Mechanisms and
Ecological Consequences of the Development of
Resistance in Insect Pests to Transgenic Plants'.
Paper Delivered to a Conference on the Environ-
mental Implications of Genetically Modified
Plants with Insect Resistance Genes, Berne,
September.

International Genetic Resources Action
Information. http://www.grain.org

ISAAA (International Service for the Acquisition of
Agri-biotech Applications) (1999). *This is ISAAA*.
Nairobi, Kenya: ISAAA. http://www.isaaa.org

Kaufman, Marc (2001) 'Biotech Corn Is Test Case
For Industry: Engineered Food's Future Hinges
On Allergy Study': *Washington Post*. 19 March.

Langridge, W. H. (2000). 'Edible Vaccines'. *Scientific
American*, September. http://www.sciam.com/
2000/0900issue/0900langridge.html

May, Robert (1999). *Genetically Modified Foods:
Facts, Worries, Policies and Public Confidence*.
Office of Science and Technology, Department
of Trade and Industry. London. UK.

Meridian Institute (2000). Plant Biotechnology:
Summary of Interviews (draft). Prepared for the
Rockefeller Foundation, 16 November.

Monsanto. http://www.monsanto.co

OECDa. http://www.oecd.org/ehs/summary.htm

OECDb. http://www.olis.oecd.org/bioprod.nsf

Osgood, Diane (2000). 'Southern Comfort: Views of
Southern NGOs on Biotechnology'. *Tomorrow*,
9/2: 10.

Pengue, Walter (2000). 'Commercial Release of
Transgenetic crops in Argentina. The Case of RR
Soybean and BT Corn'. Paper delivered to a
conference on Sustainable Agriculture in the
New Millennium, Brussels, May. Pollan, Michael.
2001. 'The Botany of Desire'. *New York Times*,
4 March.

RAFI (Rural Advancement Foundation
International). http://www.rafi.org

Research Foundation for Science, Technology and
Ecology and Vandana Shiva.
http://www.indiaserver.com/betas/vshiva

Safe Food Coalition (South Africa).
http://home.intekom.com/tm_info

Shiva, Vandana (1999). Personal communication,
London.

Soil Association. http://www.soilassociation.org

Stotzky, G. (2000). 'Release, Persistence, and
Biological Activity in Soil of Insecticidal
Proteins'. Paper delivered at a conference on The
Environmental Implications of Genetically
Modified Plants with Insect Resistance Genes,
ESF/AIGM workshop, Bern, September.

Third World Network. http://www.twnside.org.sg

UNIDO. http://www.UNIDO.org

Webb, Honey (2000). 'Labels on GM Food by 2001'.
Canberra Times, 25 July.

Women say No to GMOs.
http://www.organicsdirect.co.uk

CHAPTER 5

A DECADE OF HUMANITARIAN INTERVENTION: THE ROLE OF GLOBAL CIVIL SOCIETY

Mary Kaldor

This developing international norm in favour of intervention to protect civilians from wholesale slaughter will no doubt continue to pose profound challenges to the international community. Any such evolution in our understanding of state sovereignty and individual sovereignty will, in some quarters, be met with distrust, scepticism, even hostility. But it is an evolution we should welcome.

Why? Because despite its limitations and imperfections, it is testimony to a humanity that cares more, not less, for the suffering in its midst, and a humanity that will do more, and not less, to end it.

It is a hopeful sign at the end of the twentieth century.

Kofi Annan, Report to the United Nations General Assembly, 20 September 1999

The progress made . . . in standing up to crimes against humanity represents more than a doctrinal qualification of the prerogatives of sovereignty. Behind the advances in international justice and the increased deployment of troops to stop atrocities lies an evolution in public morality. More than at any time in recent history, the people of the world today are unwilling to tolerate severe human rights abuses and insistent that something be done to stop them. This growing intolerance of inhumanity can hardly promise an end to the atrocities that have plagued so much of the twentieth century. Some situations will be too complex or difficult for easy outside influence. But this reinforced public morality does erect an obstacle that, at least in some cases, can prevent or stop these crimes and save lives.

Human Rights Watch (2000a)

It was a French idea . . . We came over the border . . . The appeal must not come from the government but from the voice of the victims . . . The right to interfere has now been written into 150 resolutions of the United Nations. Victims are now a category of international law. So we succeeded . . . This is the revolution . . . The victim, not the government, speaking in the name of the victim—for the first time . . . We are coming back to '68. We want to change the world. We want no more Auschwitz, no more Cambodia, no more Rwanda, no more Biafra.

Bernard Kouchner, founder of Médecins Sans Frontières (Allen and Styan 2000: 825)

This chapter is about humanitarian intervention in the classic sense, that is to say, military intervention in a state, with or without the approval of that state, to prevent genocide, large-scale violations of human rights (including mass starvation), or grave violations of international humanitarian law (the 'laws of war'). It addresses the narrow question about the role of civil society in supporting or opposing the use of military force for humanitarian purposes. The wider and undoubtedly important story of the role of civil society in conflict prevention and conflict management is addressed only indirectly.

As the above quotations indicate, during the 1990s there has been a fundamental change in the norms governing the behaviour of states and international organisations. Throughout the cold war and the anti-colonial period, the principle of non-intervention expressed in Art. 2(4) of the United Nations Charter was the dominant norm in international affairs. Starting with the establishment of a safe haven in northern Iraq in 1991, and culminating in the NATO air strikes in Yugoslavia in 1999, the presumption that there is a right to use armed force in support of humanitarian objectives has become widely accepted.

This evolution is demonstrated by the increase in, and the changing character of, peace-monitoring, peacekeeping, and peace-enforcement operations. At the start of the 1990s there were only eight United Nations peacekeeping operations, involving some 10,000 troops. As of the end of 2000, there were some 15 United Nations operations involving some 38,000 military troops.[1] And a number of regional organisations were also involved in various missions concerned with conflict prevention or management. In Europe the most significant are the three NATO deployments in the former Yugoslavia (Bosnia, Kosovo, and Macedonia) authorised by the United Nations. There are also four Russian peacekeeping operations, under the umbrella of the Commonwealth of Independent States, in Tajikistan, Transdnestr, Abkhazia, and South Ossetia. In addition, the European Union has three missions and the Organisation for Security and Co-operation in Europe (OSCE) has some eleven missions, all of which involve small numbers of military personnel. In Africa, the Economic Community of West African States (ECOWAS) has been heavily involved in Sierra Leone and has conducted operations in Liberia and Guinea-Bissau. The Organisation for African Unity (OAU) also has three mainly civilian missions in Burundi, Comoros, and the Democratic Republic of Congo (SIPRI 2000; United Nations Peacekeeping Department URL). Only a few of these missions can be defined under the rubric of 'humanitarian intervention'. But their number is evidence of the growing acceptance of the use of military force for humanitarian purposes. Table 5.1 summarises the most significant interventions of the last decade in terms of the evolution of a humanitarian norm.

The changing international norms concerning humanitarian intervention can be considered an expression of an emerging global civil society. The changing norms do reflect a growing global consensus about the equality of human beings and the responsibility to prevent suffering wherever it takes place, which necessarily has to underpin a global

civil society. Moreover, this consensus, in turn, is the outcome of a global public debate on these issues. It should be stressed that a growing global consensus about the need to prevent suffering does not imply a consensus about military intervention. On the contrary, the actual experience of intervention has been disappointing and in some cases shameful. The failure to intervene to prevent the genocide in Rwanda and the failure to protect the UN-declared safe haven of Srebrenica are two particularly opprobrious moments in the history of international action. Indeed, it is hard to find a single example of humanitarian intervention during the 1990s that can be unequivocally declared a success. Especially after Kosovo, the debate about whether human rights can be enforced through military means is ever more intense.

This chapter is about the role that civil society actors played in bringing about the changing international norms and about the character of the public debate. The chapter is divided into four sections. The first section describes the actors who participate in the debate. The second section describes the evolution of humanitarian intervention, with particular emphasis on the role of civil society groups, up to the end of the 1990s. The third section summarises the character of the global public debate. The final section is about developments in 2000, in particular the military intervention(s) in Sierra Leone.

Global Civil Society Actors

The actors who have put pressure on governments and on international organisations for or against humanitarian intervention can be divided into three groups. One group comprises what are normally considered the classic actors of civil society, who often claim to speak on behalf of the victims: NGOs, social movements, and networks. The second group comprises those who tend to be closer to the elite and make use primarily of the power of words: think tanks and commissions. The third group consists of forms of communication, in particular the media: radio, television, print media, and Websites.

It should be stressed that in the debate about humanitarian intervention a key role has been played by dynamic individuals. Names like Bernard Kouchner or Fred Cuny (see Box 5.1) have resonance throughout the field of humanitarianism and undoubtedly directly or indirectly influenced government action. In the US,

---

[1] *The peak of UN operations was 1993 when some 78,000 military troops were involved. The biggest operations were UNPROFOR in Bosnia-Herzegovina and UNOSOM II in Somalia. The Balkans operations are now undertaken by NATO.*

where there has been little in the way of a grass-roots movements, individuals like George Soros, Morton Abramovitz of the Carnegie Endowment, and Aryeh Neier of Human Rights Watch and the Open Society Foundation have been very influential in the debates about various interventions. In France and in central Europe, individual intellectuals have been heavily engaged in the debate. In France, for example, Bernard Henri Levy had a powerful impact with his film about the siege of Sarajevo; and in central Europe many of the well-known former dissidents became deeply involved in the debate about intervention in Bosnia and later Kosovo.

As well as intellectuals, public personalities from the world of popular culture have added their voices to concerns about victims of war and/or starvation, thus helping to popularise humanitarian consciousness. Examples include Bob Geldof and Bandaid and Bono of U2. During the siege of Sarajevo, a number of these figures travelled to Sarajevo to support secular culture. Many of these individuals are, of course, linked to civil society organisations described below.

NGOs, social movements, networks

NGOs are professional organisations, sometimes with memberships, and often dependent on a few donors, including governments. International NGOs, that is to say, NGOs that operate across borders, tend to be based in advanced industrial countries. NGOs can be both service providers—delivering humanitarian assistance, monitoring human rights, and providing mediation services in conflicts—and advocacy groups—putting pressure on governments and international organisations. Social movements are looser organisations, often based on grass-roots groups and making use of volunteers. By and large they are campaigning groups engaged in various, often innovative, forms of protest. Because of their grass-roots nature, social movements tend to be locally based, although they can and do make coalitions across borders. Networks have been an increasingly significant phenomenon in the 1990s. They are loose coalitions of NGOs and social movements, often making use of the opportunities offered by the Internet and providing a vehicle to transmit directly the voices and arguments of Southern and Eastern groups rather than indirectly through the Northern-based NGOs.

NGOs concerned with humanitarian intervention are primarily humanitarian and human rights NGOs, although there are increasing numbers of conflict-resolution NGOs. Humanitarian NGOs were initially formed to provide relief to the victims of war, but increasingly the term has come to include the victims of all types of disasters which result in mass suffering: floods, earthquakes, and so on. These NGOs have a long history. The International Committee of the Red Cross (ICRC) was founded in 1859 by Henri Dunant after witnessing the horrors of the Battle of Solferino. The ICRC provided the impetus for the development of humanitarian law in the late nineteenth century and subsequently. It was the ICRC that pioneered some of the principles of humanitarian action such as impartiality, neutrality, and the principle of consent: principles which presupposed a notion of 'civilised' wars and 'honourable' soldiers (see Ignatieff 1998; Moorehead 1998). The wars and famines of the twentieth century and the erosion of notions of 'civilised' forms of warfare have spawned many more humanitarian NGOs. Thus, Save the Children was formed in World War II. Cooperative for American Relief Everywhere (CARE) was formed by 22 charities and trades unions in 1945 to distribute left-over American Army rations to Europe; later it shifted to the distribution of American agricultural surpluses to the Third World. Oxfam was founded in 1942 and *Médecins sans Frontières* (MSF) in 1971 during the war

The band U2 played at Sarajevo's Kosovo stadium in September 1997 (*photo:* © Reuters/Popperfoto).

The lives of two individuals—one American, Fred Cuny, and one Frenchman, Bernard Kouchner—could be said to encapsulate the story of the evolution of humanitarian intervention over the last three decades.

Both were born during World War II. Both were influenced by the student movement of the 1960s. Cuny, who had been a Republican, became active in the civil rights movement in the late 1960s. Kouchner was involved in the French *evénements* of 1968. Cuny was training to be an engineer and Kouchner was training to be a doctor.

Both went to Biafra in 1969 and were involved in the airlift that was undertaken without the permission of the Nigerian government. Kouchner, who was working for the International Red Cross, was shocked by the unwillingness of the ICRC to speak out about what was happening. 'By keeping silent, we doctors were accomplices in the systematic massacre of a population' (quoted in Allen and Styan 2000: 830). Kouchner started the International Committee Against Genocide in Biafra and started to use the media to publicise what was happening. 'We were using the media before it became fashionable . . . We refused to allow sick people and doctors to be massacred in silence and submission' (quoted in Allen and Styan 2000: 830).

Biafra, according to Cuny, was the 'mother' of all humanitarian operations. 'We still use the yardstick of Biafra to measure our performance in other disasters. It's the defining moment' (quoted in Shawcross 1995). Cuny was shocked by the lack of planning and the amateurishness of the relief effort. In 1970, he left Biafra convinced that the airlift was prolonging the war.

In 1971, Kouchner founded the NGO Médecins Sans Frontières. The aim was the rapid deployment of doctors to disaster areas, with or without official permission, with heavy reliance on the use of the media both to secure funding and to provide immunity from hostile governments. The same year Cuny founded a company, Intertect Relief and Reconstruction, which specialised in giving technical assistance and training in disaster relief to UN and volunteer agencies. Unlike MSF, which raised money from the public, the company depended on contracts from governments and international institutions. Both MSF and Intertect were involved in numerous disasters in the 1970s and 1980s—earthquakes, wars, floods, massacres, hurricanes—and gained their practical and political experiences from these events. Disaster areas included Nicaragua, Honduras, Peru, Sri Lanka, Sudan, Ethiopia, Cambodia, Bangladesh, Vietnam, El Salvador, and the Lebanon, among others. Both published books. In *Disasters and Development,* Cuny (1983) says that it was during this period that he began to understand the connection between the military and humanitarianism. 'More than anything else, the images of those planes delivering everything from food to coal fostered acceptance of the link between armed forces and humanitarian assistance and, more importantly, acceptance of the costs involved' (quoted in Weiss 1999: 17).

Kouchner's (1986) book *Charité Business* is about the relationship between the media, NGOs, and policy-makers. Indeed, it was Kouchner's emphasis on dramatic media events which led to the split in 1979 when Kouchner went on to found Médecins du Monde.

in Biafra. In the 1980s and 1990s a myriad of NGOs have been formed in response to increased 'complex emergencies' which include both famines and wars, greater public consciousness of suffering in faraway places perhaps as a result of television, and the growing tendency of governments to contract-out relief to NGOs. Many humanitarian NGOs are church-based or linked to other religions. An increasing share of official humanitarian assistance is disbursed through NGOs and, in parallel, NGOs are becoming increasingly dependent on government funds.

Human rights NGOs differ from humanitarian NGOs in that their concern is primarily with state repression and with violations of human rights, especially political and civil rights. Like humanitarian NGOs, human rights NGOs have a long history. The Anti-Slavery Society founded in 1839 is probably the oldest international human rights NGO still in existence.[2] The term 'human rights' is a post-World

---

[2] *Local anti-slavery campaigning groups existed long before the founding of the anti-slavery society in places like Manchester and Philadelphia*

The turning point for both men was the Gulf War of 1991. Kouchner had begun to promote the concept of a Droit d'Ingérence in the late 1980s. In 1988 he was appointed Minister for Health and Humanitarian Action in the French government led by Michel Rocard. He was able to promote his ideas in the United Nations and after the Gulf War pushed for the Droit d'Ingérence to help the Kurds in northern Iraq. The haven in northern Iraq did provide an important precedent in humanitarian intervention. Cuny was also there. He had convinced the US Ambassador to Turkey, Morton Abramowitz, that it was possible to bring the Kurdish refugees back to their homes in a two-month period and was given an opportunity to carry our his ideas. Subsequently, through Morton Abramowitz, Cuny was able to influence policy in Washington.

Both Cuny and Kouchner advocated military intervention in Somalia, and their voices were influential in both the US and France. Cuny favoured the creation of armed relief enclaves. Both were critical of the way the intervention was carried out. Cuny thought it was inefficient from the point of view of delivering aid. Kouchner considered the intervention to have been a success although he was critical of the American use of overwhelming force. 'There are no humanitarian catastrophes only political catastrophes . . . No! What was catastrophic was the American attitude . . . A war without prisoners, a war without dead people . . . this is just crazy' (quoted in Allen and Styan 2000: 838).

During the Bosnian war Cuny was recruited by George Soros to provide $50 million of humanitarian assistance to Bosnia. He focused on the restoration of basic utilities in Sarajevo, building a protected water purification plant and providing access to gas for heating. Kouchner was a staunch advocate of an international air offensive and became known as the proponent of 'war to end war'.

Thereafter, their careers diverged. Cuny was sent by Soros to Chechnya. After his first visit in December 1994 he said that the destruction of Grozny made Sarajevo seem like a picnic. He was convinced that he could arrange a ceasefire but he disappeared when on a trip to try to meet the Chechen leader. He was probably executed on 14 April 1995.

Kouchner was appointed UN Special Representative in Kosovo and became head of the new UN administration in Kosovo established after the NATO bombing. He left after a year and became French Minister of Health again in the government of Lionel Jospin. His record in Kosovo has been criticised but he enjoyed the full support of Kosovar Albanians.

The differences between the two men reflected their cultural backgrounds. Cuny focused on practical solutions to humanitarian crises; Kouchner focused on political solutions. Kouchner tried to develop a new language and a new ethics of humanitarianism. Cuny tried to develop new methodologies and procedures. But their differences were complementary; Kouchner's approach necessarily involved practical implementation and Cuny's search for common-sense solutions led him to politics. Both contributed in important ways, for good or for ill, to the emerging consensus about humanitarian intervention by the late 1990s.

War II invention, attributed to Eleanor Roosevelt, who objected to the 'rights of man', although the term *Menschenrechte* was always used in the Germanic languages. The official international commitment to human rights was expressed in the Universal Declaration of Human Rights (1948), the Genocide Convention (1948), and the two human rights Covenants (1966) among other treaties and declarations. As in the case of humanitarian NGOs, the 1980s and 1990s witnessed a proliferation of human rights groups and a strengthening of those that existed. Since the wars of this period also involved massive violations of human rights, these groups necessarily became more concerned with war. The best-known international NGOs are Amnesty International and Human Rights Watch, but there are thousands of smaller groups not only in advanced industrial countries but especially in the East and South.

Conflict-resolution NGOs are more recent. Well-known examples include International Alert and Conciliation Resources, based in Britain, and San

Egidio, the Vatican group, both of which have played significant roles in mediation in recent years. San Egidio, for example, was responsible for initiating peace negotiations in Mozambique, for the Education Agreement in Kosovo in 1997 (which seemed to offer a prospect for averting war), and also for bringing together the various opposition groups in Algeria. The Carter Center in the US has also been an important player in conflict mediation. There are many less well-known groups, especially women's groups, that engage in conflict resolution at local levels. Conflict-resolution groups were established in part by peace groups seeking a new direction after the end of the cold war and in part by human rights and humanitarian groups who became aware of the need for a more political approach. (For European groups, see European Platform for Conflict Prevention and Transformation URL.)

Three types of social movement have been involved in humanitarian intervention. First of all, in the countries where wars have taken place, movements supporting intervention have developed among the potential victims. Thus, an anti-war movement developed in Bosnia calling for an international protectorate before the outbreak of war; and the Kosovar resistance movement was making similar appeals throughout the 1990s (Andjelic 2000; Kaldor 1999; Independent International Commission on Kosovo 2000). Today, the Palestinian people are calling for international protection.

In the countries where outside governments have been involved, civil society actors have tended not to be movements except in the case of the former Yugoslavia. During the Bosnian war, however, a second type of movement developed, primarily in Europe. Although it had its origins in peace, human rights, and women's movements, it was a new movement in which local groups sprang up primarily to provide humanitarian assistance but also to express political positions on the Bosnian war, often with deep divisions among them.

During the Kosovo war, there were mass demonstrations against the NATO bombing or against the 'double war' (NATO bombing and Serbian President Milosevic's campaign of ethnic cleansing), especially in Serbia, Greece, and Italy.

A third type of movement, which has been influential both for and against intervention, is nationalist and fundamentalist. In this chapter I do not include non-state warring parties—paramilitary groups or warlords—as part of civil society. But the warring

Demonstrators in Sarajevo, December 1992 (*photo:* © *Reuters/Popperfoto*).

parties are often linked to organised nationalist movements or nationalist currents of opinion. These movements intensified in the 1990s in response to globalisation. In particular, diaspora groups have become increasingly significant in influencing both the character of nationalist movements and their impact on the international community (see Kaldor 1999; Smith 1996). On the whole, this type of movement jealously guards the notion of sovereignty, as in Serbia for example. But some nationalist movements favour intervention: Palestine and Kosovo are two current examples. The role of transnationally organised Islamic movements in calling for intervention in, say, Bosnia is also important.

One of the criticisms that is often made about Northern-based NGOs is that, while claiming to speak on behalf of the victims, they often drown out the victims' voices. The advantage of networks is that they provide an organisational form that allows NGOs and grass-roots organisations outside war zones to link up with local groups within the war zones. Networks may be less effective at organised lobbying but they do provide a forum through which the knowledge and views of local groups can be transmitted. This was very important during the Yugoslav wars; important examples were the Helsinki Citizens Assembly (see Box 5.2) and the Verona Forum established by the Italian Green MEP Alexander Lange. There are also a number of emerging networks in Africa: the West Africa peace-building network and the Great Lakes Policy Forum. Women's groups have played a pioneering role in developing the network form of organisation. Women in Black is an important example, which began out of solidarity with the Belgrade-based group Women in Black and has spread to other conflict regions. It organised weekly international vigils during the war in Bosnia and also increasingly engages in various conflict resolution projects (see Cockburn 2000).

Although the distinctions between humanitarian, human rights, peace, and women's groups are useful in tracing the history of these civil society organisations, in practice they are becoming less and less meaningful. Today's wars involve massive violations of human rights, including atrocities against women. In this context, peace movements may engage in solidarity actions as do the humanitarian groups or may find themselves increasingly taking on the human rights agenda. Women's groups become peace and human rights groups. Human rights groups are increasingly concerned with violations of international humanitarian law and war crimes as well as human rights violations. Humanitarian groups, traditionally non-political, find themselves adopting the causes of peace and justice.

Thus, an important development in this period has been what is sometimes known as civil society intervention, where the presence of international civil society groups, even if unarmed, constitutes a form of protection for civilians. This was the basic idea behind Peace Brigades International, formed in 1981, which began its work in Central America and now mobilises thousands of volunteers to accompany returning refugees, for example (see Mahoney and Eguren 1997). Many of the groups formed during the Yugoslav wars saw themselves carrying out similar missions.

Think tanks and commissions

While movements and NGOs raise public awareness, expert groups are often closer to governments and frame specific policy proposals. The growth during the 1980s and 1990s of think tanks and commissions addressing global issues is yet another sign of the emergence of global civil society. Think tanks like the International Crisis Group and the Institute or War and Peace Reporting, both established during the 1990s, have become significant purveyors of information and opinions. Older established think tanks concerned with defence and foreign affairs, which exist in almost every country, have also joined the debate. Similar to these think tanks are international commissions, both independent and under the auspices of the United

Nations. The Brandt, Palme, and Brundtland Commissions were important in pioneering this way of using groups of prominent individuals to make policy inputs on significant global issues. In the 1990s, international commissions concerned with various aspects of humanitarian intervention have proliferated. The Carnegie Endowment organised two commissions, one on 'Preventing Deadly Conflicts' and one on the Balkans,[3] replicating the experience of an important and pioneering Carnegie Commission on the Balkans in 1912. There have been three important reports under UN auspices concerning Rwanda, Srebrenica, and UN Peacekeeping (United Nations 1999*a*, *b*; 2000). After Kosovo, the Swedish government took the initiative in establishing an Independent International Commission to investigate the Kosovo Crisis under the Chairmanship of the South African Judge, Richard Goldstone. And more recently, the Canadian government has established a new commission to investigate the concept and practice of humanitarian intervention under the chairmanship of Gareth Evans and Mahoud Sahnoun.

As Richard Goldstone has put it in the course of an interview for the BBC in February 2001, these Commissions are an important device for increasing the transparency and public accountability of international institutions: they represent 'civil society judging governments'.

Media and websites

The importance of the international media in drawing attention to crises in far-off places is often stressed. Politicians often complain about the way their actions are media-led. Undoubtedly, at certain moments—the famine in Ethiopia in the 1980s, the discovery of detention camps in Bosnia in 1993 by ITN and the *Guardian*, the furore about the camps in eastern Zaire in the autumn of 1994—media attention has played an important role. But by and large the media have been a tool, an expression of a public debate rather than an actor in their own right. Undoubtedly, access to the media has been uneven and sometimes distorting; in particular, starvation and violence are more newsworthy than peace negotiations. Nevertheless, those civil society actors who have learned to use the media have been able to make their voices heard more effectively.

---

[3] *See Carnegie Commission on Preventing Deadly Conflict (1997) and Carnegie Endowment for Peace (1996).*

In the second half of the 1980s, parts of the West European peace movement developed a strategy of 'détente from below', making links with opposition groups in central and eastern Europe. Many of the techniques of networking—providing support to civil society groups in difficult and dangerous situations, simultaneously lobbying different governments and international institutions—were developed during this period, even before the advent of the Internet.

The Helsinki Citizens Assembly (HCA) was established in 1990 to formalise this network. The goal was to integrate Europe from below, to establish a pan-European civil society. Vaclav Havel spoke at the founding assembly which brought together over 1,000 people from all over Europe who had been involved in the dialogue, and an international secretariat was established in Prague.

The Yugoslav branch of the Helsinki Citizens Assembly was founded in Sarajevo in May 1991. The chairperson was Zdravko Grebo, a law professor from the University of Sarajevo, who had played a key role in the democratisation process in Bosnia-Herzegovina. At that time, the slogan was 'Let's Co-operate!' Whether Yugoslavia falls apart or stays together, civil society must remain united.

When federal troops entered Slovenia in June 1991, an emergency meeting of the HCA was organised in Belgrade to discuss how to prevent war. The meeting included several luminaries of the cold war oppositions, including Milovan Djilas, Adam Michnik, Bronislaw Geremek, and Ernest Gellner. Grebo warned that, if Yugoslavia disintegrated, Bosnia would also disintegrate and a war in Bosnia would be 'hell'. It was agreed to press for an international protectorate for Bosnia-Herzegovina,

"Hundreds of thousands of refugees in the former Yugoslavia could die this winter. Safe havens must be installed in Bosnia-Herzegovina immediately. It is the responsibility of each of us to save their lives."
Tadeusz Mazowiecki, UN Special Envoy to former Yugoslavia

and a series of activities was planned which laid the basis for the later war-time activism.

One of these activities was a peace caravan, which was organised in September 1991. Some 40 European activists travelled by bus through Slovenia, Croatia, Serbia, and Bosnia, making links with local anti-war activists. The caravan culminated in Sarajevo, where a human chain of 10,000 people linked the mosque, the synagogue, the Orthodox Church, and the Catholic Church. The links made during this expedition were sustained, by and large, throughout the war. Another activity was Yugofax; a monitoring service written by people from the region, which later became Balkan War Report and eventually the Institute for War and Peace Reporting.

As war in Bosnia became imminent in the spring of 1992, it was Grebo who called on people to come into the streets and tear down the barricades being erected by Serbian and Muslim paramilitary groups. Indeed, the war began when snipers fired on a citizens' demonstration of some 200,000 people, mobilised by Grebo, who were demanding the resignation of the government and the establishment of an international protectorate. Thousands more had come by bus but were prevented from entering Sarajevo by roadblocks. The official international negotiators, who were visiting Sarajevo that day, did not have time, so they said, to meet with the demonstrators. The demonstration of 12 April 1992 was the last peace demonstration of its kind; no wonder that Sarajevans were later to say that 'Europe ends in Sarajevo'.

During the war, HCA activities were of three kinds. First, the network of civic activists was maintained through meetings, conferences, workshops, newsletters, and pamphlets, as well as electronic communication. It was in Bosnia that the HCA e-mail network was first established, and indeed, at that time, it represented a pioneering kind of technology. A parallel network of municipalities was also established. A particularly important event was the Citizens and Municipal

A DECADE OF HUMANITARIAN INTERVENTION: THE ROLE OF GLOBAL CIVIL SOCIETY   Mary Kaldor

In the 1980s and 1990s, many NGOs and social movements deliberately fostered what the French call a *médiatique* strategy. MSF under Bernard Kouchner pioneered the *médiatique* approach. But it has also been taken up by other NGOs and, in the 1990s, by social movements.

Peace Conference held in Ohrid, Macedonia, in the autumn of 1992. The network was a way of expressing solidarity with the groups in the region and planning future activities.

Second, many groups collected and delivered humanitarian assistance. The Italians and the Czechs were particularly active in this respect.

Third, HCA campaigned and lobbied governments and international institutions for what was, in effect, a new kind of humanitarian intervention. This was particularly important in France, where there were some 40 local HCA groups and HCA played a key role in coordinating the movement in France, Britain, Denmark, Switzerland, Turkey, and The Netherlands. HCA pushed for an international protectorate. At Ohrid the idea of local protectorates was developed. And this was the origin of the Safe Havens campaign in early 1993, in which some 300,000 postcards calling for safe havens were sent to the negotiators and to governments from all over Europe (around one third were sent from The Netherlands).

HCA also campaigned for international administrations in Sarajevo and Mostar. And a major effort of HCA from 1994 onwards was the campaign to publicise and support the town of Tuzla, which was the only town in Bosnia-Herzegovina that had maintained a non-nationalist administration and that kept alive multicultural civic cosmopolitan values throughout the war.

In September 1994 a seminar brought NGOs and municipalities to Tuzla, which pledged all kinds of support to the town. A year later, one week after the ceasefire, HCA held its assembly bringing to Tuzla 300 activists from abroad, including 70 people from Serbia.

Undoubtedly, the HCA campaigns did contribute to the international community's policies towards Bosnia-Herzegovina. But at that time official support for humanitarian intervention was half-hearted; the safe havens were never defended effectively and there was no serious support for citizens' efforts.

The Helsinki Citizens Assembly sometimes describes itself as a family founded on certain shared values and a commitment to mutual solidarity which takes precedence over loyalty to governments or abstract principles. All the local groups are self-organised and self-financing. They gain legitimacy and visibility in their own societies from being branches of a transnational organisation with access to international policy-makers. They gain strength from international contacts and meetings through which they can develop and discuss their campaigns and projects and plan joint activities. HCA's networking involves a two-way learning process. By comparing experiences and trying to understand different local situations on the basis of the knowledge of those who live in the region, HCA develops new ideas, practical analyses, and strategies. Essentially, HCA is a mechanism for the transmission and processing of information from local activists to other activists and to institutions.

This work has not always been easy, partly because of the difficult circumstances in which some groups operate; local activists are often harassed and some have lost their lives in war. Several activists from Bosnia, Italy, and France were killed during the war in Bosnia. Another factor is the character of the organisation. HCA emerged out of the movements of the 1980s. It was never able to transform itself into an international NGO of the type demanded by donors. The latter tend to expect more emphasis on the transfer of skills from West to East than on the transfer of understanding from East to West, on the provision of services at a local level rather than campaigns at an international level, on offices rather than groups, and on professionalism rather than political mobilisation. For all these reasons HCA has found it difficult to sustain the expensive task of international networking. Nevertheless, this strange 'political animal', as the co-chair Bernard Dreano has described it, continues to exist. There is now a generation, less bound by the movement traditions of the past, that may be better able to combine individual activism with the professionalism demanded by global donors.

The media and the civil society groups have developed a sort of symbiotic relationship. As George Alagiah of the BBC put it:

Relief agencies depend upon us for publicity and we need them to tell us where the stories are. There's an unspoken understanding

Bosnian prisoners in a detention camp, Nakjaca, Bosnia, 1992 (*photo:* © *Reuters/Popperfoto*).

between us, a sort of code. We try not to ask the question too bluntly: 'Where are the starving babies'. And they never answer explicitly. But we get the pictures all the same.
(Quoted in de Waal 1997: 83)

A very important development in the 1990s was the extensive use of Websites. Many civil society organisations have Websites, which have speeded up information gathering on these issues. Websites have also provided a way in which institutions in the war zones can have more impact on the global debate. Thus the Radio B92 (URL) Website, which provided an English language digest of developments in Serbia or the Website of the independent Kosovar newspaper *Kohaditore* (URL) have been crucial sources of information about developments in former Yugoslavia. Likewise, the South Asia Citizens Web (URL) provides a local perspective on the Kashmir conflict and also a mechanism for networking within South Asia. Websites are also important sources of propaganda for nationalist and fundamentalist movements, a service often provided by more extreme groups in the diaspora.

The Evolution of Humanitarian Intervention

The idea of intervention 'to defend the rights of foreign subjects of an oppressive ruler' was advanced by Hugo Grotius in the seventeenth century (Bull 1984: 3). But the term 'humanitarian

intervention' was first used in the nineteenth century to justify interventions by European powers to protect (mainly Christian) people oppressed by the Ottoman Empire. The first instance was the intervention in Greece in 1827, which was to lead to Greek independence in 1830. This notion of humanitarian intervention clashed with the growing presumption that states had equal rights to protect their sovereignty and that interference in the affairs of other states was therefore wrong. This insistence on the importance of sovereignty and non-interference is sometimes dated back to the Treaty of Westphalia of 1648. But actually it is a more recent idea, which gained intellectual credentials in the middle of the eighteenth century in the writings of Wolff and Vattel but became widely accepted only in the twentieth century with the independence of many former colonies and the spread of communism. Newly independent and/or Communist countries regarded the doctrine of non-intervention as an important defence against what they saw as the 'constant and endemic intervention' of great powers (Bull 1984: 4).

During the cold war period, the principle of non-intervention was widely considered to take priority over humanitarian considerations. After 1945, the United Nations Charter strengthened the rules restricting the rights of states to use force. At the same time a body of law developed in the various human rights declarations and conventions which forbade states to ill-treat individuals, including their own nationals. In practice, the former overrode the latter up until the end of the 1980s (see Akehurst 1984).

There were many interventions during this period, especially by the two super-powers, but these were justified in cold war terms as interventions against communism or capitalism and usually legitimised on the grounds that outside powers were 'invited' to intervene (Vietnam, Czechoslovakia, or Afghanistan). As Nicholas Wheeler (2000) shows, there were also interventions which could be described as humanitarian, notably the Indian intervention in Bangladesh in 1971, the Vietnamese intervention in Cambodia in December 1977 which led to the fall of the Khmer Rouge, and the Tanzanian intervention in Uganda which led to the overthrow of Idi Amin in April 1979. But none of these interventions was justified in humanitarian terms.[4]

---

[4] *In the case of the Indian intervention of 1971, the Indian Ambassador to the United Nations Security Council used humanitarian arguments. He claimed that the suffering of the Bangladeshi people was sufficient to 'shock the conscience of the*

The debates in the United Nations Security Council during this period, described by Wheeler, show the strength of the non-intervention norm. Thus, in the debate over Vietnam's intervention in Cambodia, the French Ambassador Leprette said: 'The notion that because a regime is detestable foreign intervention is justified and forcible overthrow is legitimate is extremely dangerous. That could ultimately jeopardise the very maintenance of international law and order and make the continued existence of various regimes dependent on the judgement of their neighbours' (Wheeler 2000: 93). Similar arguments were put forward by other members of the Security Council. As late as 1986, the prominent international theorist, Hedley Bull, argued:

The growing moral conviction that human rights should have a place in relations among states has been deeply corrosive of the rule of non-intervention, which once drew strength from the general acceptance that states alone have rights in international law.
(Bull 1984: 183)

What were the factors that led to such a dramatic change in international norms in the late 1980s and 1990s? One was the spread of 'new' or 'post-modern' wars, especially in Africa and eastern Europe. These are wars that have evolved out of the guerrilla and counter-insurgency wars of an earlier period. They are often called 'civil' or 'internal' wars although they involve an array of global actors. They are wars in which direct fighting between the contestants is rare and most violence is directed against civilians. Indeed, techniques, such as population displacement, and various atrocities which directly violate both the laws of war and human rights are central to the strategies of these wars. They are also wars in which the manipulation of food supply, loot and pillage, and the control of valuable commodities are built into the functioning of a war economy. Not only did these wars increase in number during this period but there was also a big increase in civilian suffering, as measured by the ratio of military to civilian casualties and by the explosion

of refugees and internally displaced persons (see Kaldor 1999).

A second factor was the growth of humanitarian NGOs. The war in Nigeria in 1971 was a turning point for the humanitarian NGOs. It was the moment when the ICRC abandoned its insistence on neutrality and operating within the framework of consent. The ICRC was conscious that its insistence on neutrality had prevented the ICRC from publicly protesting about what it knew to be happening to the Jews in World War II and there were fears of genocide in Biafra. Thus the ICRC, together with more recent humanitarian NGOs influenced by the student movements of the 1960s and the interrogations about World War II, decided to organise an airlift to Biafra without the consent of the Nigerian authorities.

For many of the newer NGOs, Biafra was the defining moment. Subsequently many of the groups formed or shaped by that experience went on to respond to crises in various parts of the world: earthquakes, floods, famines, and war. In 1984, the famine in Ethiopia sparked a debate about humanitarianism and political action. Groups like Bandaid had helped to stimulate a media-orchestrated response to the famine. But other groups argued that the famine was being created deliberately as an instrument of war by Mengistu, the Ethiopian leader, and that the humanitarians were keeping Mengistu in power. MSF, which took this position, was thrown out of Ethiopia at this time. During this period the NGOs increasingly began to operate without consent, as had happened earlier in Biafra. Indeed, in Ethiopia a split developed among those NGOs that worked in non-governmental areas and those that cooperated with the government. Only the ICRC was allowed to work openly with both sides, although Save the Children managed to do so informally.

By the mid-1980s this new type of war had become increasingly important. In Mozambique and Afghanistan, official agencies increasingly began to see the advantage of NGOs as a form of non-governmental intervention and a way of working in war zones without permission. In several places, 'corridors of tranquillity' or 'humanitarian corridors' were established to provide relief. Operation LifeLine in Sudan was another particularly important episode where many of these techniques were developed, particularly through UNICEF and its programmes for immunisation of children. It was then that 'clamours for more muscular support' began to be raised.[5]

---

world'. And he asked 'what has happened to our conventions on genocide, human rights, self-determination and so on? . . . Why [are members of the Security Council] so shy about speaking of human rights? . . . What has happened to the justice part [of the UN Charter]?' (Wheeler 2000: 63). But he did not invoke these arguments to justify the intervention; instead he referred to the (outlandish) crime of 'refugee aggression'.

---

[5] Interview with Mark Bowden of Save the Children, 9 March 2001.

	Purpose	Dates	Troops involved
Northern Iraq Operation Provide Comfort	Provide safe haven for Kurds in northern Iraq. Establish no-fly zones in north and south of Iraq.	April 1991–3	20,000 troops from US, Britain and France.
Bosnia-Herzegovina	Safe havens, humanitarian corridors, no-fly zone, establishment of war crimes tribunals.	1992-5	UNPROFOR involving 23,000 troops.
Somalia	Protect food convoys and provide secure relief centres.	1992-3	UNITAF (37,000 troops led by the US) and UNOSOM II (28,000 troops).
Rwanda	Small UN force withdrawn before massacre. French led force to protect refugees after the massacre.	1994	UNAMIR I. (1,500 troops) and II (5,500 troops). Main contingents: France, Canada, and Belgium.
Haiti Operation Restore Democracy	American-led force to restore democratically elected government.	September 1994	Multi-national Force (MNF) including 21,000 US troops and 1,250 troops from the Caribbean.
Kosovo	NATO air strikes against Yugoslavia.	March–July 1999	NATO aircraft from 13 countries flew 38,400 sorties, including 10,484 strike sorties.
East Timor	Australian-led force after massive violence following referendum on independence.	September 1999	International Force for East Timor (INTERFET). Some 10,000 troops led by Australia.
Sierra Leone	Series of interventions to restore democratic government.	1994–2000	Ghurkas. Executive Outcomes, ECOMOG, UNAMSIL, British forces.

Authorisation	Global civil society groups	Comments
United Nations Security Council (UNSC) Resolution 688.	Pressure from media and human rights groups e.g. Human Rights Watch. Hesitation from humanitarian groups e.g. Oxfam.	First safe haven; provided precedent for humanitarian intervention. Initial success, but not sustained.
Various UN Security Council Resolutions, especially 770 (protection of humanitarian convoys) and 836 (safe areas).	Combination of NGOs, think tanks, local groups in Europe and inside Bosnia, networks.	Marked an important precedent but insufficiently robust. Low point was fall of Srebrenica in July 1995.
UNSC Resolution 794 authorised UNITAF UNSCR 814 authorised UNOSOM II.	Humanitarian NGOs mainly in favour. Save the Children and Africa Rights against.	Excessive use of force, failure to disarm militia. Widely considered a debacle. American soldiers killed and bodies publicly paraded.
UNSC Resolution 872 authorised UNAMIR to monitor ceasefire. Request for reinforcements when massacre began followed by decision to withdraw UNAMIR. UMNAMIR II authorised after massacre was over.	NGOs and media strongly in favour of intervention. ICRC lost 13 staff members.	Failure to intervene and prevent genocide despite request of UN Commander General Dallaire.
UNSC Resolution 940	Apparently successful operation.	Generally considered a successful intervention carried out in the US national interest.
No UN authorisation.	Civil society groups involved in transnational networks call for intervention. Demonstrations against in Greece, Italy, and Serbia.	Did not prevent ethnic cleansing of Albanians and then Serbs but did enable the return of all Albanians and end the rule from Belgrade
UNSC Resolution 1264	Civil society pressure for intervention much earlier.	Too late although effective.
UNAMSIL authorised by UNSC Resolution 1270. ECOMOG authorised by ECOWAS.	Strong civil society pressure in West Africa. International NGOs divided.	Rebels still control parts of the country.

This was the period that Bernard Kouchner, together with his colleague, the lawyer Mario Bettani, launched the idea of a *Devoir d'Ingérence* (Duty to Interfere), which later became a *Droit d'Ingérence* (Right/Law of Interference). Kouchner became French Minister of Humanitarian Action in 1988, and in the same year the United Nations General Assembly passed Resolution 43/131, which put these arrangements on a more formal footing. The resolution reaffirmed the sovereignty of states but recognised that the 'international community makes an important contribution to the sustenance and protection' of victims in emergency situations. Failure to provide humanitarian assistance 'constitutes a threat to life and human dignity'. The resolution stressed the 'important contribution' of 'intergovernmental and non-governmental organisations working with strictly humanitarian motives'. Subsequently, General Assembly Resolution 45/100 praised the Secretary-General for continuing consultations on the establishment of 'humanitarian corridors' (Allen and Styan 2000: 831–2).

A third factor in the changing international climate was the growth of human rights groups. Particularly important were the emergence of pro-democracy and human rights movements in the Third World and eastern Europe. In part, this was a consequence of the exhaustion of post- colonial and communist projects: the loss of appeal of earlier emancipatory ideas. And it part it has to be understood in the context of growing global interconnectedness and the possibility to obtain support and to make links across borders, which provided a way of opening up closed societies. In Europe and North America, the movements which evolved after the 1960s spawned human rights groups sometimes in dispute with the traditional left. In the United States, it was the coup in Chile and the growth of human rights groups in Latin America during the 1970s and 1980s that led to the emergence of transnational human rights networks (see Keck and Sikkink 1998: Ch. 3). In France, the debate about *tiermondisme* led many French intellectuals to attack the simplicities of those traditional left groups who had unquestioningly supported liberation movements in the Third World and to place increasing emphasis on democratic freedoms and human rights; the group *Libertés sans Frontières* was an expression of this line of thought. In the rest of Europe, the mass peace movement of the 1980s stimulated a debate about human rights

and the relationship of peace to justice. Some parts of the peace movements made links with eastern human rights groups and pioneered the concept of 'détente from below' and the idea of a new form of civil society intervention in support of human rights; they argued that the threat of nuclear weapons had prevented interference in support of human rights. Other parts of the peace movement insisted on non-interference, arguing that the danger of nuclear war was the overriding concern and that support for human rights could contribute to cold war rhetoric.

The 1989 revolutions gave further impetus to the human rights movements. The discourse of civil society was the discourse of the movements which toppled the communist regimes. To this was added the language of transnationalism and global responsibility that came out of the cross-border links made in the 1980s. Moreover, the revolutions seemed to discredit traditional left thinking, which was associated with notions of non-interference and of collectivism that were supposed to take priority over individual rights.

The final factor was, of course, the post-cold war global context. The end of the cold war provided an opportunity, for the first time, for concerted international action. It also allowed the 'new wars' to become more visible and a new global discourse about humanitarianism and human rights to supplant the tired cold war rhetoric.

The Gulf War of 1991 provided the first oppor-tunity to display the new international consensus. The war, of course, was not a humanitarian intervention; it was a response to the invasion of Kuwait by Iraq, and once Kuwait had been liberated a ceasefire was declared. Indeed, the war is probably better described as an American attempt to assert its new found unchallenged global hegemony: this was the essence of President Bush's 'new world order'.

In the aftermath of the war, however, there were uprisings by Kurds in the north and Shiites in the south in the expectation that Saddam Hussein would be overthrown. The uprisings were brutally suppressed. This was the moment for Kouchner and the French government to push for a *Droit d'Ingérence*. Public sympathy for the plight of the Kurds also propelled other governments, particularly in Britain and the United States, into action. The consequence was United Nations Security Council Resolution 688, which established a safe haven in northern Iraq for the Kurds. The resolution did not actually mandate the use of troops; nevertheless

In 1991, thousands of Iraq's Kurdish refugees settled in Isikveren camp, Turkey (*photo: © Reuters/Popperfoto*).

Operation Provide Comfort involved the deployment of over 20,000 troops to protect the safe haven. At the time, only the French were pushing for a *Droit d'Ingérence*. The resolution was couched in terms of the threat to 'international peace and security' posed by refugees and by the situation in the area. The term 'haven' was used in preference to 'enclaves' at the insistence of the British Ambassador, Sir David Hannay, on the grounds that 'enclaves' suggested a redrawing of boundaries. Nevertheless, the resolution did create a precedent in that it demanded that Iraq 'immediately end this repression' and 'ensure that the human and political rights of all Iraqi citizens are respected'.

Although public pressure and media exposure of what was happening in northern Iraq were important in propelling forward the proposal for a safe haven, it is interesting to note that, at the time, there were doubts among UN officials as well as NGOs operating in northern Iraq, who feared alienating the Iraqi government. According to an Oxfam staff member in the region:

> The feeling is that we can't jeopardise the good work we already have going by getting into a conflict with the Iraqi government up here . . . It's the sort of thing we ought to be doing but it would violate Oxfam's line at the moment.[6]

The relative success of the safe haven, at least initially, was to change attitudes among many NGOs.

The international troops were withdrawn in 1993 and replaced by a small UN guard and a 'residual' force based in Turkey. The Kurds have re-established a measure of autonomy (which they had enjoyed years earlier) but they remain vulnerable to Iraqi raids. The no-fly zone has not prevented the ethnic cleansing of Shiites in the south.

But the safe haven in northern Iraq did turn out to be a precedent. The genie was out of the bottle. As Adam Roberts (1996: 16) points out, the proclamation of humanitarian interests has an inevitable 'ratchet effect'.

> It is inherently difficult for major powers to proclaim humanitarian principles and policies in relation to a conflict, and then do nothing to protect the victims and/or punish their tormentors when atrocities occur. Thus an initial humanitarian involvement can lead to a more military one—a process involving awkward changes of direction. Further, it is inherently difficult to preach humanitarianism in one crisis and then not to do so in the next, however unpromising the situation and however slim the interests of outside powers.

---

[6] Washington Post, *25 April 1991*.

The war in Bosnia

After Iraq came the disintegration of Yugoslavia and the wars in Slovenia, Croatia, and Bosnia-Herzegovina. It was the war in Bosnia, which lasted from April 1992 to October 1995, which was to generate the most heated public debate about humanitarian intervention. There were many other wars in the world, and many other tragedies just as terrible as in Bosnia, as the United Nations Secretary-General, Boutros Boutros Ghali, was to point out when he visited Sarajevo in 1992. But it was the war in Bosnia and the plight of Sarajevo that captured global attention.

In Europe a mass movement developed in the wake of the war. Hundreds of groups sprang up both to collect and distribute aid and to increase awareness and make protests. In Italy, for example, the Italian Consortium for Solidarity was established in 1993 linking civil society groups and organisations. From Italy alone more than 15,000 volunteers travelled to the war zones and some 2,200 convoys were organised. But throughout Europe similar mobilisations took place, including the new democratic countries of central Europe. In the Czech Republic, for example, the People in Need Foundation (*Clovek v Tisni*) ran a television campaign and even persuaded army officers to donate part of their salaries. A particularly interesting group was Workers Aid for Tuzla, which later became International Worker's Aid. This group was started by British miners who had received support from the town of Tuzla during the 1984 miners' strike and wanted to repay their debt. Those who drove convoys or established local offices in war zones did risk their lives and a number of volunteers from several European countries were killed.

As well as collecting aid, local groups organised novel forms of protest to draw attention to the plight of Sarajevo, especially in France. In Nantes, the main square was renamed Sarajevo Square. In Strasbourg, a checkpoint was set up on one of the main bridges, arbitrarily stopping people from crossing. And in Grenoble, the sound of shelling and sirens was reproduced throughout the town at 2 a.m. to give the local inhabitants the feeling of what it was like to be in Sarajevo. In Britain, a group of well-known personalities presented bottles of dirty water to the Prime Minister's residence and to Members of Parliament to show what the people in Sarajevo were being forced to drink.

A remarkable feature of the movement was the role played by local municipalities, a development of the nuclear-free zone idea of the 1980s. Many municipalities were twinned with municipalities in the former Yugoslavia and others introduced twinning arrangements during the war. Thus, Norwich was twinned with Novi Sad and, at the height of the war, Tuzla decided to twin with Bologna. These twinning arrangements provided a mechanism for the provision of humanitarian assistance and for various other kinds of support. Particularly in Germany, The Netherlands, and Scandinavia, municipalities became an important source of relief and political support.

As well as grass-roots groups, intellectuals and cultural figures (artists, writers, actors, and actresses) played an important role in the movement. In France, prominent intellectuals became the 'voice' of the movement. In the United States, where there were fewer grass-roots movements, and in Europe, elite campaigning groups were established like Action Council for Peace in the Balkans which were to be very influential. There were also cultural festivals aimed at drawing attention to Sarajevo's secular culture; and a number of writers, film makers, and people from the world of theatre travelled to Sarajevo.

Unlike the peace movement of the 1980s, the movement against the war in Bosnia was rather fragmented. There were some Europe-wide networks, for example the Helsinki Citizens Assembly, but these by no means could claim to speak for the movement as a whole. Indeed, in political terms the movement was deeply divided and these divisions generated a debate about Bosnia that constituted a social learning process. Although there was an implicit consensus about the role of civil society in providing solidarity and a sort of unarmed protection, there were big differences about what governments and international organisations should be doing and these differences tended to reflect different analyses of the character of the war.

Public pressure led to a series of interventions by the international community: the protection of aid convoys and the establishment of humanitarian corridors, safe havens, a no-fly zone, a tribunal for war crimes committed in the former Yugoslavia, and international administrations for Sarajevo and Mostar. In retrospect, the latter two innovations were to have considerable significance. The Hague and Arusha Tribunals created a momentum for an international criminal court and the demand for the arrest of war criminals raised the issue of international law enforcement. Likewise, the establishment of international administrations paved

Body bags of victims found in mass graves after the 1995 Srebenica massacre (*photo: © Reuters/Popperfoto*).

the way for the protectorates in Bosnia and Kosovo. Again, the problem of public security in both these cases led to further demands for some form of international policing.

But despite these innovations and despite the continuing negotiation process, the war continued for three and a half years. It was brought to an end through the Dayton Agreement, which some attribute to the NATO air strikes at the end of the war and others to the fact that ethnic cleansing was virtually complete and the Serbs and Croats had, more or less, succeeded in carving out ethnically pure territories. The humanitarian innovations are widely considered to have been a failure. Despite the presence of troops, the Serbs and Croats were still able to dictate the terms of aid delivery. The safe havens of Srebrenica and Zepa fell towards the end of the war. In particular, the massacre of 8,000 men in Srebrenica was, at least for the international community, the most humiliating moment of the war.

The failure is attributed to the inadequacy of the mandate and the provision of insufficient troops. Nevertheless, there were successes that suggest the failures had more to do with the difficulty of adapting traditional military concepts than with insufficient resources. Both the British and the Danish demonstrated on occasion that more 'robust' peacekeeping could be effective even though they were reprimanded by the UN command for their actions. In Zepa, Ukrainian troops refused to hand over local people to the Serbs and in the end were able to negotiate their safe passage.

From Somalia to Kosovo

The war in Bosnia is the context in which to understand the decision of President George Bush to intervene in Somalia. The Bush Administration was under pressure to make a stronger commitment to Bosnia and to give substance to the notion of a 'new world order'. It believed that Somalia was an easier case than Bosnia and that intervention in Somalia would relieve the pressure to step up intervention in Bosnia. According to Lawrence Eagleburger, then Secretary of State:

The fact of the matter is that a thousand people are starving to death every day and that is not going to get better if we don't do something about it, and it is an area where we can affect events. There are other parts of the world where things are equally tragic, but where the cost of trying to change things would be monumental. In my view, Bosnia is one of those. (Quoted in Ramsbotham and Woodhouse 1996: 206)

After the fall of the long-time Somalian dictator, Mohammed Siad Barre, a 'new war' developed in which clan-based warlords established control over territory through displacement and atrocities inflicted by groups of fighters known as *mooryan*, often under the influence of the drug, Qat. Between November 1991 and March 1992, some 50,000 people died and 1.5 million became refugees or Internally Displaced Persons (IDPs): some 29 per cent of the pre-war population. Humanitarian NGOs were calling for intervention and drawing the media's attention to the suffering in Somalia. CARE was particularly influential and held regular meetings with the Bush administration. Fred Cuny was calling for armed protection of relief enclaves. The ICRC hired armed guards for the first time in its history. The European Commission was calling for UN convoys as early as August under the influence of European NGOs. A large advertisement in a Dutch newspaper calling for intervention was signed by several European NGOs including Oxfam. According to Eurostep, an organisation representing some 20 European NGOs, there is 'general agreement among many European NGOs that it was not sufficient to send aid without a certain level of military protection to stop piracy'[7]

A few NGOs opposed the intervention. These included Save the Children, particularly its director, Mark Bowden, and a group of individuals, including Alex de Waal and Rakiya Omaar, who broke away from Human Rights Watch because they opposed the intervention and formed Africa Rights. They believed that the negotiations carried out by the UN envoy Mahmoud Sahnoun were bearing fruit, that the immediate needs for food supply had already been solved, and that a US-led intervention could be the harbinger of a new form of imperialism (Africa Rights 1993).

United Nations Security Council Resolution 794, which was passed unanimously on 2 December 1992, was widely considered to break new ground. Even though the resolution mentions, as in 688, the threat to 'international peace and security', it was the first resolution to authorise the use of force, under Chapter VII of the UN Charter, to relieve human suffering. Many states that had opposed 688, particularly in Africa, supported 794. For Kouchner, it was a triumph: 'a fantastic step forward, a new legal base for the international Droit d'Ingérence'. The headline in *Liberation* the next day was: 'L'humanitaire s'en va t'en guerre' (Allen and Styan 2000: 838).

[7] *Interpress Service, 12 August 1992.*

Mogadishu, August 1993: A Somali points at human remains and fragments of US army cloth allegedly belonging to a US soldier (*photo: © Reuters/Popperfoto*).

The Somali intervention turned out, however, to be a debacle, as a few groups had predicted. The American-led Unified Task Force (UNITAF) succeeded at first in protecting aid convoys and providing secure relief centres but failed to disarm the militias, disappointing most local Somalis. In May UNITAF was replaced by UNOSOM II (United Nations Operation in Somalia) with an even stronger mandate. However, attacks on Pakistani troops led the American Commander Admiral Howe to engage in warfare against the clan faction responsible, led by General Aideed. Despite the use of what many considered to be excessive force, the Americans failed to capture Aideed. On the contrary, Somali militia succeeded in shooting down two American helicopters, killing 18 American soldiers and wounding 75. The bodies of the American soldiers were paraded publicly in front of international television cameras. Shortly thereafter the Clinton Administration took the decision to withdraw from Somalia.

The debacle in Somalia led to the decision to issue Presidential Decision Directive 25 in May 1994, which one author has described as a 'Somali corollary to the Vietnam syndrome' (Weiss 1999: 90). PDD 25 strictly limited American participation in future peacekeeping operations. It was invoked as pressure mounted from NGOs and the media to intervene to stop the horrifying genocide of Tutsis and tolerant Hutus that was taking place in April, May, and June 1994 in Rwanda. Between 500,000 and 1 million people were killed in 100 days. The massacre was orchestrated by the government and the army, and carried out by local officials and government-organised paramilitary groups using machetes and mobilised through 'hate radio', Radio Milles Collines.

There was at the time a small UN force of 1,500 troops, United Nations Assistance Mission to Rwanda (UNAMIR). Despite warnings from the local commander General Dallaire and proposals to seize weapons and create safe havens, the Security Council took the decision to prepare for withdrawal and to scale down the UN force. Later, when it was clear that Dallaire's warnings should have been taken seriously, the Secretary-General proposed an intervention force of 5,500; several African forces were prepared to take part but they needed American logistical support, which was not forthcoming. Indeed, the Clinton Administration actively mobilised against those governments, NGOs, and media who wanted to describe what was happening in Rwanda as 'genocide' for fear that this would oblige it to act under the 1948 Genocide Convention (see Wheeler 2000: 224–5).

At the end of August 1994, a French intervention force was dispatched. But by this time the genocide was over and the Rwandan Patriotic Front had succeeded in overthrowing the extremists in part. The French intervention was suspect because of French support for the previous regime; and all it was able to achieve was to provide safe havens for fleeing Hutus, many of whom were former militiamen engaged in the genocide.

The tragedy and disgrace of Rwanda had a powerful impact on the humanitarian NGOs and on public opinion. The ICRC lost 13 staff: it was the moment of change of heart towards humanitarian intervention. All the same, the immediate aftermath of the tragedy seems to have led to excessive enthusiasm for interventions; many humanitarian NGOs called for intervention to protect the refugee camps of eastern Zaire, which were run by former Hutu militiamen. Before a Canadian intervention force could be mobilised, however, the camps were overrun by Zairian rebels, and the refugees returned to Rwanda. It was a low point for the humanitarian NGOs. As Mark Bowden of Save the Children, one of the few NGOs to oppose intervention, put it, 'Agencies are competing for dwindling resources, competing for contracts and position and profile in the media. Philosophically, we are bankrupt. "Go and feed them" is always our response' (*Financial Times*, 3 December 1996). Only the human rights NGOs took a different tack, calling for the militia to be brought before a war crimes tribunal.

Interestingly enough, at the very moment that Rwanda was being debated, the Americans, with UN authorisation, undertook a classic humanitarian intervention in Haiti. Operation Restore Democracy was launched in July 1994 to overthrow a brutal military dictatorship that had displaced the democratically elected government. In Clinton's words, the purpose was 'to protect our interests, to stop the brutal atrocities that threaten Haitians, to secure our borders and to preserve stability and democracy on our continent ' (quoted in Weiss 1999: 184). Many NGOs were doubtful about intervention by the United States, the dominant power in the region. But perhaps the intervention in Haiti can be considered the most successful intervention of the 1990s.

During this period, there were also significant regional interventions—ECOWAS Monitoring and Observation Group (ECOMOG) in Liberia, the CIS (mainly Russia) in Tajikistan—although it would probably be misleading, especially in the Russian case, to describe them as humanitarian. An important part of the story is, of course, the wars in Chechnya in 1994–6 and since 1998. Despite the fact that these wars involved widespread violations of human rights, outside involvement was minimal even from the hardiest NGOs: it was here that Fred Cuny met his end. The fact that there was no consideration of humanitarian intervention there has been cited by opponents of intervention as evidence of its selective character. Although NGOs and movements like Soldiers Mothers and Memorial and the well-known human rights leader, Sergei Kovalev, did try to mobilise international support, none of these groups

An estimated 250,000 Rwandese refugees swept into Tanzania in 24 hours, fleeing the genocide. *(photo: © UNHCR/P. Moumtzis).*

or individuals advocated international military intervention. The war against the Kurds in Turkey is also often cited as a case of double standards since even international condemnation is rare.

The case of Kosovo was different. The crisis had been developing throughout the 1990s. From 1991, NGOs and commentators were warning of a likely war in Kosovo. After Milosevic, the Serbian president, removed the autonomy of Kosovo and imposed a form of apartheid on the province, the Kosovar Albanians organised a non-violent resistance movement including the establishment of parallel institutions, especially in health and education. They called for international intervention and the establishment of an international protectorate. It was evident that this situation could not be sustained. A turning point was the Dayton Agreement, from which the issue of Kosovo was deliberately excluded. Many Kosovars, exhausted by the parallel system, concluded that non-violence was an ineffective strategy for calling international attention to their plight. In 1997, the Kosovo Liberation Army first made its appearance with the deliberate strategy of using violence to provoke an international intervention (see Independent International Commission on Kosovo 2000).

As the conflict intensified in the spring of 1998, Western leaders began to make strong statements about the necessity for action in Kosovo. 'We are not going to stand by and watch the Serb authorities do in Kosovo what they can no longer get away with in Bosnia', said the US Secretary of State, Madeline Albright, in March. Similar pronouncements were made by the UN Secretary-General, Nato's Secretary-General, and various foreign and defence ministers. However, the method chosen to prevent war was diplomacy backed by the threat of air strikes. American leaders had drawn the—probably wrong— conclusion from Bosnia that the Dayton Agreement succeeded because of air strikes. Many groups inside Kosovo and elsewhere in Europe were calling for the deployment of ground troops to protect civilians from the ethnic cleansing that had already begun. But the Americans were unwilling to commit ground troops until a very late stage in the negotiations. When diplomacy failed, a campaign of air strikes was undertaken. At the same time, ethnic cleansing was dramatically accelerated. Over a million Kosovar Albanians, the majority of the population, were expelled from the province, and some 10,000 people were killed. Eventually, Milosevic capitulated; an international protectorate was established in Kosovo

and the refugees returned. Bernard Kouchner was chosen to head the UN Mission.

The war over Kosovo deeply divided civil society. Some groups felt the intervention was justified. Some favoured military intervention but criticised the form of intervention: the use of air strikes instead of ground troops, which could have directly protected people. Human Rights Watch (2000b), in particular, drew attention to the ways in which NATO bombings may have violated international humanitarian law.[8] For many human rights groups Kosovo was a troubling moment. Many sympathised with the plight of the Kosovars but at the same time found bombing repugnant and an inappropriate way to enforce human rights. This was especially true in eastern Europe, where bombing has always been regarded as much more unacceptable than in the West. Yet at the same time east European human rights groups were uneasy about criticising the air strikes, both because of sympathy with the Kosovars and because of the legacies of the cold war. Dimitrina Petrova (2000) writes that:

> *Human rights defenders feared that whatever they say immediately places them in one of two camps—for or against NATO. And if one is against NATO, one is enemy to democracy, etc. The black and white scheme prevailed and nuances were only possible if they were about details. Political correctness dictated unholy alliances.*

Kosovars, dumped out of trains near the F.Y.R. Macedonia, wait to cross the border (photo: © UNHCR/R. LeMoyne).

Among Palestinians almost an opposite dilemma had to be confronted. On the one hand, there was a deep and innate suspicion of any action by NATO and the United States. On the other hand, many could see the similarities between the plight of the Kosovars and their own situation. Even an organisation like Human Rights Watch was torn by the NATO bombing between those who were strongly in favour and those who felt that bombing had accelerated ethnic cleansing.[9]

Others argued more strongly that 'military humanism', the phrase coined by Noam Chomsky (1999), had become the new justification for American imperialism and the American military industrial complex following the demise of the Soviet threat. This was the predominant view among groups which viewed themselves as peace activists, for example at the Hague Peace Conference, attended by some 8,000 activists from all over the world, which took place in May during the bombing. As mentioned above, there were mass demonstrations against the bombing, or against the 'double war', in several countries.

The final intervention of the 1990s was in East Timor. The intervention in East Timor was simply too late, as many civil society groups had earlier foreseen. In reaching agreement with the Indonesian government to hold a referendum on independence in East Timor, the United Nations made the tragic mistake of leaving the Indonesian government to provide security. Subsequently, Western powers may have been too preoccupied with Kosovo as army-supported violence against the population intensified in the spring and summer of 1999. When the East Timorese voted overwhelmingly for independence, militia groups supported by the Indonesian army went on an organised rampage, killing and displacing people from their homes. It was not until the Indonesian government agreed to a United Nations military presence that an Australian-led force was able to restore order, although by then much of the damage had been done. In terms of the evolution of norms of humanitarian intervention, the courageous

behaviour of the non-military United Nations Mission in East Timor deserves mention. They refused to be evacuated from their headquarters in Dili until local staff, family members, and also Timorese who had sought refuge in the UN compound were evacuated with them. This was a notable contrast to the OSCE monitoring mission in Kosovo, which withdrew before the NATO bombing, leaving their local staff behind to be killed.

Part of the story of the 1990s is the way in which political leaders consistently learned the wrong lessons from each intervention, which then contributed to the failures of the next intervention, rather as generals tend to fight the previous war. In particular, international policy seems to have swung from inaction or inadequate action to overwhelming force, especially the use of air strikes, and back again. It seems to have been very difficult to chart a middle course. The safe haven in Iraq was initially successful but was not sustained. The intervention in Bosnia was too weak and it was (probably) wrongly concluded that air strikes had been a crucial factor in the success of the final agreement. The intervention in Somalia was supposed to compensate for the weaknesses of the mandate in Bosnia, however, the US-led force emphasised the use of overwhelming force at the expense of politics. The Somali debacle resulted in the non-intervention in Rwanda, which was probably the most serious failure of the whole period. The need to restore credibility and act forcefully led to the NATO air attacks against Yugoslavia. And the intervention in East Timor was too late.

What can be concluded from this sorry story? Is the notion of humanitarian intervention inherently flawed? Is there no middle ground between inaction and overwhelming force? Or is it still possible to adapt thinking and institutions to fit the new reality? These are the questions that confront the civil society actors concerned with this issue.

The Global Public Debate

As this story indicates, civil society actors took different positions in different conflicts, and opinions evolved throughout the period. Four broad strands of opinion can be identified, although there are overlaps and nuances that are not necessarily captured by these categories. Table 5.2 summarises the different positions and the actors. These categories parallel the those adopted in the other issue chapters in this Yearbook.

---

[8] These included cases where NATO forces: 'conducted air attacks using cluster bombs near populated areas; attacked targets of questionable military legitimacy including Serb Radio and Television, heating plants and bridges; did not take adequate precautions in warning civilians of attack; took insufficient precautions in identifying the presence of civilians when attacking convoys and mobile targets; and caused excessive civilian casualties by not taking sufficient measures to verify that military targets did not have concentrations of civilians (such as Korisa)'.

[9] Interview with Human Rights Watch, February 2001.

Table 5.2: The debate about humanitarian intervention

Position	Arguments	Civil society groups	Bosnia
Sovereignist	Believe in non-interference. Wars for national interest only.	Individual politicians, especially on right. Traditional left and nationalist groups.	War was a civil war. Should not risk lives of nationals for others in civil war. Should not jeopardise principle of non-intervention.
Just war	War is justified for humanitarian purposes. Morality is more important than legality.	Rhetoric of centre politicians and prominent intellectuals. Civil society groups among victims of large-scale human rights abuses.	War was an international war of aggression by Serbia (and Croatia) against Bosnia. Support for Bosnian government including lifting arms embargo and air strikes against Serb positions.
Humanitarian peace	Governments cannot be trusted. Humanitarian intervention is a cover for imperialism. Should be civil society intervention.	Many humanitarian and peace groups. Human rights groups divided.	Opposed military intervention. Favoured negotiation at both governmental and grass-roots levels.
Human rights enforcement	Civil society needs framework of law. Humanitarian intervention is not war but international law enforcement. Must involve direct protection of civilians and arrest of war criminals.	International human rights groups especially in Europe and North America. Also some think tanks and commissions.	Pressed for safe havens and international criminal tribunal. Wanted more robust military role on the ground in support of these objectives.

Sovereignist (rejectionists)

This is a French term which describes those people or groups who oppose humanitarian intervention either because they support the principle of non-intervention or because they believe that intervention should be carried out only in the national interest. The former are known in the international relations literature as 'pluralists' who believe in a rule-governed society of states in which an important rule is the principle of non-intervention. The principle is considered important because it promotes stability and inhibits powerful states from imposing their hegemony on weak states (see Wheeler 2000; Ramsbotham and Woodhouse

1996; Jackson 2000). The latter are known as 'realists' in the international relations literature; they believe in a Hobbesian world characterised by international anarchy where states have to act according to the dictates of survival. With the collapse of communism and the spread of democracy in Africa and Latin America, the number of sovereignists is declining. However, they are still to be found among Third World and Eastern elites, particularly in authoritarian states, and on the Western right.

Among intervening countries, an important version of the realist argument is the nationalist argument that nationals are privileged over foreigners. The job of states is to protect their own

Somalia	Kosovo	Sierra Leone
Intervention was human rights imperialism. Should not risk lives for others in civil war.	Air strikes were NATO imperialism. Should not prioritise Kosovo over relations with Russia.	Authoritarian leaders with geo-political interest in non-intervention by others.
Favoured overwhelming force against warring clans particularly Aideed.	Supported air strikes against Yugoslavia.	Support for unilateral interventions: Executive Outcomes, ECOMOG, and Britain.
Opposed military intervention. Supported efforts of UN negotiator, Mahmoud Sahnoun, to involve civil society in talks.	Against 'double war': both NATO bombing and Milosevic war against Kosovar Albanians. Supported stronger OSCE presence.	Distrust of all military forces. Interventions too one-sided. Favour civil society reconciliation.
Favoured military intervention aimed at disarming militias and providing security on the ground, not just delivering aid.	Favoured ground intervention to protect Kosovar Albanians based on more robust OSCE presence.	Favour more robust UN presence. Greater efforts to protect civilians, arrest criminals, and implement disarmament and demobilisation.

nationals and not others. Thus, for example, Samuel Huntington wrote in 1992 that 'it is morally unjustifiable and politically indefensible that members of the armed forces should be killed to prevent Somalis from fighting one another' (quoted in Weiss 1999: 90). Similar views were expressed during the Bosnian war, especially among those who understood the war as an endless continuation of ancient rivalries. Richard Goldstone (2000: 74), for example, describes meeting Edward Heath just after he had been appointed Chief Prosecutor for the Yugoslav and Rwanda Tribunals:

'Why did you accept such a ridiculous job?' Heath asked me in a friendly tone. I told him that I thought prosecuting war criminals was important, especially given the magnitude of the crimes committed in Bosnia. Heath replied to the effect that if people wished to murder one another, as long as they did not do so in his country, it was not his concern and should not be the concern of the British government. At the time, his opinion startled me. Little did I realise that he was candidly stating what many leading politicians in major Western countries were saying privately—and what many of them believe.

Among Third World and east European nationalist movements, intervention is viewed as imperialism. In Serbia and Iraq, nationalist demonstrations, undoubtedly orchestrated by the governments, were held to oppose Western intervention. Serbian opposition to sanctions and later to the bombing during the Kosovo war seems to have strengthened nationalist feelings and helps to explain the nationalist character of the post-Milosevic regime.

The imperialist argument is also shared by radical anti-globalisation groups. These groups oppose the spread of global capitalism and see the state as defending the poor. For them, Chomsky's theory of 'military humanism' is an expression of a view of the United States and NATO as the military arm of global capitalism. They point to the selective character of intervention and suggest that so-called humanitarian intervention is undertaken only in places where it suits Western interests and not elsewhere. These groups bring together remnants of the traditional left and a new generation which has not experienced the traumas of communism. Of course, it needs to be stressed that these groups overlap with the humanitarian peace position (see below); they may not be against all forms of intervention.

Just war (supporters)

The most well-known proponent of the just war position is the British Prime Minister Tony Blair, who famously proclaimed that the NATO air strikes over Kosovo represented the first 'war for human rights': 'This is a just war, based not on territorial ambitions but values' (Blair 1999). The 'just war' position differs from the human-rights enforcement position (see below) in that it combines national and humanitarian assumptions. War is between two sides and the goal of war is to defeat an enemy with minimum casualties on one's own side. Typically, the 'just war' proponents favour air strikes and the use of overwhelming force, although they also favour precision bombing to minimise 'collateral damage', that is, civilian casualties.

'Just war' proponents tend to place more emphasis on morality and military necessity than on legality. If the cause is just, they favour unilateral intervention, that is to say, intervention without UN Security Council authorisation. (According to the UN Charter, all forms of force, except self-defence, are prohibited unless authorised by the Security Council.) Although they would insist that wars should be fought according to

the 'laws of war', military necessity is considered to override the laws of war in some instances. Moreover, they privilege the lives of nationals. Thus, the lives of foreign civilians are sometimes risked in order to save the lives of soldiers.

The Blair position is supported by many intellectuals who took a similar stance during the Bosnian war, especially in France, the United States, and central Europe. They argued that the war in Bosnia was international, initiated by Serbian (and Croatian) aggression against the Bosnian state; they lobbied for military intervention and tended to favour air strikes and lifting the arms embargo on Bosnia to allow for self-defence as a way of minimising outside casualties. These groups are often the descendants of the cold war human-rights community. Kouchner belongs to this strand of opinion, as do some American intellectuals like Aryeh Neier.

Another important group that supports the just war position is the direct representatives of the victims. Civil society groups in Kosovo, Rwanda, Haiti, or East Timor supported intervention of any kind—it did not matter how or by whom the intervention was carried out nor whether it was approved by the UN Security Council. They wanted protection. The Kosovars, of course, favoured ground troops but they were grateful for the air strikes.

Humanitarian peace (alternatives)

The third strand of opinion is to be found among some humanitarian organisations and among peace groups. These groups share some of the scepticism of the sovereignists. They distrust US-led interventions because they fear a new form of Western imperialism; defending human rights becomes a new 'colonising enterprise'. They do not believe that governments, whose job is to protect the 'national interest', can act for 'noble purposes'. In addition, some of these groups are pacifist and believe that it is a fundamental contradiction to suppose that human rights can be defended by military means. Where they differ from the sovereignists is in their insistence on civil society intervention. Human rights protection, the delivery of relief, and conflict prevention and resolution, according to this view, are the job of civil society, not governments.

This debate about humanitarian peace versus just war was an important reason for the split in MSF in 1979. Kouchner and his supporters, known as the 'légitimiste' tendency, took the view that NGOs lacked the capacity to meet serious humanitarian needs. Their role was symbolic: to draw attention to the plight of victims, to mobilise the media, and to influence governments. The other group, known as the 'indépendantiste' tendency, argued that morality should not be confused with politics and that only NGOs were capable of genuinely humanitarian action (see Brauman 1996). As François Jean of MSF put it:

> We were against this principle [of humanitarian intervention] because we felt that it was mainly the right for a strong state to intervene in a weak state . . . we questioned the purity of any state undertaking so-called humanitarian intervention.
> (Allen and Styan 2000: 836)

A similar position is taken by peace groups, especially those that took on humanitarian roles, and conflict resolution groups. Groups in Germany and Italy often argued that the Bosnian war was a civil war between different nationalist groups; they opposed any form of military intervention and favoured negotiations both at a political level and at the level of civil society. Many of these groups mobilised humanitarian assistance and undertook local mediation projects. Indeed, the practice of civil society intervention in conflicts greatly increased in the 1990s not only in the former Yugoslavia but in other regions as well, especially the Transcaucasus and the Middle East. An important aspect of this civil society activity is the links that are made with local groups and the knowledge that is gained about the local situation. The argument is that civil society is better equipped than governments to undertake actions at the level of society that are needed in the new types of wars (Marcon and Pianta 2001).

Human rights enforcement (reformists)

The fourth strand of opinion is to be found among parts of the peace movement, especially those which took up human rights issues like the Helsinki Citizens Assembly, and large parts of the human rights movement. It distinguishes humanitarian intervention from war. Humanitarian intervention is a method of enforcing international law with respect to human rights and the laws of war where the state has collapsed or where the state itself violates the law. Law enforcement is different from war. It involves minimising casualties on all sides, direct

protection of the victims, and the arrest of war criminals. It scrupulously respects human rights and humanitarian law in implementing its mission. It is more like policing than war, although it may require more robust action than domestic policing. It involves impartiality in the sense that all civilians, whatever their views or ethnic background, need to be protected and, likewise, all war criminals need to be opposed whatever side they are on. But this is not the same as neutrality—a position implied by the sovereignists and the humanitarian peace groups— since one side is almost always more responsible for human rights abuses than the other. The war in Kosovo, justifiable or not, cannot be classified as a humanitarian intervention since it was a war between NATO and Yugoslavia rather than a direct intervention to protect Kosovar Albanians on the ground.

For the human rights enforcement position, legality is very important since the very concept of humanitarian intervention is based on the idea of strengthening international law. In effect, humanitarian intervention is understood as filling the enforcement gap in international law. Those who support this position would accept that, at present, there is a gap on occasion between morality and legality since the Security Council is dominated by the great powers, who can veto humanitarian intervention for reasons of self-interest. They would favour a strengthening of international law to close that gap. A thoughtful expression of this view has been elaborated by the president of the Sierra Leone Bar Association in comparing the legality of the NATO intervention in Kosovo and the ECOMOG intervention in Sierra Leone:

> Regardless of the legality, missions such as NATO's and ECOMOG's will become the norm rather the exception. The United Nations made a mortal mistake in Rwanda, when it sat back and watched genocide occur. This must never happen again . . . Increasingly, the question will not simply be whether it is legal but whether it is moral. These moral and ethical questions will increasingly force the international community to accept this exception and formulate better laws to avoid these catastrophes and better protect human rights. (Tejan-Cole 2001)

Those who favour human rights enforcement share the views of the humanitarian peace groups about the important role of civil society. But they take the view that civil society, while playing a crucial role in correcting the abuses of the state, can exist only in the framework of the rule of law. This lesson was rudely learned at the outbreak of the Bosnian war, when, in the euphoric aftermath of the 1989 revolutions, it was hoped that citizens could prevent war through mass public action. In the months leading up to the war there were demonstrations and campaigns throughout Bosnia. But the war began when snipers fired on a mass demonstration in Sarajevo, demanding the establishment of an international protectorate. In wars, civil society is the first victim, and the longer the wars are the more civil society is destroyed.

Humanitarian intervention cannot resolve conflicts. But it can create a secure environment in which civil society can be strengthened and peaceful solutions found. It was this strand of opinion, mainly to be found in western Europe and inside Bosnia, that in the case of the Bosnian war favoured a new kind of military intervention aimed directly at protecting civilians and creating space for political alternatives. Hence, it was this group that, together with some of the humanitarian NGOs, called for an international protectorate for Bosnia, and later for safe havens, for local protectorates especially in Sarajevo and Mostar, for opening Tuzla airport, and for lifting the siege of Sarajevo. Likewise, it was this group that favoured ground intervention in Kosovo.

The version of humanitarian intervention favoured by the human rights enforcers occupies the middle ground between inaction (favoured by sovereignist and humanitarian peace proponents) and overwhelming force (favoured by just war proponents). So far, no international military operation easily fits this description of humanitarian intervention. Does this mean that the human rights enforcement position is utopian? Will either the just war position or the humanitarian peace position bring us closer to coping with 'new wars'? It is certainly true that neither the legal system nor the structure and training of military forces is yet adapted to humanitarian intervention. But those who insist on human rights enforcement would argue that this has to be done. The humanitarian peace approach, they would say, can do no more than alleviate suffering. The just war position can have the opposite effect from that intended by engaging in forms of violence that are not so very different from those they are supposed to prevent; there is no such thing as a civilised war any longer if there ever was.

Intervention in 2000: The Case of Sierra Leone

There were two main new UN missions in 2000. One was the force sent to Congo to implement the ill-fated Lusaka Peace Accord, which has never been able to fulfil its mandate since none of the parties has respected the agreement (International Crisis Group 2000). The other was the intervention in Sierra Leone, which led to an additional unilateral British intervention. The war in Sierra Leone is a typical 'new war'. Events during 2000 attracted the attention of the humanitarian, peace, and human rights communities; all of the positions described above can be illustrated in relation to outside intervention. For these reasons, and because it took place in 2000, it is worth exploring the example in some detail.

Background

The war in Sierra Leone began on 23 March 1991, when the Revolutionary United Front (RUF) led by Foday Saybana Sankoh invaded Sierra Leone with a group of dissident Sierra Leoneans, Liberians, and mercenaries (Hirsch 2001). The rebels, the RUF, were led by a group of radical student leaders trained in Libya and backed by Charles Taylor of Liberia. According to one view, they were angry about the corrupt character of the patrimonial state and their exclusion from power (Richards 1996). They mobilised poor, unemployed, rural young people through a combination of fear, material inducements, and the offer of adventure. The methods of the rebels were particularly brutal: the practice of amputation in the areas they conquered is legendary.[10] Whatever their original motivations, however, the conflict increasingly became a war about 'pillage not politics' and about control of the lucrative diamond trade. The rebels were under the control of Charles Taylor and the war enabled him to gain access to the diamond fields. Diamonds have always played a central role in

---

[10] *According to Paul Richards (1996: 164), 'Rebel violence in Sierra Leone is no instructive response to population pressure but a mobilisation of youth on behalf of a small group of people angry at their exclusion from an opaque patrimonial political system serving mineral extraction interests. In working through their anger some of the cultural scar tissue from the days of the slave trade—a trade active in the forests of eastern Sierra Leone until mid-nineteenth century—is once more exposed. The upper Guinean forests continue to resonate with the seizure of young people and their induction into a world of heightened violence'.*

Sierra Leonean politics, involving a murky mixture of the various warring factions in Lebanon, Israeli 'investors', and American and Russian crime families, not to mention the Antwerp diamond traders. As Smillie, Gberie, and Hazelton (2000: 1) put it: 'The point of the war may not actually have been to win it but to engage in profitable crime under the cover of warfare'.

Since the war began, around 75,000 people have died and around half the population of 4.5 million has been displaced. All sides have recruited children and have given them drugs, particularly cocaine and marijuana. Terrible atrocities have been committed including 'amputation of limbs, ears and lips with machetes, decapitation, branding, and the gang rape of women and children' (*Conciliation Resources* 2000: 13). The first outside intervention occurred in 1993, when Gurkha Security Group, a private security company mainly made up of Nepalese Gurkhas, was hired by the government; it was forced to withdraw after suffering heavy casualties, including the murder of its American commander, Robert Mackenzie. Then in 1995 the private South African company Executive Outcomes repelled an RUF attack on Freetown. Indeed, throughout the period a number of private security companies have been present in Sierra Leone.

In 1996, as a result of pressure from civil society, elections were held and were won by Ahmed Tejan Kabbah of the Sierra Leone People's Party; this was followed by the Abidjan peace agreement. However, the following year Kabbah was overthrown in a coup by parts of the Sierra Leonean army led by Major Johnny Paul Koroma. He formed the Armed Forces Revolutionary Council (AFRC) and invited the RUF to join it. Then in February 1998, the AFRC, in turn, was overthrown by the Nigerian-led West African force ECOMOG. Despite a brutal attack on Freetown by the rebels in January 1999, the return of Kabbah paved the way for a peace agreement signed in July 1999. The agreement included a blanket amnesty as well as important positions in government for the rebels. As the then American Ambassador, John Hirsch (2001: 80), put it, 'For the democratic forces, the Lomé negotiations were a bitter and painful reversal from the international ostracism of the RUF almost two years earlier'. The Agreement was criticised by Mary Robinson, the UN High Commissioner for Human Rights, and several international NGOs, primarily for the blanket amnesty. In a letter to the UN Security Council dated 19 May 2000, Human Rights Watch requested the setting up of an International Criminal Tribunal for Sierra Leone as well as confirmation of Mary Robinson's position that the agreement cannot apply to 'crimes of genocide, crimes against humanity, war crimes, and other serious violations of international humanitarian law'.

In October 1999 the UN Security Council authorised the establishment of the United Nations Mission in Sierra Leone (UNAMSIL), which replaced the UN Observer Mission set up in 1998. At that time, up to 6,000 troops were authorised. UNAMSIL's mission was to assist the implementation of the Agreement and it included an explicit mandate, under Chapter VII of the UN Charter, to 'protect' civilians under 'imminent threat of physical violence'. In February 2000 UNAMSIL's troops were increased to 11,100 and its mandate further extended to include the provision of security at key locations in and near Freetown and at all disarmament sites. Despite the mandate, UNAMSIL was very slow to implement the disarmament and demobilisation provisions of the agreement and was considered insufficiently robust in protecting civilians. In May, the RUF attacked UN personnel; a number of troops were killed and some 500 taken hostage.

At this point, the British sent to Sierra Leone some 700 troops, who were well-trained and well-equipped and given a robust mandate; they helped to protect the capital and to create the conditions for the release of the hostages. The UN troops were also increased to 13,000. In August, eleven British soldiers were also captured by the rebels. Five were released and the remaining six were rescued in September. In the process, the notorious West Side Boys, one of the most brutal rebel groups, were rounded up. British troops later withdrew but additional reinforcements were announced in October; emphasis was placed on training the army and the police. The Indian and Jordanian contingents also withdrew after the Indian commander, Major-General Vijay Jetley, wrote a secret memorandum to the Security Council accusing Nigerian officials, including the UN Special Representative and the UNAMSIL deputy commander, of colluding with the rebels. A new ceasefire agreement was signed in November 2000.

Other measures taken by the United Nations include further strengthening of UNAMSIL, the imposition of an arms embargo and a diamond embargo on Liberia (from where rebel diamonds are exported), the introduction of diamond certification, and the establishment of a war crimes tribunal, although funds for the latter have not been secured.

23 March 1991: RUF invades Sierra Leone with support from Liberia and Burkina Faso, led by Foday Sankoh.

29 April 1992: Coup against authoritarian leader, Joseph Momoh. Formation of National Provisional Ruling Council (NPRC), led by Captain Valentine Strasser.

1993: NPRC hires mercenaries including Gurkha unit, which is later defeated.

April–July 1995: South African-led company Executive Outcomes expels the RUF from Freetown and the environs, retakes the bauxite and rutile mines, and secures the Kono diamond fields. Payment is cash and diamond concessions.

August 1995: After massive demonstrations organised by women's groups, a National Consultative Conference is held. The conference calls for elections and for a negotiated settlement.

March 1996: After Strasser is overthrown in a palace coup, elections are held. Won by former UN bureaucrat Ahmad Tejan Kabbah.

November 1996: Abidjan peace accord. Includes amnesty for RUF, transformation of RUF into a political party, disarmament and demobilisation of combatants, reduction of armed forces, and withdrawal of Executive Outcomes. (Executive Outcomes is dismissed in January because Kabbah cannot pay them.) Within a few weeks, fighting resumes.

March 1997: Sankoh is arrested in Nigeria on weapons charges.

25 May 1997: Coup by junior officers calling themselves Armed Forces Revolutionary Council (AFRC). New Leader is Major Johnny Paul Koroma. The junta suspends the constitution and invites the RUF to join them. Widespread civil disobedience and international condemnation. Thousands flee Sierra Leone, including Kabbah and many civil society activists.

February 1998: Nigerian led ECOMOG forces overthrow AFRC.

6 January 1999: RUF and AFRC attack Freetown. After two weeks of fighting in which 5,000–6,000 people die and hundreds are mutilated, ECOMOG restores control.

7 July 1999: Signing of Lomé Peace Accord. Includes power sharing between government and rebels, blanket amnesty for rebels, disarmament and demobilisation, and establishment of commissions for human rights and for truth and reconciliation. Civil society groups play an active role through parallel negotiations. Although civil society has an important role in implementation, there is great disappointment about power sharing and the blanket amnesty.

22 October 1999: UN Security Council authorises establishment of UN Mission in Sierra Leone (UNAMSIL) of up to 6,000 troops including 260 unarmed observers, under Chapter VII (Resolution 1270).

7 February 2000: UN Security Council expands UNAMSIL to 11,100 troops. Mandate expanded to provision of security at key locations in and near Freetown and at all disarmament sites.

1 May 2000: RUF seizes nearly 500 Kenyan and Zambian peacekeepers in remote locations in north and east. Britain sends 700 paratroopers to restore security in and around Freetown and to bolster morale and resolve of peacekeepers.

The role of civil society

Since 1994 and 1995 a number of civil society peace initiatives have been taken. Most of these initiatives were local but they would not have been possible, at least not on the same scale, without international support. This included support from international donors, like the US and the UK, diaspora groups, international NGOs present in Sierra Leone, and West African networks, particularly links with Nigerian civil society.

In 1996 a coalition of groups including trades unions, journalists, paramount chiefs, and well-known academics began to press for elections. Particularly

8 May 2000: Massive civil society protest in Freetown demanding release of peacekeepers. 30,000 people move towards Sankoh's house. Sankoh's bodyguards open fire, killing 19 people and injuring dozens. Sankoh flees over a back wall in women's clothing.

12 May 2000: Funeral of civilians killed in protest.

14 May 2000: Friends of Sierra Leone send letter to President Clinton calling for stronger action in Sierra Leone

17 May 2000: Sankoh captured and arrested.

19 May 2000: UN Security Council authorises further increase in strength of UNAMSIL up to 13,000 (Resolution 1299).

20 May 2000: Human Rights Watch letter to UN Security Council.

June 2000: Most hostages released after negotiations through Charles Taylor of Liberia.

5 July 2000: UN Security Council imposes an embargo on all rough diamonds from Sierra Leone unless they have a government of Sierra Leone Certificate of Origin (Resolution 1306).

22 July 2000: UNAMSIL Operation Thunderbolt frees roadblocks between Freetown and airport and attacks Occra base of West Side Boys, a paramilitary group including RUF and AFRC personnel.

14 August 2000: UN Security Council authorises the UN Secretary-General to negotiate the establishment of an independent Special Court to try persons responsible for war crimes, crimes against humanity, and violations of international humanitarian law, as well as crimes under relevant Sierra Leonean law committed on the territory of Sierra Leone (Resolution 1315).

25 August 2000: Eleven British military personnel taken hostage by West Side Boys together with one member of the Sierra Leone Army.

10 September 2000: British rescue mission releases hostages and attacks the West Side Boys' base. Some West Side Boys killed and many surrender as a result of both British attacks and Operation Thunderbolt.

20 September 2000: India announces the withdrawal of Indian troops from UNAMSIL following disagreement between Indian commander and Nigerian officials about conduct of war.

26 September 2000: US Congressional hearing on child amputees.

9–14 October 2000: UN Security Council Mission to Sierra Leone. Stresses need for a comprehensive strategy and for regional approach (S/2000/922).

10 October 2000: British government announces a package of additional measures, including military assistance to the Sierra Leone government, a rapid-reaction capability in support of UNAMSIL, and staff officers seconded to UNAMSIL.

19 October 2000: Jordan announces the withdrawal of Jordanian troops from UNAMSIL.

10 November 2000: Ceasefire signed under ECOWAS auspices in Abuja. Under agreement, RUF agrees to free movement of persons and goods throughout the country, to return seized weapons, and to disarm. UNAMSIL guaranteed free movement throughout Sierra Leone

30 March 2001: UN Security Council authorises further increase in UNAMSIL up to 17,500 troops (Resolution 1346).

important was the women's movement. Women's groups had always been active in Sierra Leone, in the churches, local communities, or Descendants groups — that is, descendants from original slave settlers. These groups were active all over the country and had an enormous mobilising potential.[11] But it was not until 1994 that they came together to establish the

Women's Forum, in order to prepare for the United Nations' Women's Conference in Beijing, with international support. This was the moment they became aware of their potential, and some of the

---

[11] *Interview with Yasmin Jusu-Sherif, a prominent member of Sierra Leone Women's movement, 27 March 2001.*

women argued for a more political stance and in particular the need for women to play a role in securing peace; as a result the Sierra Leonean women's peace movement was formed. It was felt that women were able to play a more active role because they were less threatening to the military government and therefore had more room to act. The first peace demonstration was held in January 1995. It was:

> a joyous carnival affair led by a then little-known paediatrician, Fattima Boie-Kamara ... Female professionals, previously known for standing aloof from the concerns of ordinary people, danced through Freetown, linking arms with female soldiers, petty traders, and student nurses, singing choruses. The message of the demonstrators was simple and compelling: 'Try peace to end this senseless war.' (Yasmin Jusu-Sherif in Conciliation Resources 2000: 47–9)

Previous peace groups had been considered rebel sympathisers or 'fifth columnist'. The emergence of a mass women's movement made peace a respectable option. The demand for democratisation was seen as a condition for ending the war and women played a key role in the National Consultative Conference that was held in August 1995 and prepared the way for elections. In the event, there was disappointment that the first peace agreement and the Kabbah government, in practice, excluded women.

After the coup, some 200,000 people left Sierra Leone, many of them civil society activists. Branches of the Women's Forum were established in London and in Conakry, Guinea. Nevertheless, civil society groups were to play an active role in the Lomé agreement. In addition to the women's movement, new groups were important like the Inter-Religious Council, established in 1997, and the Campaign for Good Governance led by Zainab Bangura. A Nigerian NGO, the Centre for Democracy and Development (CDD), organised a Round Table in parallel with the formal negotiations. According to Zainab Bangura:

> To my mind, more was achieved in the two-day meeting than during the entire process of negotiation. The round-table brought together two extreme positions and unveiled the arrogance of the rebels and the defiance of civil society. The two forces clashed and accepted for the first time that they would have to deal with each other. It was a reality that was

needed to cement any agreement that would come out. Both parties were confronted with what was going to happen after the signing of an agreement and the problems to be confronted in the process of peace consolidation. It also helped to bring into the open the bitterness of the war that had caused so much destruction both in terms of human life and property. The RUF needed to see and feel the bitterness of Sierra Leonean society against them to bring them down from the Ivory Tower they had created for themselves at Lomé. (Oludipe 2000: 88)

Civil society representatives were appointed to the various commissions responsible for the implementation of Lomé. The capture of UN equipment and peacekeepers was a bitter disappointment. As Zainab Bangura put it: 'When civil society groups realised that true peace was still an illusion, despite all efforts and sacrifices, they became very angry.' The consequence was a massive demonstration in Freetown, demanding the release of the peacekeepers. Some 30,000 people moved towards the house of Foday Sankoh, where his bodyguards opened fire and killed 17 people. Sankoh ran away but a few days later he was captured and arrested.

The public debate about intervention

All four global civil society positions can be identified in relation to the debate about intervention in Sierra Leone.

The *sovereignist* position is rather limited, put forward primarily by President Charles Taylor of Liberia and President Blaise Campaore of Burkina Faso. Both are authoritarian leaders supporting the rebels and engaged in the illegal diamond trade.

The dominant opinion among civil society groups inside Sierra Leone lies somewhere between *just war* and *human rights enforcement*. Civil society groups inside Sierra Leone were strongly supportive of effective outside intervention, whether or not it was authorised by the United Nations. Thus, they supported Executive Outcomes, ECOMOG, and the latest British intervention, although they have become increasingly disillusioned with UNAMSIL. When the British arrived, the main reaction of Sierra Leonean civil society, according to Kayode Fayemi of CDD was 'thank god'.[12]

---

[12] Interview, March 2001.

The failure of the two peace agreements has left civil society activists disillusioned with the possibility of a negotiated peace, while the weakness and corruption of the government have underlined the necessity for outside intervention. In an e-mail communication of 24 January 2001, Zainab Bangura explains:

The only language the RUF understands is violence. For there to be peace, the military capability of the RUF has to be reduced. This can be only done by force. This is a fact that every Sierra Leonean with the exception of the government understands. And the only people who have ever successfully subdued the RUF are the Executive Outcomes and the ECOMOG. This is why Sierra Leoneans have very fond memories of the two forces and always want them to stay . . . On the issue of neo-colonialism over 90 per cent of Sierra Leoneans believe and know that our predicament is due to mismanagement, corruption, and bad governance. The people responsible are still running the country. So there is big disdain, hatred and bitterness for the ruling class. Most people would like to see the bulk of the institutions of government run by expatriates. This tells you how despondent they are with their own people.

In other words, civil society groups inside Sierra Leone want order restored and see the rebels as the main problem. Of course, they would prefer an intervention that minimises casualties and prioritises the protection of civilians, just as the Kosovar Albanians would have preferred ground intervention to air strikes, but they prefer any kind of intervention to none.

Outside Sierra Leone, views are more mixed. Ambrose Ganda, who runs the influential Website Focus on Sierra Leone (URL), puts forward an argument that is closer to the *humanitarian peace* position. Ganda argues that the intervention is too one-sided. Basically it is propping up a corrupt government—a 'bunch of discredited, crooked and obnoxious politicians'. In theory, it should be possible to have a genuine humanitarian intervention that is non-partisan and even-handed and under UN auspices. However, in practice it is difficult to conceive of genuinely disinterested outside intervention. The UN is dominated by the great powers, which have little interest in Africa. Moreover, the mainly Nigerian UN peacekeepers at present in Sierra Leone, according to

Ganda, are interested only in diamonds. Ganda thinks that the British ought to have put their forces under UN command and to have helped to enhance the legitimacy and effectiveness of the UN forces. Instead, they are retraining an army which had earlier been involved in coups and repression. What is needed, according to Ganda, is grass-roots reconciliation on a broad scale and not elections since 'politicians prey on the prejudices and fears of the electorate to retain or gain power'.

A similar view is expressed by Christopher Clapham, an Africanist at the University of Lancaster. According to Clapham, the Lomé Agreement of 1999:

ostensibly established a coalition between an ineffectual elected government and a ruthless armed opposition with a record of reneging on agreements. It is open to the UN to send real fighting forces into situations like Sierra Leone, to kill or be killed, if the states concerned would allow it. That would be a very hazardous enterprise and unlikely to lead to the reconstruction of Sierra Leone. But at least the UN would have some idea of what it was supposed to be doing. Peacekeeping in recent conflicts is a farce, fuelled by wishful thinking. We'd be better off without it . . . No matter how tragic the loss of life, and how appalling the abuse of rights, the UN and its leading states must recognise the limitations on their capacities and come to terms with a world they cannot control. They must resist the temptation to send peacekeepers into situations where they add to the number of victims of the UN's naivety and over-ambition.[13]

Clapham argues that both intervention and efforts at negotiation have failed. The only alternative is a massive internal civil society effort at reconciliation (CDD 2000).

The final position, *human rights enforcement*, can be found among international and Nigerian NGOs. Throughout 2000, human rights groups like Human Rights Watch, Amnesty International, and Friends of Sierra Leone—a group made up of former Peace Corps volunteers in Sierra Leone—were lobbying for a more forceful UN presence. They pressed for more robust protection of civilians, for the prosecution of war

---

[13] 'Saturday Debate: Should the UN get out of Sierra Leone?', Guardian, 22 May 2000.

Freetown, Sierra Leone, March 1998: Welcome messages were daubed on the roads in February 1998 when ECOMOG peacekeepers intervened (*photo: Reuters/Popperfoto*).

British, the UN forces, and private security forces. The primary mission of an outside force is to protect civilians and to reduce and control these various soldiers and rebels. Up to now, the most that outside forces seem to be able to achieve is to freeze the status quo with the rebels still controlling the eastern diamond areas and the government with British support in control of Freetown. Under the Lomé agreement the UN forces were supposed to protect civilians from physical harm and to carry out a disarmament and demobilisation programme, which would offer fighters a more productive and stable alternative to their present employment and provide an opportunity to integrate the country. That is still the priority. Reducing the number of men in arms and the amounts of armaments requires more effectiveness and robustness than has been displayed so far. The advantage of the UN is that, at least in theory, it enjoys more legitimacy than forces closely identified with the government.

Conclusion

What is striking about the last decade is the emergence of what might be called a global humanitarian regime. It involves changing norms: a growing consensus about respect for human rights, a strengthening of international law (the International Criminal Court, international protectorates, land mines convention, universal jurisdiction for grave human rights violations, and so on), a growing readiness by governments to commit resources (money and troops) to humanitarian purposes, and above all a significant growth of global civil society groups who focus on the issue of humanitarian intervention in various ways.

The role of global civil society has been crucial in underpinning this global humanitarian regime. During the 1990s, international NGOs, think tanks, and commissions concerned with conflict prevention, management, and resolution have proliferated. Many of these groups are actively engaged on the ground in conflict zones. Equally, if not more important, has been the emergence of local grass-roots groups, as in Bosnia and Sierra Leone, which have seen the advantage of making transnational links or developing networks as a way of protecting local civic space, as a source of technical and financial assistance, and as a way of transmitting local knowledge, proposals, and ideas to global decision-makers. Global civil society has provided a direct form of protection for civilians in conflict zones,

crimes, and for the control of diamonds. They also favour a regional approach towards negotiation. Friends of Sierra Leone (URL) organised a US congressional hearing in September for child amputees.

Nigeria dominates ECOMOG and Nigerian NGOs faced real dilemmas about its role. The Nigerian dictator, General Abacha, was using ECOMOG to serve his own ambition of becoming a regional hegemon. This was costing some $1 million a day. Moreover, by using humanitarian arguments he was able to shore up his own position. At the same time there was much sympathy for the plight of the Sierra Leoneans. As Kayode Fayemi put it, 'The internal project of dislodging the military from power conflicted with the pan-African ideal of helping Africans in need which all Africans imbibe from birth'.[14] A public debate after the death of Abacha and the transition to democracy led to the withdrawal of ECOMOG and the establishment of UNAMSIL, to which the Nigerians were the main contributors.

Thus the human rights enforcement position basically entails the view that outsiders do need to provide security in Sierra Leone if the project of civil society reconciliation is to be achieved. However, that outside role has to take a specific form. At present there is a proliferation of military forces in Sierra Leone: the rebels, various government forces including militia groups such as the *kamajors*, the

---

[14] *Interview, March 2001.*

with or without the support of outside governments, and has generated a global public debate about whether, when, and how humanitarian intervention should be undertaken.

Of the four positions outlined in this chapter, three (just war, humanitarian peace, and human rights enforcement) favour humanitarian intervention, although they differ about what this means. For the just war position it can mean war; for the humanitarian peace position it means civil society intervention; and for the human rights enforcement position it means a combination of civil society intervention and a new form of international policing. Few of the conflicts of the 1990s have been resolved. Indeed, one of the characteristics of 'new wars' is that pre-conflict and post-conflict phases increasingly resemble each other. Agreements stabilise the violence but tend not to provide solutions. Moreover, the 'new wars' have a tendency to spread through criminal networks, refugees, and the virus of exclusivist ideologies. The risk is that the just war and humanitarian peace positions could end up prolonging these wars perhaps indefinitely. Air strikes and overwhelming force tend to reinforce particularist views of the world and can contribute to polarisation and destabilisation while giving the impression of action. Humanitarian peace may alleviate hunger and even sometimes protect people, but, by being ineffective, too even-handed, and sometimes vulnerable, there is a risk of discrediting the non-violent civil society position.

For human rights enforcement, the third option, to work, there needs to be a much more substantial commitment than displayed hitherto: a commitment that goes beyond rhetoric. In part it is a commitment to resources. Humanitarian intervention perhaps needs to be reconceptualised as international presence in conflict-prone areas, a presence that represents a continuum from civil society actors to international agencies up to and including international peacekeeping troops on a much larger scale than seen so far. In part it means a change in outlook, especially the training, equipment, principles, and tactics of peacekeeping troops. But above all it involves a genuine belief in the equality of all human beings; and this entails a readiness to risk the lives of peacekeeping troops to save the lives of others where this is necessary. It should be stressed that I am not talking about full-scale war, and the risks are therefore, less than in a conventional ground war; nevertheless, they exist. Neither the just war position nor the humanitarian peace position is ready to risk soldiers' lives. The former privileges the lives of soldiers; the latter is willing to risk the lives of human

rights activists but opposes the use of soldiers. Even in the most well-ordered societies, police take risks to maintain the security of ordinary citizens. The human rights enforcement position would require the same sort of commitment at an international level.

The trend towards global humanitarianism is, of course, reversible. The fourth position—the rejectionist sovereignist position—seemed to be a minority view during the 1990s. However, the new Bush administration in the US is much closer to a sovereignist position than the previous administration; and the spread of nationalist and fundamentalist political movements shows no sign of abating. An equally plausible scenario is one in which global civil society finds itself increasingly embattled both on the ground in conflict zones and in the global debate.

I should like to thank Mark Bowden, Kayode Fayemi, Yasmin Jusu-Sherif, and John Hirsch for giving interviews, and Zainab Bangura, Walid Salem, and Abdul Tejan-Cole for responding to my questions via e-mail.

References

Akehurst, M. (1984). 'Humanitarian Intervention', in H. Bull (ed.), *Intervention in World Politics*. Oxford: Clarendon Press.

Africa Rights (1993). *Somalia and Operation Restore Hope: A Preliminary Assessment*. London (May).

Allen, T. and Styan D. (2000). 'A Right to Interfere? Bernard Kouchner and the New Humanitarianism'. *Journal of International Development*, 12: 825–42.

Andjelic, N. (2000). 'Bosnia-Herzegovina: Politics and Society at the end of Yugoslavia' (Ph.D. thesis). Brighton: University of Sussex.

Blair, T. (1999). 'Doctrine of the International Community'. Chicago (23 April). http://www.primeminister.gov.uk

Brauman, R. (1996). *Humanitaire: le dilemme. Conversations pour demain*. Paris: Les Éditions Textuel.

Bull, H. (ed.) (1984). *Intervention in World Politics*. Oxford: Clarendon Press.

Carnegie Commission on Preventing Deadly Conflict (1997). *Preventing Deadly Conflict: Final Report*. Washington, DC: Carnegie Commission on Preventing Deadly Conflict.

Carnegie Endowment for Peace (1996). *Unfinished Peace: Report of the International Commission on the Balkans.* Washington, DC: Carnegie Endowment for Peace.

CDD (Centre for Democracy and Development) (2000). *Engaging Sierra Leone* (Strategy Planning Series 4). London: CDD.

Chomsky, N. (1999). *The New Military Humanism: Lessons from Kosovo.* London: Pluto Press.

Cockburn, C. (2000). 'The Women's Movement: Boundary-crossing on Terrains of Conflict', in R. Cohen and Shirin M. Rai (eds), *Global Social Movements.* London: Athlone Press.

Conciliation Resources (2000). Issue 9.

Cuny, Frederick C. (1983). *Disasters and Development.* Oxford: Oxford University Press.

de Waal, A. (1997). *Famine Crimes: Politics and the Disaster Relief Industry in Africa.* Oxford and Indiana: James Currey/Indiana University Press.

European Platform for Conflict Prevention and Transformation. http://www.euconflict.org

Focus on Sierra Leone. http://www.freespace.virgin.net/ambrose.ganda/

Friends of Sierra Leone. http://www.fosalone.org

Goldstone, R. J. (2000). *For Humanity: Reflections of a War Crimes Investigator.* New Haven and London: Yale University Press.

Hirsch, J. L. (2001). *Sierra Leone: Diamonds and the Struggle for Democracy* (International Peace Academy Occasional Papers). Boulder, CO and London: Lynne Rienner.

Human Rights Watch (2000*a*). *World Report 2000.* New York. http://www.hrw.org/reports/2000

— (2000*b*). *Civilian Deaths in the NATO Air Campaign.* New York (February). http://www.hrw.org/reports/2000/nato

Ignatieff, M. (1998). *The Warrior's Honor: Ethnic War and the Modern Conscience.* London: Chatto and Windus.

Independent International Commission on Kosovo (2000). *Kosovo Report: Conflict, International Response, Lessons Learned.* Oxford: Oxford University Press.

International Crisis Group (2000). *Scramble for the Congo: Anatomy of an Ugly War.* Brussels (20 December). http://www. intl-crisis-group.org

Jackson, Robert (2000). *The Global Covenant: Human Conduct in a World of States.* Oxford: Oxford University Press.

Kaldor, M. (1999). *New and Old Wars: Organised Violence in a Global Era.* Cambridge: Polity Press.

Keck, Margaret E. and Sikkink, Kathryn (1998). *Activists Beyond Borders: Advocacy Networks in International Politics.* Ithaca, NY and London: Cornell University Press.

Kohaditore. http://www.kohaditore.com

Kouchner, Bernard (1986). *Charité Business.* Paris: Le Pré aux clercs.

Mahoney, L. and Eguren, L. E. (1997). *Unarmed Bodyguards: International Accompaniment for the Protection of Human Rights.* Bloomfield: Kumarian Press.

Marcon, Giulio, and Pianta, Mario (2001). 'New Wars, New Peace Movements'. *Soundings: A Journal of Politics and Culture,* 17: 11–24.

Moorehead, C. (1998). *Dunant's Dreams: War, Switzerland and the History of the Red Cross.* London: Harper Collins.

Oludipe, O. (ed.) (2000). *Sierra Leone: One Year After Lomé* (One-Day Analytical Conference on the Peace Process,. London, 15 September; CDD Strategy Planning Series No. 5). London: CDD.

Petrova, D. (2000). 'The Kosovo War and the Human Rights Community'. Paper presented to LSE seminar, 18 November.

Radio B92. http://www.b92.net

Ramsbotham, O. and Woodhouse, T. (1996). *Humanitarian Intervention in Contemporary Conflict: A Reconceptualization.* Cambridge: Polity Press.

Richards, P. (1996). *Fighting for the Rainforest: War, Youth and Resources in Sierra Leone.* Oxford: International African Institute, James Currey.

Roberts, A. (1996). *Humanitarian Action in War* (International Institute of Strategic Studies, Adelphi Paper 305). Oxford: Oxford University Press.

Shawcross, William (1995). 'A Hero of our Time'. *New York Review of Books,* 30 November .

SIPRI (Stockholm International Peace Research Institute) (2000). *SIPRI Yearbook 2000: Armaments, Disarmament, and International Security.* Oxford: Oxford University Press.

South Asia Citizens Web. http://www.mnet.fr/aiindex

Smillie, I., Gberie, L., and Hazelton, R. (eds) (2000). *The Heart of the Matter. Sierra Leone:*

Diamonds and Human Security. Partnership Africa (January).

Smith, A. D. (1996). *Nations and Nationalism in a Global Era*. Cambridge: Polity Press.

Tejan-Cole, A. (2001). 'The Legality of NATO and ECOMOG Interventions'. Unpublished manuscript.

United Nations (1999a). *Report on the Fall of Srebrenica* (UN Doc. A54/549,15 November). New York: United Nations.

— (1999b). *Report of the Independent Inquiry into Actions of the United Nations During the 1994 Genocide in Rwanda* (UN Doc. S/1999/1257, 15 December). New York: United Nations.

— (2000). *Report of the Panel on United Nations Peace Operations* (UN Doc. A/55/305-S/2000/809, 21 August). New York: United Nations.

United Nations Peacekeeping Department. http://www.un.org/depts/dpko

Weiss, T. G. (1999). *Military-Civilian Interactions: Intervening in Humanitarian Crises*. Lanham, Maryland: Rowman and Littlefield.

Wheeler, N. J. (2000). *Saving Strangers: Humanitarian Intervention in International Society*. Oxford: Oxford University Press.

Part III: Infrastructure of Global Civil Society

CHAPTER 6

CONTESTED SPACE: THE INTERNET AND GLOBAL CIVIL SOCIETY

John Naughton

Introduction

The Internet offers powerful facilities for groups and organisations operating outside conventional power structures. It does this by changing the economics and logistics of information and communication. Civil society institutions were 'early adopters' of the Internet and are successfully and intensively using the network to further their goals and conduct their activities. This is not surprising given the libertarian ethos of the Net and its decentralised architecture.

However, the extent to which the Internet is being harnessed for civil society purposes is uneven. In some cases the potential of the medium has not been realised because of inequalities in access—particularly the digital divide measured in social, economic, and educational terms—government regulation or censorship, and aggressive corporate action.

We are in a transition phase in which established power structures are catching up with the libertarian and centripetal characteristics of the Net. In many cases civil society's uses of the network have been more imaginative than those of traditional institutions. But the old order is wising up. Aspects of Internet activity that only four years ago were regarded as intrinsically incapable of being regulated—for example, copyright and defamation—are rapidly being brought within the scope of national legal systems. New regulatory regimes which are intrinsically more intrusive are being implemented by legislatures across the globe, ostensibly to address the new challenges presented by the Internet but in many cases as a response to pressures from corporate lobbies and security services. And the evolution of the Internet into a mass medium has made it more vulnerable to government and corporate control.

Many of the features of the Internet which make it particularly conducive to civil society uses are a product of the network's technological architecture. But if the underlying architecture were to change, its usefulness to civil society might be reduced. There are good reasons to suppose that the rapid development of e-business poses a major threat to online freedoms because online commerce requires modification of the existing 'permissive' architecture in ways that will make it a more controlled space. It is important that civil society recognises the nature and extent of this threat, and that civil society groups formulate policies and initiatives to address it.

At the same time, other, potentially very radical Internet technologies exist or are incubating, notably public key encryption, peer-to-peer networking, the spread of persistent ('always on') broadband connectivity, and the evolution of the Web into a two-way communication medium rather than a relatively passive publication medium. By giving a new impetus to libertarian uses of the Internet, these technologies are also likely to trigger a new set of tensions between Internet 'freedoms' and regulatory pressures.

The question of whether the Internet is intrinsically a subversive technology which is immune from control by established economic and power structures is thus an open one. Recent history is not necessarily a guide to future outcomes and may even be misleading. This chapter therefore attempts to chart a contested space which is in a state of constant disequilibrium and likely to continue that way.

We begin with an outline of the architecture of the Internet and the facilities it offers to global civil society. This is followed by some illustrations of civil society uses of the Net in a number of different areas. We then consider two factors which threaten to limit the usefulness of the network in these contexts. The first is the so-called 'digital divide' and its worrying implications for those who seek to harness the Internet as a force for enlarging the space for public discussion and social action. The second is the steady encroachment of governmental and corporate agencies on the basic freedoms of the Net. Finally we examine some of the new Internet-based technologies which may tip the balance back in favour of libertarian uses of the network. The concluding section argues that global civil society has a vital stake in ensuring that the Net remains open and uncontrolled by governmental or corporate forces.

The Network

History

Although the Internet is popularly portrayed as a computer network, it is more accurately defined as 'a global network of computer networks' which operates using a set of open technological protocols of which the Transmission Control Protocol (TCP/IP) suite is the most important. The Internet works by breaking messages into small parcels of data known as packets and then passing those packets through the system until they reach their destination. TCP takes care of the disassembly of messages into packets at the transmission end and their reassembly at the receiving end. IP handles the addressing of data packets.

The current Internet[1] came into being in January 1983, having evolved from the ARPANET, a packet-switching network conceived and funded by the Advanced Research Projects Agency (ARPA) of the US Department of Defense (DoD). The ARPANET came into operation in October 1969. Although it was funded by a military budget, the prime motivation behind the network was to link research computers and researchers funded by ARPA in laboratories and universities across the US, thereby increasing the utilisation of what were at the time extremely expensive assets, namely, large mainframe computers, most of which were incompatible with one another. The prime uses of the new network were originally expected to lie in the facilitation of remote access to these time-shared mainframes and the transport of files from one location to another. One of the unexpected discoveries of the project was that the most intensive application turned out to involve the passing of messages between researchers, that is, electronic mail (Hafner and Lyon 1996: 214).

The ARPANET was a uniform system accessible only to researchers funded by ARPA. Shortly after it came into operation, a number of other computer networks came into being in the US and elsewhere. Among them were the ALOHA network in Hawaii, the Cyclades network in France, and the NPL network in the UK's National Physical Laboratory. Although all

of these non-ARPA networks also used packet-switching technology, they were functionally incompatible with one another and the DoD system. After the successful demonstration of the ARPANET as a working system in 1972, therefore, ARPA turned its attention to the problem of how to 'internetwork' these networks to create a bigger, transnational network. The solution, which originated with Vinton Cerf and Robert Kahn, evolved over the decade 1973–83 and involved the creation of a set of protocols (technical conventions) which would enable computers to act as gateways between different networks so that messages could be passed reliably from any node to any other node via an indeterminate number of routing stations (Naughton 2000: 162). These protocols eventually became a 'family' of upwards of 100 detailed standards known collectively as the 'TCP/IP suite'.

The architecture of the Net

The significance of the 'internetting' technology based on TCP/IP is that it enabled the creation of a global network with an open, permissive architecture. As there was no central control, it would not make sense to try to pre-specify the kinds of networks which would be permitted to join. Anyone could hook up a network to the emerging 'internetwork' so long as they had a gateway computer which 'spoke' TCP/IP. This principle enabled the emerging network to grow organically at an astonishing speed.

An important implication of the Cerf-Kahn design was that the overall network was essentially 'dumb'. Its only function was to pass electronic packets from one point to another: the so-called 'end-to-end' principle.[2] As far as the network was concerned, those packets might be fragments of e-mail, photographs, recorded music, or pornographic videos: they were all the same to the network and were treated identically. This indifference to content made the Internet—the term 'internetwork' was quickly shortened to the less cumbersome 'Internet'—radically different from previous communications networks which had been owned or controlled by agencies that determined the uses to which their systems could be put. In the UK and many European countries,

---

[1] The term 'Internet' is often used synonymously with other terms like 'Web'. For our purposes, the Internet is treated as the communications infrastructure along which various kinds of communications traffic—electronic mail, Web pages, digitised files (MP3, voice, video, text, and so on)—pass.

[2] The 'end-to-end argument' was articulated by network architects Jerome Saltzer, David Reed, and David Clark in 1981 as a principle for allocating intelligence within a large-scale computer network. It has since become a central principle of the Internet's design. See Stanford Center for Internet and Society (2000).

for example, the national telephone networks were owned for most of the twentieth century by national post offices, which partly explains why FAX technology was so slow to take off in the West: organisations devoted to delivering letters by hand were not disposed to promote the idea of sending letters down a telephone wire. In sharp contrast, uses and applications of the Internet were determined entirely by the ingenuity of its users and those who developed applications which could harness its message-passing capabilities. Some commentators (for example, Lessig 1999*a*) have attributed the explosion of economic activity and creativity generated by the Internet to this factor.

The other feature of the original Internet architecture which is significant for our purposes is the fact that authentication of users was not required. Each machine connected to the Net needed to have a unique 'IP' (Internet Protocol) address,[3] and all of that machine's transactions with other machines on the network could be logged. But there was—and currently still is—no provision for linking IP addresses to known individuals. This meant that the architecture facilitated anonymity: a feature famously encapsulated by the celebrated 1993 New Yorker cartoon showing two dogs in front of a computer. 'On the Internet', one is saying, 'nobody knows you're a dog'.

The implications of the architecture's facilitation of anonymity have been far-reaching. Anonymity is a two-edged sword. On the one hand it permits a wide range of reputable (and disreputable) uses of the Net because the identity-based sanctions of the real world do not apply in cyberspace. On the other hand, anonymity often enables the free expression and dissemination of views in ways that would be more difficult in real-world arenas. The architecture makes it difficult, for example, for security services to track down or silence dissidents and for corporations to identify whistle-blowers or campaigning groups disseminating critical information or hostile propaganda.

The technical architecture of the Net has thus been a prime determinant of how the network has been used. As in the physical world, architecture enables some things and prevents others. The

Table 6.1: Estimated internet user population, November 2000		
Region	Users (millions)	% of total
Africa	3.11	0.76
Asia/Pacific	104.88	25.76
Europe	113.14	27.79
Middle East	2.40	0.59
Canada and USA	167.12	41.05
Latin America	16.45	4.04
World Total	407.10	

Source: Nua Internet Surveys (URL) For country data see table R10 in part IV of this yearbook.

significant point from our point of view is that the architecture of the Net is cast in terms of technical protocols, that is to say, as computer code. And, as Lessig (1999*b*) has pointed out, there is nothing immutable about code. It is pure 'thought-stuff' and as such can be changed. This is a subject to which we will return.

Scale

The Internet is a global system in that it has nodes in virtually every country, but the density of users and connections is very uneven across the globe. It is estimated, for example, that 69 per cent of Internet users are located in North America and Europe, and that Africa, with 13 per cent of the world's population, has less than 1 per cent of the world's Internet users.

Nevertheless the scale of the network's coverage is still remarkable. Because of the 'organic' architecture created by the TCP/IP protocols, it's impossible to say how many Internet users there are, but authoritative estimates at the time of writing (February 2001) suggest numbers in the region of 400 million.

The Internet as a communications space for global civil society

Although there are arguments about its long-term significance, few doubt that the Internet represents a radical transformation of mankind's communications environment. As one well-known Net evangelist (Barlow in Barlow *et al.* 1995) has said, 'We are in the middle of the most transforming technological event since the capture of fire'. There is a widespread belief

---

[3] *A number made up of four sets of digits: for example, 255.212.12.40. Computers accessing the Net via dial-up lines are assigned temporary IP addresses from a bank held by their Internet services provider (ISP). Computers on local area networks generally access the Net through a gateway machine so that all transactions by an individual machine are logged against the IP address of the gateway computer.*

that in areas where 'information is power' the rise of the Net has to some extent levelled the playing field on which marginalised and grass-roots organisations compete with established economic, media, and governmental interests for public attention.

Most of the evidence for this is anecdotal, if only because there has as yet been little systematic empirical research on the subject. But an examination of the communications capabilities of the Internet suggests some good reasons for supposing that the conjecture is plausible.

As a communications space, the Internet:

- facilitates access to published data, information and knowledge;
- lowers the barriers to publication and enables groups and individuals to bypass traditional gatekeepers in media and publishing;
- facilitates rapid communication on a global scale;
- facilitates the sharing of information resources; and
- facilitates the formation and maintenance of 'virtual communities' of people or institutions with shared interests.

Access to published data, information and knowledge

The volume of data and information now published on the World Wide Web (WWW) is phenomenal, and indeed threatens to overwhelm the capacity of search engines and directories to index and categorise it. In February 2001, Google (URL), a leading search engine, was claiming to index 1.3 billion Web pages, which it estimated to be about half of the total number of Web pages published at that time. Other estimates of the total number of Web pages are higher. More significant than the sheer volume, however, is that fact that an increasing proportion of government, official, institutional, and corporate publications are now routinely published on the Web. Although many of these publications have previously been available in print, the practical effect of online publication has been greatly to increase the accessibility of such documents. For example, Hansard, the daily transcript of proceedings in the UK Parliament, has always been available in print to those who had the resources to purchase or physically access the printed edition, which in practice meant those with ready access to a major

library in the United Kingdom or one of the very few national libraries which have such holdings. Now Hansard is published daily on the Web, with the result that anyone anywhere in the world with a browser and an Internet connection can access the British parliamentary record. Similarly with major public documents such as the report of the inquiry into the BSE (URL) epidemic in Britain.

Much the same applies in other countries— for example, the US—where transcripts of congressional sessions, court proceedings, legal judgments and pleadings, and so on are available online. Instead of relying on local media reports, an environmental activist in Asia or Europe can now immediately access the exact text of President Bush's rejection of the Kyoto Protocol, for instance. Most significant UN publications are now published on the Web. Given that many civil society activities are about widening the scope of public debate about controversial issues and that interpretations of official data and information are a critical input to this process, online publication has been a boon for this sector. It has also much facilitated local and national activism on global issues, as activists can compare the policies of different governments and international organisations when deciding how to approach their own authorities.

Lowering barriers to publication

For many civil society applications, online publication is preferable to publication in traditional media because it is relatively inexpensive, provides global coverage, and bypasses the gatekeepers who control access to traditional media. It makes it possible, for example, to publish an attractive, full-colour pamphlet and distribute it globally at a cost which is determined almost entirely by the remuneration required by those who produce it. There is no need to set up a distribution network; and distribution costs are paid by readers. Furthermore, online publication is not limited simply to documents. Anyone with a modicum of skill and a simple recording device—for example, minidisc recorder, still camera, video camera, scanner—can create audio, photographic, or digital files which can be loaded onto a Web server and made available for download to all comers, again on a global basis—though of course there are channel capacity (bandwidth) limitations: users with slow dial-up connections will take much longer to access non-text files. The Internet thus lowers the barriers not just to document publication but also to multi-media publication.

The Internet makes it increasingly difficult for governments to maintain secrecy or prevent—for example, by legal injunction—publication within their jurisdictions. In the 1980s, for example, the British government successfully used legal methods to prevent Spycatcher—the memoirs of Peter Wright, a former MI5 officer who alleged that the security service had conspired to undermine the British Labour government led by Harold Wilson in the 1960s—from being read by British subjects, even though the book had been widely published abroad. Newspapers which attempted to publish excerpts were made subject to legal injunctions and British residents who wished to read Wright's allegations had to resort to absurd measures like making a day-trip to the Irish Republic in order to obtain a copy. This would be unimaginable today.[4] At the first sign of a British or European injunction the contents of the book would appear on a Web-server in the US where they would enjoy the protection of the First Amendment and be available to anyone with a browser and an Internet connection.

Rapid and inexpensive communication on a global scale

The Internet offers a wide range of facilities for individual and group communication and discussion.

Electronic mail and discussion lists. E-mail and discussion lists are the oldest, most popular, and lowest-tech forms of interaction on the Internet. E-mail is a classic person-to-person medium and represents the way in which most Internet users actively engage with the network. For example, one authoritative survey (The Pew Internet and American Life Project URL) estimates that 49 per cent of US Internet users send one or more e-mail messages a day.

For group purposes, the most significant development of e-mail technology is the 'list server', that is, a program, sometimes called a ListServ, which enables people to subscribe to a discussion list and receive by e-mail messages that the list owner or other subscribers have posted. When people send messages and responses to a list, an online discussion can develop. The number of discussion lists currently active is unknowable but is certainly very large[5] and they are a prime resource for civil society groups.

E-mail lists have certain characteristics which distinguish them from other kinds of Internet-based discussion systems. They are, for example:

> *typically owned by a single individual or small group. Since all messages to a list must pass through a single point, email lists offer their owners significant control over who can contribute to their group. List owners can personally review all requests to be added to a list, forbid anyone from contributing to the list if they are not on the list themselves, and even censor specific messages that they do not want broadcast to the list as a whole.*
> *(Kollock and Smith 1999: 5)*

Since most lists thus operate as 'benign dictatorships', they are often characterised by their more orderly and focused activity than other online discussion forums.

An important feature of e-mail is that it is an asynchronous medium—sender and recipient do not have to be connected at the same time in order to communicate. This means that it is particularly useful for communicating across time zones. It is also, in general, extremely quick. Most messages reach their destination inboxes in minutes or less. E-mail is, therefore, an exceedingly powerful medium for alerting large numbers of people to new developments, which is why it has enabled global civil society groups to respond rapidly to events and often to outpace and outflank established power structures. For example, Amnesty International has launched an online network, Fast Action Stops Torture (FAST URL), as part of its worldwide campaign to stop torture. When the organisation learns of an imminent threat of torture, FAST instantly sends out an alarm to its network of activists around the globe, requesting activists by the thousands to sign electronic letters of protest. In this way a threat of torture can be exposed within hours. The rationale is that exposing torture makes it more difficult to carry out.

Asynchronous conferencing systems. The Internet also provides other forms of asynchronous discussion/ conferencing systems. The most prominent is Usenet, a global system of online conferences called 'news groups' because originally they were used for circulating news about bugs and updates to managers of Unix systems; but there are proprietary equivalents run by Internet service providers (ISPs) like AOL and MSN. These allow participants to create topical groups

---

[4] *Compare, for example, the use of the Internet in 2000 by a disaffected MI5 operative, David Shayler (URL) to publicise his case.*

[5] *See http://www.liszt.com/ for a directory.*

in which a series of messages akin to e-mail messages can be strung together to form discussion 'threads'. Usenet-type systems are 'pull' media in the sense that people have to subscribe to conferences and then pull down from a News server the messages that interest them. In order to access newsgroups a user needs (1) a special 'client' program called a Newsreader, freely downloadable from the Net or provided in many e-mail programs, and (2) access to a News server (usually provided by one's ISP).

Usenet is, like the Internet itself, a self-organising system which operates on the basis of agreed protocols, in this case a standard message format. Something like 45,000 discussion groups, devoted to every conceivable specialism and interest, currently exist, each containing anything from a dozen to thousands of messages. On an average day tens of thousands of Usenet subscribers submit messages to the system. A new site 'joins' the Usenet by finding an existing site that is willing to pass along the daily 'feed', that is, the collections of messages *it* receives. No one 'owns' Usenet; there is no central authority, no institution that can police behaviour or enforce standards of behaviour. Virtually anyone can subscribe to a newsgroup, read all the messages on the conference, or contribute new messages. This makes the Usenet:

> *a more interesting and challenging social space than systems that are ruled by central authorities. Whatever order exists on the Usenet is the product of a delicate balance between individual freedom and collective good. Many newsgroups are wild, unordered places, but what is startling is how many are well organized and productive.*
> *(Kollock and Smith, 1999: 6)*

The main limitation in practice is whether your ISP agrees to carry the particular newsgroups in which you are interested. In practice this is one of the important 'choke points' which gives leverage to corporations and governments seeking to curtail online discussion.

Chat systems. So-called 'chat' systems enable various kinds of synchronous conversation. By far the most widespread technology is that of 'text chat' in which a number of people exchange typed messages in real time in a shared virtual space known as a 'chat room'. Although proprietary networks like AOL and MSN derive a considerable part of their revenues from the chat facilities they provide, the majority of chat interactions take place via the non-proprietary Internet Relay Chat (IRC). IRC (URL) has been described as 'the net's equivalent of CB radio'. Like CB, chat systems tend to have a great number of channels, that is, chat rooms. But unlike CB, which is localised in coverage, chat enables people all over the world to participate in real-time conversations.

Using an IRC 'client' program—freely downloadable from the Net—or proprietary clients provided by ISPs like AOL or MSN, participants exchange text messages interactively with other people via a chat server. Conversation consists of typed messages that are instantly sent to other participants. The fact that chat systems require a central server grants the server owner a great deal of power over access to both the system and individual channels. AOL's chat facilities, for example, are policed by staff or appointed volunteers (Lessig 1999*b*: 68). And even in the non-proprietary IRC each channel has an 'owner' who can control access (Kollock and Smith 1999:6).

In recent years, as modem speeds and the bandwidth of Internet connections have increased, systems which permit voice chat and even primitive video-conferencing have become popular. Excite Voice Chat, for example, enables users with multimedia-capable personal computers (PCs) —that is, computers equipped with sound cards, speakers/ headphones and a microphone—to hold audio conferences with up to nine other people. And systems such as Microsoft's NetMeeting enable one-to-one video-conferencing over the Net. Performance of these non-text systems is, however, critically dependent on the quality and bandwidth of participants' Internet connections.

Web-based conferencing and chat. Although the software required for accessing Usenet and Chat is relatively easy to use, downloading and installing client software represents a challenge for many Internet users. Because most users find using a Web browser relatively unproblematic, however, there is an increasing trend to providing interactive services via the Web. Thus many of the Usenet groups can be accessed via a Web interface[6] which also provides search facilities allowing one to look for topics over the entire Usenet system: facilities that are not available via the classic Newsreader client.

Instant messaging. This is a relatively new communications service that enables an Internet user

---

[6] *Available at http://www.groups.google.com*

to create what is in effect a private chat room with another individual. Typically, the Instant Messaging (IM) system alerts the user whenever somebody on her private list is online. She can then initiate a chat session with that particular individual. IM has proved remarkably popular since its introduction some years ago because it is a useful technology for keeping friends and colleagues in touch with one another. At present there are several competing IM systems and no over-arching standard, so people who want to send messages to one another must use the same instant messaging system. And of course IM technology still depends on there being a central server which brokers connections between IM subscribers.

Sharing of information resources

Because of the ease of publication discussed earlier, the Internet makes it much easier for groups and individuals to share information resources. Archives of documents and other resources can be digitised and placed on Web or File Transfer Protocol (FTP)[7] servers from which they can be accessed by anyone with the appropriate permissions.

The hyper-linking technology of the Web makes it easy for collaborating organisations to compile indexes and guides to one another's materials without having to maintain multiple archives. This facility is widely used by civil society groups.

And although the growing volume of Web pages continues to outpace the capacity of search engines to index and categorise them, there are some powerful general search engines like Google (URL) which enable users to locate a high proportion of relevant documents for many types of search. Because of growing concerns among civil society institutions about bias in indexing algorithms—that is, the procedures and criteria search engines use to rank pages (Introna and Nissenbaum 2000)—some organisations—for example, OneWorld—are now creating specialist search engines which attempt regularly to survey and comprehensively index sites in their areas of concern.

Given that information is such a vital ingredient in civil society activities, one would expect that the facilities provided by the Internet for sharing and aggregating information would be universally welcomed. But according to Jonathan Peizer this is not necessarily the case, at least in the NGO sector.

NGOs have historically survived by owning their information and that of their constituents. This constituted their value and substituted for significant financial assets. Yet this behaviour is antithetical to effectively leveraging the Internet to meet their missions. Because of resource constraints, many continue to be behind the technology curve. The technology is not intuitive, and many NGOs don't have the requisite experience with it. Consequently, many still mistakenly judge their organization's value on pre-Internet criteria and modes of operation. (Peizer 2000)

On this analysis, the challenge for NGOs is realising that information once unique to them may now be widely available over the Internet. The new information sources may be qualitatively better, worse, or similar, but if their providers are using their Internet presence effectively and developing online communities around it, they directly challenge the continued viability of groups which are not doing so.

Virtual communities

The literature on 'virtual communities'—social groups which conduct most of their relationships in cyberspace—is confused and confusing (for a survey see Wellman and Milena 1999). Much of the discussion focuses on the question of whether such communities are the same as 'real' communities, that is, social groupings, usually based on geographical location, to which people belong in the real world.

This is in part a continuation of old arguments about the impact of technology—as well as of bureaucratisation, urbanisation, and capitalism—on community. The current debate about the relationship between the Net and social life fits neatly into this tradition. The likelihood is, however, that once the 'fascination of the new' has palled we will discover that there is less of a dichotomy between online and real-world communities than is currently supposed. Even what we think of as normal, place-oriented communities 'can stretch well beyond the neighborhood' (Wellman and Milena 1999: 169). And one of the few ethnographic studies (Miller and Slater 2000) suggests that 'we need to treat Internet media as

---

[7] *One of the oldest Internet protocols, FTP provides a relatively fast and reliable way of exchanging files over the Net. Most software downloads are handled by FTP.*

continuous with and embedded in other social spaces', implying that people use the Net in ways that complement rather than disrupt their social lives. This view is supported by William Mitchell (1995), who objects to the suggestion that we must 'choose between participating in place-based communities and joining electronically supported, virtual ones—that it's one or the other. But that's just not the case. It's more accurate to say that bodily presence and telepresence now play differing, and potentially complementary roles in sustaining the connections that matter to us'.

A more productive approach might be to follow Howard Rheingold (1995), one of the earliest and most persuasive writers on the subject, and define virtual communities as 'communities of interest facilitated by computer networks'. On this definition, there are thousands, perhaps tens of thousands, of virtual communities centred on civil society activities, interests, and beliefs. The key question is whether such groupings constitute 'a way of revitalizing civil institutions through civil communications, or are they fostering a dangerous illusion of civil association that doesn't have an effect in the world where things like liberty matter' (Rheingold 1995). The experience of civil society is that virtual communities, mediated and linked by the Internet, can have real effects in terms of influencing real-world events.

Civil Society Uses of the Internet: Some Snapshots

The Internet has become a vitally important area for civil society. While more powerful political and economic interests dominate traditional media, the Internet has allowed the voices of ordinary citizens and organisations lacking strong financial resources to be heard. We live today in an era of globalisation, distinguished by the emergence of giant multinational corporations and unelected bureaucracies with the power to make decisions that have profound effects on people all over the world. The Internet, with over 200 million users worldwide, provides a unique public sphere where decisions that shape all our lives can be freely debated and considered. Global communities can be built there that are able to limit the power of corporations,

bureaucracies and governments. In a globalised world that continuously undermines localised democratic institutions the Internet provides an essential means for defending and extending participatory democracy.
(GreenNet URL)

Given the scope of global civil society, it would be unrealistic to attempt a comprehensive survey of its uses of the Internet. Instead this section provides an impressionistic snapshot by focusing on the ways in which civil society groups working in different areas have used the medium to achieve their diverse goals.

Oneworld.org: a civil society portal

OneWorld is the largest civil society 'portal' on the Internet. It was set up in 1995 by Anuradha Vittachi, a Sri Lankan journalist specialising in human rights and development issues, and Peter Armstrong, a British-born journalist who had previously worked for BBC television. Both had worked for five years previously in more conventional publishing media, including CD-ROM, and were concerned to 'harness the democratic potential of the Internet to promote human rights and sustainable development'. OneWorld's stated aim is to be 'the online media gateway that most effectively informs a global audience about human rights and sustainable development'. But it also seeks to provide a focus for cooperation between like-minded civil society groups: 'to bring together a global community working for sustainable development through interactive online partnerships of organisations and individuals sharing our vision' (OneWorld URL).

OneWorld began with 22 partner organisations and now has over 900, many of which supply material for publication in over 80 subject categories on the OneWorld site. In order to be admitted to partner status, an organisation must be working in the fields of sustainable development or human rights, or be branches, departments, or projects which work in the fields of sustainable development or human rights as part of larger organisations with wider aims. However, where the wider organisation is seen to significantly contravene the aims of the OneWorld community, for instance by using violence or advocating intolerance on the grounds of ethnicity, gender, sexual orientation, or religion, the application will be refused. At the time of writing, OneWorld was giving special priority to partnership applications from NGOs based in the South.

The OneWorld site now attracts over a million page views[8] a month and reaches Internet users in over 90 countries. The site publishes in five languages (English, German, Dutch, Italian, and French); it also serves as a hub for campaigns on such issues as climate change, the role of the IMF and the World Bank, and the digital divide; and runs seven specialist 'channels' on Third World Debt, learning, media, radio, TV, photography, and children. One of the aims of the radio and TV channels is to act as a not-for-profit news and features agency by providing informed broadcast material on sustainable development or human rights which can then be reused by partner organisations in ways that further their own local objectives.

Human rights on the Net

Since the appearance of the World Wide Web in 1993 there has been a veritable explosion of human rights (HR) information on the network. A crude search on Google using the keywords 'human rights' conducted on 16 April 2001 turned up 2,380,000 pages. A search on 'human rights campaigns' produced 346,000 pages. A very large number of NGOs are now online and publishing their materials, and international organisations have also begun to make large portions of their materials available online, making research much easier than in the past and enabling ready access to texts of legislation, treaties, resolutions, reports by special rapporteurs, and other essential documentation. Many academic and legal journals also offer at least some of their articles in online formats. The expansion of the Web, however, has also meant that finding materials is more difficult for those not already familiar with the major HR sites.[9]

One study (Case 1999) of the use of the Net by HR campaigners identified a number of distinct types of use:

- e-mail and discussion lists as a way of transmitting information reliably to individuals or large audiences;
- Web sites as publication platforms and sources of reliable information;
- combined use of e-mail and Web sites in conducting HR campaigns; and
- nurturing human rights communities both online and in the real world.

Case also discusses the limitations of the Net in HR work and the need for an international covenant to protect those who use it for such purposes.

It is clear that the Internet has been a boon for HR campaigners. Its facilities enable them to access official information easily and to publish information without going through the gatekeepers who control access to more traditional publishing media. E-mail and discussion lists enable them to communicate relatively easily with other activists, to make protests to government ministers and officials, to share information with large communities of like-minded people, and to alert other activists quickly—as, for example, in Amnesty International's FAST (URL) system discussed earlier—in the light of new or unexpected developments. Combinations of e-mail and Web publication make it easier to mount effective campaigns without the huge costs of traditional campaigning. And conferencing and chat technologies help to support virtual communities of activists.

The role of the Internet in coordinating protest

The use of the Internet by civil society campaigners such as the protesters who disrupted the 1999 meeting of the World Trade Organisation (WTO) in Seattle has become the stuff of media legend. Journalists marvelled at the sight of activists sending e-mail dispatches and streaming live video and audio reports from tear-gassed streets. But this was essentially a reflection of the *naïveté* and technological ignorance of mainstream media. Given that the Internet offers campaigners a communication system which is cheap, reliable, ubiquitous, efficient, and uncontrolled, it would be astonishing if they did *not* make extensive use of it, especially when it is clear that many governmental and corporate organisations do not!

The real significance of the events surrounding the Seattle WTO meeting lay not so much in

---

[8] *A 'page view' is the accessing of a Web page. A page view differs from a 'hit' by counting only the number of times a page has been accessed, whereas a hit counts the number of times that all the elements in a page, including graphics, have been accessed. Some Web pages can have a dozen or more graphical elements. Page views, however, have become harder to gauge, since pages can include frames that divide them into separate parts*

[9] *For an excellent guide to sources see Derechos Human Rights (URL).*

protestors' reliance on communications technology as in what the technology enabled them to do. To appreciate this one has to remember that one of the biggest challenges faced by civil society in recent decades is the way global capitalism, as manifested in bodies like the WTO, has succeeded in presenting an increasingly unified front to the world. This had rendered it apparently impervious to the counter-vailing activities of hundreds of thousands of isolated and uncoordinated opposition groups ranging from environmental campaigners to human rights and fair trade activists to trade unions and consumer groups. It was not as if (*pace* Fukuyama) opposition to the forces of economic globalisation did not exist: merely that their combined pressure was always less than the sum of the parts.

The Seattle meeting was significant because it showed how the Internet may be changing that. It demonstrated the synergistic possibilities when many of the disparate civil society groups opposed to organisations like the WTO use communications technology to coordinate their efforts. In the words of one observer, 'The Internet and e-mail enabled the predominantly small, non-profit groups with tiny budgets to orchestrate a massive protest among thousands of people in the United States and abroad. It also provided a link among about 150 chapters of various groups scattered on college campuses across the country' (Arnett 1999). What the WTO officials gathered in Seattle realised was that the opposition suddenly seemed greater than the sum of its parts.

Furthermore, the most important coordinating function of the Internet in this context is not so much tactical, as the traditional mass media assume, but strategic, that is, in enabling participating groups to exchange information, prepare position papers, lobby local legislatures, and generally lay the groundwork for more established forms of political action. In that sense a more instructive case study might be the role played by civil society groups in influencing the outcome of the negotiations over the proposed Multilateral Agreement on Investment (MAI).

The MAI is discussed more fully elsewhere in this volume (see Desai and Said, chapter 3 p. 60–61), but it does have an interesting Internet dimension. To recapitulate briefly: in 1997 the countries of the Organisation for Economic Cooperation and Development (OECD) began negotiating an agreement behind closed doors to set up a global framework of rules on investment. The aim was to prevent governments from favouring domestic investors and to remove restrictions on multinational corporations investing in developing countries. The intention was to give cross-border investors greater protections than those provided by the North American Free Trade Agreement (NAFTA) and the Uruguay Round agreements that established the WTO. The effect of the proposed Agreement would have been to erode national sovereignty over economic and fiscal policy in certain respects.

Publication of the MAI proposal on the Net prompted the formation of a loose coalition of NGOs including environmental organisations, consumer groups, trade unions and religious groups to question and attack the proposed agreement and expose its shortcomings and hidden agendas. By the end of 1998 there were vociferous campaigns against the agreement in half the OECD countries participating in the discussions and many more in developing countries most likely to be affected by it. Under the pressure of this publicity the negotiations collapsed.

Many participants and observers regard the networking of civil society opposition as decisive in bringing about this outcome. 'The story of the MAI', writes one:

> is a cautionary tale about the impact of an electronically networked global civil society. The days of negotiating international treaties behind closed doors are numbered, if not over. A much broader range of groups will have to be included in the globalization debate, and much more thought will have to be given to how non-participants will interpret international negotiations and agreements. (Kobrin 1998)

Environmental campaigning on the Net

Environmental groups were early and intensive users of the Net. One well-known directory (Kestemont 1998) lists over 620 major Web sites providing information, links, and contacts on environmental issues. A Google search on the keywords 'environmental pollution' turns up over 900,000 sites or pages. A similar search on 'global warming' returns over 400,000 hits. One on 'toxic waste' returns over half a million documents. Because much environmental campaigning requires access to scientific information, the increasing tendency of scientific researchers to publish on the Web as well as in specialist journals makes it easier for environmental groups to locate the kind of information needed to underpin campaigns or to buttress and inform arguments to be used in offline discussions with legislators and companies. There are striking similarities between the way environmental and human rights activists use the Internet to disseminate information, publicise and conduct campaigns, issue e-mail 'alerts', and put together rapid-response campaigns.

Uneven Playing Fields: Access and the Digital Divide

The Internet, as we have seen, has brought unprecedented benefits for civil society. The facilities it provides for accessing information, communicating, publishing, and organising evince a tremendous democratising potential. The network appears to promise the realisation of Thomas Paine's dream of a society in which everyone has a voice: a true Jeffersonian market in ideas. If this dream is ever to be fully implemented, however, a fundamental problem will have to be addressed and solved. This is the issue of inequality of access to the Internet: the so-called 'digital divide', the term popularly used to describe the gap between the 'information rich' and the 'information poor'. If the benefits and facilities of the Net are available only to a selected few, then its democratising potential, not to mention its economic potential, will never be realised.

At the moment, these benefits are available only to a select minority of mankind, variously estimated at between 2 per cent and 6 per cent of the global population.[10] The digital divide operates both within societies and between regions and countries. 'Current access to the Internet runs along the fault lines of national societies, dividing educated from illiterate, men from women, rich from poor, young from old, urban from rural' (UNDP 1999: 62).

But the digital divide also has an international dimension. According to the UNDP (1999), in mid-1998 the industrial countries of the world accounted for 88 per cent of all Internet users, despite having only 15 per cent of the world's population. At the time the UNDP report was published, North America, with 5 per cent of the people, had more than 50 per

cent of Internet users. And South Asia, home to 20 per cent of the world's population, had less than 1 per cent of the planet's Internet users.

These disparities are well known, as are the reasons for them. Internet access requires technological, social, and educational infrastructures which are unevenly distributed across global society. On the technological side, for example, the key element to date has been access to a telephone network. Using 'teledensity' (the number of telephones per 100 people) as a measure we find huge disparities in access, as Table 6.2 demonstrates.

The existence of a suitable communications infrastructure is a necessary but not sufficient condition for ensuring equality of access to the Internet. A broadband network connection is useless to someone who is illiterate. The ability to tap into and harness the information and communication resources of the Net is predicated on literacy and education. This implies that tackling the digital divide is not just a matter of creating telecommunications infrastructures where none previously existed, but also of developing universal literacy programmes and building up social capital generally. Of the two tasks, the former is likely to be the simpler to accomplish, especially given the development of wireless technologies which are much less resource intensive than conventional landline telephone networks. The inescapable conclusion is that the gap between the

Table 6.2: Teledensity in selected countries

Country	Teledensity (telephone mainlines per 100 people)
Monaco	99
United States	64
Italy	44
United Arab Emirates	40
Costa Rica	17
Kenya	0.8
Sierra Leone	0.4
Bangladesh	0.3
Uganda	0.2

Source: International Telecommunications Union (1998)
For more comprehensive data see table R10 in part IV of this Yearbook

---

[10] *The 1999 Report of the UN Development Program (UNDP) estimates that only 2 per cent of the world's population had Internet access in mid-1998. Higher estimates are based on a user population of 400 million.*

information rich and the information poor is unlikely to narrow in the medium-term future and may even widen as Internet penetration in industrialised societies gathers pace.

This is very bad news from any perspective. In economic terms, it means that under-developed societies will continue to be denied the economic benefits of the Net. Just to give one illustration, UNDP (1999:58) points out that the cost of sending a 40-page document from Madagascar to Côte d'Ivoire is $75 by five-day courier or $45 by 30-minute fax, whereas the same document can be sent by e-mail for about 20 cents—not to mention the fact that it can be dispatched to multiple recipients all over the world for the same cost.

The digital divide is also bad news in terms of human rights. Western countries have increasingly regarded universal access to telecommunications services as an important public goal (it was first written into US federal telecommunications law in 1934). The European Union requires countries seeking membership to implement policies and legislation aimed at enabling universal access to telecommunications services. The 1948 Universal Declaration of Human Rights declared that everyone has the right to freedom of expression and the right to 'receive and impart information and ideas *through any media* and *regardless of frontiers*' (emphasis added.) The digital divide implies that, in a world increasingly dependent on networked information, this right will be anything but universal for a large proportion of the global population.

The implications of the divide for global civil society are profoundly depressing. What it means is that the Internet is—and is likely to be for the foreseeable future—heavily dominated by the information-rich North/West and by very small elites in the South. This sombre reality clashes with the egalitarian aspirations ('All men are born free and equal in dignity and rights', to quote the Universal Declaration of Human Rights again) of global civil society. While Internet and computing technologies may have levelled the playing field for global civil society vis-à-vis governments and corporations in the industrialised world, it may actually have further tilted the playing field from South to North.

The Emperor's New Clues: The Battle to Control The Net

Governments of the Industrial World, you weary giants of flesh and steel, I come from Cyberspace, the new home of Mind. On behalf of the future, I ask you of the past to leave us alone. You are not welcome among us. You have no sovereignty where we gather.

We have no elected government, nor are we likely to have one, so I address you with no greater authority than that with which liberty itself always speaks. I declare the global social space we are building to be naturally independent of the tyrannies you seek to impose on us. You have no moral right to rule us nor do you possess any methods of enforcement we have true reason to fear . . .
(Barlow 1996)

In the beginning: anarchic creativity

The Internet, as we have seen, emerged from the ARPANET, which itself was a product of the 1960s. Although its early development was funded by the military, the network was designed and built—and for the most part used—by academic researchers who inhabited a liberal, uncommercialised organisational culture. In the decade 1983 to 1993—in other words, from the launch of the TCP/IP-based network to the release of the first graphically-oriented Web browser—the Internet was essentially an intellectual sandpit and working environment for academic researchers. Its operating costs were borne by government funding agencies like the Defense Advanced Projects Research Agency (DARPA), the US National Science Foundation (NSF), universities, or the research funding councils of other countries. Most computers on the network were based in research laboratories and offices and had fast permanent connections rather than slow dial-up links. And although there were official rules and regulations about what the network could and should be used for, in practice there was little supervision and applications were limited only by the ingenuity of users. So long as the application involved the passage of data packets, the Internet would—and did—handle it.

The result was not just an explosion in creativity (Lessig 1999*a*) but also the evolution of a freewheeling, anarchic, non-commercial, permissive ethos sometimes summarised by the phrase 'geek culture'. It was this ethos that found expression in John Perry Barlow's celebrated 'Declaration of Independence' quoted at the start of this section. Geek culture, however, went largely unnoticed in the outside world. Because there was no commercial activity on the Net, the business world paid little attention to it. And because the community of Internet users was relatively small and cloistered, governments were even less interested.

Because many civil society groups had roots in, or connections to, academia they were early and enthusiastic users of the Net. Far from being repelled by the techno-anarchism and libertarianism of the geek culture, many activists actively welcomed it, perceiving in it resonances with their own values. The result was that civil society users of the Net were often ahead of the adoption curve as progressive and imaginative groups recognised how suitable it was for their purposes.

The release of the Mosaic browser in the Spring of 1993 led to a sea change in commercial and governmental attitudes to the Net. Mosaic was significant because it made it easier to place pictures on Web pages. Where there were pictures, there was the possibility of entertainment. And where there was entertainment there was the prospect of commercial profit, especially when it was perceived that the Web was the 'fastest-growing communications medium in history' (Naughton 2000: 27), reaching its first 50 million users in four years—as compared with 36 years for radio and 13 for television. It began to dawn in the minds of legislators and businesspeople that this phenomenon was too important to be left to geeks.

The initial intrusions of business and government into the Internet were clumsy and ill-conceived and appeared to confirm the contemptuous disdain of the Internet community towards anyone with a profiteering or regulatory mindset. A kind of complacent arrogance took hold, based on the assumption that cyberspace was somehow different in kind from 'real' space, that it was intrinsically subversive of established ways of doing things, and that it lay beyond the reach of conventional control structures. Within the cyberlibertarian community, for example, it was widely believed that censorship would always be impossible on the Net. John Gilmore's (1996) observation that 'the Internet interprets censorship as damage and routes around it' captured this sentiment precisely. This conjecture may have

been reasonable at the time, but events have not borne it out: the Internet is potentially more susceptible to political and commercial control than was once thought. Cyberspace will not remain a 'digital commons' without vigorous political action to defend its freedoms. Left to their own devices, the forces of official regulation and commercial exploitation will gradually enclose the common. And this will have significant implications for global civil society.

The ambivalence of power: governments and the Net

All governments, including those in Western democracies, are ambivalent about the Net. On the one hand, they see it as a symbol of modernity and an engine for economic growth which may change the balance of economic advantage in their country's favour. On the other hand, they perceive it as a potentially destabilising force, undermining traditional political and legal structures, facilitating subversion, and eroding official control of what is published and read within their jurisdictions. They are also concerned at the potential erosion of their tax bases as a result of information goods crossing their frontiers as undetected (and untaxed) bitstreams.

Authoritarian responses. Governments differ greatly in the ways they react to what they see as the Internet's 'threats'. Authoritarian regimes generally attempt directly to control their populations' access to, and use of, the Net. A report by Reporters Sans Frontières (RSF) has identified 45 nations which impose blocking and filtering or all-out bans on Internet access (Reporters Sans Frontières 2000). Of the 45 nations, RSF said 20 could be described as real 'enemies of the Internet' for their actions. They are: the countries of central Asia and the Caucasus (Azerbaijan, Kazakhstan, Kirghizia, Tajikistan, Turkmenistan, and Uzbekistan), Belarus, Burma, China, Cuba, Iran, Iraq, Libya, North Korea, Saudi Arabia, Sierra Leone, Sudan, Syria, Tunisia, and Vietnam. Many of the 20 nations are singled out for restrictions that make all Internet users access the network through a single, state-run ISP. These nations include Belarus, the nations of central Asia, Sudan, and Tunisia. The report singled out China for its close monitoring of Internet use despite the rapid pace with which Internet use is growing in that country. According to the *Economist* (2001: 25), China 'has essentially covered its territory with an Intranet isolated from the rest of the world by software that blocks access to sites with unwanted content. Although clever surfers can tunnel through the "Great Firewall of China", it keeps the majority from straying too far online'. Most Chinese, in any case, access the Internet from work or public places where the state can control the software and track what they do online.

Other nations criticised for government-controlled filtering of the Internet included Iran, where, according to RSF, medical students are unable to access Web sites dealing with anatomy and where Internet access via any of Saudi Arabia's private ISPs goes through government filters that seek to maintain Islamic values.

The situation is even worse in other countries. The RSF report claimed that Internet access in Burma is available only through a state-run ISP and anyone who owns a computer must declare it to the government or face the possibility of a 15-year jail sentence if the machine is discovered. In Vietnam all Internet use has to be approved by the government through permits from the interior ministry and access is via state-run ISPs. And citizens of Iraq, Libya, North Korea, and Syria have no direct access to the Internet and even the official sites of the governments of these countries are maintained on servers overseas.

Pre-emptive legislation. More liberal administrations aim to reassert control by passing legislation which defines certain kinds of online activities as illegal, and then relying on the 'force of law' and the reluctance of ordinary citizens and ISP companies to become martyrs for liberty or freedom of speech to bring about the desired level of regulation. This is the approach favoured, for example, by the UK government, as demonstrated by its Regulation of Investigatory Powers Act 2000 (RIPA), which gives sweeping powers to the Home Secretary—that is, the minister of the interior—to intercept and read e-mail and other online traffic. RIPA gives the authorities the power to require an individual, on pain of imprisonment, to surrender the plaintext of an encrypted message or the key needed to decrypt it. A further provision makes it an offence punishable by five years in prison to reveal to a third party that she or he has been served with a decryption notice. The Act allows the Home Secretary to require ISPs to install a monitoring computer which is hardwired to a surveillance centre at MI5 headquarters, thereby enabling the authorities to gather *all* the bit traffic

flowing through the servers of bugged ISPs and, when armed with the appropriate statutory order, to read the text of messages encoded in those monitored packets. It also gives the authorities the power to monitor an individual's 'clickstream', that is, the log of sites visited by that person on the Web, without having to seek a warrant.

RIPA has been described by the Director of the Foundation for Information Policy Research as 'the most draconian Internet surveillance law in the world' (Naylor 2001: 58). But although it is a piece of domestic UK legislation, it raises a number of wider issues which are of general relevance.

First, the fact that such an illiberal measure passed through the UK Parliament with relatively little difficulty and virtually no public debate stunned the UK Internet community. What it highlighted was the extent of legislators' ignorance of the issues involved in Internet regulation and the lack of public awareness of what was at stake. This is likely to be a pattern for the future in relation to Internet regulation, in that governments—and, on occasion, industry lobbies—will seek to make pre-emptive legislative strikes ahead of public opinion and before civil society activists can raise public awareness. Environmental campaigners have long experience of this official strategy.

Second, RIPA highlights the extent to which the Internet community underestimated the efficacy of new legislation in achieving anti-libertarian ends. All a sovereign government has to do is to pass legislation which defines specified activities as illegal. Unless the proposed restrictions are widely perceived as intolerable by the populace, they will be adhered to by the vast majority of people and by all companies involved in the area. The fact that some activists may become conscientious objectors or that others will find ingenious technological fixes which circumvent or defeat the proposed restrictions counts for little in the grand scheme of things. Governments would have found it difficult to impose their will on the original Internet community of researchers, programmers, and libertarians because they were less susceptible to pressure and technically adept at circumventing repressive measures; but the metamorphosis of the Net into a mass medium has transformed the possibilities for regulation and official intimidation.

Third, RIPA highlights the fact that the ISP has become a key choke-point in regulatory terms. All Internet users have to go through a service provider in order to gain access to the Net. The vast majority of ISPs are private or public companies whose directors are obliged to obey the law and do their best to maximise shareholders' returns. This means that as corporate bodies they are disinclined to challenge legislation or legal action on principle. They see themselves as businesses and wish to be regarded, legally speaking, as common carriers rather than members of the Fourth Estate. Legislation such as RIPA which targets ISPs and requires them to cooperate with duly authorised surveillance measures is therefore likely to be very effective.

Fourth, RIPA is particularly revealing in the way it strikes at encryption: the technology that the Internet community has traditionally regarded as the ultimate guarantor of libertarian freedoms. Given that plain-text communications over the Net are intrinsically insecure, encryption is the only way of guaranteeing that private communications remain private. One could argue that, in the emerging online world, access to encryption tools becomes a basic human right and any infringement of that right must be circumscribed by law and a respect for the right to privacy enshrined in Article 8 of the European Convention on Human Rights and Fundamental Freedoms.

Historically, cryptography was something over which the state exerted total control. But the development of public key cryptography by university researchers in the 1980s created fresh waves of institutional paranoia about the subject (Levy 2000). The problem, as seen by governments, was that public key cryptography gave companies and private individuals access to strong encryption, with the result that law-enforcement, security, and surveillance services might therefore find themselves at a disadvantage with respect to the citizenry.

Most governments seem to have conceded that, technically speaking, the encryption genie has escaped from the bottle. In the Internet community this concession was interpreted as a historic victory. But such celebrations may be premature. RIPA suggests that instead of trying to crack codes surreptitiously governments will concentrate instead on putting legal pressure on individuals and companies. And the chances are that this approach will be highly effective: how many people will make a principled refusal to surrender a decryption key when the consequence of doing so is a two-year prison term?

The encryption issue is particularly important for civil society groups, some of which use the Net precisely as a way of short-circuiting or outflanking corporations and governments. Common sense suggests that they should encrypt their more sensitive communications. Yet doing so may leave them vulnerable to pressures under measures like RIPA. The old assumption—that strong encryption provided everyone with the only tool necessary to protect their privacy—has given way to the realisation that the tool has to be embedded in a politico-legal system which balances rights and responsibilities in some reasonable and accountable way.

The unexpectedly long arm of the law. The heady days when people believed that the Internet's transcendence of national boundaries would render it immune to conventional legal pressures is giving way to a more realistic appraisal of the power of legal codes to control online behaviour and to a more informed appraisal of the power of the nation state. As with encryption, the legal system seeks out critical points in the system and applies pressure on them. Once again, the ISP is a key target. In 2000, for example, a university teacher sued Demon Internet, a British ISP, because it had continued to relay Usenet news-groups in which allegedly defamatory comments about him were posted, despite previous complaints from him. Demon lost the case and then appealed, but withdrew from the appeal at the last minute, paid damages to the plaintiff—and established a legal precedent in the UK. This says that an ISP is legally bound to remove Usenet postings (or Web sites) if an individual alleges that material published therein is defamatory (Akdeniz 1999).

This has opened up an interesting can of worms; and the effects of this precedent are being felt already by campaigning civil society organisations. For example, a London pressure group campaigning for imaginative use of a disused power station castigated the new owners of the property for failing to proceed quickly with their plans for rejuvenating the building. A letter from the owners' solicitor to the ISP hosting the pressure group's Web site was sufficient to persuade the service provider to pull the site, 'just to be on the safe side'. Use of the law for purposes like this, which are essentially intimidatory, is certain to increase and is likely to cramp the freedoms of many campaigning organisations.

Other examples of the powers of national or international legislation to influence online behaviour include: the decision of a French court to require Yahoo!, an American company, to filter its auction sites selling Nazi memorabilia so that French Web users could not access them; new EU laws which enable European consumers to sue EU-based Internet sites in their own countries; the endorsement by the US of the Council of Europe's Cybercrime treaty, which aims to harmonise laws against hacking, online fraud, and child pornography; and the way the US Digital Millennium Copyright Act has been used to intimidate, for example, authorities at Oxford University into deleting the Web pages of a student who was pretending to publish on his site the code of DeCSS, a computer program written to enable DVD disks to be played on computers running the Linux operating system.

What these developments suggest is that the early heady rhetoric about the futility of attempts to apply geographically-based legal regulation to non-geographical online activities was unduly optimistic and complacent. The truth is that, as Goldsmith has argued, libertarians have tended to 'overstate the differences between cyberspace transactions and other transnational transactions' and to 'underestimate the potential of traditional legal tools and technology to resolve the multi-jurisdictional regulatory problems implicated by Cyberspace' (Goldsmith 1999). Or, as the Economist (2001: 27) puts it, 'The Internet could indeed become the most liberating technology since the printing press—but only if governments let it'.

The Politics of Architecture: The 'Invisible Hand' of E-Commerce

As we noted earlier, many of the features of the Internet which make it particularly conducive to civil society applications are a product of the network's technological architecture. But if the underlying architecture were to change, then its usefulness to civil society might be reduced. There are compelling reasons to suppose that the rapid development of e-business poses a major threat because online commerce requires modification of the existing 'permissive' architecture in ways that will make it a more controlled space.

The problem is that a space in which 'nobody knows you're a dog' is not an environment in which one can safely trade. E-commerce requires security, authentication, and confirmation of transactions. An online trader needs to know with whom he or she is dealing; messages and transactions have to be secure from surveillance and interference; contracts have to

be legally enforceable and incapable of arbitrary repudiation; ways have to be found for appending 'digital signatures' which have legal validity to electronic documents; and so on.

Technical solutions exist for all of these requirements, though many of them are currently rather clumsy. But the economic imperatives of online commerce are so urgent that significant improvements in the necessary protocols are under way. An entire new technical architecture to facilitate e-commerce is being created, in other words, ready to be grafted onto the older, libertarian architecture of the Net. And therein lies the danger.

The implication is that the Internet in 2005, say, could look very different from the Internet as it was in 1995. The old, libertarian layer will still exist, but a new layer—the e-commerce stratum—will sit above it. And the values implicit in the architecture of this new layer will be radically different from those embodied in the old one.

The key difference will be that the new layer will adapt the technical facilities of the old layer to eliminate anonymity and erode privacy. To understand how this will happen, you have to know something about how the Net operates. At present, every machine on the network has a unique address for the duration of its connection, and every transaction that machine conducts leaves a record. When an individual requests a Web page from a site, for example, the address of the requesting machine and the nature of its request are logged by the server. Anyone who runs a Web site can therefore find out the address of every machine which has accessed his or her site.[11] What they cannot ascertain, however, is the identity of the persons who initiated those accesses.

But the new e-commerce layer could change all that. It would enable sites, for example, to refuse access to people who refused—or were unable—to provide a digital signature authenticating their identity. Once admitted, everything those authenticated visitors did—which Web pages they viewed and for how long, which items they purchased, what they appeared to be most interested

---

[11] As noted earlier, computers attached to a local area network may access the Net via a single 'gateway' machine whose IP address is the one that will show up in server logs. But the principle of machine traceability remains because in general it will be possible to identify an individual machine from an examination of server and gateway logs of the kind that might be demanded during a legal discovery process.

in, and so on—can be logged against their real identities. And of course the information thus gathered could be sold or disclosed to other agencies—and all without the subjects' knowledge or consent. And because all the data gathered within such a layer would be in machine-readable form, it would be technologically and economically feasible to compile massive databases on the online behaviour of named individuals.

This possibility will be further reinforced by forthcoming changes to the Internet's address space. The explosive growth of the Net means that the world is rapidly running out of Internet addresses. Accordingly, a new version of the address protocol—IPv6—is now being implemented. This provides a vast address space but also includes a provision for an expanded IP number, part of which is the unique serial number of each computer's network-connection hardware, thereby making it possible in principle to track the online behaviour of every connected device.

The erosion of privacy implicit in such systems is an obvious danger. Less obvious, perhaps, is their potential for limiting access and widening the 'digital divide' between those who have a foothold in the new economy and those who do not. Apologists for the new e-commerce layer point out that nobody will be forced to have a digitally-authenticated signature and that they don't have to visit any site which requires one. True. Neither is there an obligation on anyone to have a credit card; but try renting a car or checking into an hotel nowadays without one.

Add to the authentication threat the provisions for digital copyright which the publishing industries are demanding from legislatures around the world, and one can see the makings of an Orwellian nightmare. When the Web first took off and it became easy to copy any text and distribute it globally, publishers—and in some cases authors—feared that it spelled ruination for them. It was, they argued, a charter for intellectual piracy, the equivalent of putting a photocopier and a printing press into every home. It hasn't turned out like that, but one can see why they were alarmed because, with an anonymous Net, everything they feared was technically possible.

But spool forward a few years and change the architecture and an entirely new scenario presents itself. Suddenly the balance of power has shifted. Every document published on the Web can be encrypted, so that only readers who have paid for a decryption key can access it. Alternatively, an unencrypted document can have a secret 'digital watermark' embedded in it, enabling publishers to tell at once whether a given digital copy is a legitimate, paid-for version or a pirated one. And even if the document is published free, unencrypted, and unmarked, on a Net where authentication protocols are in place the publisher could determine the precise identity of every single person who accesses the document online—and sell that information to other customers or abuse it in other ways. With such an architecture, the practice of anonymous reading—one of the great bulwarks of intellectual freedom—could be rendered impossible, at least in relation to online documents.

The inescapable implication is that cyberspace—the most open, uncensored and unregulated public space in human history—could easily become the most controlled environment imaginable. Or, to use Lessig's (1999*b*: 6) phrase, 'the invisible hand of cyberspace is building an architecture that is quite the opposite of what it was at cyberspace's birth. The invisible hand, through commerce, is constructing an architecture that perfects control'.

New Technologies—and New Possibilities?

The history of disruptive technologies—think of the automobile—is often one of ongoing dialectical struggle between technical innovation and social control. New developments create new possibilities, and with them new threats to the established order; there follows a period of chaos, innovation, and change while the old order is thrown into apparent disarray; then, after a burst of institutional reform and adaptation, a measure of social control is reasserted over the disruptive technology. And so the process goes on.

Looking at the Internet from this perspective, we can see a similar pattern. We are currently living through a period in which the established order, after a relatively brief period of denial and confusion, appears to be asserting control over the technology. But at the same time new technologies are emerging which may once again prove disruptive. Many of these technologies fall under the general banner of 'peer-to-peer' networking. To understand their potential significance, it's helpful to portray the development of the network in three phases. Let us call them Internet 1.0, 2.0, and 3.0.

Internet 1.0

From its inception in 1983 to about 1994, the entire Internet had a single model of connectivity. There were relatively few dial-up connections. Machines were assumed to be always on, always connected, and assigned permanent IP addresses. The Domain Name System (DNS)—the system which relates domain names like www.cnn.com to a specific Internet address (in this case 207.25.71.30)—was designed for this environment, where a change in IP address was assumed to be abnormal and rare, and could take days to propagate through the system. Because machines had persistent connections and fixed addresses, every machine on the network could function as a server. It was a genuine network of *peers*, that is, machines of equal status.

Internet 2.0

The World Wide Web was invented at CERN by Tim Berners-Lee in 1990, but the first popular Web browser was *Mosaic*, created at the National Center for Supercomputing Applications at the University of Illinois in 1993. With the appearance of *Mosaic* and the subsequent appearance of the Netscape browser in 1994, Web use began to grow very rapidly (Naughton 2000: 248) and a different connectivity model began to appear. To run a Web browser, a PC needed to be connected to the Internet over a modem, with its own IP address. This created a second class of connectivity because PCs did not have persistent connections and would enter and leave the network frequently and unpredictably.

Furthermore, because there were not enough unique IP addresses available to handle the sudden demand generated by *Mosaic* and Netscape, ISPs began to assign IP addresses dynamically, giving each PC a new, temporary IP address for the duration of each dial-up session. A subscriber might therefore be assigned a different IP address every time she logged on to the Net. This instability prevented PCs from having DNS entries and therefore precluded their users from hosting any data or Net-facing applications locally, that is, from functioning as servers. They were essentially clients: machines which requested services (files, Web pages, and so on) from servers.

For a few years, the connectivity model based on treating PCs as dumb clients worked tolerably well. Indeed, it was probably the only model that was feasible at the time. Personal computers had not been designed to be part of the fabric of the Internet, and in the early days of the Web the hardware and unstable operating systems of the average PC made it unsuitable for server functions.

Internet 2.0 is still the model underpinning the Internet as we use it today. It is essentially a two-tier networked world made up of a minority of 'privileged' machines—servers within the DNS system with persistent, high-speed connections and fixed IP addresses—providing services to a vast number of dial-up machines which are essentially second-class citizens because they cannot function as servers and have an IP address only for the duration of their connection to the Net. Such a world is, as we have seen, potentially vulnerable to governmental and corporate control for, if everything has to happen via a privileged server and servers are easy to identify, then they can be targeted for legal and other kinds of regulation.

Internet 3.0: a distributed Peer-to-Peer network?

Internet 2.0 made sense in the early days of the Web. But since then the supposedly 'dumb' PCs connected to the Net have become immeasurably more powerful and the speed and quality of Internet connections have steadily improved, at least in the industrialised world. On the software side, not only have proprietary operating systems improved but the Open Source—that is, free—software movement has produced increasingly powerful operating systems (for example, Linux) and industrial-strength server software (for example, the Apache Web server program which powers over half the world's Web sites even on commercial servers). As a result, it has become increasingly absurd to think of PCs equipped in this way as second-class citizens.

It is also very wasteful to use such powerful machines simply as life-support systems for a Web browser. The computing community realised quite quickly that the unused resources existing behind the veil of second-class connectivity might be worth harnessing. According to Shirky (2001: 23), the world's Net-connected PCs presently possess an aggregate 10 billion MHz of processing power and 10,000 terabytes (trillions of bytes) of storage. And this is a conservative estimate because it assumes only 100 million PCs among the net's 300 plus million users, and only a 100 MHz processor and 100 Mb drive on the average PC.

Early attempts to harness these distributed resources were projects like SETI@Home (URL) in which PCs around the globe analysed astronomical data as a background task when they were connected to the Net. More radical attempts to harness the power of the network's second-class citizens have been grouped under the general heading of 'peer-to-peer' (P2P) networking. This is an unsatisfactory term because, strictly speaking, the servers within the DNS system have always interacted on a peer-to-peer basis, but it has been taken up by the mass media and is likely to stick.

The best available definition of P2P is Shirky's description of it as 'resource-centric addressing for unstable environments'. In this view:

P2P is a class of applications that takes advantage of resources—storage, processing cycles, content, human presence—available at the edges of the Internet. Because accessing these decentralized resources means operating in an environment of unstable connectivity and unpredictable IP addresses, P2P nodes must operate outside the DNS system and have significant or total autonomy from central servers. (Shirky 2001: 22)

The most widely-known P2P application to date is Napster (see Box 6.1). Although Napster may fade away following its failure to win the legal battle over the propriety of its service, it has served as a seminal influence in several ways. First, it triggered a realisation that PCs on the periphery of the Net might be capable of more ambitious things than merely requesting Web pages from servers. Second, it overturned the publishing model of Internet 2.0: the idea that content had always to be obtained from the magic circle within the DNS system. Instead Napster pointed to a radically different model, which Shirky (2000) calls 'content at the edges'. The current content-at-the-centre model, he writes, 'has one significant flaw: most Internet content is created on the PCs at the edges, but for it to become universally accessible, it must be pushed to the center, to always-on, always-up Web servers. As anyone who has ever spent time trying to upload material to a Web site knows, the Web has made downloading trivially easy, but uploading is still needlessly hard'.

Napster relied on several networking innovations to get around these limitations. First, it dispensed with uploading and left the files on the PCs, merely brokering requests from one PC to another: the MP3 files did not have to travel through any central Napster server; second, PCs running Napster did not need a fixed Internet address or a permanent connection to use the service; and third, it ignored the reigning paradigm of client and server. Napster made no distinction between the two functions: if you could receive files from other people, they could receive files from you as well.

Finally, Napster pointed the way to a networking architecture which re-invents the PC as a hybrid client-plus-server while relegating the DNS-governed centre of the Internet, where all the action had hitherto taken place, to nothing but brokering connections.

Because of its reliance on a central server, Napster proved vulnerable to legal measures. But other, genuinely distributed P2P technologies now exist which may be less susceptible to challenge. Gnutella (URL), Freenet (URL), and Publius (URL), for example, are three file-distribution systems which use the resources of machines at the edge of the Internet to store and exchange files without relying on any centralised resource.[12]

From a civil society perspective, Publius (Waldman, Cranor, and Rubin 2001) is particularly interesting. It is a Web publishing system designed to be very resistant to censorship and to provide publishers with a high degree of anonymity. It was originally developed by programmers working for AT&T and named after the pen name used by the authors of the Federalist Papers: Alexander Hamilton, John Jay, and James Madison. This collection of 85 articles, published pseudo-nymously in New York State newspapers in 1787–88, was influential in persuading New York voters to ratify the proposed United States constitution.

Publius encrypts and fragments documents, then randomly places the pieces, or keys, on to the servers of volunteers in a variety of locations worldwide. The volunteers have no way of knowing what information is being stored on their servers. Software users configure their browser to use a proxy, which will bring the pieces of the document back together. Only a few keys out of many possibilities are needed to reconstruct a document. The inventors of the system claim that even if 70 per cent of the Publius sites are shut down, the content is still accessible. Only the publisher is able to remove or alter the information (Waldman, Cranor, and Rubin 2001: 153).

It is impossible to know at this stage whether P2P technologies will indeed 'turn the Internet inside out', as (Shirky 2000) has put it. But they already offer potentially powerful tools to groups which are interested in the free exchange of ideas and files online, especially if those ideas or files are likely to be controversial. Rubin, for example, has declared that his greatest hope is that Publius will become an instrument for free speech, a tool that could enable dissidents living under oppressive governments to speak out without fear of detection or punishment

(quoted in Shreve 2000). Having said that, we must remember that, as ever, technology is a necessary but not sufficient condition for liberation. The benefits of P2P will not be evenly distributed. It will work for groups in countries that are neither too poor nor too completely totalitarian to allow some access. Thus, P2P has potential for Singapore and Malaysia but much less for, say, Zimbabwe or North Korea. Libertarianism may have discovered a new tool kit. But economic, social, political, and cultural factors will determine who gets to use it.

Conclusion

This chapter has argued that the Internet offers valuable facilities to global civil society and has shown that these facilities have been imaginatively used by many groups outside the corporate and governmental worlds to foster understanding and action on human rights, sustainable development, the environment, and other important issues. We have also seen that the democratising potential of the Net is undermined by the digital divide and that the chasm between the 'information rich' in the industrialised countries and the 'information poor' in the rest of the world is alarmingly wide. What this means is that measures to understand and redress the imbalance ought to be an integral part of debates on economic, social, and cultural development.

Thus far, global civil society has been almost entirely instrumental in its attitudes to the Internet. It has assumed that the network is a 'given' and that the only challenge is to make effective use of it. This view is profoundly misguided. The Internet is the way it is—open, permissive, uncontrolled by governments and corporations—because of the values embodied in its technical architecture. These values resonate with those of global civil society. But there are powerful forces, representing very different values, which are pressing to change the architecture to make the system much more closed and controllable. Such changes would be disastrous for those who seek to use the Net for informing, communicating, and campaigning against governmental and corporate power. The danger is that civil society groups might one day discover that the network has evolved into something less congenial to their needs and purposes.

In some ways, what we are discovering is not how different cyberspace is from the real world but how

---

[12] Oram (2001) contains useful articles by developers of all three systems.

alike the two spaces are. Many of the tensions between civil society and corporate and governmental power that characterise the real world are beginning to manifest themselves in the virtual one. And this is true not just in relation to security, surveillance, control, and intellectual property but also in terms of software and infrastructure. It is vital, for example, to ensure that the Internet continues to be based on open, non-proprietary protocols and that companies like Microsoft are not allowed to leverage their market power to dominate the system. And it is important to realise that the values which drive the Open Source movement resonate powerfully with the values which motivate civil society groups (Di Bona, Ockman, and Stone 1999; Bollier 1999).

Mitch Kapor, one of the founders of the Electronic Frontier Foundation, articulated an important truth in his famous observation that 'architecture is politics' (Kapor 1990). So it is. And so too is software because that is the material from which the Internet is constructed. Global civil society has a vital stake in ensuring that the values which shaped the original Internet remain at the heart of its evolving architecture. The struggle to keep it open, free, permissive, and uncontrolled is too important to be left just to geeks and engineers.

References

Akdeniz, Y. (1999). 'Case Analysis: Laurence Godfrey v. Demon Internet Limited'. *Journal of Civil Liberties*, 4: 260–7.

Arnett, Elsa C. (1999). 'Seattle Protests Put a New Activism in Play'. *San Jose Mercury News*, 3 December. Available at http://www. /globalexchange.org/wto/sjmerc120399.html

Barlow, John Perry (1996). A Declaration of the Independence of Cyberspace. http:// www.eff.org/~barlow/Declaration-Final.html

—, Birkerts, Sven, Kelly, Kevin, and Slouka, Mark (1995). 'What are we doing online?'. *Harper's*, August.

Bollier, David (1999). 'The Power of Openness: A Critique and a Proposal for the H2O Project'. Available at http://www.opencode.org/h2o/, 10 March.

BSE. http://www.bse.org.uk

Case, Alyssa (1999). 'The Role of the Internet in Human Rights Development' (M. Phil. dissertation). Cambridge: Centre for International Studies, University of Cambridge.

Derechos Human Rights. http://www.derechos.org /human-rights/manual.htm

Di Bona, Chris, Ockman, Sam, and Stone, Mark (eds) (1999). *Open Sources: Voices from the Open Source Revolution*. Sebastapol: O'Reilly and Associates.

Economist (2001). 'The Internet and the Law: Stop Signs on the Web'. 13 January.

FAST. http://www.amnestyusa.org/stoptorture/ fast/fastindex.html

Freenet. http://www.freenet.sourceforge.net

Gilmore, John (1996). *New York Times*, 15 January.

GreenNet, 'The Civil Society Internet Charter'. http://www.gn.apc.org/action/csir/charter.html.

Goldsmith, Jack L. (1999). 'Against Cyberanarchy'. University of Chicago Law School, Occasional Paper No. 40, August 13. Available at http:// www.law.uchicago.edu/Publications/Occasional/ 40.html

Gnutella. http://www.gnutella.wego.com

Google. http://www.google.com

Hafner, Katie and Lyon, Matthew (1996). *Where Wizards Stay Up Late: The Origins of the Internet*, New York: Simon and Schuster.

International Telecommunications Union (1998). http://www.itu.int/sg3focus/teledensityA.htm

Introna, Lucas and Nissenbaum, Helen (2000). 'The Public Good Vision of the Internet and the Politics of Search Engines', in Richard Rogers (ed.), *Preferred Placement: Knowledge Politics on the Web*. Maastricht: Jan Van Eyck Editions.

IRC. http://www.mirc.com/irc.html

Kapor, Mitch (1990), 'The Software Design Manifesto', Available online at http:// www.kei.com/homepages/mkapor/Software_ Design_Manifesto.html

Kestemont, B. (1998). 'Best Environmental Directories', available at http://www.ulb.ac.be/ceese/meta/cds.html

Kobrin, Stephen (1998). 'The MAI and the Clash of Globalizations'. *Foreign Policy*, 112/Fall.

Kollock, Peter and Smith, Marc A. (1999). 'Communities in Cyberspace', in Marc A. Smith and Peter Kollock (eds), *Communities in Cyberspace*. London: Routledge.

Lessig, Lawrence (1999*a*). 'Open Code and Open Societies: The Values of Internet Governance' (1999 Sibley Lecture, 16 February). Athens: University of Georgia.

— (1999*b*). *Code and Other Laws of Cyberspace*. New York: Basic Books.

Levy, Stephen (2000). *Crypto: Secrecy and Privacy in the New Code War*. London: Allen Lane.

Miller, Daniel and Slater, Don (2000). *The Internet: An Ethnographic Approach*. Oxford: Oxford University Press.

Mitchell, William (1995). 'Public Life in Electropolis: Dialog on Virtual Communities'. http:// www. feedmag.com/95.08dialog/95.08dialog1.html

Naughton, John (2000). *A Brief History of the Future: The Origins of the Internet*. London: Phoenix.

Naylor, Lisa (2001). 'The Wrong Arm of the Law'. *The Industry Standard Europe*, 8/ March: 58–9.

Nua Internet Surveys. http://www.nua.ie

OneWorld. http://www.oneworld.net/about/ partnership_principles.shtml

Oram, Andy (ed.) (2001). *Peer-to-Peer: Harnessing the Power of Disruptive Technologies*. Sebastapol: O'Reilly and Associates.

Peizer, Jonathan (2000). 'Bridging The Digital Divide: First You Need The Bridge'. http://www.mediachannel.org/views/oped/ peizer.shtml, 21 June.

The Pew Internet and American Life Project. http://www.pewinternet.org/reports/ chart.asp?img=6_daily_activities.jpg

Publius. http://www.publius.cdt.org

Reporters Sans Frontières (2000). 'The Enemies of the Internet'. http://www.rsf.fr/uk/html/internet/ennemis.html

Rheingold, Howard (1995). 'Public Life in Electropolis: Dialog on Virtual Communities'. http://www.feedmag.com/95.08dialog/ 95.08dialog1.html

SETI@Home. http://www.setiathome.ssl. berkeley.edu

Shayler, David. http://www.guardianunlimited.co.uk/shayler/

Shirky, Clay (2000) 'Content Shifts to the Edges'. http://www.shirky.com/writings/content.html, April.

— (2001). 'Listening to Napster', in Andy Oram (ed.), *Peer-to-Peer: Harnessing the Power of Disruptive Technologies*. Sebastapol: O'Reilly and Associates.

Shreve, Jenn (2000). 'Avi Rubin: Publius' Public Crusade'. *The Industry Standard*, 13 September. Available at http://www.thestandard.com/ article/0,1902,18487,00.html

Stanford Center for Internet and Society (2000). 'The Policy Implications of End-to-End', 1 December. Proceedings available online at http://lawschool.stanford.edu/e2e/

UNDP (1999). *Human Development Report 1999*. New York: United Nations.

Waldman, Marc, Cranor, Lorrie Faith, and Rubin, Avi (2001). 'Publius', in Andy Oram (ed.), *Peer-to-Peer: Harnessing the Power of Disruptive Technologies*. Sebastapol: O'Reilly and Associates.

Wellman, Barry and Milena, Gulia (1999). 'Virtual Communities as Communities', in Marc A. Smith and Peter Kollock (eds), *Communities in Cyberspace*. London: Routledge.

CHAPTER 7

PARALLEL SUMMITS OF GLOBAL CIVIL SOCIETY

Mario Pianta

The Rise of Summits

In recent decades supranational decision-making has greatly expanded, both as a result of the formal transfer of power to old and new inter-governmental organisations, such as the European Union and the World Trade Organisation (WTO), and because of the emergence of *informal* supranational powers through inter-state agreements or cooperation, such as the G7/G8.

This new supranational decision-making power has remained hidden and unaccountable to democratic processes, and exercised largely by specialised government officials and international 'technocrats'. Its most visible side has become, in the last two decades, a model of high-profile collective action on global issues by states and inter-governmental organisations: the international summit.

Summits represent an important institutional innovation in the world system, combining the legitimacy of supranational organisations, the flexibility of informal meetings of states, and public displays of concern and action on current global problems. Summits have become more frequent and influential, with far-reaching policy consequences at the national level. In a world dominated by media and instant communication, where global problems are immediately visible everywhere, summits are often the media-oriented events which 'show' that the powers-that-be are addressing them. Moreover, they are the visible part of the growing *informal* decision-making power on supranational issues.

Summits are now a key element of the emerging governance system of an increasingly globalised world; they have widely differing natures, but their roles and activities include the following tasks, many of which may be combined in the same summit.

Framing the issue. Summits define the issues of supranational relevance. The United Nations Conference on Environment and Development in Rio de Janeiro in 1992 has defined the nature of, and solutions to, environmental problems as we understand them.

Rule-making. Summits define the rules for national policies in internationally relevant fields, from security to trade, from the environment to new technologies. The World Trade Organisation (WTO) conference in Singapore in 1998 has defined the rules of a new liberalised trading system.

Policy guidelines. Summits define the direction to be taken by policies at the national level. The decisions of the International Monetary Fund (IMF) on financial rules and lending have directed national policies towards deregulation of financial flows, privatisation of public enterprises, and reduction of social expenditure.

Enforcement. Summits may make decisions with major effects on individual countries, especially less powerful ones. G8 summits regularly address major international crises and agree on action to be taken against particular countries, such as diplomatic pressure, embargoes, or military action, often ignoring the legitimate body for addressing international crises, the Security Council of the United Nations.

It could be argued that this is what inter-governmental cooperation has always been supposed to do. But what is new in recent decades is the extension in the range of issues addressed by summits; the greater policy impact of their decisions; their frequency, which makes them a part of institutionalised decision-making; and their high media profile, in contrast to secretive diplomacy. In short, they are a crucial part of the shift in the balance of power from national to international decision-making. While there may be good reasons for transferring power to the supranational level in order to address increasingly global problems, this shift is not unproblematic.

The range of activities carried out by summits spans the prerogatives of political power that have historically emerged in states. But what is missing is the democratic process that developed at the state level in order to extend participation and representation of citizens and social groups, and legitimise the decisions taken. In fact, the officials attending summits are either professional diplomats or—mostly unelected—government officials.

Moreover, the rules and nature of most summits, with the partial exception of the UN, reflect a strong imbalance of power among states, with rich Western countries, especially the United States, dominating many decision-making processes. While summits' decisions always follow, at least indirectly, from actions of governments, which are supposed to be accountable to their citizens, most summits fail the test of democratic legitimacy. This is true both of the distribution of power among the players involved—the governments of countries included or excluded from decisions—and of the relationship between decision-makers, society, citizens, and more generally those affected by the decisions taken (see Strange 1996; Archibugi, Held, and Koehler 1998).

The proliferation and the new power of summits raise problems not only of method—democracy and legitimisation—but also of content. What are the issues discussed at summits, and what are the strategies pursued by states, inter-governmental organisations, and other key actors?

The rise of summits is associated with the globalisation process and reflects contrasting projects of globalisation. Two main ones can be identified: first, the model of *neo-liberal globalisation;* and second, the model of *globalisation of rights and responsibilities.*

The project of neo-liberal globalisation has emerged as the dominant force in supranational decision-making and has shaped many of the changes in global economic and political issues, as well as the agenda of many summits, namely, those of the G7/G8, the WTO, the IMF, and World Bank meetings. As Richard Falk puts it, 'the characteristic policy vectors of neo-liberalism involve such moves as liberalisation, privatisation, minimising economic regulation, rolling back welfare, reducing expenditures on public goods, tightening fiscal discipline, favoring freer flows of capital, strict controls on organised labor, tax reductions and unrestricted currency repatriation', amounting to a form of 'predatory globalisation' (Falk 1999: 2).

Unregulated markets, dominated by multinational corporations and private financial institutions, mostly based in the West, have been the driving force of economic growth and international integration, reducing the space for autonomous state policies in most fields. We could argue that neo-liberal globalisation has institutionalised the overwhelming power of economic mechanisms—markets and firms—over human rights, political projects, social needs, and

environmental priorities. It is no surprise that in recent decades political activity has lost much of its relevance and appeal; social inequalities have become dramatic; and the environmental crisis has deepened (see UNRISD 1995; UNDP 1999; Chomsky 1999).

The political framework for neo-liberal globalisation was prepared in the early 1980s by the policies of Margaret Thatcher in Britain and Ronald Reagan in the United States. In the aftermath of the collapse of the Soviet system in 1989–90, building on an unrivalled military supremacy, political power, and cultural dominance, the neo-liberal project of globalisation has become the new face of the hegemony of the United States.

A second important project of *globalisation of rights and responsibilities* has emerged with efforts to bring about a universalisation of human, political, and social rights and to face the responsibilities that countries, governments, and peoples have towards emerging global problems. Such a project has largely shaped the agenda of UN summits on human rights, the environment, women, food, and the International Criminal Court. It has led to declarations of principles, opened up democratic processes, influenced national policies, and promoted inter-state cooperation in these fields at the global or regional level (Europe is a major example).

The *neo-liberal* project and that based on *rights and responsibilities* point in alternative directions that the process of globalisation may take. The latter has built on key shared values, framing the issues of global concern and stressing the need for appropriate global regulations. So far, however, it is the former which has set the rules for the global economy and has had a dominant influence on policy-making around the world.

The Reaction of Global Civil Society

Few states have resisted the sweeping changes of globalisation, and most policy responses by governments have aimed at increasing national advantage in the new global setting. State-centred politics and the activities of established political forces have remained largely confined within the horizon of nation states.

However, governments and inter-governmental organisations are not the only actors on the global scene. Economic forces and firms have played a key role in the project of neo-liberal globalisation.

Conversely, resistance to these developments and alternative projects have emerged in the sphere of civil society, whose activities have become increasingly international. For the purposes of this chapter, the emerging global civil society has to be conceptualised, with all its ambiguities and blurred images, as the sphere of cross-border relations and collective activities outside the international reach of states and markets.

Key players in the emerging global civil society have been the social movements and networks of organisations active on international issues. Their origins lie in the social movements developed around the themes of peace, human rights, solidarity, development, ecology, and women's issues. Starting with their own specific issues, they have developed an ability to address problems of a global nature, build information networks, stage actions, find self-organised solutions across national borders, interacting also in original ways with the new sites of supranational power (see Lipschutz 1992; Keck and Sikkink 1998; Waterman, 1998; Della Porta, Kriesi, and Rucht 1999; Florini 2000; Cohen and Rai 2000; O'Brien *et al.* 2000).

Originating in poorly organised social movements, and addressing the most pressing issues of the time, strong civil society organisations that are increasingly engaged in international activities have emerged in most countries. Despite extreme heterogeneity and fragmentation, much of the activity in the sphere of global civil society consists of what Richard Falk (1999: 130) has termed *'globalisation from below'*, a project whose 'normative potential is to conceptualise widely shared world order values: minimising violence, maximising economic well-being, realising social and political justice, and upholding environmental quality'.

While the values embodied in global civil society remain a long way from representing a coherent alternative, they have been powerful enough to confront the dominant visions of global order, resisting the project of neo-liberal globalisation and influencing the project of globalisation of rights and responsibilities. This chapter examines these interactions by focusing on the challenges posed by global civil society to the most visible sites of supranational decision making: international summits.

The Invention of Parallel Summits

In order to confront the new power of summits of states and inter-governmental organisations, civil society organisations have invented parallel summits, events which could challenge the legitimacy of government summits, confront official delegates, give visibility to the emerging global civil society, resist neo-liberal policies, and propose alternative solutions to global problems. Parallel summits are defined here as events:

- organised by national and international civil society groups with international participation, independently of the activities of states and firms;
- coinciding with or related to official summits of governments and international institutions (with few major exceptions);
- addressing the same fundamental problems as official summits, with a critical perspective on government and business policies;
- using the means of public information and analysis, political mobilisation and protest, and alternative policy proposals; and
- with or without formal contacts with the official summits.

This chapter focuses on the past 20 years. But government summits and international civil society conferences are as old as globalisation itself. Charnovitz (1997) has shown that, from the late nineteenth century to the 1920s, the establishment of supranational bodies such as the League of Nations and of scores of inter-governmental organisations was accompanied by equally flourishing international non-governmental organisations and civil society conferences. At several official summits and in the operation of the League of Nations, civil society groups were often able to articulate proposals on a wide range of themes including peace, national liberation, and economic, social, and women's rights; in some cases they were even involved in official activities, opening the way for the formal recognition of NGOs in the Charter of the United Nations in 1945.

During most of the cold war years the space for international civil society activities was constrained and shaped by state power and policies. The international mobilisation of civil society mainly took the form of trying to influence government policies on decolonisation, national self-determination, peace, human rights, development, and the environment. The political movements of the 1960s and 1970s challenged the political and economic order at the national and the international levels with a transformative perspective still focused on state power. A major exception was the rise of the women's movement, which opened the way for new forms of politics, social practices, and culture based on identity (see Arrighi, Hopkins, and Wallerstein 1989).

In the 1980s the new social movements on peace, ecology, and feminism gave new directions to the pressure for change of previous decades. They concentrated on specific issues which had to do less with state power and more with global challenges, often marked by a lack of adequate supranational institutions.

The rapid growth of NGOs turned the movements' advocacy into practical projects and alternative policy proposals, demanding a voice in existing global forums. NGOs have found a substantial opening in the UN system, in ECOSOC, and other activities. However, this official recognition of civil society work at the international level has led to very modest results in terms of visibility, relevance, and impact on the operation of the international system (see Gordenker and Weiss 1995, and the contributions in the same special issue of *Third World Quarterly;* Otto 1996; Lotti and Giandomenico 1996).

A new wave of state summits began in the mid-1970s, spurred by far-reaching political change—East-West détente, the completion of decolonisation, and a new attention to human rights—and by economic developments—the end of the Bretton Woods international monetary system, the oil shocks, and the emergence of the North-South divide. Existing intergovernmental organisations, starting with the UN, played a renewed and broader role, and other forums were established; the first G5 meeting was held in 1975.

As global issues and supranational decision-making power became increasingly important, attention and action by civil society also increased. Moving on from traditional efforts to put pressure on nation-states, attention started to focus on global problems and on the failure of states to address them in events such as summits. Symbolic actions, at first small in scale and poorly organised, were followed by more systematic international work by civil society organisations, resulting in explicit challenges to the legitimacy and policies of summits. The evolution of modern parallel summits is summarised below.

1980–1987: The pioneering years

Each global issue has its own history of antecedents to parallel summits. Several streams of activism have monitored and flanked UN meetings on the environment, development, women, and human rights since the 1970s. In 1972 the UN Conference on the Human Environment held in Stockholm saw the participation of a few hundreds NGOs active both inside and outside the official meeting (Conca 1995). In 1975 the First World Conference on Women held in Mexico City launched the UN Decade for Women, and was followed by one in 1980 in Copenhagen and another one 1985 in Nairobi; in all events large NGO forums were held (Alter Chen 1995). Global summits of this type, with the UN system and states allowing some room for civil society voices, were possible because of the urgency of environmental problems and of the women's movement demands, and because these issues did not challenge the cold war ideologies of the time.

On the more controversial political and economic issues, civil society had to organise its international activities independently of the operation of states, the UN, and other international institutions. So the peace movement in 1981 started to organise the European Nuclear Disarmament Conventions. Public opinion tribunals were regularly held on peace, human, economic, and social rights since the one on War Crimes in Vietnam organised by Bertrand Russell in 1967 (see Box 7.1).

The first gathering of The Other Economic Summit (TOES) to coincide with a G7 meeting was organised in 1984 by the New Economics Foundation of London, in association with the Right Livelihood Awards, a sort of 'alternative Nobel Prize' which has been awarded since 1980. At first small conferences and media events, with a strong alternative development and environmental focus, TOES have since been regularly organised in cooperation with different international networks and civil society coalitions of the country hosting the G7 summit.

1988–1991: The political transition

After the first small-scale initiatives, a major change occurred in 1988 at the IMF-World Bank meeting in West Berlin, where the German and European New Left organised alternative conferences and a street demonstration with 80,000 people (Gerhards and Rucht 1992). Also, an international People's Tribunal

Denouncing major violations of human rights to world public opinion has long been the aim of public opinion tribunals. They rarely coincide with official summits or with visible decision making by the powers responsible for such violations. They do not involve large conferences or street demonstrations. Still, they have played an important role in behaving *as if* a global civil society existed, with the moral authority to identify and judge major problems not addressed by international law.

The first important Tribunal was that against war crimes in Vietnam, established in 1967 by the British philosopher and peace leader Bertrand Russell, and chaired by French philosopher Jean Paul Sartre. Modelled on the principles used in the Nuremberg Trials against Nazi war criminals, with judges chosen from prominent international lawyers and civil society figures, it held sessions in Stockholm and Roskilde in May and November 1967. In the midst of worldwide opposition to the Vietnam war, it provided evidence of war crimes and influenced public opinion.

Many years later, the Italian Socialist politician Lelio Basso, who had authored the final report on Vietnam, established the Russell Tribunal II on Latin America, in order to denounce human rights violations by military regimes in Brazil, Chile, and other Latin American countries. The new Tribunal held three sessions in Rome, Brussels, and Rome again between 1974 and 1976. In the latter session, it was proposed to make the Tribunal a permanent body, called the *Permanent Peoples' Tribunal,* based on a 'Universal Declaration of the Rights of Peoples' launched in Algiers in 1976, and it was finally established in 1979 by the Lelio Basso International Foundation for the rights and liberation of peoples in Rome.

Since its foundation, the Tribunal has met 29 times, involving dozens of judges selected from well-known experts and Nobel laureates (among them Elmar Altvater, Antonio Cassese, Richard Falk, Ruth First, Eduardo Galeano, Sean MacBride, Adolfo Peres Esquivel, Francois Rigaux, George Wald). The Tribunal examines cases of violation of rights of individuals and peoples, raised by civil society groups, where there is a lack of appropriate protection from international law (see Fondazione Internazionale Lelio Basso 1998). The sessions of the Tribunal have included:

- questions of national liberation (Western Sahara, 1979; Eritrea, 1980; East Timor, 1981);
- foreign aggressions (Afghanistan I, 1981 and II, 1982; Nicaragua, 1984);

- issues of internal democratic self-determination (Argentina, 1980; Philippines, 1980; El Salvador, 1981; Zaire, 1982; Guatemala, 1983);
- general human rights issues (the Armenian genocide, 1984; Puerto Rico, 1989; Brazilian Amazon, 1990; Latin America, 1991; Tibet, 1992; the conquest of the Americas, 1992; asylum rights in Europe; children's rights, 1995; two sessions on the States of former Yugoslavia, 1995; children's rights in Brazil, 1999); and
- economic, social, and environmental rights (two sessions on the IMF and the World Bank, in coincidence with their summits in West Berlin in 1988 and Madrid in 1994; two sessions on the Bhopal case, 1992, 1994; Chernobyl, 1996; the rights of textile workers, 1998; Elf in Africa; transnational corporations and human rights, 2000).

Evolution is evident, from problems associated to peoples' rights to self-determination in the post-colonial world to attention to human, social, and economic rights endangered by the national and supranational powers, challenged also by parallel summits.

A similar Public Opinion Tribunal was organised in December 2000 in Tokyo by the Women's International War Crimes Tribunal 2000 concerning Japanese military sexual slavery in Asian countries in the 1930s and 1940s. It considered the criminal liability of the Japanese political and military authorities, and the responsibility of the state of Japan for rape and sexual slavery as crimes against humanity. Close to 500 people, mainly women from Asian and Pacific countries, including surviving victims, participated to the Tribunal; it was preceded by a hearing on crimes against women in recent wars in all continents and by symbolic demonstrations in Japan and Germany. The Japanese government was invited to participate, but did not attend the trial, which obtained considerable media attention. The Tokyo Tribunal was important for its well-organised ability to break a decade-old silence on Asian 'comfort women' and to highlight the gender dimension of international justice.

The symbolic nature of the Tribunals can be seen as a prophetic anticipation of the creation in 1998 of the Statute for an International Criminal Court, which may in future investigate and genuinely prosecute the kinds of cases that were formerly raised by Public Opinion Tribunals.

was held on the responsibilities of the IMF and World Bank for the underdevelopment of the South.

This was a major development in the political experiences of social movements, as the left movements of the 1970s and 1980s made the key institutions of globalisation the objects of their protest. For large numbers of activists previously involved in radical politics or in the peace and ecological movements of the 1980s, this attention to global issues represented a key turning point.

The next step was the development of international networks. A major advance occurred in 1990 alongside the meeting of the IMF and World Bank. At the parallel summit organised by the Bank Information Center in Washington, for the first time civil society organisations of North and South worked together on how to resist IMF and World Bank policies. This cooperation, with various degrees of intensity and effective integration, has since been a continuing characteristic of parallel summits.

The end of the cold war and the dissolution of the Soviet system created a great opening for such events, and several initiatives were taken by the emerging global civil society. In the arena of peace, a parallel summit challenged the *raison d'être* of NATO at its 40th anniversary celebration in Rome in 1989. In these years, the last Conventions for European Nuclear Disarmament took place, independently of official political or military summits, and the first meetings of the Helsinki Citizens Assembly occurred (see Box 7.2). They brought together peace and human rights activists from eastern and western Europe, and developed an alternative agenda to the nationalist revival which later led to tragic wars in the Balkans and in the republics of the former Soviet Union (see Kaldor 1999; Marcon and Pianta 2001). Similar developments took place on the environmental front, and on other specific issues, linking past mobilisations to current challenges on a global scale.

1992–1995: The institutional expansion

The strongest development of parallel summits has emerged with the large UN thematic conferences of the early 1990s, designed to chart the agenda for the twenty-first century on issues of increasing global relevance, focusing on the universalisation of rights.

The 1992 Rio Conference on Environment and Development and the parallel summit taking the form of an NGO Forum were unprecedented in their size, media resonance, and long-term impact on ideas and

policies, and for the emergence of a global civil society involved in building networks, developing joint strategies, and confronting states and international institutions (see Conca 1995; Van Rooy 1997).

In 1993 the UN conference on human rights in Vienna saw the participation of thousands of civil society activists, and addressed a key issue, long neglected by states in the cold war (see Gaer 1995; Smith, Pagnucco, and Lopez 1998). In 1994 the Cairo conference on population led civil society groups to forge new links on the conditions of women, families, and societies in the North and South.

Finally, 1995 was a crucial year for the emergence of global civil society. The Copenhagen Conference on Social Development and the Beijing conference on Women, both with sizeable NGO forums integrated in the official programme, were points of no return for the visibility, relevance, and mobilisation of global civil society. Several thousand NGOs participated to the events in Copenhagen and Beijing, gaining attention from official delegations, influencing the agenda and the final documents, and—equally important—becoming involved in large-scale civil society networks. The key issue of the Social Development conference was the need to combine economic growth with improvements in social conditions; its policy implications were clearly at odds with the neo-liberal prescriptions to contain social expenditure and public action. The Conference on Women addressed many aspects of women's conditions in North and South, including gender roles, family structures, reproductive rights, and social and economic activities; it called for a wide range of actions, from individual self-help to international commitments by states (on environmental, social, and women's issues, see the case studies in Keck and Sikkink 1998; Florini 2000; Cohen and Rai 2000; O'Brien *et al.*, 2000; and Uvin 1995; on women see also Alter Chen 1995; Petchesky 2000).

Alongside these major events, the parallel summits at G7 meetings continued in Munich and Tokyo; in Naples in 1994 conferences and street demonstrations took place; in Halifax in 1995 the Halifax initiative of Canadian civil society was inaugurated. In Madrid in 1994 for the 50th anniversary of the foundation of the IMF and World Bank, a major parallel summit was organised around the catch-cry '50 Years is Enough'.

1996–1999: Consolidation and diffusion

Parallel summits at the end of the 1990s consolidated their networks across national borders and ventured

The peace movement of the 1980s had a major international orientation, bringing together the European countries involved in the planned deployment of Intermediate Nuclear Forces (the 'Euromissiles', Cruise and Pershing II), the US Freeze campaign, activists in Asia and the Pacific, and reaching out to civil society and independent peace groups in eastern Europe. The key events building such international connections were the Conventions of European Nuclear Disarmament, started in Brussels in the summer of 1981 (confronting the NATO headquarters) and held every year for a decade all over Europe in cities such as Amsterdam, Perugia, Coventry, Paris, and, after the end of the cold war, Moscow in 1991. They were organised by the UK END group, led by Edward P. Thompson, the British historian, and Mary Kaldor, and a well established network of European peace organisations. Conventions included conferences, peace actions, and demonstrations, each attended by thousands of people from dozens of countries. They shared with parallel summits the combination of efforts for 'internal' strengthening of the peace movement (making links, discussing issues and strategies), and the 'external' objective of influencing governments' security policy.

As the opening to civil society activities proceeded in eastern Europe, new networks emerged. The Helsinki Citizens Assembly, based in Prague, developed links among dozens of human rights, civic, and peace groups in eastern and western Europe, paralleling within society the process opened among states by the Helsinki Final Act of 1976. Bringing together intellectuals, policy-makers, and civic leaders, it organised several conferences—the first in Bratislava in 1991, then in Ohrid, Macedonia, in 1993 and in Tuzla, Bosnia, in 1995—attended by hundreds of people, building a common alternative to the outbursts of nationalism which have caused a decade of conflict in the Balkans and in the Caucasus (see Kaldor 1999; Marcon and Pianta 2001).

The largest peace conference, with 10,000 participants, including thousands of organisations from all over the world, and representatives from the UN and several governments, was held in May 1999 in the Hague. Organised by the Hague Appeal for Peace and bringing together all major international networks, the meeting filled a gap in the series of UN thematic conferences and provided an unprecedented global venue for declaring that peace is a human right and that 'it is time to abolish war'.

Why were such events not organised to coincide with meetings of the UN, NATO, the Organisation for Security and Cooperation in Europe (OSCE), or European governments? A mass social movement such as the peace movement has an autonomous dynamic setting its own calendar, agenda, and timing; important decisions are still, at least formally, in the hands of states and the domestic political sphere may still appear relevant to policy making, while the most powerful decision makers—NATO, the governments of the superpowers or of states at war—are simply too remote from the reach of civil society; in fact, the nature of military power—closely guarded by generals and military alliances, inaccessible, and arbitrary—makes it the most difficult one to confront at the international level. Still, the claims from peace movements—that political and military power has to be accountable to global society and that new arms races and wars lack legitimacy—are fundamental arguments similar to those made in parallel summits.

into an increasing range of issues, with a diversity of forms of organisations and types of events. They steadily built up their strength, which became evident in Seattle in December 1999, when they challenged the WTO summit.

G7 parallel summits mobilised increasing numbers of people in Lyon in 1996, Denver in 1997, Birmingham in 1998, and Cologne in 1999. The issue of Third World debt, raised by the worldwide campaign Jubilee 2000, became a major focus for mobilisation that took highly original forms (Pettifor 1998). The IMF-World Bank summits encountered a small parallel summit even in Hong Kong in 1997, as did the World Economic Forum in Davos (Houtart and Polet 1999).

Parallel summits in this period started to extend to major regional gatherings, including meetings of

As the United Nations celebrated its 50th year in 1995, an unconventional parallel summit was held in Perugia, Italy, with the first meeting of the Assembly of the Peoples' United Nations, a conference with civil society representatives from more than 100 countries, each invited by a local authority. The Assembly heard witnesses of world problems and called for reform and democratisation of the United Nations. Organised by Tavola della Pace (Peace Roundtable), coordinating 500 Italian local and national groups and 350 local authorities, the Assembly has since then been convened every other year with the same format, focusing in 1997 on economic justice, in 1999 on the role of global civil society—arguing that *a different world is possible*—and in 2001 on *globalisation from below*. Before each Assembly delegates visited hundreds of local authorities in an experiment to link global issues and local education, and dozens of conferences and workshops were organised all over Italy on specific issues. A major event which has ended every session of the Assembly has been the 15-mile march from Perugia to Assisi, a historic peace movement route, attended on average by 50,000 people. An extraordinary march by 100,000 people was held in May 1999 against Serbian repression and NATO bombing in Kosovo (Lotti and Giandomenico 1996; Pianta 1998; Lotti, Giandomenico, and Lembo 1999).

This experience has resulted from the need of global civil society to convene, exchange knowledge, share a common language and world view, disseminate information on ongoing activities,

Assembly of the Peoples' United Nations, 1999.
© Archivio Tavola della Pace

integrate the different agendas of single-issue campaigns, and deliberate on common priorities. More initiatives of this sort are emerging, either self-organised or developing around institutional events such as the Millennium Forum of NGOs at the United Nations, or loosely related to official summits such as the World Social Forum in Porto Alegre (see Box 7.4). These increasingly large conferences are likely to become a permanent aspect of the world social and institutional landscape, asserting the existence and autonomy of global civil society.

the European Council (such as People's Europe in the UK in 1998) and of North American and Pacific organisations. Within UN activities, NGO events marked the FAO Rome World Food summit in 1996 and the conference establishing the International Criminal Court in Rome in 1998.

A major 'parallel' summit without an official summit was the Hague Appeal for Peace conference of 1999, held during NATO intervention in Kosovo, which gathered 10,000 participants from all over the world and involved several governments (see Box 7.2).

Another set of 'parallel' global civil society summits held independently of official summits were

the Assemblies of the Peoples of the United Nations organised in 1995, 1997, and 1999 in Perugia, Italy (see Box 7.3), which brought together representatives of grass-roots groups from more than 100 different countries to discuss issues such as the reform of the United Nations, economic justice, and a stronger role for global civil society; each event included a 15-mile peace march to Assisi with 50,000 people taking part (Pianta 1998; Lotti, Giandomenico, and Lembo 1999).

Finally, in December 1999, the parallel summit and the street protests in Seattle against the ministerial meeting of the WTO marked the peak of these years of consolidation. Seattle was the

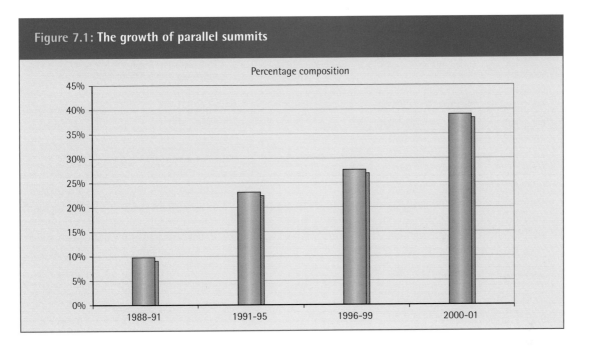

Figure 7.1: The growth of parallel summits

Percentage composition

culmination of a long process, not a sudden outburst of anti-globalisation sentiment. It captured the attention of the media, the imagination of people, and—at last—the attention of policy-makers because it had both the arguments and the strength to disrupt the official summit. The failure of the WTO ministerial meeting to launch a new comprehensive Millennium Round of trade liberalisation was equally due to the strong divisions between the US, Europe, and countries of the South. Still, in the perception of social activists, public opinion, and trade officials themselves, this was the first time a parallel summit had a major, direct impact on the conduct and outcome of the official summit (see St Clair 1999; Gunnel and Timms 2000; Kaldor 2000; on trade see also Charnovitz 1994; Marceau and Pedersen 1999; Scholte *et al.*1999).

2000 and after: frequency and radicalisation

The example of Seattle led in 2000 to a dramatic proliferation of actions combining in the same way alternative proposals on global problems and street protests against international decision-makers, developing a radical challenge to the project of neo-liberal globalisation. The World Economic Forum at Davos, the European Councils in Lisbon and Nice, the UN Millennium forum of NGOs in New York, the Okinawa G8 summit, the Prague IMF-World Bank

conference, followed in 2001 by the Porto Alegre World Social Forum and the Genoa Social Forum at the G8 summit, have filled the agenda of global civil society on a monthly basis (see Box 7.4).

They have been characterised by mass partici-pation, a radicalisation of their actions, very high media attention, a greater impact on the official summits, as well as by growing police repression. Global civil society is now an active subject on the world scene and government policies and inter-national institutions cannot afford to ignore it. The responses to demands for a different direction in the process of globalisation will test the ability of existing institutions to respect democracy and assure the effective governance of global problems.

Analysis of parallel summits

What lies behind the evolution of parallel summits set out in the concise overview in previous section? A survey was undertaken specifically for this chapter in order to investigate and report on the nature of parallel summits, the events that occurred, their forms of organisation, and their impact. A questionnaire was circulated to hundreds of civil society organisations; and dozens of newspapers, journals, NGO publications, and web sites were monitored in order to gather systematic information. From the findings, 61 cases of parallel summits have been selected, which are

Seattle. On 30 November 1999, the opening of the WTO ministerial conference in Seattle was blocked by day-long street demonstrations. Sit-ins by civil disobedience groups, protest actions, and a large trade union march brought to Seattle 60,000 people, organised by about 700 groups, including environmental, student, solidarity, labour, and other grassroots organisations. Minor violence against property also occurred, with windows smashed by small extremist groups. Police responded brutally to the non-violent protest, made hundreds of arrests, and in the evening a curfew was declared. The key demands of WTO critics were stated in the platform 'Stop Millennium Round', signed by 1,400 organisations from all over the world. Teach-ins and workshops preceded the protest, highlighting the negative effects of the current trading order, demanding rules more favourable to poor countries and to environmental and social needs, and calling on the WTO to open itself to global civil society. Seattle showed the extent and determination of the protest against a pillar of neo-liberal globalisation, obtained worldwide visibility through the media, and struck a chord in global public opinion. At the same time, the divisions between the US, Europe and Southern countries prevented the launch of the Millennium Round of new trade liberalisation talks. The resulting message was that the protest was possible, visible, and remarkably effective.

While other parallel summits had involved greater participation, the combination of unprecedented media coverage and perceived effectiveness had a dramatic effect on the initiative of global civil society. A few weeks later, in January 2000, the still-shocked business and political leaders invited at the World Economic Forum in Davos, Switzerland, were confronted by an alternative workshop and new street protests.

Washington DC. In April 2000 the targets of a parallel summit were the IMF and World Bank, gathered in their spring meeting; after workshops and conferences, 20,000 protesters, under strong police control, voiced their criticism of official financial and economic policies.

The United Nations. In May New York hosted a major UN event, the Millennium Forum of NGOs, with 1,200 participants, opening the door to civil society views on world problems and UN activities; alongside a highly detailed document, the outcome, however, was an ineffective debate with no follow-up and no impact on the special UN General Assembly held in the autumn. At the same time in New York, a parallel summit monitored the Nuclear Proliferation Treaty conference. Equally disappointing, in June, in Geneva and New York, were the follow-up meetings, five years on, of the UN summits on social development and women; they were marked by little commitment by governments and lively NGO meetings.

Asia, Africa, and Australia. July saw minor initiatives against the G8 summit in the remote Japanese island of Okinawa, while, on the other side of the world, thousands of civil society activists met in Durban, South Africa, for the Aids conference; even in the official Aids summit the interests of pharmaceutical multinationals were boldly confronted by African governments and social organisations. Other parallel summits held later in Africa included a Dakar conference on African debt in December and a Tanzanian meeting on IMF policies in February 2001. In September 2000, in Australia a major event was the protest against the Melbourne session of the World Economic Forum; after a week of workshops on global and local issues, with a bitter media campaign against the protest, the summit was confronted by a street demonstration with 10,000 people; clashes with the police occurred at its fringe.

Prague. Back in Europe, an important parallel summit was held at the end of September 2000 at the autumn meeting of the IMF-World Bank in Prague. 20,000 protesters from all over Europe, including groups prepared to carry out civil disobedience and violence against property, were confronted by strong police repression. After a busy programme of alternative conferences, the heads of the IMF and the World Bank in Prague had to accept for the first time a public debate with civil society representatives (see chapter 3 by Desai and Said in this Yearbook).

The European Union. The European Council has also become the target of regular protest. In spring 2000 in Lisbon, while governments talked of plans for an 'e-Europe', alternative conferences and street marches demanded a social Europe. An EU conference on peace and reconstruction in the Balkans was met by a parallel conference in May in Ancona. The European Council held in Nice in December 2000 to approve the new European Charter of Fundamental Rights, was met by a similar combination of alternative workshops denouncing the lack of democratic policy-making in Europe, street protests with about 50,000 people, and equally strong police controls.

On the environmental front, world governments met in the Hague in November and failed to agree on actions on climate change; a parallel summit there discussed the issues and put forward new proposals.

Porto Alegre. In January 2001 the first World Social Forum was held in Porto Alegre. The key organisers of such an original event were Brazilian progressive organisations (the municipality of Porto Alegre, the Workers' Party, trade unions, and Sem Terra, the movement of landless peasants) and Attac, a French-based network with organisations in dozens of countries, demanding a Tobin Tax on currency trans-actions and challenging neo-liberal globalisation. Timed to coincide with the World Economic Forum in Davos (where new protests and strong police repression took place anyway), the event at Porto Alegre attracted 20,000 activists from all continents (but a weak US contingent, see Klein 2001) and demanded democracy in the management of globalisation and a return for the role to national governments (there were two French government ministers at the events), under the now recurrent slogan *'a different world is possible'.*

The Americas. Civil society in North and South America has also been busy confronting the plans for a Free Trade Area of the Americas (FTAA), discussed by heads of state in April 2001 in Quebec. The parallel summit there, launched by the Continental Social Alliance, attracted 2,000 delegates to a Peoples' Summit discussing human, social, and trade union rights, and 20,000 participants to street demon-strations in the midst of very strict police measures.

The trade negotiators had been met by criticism and street protests two weeks beforehand in Buenos Aires, as Argentina was afflicted by a deepening financial crisis after a general strike against the policies imposed by the IMF.

Italy. Porto Alegre has inspired the name of the Italian coalition organising the G8 parallel summit in Genoa, in July 2001. The Genoa Social Forum saw a flurry of alternative conferences and demonstrations, attracting a hundred thousand participants from all over Europe. A rehearsal of the events was carried out in March with parallel initiatives marking the Naples Global Forum on governance, where violent street clashes took place between groups of protesters and the police.

This breath-taking sequence of parallel summits after Seattle shows the extension and radicalism of ongoing protest, which continues to be met by a refusal by existing powers to open up to the demands of global civil society. To the conferences, media events, and occasional marches which made up parallel summits in the past, systematic large-scale street demonstrations have now been added, with increasing civil disobedience and isolated acts of violence used by a small number of participants. This combination of closely held undemocratic power and radicalising protest, however, has started a perverse spiral of police repression and aggressive protest which has put in danger the effective right to demonstrate in many cities. Media coverage of parallel summits concentrates on violent episodes rather than on the issues at stake, and power-holders try to portray all protest as actions by 'anti-globalisation' extremists. The strategy pursued by governments, international institutions, and media aims at reducing the space for contestation, delegit-imising protest against summits, and turning a fundamental issue of democracy and accountability into one of public order. These developments leave little room for optimism about the possibility of more democratic and inclusive forms of global governance.

Information on parallel summits can now be found regularly in, among other publications, The US magazine *The Nation*, in the French monthly *Le Monde Diplomatique*, and in the Italian daily *Il Manifesto*.

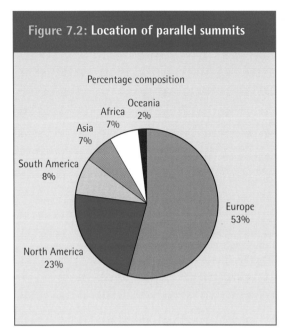

Figure 7.2: Location of parallel summits

Percentage composition

Oceania 2%
Africa 7%
Asia 7%
South America 8%
North America 23%
Europe 53%

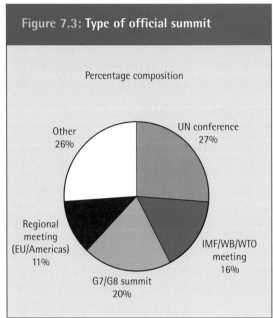

Figure 7.3: Type of official summit

Percentage composition

Other 26%
UN conference 27%
Regional meeting (EU/Americas) 11%
IMF/WB/WTO meeting 16%
G7/G8 summit 20%

considered representative of the range of events, topics, and locations. The results are presented here, shedding new light, in a systematic way, on the emergence of parallel summits, on the forces at play, and on the role of global civil society.

Figure 7.1 shows the distribution over time of the selected parallel summits, following the periodisation presented above. The four years 1988–91 account for only 10 per cent of all events, as parallel summits slowly emerged on the political scene. From 1992 to 1995 the institutional expansion associated with the large UN thematic conferences accounted for nearly a quarter of events, often on a very large scale. A slightly higher share is found in the following four years 1996–9, culminating in the Seattle protest. Since then the number of events has risen dramatically: 40 per cent of all events took place in 2000 or in the first six months of 2001.

Figure 7.2 shows the location of parallel summits; over half have been held in Europe, close to a quarter in North America, and smaller proportions in South America, Asia (where the events are likely to be under-represented), Africa, and Oceania. Such a geographical distribution may also give some indication of the origin of those who attended parallel summits, as the large majority of participants comes from the country where the event is held or from neighbouring ones.

Figure 7.3 shows the types of summit with which the parallel events were associated. More than a quarter of them were UN conferences, one-fifth G7/G8 summits, slightly fewer were IMF, World Bank, or WTO meetings, followed by regional meetings in Europe or North America. The wide range of events is shown by the one-quarter of cases developed around 'other' conferences, including peace and environmental meetings.

Figure 7.4 shows that parallel summits have been organised by coordinating bodies including national civil society groups of the hosting country, in 80 per cent of cases involving also international NGOs. In a third of cases local groups were also active, with a lesser involvement by trade unions, local authorities, and other forces such as professional organisations, official institutions, and specific networks. The building of cross-border links among organisations—discussing agendas, providing knowledge and building partnerships—clearly emerges as the dominant process in the preparation of parallel summits.

Who are the organisers of parallel summits? To this question multiple responses were possible and totals therefore do not add up to 100 per cent. Figure 7.5 shows that two-thirds of events have resulted from the work of civil society organisations active in economic issues (trade, finance, debt, and so on) and development. A third flow from actions by human rights and environmental groups, a quarter from

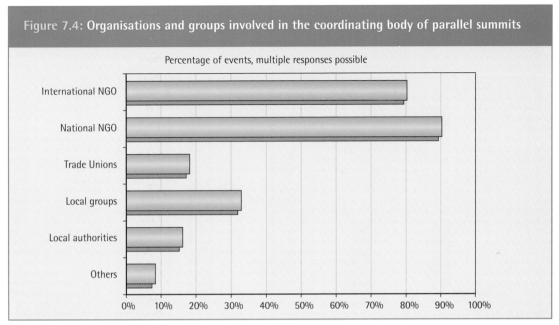

Figure 7.4: Organisations and groups involved in the coordinating body of parallel summits

Percentage of events, multiple responses possible

- International NGO
- National NGO
- Trade Unions
- Local groups
- Local authorities
- Others

0% 10% 20% 30% 40% 50% 60% 70% 80% 90% 100%

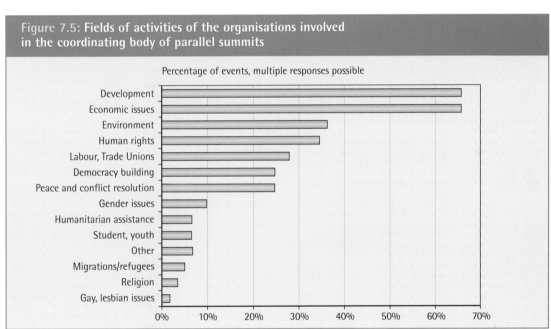

Figure 7.5: Fields of activities of the organisations involved in the coordinating body of parallel summits

Percentage of events, multiple responses possible

- Development
- Economic issues
- Environment
- Human rights
- Labour, Trade Unions
- Democracy building
- Peace and conflict resolution
- Gender issues
- Humanitarian assistance
- Student, youth
- Other
- Migrations/refugees
- Religion
- Gay, lesbian issues

0% 10% 20% 30% 40% 50% 60% 70%

trade unions, peace organisations, and campaigners for democracy. Other organisations have been involved in up to 10 per cent of parallel summits.

We may perhaps link this evidence with the two main challenges posed by parallel summits identified above: on the one hand, resistance to neo-liberal globalisation is likely to be the focus of the parallel summits organised by groups active on economic, development, and trade union issues; on the other hand, pressure for the globalisation of rights and responsibilities may characterise those organised by human rights, environment, peace, and democracy activists. As multiple answers were possible here, further analysis has been carried out by assigning each parallel summit to one of the two groups considered above. Figure 7.6 shows the evolution over time of the events where economic globalisation or global rights could be identified as the dominant issue.

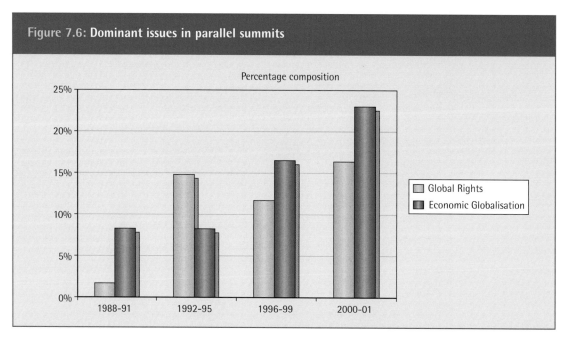

Figure 7.6: Dominant issues in parallel summits

Percentage composition

- Global Rights
- Economic Globalisation

1988–91   1992–95   1996–99   2000–01

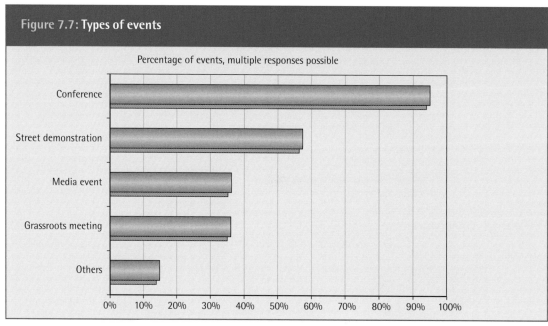

Figure 7.7: Types of events

Percentage of events, multiple responses possible

Conference

Street demonstration

Media event

Grassroots meeting

Others

0% 10% 20% 30% 40% 50% 60% 70% 80% 90% 100%

Two opposite patterns emerge. Economic globalisation issues start in the late 1980s with a higher but stable relevance, then grow rapidly in the late 1990s and even more after 2000. Global rights issues, after a weak start, become the most important theme in the 1992–5 period of 'institutional expansion' marked by the large UN conferences, and remain more or less stable in terms of overall relevance up to the present, sharing the upward dynamics after 2000.

This succession of themes reflects, on the one hand, the urgency of issues and the internal dynamics of the actors and movements involved and, on the other hand, the opportunities offered by the agenda of official conferences. Confronting neo-liberal globalisation is at present the most important issue emerging from parallel summits, but it goes hand-in-hand with demands for global rights and responsibilities.

Figure 7.8: Number of participants in the events of parallel summits

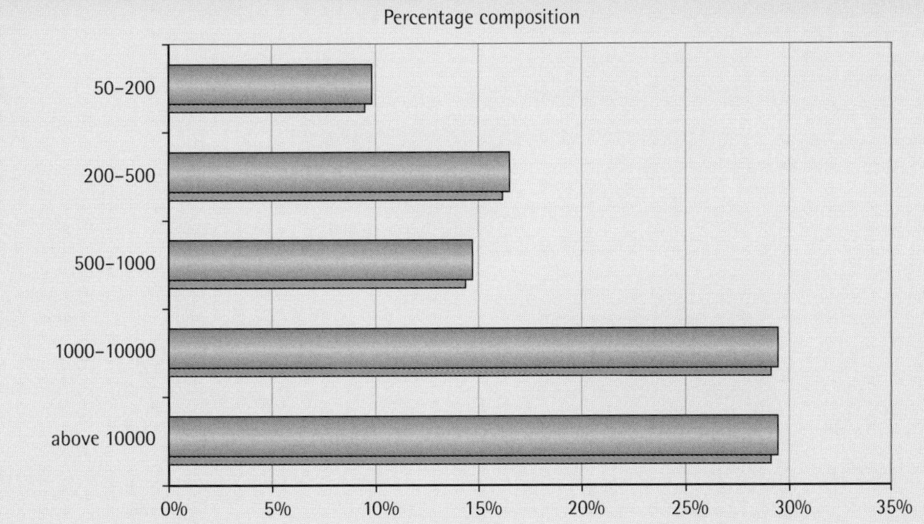

Percentage composition
50–200
200–500
500–1000
1000–10000
above 10000
0%
5%
10%
15%
20%
25%
30%
35%

Figure 7.9: Types of keynote speakers

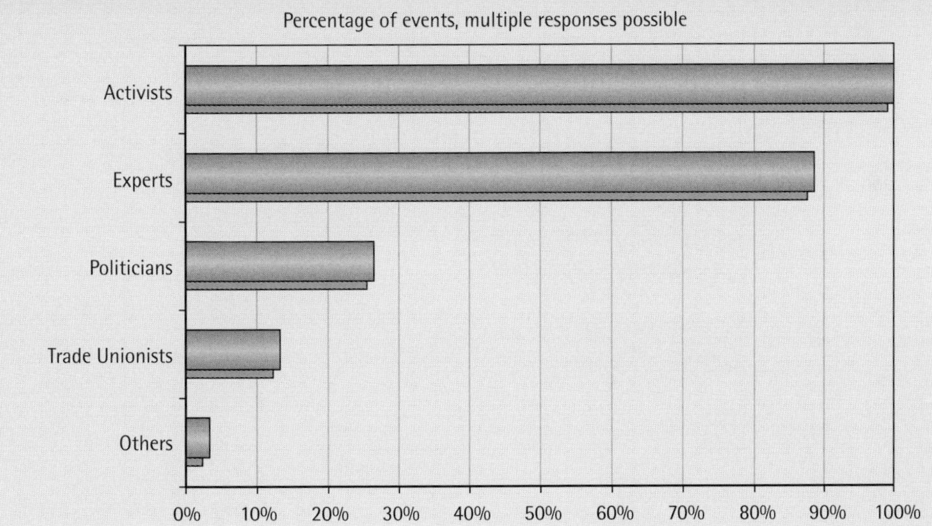

Percentage of events, multiple responses possible
Activists
Experts
Politicians
Trade Unionists
Others
0%
10%
20%
30%
40%
50%
60%
70%
80%
90%
100%

What type of event is a parallel summit? Figure 7.7 shows that it is always a conference, associated with street demonstrations in half of the cases or with media events and grass-roots meetings in a third of them. Symbolic events, meetings with institutions, street theatre, and other actions complete the picture of the activities undertaken in parallel summits.

Figure 7.8 shows that parallel summits involving more than 10,000 people and those involving between 1,000 and 10,000 people in each case amount to nearly 30 per cent of the total, suggesting that parallel summits are not an élite affair and that street demonstrations, when organised, are significant protests. It may be added that participation has clearly grown in more recent years (see Box 7.4). On the other hand, a third of parallel

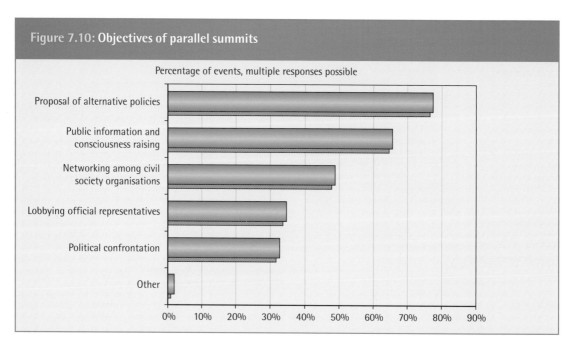

Figure 7.10: Objectives of parallel summits

Percentage of events, multiple responses possible

- Proposal of alternative policies
- Public information and consciousness raising
- Networking among civil society organisations
- Lobbying official representatives
- Political confrontation
- Other

0% 10% 20% 30% 40% 50% 60% 70% 80% 90%

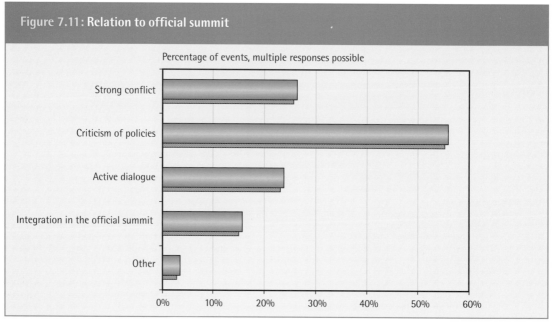

Figure 7.11: Relation to official summit

Percentage of events, multiple responses possible

- Strong conflict
- Criticism of policies
- Active dialogue
- Integration in the official summit
- Other

0% 10% 20% 30% 40% 50% 60%

summits have between 200 and 1000 participants and a few have involved an even smaller number of people.

As shown in Figure 7.9, activists are always the key players and speakers at parallel summits, in close cooperation with experts brought in for educational, visibility, and strategy-making purposes. Parallel summits in three-quarters of cases do not need politicians (or else politicians are not interested in such events) and even fewer involve participation by trade unionists, in spite of the potential for alliances indicated in a few important cases. Again, a variety of other actors are involved, from poor farmers to official representatives, in specific events.

Figure 7.10 shows that parallel summits mainly propose alternative policies (in three-quarters of cases), disseminate public information (two-thirds) or address the need for networking among civil society

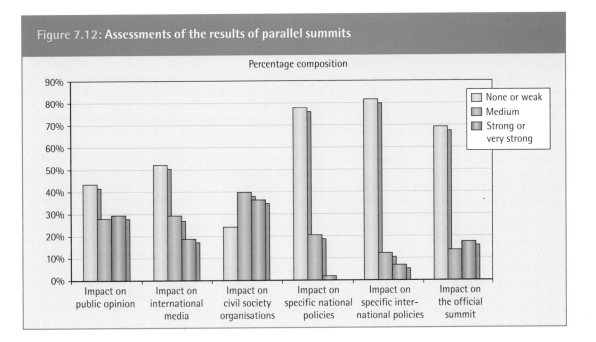

Figure 7.12: Assessments of the results of parallel summits

organisations (half). This is a systematic pattern in the objectives of parallel summits (as confirmed also in other surveys: see Benchmark Environmental Consulting 1996) which indicates the two parallel needs of such events: building up the 'internal' strength of global civil society and making more effective its 'external' activity, based on the development of alternative proposals. Following from this, both in logic and in importance of the listed objectives, is the relationship to political power, whether in the form of lobbying officials or in the more radical form of political confrontation (one-third of events each). The relatively low relevance of lobbying official representatives may be due to the declining frequency of UN-type summits open to civil society lobbying and to the resistance to such a relationship from other international institutions, but also to the emergence of a broader agenda of civil society, increasingly autonomous from that of official summits; again this confirms a previous finding of NGO surveys (Benchmark Environmental Consulting 1996). Interestingly enough, no other objective has emerged as a relevant one.

The issue of lobbying brings us to the type of relationship with the official summit, shown in Figure 7.11. The main mode of interaction is the criticism of policies, typical of more than half the parallel summits. A quarter of events engage in active dialogue and a quarter in strong conflict. Less

frequent is integration in the official summit, confirming the lack of opportunity for civil society to be formally included—as has happened in a few UN conferences—in the activities of official summits.

What is interesting from these results is that widely differing modes of interaction coexist in the same event. Strong conflict may be associated with active dialogue; even when there is integration in the official summit, criticism and conflict occur as well.

The outlook still appears open for the integration (or co-option) of parallel activities into the operation of international institutions. The activities of global civil society so far have usually avoided both passive integration into the machinery of global governance and isolation in a ghetto of ineffective radical protest. The responses from international institutions and states will be crucial to the future evolution of these activities of global civil society.

It is very difficult to assess the results of parallel summits. They have been judged either by the organisers of the events or, when information has been available, on the basis of media reports, and clearly these results have to be treated with great caution.

The strongest impact of parallel summits is on global civil society itself, where three-quarters of events were judged to have a medium or strong effect; the impact on public opinion follows with an

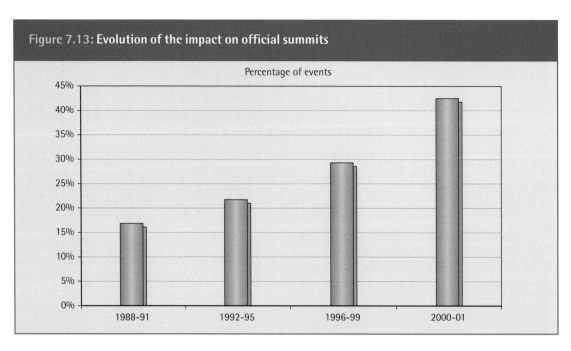

Figure 7.13: Evolution of the impact on official summits

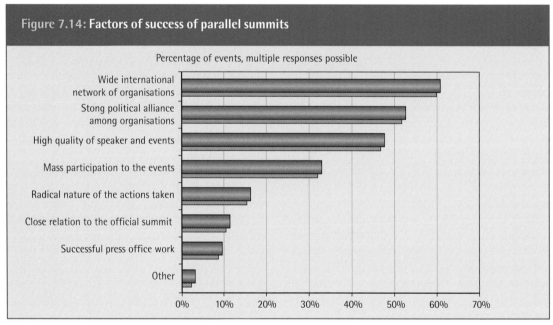

Figure 7.14: Factors of success of parallel summits

even distribution of weak, medium, and strong results, while parallel summits are judged to be less successful with international media (Figure 7.12). This may confirm the priority given to 'internal' build-up and networking within civil society, and the successes obtained in this regard. The lesser impact on the media may be associated with their long-standing lack of interest, if not hostility—although after Seattle

parallel summits have become major news stories—to the difficult and sometimes specialist nature of the issues involved, and to the summits' lack of resources for carrying out activities targeted at mainstream media and the general public.

The impact of parallel summits on specific national and international policies has been very weak, with few results, especially at the international

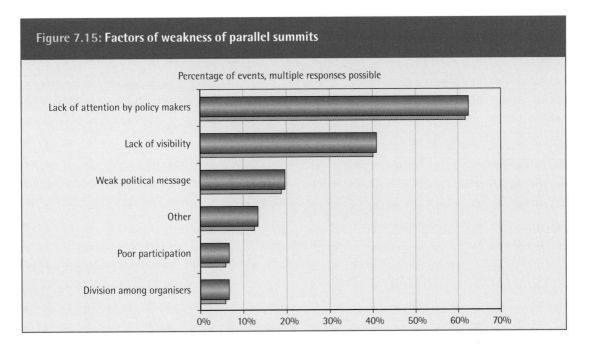

Figure 7.15: Factors of weakness of parallel summits

Percentage of events, multiple responses possible

level. While the overall impact on official summits is similarly low, the percentage of strong results is higher. Parallel summits have long been ignored by official ones or were not interested in affecting them. On the other hand, Figure 7.13 shows how events with medium or strong impact on official summits have evolved over time. A steady rise of their influence is visible, with 40 per cent of parallel summits in 2000–1 leaving their mark on the government conference.

An important factor in affecting official summits is the possibility of building alliances, outside civil society, with sympathetic governments of selected countries—frequently referred to as 'like-minded'—or with particular international institutions (essentially of the UN family), or of exploiting the divisions among governments on major issues.

Finally, the evaluation of the major strengths and weaknesses of parallel summits suggests that different factors are relevant. Figure 7.14 shows that the wide international network of organisations, the strong political alliance among them, and the high quality of speakers and events are ranked as the most important factors making for success in half or more of the cases. Mass participation is counted as a success in a third of parallel summits (half of which had planned a demonstration, see Figure 7.7) while radical protest emerges as less important. In a small number of specific cases, factors making for success include a close relationship to official summits and

press office work, which are not present in most parallel summits.

The 'internal' strategy of building global civil society activities appears to be considered successful when a strong cross-border political alliance is developed among the actors of different countries. The building up of learning and competences through high-quality presentations and debate is important in this process, and it can be used either for 'internal' strengthening of networks or for the 'external' objectives of assuring mass mobilisation or effective lobbying of official decision makers.

The weaknesses of parallel summits, shown in Figure 7.15, stem mainly from the lack of attention of policy-makers (or the failure to make them listen to civil society) in almost two-thirds of events, and from the lack of 'external' visibility (40 per cent of cases). A much lower number of responses point out 'internal' weakness in developing an adequate political message, divisions among organisers, or poor participation. Clearly these factors are much more relevant than is apparent from the survey of organisers or from often superficial media reports; divisions among organisers have been highly visible in several recent events and are likely to grow as parallel summits become larger and more important.

The overall picture of parallel summits which emerges from these data has important similarities with the findings of a survey of 520 individuals who participated in international government conferences representing non-governmental organisations, largely focusing on UN meetings, in particular the Copenhagen Social Summit of 1995 (Benchmark Environmental Consulting 1996). The objectives for participation were equally divided between making links with other NGOs and influencing governments, confirming the combination of 'internal' concerns for strengthening cross-border civil society activities and the 'external' aim of changing state policies. Also, in the ex post facto evaluation of the impact of participation, the survey found that a major result was networking and discussion with other NGOs, although the dominance of larger, English-language and Northern NGOs was felt (Benchmark Environmental Consulting 1996:17). Other important outcomes were a clearer definition of problem areas, followed at some distance by contacts with their own government and UN officials (Benchmark Environmental Consulting 1996: Chs 3–4).

In relation to decision makers, two models of action emerged from the Benchmark survey: the lobbying model extended to the international arena, and demands for a new model of inclusive global governance open to NGOs. While the former is relevant to selected cases, greater interest has emerged in the latter, with a variety of approaches among NGO actors: 'whereas some of these players are willing to work within the existing script for democratic decision making, others reject it and are working towards other forms of democratic governance' (Benchmark Environmental Consulting 1996: 4; see also Krut 1997). The growth of parallel summits can be interpreted as an outcome of the latter strategy.

Still, many questions along this road remain unanswered. The major ones are the representativeness of NGOs and the democratic procedures to be established for decision-making. Both issues emerged as problematic in the Benchmark survey and have not been addressed directly by parallel summits either. As long as parallel summits do not claim formal representation of global constituencies, or make substantial deliberation beyond occasional final documents, these problems may be lived with. The ability of global civil society to provide a solution, however, will be crucial for identifying more democratic forms of global governance.

A smaller survey was carried out in 1995 on 100 civil society representatives participating in the first Assembly of the Peoples' UN in Perugia (see Box 7.3) coming from Europe, the Americas, Africa and Asia plus Australia in similar proportions. The main areas

of activism and concern by the respondents were human rights (almost 30 per cent), peace, and economic and development issues (about a quarter each). As the focus of the Assembly was on the reform of the UN, questions were asked on civil society's views on the UN and its reform. Half of respondents had positive views on the UN system, a third had negative or very negative ones; the UN activities which were most appreciated included the protection of human rights and peacekeeping, followed at a distance by economic development and help in peoples' self-determination. Military interventions met with the greatest disapproval, followed by the power of the Security Council, superpower dominance, and bureaucratic ineffectiveness.

In the views of these representatives of global civil society, the most urgent reforms of the UN include reducing the power of the Security Council and eliminating the veto power of some of its members; democratising UN structures, including peoples' representatives; and creating a second assembly of the UN. Open questions on the ways in which global civil society could strengthen its role in the UN system were also asked, and the responses pointed out the need for a greater voice and role for NGOs in decision-making, more democratic representation and an NGO assembly at the UN, and direct participation of NGOs in UN-sponsored projects (Lotti and Giandomenico 1996: 170–6).

The Lessons from Parallel Summits

From this analysis of parallel summits, a number of key issues emerge which are likely to be crucial in shaping our understanding and future developments.

Global civil society, social movements, and politics

What is the social base of initiatives such as parallel summits, which have challenged global powers? The hundreds of thousands of individuals and the thousands of organisations which have been actively involved in the events documented here have in common a broad set of values and policy objectives; yet they remain highly heterogeneous in terms of interests, capabilities, focus of concern, approach to power and politics, national perspective, global awareness, and world view.

Demographic aspects also should not be disregarded. The Benchmark survey of participants from NGOs to international conferences found that 58 per cent of respondents were male; 40 per cent of the total were over 50 years of age, 33 per cent in their 40s, 25 per cent in their 30s, only 12 per cent under 30. Participants to parallel summits are likely to be, especially in recent years, substantially younger than this group of NGO professionals, but they are likely to share high levels of education, knowledge of foreign languages, and a middle-class background.

How can we conceptualise such a complex combination of commonalities and differences? The concept of an emerging global civil society is of great help in this regard. It identifies a sphere of cross-border relationships among heterogeneous actors who share civil values and concern for global issues, communication and meanings, advocacy actions, and self-organisation experiments. This is not a sphere which can be expected to produce well-defined social actors, common behaviour, or widely agreed political strategies and practices. What it is producing is a challenge to the inability of the current inter-state system to address global problems in a legitimate, democratic, and effective way. This is essentially what parallel summits have been about. Global civil society wants to bring back into the public arena the supranational power appropriated by unaccountable inter-governmental organisations and powerful states, multinational firms and banks, technocrats and officials, which is visibly exercised in places like international summits. But how can global civil society establish itself in the face of political and economic power? The rules, procedures, permanent structures, and activities which can strengthen and empower a cross-border civil society are difficult to define, develop, and to make effective.

How social actors organise for the purpose of recovering power over global issues is a different question, leading to a search for the ways in which individuals and groups act on these issues within global civil society. It means identifying the *social movements and networks* operating across borders, their social dynamics, forms of organisation, action, and impact (see Keck and Sikkink 1998; Pianta 1998; Klein 2000; Cohen and Rai 2000).

What should be done with this reclaimed power is yet another issue, bearing on the *political sphere* and calling into question the political projects of social movements and other forces.

The lessons we can draw from the analysis of parallel summits is that they have been the stage on which emerging global social movements are struggling to organise, confront global powers, and develop their own political project.

The typology of movements—*rejectionist, reformative, supportive, and alternative*—used by other chapters of this Yearbook can be considered here in order to summarise their social and political orientation and adapt it to the case of parallel summits.

The type of events considered here—defined above as international civil society events addressing the same issues as official summits, with a critical perspective on government and business policies—means that *supportive* positions are largely irrelevant in our case.

Most of the *rejectionist* or *isolationist* movements have traditionally not been interested in building cross-border networks for confronting globalisation on its high-profile terrain, that of official summits. Only with the recent radicalisation of protest at summits after Seattle have such forces begun to be involved in parallel events. Yet the use of the general label 'anti- globalisation movements' for activism in Seattle, Prague, Porto Alegre, or Genoa is highly inappropriate and misleading.

It was argued above that 'globalisation from below' is the broad project shared by the largest part of the forces which have been active in parallel summits. It is a project that rejects the strategy of neo-liberal globalisation and seeks to influence the possibility of a globalisation of rights and responsibilities.

Reformative movements, on the other hand, tend to accept the broad institutional setting and concentrate on changes in procedures and policies. A part of the NGO world has clearly joined parallel summits with such an approach, emphasising the opportunities for integration and dialogue with the more open inter-governmental organisations. But a large part of the agenda of parallel summits raises fundamental questions about the legitimacy and power of the present institutional setting, and seeks change which cannot be reduced to a return to national sovereignties.

Alternative movements combine two contrasting attitudes: while they refuse to accept the existing institutions and centres of global power, they concentrate on building separate, alternative arrangements and mechanisms whose viability is important in environmental and community issues, but much less so when human rights, peace, or the global economy are at stake. They are therefore unlikely to consider parallel summits as a high priority in their activity, although they have often been a significant presence.

The notion of *radical* movements may be more effective in identifying a broad part of the social forces involved in parallel summits, making clear their engagement on the same issues as those defined by supranational powers but outside the institutional framework they offer for addressing global problems. The struggle between the project of 'globalisation from below' and the neo-liberal one is clearly of a radical nature; the efforts to influence a globalisation of rights and responsibilities may include a reformative approach.

Moreover, we should bear in mind that the social forces involved in parallel summits are highly dynamic, and positions and strategies may evolve rapidly. The division between moderate reformers and radical critics, which is partly already there, is likely to develop further. However, the current structure of parallel summits and the profile of these movements do not lend themselves easily to such a split; for example, some of the radical critics are Christian-based organisations, not left extremists. A likely strategy by international institutions is to attempt to integrate the former in some loose form of involvement in global governance, and to marginalise the latter, portraying them as dangerous rebels on which greater repression could be exerted (see Box 7.4). The behaviour of authorities in Seattle in 1999, in Prague in 2000, and in Italy in 2001 would suggest that this has become a dominant strategy by states and supranational powers.

A second division at parallel summits may develop between the social forces and movements more concerned with the specific issue of their activity and those struggling to broaden the agenda. While these differences of orientation are always present, the current dynamic is clearly towards a broadening of the vision and action, raising the political profile of parallel summits. This may be resisted by some organisations more concerned with the effectiveness of their action on specific issues.

A third, obvious division at parallel summits has occasionally emerged between Northern and Southern civil society organisations. Official (and parallel) summits are largely concentrated in the North, where civil society has much greater resources to confront them. The hegemony by Northern NGOs on parallel summits, however, is likely to be challenged by increasingly active and assertive civil society groups from the South, as already shown in the Porto Alegre World Social Forum.

The co-evolution of official and parallel summits

What do these perspectives mean for the future of parallel summits? In order to explore the possible development of global civil society action, it is useful to go back to the different activities carried out in summits, outlined in the opening section, and consider the possible outcomes in terms of integration, critical dialogue, and open conflict with global civil society. Building on the evidence of the survey and on recent events, Table 7.1 speculates on the types of possible interaction between official and parallel summits, distinguishing between the dynamics of summits associated to the project of *neo- liberal globalisation* and those reflecting the *globalisation of rights and responsibilities.*

A strategy of integration in official summits is much more likely in events associated to the latter project, where international organisations and civil society may cooperate because they share an interest in strengthening global approaches and in reducing the power of states. Summits associated to *neo-liberal globalisation*, on the other hand, reflect a project where global civil society has no place; the international institutions which have been key players in this field, the IMF and the WTO, have been particularly closed to NGOs, and more conflictual outcomes could be expected.

In any event, a strategy of integration would require much extended access for civil society, in the usual form of accreditation of NGOs, in the arrangement for NGO forums or liaison activities, or with more radical innovations in global governance processes assuring that global civil society has a 'voice' and a 'vote' in global decision-making. However, while some states and inter-governmental organisations may be prepared to give it some voice, almost no one would give global civil society any form of vote.

Official summits in charge of framing issues, rather than taking decisions, are more likely to be open to the voice of global civil society, as in the case of the large UN thematic conferences, a key example of *globalisation of rights and responsibilities.* This may lead to formal integration or critical dialogue, while in the case of summits linked to *neo-liberal globalisation* critical dialogue and conflict are likely to emerge.

International institutions and summits in charge of rule-making or setting policy guidelines are unlikely to formally integrate the voice and the vote of global civil society; in the summits associated to neo-liberal globalisation both critical dialogue and conflict may result, while in those where rules on global rights are discussed critical dialogue is the most likely outcome, but integration may also be possible, depending on the issues at stake and on the degree of openness of the institution.

Summits with enforcing power tend to be closed to civil society influence, exclude integration, and resist critical dialogue, leaving conflict as the most likely outcome in their relation to parallel summits.

As the dynamics of global governance are in flux, and new institutions and procedures have to emerge in this field, it is important to keep in mind that institutional choices in the architecture of global decision-making will have an impact on its relationship with global civil society. The fundamental challenge in terms of institutional architecture is to find ways to open supranational decision-making power on setting policy guidelines and enforcement to civil society also. The accountability of such decisions taken by states and international institutions remains a crucial test of the democratic nature of the international order.

The question of politics

The analysis of parallel summits has suggested that the ability to develop strong political alliances among organisations is an important factor in their success. As most civil society organisations move from the experience of working on single issues and have the objective of extending international networking, the issues of how different social forces, issues, and policy interests are brought together becomes crucial. This has historically been the task of politics, and it should be evident that when global civil society challenges the political project of neo-liberal globalisation, or supports a project of globalisation of rights and responsibilities, it has inevitably to engage the political sphere.

This, by the way, is also the result of the spectacular failure of traditional national politics—in terms of the operation of political processes and activities of political parties—to understand and act on behalf of broad sections of society on the problems raised by globalisation.

Clearly, the most self-aware players in parallel summits have no doubt about the political nature of their challenge. But addressing the question of politics may not be easy for global civil society. How far can civil society organisations substitute for political processes (in particular, mediation among differences, extension of consensus- building), without losing their nature and effectiveness? In other words, what are the boundaries between public interest advocacy and overall policy integration? The ability of parallel summits to evolve from contesting the single issues of official ones towards developing broader, independent political agendas will be a crucial part of the answer.

The road towards politics makes the issue of representation more thorny. Business and government critics of civil society have regularly challenged its right to 'represent' public interests, to speak in the name of subjects without voice or power, of nature, or of fundamental values. The stronger response to such arguments has so far been that civil society organisations do not claim to have exclusive representation of these interests (anybody could start a new civil society group and be active on the same issue with a different agenda), and have no 'vote' in global decision-making. This means that they do not need to behave as representative and accountable democratic bodies in the way that is required for exclusive representation and decision-making power (for example, in the case of government policy-making). As broader political concerns emerge in the actions of civil society organisations, and as their power to influence decisions grows, how far can they go without coming to terms with the problem of representation and legitimacy? In other words, what are the boundaries between public interest advocacy and a more systematic representation of interests? The ability of parallel summits to reach formal agreements among global civil society organisations and to make decisions concerning their own govern- ance will be the first steps in addressing these questions.

Equally difficult could be the road towards *policies*. How far can civil society organisations be involved in or co-opted into global governance mechanisms, identifying specific policies and procedures, without losing their independence and credibility? In other words, what are the boundaries between public interest advocacy and policy implementation? The ability of parallel summits to point out specific policy solutions and open, effective implementation procedures will be crucial for progress in this direction.

Table 7.1: The dynamics of official and parallel summits

Type of relations between parallel and official summits	Type of summit			
	Framing the issue	Rule-making	Policy guidelines	Enforcement
Summits associated with neo-liberal globalisation				
Integration	Possible	Unlikely	Highly unlikely	Impossible
Critical dialogue	Highly Likely	Likely	Likely	Highly unlikely
Conflict	Likely	Likely	Highly likely	Highly likely
Summits associated with globalisation of rights and responsibilities				
Integration	Likely	Possible	Unlikely	Highly unlikely
Critical dialogue	Highly likely	Highly likely	Likely	Likely
Conflict	Possible	Likely	Likely	Highly likely

The response from power

Finally, the evolution of the actions of global civil society on global issues will depend on the ability of the existing power centres to recognise, respond to, adapt, and integrate them.

International institutions are faced with many alternative courses of action. They may resist all pressure, sticking to the formal mandate they have from states, and introducing only cosmetic improvements to their policies and image. This is more likely to happen in large organisations with enforcement and policy guideline-setting powers; this would lead to a radicalisation of conflict with global civil society. The IMF and the WTO are typical cases. The WTO decision to hold the 2001 ministerial conference in Qatar, as far as possible from the reach of global civil society, clearly shows that this is the course it has chosen.

A second option for international institutions may be reforming their own rules, procedures, and policies, meeting some requests of civil society, and integrating and coopting some organisations. This is more likely in activities of 'framing the issues' and in organisations without enforcement power. Most UN bodies fall into this category, perhaps also the World Bank, although political and bureaucratic resistance may strongly limit progress in this direction.

A third option is that international bodies contribute to a more radical rethinking of the problems of global governance and join with global civil society groups in redesigning the institutional tools for addressing them. This may be more likely in fields where the institutional architecture at the global level is still fragmented and in flux, often meeting the opposition of states which resist passing authority to international institutions, as in the cases of the environment or the International Criminal Court, where inter- governmental organisations and NGOs have often teamed up to confront states. A similar cooperation, if not alliance, is emerging in the case of UN agencies such as UNHCR, UNDP, UNICEF, and UNEP, which rely on NGOs to carry out their mission.

The players, however, are not just global civil society and international institutions. States do continue to have a key role, but they have largely failed to play it seriously. State institutions so far have been moderate supporters of the neo-liberal project of globalisation, and, by and large, passive listeners to the calls for a globalisation of rights and responsibilities. On these challenges they have not been directly pressed to change by civil society, which has given priority to proposals and action at the international level, where key decisions are made. Will this position of states change, at least in some countries more responsive to civil society? Will the national political sphere recover some of its natural role as the place for democratic debate and decision making on values and policy priorities? Well-structured national political processes might be an important means of channelling the pressure of civil society in a constructive way. But these are unlikely developments in most countries.

It is more likely that the central contest will continue to be that between supranational powers and the emerging global civil society. While the ability of the global governance system to operate effectively and respond to pressure for change remains uncertain, we can be sure that parallel summits are here to stay for an extended period, and so are the broad social forces which have invented them.

I thank Federico Silva for excellent research assistance and analysis of data; Marlies Glasius, Mary Kaldor, and the other authors of the Yearbook for their advice and criticism; Franck Amalric, Sergio Andreis, Daniele Archibugi, Carlo Donolo, Martin Koehler, Giulio Marcon, Francesco Martone, and Wolfgang Sachs for their comments; and the dozens of people in all continents who have provided basic information for making this survey of parallel summits possible.

References

Alter Chen, M. (1995). 'Engendering World Conferences: The International Women's Movement and the United Nations'. *Third World Quarterly*, 16: 477–93.

Archibugi, D., Held, D., and Kohler, M. (ed.) (1998). *Reimagining Political Community: Studies in Cosmopolitan Democracy*. Cambridge: Polity Press.

Arrighi, G., Hopkins T. K., and Wallerstein, I. (1989). *Antisystemic Movements*. London: Verso.

Benchmark Environmental Consulting (1996). *Democratic Global Civil Governance. Report of the 1995 Benchmark Survey of NGOs* (UD Evaluation Report 4.96). Oslo: Royal Ministry of Foreign Affairs.

Charnovitz, S. (1994). 'The World Trade Organization and Social Issues'. *Journal of World Trade*, 28/1: 17–33.

— (1997). 'Two Centuries of Participation: NGOs and International Governance'. *Michigan Journal of International Law*, 18/2: 183–286.

Chomsky, N. (1999). *Profits over People: Neoliberalism and Global Order*. New York: Seven Stories Press.

Cohen, R. and Rai, S. (ed.) (2000). *Global Social Movements*. London: The Athlone Press.

Conca, K. (1995). 'Greening the United Nations: Environmental Organizations and the UN System'. *Third World Quarterly*, 16: 441–57.

Della Porta, D., Kriesi, H., and Rucht, D. (ed.) (1999). *Social Movements in a Globalizing World*. London: Macmillan.

Falk, R. (1999). *Predatory Globalisation: A Critique*. Cambridge: Polity Press.

Florini, A. M. (ed.) (2000). *The Third Force: The Rise of Transnational Civil Society*. Tokyo and Washington: JCIE and CEIP.

Fondazione Internazionale Lelio Basso (1998). *Tribunale permanente dei popoli. Le sentenze: 1979-1998*. Lecco: Stefanoni.

Gaer, F. D. (1995). 'Reality Check: Human Rights Non Governmental Organizations Confront Governments at the United Nations'. *Third World Quarterly*, 16: 389–403.

Gerhards, J. and Rucht, D. (1992). 'Mesomobilization: Organizing and Framing in Two Protest Campaigns in West Germany'. *American Journal of Sociology*, 98: 555–95.

Gordenker, L. and Weiss, T. G. (1995). 'Pluralising Global Governance: Analytical Approaches and Dimensions'. *Third World Quarterly*, 16: 357–87.

Gunnel, B. and Timms, D. (ed.) (2000). *After Seattle: Globalization and its Discontents*. London: Catalyst.

Houtart, F. and Polet, F. (ed.) (1999). *L'autre Davos. Mondialisation des résistances et des luttes*. Paris-Montréal: L'Harmattan.

Kaldor, M. (1999). 'The Ideas of 1989: The Origins of the Concept of Global Civil Society'. *Transnational Law and Contemporary Problems*, 9: 475–88.

— (2000). 'Civilising Globalisation? The Implications of the "Battle in Seattle"'. *Millennium: Journal of International Studies*, 29: 105–14.

Keck, M. E. and Sikkink, K. (1998). *Activists beyond Borders: Advocacy Networks in International Politics*. Ithaca and London: Cornell University Press.

Klein, N. (2000). *No Logo*. London: Flamingo.

— (2001). 'A Fete for the End of the End of History'. *The Nation*, 19 March.

Krut, R. (1997). *Globalization and Civil Society: NGO Influence in International Decision Making*. Geneva: UNRISD.

Lipschutz, R. D. (1992). 'Reconstructing World Politics: The Emergence of Global Civil Society'. *Millennium: Journal of International Studies*, 21: 389–420.

Lotti, G. and Giandomenico, N. (eds) (1996). *L'Onu dei popoli*. Turin: Edizioni Gruppo Abele.

— and Lembo, R. (eds) (1999). *Per un' economia di giustizia*. Perugia: Tavola della Pace.

Marceau, G. and Pedersen, P. N. (1999). 'Is the WTO Open and Transparent? A Discussion of the Relationship of the WTO with Non-governmental Organisations and Civil Society's Claims for More Transparency and Public Participation'. *Journal of World Trade*, 33/1: 5–49.

Marcon, G. and Pianta, M. (2001). 'New Wars and New Peace Movements'. *Soundings: A Journal of Politics and Culture*, 17: 11–24.

O'Brien, R., Goetz, A. M., Scholte, J. A., and Williams, M. (2000). *Contesting Global Governance: Multilateral Economic Institutions and Global Social Movements*. Cambridge: Cambridge University Press.

Otto, D. (1996). 'Nongovernmental Organizations in the United Nations System: The Emerging Role of International Civil Society'. *Human Rights Quarterly*, 18: 107–41.

Petchesky, R. (2000). *Reproductive and Sexual Rights: Charting the Course of Transnational Women's NGOs* (Occasional Paper 8). Geneva: UNRISD.

Pettifor, A. (1998). 'The Economic Bondage of Debt—And the Birth of a New Movement'. *New Left Review*, 230: 115–22.

Pianta, M. (1998). 'Imagination Without Power. Notes on Contemporary Social Movements in Italy'. *Soundings: A Journal of Politics and Culture*, 10: 40–50.

Scholte, J. A. with O'Brien, R. and Williams, M. (1999). 'The WTO and Civil Society'. *Journal of World Trade*, 33/1: 107–23.

Smith, J., Pagnucco, R. with Lopez, G. A. (1998). 'Globalizing Human Rights: The Work of Transnational Human Rights NGOs in the 1990s'. *Human Rights Quarterly*, 20: 379–412.

St Clair, J. (1999). 'Seattle Diary: It's a Gas, Gas, Gas'. *New Left Review*, 238: 81–96.

Strange, S. (1996). *The Retreat of the State*. Cambridge: Cambridge University Press.

Uvin, P. (1995). 'Scaling Up the Grass Roots and Scaling Down the Summit: The Relations between Third World Nongovernmental Organizations and the United Nations'. *Third World Quarterly*, 16: 495–512.

UNDP (United Nations Development Programme) (1999). *Human Development Report 1999—Globalization*. Oxford: Oxford University Press.

UNRISD (United Nations Research Institute for Social Development) (1995). *States of Disarray: The Social Effects of Globalization*. Geneva: UNRISD.

Van Rooy, A. (1997). 'The Frontiers of Influence: NGO Lobbying at the 1974 World Food Conference, the 1992 Earth Summit and Beyond'. *World Development*, 25/1: 93–114.

Waterman, P. (1998). *Globalisation, Social Movements and the New Internationalism*. London: Mansell.

CHAPTER 8

FUNDING GLOBAL CIVIL SOCIETY ORGANISATIONS

Frances Pinter

Introduction

The funding of civil society organisations (CSOs) that operate globally or even regionally is considerably more complex than the funding of local CSOs. For a number of reasons, what happens at the international or global level is not simply a mirror image of what goes on at the local or state level. This chapter seeks to highlight some of the differences between the local and the global, and offers suggestions for further research. It does not discuss the whole array of resources employed by CSOs, such as social capital, information, reputation, and so forth, though the need to do so in subsequent studies is discussed in the conclusion.

The term 'civil society organisation' is used here as an umbrella concept that includes NGOs, social movements, and grass-roots organisations. A global CSO is not necessarily global in the sense of having representation in all four corners of the globe, but may also include regional and bilateral cross-border initiatives. Collecting data on such a diverse range of bodies is a formidable challenge, as this chapter will demonstrate. Most data sources are national rather than international and focus on subsets based on definitions that do not work well in a cross-border context.

The environment in which funds for global CSOs are raised and through which funds must move is by definition multinational. At an operational level, global civil society organisations are more expensive to fund than local civil society groups. Money needs to be found for travel and long-distance communication costs. Variable exchange rates and currency risks need to be taken into account. Fundraising tends to be more difficult as issues may be perceived as irrelevant to the localities where the money is raised. More complex fundraising strategies are often employed. Each country has its own methods of funding civil society bodies and its own traditions of sharing financial burdens between the state and the individual. The regulatory and institutional arrangements for civil society bodies, whether local or global, affect the

funding capacity of the state and its people. The state also plays an important part in both resourcing transnational activities and facilitating—or hindering—the flow of funds between countries through their various tax regimes.

The political agendas of the larger funding bodies can be difficult to influence and are often at odds with grass-roots organisations (Edwards 1999). Foundations, particularly a handful of larger American ones, along with the main multilateral donor agencies, play a significant role in determining the activities of NGOs worldwide, yet they are subject to no democratic controls. While the number of funders may be potentially greater much funding is actually derived from a limited pool of big participants.

Methodological health warnings

It is useful at this point to distinguish between (1) sources of funding, (2) types of bodies funded, (3) forms of funding, (4) types of activities funded, and (5) core issue areas funded. This chapter focuses primarily on the sources of funding and types of bodies funded, with some reference to forms of funding.

The forms of funding include grants, support for operating programmes—these are programmes conducted primarily by the funding body's internal staff—loans, programme-related investments, venture philanthropy, membership fees, subscriptions, donations, income-generating activities, in-kind donations, and volunteer work. Grass-roots organisations and social movements tend to rely on more meagre resources; social movements usually depend on their own members and their friends and families. The more formal the organisation, the more formal is the source of funding. Large multinational NGOs tend to find it easier than grass-roots organisations to raise funds from the larger donors.

Significant methodological difficulties arise with attempts to identify types of activity. Much of what is funded is a mixture of different kinds of activities. Some organisations need funds only for advocacy and activism. This includes primarily salaries (for some only), overheads and travel, and communications and promotional expenses. Other types of bodies receive funds and act as intermediary organisations that carry out projects on a contractual basis, for example to deliver services—such as rural health; or to dispense aid, for example, disaster relief to smaller organisations on the ground. The chain of intermediaries can be a long one, giving rise to disputes over the allocations of funding. Confusion may also arise when, for example, NGOs take a slice of a grant and effectively charge a management fee when acting as intermediaries.

Dissecting the global from the local is a formidable challenge. However, a starting point might be to look at the methodology employed in comparative studies of nationally based non-profit organisations which constitute a large part of civil society. The Johns Hopkins Comparative Nonprofit Sector Project, covering 22 countries, provides some useful parameters for identifying the non-profit sector. The International Classification of Nonprofit Organisations (ICNPO) was conceived and designed to be consistent with the International Standard Industrial Classification (ISIC) developed by the United Nations (Table 8.1). The organisations included share five common features: they are (1) collections of people that are institutionalised to some degree, (2) private, (3) non-profit-distributing, (4) self-governing, and (5) voluntary in the sense that they are not statutory bodies and time and/or money are voluntarily donated to them.

In the study of global civil society organisations, the above definition might need to be stretched somewhat to include social movements and grassroots organisations as collections of people who are not necessarily 'institutionalised to some degree' but rather devote a portion of their time to a cause, which may have some full- or part-time organisers, but which can consist of considerably larger groups of people with strong commitments to the cause.

Tracking funding flows across borders, to formal NGOs, social movements, and grass-roots organisations is also problematic. Such statistics as exist are often simply totals of national statistics. Funds may be double-counted because of the circuitous routes that money can take; or, with the use of offshore vehicles, they may not be captured at all. With electronic fund transfers, tracking has become both simpler and more difficult as funds leapfrog from one jurisdiction to another at the click of a mouse. The UN System of National Accounts, a much utilised

statistical resource, is an inadequate data source for such cross-border studies because NGO and foundation flows are lumped together within the residual 'household' category, which includes too many other flows to provide accurate figures for the civil society sector.

Some of the problems associated with data collection are evident from even a cursory glance at national statistics. For example, American foundations are reported to have disbursed a total of over $23 billion in 2000 (11 per cent of which is for international work). This figure is based on data collected by the US-based Foundation Center (URL), assembled primarily from the yearly and monthly information (Form 990-PF) submitted to and collected by the Internal Revenue Service. The study is augmented by annual reports, other foundation publications, and questionnaires mailed out to over 18,000 larger foundations (Renz, Samson-Atienza, and Lawrence 2000). Nevertheless, it takes into account only fund flows reported inside the US. Other countries employ similar methods. Newer foundations that source funds from around the world with a view to giving globally may have no need whatsoever to bring funds through the US or any other home country. Many foundations produce consolidated reports on their giving on a geographical basis but provide less comprehensive information on the geographical origins of their funds.

The Foundation Center's method of recording data does not account for grants made from one foundation to another. For example, it reported $124.6 million of giving by the New York based Open Society Institute (URL) and $108.8 million from the Soros Foundation (Renz, Samson-Atienza, and Lawrence 2000: 48). The total given in the table of the top 50 givers includes both sums. However, the body of the text makes it clear that the $108.8 million was given from the Soros Foundation to the Open Society Institute, which acted as an intermediary for onward giving. Re-granting of funds, for example from one large foundation on to several smaller foundations, is a common practice worldwide. There is no way of identifying how many of the funds flowing through foundations are in effect double-counted as a result of re-granting.

In *Cross-border Philanthropy*, which draws its data from the Johns Hopkins Comparative Non-profit Sector Project, Helmut Anheier and Stefan List address many of the methodological problems associated with such research. The survey concludes that, in addition to flows from institutional actors, those from non-institutional units such as individuals, unincorporated enterprises, or informal associations need to be taken into account (Anheier and List 2000: 16). The less formal the source, the more difficult it becomes to identify it and then separate the global from the local.

A variety of funding methods support the operations of civil society organisations. Transfers of funds for which no formal 'exchange' is expected include donations and grants. Where an exchange such as the sale of goods or services has occurred, there is a transaction, as when an NGO sells a T-shirt and funds some of its operation out of the profits. An NGO may operate on a 'not-for-profit' basis—that is, it does not distribute profits to shareholders—but it may have a trading arm that generates income. Contributions of an 'in-kind' or voluntary nature are usually treated as transfers since no tangible transaction has taken place, though some may argue that the satisfaction derived from making a non-financial donation does, in effect, constitute a transaction. The significance of the distinction between transfers and transactions will become clearer later on when the role of intermediaries in the funding process is examined.

Most global civil society organisations operate primarily on a not-for-profit basis. The mix of fees and charges, public-sector funding, and philanthropic donations in the not-for-profit sector varies considerably from country to country. However, it would be incorrect to equate global civil society with the not-for-profit sector. A growing number of for-profits established by social entrepreneurs are committed to creating a public good through the operational vehicle of a commercial entity (see Changemakers URL). The increasingly blurred boundary between public and market delivery of goods and services affects the study of how CSOs go about raising and employing funds.

With a potential multitude of sources of funding and of constituencies of recipients of funding, funders, and funded must come to terms with a multiplicity of tax regimes that affect the movement of funds. The net amount left for a cause in a neighbouring country after taxation may be considerably less than the amount that could be generated locally. However, before looking at some of these technicalities it would be useful to glance briefly at the history of global civil society funding.

The History of Global Civil Society Funding

The history of global civil society shapes the context from which today's donors have emerged. Before the mid-nineteenth century, religious organisations were the main funders of civic works. Missionaries were motivated by philanthropy and a desire to make converts to Christianity. Originally their charitable works focused on education and health. In many ways these men and women of God were the first development project managers, setting up schools and clinics in countries far from home. Towards the latter part of the nineteenth century organisations emerged such as the Red Cross, founded in 1864, initially as religiously sponsored relief organisations, though they subsequently became increasingly independent. Such organisations relied on volunteers and contributions from individuals around the world to deal with problems of natural and man-made disasters wherever they occurred. The Anti-Slavery Society founded in 1839 was probably one of the first human rights international NGOs (Risse 2000: 188), though it may not have considered itself as such.

Women formed cross-border links over a variety of causes. The international suffrage movement began shortly after the women's peace movement in the second half of the nineteenth century. The socialist feminism campaigns began in the late nineteenth century, as did the international temperance movement. Between the two world wars women founded international bodies championing the causes of newly emerging institutions that were intended to deal with matters such as equal employment rights. Many of these movements were funded by local fundraising initiatives and membership fees paid by affiliated national bodies.

International trade union co-operation also began around the mid-nineteenth century, with the first International Trade Union Federation following on in 1901 and the first World Federation of Trade Unions established in Paris in 1945. The cold war caused a split in the WFTU in 1949, when Western trade unions formed the International Confederation of Free Trade Unions. These and other trade union bodies engaged in various charitable works around the world.

After the Second World War the post-Bretton Woods institutions such as the World Bank and the International Monetary Fund found themselves in need of implementation partners. The 'development industry' to some extent discovered civil society almost by accident. Those involved in funding aid and assistance came to rely more and more on local NGOs to implement their projects. At times this counterbalanced authoritarian and corrupt states; in other instances it led to a weakening of already marginalised states. Such interventions often had unintended consequences. Projects were launched and funded that required skilled people for their implementation. NGOs mushroomed as employment opportunities presented themselves. Huge sums of development money in the region of $50 billion a year (see Table 8.2) spawned a correspondingly large implementation infrastructure. There are now thousands of organisations, large and small, that, whether for ideological or for practical tax reasons, prefer to work as not-for-profit entities. These organisations often compete with for-profit companies and consultants offering the same services. However, the NGOs' not-for-profit status usually, though not always, provides them with a perceived moral advantage.

In the 1960s young people across Europe and America felt uneasy with the emergent status quo, as reflected in student demonstrations. The war in Vietnam attracted unprecedented international protest. The founding of Amnesty International in the 1960s spawned numerous country committees and, in the 1970s, organisations with a wider human rights brief. Other movements galvanised around the inequities of the development process and the degradation of the environment. The funding for these movements was ad hoc and small-scale, though these issues, being cross- border by nature, generated transnational responses at both the intergovernmental and the civil society levels.

The aftermath of the cold war changed the environment in which civil society operated. The fall of the Berlin Wall was to create a completely new configuration of relationships. First, an indigenous civil society emerged in the post- communist bloc, which would have been inconceivable before the events of 1989–90. Second, related but not solely due to the fall of communism, the globalisation of capital and financial markets created a more favourable regulatory environment for funding transfers that also benefited NGOs. Third, improved information and communications technologies (ICTs) made access to information cheaper and faster, thus enabling groups that had previously operated in ignorance of one another to link up, create leverage, and improve the quality of information employed. The

benefits of ICT are abundantly evident and dealt with elsewhere in this volume.

The final quarter of the twentieth century saw an explosion of NGOs, with over 40,000 international NGOs registered with the Union of International Associations (URL) by the year 2000. The increasing number of democratic countries suggests that self-organising organisations will grow rather than contract. The position of global CSOs in this increasingly complex array of participants is likely to attract more attention.

Who Funds?

This section looks at the sources of funding available to global CSOs. They include individuals, the state—at the national and the local levels—providing grants and contracts as well as tax concessions, multilateral agencies providing loans and grants, bilateral aid programmes, foundations—state, private and corporate—religious organisations, and trade unions. Recipients of funding usually seek support from more than one source within and across these categories.

Individuals: donating money and time

Contributions from individuals, whether in the form of money or of time, are a significant factor in the operations of any NGO. This is especially so for social movements and grass-roots organisations that rely on informal means of fundraising. Some countries keep national statistics on giving, but even these do not reflect the funds raised informally by committed activists at grass-roots levels. Cake sales, jumble sales, and raffles are all part of their stable of fundraising techniques. Celebrities offer their time and names free of charge. Musicians, actors, and comedians are willing to perform, artists donate their works to causes close to their hearts. Activists often use their own funds or contributions from their friends and families to cover the costs of travel, communications, and publicity.

Most advocacy campaigns begin with a single individual or small group committed to a cause and donating their own resources to turning an idea into an organisation. For instance, Peter Eigen, a World Bank regional director for East Africa, took early retirement from his secure job to form Transparency International (TI) when he could no longer tolerate the complacency he found towards corruption (Galtung

Table 8.1: Giving and volunteering, selected countries, by INCPO group, by country, 1991, 1992

ICNPO major group	Percentage of respondents giving in:			Percentage of respondents volunteering in:		
	US	Germany	France	US	Germany	France
Culture & Recreation	15.7	8.9	2.4	12.5	6.4	8.7
Education & Research	21.1	1.8	8.0	15.4	0.6	2.0
Health	32.9	13.2	23.2	12.9	1.0	1.7
Social Services	49.6	13.1	9.8	26.8	0.9	3.3
Environment	16.3	9.4	1.7	8.6	0.9	1.0
Civic & Advocacy	12.0	2.8	2.2	4.7	1.8	0.7
Philanthropy	16.2	1.0	1.3	8.7	0.4	0.3
International Activities	3.5	14.8	6.7	2.3	0.3	0.7
Business Associations	16.0	1.5	1.5	7.1	0.6	1.2
Religious without church tax	51.3	23.9	9.1	26.8	3.1	2.0
Religious with church tax	-	over 90%	-	-	-	-
Other	2.8	2.5	1.1	2.7	0.6	1.4

Percentages do not add to 100% because multiple answers were allowed.

Source: The Johns Hopkins Comparative Nonprofit Sector Project (Salamon *et al.* 1996: 57).

2000). It was several years before his organisation could afford to pay professional staff. TI now operates on a $5 million annual budget. Individual giving in the form of donations and membership dues plays a significant role not only in providing much-needed cash but also in demonstrating the presence of a constituency of concern for a particular cause. Greenpeace (URL), for example, raises 81 per cent of its funding from donations of less than $1,000.

Reported patterns of giving vary from country to country. The causes supported also vary. US giving is directed primarily to causes close to home with only 1.2 per cent allocated to international affairs (Giving USA URL). In the UK three of the top twelve national charities are devoted to overseas aid (Wright 2000). These and other patterns reflect a variety of cultural and historical differences.

Individuals are also a source of funding foundations. In addition to establishing foundations, they may give directly in order to fund projects or add to a foundation's endowment, which then provides an income stream. In some cases individual donations are earmarked specifically for investment purposes only. For example, the World Scout Foundation received over 2 million Swiss francs in 1999 to augment its endowments. Again, patterns differ from country to country. Some of the differences in preferences between nations are captured in Table 8.1, which compares giving and volunteering patterns in three countries based on the ICNPO categories. Any

Table 8.2: Major aid flows: net flows from major donor countries ($m)

Country	1993	1998
Australia	953	960
Austria	544	456
Belgium	810	883
Canada	2,400	1,691
Denmark	1,340	1,704
Finland	355	396
France	7,915	5,742
Germany	6,954	5,581
Ireland	81	199
Italy	3,043	2,278
Japan	11,259	10,640
Luxembourg	50	112
Netherlands	2,525	3,042
New Zealand	98	130
Norway	1,014	1,321
Portugal	235	259
Spain	1,304	1,376
Sweden	1,769	1,573
Switzerland	793	898
United Kingdom	2,920	3,864
United States	10,123	8,786
Total	56,486	51,888

Source: OECD (2000)

campaign wishing to mobilise resources across borders needs to take such national diversity into account.

Volunteers have been a feature of civil society for centuries. The incidence of citizen participation in charitable causes tells us a great deal about how societies choose to organise themselves. While this chapter does not cover the role of volunteers as such, a few general comments on the relationship between volunteering and funding need to be made. Levels of employment affect the amount of time that people are prepared to donate, though the relationship between the two is not straightforward and varies with the socio-cultural context. The numbers of volunteers working alongside the paid workforce in developed countries is likely to increase as the cohort of 'retired' people grows. In the late 1990s the share of adults volunteering in Europe ranged from a high of 38 per cent in The Netherlands to a low of 12 per cent in Slovakia (Anheier and Salamon 1999: 53). The World Values Survey demonstrates an increase in volunteers in organisations concerned with global issues. For example, the number of volunteers worldwide devoting time to environmental NGOs increased by 50 per cent in less than ten years. Many northern countries finance the subsistence cost of volunteers (Anheier and Salamon: 1999). Any large-scale study of resourcing global CSOs will need to account for volunteering. The importance of volunteering was underlined in 1997 when the UN declared the year 2001 to be the United Nations Year of Volunteering. Over 100 countries now celebrate 5 December as International Volunteer Day.

ICT and giving

Giving has never been easier. Developments in ICT have made possible specialist websites that facilitate donations. Donors, institutional funders, and charities become better informed, more effective, and more efficient as the process of fundraising for, and giving to, causes abroad becomes much simpler. GuideStar (URL), for example, was established in 1994 in an attempt to bring about greater transparency and accountability by making available information about the operations and finances of non-profit organisations. A service provided by GuideStar is to match donors with charities so as to lower fundraising costs. An online facility for making donations is available. The service is free to donors while its operational costs are supported by large private and corporate foundations. It has entered into partnerships with bodies that provide similar and complementary services such as Helping.org, which is based inside the AOL Foundation. Corporate and private foundations as well as bodies such as the Digital Divide Working Group provide additional financial support. Another model demonstrating corporate involvement is thehungersite.com. For each click on the site advertisers donate one cup of staple food to poverty programmes around the world.

Diasporas

A source of funding that is elusive, at least in terms of tracking flows, is the increasingly active national diasporas around the world. While much of this funds basic needs, some is directed towards building civil society. In the 1990s, for example, Kosovar communities abroad agreed to remit 3 per cent of their income to Kosovo to help mitigate the deprivations caused by the Milosevic regime. The disbursement of the funds for education and health required the building of an infrastructure that enjoyed the support of the population at large. While diaspora funding for home countries has been prevalent throughout the centuries, no concrete statistics are available for this subset.

The state

State support at the national and local levels provides grants (transfers) and contracts (transactions), either directly to specific organisations or through intermediaries. This constitutes an important source of funding for CSOs. Governments and organs of the state in democratic societies recognise the value of independent contributions. Civil society is increasingly appreciated both as service providers and as independent commentators on policy. Independent think tanks, for example, are more visible than ever before in contributing to policy analysis.

Local authorities are increasingly willing, budgets permitting, to fund international links such as city twinning programmes, which despite cynical commentary do not always reflect economic benefits but are often the result of civic initiatives. Local municipalities are also quick to recognise marketing opportunities by joining global causes. As early as the 1980s in the United Kingdom, grass-roots trade union activists received considerable financial support from the radical Greater London Council to help them develop links with their counterparts in other European countries working for transnational companies such as Kodak, Ford, and Unilever (Mackintosh and Wainwright 1987). Porto Allegre in Brazil burst forth on to the global map when, early in 2001, it hosted the Global Social Forum, a parallel summit held at the time of the World Economic Forum in Davos.

States may make substantial contributions to NGOs through favourable tax treatment of not-for-profits. Since most NGOs take on a legal status in whichever jurisdiction they are registered, decisions on where to locate global or regional CSO offices may in part be influenced by tax regimes. Some of the issues surrounding the legislative and tax environments that facilitate and or restrict cross-border activities are examined later in this chapter.

Bilateral aid

Bilateral aid has always been motivated by self-interest tempered with a dash of idealism. Historically much bilateral aid has been in the name of helping the poor but has been structured in such a way as to bring benefits to the donor. Table 8.2 shows that most countries providing bilateral assistance reduced their expenditures between the first half and second half of the 1990s. Some of the shortfall is being made up by private foundations and multilateral agencies, but the contraction of funds has political implications which are widely discussed in the development literature.

With the end of the cold war, democracy took on a greater significance. Its role in promoting stable market economies led to substantial bilateral-aid funds being devoted to democracy building. This has been an important development for the recipients of bilateral aid. USAID's funding for democracy assistance, for example, rose from $165.2 million in 1991 to $637.1 in 1999 (Carothers 1999: 49). Within that budget, support for civil society also grew in the same period from $56.1 million to $230.8 million. In 1999 $146.9 million was spent on rule-of-law projects, $203.2 million on governance, and $58.9 million on elections and political processes. Over $100 million was allocated for democracy building from a number of other departments and agencies such as the US Information Agency, the State, Defense and Justice Departments, the National Endowment for Democracy, the Asia Foundation, and the Eurasia Foundation. Table 8.3 shows the allocation by region over a nine-year period.

Thomas Carothers (1999: 210) describes the international civil society assistance priorities of the US and other Western countries as follows:

> NGOs dedicated to advocacy on what aid providers consider to be sociopolitical issues touching the public interest including election monitoring, civic education, parliamentary transparency, human rights, anticorruption, the environment, women's rights and indigenous people's rights. Three other areas of U.S. democracy assistance—civic education, media assistance and aid to labour unions—also represent efforts for the development of civil society, though when US aid providers use the term 'civil society assistance' they are usually referring specifically to their work with advocacy groups.

Two US-funded public foundations, the Inter-American Foundation and the African Development Foundation, were established specifically to channel funds to developing country NGOs. The Asia Foundation, which conducts similar activities in Asia, uses a different funding model that combines funds from public and private sources.

Bilateral aid is increasingly administered through NGOs. In 1999 Norway channelled 24 per cent of its bilateral aid through NGOs, Sweden 29 per cent, Finland 11 per cent. The Canadian International Development Agency (CIDA) established a separate division in 1975 devoted to supporting international NGO bodies that worked towards strengthening developing countries. Other countries have similar units.

Table 8.4 tracks 28 countries' official development assistance over a decade and provides information on the extent of their reliance on NGOs for disbursements.

Multilateral agencies

Most funding for global CSOs, broadly defined, emanates one way or another from the 'development industry' and is led by the multilateral agencies. Distinguishing projects that build bridges from those that build civil society does not always aid analysis. Many of the projects that rely on NGOs for delivery contribute to capacity building and networking which is crucial to global CSOs. According to the United Nations Development Program (UNDP), '250 million people are now "reached" by NGOs (as opposed to

Table 8.3: USAID funding for democracy: assistance by region, fiscal years 1991–1999 ($m)

Year	Latin America	Eastern Europe and the former Soviet Union	Sub-Saharan Africa	Asia and the Middle East	Global
1991	83.5	22.0	30.6	27.7	1.4
1992	101.2	43.1	55.3	22.0	3.2
1993	132.8	68.6	72.3	30.4	11.4
1994	75.4	156.4	102.9	35.6	10.3
1995	110.0	136.8	70.8	80.0	38.0
1996	67.3	119.8	85.9	83.2	31.0
1997	65.9	107.3	67.4	64.2	17.4
1998	82.2	216.3	96.9	112.4	23.9
1999*	86.8	288.4	123.4	111.5	27.0

* 1999 figures are budgeted expenditures rather than actual expenditures.

Source: USAID Democracy/Governance Information Unit (Carothers 1999).

Table 8.4: Overseas development aid distributed through NGOs

	Net official development assistance (ODA) disbursed		Share of ODA through NGOs[a] (%)	Ranking by % of GNP	Ranking by % disbursed through NGOs
	Total (US$m) 1997	As % of GNP 1997	1995/96	1997	1995/1996
Canada	2,045	0.34	8.5	7	4
Norway	1,306	0.86	–	2	
United States	6,878	0.09	8.6	16	3
Japan	9,358	0.22	2.1	14	8
Belgium	764	0.31	0.3	9	15
Sweden	1,731	0.79	6.0	4	5
Australia	1,061	0.28	0.6	10	13
Netherlands	2,947	0.81	9.2	3	2
United Kingdom	3,433	0.26	2.0	11	9
France	6,307	0.45	0.2	6	16
Switzerland	911	0.34	5.8	7	6
Finland	379	0.33	0.7	8	12
Germany	5,857	0.28	2.6	10	7
Denmark	1,637	0.97	0.5	1	14
Austria	527	0.26	0.5	11	14
Luxembourg	95	0.55	12.5	5	1
New Zealand b	154	0.26	2.0[b]	11	9
Italy	1,266	0.11	1.0	15	10
Ireland	187	0.31	0.1	9	17
Spain	1,234	0.23	–	13	
Portugal	250	0.25	0.8	12	11
Total	48,324	0.22	3.4		

[a]On a disbursement basis.   [b]Data refer to 1994.   *Source:* UNDP (2000).

Table 8.5. Patterns in World Bank–NGO operational collaboration, fiscal years 1987–1998

	Total 1987–95			1998		
By region[a]	Number of projects	Percentage of projects run through NGOs	Ranking as percentage of projects run through NGOs	Number of projects	Percentage of projects run through NGOs	Ranking as percentage of projects run through NGOs
Africa	680	34	1	59	54	2
East Asia and Pacific	378	20	4	45	51	4
South Asia	239	33	2	25	73	1
Europe and Central Asia	225	16	5	69	37	6
Latin America and the Caribbean	443	24	3	68	51	5
Middle East and North Africa	180	12	6	20	52	3
Total	2,145	25		286	50	
By sector						
Agriculture	443	41	4	47	74	5
Education	190	29	6	36	63	7
Electric power and energy	165	5	12	15	40	10
Environment	74	42	3	18	78	4
Finance	109	2	14	17	6	14
Health, population and nutrition	134	66	2	24	79	3
Industry	86	27	7	2	33	11
Mining	16	12	10	4	100	1
Multisector	190	4	13	19	30	12
Oil and gas	53	26	8	2	–	
Public sector management	141	7	11	28	24	13
Social sector	60	92	1	12	80	2
Telecommunications	37	–		3	–	6
Transportation	233	7	11	27	71	
Urban development	113	37	5	19	55	9
Water supply and sanitation	101	16	9	13	62	8
Total	2,145	25		286	50	

[a] refers to percentage of NGO-involved projects in all World Bank-approved projects in the region. *Source:* World Bank (1999).

100 million in the 1980s) and their rising budget of $7.2 billion is equivalent to 13 percent of net disbursements of official aid' (Pearce 1997: 268). The lead agencies such as the World Bank have been looking increasingly to engage in partnerships rather than acting alone, even though such relationships inevitably involve cultural clashes. Many NGOs question the value of such collaboration. The World Bank (1998) claims that half of its operations involve NGO participation in some capacity. Table 8.5 indicates

Table 8.6: EU budget headings with some element of funding for civil society

Budget heading	Appropriation 2000 (Euros)
Education, vocational training and youth	481,500,000
Culture and audiovisual media	111,500,000
Information and communication	104,000,000
Social dimension and employment	144,615,000
Environment	157,700,000
Consumer protection	22,500,000
Trans-European networks	688,000,000
Areas of freedom, security and justice	68,700,000
Research and technological development	3,630,000,000
Pre-accession strategy	3,166,710,000
Food and humanitarian aid	935,996,000
Cooperation with developing countries	905,738,000
Cooperation with Mediterranean and Middle East countries	1,142,923,000
Cooperation with C&EE, Balkans & NIS	941,769,000
Other external cooperation measures	356,850,000
European initiative for democracy and human rights	95,373,000

Source: European Commission (2000).

the patterns of World Bank-NGO collaborations, which display considerable diversity.

The other development banks, such as the European Bank for Reconstruction and Development, the African Development Bank, the Asian Development Bank, and the Inter-American Development Bank Group, as well as sub-regional financial institutions such as the Islamic Development Bank, also engage with NGOs. Most of their grants are for technical assistance, advisory services, and project preparation, though some also run scholarship programmes.

Regional bodies

Regional bodies also engage with civil society. The extent to which trans-border activities are supported depends on the issues concerned and the strategic objectives of the funding body. OPEC may fund a few

educational projects, but this is not central to its aspirations. The European Union, however, sees funding of multinational education and research as central to its mission of furthering European integration. The introduction of line items such as human rights in its general budget is a relatively new phenomenon. Table 8.6 demonstrates that a fair proportion of the EU's budget for 2000 of nearly 90 billion euros was devoted to activities that either fostered the development of cross-border civil society activities or employed the services of NGOs—some of which are trans-border CSOs—in their delivery.

Foundations: private and corporate

There are now hundreds of thousands of foundations worldwide whose historical development goes back several centuries. The largest private and corporate foundations are now so big that they themselves are becoming significant players on the world stage. Clearly, typical community foundations—usually local grant-making entities that receive funds and endowments from a number of sources—bear little resemblance to the likes of the Ford Foundation, one of the largest privately endowed independent foundations. However, there are some structural similarities. Foundations are usually asset-holding bodies. They are concerned with charitable or philanthropic causes. Their organisational structures vary; and here it is useful to distinguish between operating and grant-making foundations, since the former are more involved in carrying out intended activities than the latter (Anheier and Toepler 1999:163). Foundations may make grants to other bodies or deliver services themselves.

Foundations range in size from the very small, handling only a few thousand dollars a year, to the largest—currently the Bill and Melinda Gates Foundation with an endowment currently standing at $22 billion. Each country has its own laws on how foundations must be structured, how funds may be disbursed, and what activities they may undertake. In the newer democracies laws governing foundations have either just been introduced or recently been considerably amended under pressure to ensure transparency and accountability. In the first few years after the collapse of communism, many of these laws of central and eastern Europe countries were very loose and encouraged tax evasion. The second generation of legislation in the late 1990s was a great improvement.

Foundations may provide grants to one another, either as part of a co-funding arrangement or as subcontracted agents. Like corporations, they enter into partnerships and alliances. Sometimes joint funding decisions are taken simply to minimise risk. Close to four-fifths of the grant makers surveyed by the US-based Foundation Center in 2000 reported partnering with other donors (Renz, Samson-Atienza, and Lawrence 2000). This tendency is leading to increasingly standardised procedures of decision-making, with foundations often using the same advisers.

There is a certain degree of overlap of 'good causes' funded by some of the wealthiest foundations in the world. Many of the issues themselves are global, the environment, for example, and foundations can effectively fund globally even if the organisations they fund are themselves local. New forms of support include programme-related investments, whereby a foundation may make what appears to be commercially based investments—with an expected return on capital and exit route—in business ventures that further the social causes served by the foundation. Venture philanthropy, though lacking a commonly agreed definition, is another new form of funding. It refers to a hybrid concept marrying high-risk investment approaches with altruistic actions. Venture capitalism usually refers to investments in the form of equities or loans accompanied by professional guidance, usually to start-ups or relatively new companies. Philanthropy is associated with the giving of money or time to good works. Venture philanthropy, then, might be defined as the act of investing capital in businesses that have a social purpose and where a capital return is desirable but not paramount. However, many foundations use the term loosely to designate grant programmes that concentrate on projects that are high-risk in terms of their likelihood of achieving their stated objectives. An example of the first definition of venture philanthropy is the Markle Foundation (URL) that has taken equity stakes in dotcoms that are expected to produce socially useful services. Zoe Baird, Markle's President, has defended her foundation's position in the face of public attack as being the most efficient way of encouraging companies to focus more on public rather than private goods.

Hybrid models, mixing the philanthropic with the business *modus operandi*, are becoming increasingly popular with foundations willing to finance pro-gramme-related investments, while NGOs are becoming more comfortable adopting a multiplicity of approaches to accomplishing their mission. MamaCash (URL) is an interesting example in terms of both its geographical focus and its mix of support for both not-for-profit and for-profit activities. In The Netherlands, its home country, MamaCash provides guarantees for bank loans to support women entrepreneurs as well as grants and loans for local feminist cultural and social projects. At the same time grants are provided to groups concerned with women's issues in the southern hemisphere as well as central and eastern Europe. Although the average grant size is small at less than $3,000, this body has concentrated on providing seed money for groups that encounter difficulties in raising first-round funding because of the controversial nature of the issues they wish to address. MamaCash relies on private donations and loans from individuals and carefully guards its independence.

The growth of both private—that is, established through individual wealth—and corporate—established by a company—foundations has followed the rapid growth in wealth creation of the 1990s. US foundations' endowments nearly doubled between 1994 and 1999 to $385 billion (Lawrence, Camposeco, and Kendzior 2000: 3). Foundation giving also increased from $11.3 billion to $22.8 billion during those five years (Lawrence, Camposeco and Kendzior 2000: 1) and rose to $27.6 billion in 2000 (Renz and Lawrence 2001:3). The largest percentage increase in the late 1990s was in corporate giving—18 per cent in 1998—though a slowdown followed the stock-market trend in 2000 with corporate giving rising by only 9 per cent (Renz and Lawrence 2001: 4). As capital and markets have become global so too have the interests of foundations, particularly the large US ones. This is less so of other developed countries such as Germany, which has concentrated primarily on domestic issues.

Of total US foundation giving in the 1990s, just over 11 per cent was allocated to international activities. Unsurprisingly, the largest foundations devoted a higher percentage—14 per cent—of their giving to international projects (Renz and Lawrence 2001). However, the giving of funds to domestic NGOs for foreign projects increased at a greater pace than giving directly overseas—65 per cent versus 57 per cent. Highlights from the Foundation Center's report provide some insight into the changes in funding patterns that occurred towards the end of the 1990s. It remains to be seen whether this trend continues. Based on a sample of 1,020 foundations in 1994 and 1,009 in 1998, the survey included grants of $10,000 or more and covered over half of all foundation giving in the US each year and an

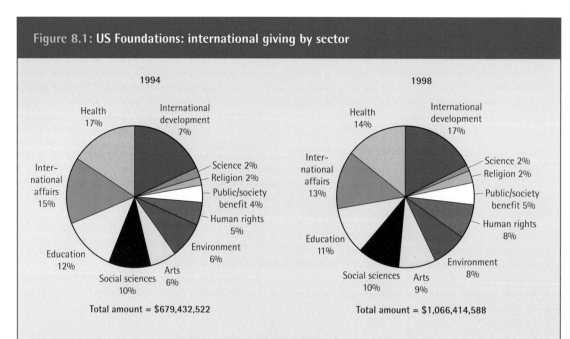

Figure 8.1: US Foundations: international giving by sector

1994

Health 17%

International development 7%

Science 2%

Religion 2%

Public/society benefit 4%

Human rights 5%

Environment 6%

Arts 6%

Social sciences 10%

Education 12%

International affairs 15%

Total amount = $679,432,522

1998

Health 14%

International development 17%

Science 2%

Religion 2%

Public/society benefit 5%

Human rights 8%

Environment 8%

Arts 9%

Social sciences 10%

Education 11%

International affairs 13%

Total amount = $1,066,414,588

The public/society benefit category includes grants for public affairs, philanthropy, and general grants to promote civil society. Civil society grants are also found in other categories, such as human rights and international development.

Based on sample of grants of $10,000 or more from 1,020 foundations for 1994 and 1,009 foundations for 1998.

Source: Renz, Samson-Atienza, and Lawrence (2000).

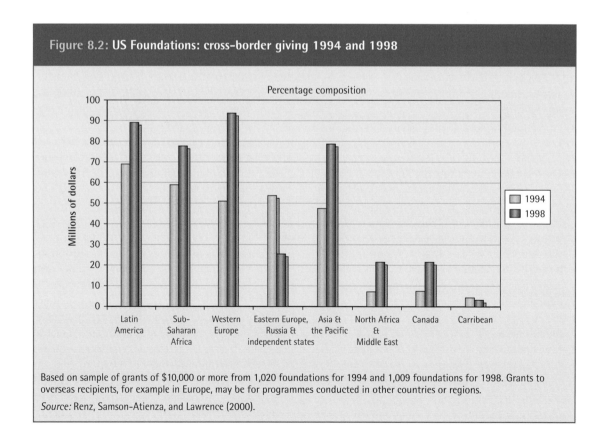

Figure 8.2: US Foundations: cross-border giving 1994 and 1998

Percentage composition

Millions of dollars

Latin America · Sub-Saharan Africa · Western Europe · Eastern Europe, Russia & independent states · Asia & the Pacific · North Africa & Middle East · Canada · Carribean

☐ 1994
■ 1998

Based on sample of grants of $10,000 or more from 1,020 foundations for 1994 and 1,009 foundations for 1998. Grants to overseas recipients, for example in Europe, may be for programmes conducted in other countries or regions.

Source: Renz, Samson-Atienza, and Lawrence (2000).

Box 8.1: The Soros Foundations Network

The profile of the Soros Foundations Network is an unusual one, but as a major player in the international arena it warrants special attention. Established in the 1980s by one individual, the billionaire financier George Soros, it is funded primarily out of his current income and a number of charitable entities established by the Soros family. Some of the programmes receive additional funds from the US government—particularly scholarships—and from other donors. Partnershipping with multilateral and bilateral agencies as well as NGOs on a programmatic level is encouraged throughout the network which is made up of nationally governed and staffed foundations now in 31 countries, primarily in central and eastern Europe, the former Soviet Union, and Africa, as well as Haiti and Guatemala. In addition, the flagship foundations of the OSI of New York and the OSI of Budapest offer a selection of 'network' programmes that draw on a central pool expertise and are coordinated through a number of advisory boards. National foundations are encouraged to draw on these centralised internal resources.

Source: Open Society Institute (1999).

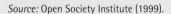

Total amount = $560,000,000

(Pie chart: Culture, recreation 24%; Education, research 27%; Health 6%; Social services 8%; Development & housing 6%; Civic & advocacy 13%; Other 16%)

While the distinctive mission of George Soros has been to create 'open societies' out of formerly authoritarian ones, the need to leverage and scale-up innovative models has necessitated working increasingly in partnerships with other donors that have a greater developmental focus, not only because of cost but also as a way of encouraging changes to take root by spreading the commitment across a broader base.

---

estimated two-thirds of the total international giving by all foundations. Changes in programmatic focus for the US foundations over the decade were as follows:

1. The main areas of substantial growth in giving were in international development, health, international affairs, and education. These were followed by human rights, public/social benefit, arts and culture, and religion.
2. Continued growth was reported in micro-enterprise development, human services, reproductive health care, pre-collegiate and adult education, refugee issues, civil rights, civil participation, and the non-profit sector and philanthropy.
3. New areas of growth include programmes on Aids, child health, disaster relief and humanitarian aid, climate change and pollution control, forest protection, and the impact of globalisation

The comparative growth and decline of individual areas of interest can be seen in Figure 8.1.

The changing international funding environment is also shown in Figure 8.2. Foundations felt that partnerships between grantmakers and other international funding organisations would increase, as would funding directly overseas. The increase in interest in giving abroad appears to be a result of globalisation, the decline in US government funding, and the rapid growth of foundation endowments.

The variations in growth patterns need to be further examined. However, the significant increase in funds directed to Western Europe may be explained by a greater willingness of US foundations to use West European NGOs as intermediaries, while the drop in interest in central and eastern Europe, Russia, and the Independent States reflects a correction after the first influx of funds following the fall of communism.

There does appear to be a convergence around a handful of key issues which some have interpreted cynically as the 'Washington consensus'. Certainly,

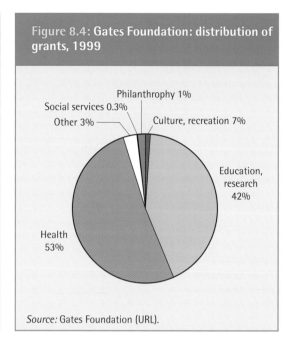

Figure 8.3: International programmatic trends of top twelve US foundations providing international grants, 1998

Other 2%
Arts 7%
International affairs 13%
Education 9%
Science 2%
Social sciences 11%
Health 15%
Human rights 10%
Public/society benefit 4%
International development 18%
Environment 9%

Source: Renz, Samson-Atienza, and Lawrence (2000).

Figure 8.4: Gates Foundation: distribution of grants, 1999

Philanthrophy 1%
Social services 0.3%
Other 3%
Culture, recreation 7%
Education, research 42%
Health 53%

Source: Gates Foundation (URL).

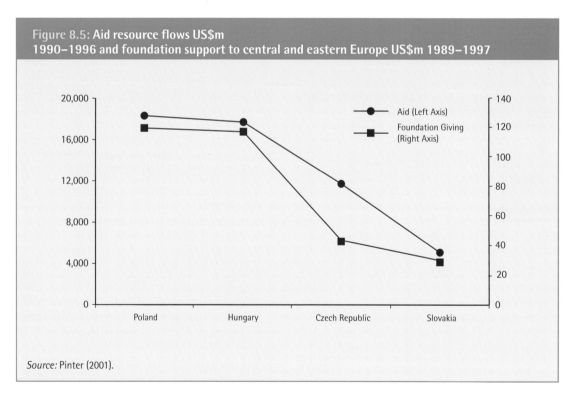

Figure 8.5: Aid resource flows US$m 1990–1996 and foundation support to central and eastern Europe US$m 1989–1997

Aid (Left Axis)
Foundation Giving (Right Axis)

Poland   Hungary   Czech Republic   Slovakia

Source: Pinter (2001).

improved communications and increased attendance at international conferences have enabled foundations to watch more closely one another's interests. The large amount of American money pouring into this arena is setting the standards and procedures followed by these and other donors. The degree of overlap of funded areas is demonstrated in Figure 8.3.

The core issues addressed by these bodies include human rights, the environment, biotechnology, humanitarian interventions, anti-capitalism/globalisation, democracy building, civil society building, arts and culture, the media, and health. Not reflected in these Foundation Center headings or in the main ICNPO listing is the importance of programmes and campaigns associated with gender issues, which in fact cut across many of the main sectors.

Corporate foundation giving in America grew faster than any other foundation sector in the late 1990s. The interests of corporate foundations in the globalisation process would suggest that a further coupling of the public and private can be expected in the early twenty-first century.

Many multinationals have identified areas in which acting in the public interest can be beneficial for themselves as well. Pharmaceutical companies, for example, spawned foundations that list in their annual report 'in-kind' drug donations from their parent companies. Cynics argue that this is actually just a marketing exercise with tax and goodwill benefits attached. While the intentions of some individuals involved may be sincere, it is obvious that, by giving away, for example, the hardware and software products of their parent companies, corporate foundations can help seed under-developed markets. The American Express Foundation explicitly states in its 1999 Annual Report 'many of our major philanthropic efforts are tied directly to the company's long-term business objectives' (American Express 2000: 3).

Attention is focused presently on the activities of the William and Melinda Gates Foundation (URL) that topped up its endowment funds to over $22 billion in 2000. Although programme development is still at an early stage, indications of priorities are clear. The distribution of funds in 1999 is shown in Figure 8.4. However, this does not reflect the growing concern Bill Gates has expressed over health provisions for the poorest people in Africa, which will be evident in later reports.

Foundation support internationally, whether private or corporate, often follows the same path as multilateral and bilateral aid. This occurred in central Europe in the 1990s as is illustrated in Figure 8.5.

Religious organisations

In recent years religious bodies have shifted their emphasis to include poverty reduction, agricultural development, provision of finance through small loan schemes, birth control—for and against—and, significantly, human rights and emergency relief programmes. Like many other funding bodies, religious organisations both disburse their own funds raised through donations and act as implementing agents for other funders.

In addition to the large numbers of locally sponsored and cross-border projects, a number of bodies bring state-based churches together within international networks. For example, the World Council of Churches represents more than 330 churches, denominations, and fellowships in 100 countries representing 400 million Christians. Actions by Churches Together is an alliance of churches and relief agencies that deal with emergencies in more than 50 countries. The World Alliance of Reformed Churches links more than 75 million Christians in over 100 countries. The Lutheran World Federation has 128 member churches in 70 countries representing 58 million Lutherans. Many nationally based religions have strong congregations around the world, such as the Russian Orthodox Church and the Armenian Church, all of which redistribute resources. Federations of Islamic religious groups play an active role in social and educational welfare. These umbrella groups facilitate the movement of funds across borders for the various causes endorsed and supported by religious bodies.

While the amount of funding for cross-border activities by religious bodies is difficult to ascertain, the Johns Hopkins study provides indicators of religious giving and volunteering as a percentage of total giving and volunteering. Table 8.7 demonstrates that religious giving and volunteering constitutes a sizeable proportion in each of the three countries surveyed. Whereas much of this is for local causes, a substantial portion is devoted to disaster relief around the world.

Trade unions

By 1999, the International Confederation of Free Trade Unions (ICFTU), much the largest trade union federation, had 213 member organisations in 143 countries, with a combined membership of 124 million employees. Although individual unions can join, most affiliates are national union centres. The main bulk of funding comes from affiliation fees from member organisations, based on the number of affiliated members. Some income also comes from publications sales, though this has been in decline since the 1980s, perhaps partly due to use of the Internet (Gordon and Turner 2000: 83–4).

Table 8.7: Religious giving and volunteering indicators, selected countries, 1991 and 1992

Dimension	United States	Germany		France
		With church tax	Without church tax	
Sum of religious giving as % of total sum of giving	60.4	80.21	33.1	22.1
Religious giving as % of annual income of givers	0.95	0.80–0.92	0.33	0.08
Average total sum of religious donations for givers previous 12 months	$800	–	$119	$107
Median total sum of religious donations for givers previous 12 months	$300	–	$40	$40
Sum of religious volunteering as % of total sum of volunteer hours	27.5	23.1	–	5.8
Average total sum of religious volunteer hours for volunteers previous 12 months	363	223	–	106

Source: The Johns Hopkins Comparative Nonprofit Sector Project (Salamon *et al.* 1996: 56).

Income for ICFTU's 'International Solidarity Fund' comes from special appeals, both general and for ear-marked projects. The ICFTU has also become increasingly reliant on grants from various public agencies (Gordon and Turner 2000: 91–2).

International cooperation also takes place on the industry or sector levels through International Trade Secretariats. As with the general federations, funds come from affiliation fees from member unions. However, they also receive grants from public agencies and private foundations

Who is funded?

The kinds of groups, organisations, and entities falling within the global civil society arena and funded by the sources discussed above may be large, well-established multinational NGOs or they may be small NGOs housed in one-room offices. They are sometimes more and sometimes less than inter-national non-governmental organisations (INGOs),

a category that the Union of International Associations (URL) prefers to call 'transnational association networks'. NGOs may be societally sponsored or established by governments, in which case they may be referred to as government organised NGOs (GONGOs); as multinational NGOs (MANGOs), referred to by some as 'manipulated' NGOs; or as government regulated and initiated NGOs (GRINGOs). NGOs may also be sponsored by Inter-Governmental Organi-sations (IGOs). The official purpose of an NGO is outlined in its constitution, but its ultimate course is influenced by its members and backers. While all claim to be independent, many serve only the interests of their sponsors.

Other funded bodies including social movements, a looser form of organisation, also come in a variety of shapes and sizes. Grass-roots organisations, while tending to be local, sometimes employ a network of international alliances to further their causes. Grass-roots organisations are most likely to receive local funding from individuals, businesses, and municipalities. Their resources are almost always stretched and, like social movements, they live a hand-to-mouth existence, receiving much in-kind support such as use of computers and telecommunications facilities. NGOs vary in size, of course, but usually have easier access to funding from more established bodies than do social movements. Social movements are considered by some funders to be too radical and too chaotically run. Grass-roots bodies tend to be more firmly rooted than social movements and therefore able to find more stable sources of funding. NGOs tend to be better equipped to attract funding from foundations of all kinds as well as the state, often through competitive processes requiring the submission of formal written applications. Increasingly the larger NGOs are relying on professional fundraising staff.

Bilateral aid programmes work alongside the multilateral agencies, as both engage with NGOs. How civil society organisations might operate within this context is described by Muduuli (2000) as follows—which applies equally to global CSOs:

1. influencing policy formulation through advocacy dialogue, research, and analysis;
2. participating in formulation of sector plans as researchers, stakeholders; and beneficiaries;
3. providing delivery of socio-economic services and implementing public programmes;
4. influencing public expenditure prioritisation, resource mobilisation, allocation and utilisation; and
5. monitoring and evaluating public expenditure and programmes.

Some of the funding of the above may be built into project costs, but funds are scarce for all but item three of the list. CSO project managers often find themselves turning to private foundations to cover the salary costs involved in influencing policy formulation, participating in planning, influencing prioritization, and monitoring.

These organisations' core activities include advocacy, activism, conflict resolution, humanitarian relief, educational/capacity building/training, and facilitating the use of digital communications. The make-up of different types of funding depends not only on the issue area addressed but also on the kind of activity pursued. Not-for-profit income-generating activity in the educational field provides a higher proportion of revenue than, say, selling T-shirts to support an advocacy endeavour on banning landmines.

While much global civil society activism is resourced through voluntary contributions of time, there are recurring costs that are fairly typical of most organisations. These include salaries for paid staff, premises—usually rented rather than purchased—office overheads, computers, telecommunications, information content—that is, books, reports, subscriptions, and Internet access—travel, training and capacity building, and public relations campaigns. The cost of many of these activities has dropped in recent years. Air travel in real terms has decreased by about 70 per cent (*Economist* 2001: 5) and ICT has enabled cash-poor organisations to launch campaigns on the web for a fraction of the cost of a paper campaign.

Whatever combination of funding sources is pursued, all civil society actors face the three main issues of independence, sustainability, and accountability.

Independence

From an anthropological point of view no organisation can ever truly retain its independence. A 'resource dependency perspective' developed by Pfeffer and Salancik is summarised by David Lewis (2001: 87) as follows:

> *The theory is based on the idea that instead of seeing organisations as relatively autonomous, the environment is a strong constraining influence which limits room for manoeuvre. All organisations depend on the environment for the resources they need and to do this they must continuously negotiate and exchange, and in this sense are to a large degree 'externally controlled'. Organisations try to reduce this dependency by controlling the flow of information about themselves to outsiders and by diversifying their sources of resources.*

The above is as true for NGOs as it is for corporations. While there has been an increase in income-generating activities across the whole spectrum of NGOs, advocacy groups rely mainly on spreading their dependency across a wide enough range of donors to ensure their independence.

Amnesty International (AI), for example, was launched in 1961 with 1,000 offers of support. Today it has over a million members, subscribers, and regular donors in more than 160 countries and territories. There are more than 5,300 local youth, student, and professional AI groups registered with the International Secretariat. Nationally based sections exist in 56 countries. Amnesty International does not accept funding from governments for its work investigating and campaigning against human rights violations. The International Secretariat's budget is in the region of $25 million, though this is only part of its worldwide funding (Amnesty International URL). This money is raised through membership fees and donations from trusts, foundations and companies. Human Rights Watch, with a core budget of $12.5 million also does not accept government funding. However, it relies more heavily on foundation grants rather than membership fees or individual donations (Human Rights Watch URL). Such broadly based bodies devote substantial resources to soliciting and then servicing their membership.

Campaigning globally on environmental issues, Greenpeace relies on a broad funding base for its legitimacy as much as for its financing. In 1999, 2.5 million donations were received, amounting to 126 million Euros. It does not accept contributions from governments or corporations. Money flows from the periphery to the centre as grants from the 25 national offices received by Greenpeace International's head office amounted to just over 25 million euros, while grants to the national branches from head office amounted to 4.5 million euros. Income from merchandising and licensing is in the region of 2 million euros and is a potentially growing source of revenue (Greenpeace URL). Friends of the Earth, founded in 1971, has also grown dramatically; it now has over 5,000 local activist groups and a combined budget of $200 million (Friends of the Earth URL). Even with 700 full-time staff members, much of its campaign work is carried out by volunteers.

The degree to which an organisation is independent of its financial backers depends, in part, on the amount of support it receives from volunteers and in-kind contributions. In many ways the more established and dependent an NGO is on outside finance, the more vulnerable it can become to changes in funding fashions. Relative dependency on financial resources varies according to the task at hand and the nature of the organisation to be funded. However, funding is only one, albeit important, component of the resourcing of any kind of activity. The appropriateness or viability of non-financial resources as substitutes or complements to financial resources depends on the structure of the organisation, what it intends to achieve and how, and the overall cultural climate surrounding the particular issue area. For example, in general the greater the local support for the effort, the less funding is required for advocacy campaigns. Other patterns of funding are necessary if highly paid experts need to be brought and bought in. The more global the coverage the more money needs to be spent on communications, both virtual and physical.

The question from whom organisations are independent varies from region to region. For example, in the transition countries of central and eastern Europe the rapid retreat of the state created a dramatic shortfall of funding in many areas. Substitution came primarily from foreign donors who then created a different kind of dependency relationship. After a few years of gratitude resentment set in. The same ingenuity that commandeered resources from the state was and is being employed in attempts to maintain the flow of foreign funds, even as the former Soviet bloc has fallen out of fashion with some donors.

Historically, northern NGOs (NNGOs) were the implementing agencies of choice for multilateral donors. These NNGOs would often subcontract components of projects to southern NGOs (SNGOs). Recently there has been a shift towards contracting directly with SNGOs. The rationale behind this is that the process itself assists in the building of local civil society; and, of course, it costs far less. Some argue that this can lead to an unhealthy dependency when NGOs act on behalf of funders with whose ideology they disagree. In trying to attract the business, NGOs risk losing their focus as independent commentators and promoters of alternative perspectives (Hulme and Edwards 1997). Conversely, as the donors become more dependent on NGOs for delivery, donor policies may to some extent be influenced by the NGOs themselves.

Sustainability

Sustainability as a concept may be applied to a project or programme that is sustained by its beneficiaries. In commerce the cost of creating and delivering products to the market is 'sustained' by the customers' willingness and ability pay for them. But who are the beneficiaries of the actions of global civil society? NGOs can mistakenly be thought of as the beneficiaries of the funds they receive, and herein lies the crux of the problem in defining what is and is not sustainable. The causes represented by NGOs are not the same as the organisations themselves. There is always a danger that organisations perpetuate themselves out of self-interest rather than for the sake of their original mission. The most successful organisation can fail to make itself redundant once its goals are achieved. The natural lifespan of a CSO depends on different factors from those that determine the lifespans of governments or businesses.

Social movements also face transformation questions. They may redefine themselves, as has been the case with many anti-apartheid groups. In central and eastern Europe many of the underground movements of the 1980s found it very difficult to adjust to the less idealistic and more materialistic 1990s. In the early 2000s many are still mourning the fragmentation of their old groups. However, others have grown up in their wake and a new generation of tougher, more pragmatic, and more highly structured NGOs has emerged.

Actors within the civil society sector are looking for ways of becoming self-sustainable, and to this end NGOs have adopted many of the business models stemming from the commercial world. Funds are increasingly raised through the provision of goods and services. Generating revenue from market activities rather than relying solely on membership contributions or donations from foundations, the state, or multilateral organisations may, to some extent, increase sustainability and independence. While the mission itself dictates to some degree the mode of operation, the will to survive causes CSOs to transform themselves from advocacy groups into consultants and subcontracted project managers.

The matching of funder and funded is as complex as any mating game. One cynical report argues that some NGOs will simply define their mission to agree with whatever a funder wants (Economist 2000). On a practical level CSOs do have to conform to certain requirements. Funders tend to operate with strict funding cycles. Applications need to be submitted by certain dates. Immediate needs often cannot be met because of waiting times for decisions to be made. The identity of the funder(s) also makes a difference. The source of support can determine the CSO's legitimacy and thus its effectiveness in influencing policy and accomplishing its objectives.

Accountability

The definition of accountability has broadened considerably since it applied solely to financial accounting practices, and now reflects the spread of the democratic process at all levels of society. Citizens worldwide are increasingly demanding that their elected leaders and the bureaucracies that serve them show a greater degree of accountability for their actions. In turn, questions have emerged about the accountability of civil society, in particular with regard to its mandate and to whom it is responsible.

Within the jurisdiction of the state, laws regulate the actions of civil society, but the power and influence of global civil society actors seem to be beyond the control of any individual state. Mechanisms for incorporating democratic values and involving all stakeholders in decision-making are as yet relatively undeveloped. The ideal may be unattainable because of purely logistical constraints, but greater transparency and clearer representations are being promoted more widely than ever. There is always the danger that NGOs administering funds are more accountable to their donors than to their beneficiaries (Edwards 2000: 209). However, with full disclosures, public debate, and more democratic governance it may be possible to generate more trust. Accountability will continue to be an issue at all levels, among the funders and the funded.

Legislative and Tax Environments: The State— Friend or Foe?

The legislative and tax environments affect all fund flows, whether emanating from development agencies, foundations, or individual contributors. This is particularly true for cross-border flows that not only are subject to a variety of legal regulations but also may experience practical difficulties, as with electronic transfers to countries with underdeveloped banking systems. In some instances the banks simply do not function at all, as in Kosovo just after the war of 1999. In rare instances

a well-known global CSO can maintain its existence without locating itself physically in any state. When the Campaign to Ban Landmines received a Nobel Peace prize it transpired that it did not have a bank account (Florini 2000: 143). It was simply a coalition of over a thousand CSOs worldwide working towards the same goal and brought together by the drive of a few individuals.

Both private and corporate foundations are increasingly taking advantage of differing tax and legal environments around the world in order to stretch their philanthropic funds. Increasingly popular are offshore sites from which funds may be easily disbursed; many choose to register in Liechtenstein and Switzerland with their favourable tax environments. At the same time some organisations such as Amnesty International have chosen to forgo the legal and tax benefits of charitable status for fear that such status might compromise their political independence.

Taxation and legislative policies do affect the ability of foundations to give to causes outside their home country. In many countries, the taxation of charities and donations encourages domestic programmes only; giving to foreign- registered NGOs is almost never tax-deductible. Only occasionally do bilateral treaties covering double taxation reduce these losses. Foundations may risk their tax status unless they ensure the charitable nature of the recipients of their grants; and this is more difficult to control when giving abroad.

Many governments are suspicious of CSOs and voluntary organisations. They suspect that NGO growth, particularly in the service provision sector, may erode their tax base. This is despite the advantages of encouraging voluntary organisations to take over some of the burdens of the state, often resulting in net cost savings. Non-profit legislation is less advanced in developing countries; and restrictions on incoming money flows often hinder rather than encourage increased flows from abroad. Many organisations establish legal entities within a number of the wealthier countries so as to offer the best tax advantage to potential givers from these countries, even though the ultimate recipient may be outside the country.

A healthy balance in NGO legislation is described below by John Clark (1997: 54). Not many countries have achieved this lofty state:

Government-imposed NGO regulations and reporting requirements must strike a balance between nurturing NGO growth, and guarding against corruption, management ill-discipline and other malpractice. Restrictive laws and procedures designed for the political control of NGOs clearly hamper legitimate NGOs. Fiscal policies should be transparent and even-handed, providing incentives for legitimate NGO activities (conforming with State development priorities). Tax concessions may be used to encourage indigenous philanthropy and income generating activities of NGOs. And legitimate NGOs should be able to receive foreign funds and donated goods without onerous bureaucratic delays. There should be no arbitrariness, bias or 'rent seeking' in the awarding of these privileges.

Some developed countries are only just beginning to establish NGO-friendly laws. Until Japan passed its Law to Promote Specified Nonprofit Activities in 1998, 90 per cent of Japanese NGOs remained unincorporated, resulting in all financial transactions being carried out in the names of individuals rather than organisations (Florini 2000:169).

The extent to which the state can set the regulatory framework for the cross-border flow of goods, services, and capital is contested, though the discussion is about degrees rather than absolutes (Higgott, Underhill, and Bieler 2000). NGOs serving global causes certainly benefit from more liberal regimes.

Conclusion

The earlier sections of this chapter focused on funding. But money alone does not create civil society. Human, social, organisational, informational, and financial resources provide a finely balanced mix that fuels global CSOs. Depending on whether it is lubricating the parts or firing the engine, different types of oil are required. The permutations are infinite, but the components are still of the same raw ingredients. New forms of renewable energy, in attempts to achieve sustainability, have become part of the global civil society resource kit and the advantages of recyclable resources are becoming increasingly apparent.

The dangers of focusing too heavily on financial resources were brought forcibly home in a paper presented by the former Chief Economist of the World Bank, Joseph Stiglitz, at the Bank's Annual Conference on Development Economics in 1999,

which focused on the failure to build social and organisation capital in the former communist bloc countries:

Arrow, Hirshman, Putnam, Fukuyama, and others have argued that the success of a market economy cannot be understood in terms of narrow economic incentives: norms, social institutions, social capital, and trust play critical roles. It is this implicit social contract, necessary to a market society, that cannot be simply legislated, decreed, or installed by a reform government. Some such 'social glue' is necessary in any society. One of the most difficult parts of a transformation, such as the transition from socialism to a market economy, is the transformation of the old 'implicit social contract' to a new one. (Stiglitz 1997: 8)

What Stiglitz is saying is that strategic funding alone cannot accomplish change. Whether at the abstract level of a general social contract or in the detail of how individuals behave in the associations they create, the social 'glue' of norms and trust must be in place if there is to be any life in the organisation or institution. This became a powerful, though not always heeded, lesson for both governments and foundations alike as they watched billions of dollars originally intended to assist the transition in the post-communist bloc disappear into Swiss bank accounts. It was an expensive demonstration of what happens in societies where there is no social glue to hold them together.

In a world of increasingly dense networks that engage more and more in communicating with one another, there appears to be a growing convergence around a handful of core issues among the major donors. The causes around which advocacy and activist groups have emerged, such as human rights, environmental issues, poverty alleviation, better access to health and education, and gender rights have given hope to some that a cultural cosmopolitan consensus (Held et al.1999) is emerging. Others see a bleaker world in the making that is totally subservient to the dictates of global capitalism.

At this stage it may be said that even if the perimeters of this new global civil society were clearer, it would still be impossible to quantify accurately how much money is flowing into this arena and what effect it is having. While the general shape of the funding community can be sketched, the actual total amounts flowing into the civil society space through global and regional CSOs are difficult to determine. It has been noted that over $7 billion of development funds flow through NGOs—but not all for civil society projects; that over $2 billion of US foundation giving is international—not all for and through CSOs; and that nearly $700 million of USAID was devoted to democracy building in 1999 alone. However, this is only a part of what is being spent worldwide on a cross-border basis that funds global civil society activities. The funding level we see is in the billions of dollars rather than millions or hundreds of millions. More studies need to be carried out at all levels, to create workable typologies and to demarcate clearly what is global from what is local. Comparative work to establish how funding patterns vary from region to region is also needed.

This chapter has tried to introduce the main issues around identifying and measuring the funding of organisations and movements that qualify as actors in the global civil society space. There is clearly a need to engage in further research, of both an empirical and a theoretical nature, related to the questions surrounding all aspects of resourcing, and not just funding. More fundamental questions on the nature of the economies in which global civil society is embedded need to be raised. Do healthy local civil societies attract more or less outside funding than less healthy ones? More in-depth comparative case studies need to look at how foreign funds influence local civil society and vice versa. It is to be hoped that the concept will in time be brought into sharper focus. The data, however, will in all likelihood still be problematic as the primary units of analysis remain nation-state based. More imaginative research approaches will be required to overcome this difficulty.

I would like to thank Jerzy Celichowski and Andy Roberts for their assistance in assembling the data for this chapter.

References

American Express (2000). *Annual Report.* New York: American Express.

Amnesty International. http://www.amnesty.org

Anheier, Helmut K. and List, Regina (ed.) (2000). *Cross-border Philanthropy: An Exploratory Study of International Giving in the United Kingdom, United States, Germany and Japan.* Baltimore, MD: Institute for Policy Studies, Johns Hopkins University; London: Center for Civil Society Studies.

— and Salamon, Lester M. (1999). 'Volunteering in Cross-National Perspective: Initial Comparisons'. *Law and Contemporary Problems,* 62/4: 43–66.

— and Toepler, Stefan (ed.) (1999). *Private Funds, Public Purpose: Philanthropic Foundations in International Perspective.* New York, Boston, Dobrecht, London, Moscow: Kluwer Academic/Plenum Publishers.

Carothers, Thomas (1999). *Aiding Democracy Abroad: The Learning Curve.* Washington, DC: Carnegie Endowment for International Peace.

Changemakers. http://www.changemaker.net

Clark, John, 'The State, Popular Participation and the Voluntary Sector', in David Hulme and Michael Edwards (ed.) (1997). *NGOs, States and Donors: Too Close for Comfort?* New York: St Martin's Press.

Economist (2000). 'NGOs: Sins of the Secular Missionaries'. 29 January.

— (2001). 'Air Travel'. 10 March.

Edwards, Michael (1999). *Future Positive: International Co-operation in the 21st Century.* London: Earthscan.

— (2000). *NGO: Rights and Responsibilities: A New Deal for Global Governance.* London: Foreign Policy Centre/NCVO.

Florini, Ann M. (ed.) (2000). *The Third Force: The Rise of Transnational Civil Society.* Washington, DC: Carnegie Endowment for International Peace.

Foundation Center, NY. http://www.foundationcenter.org

Friends of the Earth. http://www.foei.org

Galtung, Fredrik (2000). 'A Global Network to Curb Corruption: The Experience of Transparency International', in Ann M. Florini (ed.), *The Third Force: The Rise of Transnational Civil Society.* Washington, DC: Carnegie Endowment for International Peace.

Gates Foundation. http://www.gatesfoundation.org

Giving USA. http://www.aafrc.org/giving

Greenpeace. http://www.greenpeace.org

GuideStar. http://www.guidestar.org

Held, David, McGrew, Anthony, Goldblatt, David, and Perraton, Jonathan (1999). *Global Transformations: Politics, Economics and Culture.* Cambridge: Polity Press.

Higgott, Richard A., Underhill, Geoffrey, and Bieler, Andreas (ed.) (2000). *Non-State Actors and*

Authority in the Global System. London: Routledge.

Hulme, David and Edwards, Michael (ed.) (1997). *NGOs, States and Donors: Too Close for Comfort?* New York: St Martin's Press.

Human Rights Watch. http://www.hrw.org

Lawrence, Steven, Camposeco, Carlos, and Kendzior, John (ed.) (2000). *Foundation Yearbook: Fact and Figures on Private and Community Foundations.* New York: The Foundation Center.

Lewis, David (2001). *Management of Non-Governmental Development Organizations: An Introduction.* London: Routledge.

Mackintosh M. and Wainwright, H. (1987). *A Taste of Power: The Politics of Local Economics.* London: Verso.

MamaCash. http://www.mamacash.org.

Markle Foundation. http://www.nypost.com/news/27330.htm

Muduuli, M. C. (2000). Paper delivered at Donor Policy Synergy and Coordination Workshop. Glasgow, 25–6 May.

OECD (2000). *World Development Indicators.* Paris: OECD.

Open Society Institute (1999). http://www.soros.org

Pearce, Jenny, (1997). 'Between Co-operation and Irrelevance? Latin American NGOs in the 1990s', in David Hulme and Michael Edwards (ed.). *NGOs, States and Donors: Too Close for Comfort?* New York: St Martin's Press

Pinter, Frances, (2001) 'The Role of Foundations in the Transformation Process in Eastern Europe', in Andreas Schlüter, Volker Then and Peter Walkenhorst (ed.) *Foundations in Europe: Society, Management and Law.* London: Directory of Social Change.

Renz, Loren and Lawrence, Steven. (2001) *Foundation Growth and Giving Estimates, 2000 Preview.* New York: The Foundation Center.

—, Samson-Atienza, Josefina, and Lawrence, Steven (2000). *International Grantmaking 11.* New York: The Foundation Center.

Risse, Thomas (2000). 'The Power of Norms versus the Norms of Power: Transnational Civil Society and Human Rights', in Ann M. Florini (ed.). *The Third Force: The Rise of Transnational Civil Society.* Washington, DC: Carnegie Endowment for International Peace.

Salamon, Lester M., Anheier, Helmut K., and Sokolowski, Wojciech and Associates (1996). *The Emerging Sector: A Statistical Supplement.* Baltimore: The Johns Hopkins Comparative Nonprofit Sector Project.

Stiglitz, Joseph E., (1997) 'Wither Reform? Ten Years of the Transition'. http://www.worldbank.org/research/abcde/pdfs/stiglitz.pdf. 28–30 April.

UNDP (United Nations Development Programme) (2000). *Human Development Report.* New York and Oxford: Oxford University Press.

UNHCR. http://www.unhcr.ch

Union of International Associations. http://www.uia.org

World Bank (1998). *Annual Report.* Washington, DC: World Bank.

— (1999). *Annual Report.* Washington, DC: World Bank.

Wright, Karen (2000) *Generosity vs Altruism: Philanthropy and Charity in the US and UK.* London: Centre for Civil Society, London School of Economics.

Part IV: Records of Global Civil Society

MEASURING GLOBAL CIVIL SOCIETY

Helmut Anheier

Really to impress the mind a concept has first to take visual shape.
J. Huizinga, *The Waning of the Middle Ages*

Introduction

As the opening chapter of this *Yearbook* edition suggested, global civil society is both an emerging reality and an emerging concept. As a term, it is neither easily understandable nor communicable. Global civil society remains a fuzzy concept, located uncomfortably in the conceptual map of modern social science. How, then, given these difficulties, could global civil society at all be measured?

At a fundamental level, the difficulty social scientists and policy-makers have with the term 'global civil society' reflects the increasing inadequacy of national and international statistical systems to come to terms with the informational requirements of globalisation. The current 'statistical world order' continues to assume equivalence between nation state, domestic economy, and national society. This equivalence is fundamentally challenged by globalisation.

The process of globalisation has created, and continues to create, new institutions and organisational forms (Castells 1996; Giddens 1990; Held *et al.* 1999). This set of institutions and forms includes different types of international governments, international power relations, transnational corporations, international non-governmental organisations and networks of many kinds, and phenomena such as global cities, global broadcasting systems, and the Internet. It also creates dispersed yet internationally connected communities based on ethnicity, shared values, professional background, or some other kind of common interest. For Shaw (2000: 11–12) globalisation involves more than the expansion of a global infrastructure of organisations and networks: it involves also the development of a 'common consciousness of human society on a world scale'. Many of the emerging forms, values, and orientations of global civil society are only inadequately captured, if at all, by the conventional statistical machinery in place.

Scholte (1999), Shaw (2000: 68–70), and Beck (2001) use the term 'methodological nationalism' to describe the tendency of much modern social science to remain wedded to, and caught in, categories more applicable to the nineteenth century notion of the industrial nation state than to the more complex world of globalisation. A consequence directly relevant to the purpose of measuring global civil society is the profound impact national statistical systems have on what kind of statistics are collected, analysed, and reported, and what remains outside the remit of official economic and social accounts. Importantly, this applies to the international level too, as international statistical agencies typically rely on data supplied by national statistical offices. Even though some UN agencies collect their own statistics, the conventional model of generating international data uses information provided by national statistical offices and similar agencies.

The capacity of the international community to generate its own data outside the realm of national systems thus remains severely limited. A major consequence of the primacy of methodological nationalism is a 'statistical world order' that systematically disregards whatever does not fit the framework of domestic economy, sovereign national polity, and national society. As a result, international statistical systems are ever more at odds with the reality of an increasingly globalised world, as the examples set out below illustrate.

The economic activities of transnational corporations (TNCs) are split up across the numerous domestic economies in which they do business, even though the economic scale of some of these corporations, taken as a whole, is larger than the gross domestic product of many of the countries in which they operate. Yet other than in special reports directed at experts (for example, UNCTAD 2000; van Tulder *et al.* 2001; Castells 1996) or country-specific listings (for example, *Fortune*, the US business magazine, and its annual list of the largest US corporations as the

Fortune 500), relatively little systematic statistical data is published and available on a regular basis on the world's larger corporations *as a whole* (see Sklair 1995: 104–19). The glaring gap in data includes core areas such as total labour-force characteristics, production and distribution chains, and other essential information to understand the workings of a globalised economy. Indeed, in the absence of more systematic efforts that go beyond the information needs of financial markets, it is frequently left to activists and advocacy organisations to point out the complex network and frequently problematic nature of a globalised economy and its interactions with national politics and societies.

An even worse assessment could be reached for information on international NGOs and transnational associations.[1] They, too, are treated as domestic economic agents for measurement purposes, thereby losing an essential aspect of their very *raison d'être*, that is, their transnationality and the fact that, like transnational corporations, they are increasingly less bound by the artificial boundaries of national statistics. What is more, if we move from the level of formal organisations like the Federation of Red Cross and Red Crescent Societies, Amnesty International, or GreenPeace to informal networks among activists and concerned citizens, the data situation becomes even more patchy and unsystematic. It is perhaps only a slight overstatement to assert that, for the first time in human history, interpersonal and inter-organisational networks are emerging at a global scale and are increasingly achieving global range. Yet much of this process and many of the contours of such networks remain unmeasured and go unreported (see Chapter 1).

These examples point to the basic methodological problem for generating global statistics: how to establish new units of analysis beyond the nation state, or how to go beyond the methodological nationalism of the current system? The information presented in this section is just the first step toward addressing this question.

Of course, any data effort that relies on the availability of high-quality and comparable information across many different countries and regions

faces considerable challenges. As will become clear below, for few topics could the data situation be more precarious than it presently is for global civil society. At the same time, a rich body of information, however inadequate and incomplete still, is increasingly becoming available internationally. This is due in large measure to the efforts of organisations like the World Bank, the United States Statistics Division, the United Nations Development Programme (UNDP), the International Labour Organisation (ILO), UNESCO, regional institutions like EUROSTAT, and more specialised agencies like the Union of International Associations. Moreover, particular projects like the World Bank's project on governance (Kaufmann, Kraay, and Zoido-Lobatón 1999*a*, *b*) and social capital (Dasgupta and Serageldin 2000), Transparency International (1999/2000), the European and World Value Surveys (Inglehart, Basañez, and Moreno 1998), and the Johns Hopkins Comparative Nonprofit Sector Project (Salamon *et al.* 1999) have made critical contributions to improve the international data situation in hitherto neglected areas.

Unfortunately, the improvement of data coverage and quality is not happening in equal measure across countries and regions. While some gaps are being filled, many remain, and some are indeed becoming wider, particularly in many developing countries. According to UNDP (2000: 141), 'despite the considerable efforts of international organisations to collect, process, and disseminate social and economic statistics and to standardise definitions and data collection efforts, many problems remain in coverage, consistency, and comparability of data across countries and over time' (see also Development Cooperation Directorate, OECD, 2001). For example, the report states that for 66 developing countries, or about one-third of all countries worldwide, no recent data on the incidence of poverty are available. What is more, over 90 countries have no data on youth literacy, and over 60 countries cannot supply adequate data on underweight children younger than five years of age.

With data on such basic indicators as poverty, literacy, or child welfare missing for a substantial number of the world's countries, how realistic is it to assume that data will be available for global civil society on a systematic and comparable basis? The challenge implicit in this question will be addressed, at least initially, in the following pages. In summary,

---

[1] *The Union of International Associations (1905–1999/2000) in Brussels is the only institution in the world that systematically collects data on the number, location, size, and activities of international non-governmental organisations. Its handful of staff equals that of a municipal statistical office in a medium-sized city in OECD countries.*

the objective is to come up with a set of indicators, measures, and data that

- describe the context in which global civil society develops and exists, that is, globalisation of the economy, human rights, and communication patterns;
- portray the infrastructure of global civil society in terms of organisations, associations, and networks;
- depict the values and activities of the people participating in, and thereby creating, global civil society; and
- explore, pending a closer examination of data availability and patterns, the possibility of developing a Global Civil Society Index for future editions of the Yearbook. This index would allow for a comparative ranking of countries in terms of their participation and inclusion in global civil society.

Making an Abstract, Emerging Concept Operational

Measuring global civil society involves several major challenges: identifying the appropriate unit of analysis, dealing with the aggregation problem, selecting appropriate indicators and measures, and finding available data. We will address each in turn, in the full understanding that we have been able to suggest only initial responses to these basic problems.

Challenges

1 What is the *unit of analysis* for global civil society, and how can we establish conceptual and empirical boundaries for the purpose of identifying and measuring central dimensions? How does the concept relate to adjacent notions and terms in the social sciences such as 'globalisation', 'information society', 'social capital', 'third sector', and 'social movements'? Global civil society is too abstract a concept for direct observation (see below); for measurement purposes, it seems best to focus on *identifiable elements* that 'carry' the essential characteristics of interest. This refers to organisational entities—number, activities, and growth (Tables R19–R24)—on the one hand, and individuals—values and activities (Tables R25–R32)—on the other. In addition, we put the elements of global civil

society in the context of related phenomena such as globalisation and the international rule of law (Tables R1–R18). In most cases, however, because of the aggregation problem (see next point), the country becomes the *de facto* unit of analysis.

How can the *aggregation problem* be solved? Most data are nation-based, which creates at least a potential mismatch between unit of observation (for example, organisation) and the *de facto* unit of analysis (country). If global civil society is qualitatively different from national and international units of analysis, then it cannot simply be the additive score of nation-based observations. The problem is primarily one of prevailing practices whereby data are aggregated and reported at national levels, and cannot be disaggregated and reconstituted at the supra-national level. This is the consequence of Scholte's (1999) and Beck's (2001) 'methodological nationalism' that plagues the modern social sciences. In some cases, however, it is possible to move beyond the unit of the national state (Table R3 on TNCs; Table R23 on the purposes of INGOs; Table R32 covering the language abilities of INGO leaders).

2 What actual *indicators and measures* are best suited for portraying the central dimensions of global civil society? Obviously, these measures range from economic, political, and social indicators to more qualitative assessments of global legal issues such as human rights, conflicts, and global governance. We examined a wide range of indicators for each dimension and unit of analysis and selected those that are closest to the intended meaning of the concept (see below; for example, 'density measures' of international NGO distribution across countries as an indicator of the organisational infrastructure of global civil society: Tables R19 and R20), relatively uncontroversial and established (trade data to measure economic globalisation: Table R1), widely available and for many countries (for example, human rights measures: Table R12).

3 What is the data coverage and availability? Much of the *data* needed to report on global civil society may not be readily available or not exist at all. Moreover, parts of the data may be qualitative and even involve value judgements of one kind or another. As in the case of indicators, we explored a broad range of potential data sources. In most cases, however, appropriate data could be found, although with limited country coverage and other

aspects that reduce comparability.[2] For example, some of the population survey data used to measure cosmopolitan values reported in Table R25 are available for some developing countries only, and may not be fully representative of the rural population or the poor. For other indicators, as in the case for *solidarity* (helping immigrants: Table R27; and concern about the living conditions of humankind in Table R28), data are available for European countries only.

Assumptions

Like the approach underlying the Human Development Index (UNDP 2000) and Desai's (1994) Political Freedom Index, the measurement of global civil society rests on the premise of parsimony and emphasises a select number of indicators that can be operationalized, are measurable, and have a reasonable degree of data availability. This approach implies that highly complex and demanding models are of little use when indicators cannot be observed and when data are not readily available; moreover, complex models can be difficult to communicate to diverse audiences. Specifically, and in the light of the conceptual discussion in Chapter 1, we proceed from four assumptions.

Assumption 1: Any measurement of global civil society will be simpler and less perfect than the richness, variety, and complexity of the concept it tries to measure.[3] As an analytic and operational concept, global civil society must necessarily abstract from historical and current variations in its development, and disregard important cultural, political, and social differences among countries and regions. Guided by the conceptual literature in the field, the information presented in the tables aims to provide the essential characteristics of global civil society and its context, and not its full variety and subtlety (see below).

Assumption 2: Global civil society is a multifaceted, emerging phenomenon, and its operationalisation must take account of this

essential characteristic. As the essence of global civil society may vary with theoretical approach, disciplinary outlook, or policy-related interests, the profile should be based on a broad approach that emphasises various aspects of the concept and takes account of different dimensions and orientations. For example, while the operational definition of global civil society proposed here (see Chapter 1 and below) excludes market institutions, others, like Keane (1998), argue that it should include transnational corporations. Analysts are similarly divided over whether institutions like the rule of law and the media should be included. We decided nonetheless to include relevant tables covering these aspects.

Assumption 3: Global civil society is essentially a normative concept. Global civil society is not a value-free concept but rests on the normative expectations of a more humane and inclusive world (see Kaldor, forthcoming) and the possibility of an ethical consensus (Küng 1998). The normative aspect is included in conceptions of global civil society that stress the emerging 'awareness of a common framework of worldwide human society' (Shaw 2000: 12) that becomes increasingly dominant over local and national understandings. In this sense, the emergence of a global civil society is part of a civilising process that elevates from national and regional contexts to the global level aspirations for human rights and the rule of law, peace, sustainability, and social justice as well as values like non-violence, tolerance, solidarity, compassion, and stewardship of the environment and cultural heritage. These aspirations and the norms they imply, however, are contested, and little agreement exists across the diverse audiences of researchers, policy-makers, and activists as to their acceptability, meanings, and implications.

Assumption 4: The operationalisation and measurement of global civil society has a strategic-developmental dimension. We view the current profile of global civil society as an evolving system that can be perfected over time. Feedback received from the social science and policy communities will help improve the data situation so that future editions of the *Yearbook* can build on each other. Moreover, the profile of global civil society should lend itself to policy-relevant analysis and be of use to policy-makers and social scientists in diverse settings.

---

[2] *Taken together, the data situation points to a significant need to fill the most glaring gaps through primary research; moreover, some data currently available will not be updated until 2005–8: for example, the European and World Value Surveys (Inglehart, Basañez, and Moreno 1998.)*

[3] *On the concepts of civil society and global civil society and the rich intellectual traditions they embody, see Chapters 1 and 2 in this volume; see also Cohen and Arato (1997); Kaldor (forthcoming); Keane (1998).*

Initial operationalisation

In Chapter 1 we suggested that global civil society is closely linked to the overarching concept of globalisation, defined as the functional integration of internationally dispersed activities (Dicken 1998; Held *et al.* 1999). By 'global civil society' we depict the socio-sphere of ideas, values, institutions, organisations, networks, and individuals located primarily outside the institutional complexes of family, state, and market and operating beyond the confines of national societies, polities, and economies. This definition, more fully discussed in Chapter 1, serves operational purposes only, and is suggested with due recognition of the existence and legitimacy of different definitions and normative assumptions. The *elements* of global civil society are:

- *Organisations, associations, and networks as the infrastructure of global civil society* (for example, Giddens 1990; Castells 1996; Dicken 1998; Held *et al.* 1999). What are the organisations that relate to global civil society (for example, national, regional, and international governments; TNCs) or are integral parts of it (for example, international NGOs; other civil society organisations, social movements operating across borders, and transnational networks)? What networks exist in global civil society (social movements, professional networks, activists' networks, partnerships like twinning programmes, Internet groups, and forums)?
- *Individuals: awareness, values, participation, and identity* (for example, Shaw 2000; Keck and Sikkink 1998; Kaldor, forthcoming). What are the characteristics of individuals who create, participate in, or otherwise act in global civil society (for example, activists, members, global civil leaders; internationally mobile professionals, staff of international NGOs)? Are individual awareness and identities related to 'global communities' and the notion of global citizenry? How widespread are values of civility, including tolerance, solidarity, and compassion?

Following Held *et al.* (1999: 17–27), we suggested that some of the major contours of global civil society can be described by three related characteristics:

- *extensity* as a measure of the geographical stretching of activities, indicated by the number of 'nodes' (organisations, associations, informal networks, activists, and participants) that constitute the overall spread of the network. Extensity refers to the range of global civil society;
- *intensity* of the overall density of the network in terms of the number and types of connections involved among the various 'nodes'. Intensity indicates how densely the elements of global civil society are connected amongst each other; and
- *velocity* of the overall network as measure of the frequency to which connections are made or used among network nodes. Velocity refers to the volume of interactions among global civil society actors and organisations.

Table M1 relates the contours of global civil society to the two basic units of analysis: *organisations* and the infrastructure they generate on the one hand, and *individuals* and their values and activities on the other. Data coverage is far from ideal for each of the six fields, but it is better for extensity than for intensity measures and worst for velocity indicators. The true challenge, however, is found in the field of impact measures of global interconnectedness, the fourth element identified by Held *et al.* (1999) in developing a framework for the analysis if globalisation. Unfortunately, virtually no data are available for this dimension at present; it is therefore not covered in the tables that follow. Ideally, impact measures should go beyond changes

Table M1: Contours of global civil society		
	Organisational infrastructure	**Individual participation and identity**
Extensity	e.g. number of reach of connections among organisational entities	e.g. number of reach of connections among network members
Intensity	e.g. density and multiplexity of connections	e.g. forms of participation and types of interactions
Velocity	e.g. volume of contacts and flows	e.g. volume of contacts and interactions

in global civil society—range, density, and velocity—and include policy changes of governments and businesses as well.

Of course, as we suggested in Chapter 1, there is more to global civil society than the network of institutions, organisations, and activists. Defining global civil society as a socio-sphere goes beyond the notions of network or infrastructure. As Kaldor (forthcoming) and Shaw (2000) suggest, global civil society includes aspects of civility and value dispositions. For this reason, we also include value-related aspects, normative expectations, and questions of awareness and personal identity in our approach to measure global civil society.

As we argued in Chapter 1, the extensity, intensity, and velocity of global civil society, and the values, awareness, and motivations associated with it are not phenomena *sui generis* but the reflection of other processes. In other words, global civil society exists and develops in a particular context constituted by a general trend towards globalisation of the economy and a thickening of the international rule of law. This process takes place in most institutional fields, be they the economy, communications and media, religion, or education and research, among others (see Beynon and Dunkerley 2000; Dicken 1998; Held *et al.* 1999), and involves both proponents and opposition. Like civil society, some institutions and organisations in these fields are assuming global

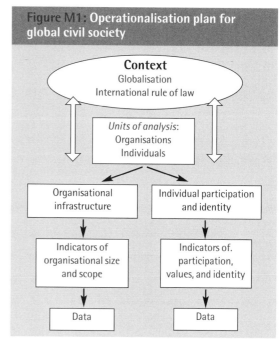

Figure M1: Operationalisation plan for global civil society

characteristics and are closely related to the emergence of global civil society itself. A second and related process is the expansion and consolidation of an international system of the rule of law laying down rules in the field of human rights, international criminal law, and environmental law that directly protect and empower citizens. In other words, global civil society consists of two basic units of analysis:

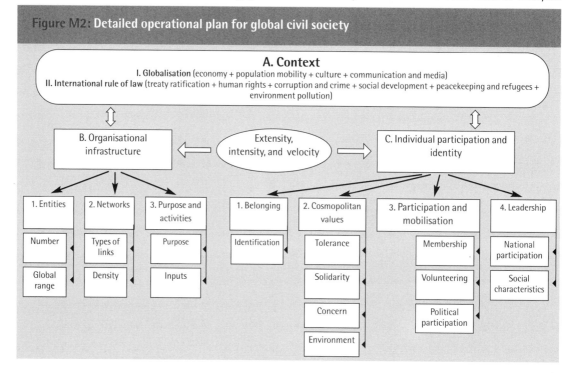

Figure M2: Detailed operational plan for global civil society

organisations—associations, networks, and so on—and *individuals* in the context of a larger globalisation process (Figure M1):

Figure M2 offers a more detailed view of the operationalisation of global civil society suggested here. For each unit of analysis (organisations, individuals) a range of indicators further specifies core dimensions and, for some cases, additional characteristics. For example, to measure the organisational infrastructure of global civil society, we differentiate between the number of entities (*intensity*: organisations, associations, networks, and other organisational forms), the networks they form at the global level (*extensity*: different types of ties, density measures), and their purpose (*multiplexity*: culture, education, advocacy, and so forth) and economic scale (*velocity*: employment, expenditures, revenue structure).

The tables in this section present the result of this operationalisation process and provide empirical information on key elements and dimensions of global civil society (references to the relevant box in Figure M1 are included in parentheses):

Globalisation as Context

Economy:

- What is the extent of global economic links and the globalisation of domestic economies, and what is the scale, direction, and growth of merchandise trade (Global economy, trade, Tables R1 and R2)?
- What is the scale of the largest 100 transnational corporations (Transnationality, Table R3)?

Population mobility:

- What is the magnitude of the student exchanges among different world regions (Foreign students, Table R4)?
- What is the scale and direction of labour migration (Foreign labour, Table R5)?
- What are the size and patterns of international travel and tourism (Travel, Table R6)?

Culture:

- What is the magnitude of trade in cultural goods (Cultural trade, Table R7)?
- What are the major world languages and religions (Languages, Table R8)?

Communication and media:

- What is the scale and patterns of international phone, TV, radio, newspaper and Internet use (Media, communication, Tables R9 and R10)?

Rule of law:

- What is the extent of international treaty ratification (Treaty ratification, Table R11)?
- To what extent are human rights respected and violated (Human rights, Table R12)?
- What is the level of corruption in different parts of the world and how widespread is serious crime such as homicide and assault (Corruption, crime, Tables R13 and R14)?

Peace-keeping and refugees:

- What is the magnitude and flow of refugees in terms of host countries and country of origin (Refugees, Table R15)?
- Which countries participate in peace-keeping efforts and where are the world's armed conflicts (Peacekeeping, Table R16)?

Social and environmental development:

- What is the range of social development in different parts of the world for measures such as literacy, child mortality, and income inequality (Social justice, Table R17)?
- What is the extent of energy consumption per capita and relative to GDP (Energy consumption, Table R18)?

Organisational Infrastructure

Entities:

- How many international non-governmental organisations are there (Number, Table R19)?
- What is their global reach in terms of membership (Global range, Table R20)?

Networks:

- What links international non-governmental organisations and what kind of networks do they form (Types of links, Density, Table R21)?

- What is the nationality of, and network among, international organisation leaders (Nationality and Types of links, Table R22)?

Purpose and activities:

- In what areas do international non-governmental organisations operate, and what is their purpose (Purpose, Table R23)?
- What is the economic weight of international non-governmental organisations in terms of employment, expenditures, and revenue structure (Inputs, Table R24)?

Individual Participation and Identity

Belonging:

- To what extent do people primarily identify with a particular locality, region or nation as opposed to the world at large (Identification, Table R25)?

Cosmopolitan values:

- How widespread are cosmopolitan values such as tolerance of other races, immigrants and 'foreigners' among the world population (Tolerance, Table R26)?
- To what extent do people regard it as their moral duty, or in the interest of society, to help others, in particular those in need and irrespective of national origin, race, and religion (in this case, immigrants) (Solidarity, Table R27)?
- To what degree are people concerned about the living conditions of humankind relative to their concern for neighbourhood, region, or country (Compassion, Table R28)?
- Are people willing to give up part of their income to aid the environment (Environment, Table R29)?

Participation and mobilisation:

- What is the proportion of people who are members of typical global civil society organisations (Memberships, Table R30)?
- What is the share of people volunteering in and for typical global civil society organisations (Volunteering, Table R30)?

- To what extent are people willing to participate in political events (Political participation, Table R31)?

Leadership:

- What are other social characteristics like gender, age, language and educational background of international organisation leaders (Social Characteristics, Table R32

The list above and the tables that follow make easily apparent that currently available data do not cover several core dimensions and relationships of global civil society. This is most critically the case for the link between the organisational infrastructure of global civil society and the value patterns among individuals in terms of civility or belonging. In other cases, the data presented on global civil society would gain significantly in meaning if they could be contrasted with similar data for global businesses and international organisations. For example, the socio-demographic characteristics of leaders in international NGOs cannot be compared with those for the management staff of TNCs as no comparable data are available. Together with data on IGO staff, these three components would offer a social profile of the emerging group of global professionals.

Moreover, some data are proxy measures at best. Take for example the data reported from various population surveys as part of the European and World Value Surveys (Inglehart, Basañez, and Moreno 1998). The questions about behaviour such as political activism and volunteering are based on the respondents' recall and may only approximate rather than measure such behaviour directly. More generally, the following core areas are missing from the table programme at present:

- social movements, grass roots groups, and loose networks (see Buechler 2000; Cohen and Rai 2000; Smith 1997). The data reported here focus on registered INGOs and miss perhaps the most dynamic part of emerging global civil society: locally based yet internationally connected networks of people and activists;
- the types and frequency of activities in global civil society such as political actions, particular those using the Internet as a mobilisation and information tool;

- the relationship between world cultures and religions on the one hand and global civil society on the other (see Huntington 1996; Barber 1995);
- patterns of social, cultural and political innovation and diffusion in global civil society (see Meyer *et al.* 1997);
- patterns of social inclusion and exclusion in global civil society; and
- the 'dark side', or global 'uncivil' society such as crime, terrorists, supremacists, and fundamentalists, and the movements, networks, and organisations they create and operate.

Towards A Global Civil Society Index?

We suggested above the possibility of developing a Global Civil Society Index for future editions of *Yearbook*. This index would allow for a comparative ranking of countries in terms of their participation and inclusion in global civil society. While it may be premature to present the preliminary result of this exploration for this edition, it is nonetheless useful to outline some of the thinking behind it. Similar to the Human Development Indicator developed by UNDP, the Global Civil Society Index would be a composite measure of three independent component indicators, each measuring a distinct aspect: civility, infrastructure, and participation. Specifically:

- *civility* would itself be a combined measure of cosmopolitan values such as tolerance, concern for humankind, and solidarity with and compassion towards those in need (see Kaldor, forthcoming; Shaw 2000). Most likely, data for these measures will come from sources like the World Value Survey (Inglehart, Basañez, and Moreno 1998). Yet the challenge in measuring civility lies in the implicit value judgements that might necessarily be involved: whose values are counted and whose not, and what priorities exist among values, for example between concern for humankind and concern for the environment?
- *infrastructure* would refer to the density of international NGOs and associations in a particular country (see Castells 1996; Dicken 1998; Held *et al.* 1999). The infrastructure measure would be closely related to the extensity and intensity measures discussed above, and likely be based on data provided by the Union of International

Associations, yet this would leave out other forms of associations like informal networks among professionals or activists; and
- *participation* would measure individual involvement in, and voluntary work for organisations, associations, or networks related to global civil society (see Keck and Sikkink 1998), and would complement organisation-based extensity and intensity indicators. This would link the global civil society to aspects of social capital (Dasgupta and Serageldin 2000). One indicator would be membership in international associations and networks, yet the very notion of membership is culture-bound even within OECD countries. Others are political participation and action. An additional measure would be a cross-national communication indicator for individuals.

The actual construction and testing of the Index is yet to take place, and its final form and calculation will depend on data availability and the distributional properties of the different variables that come into focus.

References

Beck, Ulrich (2001). 'The Postnational Society and its Enemies'. Public lecture, London School of Economics and Political Science, 24 February.

Barber, Benjamin (1995). *Jihad vs. McWorld*. New York: Times Books.

Beynon, John and Dunkerley, David (eds.) (2000). *The Globalization Reader*. London: Athlone Press.

Buechler, Steven M. (2000). *Social Movements in Advanced Capitalism*. Oxford: Oxford University Press.

Castells, Manuel (1996). *The Rise of Network Society*. Oxford: Blackwell.

Cohen, Jean L. and Arato, Andrew (1997). *Civil Society and Political Theory*. Cambridge: Cambridge University Press.

Cohen, Robin and Rai, Shirin M (eds) (2000). *Global Social Movements*. London: Athlone Press.

Dasgupta, P., and Serageldin, I. (2000). *Social Capital: A Multifaceted Perspective*. Washington, DC: World Bank.

Desai, M. (1994). *Measuring Political Freedom* (Discussion Paper 10). London: Centre for the

Study of Global Governance, London School of Economics.

Development Cooperation Directorate (OECD) (2001). *Partnerships in Statistics for Development in the 21st Century*. Paris: OECD. http://www.paris21.org

Dicken, Peter (1998). *Global Shift: Transforming the World Economy*. London: Chapman.

Giddens, Anthony (1990). *The Consequences of Modernity*. Cambridge: Polity Press.

Held, David, McGrew, Anthony, Goldblatt, David, and Perraton, Jonathan (1999). *Global Transformations*. Cambridge: Polity Press.

Huntington, Samuel (1996). *The Clash of Civilisations and the Remaking of World Order*. New York: Simon and Schuster.

Inglehart, R., Basañez, M., and Moreno, A. (1998). *Human Values and Beliefs: A Cross-Cultural Sourcebook: Political, Religious, Sexual, and Economic Norms in 43 Societies: Findings from the 1990–1993 World Values Survey*. Ann Arbor: The University of Michigan Press,

Kaldor, Mary (forthcoming). *Global Civil Society*. Cambridge: Polity Press.

Kaufmann, D., Kraay, A., and Zoido-Lobatón, P. (1999*a*). *Governance Matters* (World Bank Policy Research Working Paper 2196). Washington, DC: World Bank. http://www.worldbank.org/wbi/governance/pdf/govmatrs.pdf.

— (1999*b*). *Aggregating Governance Indicators* (World Bank Policy Research Working Paper 2195). Washington, DC: World Bank. http://www.worldbank.org/wbi/governance/pdf/agg_ind.pdf

Keane, J. (1998). *Civil Society: Old Images, New Visions*. Cambridge: Polity Press.

Keck, Margaret E. and Sikkink, Kathryn (1998). *Activists Beyond Borders*: *Advocacy Networks in International Politics*. Ithaca, NY: Cornell University Press.

Küng, Hans (1998). *A Global Ethic for Global Politics and Economics*. Oxford: Oxford University Press.

Meyer, John, Boli, John, Thomas, George, Ramirez, Fransisco O. (1997). 'World Society and the Nation State'. *American Journal of Sociology*, 103/1: 144–81.

Salamon, L. M., Anheier, H. K., List, R., Toepler, S., Sokolowski, S. W. and Associates (1999). *Global Civil Society: Dimensions of the Non-profit Sector*. Baltimore, MD: Center for Civil Society Studies, Institute for Policy Studies, Johns Hopkins University.

Scholte, Jan-Aart (1999). 'Globalisation: Prospects for a Paradigm Shift', in M. Shaw (ed.), *Politics and Globalisation*. London: Routledge.

Shaw, Martin (2000). *Theory of the Global State: Global Reality as an Unfinished Revolution*. Cambridge: Cambridge University Press.

Sklair, Leslie (1995). *Sociology of the Global System*. Baltimore, MD: Johns Hopkins University Press.

Smith, Jackie (ed.) (1997). *Transnational Social Movements and World Politics: Solidarity Beyond the State*. Syracuse, NY: Syracuse University Press.

Transparency International (TI) (1999–2000). *The 2000 Corruption Perceptions Index* (CPI). http://www.transparency.de/documents/cpi/2000/cpi2000.html#cpi (see also http://www.transparency.de/documents/cpi/2000/methodology.html for methodology; and http://www.gwdg.de/~uwvw/ for previous years).

UNCTAD (2000). *World Investment Report, 2000: Cross-border Mergers and Acquisitions and Development*. Geneva: UNCTAD.

UNDP (2000). *Human Development Report 2000: Human Rights and Human Development*. New York: United Nations. http://www.undp.org/hdr2000/english/book/back1.pdf

Union of International Associations (1905–1999/2000). *Yearbook of International Organizations*. Munich: K. G. Saur.

Van Tulder, R., van den Berghe, D., and Muller, A. (2001). *Erasmus Scoreboard of Core Companies: The World's Largest Firms and Internationalization*. Rotterdam: Rotterdam School of Management.

Zerubavel, Eviatar (1991). *The Fine Line: Making Distinctions in Everyday Life*. New York: Free Press.

TABLE PROGRAMME

Table Notes

Sources and explanatory notes

Brief references to sources are found at the end of each table. All major terms used in the tables are briefly defined in the Glossary. As will become clear, comparative information is not available for some countries and variables. A blank entry indicates that the data are not available, not comparable, or otherwise of insufficient quality to warrant reporting.

To improve readability of the data and to facilitate interpretation, each table is preceded by a brief description of the information presented and points to some of the key findings.

Time periods

Dependent on data availability, data are reported for 1990 and 2000 or the closest years possible, as indicated.

Countries

Countries in these tables are independent states with more than 100,000 inhabitants. Country names are used for the sake of brevity and common usage. It is not the intention of the editors to take a position with regard to the political or diplomatic implications of geographical names or continental groupings used.

China, Hong Kong, Macao, Taiwan, and Tibet
Hong Kong became a Special Administrative Region (SAR) of China in 1997 after formal transfer from the UK. Macau became a Special Administrative Region (SAR) of China in 1999 after formal transfer from Portugal. Data for China before these dates do not include Hong Kong and Macao; thereafter they do tunless otherwise stated. Tibet was annexed by The People's Republic of China following its establishment in 1949. Data for Tibet are included in those for China and Tibet. Taiwan became the home of Chinese nationalists fleeing communist rule on the mainland and claims separate status from China. No data are given for Taiwan, which is not recognised by the United Nations as an independent country.

Czechoslovakia
Czechoslovakia ceased to exist (by UN terms) on 31 December 1992. Its successor states, the Czech Republic and the Slovak Republic, became UN members in 1993. As no fruitful comparisons can be made, no 1990 data are given for Czechoslovakia.

Ethiopia and Eritrea
Eritrea became independent from Ethiopia in 1993. Data for Ethiopia until 1993 include Eritrea, later data do not.

Germany
The Federal Republic of Germany and the German Democratic Republic were unified in 1990. Data for 1990 concern only former West Germany (FRG), later data include both.

Indonesia and East Timor
The Indonesian occupation of East Timor ended in late 1999. All data for Indonesia and East Timor include East Timor unless otherwise indicated. All data for Indonesia also include Irian Jaya (West Papua), the status of which has been in dispute since the 1960s.

Israel and the Occupied Territories
Data for Israel include both the Occupied Territories and territories administered by the Palestinian Authority. In Tables R19–23 and R32, they include territories identified by INGOs as 'Palestine', 'Cisjordania', 'Gaza', 'Jerusalem', and 'West Bank'.

Morocco and the Western Sahara
The Western Sahara (formerly Spanish Sahara) was annexed by Morocco in the 1970s. Data are amalgamated for 'Morocco and the Western Sahara'.

USSR

The Union of Soviet Socialist Republics (USSR) dissolved in 1991 into Armenia, Azerbaijan, Belarus, Georgia, Kazakhstan, Kyrgyzstan, Republic of Moldova, Russian Federation, Tajikistan, Turkmenistan, Ukraine, and Uzbekistan. Data for the Russian Federation concern only the Russian Federation, except where they are indicated to refer to the USSR.

Yemen

Yemen and Democratic Yemen (formerly both UN members) merged under the name 'Yemen' in 1990. Data from 1990 onwards concern the unified country.

Yugoslavia

The Socialist Federal Republic of Yugoslavia dissolved in 1991 into Bosnia and Herzegovina, the Republic of Croatia, the Republic of Slovenia, the Former Yugoslav Republic of Macedonia, and the Federal Republic of Yugoslavia. For 1990, data for Yugoslavia include all the constituent States. For later dates, Yugoslavia includes data for 'Yugoslavia' or 'Serbia and Montenegro' or aggregates thereof.

Table R1 Global economy

This table presents data on the globalisation of domestic economies using three indicators: total trade; stock of foreign direct investment; and receipts of overseas development assistance. All three indicators are expressed as a percentage of GDP, and the table also reports changes over time between 1990 and 1998, the latest figures available. The table shows the extent to which different national economies are part of the emerging global economy, and where economic growth or contraction processes have been most pronounced over the last decade in this respect. The tables confirm that economies are becoming increasingly interconnected, a process that coincides with the emergence of global civil society. It shows significant increases in trade and direct investments, and decreases in overseas development assistance between 1990 and 1998.

| | Trade | | | Foreign direct investment | | | Development aid | | |
| | Total trade in % GDP | | Percentage change | Inward plus outward FDI stock in % GDP | | Percentage change | Overseas development assistance in % GDP | | Percentage change |
Country	1990	1998	1990–1998	1990	1998	1990–1998	1990	1998	1990–1998
Albania	38	42	0.1		14.9		0.5	7.8	13.9
Algeria	48	47	0.0	2.4	3.5	0.5	0.4	0.9	1.0
Angola	60	93	0.6	13.2	69.6	4.3	3.3	8.2	1.5
Argentina	15	23	0.5		18.0		0.1	0.0	-0.8
Armenia	81	71	-0.1	10.7	19.3	0.8	0.0	7.3	
Australia	34	42	0.2	35.5	45.2	0.3			
Austria	79	168	1.1	8.9	19.5	1.2			
Azerbaijan		83			79.4			2.3	
Bahamas				60.2	52.0	-0.1	0.1		
Bahrain	222			31.8	122.2	2.8	4.0	0.9	-0.8
Bangladesh	20	33	0.7		1.5		6.9	2.8	-0.6
Barbados	101	130	0.3	11.2	13.2	0.2	0.2		
Belarus	90	130	0.4		3.3			0.1	
Belgium & Luxembourg	137			48.0	111.9	1.3			
Belize	125	102	-0.2	17.7	32.2	0.8	7.6	2.3	-0.7
Benin	52	55	0.1	8.6	20.1	1.3	14.8	9.2	-0.4
Bhutan	61	76	0.2				17.7	15.0	-0.2
Bolivia	47	49	0.0	21.3	44.9	1.1	11.8	7.5	-0.4
Botswana	106	69	-0.3	51.8	31.3	-0.4	4.0	2.3	-0.4
Brazil	15	18	0.2	8.5	18.5	1.2	0.0	0.0	0.3
Brunei				0.8	4.2		0.1	0.0	-1.0
Bulgaria	70	91	0.3		12.3		0.1	1.9	23.7
Burkina Faso	38	44	0.2	1.4	4.9	2.5	12.0	15.5	0.3
Burundi	36	28	-0.2	2.6	3.6	0.4	23.6	8.8	-0.6
Cambodia	19	78	3.1	13.4	22.3	0.7	3.8	11.8	2.1
Cameroon	37	51	0.4	10.7	14.3	0.3	4.2	5.2	0.2
Canada	52	84	0.6	34.5	50.8	0.5			
Cape Verde	56	82	0.5	1.7	22.3	12.1	31.8	26.5	-0.2
Central African Republic	42	41	0.0	7.6	14.7	0.9	17.1	11.6	-0.3
Chad	42	51	0.2	17.3	27.5	0.6	18.2	10.0	-0.4
Chile	66	56	-0.2	33.8	52.1	0.5	0.4	0.1	-0.6
China & Tibet	32	39	0.2	7.7	30.0	2.9	0.6	0.3	-0.6
Colombia	36	34	-0.1	13.2	22.6	0.7	0.2	0.2	-0.3
Comoros	51	59	0.2	6.4	15.6	1.4	18.1	17.8	0.0
Congo, Dem. Rep.	59			1.8	2.9	0.6	10.5	2.0	-0.8
Congo, Rep.	99	135	0.4	20.1	30.4	0.5	9.4	3.9	-0.6

233

Country	Trade			Foreign direct investment			Development aid		
	Total trade in % GDP		Percentage change	Inward plus outward FDI stock in % GDP		Percentage change	Overseas development assistance in % GDP		Percentage change
	1990	1998	1990–1998	1990	1998	1990–1998	1990	1998	1990–1998
Costa Rica	76	100	0.3	26.1	41.1	0.6	4.2	0.3	-0.9
Côte d'Ivoire	59	82	0.4	9.0	25.1	1.8	7.5	7.8	0.0
Croatia		89			17.8			0.2	
Cyprus	109			20.8	22.0	0.1	0.7	0.4	-0.5
Czech Republic	88	121	0.4	4.3	27.6	5.4	0.0	0.8	19.0
Denmark	67	71	0.1	12.4	37.1	2.0			
Dominican Republic	78	70	-0.1	8.1	18.5	1.3	1.5	0.8	-0.5
Ecuador	60	62	0.0	15.2	28.2	0.9	1.6	1.0	-0.4
Egypt	53	40	-0.2	26.0	20.9	-0.2	12.9	2.2	-0.8
El Salvador	50	59	0.2	4.4	9.9	1.3	7.4	1.5	-0.8
Equatorial Guinea	102	275	1.7	19.2	121.5	5.3	49.2	6.2	-0.9
Eritrea		110						20.6	
Estonia		169			39.5			1.8	
Ethiopia	20	43	1.2	1.5	7.4	3.9	15.0	10.0	-0.3
Fiji	130	131	0.0	37.1	44.4	0.2	3.7	2.4	-0.4
Finland	48	73	0.5	12.1	36.5	2.0			
France	45	52	0.2	16.4	27.6	0.7			
Gabon	77	91	0.2	23.0	38.8	0.7	2.5	0.9	-0.6
Gambia	131	113	-0.1	11.2	28.6	1.6	34.0	9.3	-0.7
Georgia	86	42	-0.5		4.9			3.1	
Germany		57		16.0	26.6				
Ghana	43	63	0.5	5.4	18.3	2.4	9.8	9.3	0.0
Greece	45			17.9	19.0	0.1			
Guatemala	46	46	0.0	22.7	16.0	-0.3	2.7	1.2	-0.5
Guinea	62	45	-0.3	2.5	5.0	1.0	11.3	10.3	-0.1
Guinea-Bissau	47	50	0.1	3.3	13.2	3.0	55.4	50.3	-0.1
Guyana	143	203	0.4		73.9		61.5	14.0	-0.8
Haiti	45	41	-0.1	5.0	4.7	-0.1	5.7	10.5	0.9
Honduras	76	98	0.3	12.5	17.6	0.4	16.2	6.2	-0.6
Hungary	60	102	0.7	2.3	35.5	14.4	0.2	0.5	1.1
Iceland	67			1.9	9.7	4.1			
India	17	25	0.5	0.5	3.6	6.2	0.4	0.4	-0.2
Indonesia & East Timor	50	98	1.0	34.0	79.7	1.3	1.6	1.5	-0.1
Iran	46	28	-0.4	1.0	0.5	-0.5	0.1	0.1	0.7
Iraq							0.1		
Ireland	111	165	0.5	17.0	45.1	1.7	0.0	0.0	
Israel & Occupied Territories	80	75	-0.1	6.0	17.9	2.0	2.7	1.1	-0.6
Italy	40	50	0.3	10.5	22.9	1.2			
Jamaica	108	112	0.0	18.1	39.6	1.2	7.1	0.3	-1.0
Japan	21	22	0.0	7.1	7.8	0.1			
Jordan	155	120	-0.2	18.0	17.6	0.0	24.3	7.1	-0.7
Kazakhstan		66			35.7			1.0	
Kenya	58	57	0.0	8.5	9.1	0.1	14.7	4.2	-0.7
Korea, Rep.	59	85	0.4	2.9	12.6	3.3	0.0	0.0	-1.8
Kuwait	103	92	-0.1	20.0	8.2	-0.6	0.0	0.0	-0.2
Kyrgyzstan	79	87	0.1		20.5			13.1	

Country	Trade Total trade in % GDP 1990	1998	Percentage change 1990–1998	Foreign direct investment Inward plus outward FDI stock in % GDP 1990	1998	Percentage change 1990–1998	Development aid Overseas development assistance in % GDP 1990	1998	Percentage change 1990–1998
Laos	36	9	-0.8	1.6	42.6	25.6	17.3	23.0	0.3
Latvia	97	109	0.1		29.7			1.5	
Lebanon	118	62	-0.5	1.9	3.1	0.6	7.5	1.4	-0.8
Lesotho	129	158	0.2	23.9	279.0	10.7	13.8	6.2	-0.6
Lithuania	113	106	-0.1	4.4	15.3	2.5		1.2	
Macedonia		98			5.5			3.7	
Madagascar	44	50	0.1	3.4	5.6	0.6	13.6	13.4	0.0
Malawi	60	74	0.2	10.2	23.4	1.3	28.6	24.4	-0.1
Malaysia	151	207	0.4	30.3	89.6	2.0	1.1	0.3	-0.7
Maldives	130			17.1	23.2	0.4	16.8	8.1	-0.5
Mali	51	58	0.1	2.5	14.3	4.7	20.0	13.1	-0.3
Malta	184	182	0.0	20.1	44.6	1.2	0.2	0.6	3.0
Mauritania	96	95	0.0	5.2	12.2	1.3	22.0	18.0	-0.2
Mauritius	138	130	-0.1	6.2	11.2	0.8	3.4	1.0	-0.7
Mexico	38	64	0.7	8.7	15.7	0.8	0.1	0.0	-0.9
Moldova	100	122	0.2		18.4		0.0	2.0	
Mongolia	64	105	0.6		8.4		0.0	20.5	
Morocco & Western Sahara	48	44	-0.1	3.5	13.8	2.9	4.2	1.5	-0.6
Mozambique	44	42	0.0	2.0	14.4	6.2	42.3	28.2	-0.3
Myanmar	7								
Namibia	111	126	0.1	87.1	49.3	-0.4	4.9	5.7	0.2
Nepal	32	58	0.8		2.1		11.5	8.3	-0.3
Netherlands	104	127	0.2	64.3	116.9	0.8			
New Zealand	55	62	0.1	26.0	77.2	2.0			
Nicaragua	71	111	0.6	11.3	39.0	2.5	33.6	31.6	-0.1
Niger	37	40	0.1	14.1	27.8	1.0	16.3	14.4	-0.1
Nigeria	72	55	-0.2	62.2	81.4	0.3	1.0	0.5	-0.5
Norway	75	72	0.0	11.3	39.3	2.5			
Oman	83			16.9	17.0	0.0	0.6	0.0	-1.0
Pakistan	39	36	-0.1	5.4	15.1	1.8	2.9	1.7	-0.4
Panama	72	77	0.1	118.1	141.4	0.2	2.0	0.3	-0.9
Papua New Guinea	90	138	0.5	49.3	43.8	-0.1	13.3	10.3	-0.2
Paraguay	51	94	0.8	9.1	20.2	1.2	1.1	0.9	-0.2
Peru	24	29	0.2	4.2	12.9	2.1	1.3	0.8	-0.3
Philippines	61	116	0.9	7.7	16.9	1.2	2.9	0.9	-0.7
Poland	48	58	0.2	0.4	15.9	38.8	2.4	0.6	-0.8
Portugal	75	72	0.0	14.8	29.4	1.0			
Qatar					6.0		0.0	0.0	-1.0
Romania	43	60	0.4	2.2	10.7	3.9	0.6	0.9	0.5
Russian Federation	36	58	0.6		7.6		0.0	0.4	7.7
Rwanda	20	28	0.4	8.2	11.8	0.4	11.3	17.4	0.5
Samoa	96			5.4	15.7	1.9	31.8	20.5	-0.4
Sao Tome & Principe	102	116	0.1				122.2	77.8	-0.4
Saudi Arabia	82	67	-0.2	23.2	24.0	0.0	0.0	0.0	-0.5
Senegal	56	71	0.3	5.8	15.5	1.7	14.9	10.8	-0.3
Sierra Leone	41	53	0.3				7.6	16.9	1.2

Country	Trade Total trade in % GDP 1990	Trade Total trade in % GDP 1998	Trade Percentage change 1990–1998	Foreign direct investment Inward plus outward FDI stock in % GDP 1990	Foreign direct investment Inward plus outward FDI stock in % GDP 1998	Foreign direct investment Percentage change 1990–1998	Development aid Overseas development assistance in % GDP 1990	Development aid Overseas development assistance in % GDP 1998	Development aid Percentage change 1990–1998
Singapore	397	287	-0.3	97.2	141.9	0.5	0.0	0.0	-1.3
Slovakia	62	139	1.2	0.6	15.3	24.5	0.0	0.8	16.0
Slovenia		115			17.3			0.2	
Solomon Islands	120			32.8	54.7	0.7	21.7	14.6	-0.3
Somalia	48						59.2	0.0	-1.0
South Africa	43	50	0.2	22.7	38.2	0.7		0.4	
Spain	38	57	0.5	16.6	34.0	1.0			
Sri Lanka	68	78	0.1	8.6	13.4	0.6	9.3	3.2	-0.7
St. Lucia	157	133	-0.2	75.7	97.4	0.3	3.3	1.1	
St. Vincent & Grenadines	143	121	-0.2	24.4	102.6	3.2	8.0	6.8	
Sudan				0.2	4.9	23.5	6.5	2.3	-0.7
Suriname	56						20.0	8.1	-0.6
Swaziland	153	196	0.3	43.6	48.4	0.1	5.9	2.2	-0.6
Sweden	59	85	0.4	26.9	63.8	1.4			
Switzerland	72	76	0.1	29.5	95.6	2.2			
Syria	55	69	0.3		2.1		5.9	1.0	-0.8
Tajikistan					7.6			4.9	
Tanzania	48	43	-0.1	2.2	9.9	3.5	29.2	12.4	-0.6
Thailand	76	101	0.3	10.1	19.2	0.9	0.9	0.6	-0.4
Togo	79	74	-0.1	16.9	31.3	0.9	16.3	8.6	-0.5
Trinidad & Tobago	71	98	0.4	41.7	93.7	1.2	0.4	0.2	-0.4
Tunisia	94	88	-0.1	59.1	59.5	0.0	3.3	0.8	-0.8
Turkey	31	53	0.7	0.9	4.3	3.8	0.8	0.0	-1.0
Turkmenistan					33.3			0.7	
Uganda	27	30	0.1		12.9		15.8	7.0	-0.6
Ukraine	56	83	0.5		6.8		0.3	0.9	1.9
United Arab Emirates	106			2.5	4.4	0.8			
United Kingdom	51	56	0.1	44.2	59.2	0.3			
United States	21	25	0.2	14.9	21.0	0.4			
Uruguay	46	44	0.0	11.0	8.4	-0.2	0.7	0.1	-0.8
Uzbekistan	77	45	-0.4	0.0	5.6			0.7	
Vanuatu	123			71.9	137.8	0.9	30.7	18.4	-0.4
Venezuela	60	40	-0.3	9.3	25.6	1.8	0.2	0.0	-0.8
Vietnam	60			4.5	54.5	11.1		4.3	
Yemen	35	88	1.5	1.2	30.6	24.5	8.6	7.9	-0.1
Zambia	72	68	-0.1	29.8	52.8	0.8	16.0	11.1	-0.3
Zimbabwe	46	94	1.0				4.0	4.7	0.2
World	72	81	0.2	18.1	32.8	2.7	10.5	6.4	0.4

Sources: World Bank, *World Development Indicators 2000* (CD-Rom); UNCTAD, *World Investment Report 2000* (Geneva: United Nations, 2000), Annex B.

Table R2 Direction and growth of world trade

Following Table R1, this table shows flows of import and export trade within and among major world regions. The table reports these data for high-income importers and low- to middle-income importers separately, both as a percentage of world trade in 1998 and as an annual growth rate for the period 1988–98. This table shows significant growth, but also the unevenness of economic globalisation as measured by trade flows.

Direction of trade % of world trade, 1998	European Union	Japan	United States	Other industrial	All industrial	Other high-income	All high-income
Source of imports							
High-income economies	32.0	2.8	11.0	7.6	53.4	5.2	58.5
Industrial economies	30.6	2.1	9.1	7.3	49.1	4.0	53.1
European Union	24.7	0.6	3.2	3.4	32.0	1.4	33.4
Japan	1.3		2.2	0.4	3.9	1.3	5.1
United States	2.8	1.1		3.3	7.1	1.1	8.1
Other industrial economies	1.8	0.4	3.7	0.3	6.2	0.3	6.5
Other high-income economies	1.4	0.7	1.9	0.3	4.3	1.1	5.4
Low- and middle-income economies	6.1	1.9	5.6	0.9	14.4	2.6	17.0
East Asia & Pacific	1.6	1.4	2.0	0.5	5.5	2.2	7.6
Europe & Central Asia	2.3	0.1	0.2	0.1	2.7	0.1	2.8
Latin America & Caribbean	0.7	0.1	2.7	0.1	3.7	0.1	3.7
Middle East & N. Africa	0.7	0.2	0.2	0.0	1.1	0.1	1.2
South Asia	0.3	0.0	0.2	0.0	0.6	0.1	0.7
Sub-Saharan Africa	0.5	0.1	0.2	0.0	0.8	0.1	0.9
World	**38.0**	**4.7**	**16.6**	**8.5**	**67.8**	**7.8**	**75.6**

Nominal growth of trade annual % growth, 1988-1998	European Union	Japan	United States	Other industrial	All industrial	Other high-income	All high-income
Source of imports							
High-income economies	5.9	4.0	6.3	7.4	6.0	8.3	6.2
Industrial economies	5.8	3.7	6.1	7.4	6.0	7.4	6.1
European Union	6.0	5.0	6.8	8.0	6.2	9.1	6.3
Japan	3.2		2.9	0.8	2.8	6.3	3.5
United States	6.5	4.4		7.9	6.8	7.5	6.9
Other industrial economies	4.0	0.5	8.1	6.8	6.0	5.3	6.0
Other high-income economies	8.6	5.0	7.0	6.8	7.0	12.5	8.0
Low- and middle-income economies	8.2	5.5	11.6	9.9	9.0	10.5	9.2
East Asia & Pacific	13.1	7.1	11.2	13.9	10.7	11.6	10.9
Europe & Central Asia	10.4	-1.6	14.0	10.0	10.2	13.5	10.3
Latin America & Caribbean	4.5	1.6	14.0	7.3	10.4	6.2	10.2
Middle East & N. Africa	2.6	4.5	1.1	0.2	2.5	0.1	2.2
South Asia	10.3	1.6	12.9	9.1	10.0	13.1	10.5
Sub-Saharan Africa	3.6	1.3	4.3	2.1	3.5	12.3	3.9
World	**6.2**	**4.6**	**7.8**	**7.6**	**6.6**	**9.0**	**6.8**

Low- and middle-income importers

Direction of trade % of world trade, 1998	East Asia & Pacific	Europe & Central Asia	Latin America & Caribbean	Middle East & N. Africa	South Asia	Sub-Saharan Africa	All low- & middle-income	World
Source of imports								
High-income economies	5.8	3.8	4.4	1.7	0.7	0.9	17.3	75.8
Industrial economies	3.6	3.7	4.2	1.6	0.5	0.8	14.4	67.5
European Union	1.0	3.2	1.1	1.0	0.2	0.6	7.2	40.5
Japan	1.3	0.1	0.4	0.2	0.1	0.1	2.0	7.1
United States	1.0	0.2	2.6	0.3	0.1	0.1	4.3	12.5
Other industrial economies	0.4	0.1	0.1	0.1	0.1	0.0	0.9	7.3
Other high-income economies	2.2	0.1	0.2	0.1	0.2	0.1	2.9	8.3
Low- and middle-income economies	2.1	2.0	1.5	0.6	0.5	0.5	7.1	24.2
East Asia & Pacific	1.4	0.3	0.3	0.2	0.2	0.1	2.5	11.1
Europe & Central Asia	0.1	1.5	0.1	0.1	0.0	0.0	1.9	4.7
Latin America & Caribbean	0.1	0.1	1.1	0.1	0.0	0.0	1.4	5.1
Middle East & N. Africa	0.3	0.1	0.0	0.1	0.1	0.0	0.7	1.9
South Asia	0.1	0.0	0.0	0.0	0.1	0.0	0.2	1.0
Sub-Saharan Africa	0.1	0.0	0.0	0.0	0.0	0.2	0.4	1.3
World	7.9	5.8	5.9	2.3	1.1	1.4	24.4	100.0

Nominal growth of trade annual % growth, 1988-1998	East Asia & Pacific	Europe & Central Asia	Latin America & Caribbean	Middle East & N. Africa	South Asia	Sub-Saharan Africa	All low- & middle-income	World
Source of imports								
High-income economies	8.8	12.3	11.4	3.9	4.0	2.8	8.7	6.7
Industrial economies	7.2	12.2	11.3	4.0	2.3	2.7	8.3	6.5
European Union	8.7	14.1	10.6	3.7	2.6	2.6	8.9	6.7
Japan	5.7	0.0	8.6	2.1	0.2	-0.6	4.9	3.9
United States	8.8	6.8	12.5	5.6	1.8	6.0	10.1	7.9
Other industrial economies	5.2	2.8	5.6	5.0	5.5	3.2	4.7	5.8
Other high-income economies	12.0	19.0	13.9	2.7	10.2	3.3	11.2	9.0
Low- and middle-income economies	15.3	6.0	14.1	2.8	10.2	10.2	9.7	9.4
East Asia & Pacific	19.0	11.8	23.2	7.0	12.7	10.0	15.8	11.9
Europe & Central Asia	3.8	6.8	14.1	-1.1	-2.2	4.7	5.7	8.2
Latin America & Caribbean	5.8	0.8	13.9	5.0	9.8	5.9	10.9	10.4
Middle East & N. Africa	16.5	-2.9	-3.2	0.5	8.8	10.2	5.1	3.1
South Asia	13.3	-3.1	28.6	7.3	13.7	15.9	8.4	9.9
Sub-Saharan Africa	11.9	3.6	11.0	11.5	25.0	11.6	11.6	5.8
World	10.1	9.7	12.0	3.6	6.1	4.7	9.0	7.3

Source: World Bank, *World Development Indicators 2000* (CD-ROM).

Table R3 Transnationality of top 100 TNCs

This table lists the name and global headquarter country for the 100 largest transnational corporations (TNCs), and then presents data on their size and foreign share of assets, sales, and employment. In addition, the table shows the ranks and degree of transnationality of each TNC, with the most transnational companies at the top, where higher index numbers (and lower rank numbers) indicate an overall greater share of transnationality. The table suggests the importance of TNCs and the globalised economy they create as one major reference point for the development of global civil society—from activists protesting against certain corporate practices and the emergence of corporate cultures, to the growing numbers and influence of a highly mobile groups of managers and professionals working for TNCs.

Ranking by: TNI* Corporation	Country	Assets Foreign	Total	% Foreign	Sales Foreign	Total	% Foreign	Employment Foreign	Total	% Foreign	TNI (%)
1 Seagram Company**	Canada	18.8	22.2	84.7	9.1	8.7	104.6		24,200		94.8
2 Thomson Corporation	Canada	12.1	12.5	96.8	5.8	6.2	93.5	36,000	39,000	92.3	94.6
3 Nestle SA	Switzerland	35.6	41.1	86.6	51.2	52	98.5	225,665	231,881	97.3	94.2
4 Electrolux AB	Sweden		10.3	0.0	13.8	14.5	95.2	89,573	99,322	90.2	92.7
5 British American Tobacco Plc	United Kingdom	10.5	12.4	84.7	13.8	15.3	90.2	99,204	101,081	98.1	91
6 Holderbank Financiere Glarus	Switzerland	11.6	12.8	90.6	7	8	87.5	37,779	40,520	93.2	90.5
7 Unilever	Netherlands/ United Kingdom	32.9	35.8	91.9	39.4	44.9	87.8	240,845	265,103	90.8	90.1
8 ABB	Switzerland		32.9	0.0	23.1	27.7	83.4	154,263	162,793	94.8	89.1
9 SmithKline Beecham Plc	United Kingdom	10.4	15	69.3	12.4	13.4	92.5	50,900	59,500	85.5	82.3
10 SCA	Sweden	7	9.7	72.2	7	7.7	90.9	25,346	32,211	78.7	80.8
11 Rio Tinto Plc	United Kingdom/ Australia	12.4	16.1	77.0	7.1	7.1	100.0	22,478	34,809	64.6	80.4
12 News Corporation	Australia	22.9	33.6	68.2	10.5	11.7	89.7		50,000		78.7
13 Roche Holding AG	France	21.2	40.6	52.2	16.7	17	98.2	57,142	66,707	85.7	78.7
14 Philips Electronics	Netherlands	19	32.8	57.9	32.1	33.9	94.7	189,210	233,686	81.0	77.8
15 L'Air Liquide Groupe	France		10.6	0.0	5.1	6.8	75.0	20,306	28,600	71.0	77
16 Akzo Nobel NV	Netherlands	10.1	14	72.1	11.6	14.6	79.5	67,800	85,900	78.9	76.8
17 Diageo Plc	United Kingdom	27.9	46.3	60.3	10.5	12.4	84.7	65,393	77,029	84.9	76.7
18 Michelin	France		15	0.0	12.3	14.6	84.2	87,160	127,241	68.5	76
19 Exxon Corporation	United States	50.1	70	71.6	92.7	115.4	80.3		79,000		75.9
20 Glaxo Wellcome Plc	United Kingdom	10.8	15.5	69.7	10.9	13.3	82.0	42,562	56,934	74.8	75.5
21 BP AMOCO	United Kingdom	40.5	54.9	73.8	48.6	68.3	71.2	78,950	98,900	79.8	74.9
22 Stora Enso Oys	Finland	11.5	18	63.9	10.8	11.7	92.3	25,189	40,987	61.5	72.8
23 Hoechst AG	Germany	21.2	33.5	63.3	21	26.2	80.2		96,967		71.6
24 Nortel Networks	Canada	14.3	19.7	72.6	12.2	17.6	69.3		75,052		70.8
25 Coca-Cola Company	United States	14.9	19.2	77.6	11.9	18.8	63.3		29,000		70.6
26 Rhone-Poulenc SA	France		28.4	0.0	12	14.7	81.6	36,421	65,180	55.9	69.1
27 Total Fina SA	France		27	0.0	20.8	28.6	72.7	35,100	57,166	61.4	69
28 Cable and Wireless Plc	United Kingdom	17.7	28.5	62.1	8.8	13.2	66.7	37,426	50,671	73.9	67.5
29 Danone Groupe SA	France	10.3	17.6	58.5	8.8	14.4	61.1	58,602	78,945	74.2	64.6
30 Compart Spa	Italy	10.2	21.6	47.2	10.5	15	70.0	24,097	33,076	72.9	63.4
31 Montedison Spa	Italy		19.4	0.0	9.9	14.3	69.2	20,050	28,672	69.9	63.1

US$ billions and number of employees, 1998

Ranking by: TNI*			Assets			Sales			Employment			
	Corporation	Country	Foreign	Total	% Foreign	Foreign	Total	% Foreign	Foreign	Total	% Foreign	TNI (%)
32	Royal Ahold NV	Netherlands		13.3	0.0	20.9	29.4	71.1	133,716	279,255	47.9	62.9
33	Bayer AG	Germany	21.4	34.3	62.4	21.9	31.1	70.4	80,900	145,100	55.8	62.8
34	Renault SA	France	23.6	43.2	54.6	25.4	39.8	63.8	92,854	138,321	67.1	61.8
35	Crown Cork & Seal	United States	8	12.5	64.0	5	8.3	60.2		38,459		61.8
36	McDonald's Corporation	United States	12	19.8	60.6	7.5	12.4	60.5		284,000		60.7
37	Ericsson LM	Sweden	9.6	20.7	46.4	17.8	22.8	78.1	58,688	103,667	56.6	60.4
38	Honda Motor Co Ltd	Japan	26.3	41.8	62.9	29.7	51.7	57.4		112,200		60.2
39	Imperial Chemical Industries	United Kingdom	7.2	14.9	48.3	10.9	15.1	72.2		59,100		60.2
40	BMW AG	Germany	22.9	35.7	64.1	26.8	37.7	71.1	53,107	119,913	44.3	59.9
41	Sony Corporation	Japan		52.5	0.0	40.7	56.6	71.9	102,468	173,000	59.2	59.3
42	Alcatel	France	16.7	34.6	48.3	14.5	23.6	61.4	80,005	118,272	67.6	59.1
43	Mobil Corporation	United States		42.8	0.0	29.7	53.5	55.5	22,100	41,500	53.3	58.6
44	Bridgestone	Japan	7.4	14.7	50.3	11.3	17.1	66.1		97,767		58.2
45	Royal Dutch/ Shell Group	Netherlands/ United Kingdom	67	110	60.9	50	94	53.2	61,000	102,000	59.8	58
46	BASF AG	Germany		30.4	0.0	24.2	32.4	74.7	46,730	105,945	44.1	57.9
47	Volvo AB	Sweden		25.2	0.0	23.8	26.3	90.5	35,313	79,820	44.2	57.4
48	Robert Bosch GmbH	Germany		21.9	0.0	19.6	30.2	64.9	94,180	189,537	49.7	56.3
49	Carrefour SA	France	10.3	20.3	50.7	17.2	30.4	56.6	86,846	144,142	60.3	55.9
50	Viag AG	Germany		34.8	0.0	16.3	27.9	58.4	41,990	85,694	49.0	55.3
51	Volkswagen Group	Germany		70.1	0.0	52.3	80.2	65.2	142,481	297,916	47.8	53.8
52	Siemens AG	Germany		66.8	0.0	45.7	66	69.2	222,000	416,000	53.4	53.6
53	Hewlett-Packard	United States	17.6	33.7	52.2	25.2	46.5	54.2		124,600		53.2
54	IBM	United States	43.6	86.1	50.6	46.4	81.7	56.8	149,934	291,067	51.5	53
55	Canon Electronics	Japan	7.4	23.4	31.6	17.8	24.4	73.0	41,834	79,799	52.4	52.3
56	Elf Aquitaine SA	France	20.7	43.2	47.9	21.8	37.9	57.5	42,000	85,000	49.4	51.6
57	Dow Chemical	United States	10.4	23.8	43.7	11	18.4	59.8	19,125	39,029	49.0	50.8
58	Mitsubishi Motors	Japan	8.4	25.4	33.1	16.8	29.1	57.7	18,251	29,945	60.9	50.6
59	DaimlerChrysler	Germany	36.7	159.7	23.0	125.4	154.6	81.1	208,502	441,502	47.2	50.4
60	Toyota	Japan	44.9	131.5	34.1	55.2	101	54.7	113,216	183,879	61.6	50.1
61	Broken Hill Proprietary	Australia	8	20.6	38.8	8.7	12.6	69.0	20,000	50,000	40.0	49.3
62	Motorola Inc	United States	14	31	45.2	14	31.3	44.7	66,800	141,000	47.4	45.8
63	Suez Lyonnaise Des Eaux	France		84.6	0.0	12.9	34.8	37.1	126,500	201,000	62.9	45.6
64	Mannesmann AG	Germany		20.3	0.0	10.8	21.2	50.9	43,821	116,247	37.7	44.4
65	Peugeot SA	France	15.9	39.8	39.9	24.4	37.5	65.1	43,300	156,500	27.7	44.2
66	Johnson & Johnson	United States		26.2	0.0	11.1	23.7	46.8		93,100		43
67	Nissan Motor Co Ltd	Japan	21.6	57.2	37.8	25.8	54.4	47.4		131,260		42.6
68	Compaq Computer Corp.	United States	7	21.7	32.3	16.4	31.2	52.6		71,000		42.6
69	Du Pont (E.I) de Nemours	United States	16.7	38.5	43.4	11.7	24.8	47.2	35,000	101,000	34.7	41.7
70	ALCOA	United States		17	0.0	6.6	15.3	43.1		103,500		41.7
71	Procter & Gamble	United States	10	31	32.3	17.9	37.2	48.1		110,000		40.3
72	Matsushita Electric	Japan	12.2	66.2	18.4	32.4	63.7	50.9	133,629	282,153	47.4	38.9

US$ billions and number of employees, 1998

Ranking by: TNI*			Assets			Sales			Employment			
	Corporation	Country	Foreign	Total	% Foreign	Foreign	Total	% Foreign	Foreign	Total	% Foreign	TNI (%)
73	Wal-Mart Stores	United States	30.2	50	60.4	19.4	137.6	14.1		910,000		37.2
74	RJR Nabisco Holdings	United States		28.9	0.0	5.6	17	32.9		74,000		36.9
75	General Electric	United States	128.6	355.9	36.1	28.7	100.5	28.6	130,000	293,000	44.4	36.3
76	Ford Motor Company	United States		237.5	0.0	43.8	144.4	30.3	171,276	345,175	49.6	35.4
77	Texas Utilities Company	United States	15.8	39.5	40.0	4	14.7	27.2	8,300	22,055	37.6	35
78	Mitsui & Co Ltd	Japan	17.3	56.5	30.6	46.5	118.5	39.2		7,288		34.9
79	Fujitsu Ltd	Japan	12.2	42.3	28.8	15.9	43.3	36.7	74,000	188,000	39.4	34.9
80	ENI Group	Italy		48.4	0.0	12	33.2	36.1	24,602	78,906	31.2	34.1
81	Mitsubishi Corporation	Japan	21.7	74.9	29.0	43.5	116.1	37.5	3,668	11,650	31.5	32.7
82	Fiat Spa	Italy	14.2	76.1	18.7	19.4	51	38.0	87,861	220,549	39.8	32.1
83	Vivendi	France		57.1	0.0	11.5	35.3	32.6	94,310	235,610	40.0	31.5
84	Merck & Co	United States	9.3	31.9	29.2	6.6	26.9	24.5	22,800	57,300	39.8	31.1
85	General Motors	United States	73.1	246.7	29.6	49.9	155.5	32.1		396,000		30.9
86	Telefonica	Spain	13.8	42.3	32.6	6.1	20.5	29.8	27,802	101,809	27.3	29.9
87	Petroleos de Venezuela SA	Venezuela	7.9	48.8	16.2	11	25.7	42.8	6,026	50,821	11.9	23.7
88	VEBA Group	Germany		52.2	0.0	14.7	49	30.0	39,220	116,774	33.6	28.2
89	Sumitomo Corporation	Japan	15	45	33.3	17.6	95	18.5		5,591		26.3
90	Marubeni Corporation	Japan	10.6	53.8	19.7	31.4	98.8	31.8		8,618		25.8
91	Chevron Corporation	United States	16.9	36.5	46.3	2	29.9	6.7	8,956	39,191	22.9	25.3
92	Nissho Iwai	Japan	14.2	38.5	36.9	9.1	71.6	12.7		4,041		24.9
93	Toshiba Corporation	Japan	6.8	48.8	13.9	14.5	44.6	32.5		198,000		23.3
94	Atlantic Richfield	United States		25.2	0.0	1.6	10.3	15.5	4,300	18,400	23.4	22.5
95	RWE Group	Germany	10.8	57.2	18.9	8.2	41.2	19.9	42,681	155,576	27.4	22.1
96	Itochu Corporation	Japan	15.1	55.9	27.0	18.4	115.3	16.0		5,775		21.5
97	Hitachi Ltd	Japan	12	76.6	15.7	19.8	63.8	31.0	58,000	331,494	17.5	21.4
98	Southern Company	United States	9.6	36.2	26.5	1.8	11.4	15.8		31,848		21
99	GTE Corporation	United States	7.3	43.6	16.7	3.3	25.7	12.8	22,000	120,000	18.3	16
100	SBC Communications	United States		75	0.0		46.2	0.0		200,380		13.5
Average					36.1			58.1			56.2	

*TNI = Transnationationality Index (avg. of the ratios of foreign to total assets, sales and employment).

**Value obtained for foreign sales is greater than that of total sales, these figures appear as found in original source.

Source: UNCTAD, World Investment Report 2000 (Geneva: United Nations, 2000), Annex B.

Table R4 Foreign students

This table indicates the number of students studying abroad from major world regions, and the respective host region. However, these data are incomplete, missing some major countries like India and Brazil. Foreign students are major transmitters of knowledge and ideas, and interlocutors among cultures. A growing practice of studying abroad may therefore be one catalyst of the emergence and spread of global civil society.

1996 Region of origin	More developed regions	Countries in transition	Less developed regions	Host region* Sub-Saharan Africa	Arab States	Latin America/ Caribbean	Eastern Asia/ Oceania	Southern Asia	World
More developed regions of which:	438,503	18,054	19,834	16	214	939	16,708	5	476,391
Northern America	52,316	655	4,518	5	42	260	4,157	2	57,489
Asia/Oceania	68,860	2,030	10,200		51	5	9,976	2	81,090
Europe	317,327	15,369	5,116	11	121	674	2,575	1	337,812
Countries in transition	76,451	98,444	5,375	3	320	4	582	111	180,270
Less developed regions of which:	702,194	36,459	94,573	7,953	50,109	14,478	14,385	557	833,226
Sub-Saharan Africa	79,554	8,072	16,443	7,947	4,772	2,747	446	19	104,069
Arab States	101,241	14,190	48,687	7	46,385	344	334	213	164,118
Latin America/Caribbean	74,364	1,732	11,698		30	11,416	247		87,794
Eastern Asia/Oceania	324,637	3,948	12,970		369	140	12,316	75	341,555
Southern Asia	79,920	7,331	3,812	5	908	29	1,037	249	91,063
Least developed countries	53,748	10,041	12,403	2,047	6,671	1,945	654	194	76,192
Unspecified	39,898	1,819	18,701	7,039	4,661	3,142	797	4	60,418
World	1,257,046	154,776	138,483	15,011	55,304	18,563	32,472	677	1,550,305

* Reports data only for 77 major host countries; major host countries such as Brazil and India are not included.

Source: UNESCO, *World Education Report 2000: The Right to Education: Towards Education for All Throughout Life* (Paris: UNESCO Publishing, 2000).

Table R5 Foreign labour and population (OECD)

Labour migration has increased in recent years. This includes not only the movement from the developing world to low-paying jobs in high-income countries but also professionals and the highly educated. Both types of migration strengthen the interconnectedness of their countries of origin with their countries of residence. Unfortunately, few comprehensive statistics are available. The table shows the foreign population and labour force as well as the overall foreigner inflow for selected OECD countries and the significant share of foreign workers in most major OECD countries.

| | Foreign population | | | | Foreign labour | | Inflow of foreign population | | | |
| | In thousands | | % of population | | % of labour force | | In thousands | | % of population | |
Country	1990	1997	1990	1997	1990	1997	1990	1997	1990	1997
Australia	3,753	3,908	22.3	21.1	25.7	24.8	121	86	0.7	0.5
Austria	456	733	5.9	9.1	7.4	9.9				
Belgium	905	903	9.1	8.9		7.9	51	49	0.5	0.5
Canada	4,343	4,971	16.1	17.4	18.5	18.5	214	216	0.8	0.7
Denmark	161	250	3.1	4.7	2.4		15		0.3	
Finland	26	81	0.5	1.6			7	8	0.1	0.2
France	3,597	3,597	6.3			6.2	6.1	102	102	0.2	0.2
Germany	5,343	7,366	8.4	9.0	7.1		842	615	1.1	0.7
Ireland	80	114	2.3	3.1	2.6	3.4				
Italy	781	1,241	1.4							
Japan	1,075	1,483	0.9	1.2		0.2	224	275	0.2	0.2
Luxembourg	113	148	29.4	34.9	45.2	55.1	9	10	2.4	2.3
Netherlands	692	678	4.6		3.1	2.9	81	77	0.5	0.5
Norway	143	158	3.4	3.6	2.3	2.8	16	22	0.4	0.5
Portugal	108	175	1.1	1.8	1.0	1.8				
Spain	279	609	0.7	1.5	0.6	1.1				
Sweden	484	522	5.6	6.0	5.4	5.2	53	33	0.6	0.4
Switzerland	1,100	1,341	16.3	19.0	18.9	17.5	101	73	1.5	1.0
United Kingdom	1,723	2,066	3.2	3.6	3.3	3.6		237		0.4
United States	19,767	25,779	7.9	9.7	9.4	11.6	1,537	798	0.6	0.3
Average	2,246	2,806	7	9	10	11	241	186	1	1

Source: World Bank, *World Development Indicators 2000* (CD-ROM).

Table R6: Air travel and international tourism

This table offers data on air transport and international tourism for 1988 and 1998, and also presents the percentage change for this time period. The lower part of this table shows tourism figures aggregated by region and type of economy. The massive expansion of tourism and air transport establishes connections among different cultures and peoples, and creates economic as well as social ties. Air travel also facilitates global activism.

Country	Air transport — Passengers carried (thousands) 1988 Total	Per capita	1998 Total	Per capita	% change 1988–1998	International tourism — Inbound tourists (thousands) 1980 Total	Per capita	1998 Total	Per capita	% change 1980–1998	Outbound tourists (thousands) 1980 Total	Per capita	1998 Total	Per capita	% change 1980–1998
Afghanistan	201	0.01	53	0.00	-0.7										
Albania			21	0.01		4	0.00	27	0.01	5.8			18	0.01	
Algeria	3,655	0.15	3,382	0.11	-0.1	946	0.05	678	0.02	-0.3	698	0.04	1,377	0.05	1.0
Angola	750	0.08	553	0.05	-0.3			52	0.00				3	0.00	
Argentina	5,069	0.16	8,447	0.23	0.7	1,120	0.04	4,860	0.13	3.3			5,522	0.15	
Armenia			365	0.10				32	0.01						
Australia	18,816	1.12	30,186	1.61	0.6	905	0.06	4,167	0.22	3.6	1,217	0.08	3,161	0.17	1.6
Austria	1,965	0.26	5,872	0.73	2.0	13,879	1.84	17,352	2.15	0.3	3,525	0.47	13,263	1.64	2.8
Azerbaijan			669	0.08				170	0.02				232	0.03	
Bahamas	1,066	4.26	701	2.38	-0.3										
Bahrain	698	1.43	1,207	1.88	0.7										
Bangladesh	1,005	0.01	1,153	0.01	0.1	57	0.00	172	0.00	2.0			992	0.01	
Belarus			226	0.02				355	0.03				969	0.09	
Belgium	2,605	0.26	8,748	0.86	2.4	3,777	0.38	6,179	0.61	0.6	9,565	0.97	7,773	0.76	-0.2
Benin	104	0.02	91	0.02	-0.1	39	0.01	152	0.03	2.9			420	0.07	
Bhutan	8	0.01	36	0.05	3.5										
Bolivia	1,267	0.20	2,116	0.27	0.7	155	0.03	434	0.05	1.8			298	0.04	
Bosnia & Herzegovina			50	0.01				100	0.03						
Botswana	58	0.05	124	0.08	1.1	236	0.26	740	0.47	2.1			460	0.29	
Brazil	17,011	0.12	28,091	0.17	0.7	1,271	0.01	4,818	0.03	2.8	427	0.00	4,598	0.03	9.8
Brunei	279	1.12	877	2.78	2.1										
Bulgaria	2,164	0.24	828	0.10	-0.6	1,933	0.22	3,000	0.36	0.6	759	0.09	3,059	0.37	3.0
Burkina Faso	126	0.01	102	0.01	-0.2	38	0.01	140	0.01	2.7					
Burundi	11	0.00	12	0.00	0.1	34	0.01	14	0.00	-0.6			16	0.00	
Cambodia								576	0.05				41	0.00	
Cameroon	582	0.05	278	0.02	-0.5	86	0.01	135	0.01	0.6	14	0.00			
Canada	22,379	0.82	24,653	0.81	0.1	12,876	0.52	18,837	0.62	0.5	12,833	0.52	17,648	0.58	0.4
Cape Verde	176	0.53	236	0.57	0.3										
Central African Republic	124	0.04	91	0.03	-0.3	7	0.00	20	0.01	1.9					
Chad	86	0.02	98	0.01	0.1	7	0.00	11	0.00	0.6			10	0.00	
Chile	1,144	0.09	5,150	0.35	3.5	420	0.04	1,757	0.12	3.2	379	0.03	1,351	0.09	2.6
China & Tibet	17,000	0.02	53,234	0.04	2.1	3,500	0.00	25,073	0.02	6.2			8,426	0.01	
Colombia	5,460	0.16	9,290	0.23	0.7	553	0.02	841	0.02	0.5	781	0.03	1,140	0.03	0.5
Congo, Dem. Rep.	216	0.01				23	0.00	32	0.00	0.4					
Congo, Rep.	220	0.10	241	0.09	0.1	48	0.03	44	0.02	-0.1					
Costa Rica	401	0.14	1,170	0.33	1.9	345	0.15	943	0.27	1.7	133	0.06	330	0.09	1.5
Côte d'Ivoire	191	0.02	162	0.01	-0.2	194	0.02	301	0.02	0.6			5	0.00	

| Country | Air transport Passengers carried (thousands) | | | | | International tourism | | | | | | | | | |
| | 1988 Total | 1988 Per capita | 1998 Total | 1998 Per capita | % change 1988–1998 | Inbound tourists (thousands) | | | | | Outbound tourists (thousands) | | | | |
						1980 Total	1980 Per capita	1998 Total	1998 Per capita	% change 1980–1998	1980 Total	1980 Per capita	1998 Total	1998 Per capita	% change 1980–1998
Croatia			828	0.18				4,112	0.91						
Cuba	964	0.09	1,138	0.10	0.2	101	0.01	1,390	0.13	12.8	7	0.00	55	0.00	6.9
Cyprus	697	1.04	1,346	1.79	0.9										
Czech Republic	1,154	0.11	1,601	0.16	0.4			16,325	1.59						
Denmark	4,377	0.85	5,947	1.12	0.4	1,619	0.32	2,073	0.39	0.3			4,972	0.94	
Djibouti	125	0.25							0.00						
Dominican Republic	351	0.05	34	0.00	-0.9	383	0.07	2,309	0.28	5.0	257	0.05	354	0.04	0.4
Ecuador	684	0.07	1,919	0.16	1.8	243	0.03	511	0.04	1.1			330	0.03	
Egypt	3,192	0.06	3,895	0.06	0.2	1,253	0.03	3,213	0.05	1.6	1,180	0.03	2,921	0.05	1.5
El Salvador	449	0.09	1,694	0.28	2.8	118	0.03	542	0.09	3.6	464	0.10	868	0.14	0.9
Equatorial Guinea	28	0.08	21	0.05	-0.3										
Eritrea								188	0.05						
Estonia			297	0.20				825	0.57				1,659	1.14	
Ethiopia	593	0.01	790	0.01	0.3	42	0.00	91	0.00	1.2	25	0.00	140	0.00	4.6
Fiji	382	0.53	516	0.65	0.4										
Finland	4,010	0.81	6,771	1.31	0.7	1,273	0.27	1,858	0.36	0.5	291	0.06	4,743	0.92	15.3
France	30,667	0.54	42,232	0.72	0.4	30,100	0.56	70,000	1.19	1.3	7,930	0.15	18,077	0.31	1.3
Gabon	383	0.41	467	0.40	0.2	17	0.02	192	0.16	10.3					
Gambia						22	0.03	91	0.07	3.1					
Georgia			110	0.02				317	0.06				433	0.08	
Germany	17,895	0.23	49,280	0.60	1.8	11,122	0.14	16,511	0.20	0.5	22,473	0.29	82,975	1.01	2.7
Ghana	248	0.02	210	0.01	-0.2	40	0.00	335	0.02	7.4					
Greece	6,660	0.66	6,403	0.61	0.0	4,796	0.50	10,916	1.04	1.3	1,374	0.14	1,935	0.18	0.4
Guatemala	99	0.01	506	0.05	4.1	466	0.07	636	0.06	0.4	178	0.03	391	0.04	1.2
Guinea	27	0.00	36	0.01	0.3			99	0.01						
Guinea-Bissau	21	0.02	20	0.02	0.0										
Guyana	135	0.17	126	0.15	-0.1										
Haiti	0	0.00				138	0.03	150	0.02	0.1					
Honduras	482	0.10				122	0.03	318	0.05	1.6			202	0.03	
Hungary	1,176	0.11	1,749	0.17	0.5	9,413	0.88	15,000	1.48	0.6	5,164	0.48	12,317	1.22	1.4
Iceland	845	3.34	1,593	5.81	0.9										
India	12,863	0.02	16,521	0.02	0.3	1,194	0.00	2,359	0.00	1.0	1,017	0.00	3,811	0.00	2.7
Indonesia & East Timor	8,824	0.05	12,614	0.06	0.4	527	0.00	4,606	0.02	7.7	635	0.00	2,200	0.01	2.5
Iran	4,487	0.08	9,200	0.15	1.1	156	0.00	1,008	0.02	5.5	428	0.01	1,354	0.02	2.2
Iraq	1,113	0.06				1,222	0.09	51	0.00	-1.0	443	0.03			
Ireland	3,676	1.05	10,401	2.81	1.8	2,258	0.66	6,064	1.64	1.7	669	0.20	3,053	0.82	3.6
Israel & Occupied Territories	1,895	0.42	3,699	0.45	1.0	1,116	0.29	1,942	0.24	0.7	513	0.13	2,983	0.36	4.8
Italy	15,649	0.28	27,463	0.48	0.8	22,087	0.39	34,829	0.60	0.6	23,994	0.43	14,327	0.25	-0.4
Jamaica	1,189	0.50	1,454	0.56	0.2	395	0.19	1,225	0.48	2.1					
Japan	62,088	0.50	101,701	0.80	0.6	1,317	0.01	4,106	0.03	2.1	5,224	0.04	15,806	0.13	2.0
Jordan	1,226	0.40	1,187	0.26	0.0	393	0.18	1,256	0.28	2.2	720	0.33	1,347	0.30	0.9
Kazakhstan			566	0.04											
Kenya	721	0.03	1,138	0.04	0.6	372	0.02	894	0.03	1.4			350	0.01	

Country	Air transport — Passengers carried (thousands)					International tourism									
						Inbound tourists (thousands)					Outbound tourists (thousands)				
	1988		1998			1980		1998			1980		1998		
	Total	Per capita	Total	Per capita	% change 1988–1998	Total	Per capita	Total	Per capita	% change 1980–1998	Total	Per capita	Total	Per capita	% change 1980–1998
Korea, Dem. Rep.	218	0.01	64	0.00	-0.7			130	0.01						
Korea, Rep.	9,826	0.23	27,109	0.58	1.8	976	0.03	4,250	0.09	3.4	339	0.01	3,067	0.07	8.0
Kuwait	1,557	0.76	2,241	1.20	0.4	108	0.08	79	0.04	-0.3	230	0.17			
Kyrgyzstan			620	0.13				59	0.01				32	0.01	
Laos	48	0.01	124	0.02	1.6			200	0.04						
Latvia			229	0.09				567	0.23				1,961	0.80	
Lebanon	493	0.14	716	0.17	0.5			631	0.15				1,650	0.39	
Lesotho	63	0.04	28	0.01	-0.6	73	0.05	150	0.07	1.1					
Liberia	46	0.02													
Libya	1,581	0.37	571	0.11	-0.6	126	0.04	32	0.01	-0.7	95	0.03	650	0.12	5.8
Lithuania			259	0.07				1,416	0.38				3,241	0.88	
Luxembourg	294	0.78	701	1.64	1.4				0.00						
Macedonia			489	0.24											
Madagascar	387	0.03	601	0.04	0.6	13	0.00	121	0.01	8.3			35	0.00	
Malawi	116	0.01	158	0.01	0.4	46	0.01	205	0.02	3.5					
Malaysia	7,684	0.43	13,654	0.62	0.8	2,105	0.15	5,551	0.25	1.6	1,738	0.13	25,631	1.16	13.7
Maldives	8	0.04	247	0.94	29.9										
Mali			91	0.01		27	0.00	83	0.01	2.1					
Malta	481	1.37	1,159	3.07	1.4										
Mauritania	216	0.11	250	0.10	0.2										
Mauritius	384	0.37	848	0.73	1.2	115	0.12	558	0.48	3.9	33	0.03	143	0.12	3.3
Mexico	11,412	0.14	17,717	0.18	0.6	11,945	0.18	19,810	0.21	0.7	3,322	0.05	9,803	0.10	2.0
Moldova			118	0.03				20	0.00				35	0.01	
Mongolia			240	0.09		195	0.12	135	0.05	-0.3					
Morocco & Western Sahara	1,267	0.05	3,012	0.11	1.4	1,425	0.07	3,243	0.12	1.3	578	0.03	1,359	0.05	1.4
Mozambique	235	0.02	201	0.01	-0.1										
Myanmar	516	0.01	333	0.01	-0.4	38	0.00	201	0.00	4.3					
Namibia			214	0.13				560	0.34						
Nepal	988	0.05	754	0.03	-0.2	163	0.01	435	0.02	1.7	23	0.00	110	0.00	3.8
Netherlands	7,860	0.53	18,676	1.19	1.4	2,784	0.20	9,320	0.59	2.3	6,749	0.48	12,860	0.82	0.9
New Zealand	5,094	1.50	8,655	2.28	0.7	465	0.15	1,485	0.39	2.2	454	0.15	1,166	0.31	1.6
Nicaragua	87	0.02	51	0.01	-0.4			406	0.08				422	0.09	
Niger	111	0.01	91	0.01	-0.2	20	0.00	19	0.00	-0.1			10	0.00	
Nigeria	995	0.01	313	0.00	-0.7	86	0.00	739	0.01	7.6					
Norway	8,261	1.95	14,292	3.22	0.7	1,252	0.31	2,829	0.64	1.3	246	0.06	3,120	0.70	11.7
Oman	776	0.49	1,849	0.80	1.4	60	0.05	612	0.27	9.2					
Pakistan	4,889	0.05	5,414	0.04	0.1	299	0.00	429	0.00	0.4	104	0.00			
Panama	382	0.16	860	0.31	1.3	392	0.20	431	0.16	0.1	113	0.06	211	0.08	0.9
Papua New Guinea	887	0.24	1,110	0.24	0.3	40	0.01	67	0.01	0.7			63	0.01	
Paraguay	249	0.06	222	0.04	-0.1	302	0.10	350	0.07	0.2			498	0.10	
Peru	2,737	0.13	2,775	0.11	0.0	373	0.02	833	0.03	1.2	127	0.01	577	0.02	3.5
Philippines	5,720	0.09	6,732	0.09	0.2	1,008	0.02	2,149	0.03	1.1	461	0.01	1,817	0.02	2.9
Poland	1,600	0.04	2,213	0.06	0.4	5,664	0.16	18,780	0.49	2.3	6,852	0.19	49,328	1.28	6.2
Portugal	3,025	0.30	7,023	0.70	1.3	2,730	0.28	11,295	1.13	3.1			2,425	0.24	

Country	Air transport — Passengers carried (thousands) 1988 Total	1988 Per capita	1998 Total	1998 Per capita	% change 1988–1998	International tourism — Inbound tourists (thousands) 1980 Total	1980 Per capita	1998 Total	1998 Per capita	% change 1980–1998	Outbound tourists (thousands) 1980 Total	1980 Per capita	1998 Total	1998 Per capita	% change 1980–1998
Qatar	698	1.65	1,207	1.63	0.7				0.00						
Romania	1,323	0.06	908	0.04	-0.3	3,270	0.15	2,966	0.13	-0.1	1,711	0.08	6,893	0.31	3.0
Russian Federation								15,805	0.11				11,711	0.08	
Rwanda	12	0.00				30	0.01	2	0.00	-0.9					
Sao Tome & Principe	22	0.20	25	0.18	0.1										
Saudi Arabia	9,880	0.65	11,816	0.57	0.2	2,475	0.26	3,700	0.18	0.5					
Senegal	135	0.02	121	0.01	-0.1	186	0.03	352	0.04	0.9					
Sierra Leone	44	0.01	0	0.00	-1.0	46	0.01	50	0.01	0.1					
Singapore	6,047	2.28	13,331	4.21	1.2	2,562	1.12	5,631	1.78	1.2			3,745	1.18	
Slovakia			107	0.02				896	0.17				414	0.08	
Slovenia			460	0.23				977	0.49						
Solomon Islands	69	0.22	94	0.23	0.4										
Somalia	105	0.01													
South Africa	5,126	0.15	6,480	0.16	0.3	700	0.03	5,898	0.14	7.4	572	0.02	3,080	0.07	4.4
Spain	18,983	0.49	31,594	0.80	0.7	22,388	0.60	47,749	1.21	1.1	18,022	0.48	13,203	0.34	-0.3
Sri Lanka	694	0.04	1,213	0.06	0.7	322	0.02	381	0.02	0.2	138	0.01	518	0.03	2.8
Sudan	534	0.02	499	0.02	-0.1	25	0.00	39	0.00	0.6			200	0.01	
Suriname	135	0.34	278	0.67	1.1										
Swaziland	47	0.06	41	0.04	-0.1										
Sweden	10,212	1.20	11,878	1.34	0.2	1,366	0.16	2,568	0.29	0.9	2,941	0.35	11,422	1.29	2.9
Switzerland	7,484	1.13	14,299	2.01	0.9	8,873	1.40	10,900	1.53	0.2	4,451	0.70	12,213	1.72	1.7
Syria	342	0.03	685	0.04	1.0	1,239	0.14	1,267	0.08	0.0	1,189	0.14	2,750	0.18	1.3
Tajikistan			592	0.10				511	0.08						
Tanzania	410	0.02	220	0.01	-0.5	84	0.00	450	0.01	4.4			150	0.00	
Thailand	6,236	0.11	15,015	0.25	1.4	1,859	0.04	7,843	0.13	3.2	497	0.01	1,412	0.02	1.8
Togo	70	0.02	91	0.02	0.3	92	0.04	94	0.02	0.0					
Trinidad & Tobago	1,296	1.07	804	0.63	-0.4	199	0.18	347	0.27	0.7	206	0.19	250	0.19	0.2
Tunisia	1,210	0.15	1,859	0.20	0.5	1,602	0.25	4,718	0.51	1.9	478	0.07	1,526	0.16	2.2
Turkey	3,497	0.06	9,949	0.16	1.8	921	0.02	8,960	0.14	8.7	1,795	0.04	4,601	0.07	1.6
Turkmenistan			521	0.11				300	0.06				357	0.08	
Uganda	61	0.00	100	0.00	0.6	36	0.00	238	0.01	5.6					
Ukraine			1,066	0.02				6,208	0.12				10,326	0.21	
United Arab Emirates	1,330	0.78	5,264	1.93	3.0	300	0.29	2,184	0.80	6.3					
United Kingdom	37,573	0.66	61,940	1.05	0.6	12,420	0.22	25,745	0.44	1.1	15,507	0.28	50,872	0.86	2.3
United States	454,203	1.84	588,171	2.18	0.3	22,500	0.10	46,395	0.17	1.1	22,721	0.10	52,735	0.20	1.3
Uruguay	386	0.13	557	0.17	0.4	1,067	0.37	2,163	0.66	1.0	640	0.22	654	0.20	0.0
Uzbekistan			1,560	0.06				272	0.01						
Vanuatu	19	0.13	89	0.49	3.7				0.00						
Venezuela	8,384	0.44	3,737	0.16	-0.6	215	0.01	837	0.04	2.9	747	0.05	524	0.02	-0.3
Vietnam	88	0.00	2,304	0.03	25.2			1,520	0.02				168	0.00	
Yemen	636	0.06	765	0.05	0.2	39	0.00	88	0.01	1.3					
Zambia	304	0.04	49	0.01	-0.8	87	0.02	362	0.04	3.2					
Zimbabwe	525	0.06	789	0.07	0.5	243	0.03	1,984	0.17	7.2	326	0.05	123	0.01	-0.6

International tourism

| | Inbound tourists (thousands) | | | | | | | Outbound tourists (thousands) | | | | | | |
| | 1980 | | | 1998 | | | | 1980 | | | 1998 | | | |
	Total	Per capita	%	Total	Per capita	%	% change 1980–1998	Total	Per capita	%	Total	Per capita	%	% change 1980–1998
World	266,338	0.06	100.0	634,659	0.98	100	138.3	158,991	0.04	100	442,737	0.14	100.0	178.5
Low income	8,348	0.00	3.1	45,439	0.02	7.2	444.3	2,121	0.00	1.3	14,957	0.02	3.4	605.2
Excl. China & India	3,654	0.00	1.4	17,877	0.03	2.8	389.2	1,104	0.00	0.7	2,720	0.02	0.6	146.4
Middle income	62,781	0.06	23.6	198,850	0.22	31.3	216.7	33,235	0.03	20.9	161,250	0.22	36.4	385.2
Lower middle income	21,407	0.03	8.0	75,412	0.12	11.9	252.3	9,147	0.01	5.8	38,237	0.15	8.6	318.0
Upper middle income	41,374	0.09	15.5	123,438	0.38	19.4	198.3	24,088	0.06	15.2	123,013	0.36	27.8	410.7
Low & middle income	71,129	0.02	26.7	244,289	0.13	38.5	243.4	35,356	0.01	22.2	176,207	0.15	39.8	398.4
East Asia & Pacific	10,546	0.01	4.0	52,938	0.05	8.3	402.0	3,678	0.00	2.3	40,661	0.15	9.2	1005.5
Europe & Central Asia	21,205	0.05	8.0	97,306	0.29	15.3	358.9	15,522	0.04	9.8	92,965	0.37	21.0	498.9
Latin America & Carib.	22,886	0.06	8.6	51,623	0.15	8.1	125.6	9,907	0.03	6.2	27,911	0.08	6.3	181.7
Middle East & N. Africa	11,096	0.06	4.2	22,267	0.13	3.5	100.7	4,620	0.03	2.9	8,632	0.15	1.9	86.8
South Asia	2,086	0.00	0.8	4,182	0.01	0.7	100.5	1,259	0.00	0.8	5,358	0.01	1.2	325.6
Sub-Saharan Africa	3,310	0.01	1.2	15,973	0.06	2.5	382.6	370	0.00	0.2	680	0.04	0.2	83.8
High income	195,209	0.25	73.3	390,370	0.65	61.5	100.0	123,635	0.16	77.8	266,530	0.68	60.2	115.6
Europe EU	113,018	0.41	42.4	221,946	0.78	35.0	96.4	68,933	0.25	43.4	141,098	0.80	31.9	104.7
U.S. & Canada	35,376	0.31	13.3	65,232	0.40	10.3	84.4	35554	0.31	22.4	70383	0.39	15.9	98.0
Japan	1,317	0.01	0.5	4,106	0.03	0.6	211.8	5224	0.04	3.3	15806	0.13	3.6	202.6
Australia & New Zealand	1,370	0.11	0.5	5,652	0.31	0.9	312.6	1671	0.11	1.1	4327	0.24	1.0	158.9

Sources: World Bank, *World Development Indicators 2000* (CD-ROM); International Civil Aviation Organization, *Civil Aviation Statistics of the World,* 23rd ed. (Montreal: ICAO, 1999)

Table R7: Trade in cultural goods

This table presents the country share of the total monetary value of imports, exports, and trade balance of cultural goods for 1990 and 1998. Cultural goods are largely the carriers and receivers of political, artistic, entertainment, and otherwise culture-related content. Rather than showing Americanisation or Westernisation, it shows how much cultural products are part of geographically dispersed production and distribution processes with growth concentrated in developing countries. The table shows only legally traded goods; it does not account for pirated import, which is common in many countries.

	1990			1998		
	% of world import	% of world export	Balance	% of world import	% of world export	Balance
Argentina	0.1	0.1	0.0	0.6	0.2	-0.4
Australia	1.9	0.3	-1.6	1.8	0.4	-1.4
Austria	2.0	1.4	-0.6	1.5	2.3	0.8
Belgium & Luxemburg	3.0	2.6	-0.3	2.6	2.8	0.2
Bolivia	0.0	0.0	0.0	0.0	0.0	0.0
Brazil	0.3	0.1	-0.2	0.6	0.1	-0.6
Cameroon	0.2	0.0	-0.2	0.0	0.0	0.0
Canada	4.9	1.3	-3.6	4.9	2.4	-2.5
Chile	0.1	0.0	-0.1	0.3	0.2	-0.1
China & Tibet	1.6	3.9	2.3	1.1	9.5	8.5
Colombia	0.0	0.2	0.1	0.2	0.2	-0.1
Costa Rica	0.1	0.0	-0.1	0.1	0.0	-0.1
Croatia	0.0	0.0	0.0	0.1	0.0	-0.1
Cyprus	0.1	0.0	-0.1	0.1	0.0	-0.1
Czech Republic	0.0	0.0	0.0	0.6	0.7	0.1
Denmark	1.0	1.2	0.2	0.9	0.9	0.0
Ecuador	0.0	0.0	0.0	0.1	0.0	-0.1
Egypt	0.1	0.0	-0.1	0.1	0.0	-0.1
Finland	0.7	0.4	-0.3	0.4	0.6	0.2
France	8.0	6.7	-1.2	5.1	4.9	-0.2
Germany	7.7	13.8	6.1	6.9	10.3	3.4
Greece	0.3	0.1	-0.2	0.4	0.1	-0.3
Guatemala	0.0	0.0	0.0	0.1	0.0	-0.1
Hungary	0.0	0.0	0.0	0.6	0.3	-0.3
India	0.1	0.1	-0.1	0.0	0.0	0.0
Indonesia	0.1	0.1	0.0	0.1	0.1	0.1
Ireland	0.7	2.4	1.7	0.9	4.8	3.9
Israel & Occupied Territories	0.2	0.1	-0.1	0.3	0.2	-0.2
Italy	2.9	3.4	0.5	2.5	3.1	0.6
Japan	8.6	7.4	-1.2	4.0	7.4	3.4
Korea, Rep.	0.6	3.2	2.7	0.6	1.4	0.8
Kuwait	0.1	0.0	0.0	0.0	0.0	0.0
Libya	0.1	0.0	-0.1	0.0	0.0	0.0
Lithuania	0.0	0.0	0.0	0.1	0.0	0.0
Malaysia	0.3	0.4	0.1	0.3	0.6	0.3
Malta	0.0	0.1	0.1	0.0	0.1	0.1
Mexico	0.8	0.5	-0.3	1.6	1.9	0.3
Morocco & Western Sahara	0.1	0.0	-0.1	0.0	0.0	0.0
Netherlands	3.9	4.6	0.7	2.8	4.2	1.4
New Zealand	0.5	0.1	-0.4	0.3	0.1	-0.2
Norway	0.8	0.2	-0.6	0.8	0.2	-0.6
Panama	0.0	0.0	0.0	0.1	0.0	-0.1

	1990			1998		
	% of world import	% of world export	Balance	% of world import	% of world export	Balance
Paraguay	0.1	0.0	-0.1	0.0	0.0	0.0
Peru	0.1	0.0	-0.1	0.2	0.0	-0.1
Philippines	0.1	0.1	0.0	0.2	0.2	0.1
Poland	0.0	0.0	0.0	0.6	0.4	-0.2
Portugal	0.4	0.1	-0.3	0.5	0.1	-0.4
Romania	0.1	0.1	0.0	0.1	0.1	-0.1
Russian Federation	0.0	0.0	0.0	0.7	0.7	0.0
Saudi Arabia	0.3	0.0	-0.3	0.0	0.0	0.0
Singapore	1.5	1.4	-0.1	2.0	2.4	0.4
Slovakia	0.0	0.0	0.0	0.2	0.2	0.0
Slovenia	0.0	0.0	0.0	0.1	0.1	0.0
South Africa	0.0	0.0	0.0	0.5	0.1	-0.4
Spain	2.0	1.5	-0.5	1.9	2.1	0.3
Sweden	1.7	1.0	-0.7	1.0	0.7	-0.3
Switzerland	4.2	4.6	0.4	3.6	2.7	-0.9
Thailand	0.3	0.8	0.5	0.0	0.0	0.0
Tunisia	0.0	0.0	0.0	0.1	0.0	0.0
Turkey	0.1	0.1	-0.1	0.3	0.1	-0.1
United Kingdom	11.7	14.2	2.6	10.2	11.9	1.7
United States	20.1	17.8	-2.3	27.0	16.9	-10.1
Venezuela	0.1	0.1	0.0	0.2	0.0	-0.2
Developing countries	12.5	14.3	1.8	19.6	20.9	1.3
Developed countries	87.5	85.7	-1.8	80.4	79.1	-1.3

Cultural goods here include: books; newspapers & periodicals; other printed matter; sound recordings & media; paintings, drawings & pastels; original engravings, prints & lithographs; original sculptures & statuary; stamps, coins, jewellery & antiques; games.

* Countries with values of zero for all categories have not been included in this analysis

Source: UNESCO, International Flows of Selected Cultural Goods 1980-1998, Statistical Annexes (CD-ROM, 2000).

Table R8 World languages and web languages

These tables and figures offer information on the distribution of languages by geographical region (**Figure R1**) and the scale of major language groups. English, while not the not the most frequent language in terms of native speakers (which is Chinese, Table R8c), is the primary language of the Internet (**Figure R2**) and the second language for a sizeable portion of the world population (Table R8a and R8b). Figure R2 also shows that other European languages too, while representing a mere 3% of the world's languages, contribute more than 90% to web content. It is likely, therefore, that people who can speak English and/or other European languages are overrepresented in global civil society.

R8a English speakers

Countries	L1 = Native speakers	L2 = Second language speakers
Australia	15,316,000	2,084,000
Bahamas	250,000	25,000
Bangladesh		3,100,000
Barbados	265,000	
Belize*	135,000	30,000
Bhutan		60,000
Botswana		620,000
Brunei*	10,000	104,000
Cameroon		6,600,000
Canada	19,700,000	6,000,000
Dominican Republic		12,000
Fiji		160,000
Gambia		33,000
Ghana		1,153,000
Guyana	700,000	30,000
India*	320,000	37,000,000
Ireland	3,334,000	190,000
Jamaica	2,400,000	50,000
Kenya		2,576,000
Lesotho		488,000
Liberia*	60,000	2,000,000
Malawi		517,000
Malaysia*	375,000	5,984,000
Malta		86,000
Mauritius		167,000
Micronesia, Fed.		15,000
Namibia*	13,000	300,000
Nepal		5,927,000
New Zealand	3,396,000	150,000
Nigeria		43,000,000
Pakistan		16,000,000
Papua New Guinea*	120,000	28,000,000
Philippines*	15,000	36,400,000
Rwanda		24,000
Samoa		86,000
Sierra Leone	450,000	
St Lucia	29,000	22,000
St Vincent & Grenadines	111,000	

R8a English speakers continued

Countries	L1 = Native speakers	L2 = Second language speakers
Singapore*	300,000	1,046,000
South Africa*	3,600,000	10,000,000
Solomon Islands		135,000
Sri Lanka*	10,000	1,850,000
Suriname	258,000	150,000
Swaziland		40,000
Tanzania		3,000,000
Trinidad & Tobago	1,200,000	
Uganda		2,000,000
United Kingdom	56,990,000	1,100,000
United States*	226,710,000	30,000,000
Vanuatu		160,000
Zambia*	50,000	1,000,000
Total**	337,297,000	282,979,000

*indicates territories in which English is used as a native language, but where there is greater use of English as a second language or significant use of another language.

**world total encompasses figures taken from additional small countries not included in this analysis

Sources: David Graddol, *The Future of English?: A Guide to Forecasting the Popularity of the English Language in the 21st Century* (The British Council, 1997, 2000). http://www.britishcouncil.org/english/pdf/future.pdf; B. F.Grimes (ed.), *Ethnologue: Languages of the World* (Dallas: Summer Institute of Linguistics, 1996)

R8b Countries in transition from EFL (English as a Foreign Language) to L2

Argentina	Nepal	Sweden
Belgium	Netherlands	Switzerland
Costa Rica	Nicaragua	United Arab
Denmark	Norway	Emirates
Ethiopia	Panama	
Honduras	Somalia	
Lebanon	Sudan	
Myanmar	Suriname	

R8c Speakers of major languages

Language	engco model***	Ethnologue***
Chinese	1.113	1.123
English	372	322
Hindi/Urdu	316	236
Spanish	304	266
Arabic	201	202
Portuguese	165	170
Russian	155	288
Bengali	125	189
Japanese	123	125
German	102	98
French	70	72
Italian	57	63
Malay	47	47

*** See glossary

Figure R1: Languages of the world

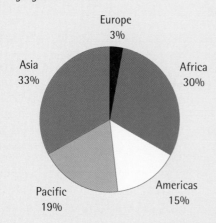

Source: Grimes, B.F., ed. *Ethnologue: Languages of the World*, Summer Institute of Linguistics, Dallas, 1996.

Figure R2: Languages of the Web

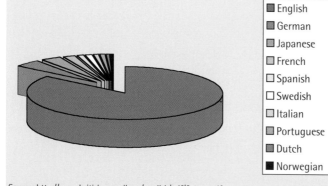

- English
- German
- Japanese
- French
- Spanish
- Swedish
- Italian
- Portuguese
- Dutch
- Norwegian

Source: http://www.britishcouncil.org/english/pdf/future.pdf

Table R9 Media

This table shows the daily newspaper circulation, the number of radios, television sets, and cable subscribers per thousand of population. It gives an indication of people's exposure to different media, although it does not show the number of sources within each medium.

figures are per thousand of population Country	Daily news-papers 1996	Radios 1997	Television sets 1998	cable subscribers 1998	Country	Daily news-papers 1996	Radios 1997	Television sets 1998	cable subscribers 1998
Albania	36	217	109	0	Eritrea		91	14	
Algeria	38	241	105	0	Estonia	174	693	480	15.1
Angola	11	54	14		Ethiopia	1	195	5	
Argentina	123	681	289	163.1	Finland	455	1,496	640	175.7
Armenia	23	224	218	0.4	France	218	937	601	27.5
Australia	293	1,376	639	43.6	Gabon	29	183	55	
Austria	296	753	516	139.1	Gambia	2	168	3	
Azerbaijan	27	23	254	0.1	Georgia		555	473	2.8
Bangladesh	9	50	6		Germany	311	948	580	214.5
Belarus	174	296	314		Ghana	14	238	99	
Belgium	160	793	510	367.3	Greece	153	477	466	1.2
Benin	2	108	10		Guatemala	33	79	126	28.5
Bolivia	55	675	116		Guinea		47	41	0
Bosnia & Herzegovina	152	248	41		Guinea-Bissau	5	44		
Botswana	27	156	20		Haiti	3	55	5	
Brazil	40	444	316	16.3	Honduras	55	386	90	
Bulgaria	257	543	398	28.8	Hungary	186	689	437	146.5
Burkina Faso	1	33	9		India		121	69	18.8
Burundi	3	71	4		Indonesia & East Timor	24	156	136	
Cambodia	2	127	123		Iran	28	265	157	0
Cameroon	7	163	32		Iraq	19	229	83	
Canada	159	1,077	715	263.8	Ireland	150	699	403	171.1
Central African Republic	2	83	5		Israel & Occupied Territories	290	520	318	184
Chad	0	242	1	0	Italy	104	878	486	2.8
Chile	98	354	232	44.8	Jamaica	62	480	182	73.1
China & Tibet		333	272	40	Japan	578	955	707	114.8
Colombia	46	581	217	16.7	Jordan	58	287	52	0.1
Congo, Rep.	8	124	12		Kazakhstan		384	231	
Congo, Dem. Rep.	3	375	135		Kenya	9	104	21	
Costa Rica	94	271	387	13.8	Korea, Dem. Rep.	199	147	53	
Côte d'Ivoire	17	164	70	0	Korea, Rep.	393	1,033	346	138.3
Croatia	115	336	272		Kuwait	374	660	491	
Cuba	118	353	239	0	Kyrgyzstan	15	112	45	
Czech Republic	254	803	447	77.1	Laos	4	143	4	
Denmark	309	1,141	585	248.4	Latvia	247	710	492	58
Dominican Republic	52	178	95	15.5	Lebanon	107	906	352	1.4
Ecuador	70	419	293	11.7	Lesotho	8	49	25	
Egypt	40	324	122		Libya	14	233	126	0
El Salvador	48	464	675						

Table R9 continued Country	Daily news-papers 1996	Radios 1997	Television sets 1998	cable subscribers 1998	Country	Daily news-papers 1996	Radios 1997	Television sets 1998	cable subscribers 1998
Lithuania	93	513	459	67.5	Senegal	5	142	41	
Macedonia	21	200	250		Sierra Leone	4	253	13	0
Madagascar	5	192	21		Singapore	360	822	348	49.5
Malawi	3	249	2		Slovakia	185	580	402	105.1
Malaysia	158	420	166	5.2	Slovenia	199	406	356	150.5
Mali	1	54	12	0	South Africa	32	317	125	
Mauritania	0	151	91		Spain	100	333	506	11.8
Mauritius	75	368	226		Sri Lanka	29	209	92	0
Mexico	97	325	261	15.7	Sudan	27	271	87	0
Moldova	60	740	297	17.6	Sweden	445	932	531	221.4
Mongolia	27	151	63	10.8	Switzerland	337	1,000	535	352.7
Morocco &					Syria	20	278	70	
Western Sahara	26	241	160		Tajikistan	20	142	285	
Mozambique	3	40	5		Tanzania	4	279	21	0
Myanmar	10	95	7		Thailand	63	232	236	10.1
Namibia	19	144	37		Togo	4	218	18	
Nepal	11	38	6	0.2	Trinidad &				
Netherlands	306	978	543	378.3	Tobago	123	534	334	
New Zealand	216	990	508	1.3	Tunisia	31	223	198	
Nicaragua	30	285	190	40.2	Turkey	111	180	286	9.2
Niger	0	69	27		Turkmenistan		276	201	
Nigeria	24	223	66		Uganda	2	128	27	
Norway	588	915	579	160.1	Ukraine	54	884	490	15.7
Oman	29	598	595	0	United Arab				
Pakistan	23	98	88	0.1	Emirates	156	345	294	
Panama	62	299	187		United Kingdom	329	1,436	645	45.9
Papua New Guinea	15	97	24		United States	215	2,146	847	244.3
Paraguay	43	182	101		Uruguay	293	607	241	
Peru	84	273	144	14.1	Uzbekistan	3	465	275	
Philippines	79	159	108	8.2	Venezuela	206	468	185	25.8
Poland	113	523	413	83.3	Vietnam	4	107	47	
Portugal	75	304	542	59.8	Yemen	15	64	29	
Romania	300	319	233	119.2	Yugoslavia	107	297	259	
Russian Federation	105	418	420	78.5	Zambia	12	121	137	
Rwanda	0	102	0		Zimbabwe	19	93	30	
Saudi Arabia	57	321	262		World	100	418	247	55.8

Sources: International Telecommunications Union, *World Telecommunication Development Report 1999* (Geneva: ITU, 1999); UNESCO, S*tatistical Yearbook 1999* (Paris: UNESCO, 1999).

Table R10 Communication

This table shows the number of telephone mainlines and mobile phones and the number of international outgoing call minutes per subscriber. It also gives the number of personal computers per thousand of population, the number of Internet hosts per ten thousand of population, and the number of estimated users as percentage of the population. It shows the extent to which people communicate with each other by technological means, with column three indicating cross-border communication.

Country	Telephone mainlines per thousand of population 1998	Mobile phones per thousand of population 1998	International outgoing calls minutes per subscriber 1998	Personal computers per ten thousand of population Jul-99	Internet hosts per ten thousand of population 1998	Estimated Internet users as % of population 1999/2000
Albania	31	1	425	2		0.1
Algeria	53	1	76	14	0.0	0.1
Angola	6	1	385	8		0.1
Argentina	203	78	45	443	27.9	2.4
Armenia	157	2	102	42	1.9	0.9
Australia	512	286	125	4,116	477.9	43.9
Austria	491	282	313	2,334	252.0	36.9
Azerbaijan	89	8	94		0.2	0.1
Bahamas						5.1
Bahrain						6.0
Bangladesh	3	1	111			0.0
Barbados						2.2
Belarus	241	1	71		0.8	0.1
Belgium	500	173	270	2,860	266.9	36.3
Belize						4.8
Benin	7	1	296	9	0.0	0.2
Bhutan						0.0
Bolivia	69	27	45	75	0.5	0.4
Bosnia & Herzegovina	91	7	285		1.4	0.1
Botswana	65	15	432	255	6.0	0.8
Brazil	121	47	27	301	18.5	5.7
Brunei						1.2
Bulgaria	329	15	31		11.9	2.6
Burkina Faso	4		212	7	0.2	0.0
Burundi	3		140			0.0
Cambodia	2	6	309	9	0.1	
Cameroon	5		335			0.1
Canada	634	176	230	3,300	423.0	42.8
Cape Verde						1.3
Central African Republic	3		431			0.0
Chad	1		376			0.0
Chile	205	65	85	482	21.5	4.1
China & Tibet	70	19	20	89	0.5	1.3
Colombia	173	49	32	279	7.5	1.5
Comoros						0.1
Congo, Rep.	8	1				0.0
Congo, Dem. Rep.			36			
Costa Rica	172	28	116	391	10.4	4.0
Côte d'Ivoire	12	6	337	36	0.3	0.1

Country	Telephone mainlines per thousand of population 1998	Mobile phones per thousand of population 1998	International outgoing calls minutes per subscriber 1998	Personal computers per ten thousand of population Jul-99	Internet hosts per ten thousand of population 1998	Estimated Internet users as % of population 1999/2000
Croatia	348	41	176	1,116	25.9	2.1
Cuba	35		75		0.1	0.5
Cyprus						10.6
Czech Republic	364	94	91	973	85.6	3.4
Denmark	660	364	167	3,774	540.3	48.4
Djibouti						0.2
Dominican Republic	93	31	201		7.6	
Ecuador	78	25	76	185	1.4	0.2
Egypt	60	1	32	91	0.3	0.7
El Salvador	80	18	135		1.2	0.7
Equitorial Guinea						0.1
Eritrea	7		119		0.0	0.0
Estonia	343	170	151	344	174.7	21.6
Ethiopia	3		72		0.0	0.0
Fiji						0.9
Finland	554	572	142	3,492	1,116.8	43.9
France	570	188	100	2,078	110.6	15.3
Gabon	33	8	494	86	0.0	0.4
Gambia	21	4	216		1.6	0.0
Georgia	115	11	73	26	0.0	0.4
Germany	567	170	101	3,077	174.0	24.3
Ghana	8	1	208	16	0.1	0.1
Greece	522	194	124	519	59.6	12.4
Guatemala	41		113			0.5
Guinea	5	3	422	26		0.1
Guinea-Bissau	7		33		0.1	0.1
Guyana						0.4
Haiti	8		205			0.1
Honduras	38	5	195	76	0.2	0.3
Hungary	336	105	70	589	93.1	6.4
Iceland						52.1
India	22	1	20	27	0.2	0.5
Indonesia & East Timor	27	5	58	82	0.8	0.2
Iran	112	6	24	319	0.1	0.2
Iraq	31					
Ireland	435	257	463	2,717	156.7	27.5
Israel & Occupied Territories	471	359	128	2,172	187.4	17.1
Italy	451	355	104	1,734	68.3	23.3
Jamaica	166	22	183	394	1.0	2.3
Japan	503	374	28	2,372	163.8	30.5
Jordan	86	12	239	87	1.2	1.9
Kazakhstan	104	2	113		1.4	0.4
Kenya	9		107	25	0.2	0.2
Korea, Dem. Rep.	47					
Korea, Rep.	433	302	30	1,568	55.5	34.6
Kuwait	236	138	405	1,049	23.8	5.0
Kyrgyzstan	76		84		4.1	0.2

Country	Telephone mainlines per thousand of population 1998	Mobile phones per thousand of population 1998	International outgoing calls minutes per subscriber 1998	Personal computers per ten thousand of population Jul-99	Internet hosts per ten thousand of population 1998	Estimated Internet users as % of population 1999/2000
Laos	6	1	301	11		0.0
Latvia	302	68	75		50.9	9.7
Lebanon	194	157	113	392	7.0	6.4
Lesotho	10	5	2		0.1	0.1
Liberia						0.0
Libya	84	3	93			0.2
Lithuania	300	72	46	540	30.5	6.2
Luxembourg						21.7
Macedonia	199	15	127		4.4	1.5
Madagascar	3	1	197	13	0.1	0.1
Malawi	3	1	341			0.1
Malaysia	198	99	172	586	23.5	6.9
Maldives	3		444			0.1
Mali				7	0.0	0.1
Malta						10.2
Mauritania	6		427			0.1
Mauritius	214	53	113	871	4.6	4.7
Mexico	104	35	132	470	23.0	2.5
Moldova	150	2	81	64	2.4	0.3
Mongolia	37	1	34	54	0.0	0.1
Morocco & Western Sahara	54	4	119	25	0.3	0.4
Mozambique	4		251	16	0.1	0.1
Myanmar	5		83			
Namibia	69	12	543	186	11.7	0.6
Nepal	8		95		0.1	0.1
Netherlands	593	213	173	3,176	403.5	45.8
New Zealand	479	203	235	2,821	476.2	39.0
Nicaragua	31	4	266	78	2.2	0.4
Niger	2		322	2	0.0	0.0
Nigeria	4		113	57		0.1
Norway	660	474	176	210	2.9	52.6
Oman	92	43	425	3,734	754.2	2.0
Pakistan	19	1	30	39	0.2	0.9
Panama	151		119			1.6
Papua New Guinea	11	1	572		0.5	0.0
Paraguay	55	41	131	960	2.4	0.4
Peru	67	30	52	181	3.1	1.5
Philippines	37	22	106	151	1.3	0.6
Poland	228	50	68	439	40.9	7.3
Portugal	413	309	114	813	59.4	7.0
Qatar						6.2
Romania	162	29	36	102	9.0	2.7
Russian Federation	197	5	36	406	13.1	6.3
Rwanda	2	1	421			0.0
Samoa						0.3
Sao Tome & Principe						0.3
Saudi Arabia	143	31	324	496	1.2	1.4

Table R10 continued

Country	Telephone mainlines per thousand of population 1998	Mobile phones per thousand of population 1998	International outgoing calls minutes per subscriber 1998	Personal computers per ten thousand of population Jul-99	Internet hosts per ten thousand of population 1998	Estimated Internet users as % of population 1999/2000
Senegal	16	2	225	114	0.3	0.3
Sierra Leone	4		230		0.1	0.0
Singapore	562	346	695	4,584	322.3	44.6
Slovakia	286	87	100	651	38.8	12.9
Slovenia	375	84	157	2,509	99.3	23.0
Solomon Islands						0.6
South Africa	115	56	79	474	33.4	4.2
Spain	414	179	111	1,448	76.8	13.7
Sri Lanka	28	9	75	41	0.5	0.3
St. Lucia						3.2
St. Vincent & the Grenadines						1.7
Sudan	6		114	19		0.0
Swaziland						0.3
Sweden	674	464	169	3,614	581.5	56.4
Switzerland	675	235	396	4,218	371.4	33.1
Syria	95		70	17		0.1
Tajikistan	37		45		0.2	0.0
Tanzania	4	1	917	16	0.1	0.1
Thailand	84	32	58	216	4.5	1.7
Togo	7	2	242	68	0.2	0.2
Trinidad & Tobago	206		251			2.6
Tunisia	81	4	150	147	0.1	1.2
Turkey	254	53	38	232	8.1	3.1
Turkmenistan	82	1	43		0.6	0.0
Uganda	3	1	112	15	0.1	0.1
Ukraine	191	2	52	138	4.6	0.4
United Arab Emirates	389	210	956	1,062	39.4	17.1
United Kingdom	557	252	177	2,630	1,122.6	33.6
United States	661	256	136	4,586	1,508.8	55.8
Uruguay	250	60	97	912	270.6	7.5
Uzbekistan	65	1	42		0.1	0.0
Vanuatu						1.6
Venezuela	117	87	62	430	4.0	1.7
Vietnam	26	2	32	64		0.1
Yemen	13	1	116	12	0.0	0.1
Yugoslavia	218	23	95	188	7.7	
Zambia	9	1	174		0.5	0.2
Zimbabwe	17	4	278	90	1.2	0.3
World	146	55	113m	706	94.5	

Sources: International Telecommunications Union (ITU), *World Telecommunication Development Report* 1999; Internet Software Consortium (http://www.isc.org); NUA Publish (http://www.nua.ie)

Table R11 Ratification of treaties

This table is a 'tracking sheet' to indicate which countries have ratified which and how many of the various international treaties, and which countries have not. The table also offers information on how many countries have ratified each particular treaty. The information in this table provides an overview of the reach and density of some of the most important international treaty regulations. Global civil society is dependent on the international rule of law as well as being one of the main actors pushing for the adoption and enforcement of international law.

2000 Country	ICESCR	ICCPR	CCPR-OP1	CCPR-OP2	CERD	CEDAW	CAT	Gen	ILO 87	CSR	ICC	CWC	BWC	BC	CBD	LMC	VCPOL	UNFCCC	KP	Geneva	Prot 1	Prot2	Total
Afghanistan	*	*			*		*	*					*		*	*				*			9
Albania	*	*			*	*	*	*	*	*	*	*		*	*		*	*	*	*	*	*	18
Algeria	*	*	*		*		*	*	*	*		*		*	*		*	*	*	*	*	*	17
Angola	*	*	*			*			*	*				*	*		*	*		*	*		12
Argentina	*	*	*		*	*	*	*	*	*	*	*	*	*	*		*	*	*	*	*	*	19
Armenia	*	*	*		*	*	*		*	*		*	*	*	*		*	*	*	*	*	*	18
Australia	*	*	*	*	*	*	*	*	*	*		*	*	*	*	*	*	*	*	*	*	*	22
Austria	*	*	*	*	*	*	*	*	*	*	*	*	*	*	*	*	*	*	*	*	*	*	22
Azerbaijan	*			*				*		*		*	*	*	*		*	*	*	*	*	*	11
Bahamas					*	*		*			*	*	*	*	*		*	*	*	*	*	*	15
Bahrain					*			*	*	*			*	*	*		*	*	*	*	*	*	13
Bangladesh	*	*			*	*	*	*	*	*		*	*	*	*		*	*	*	*	*	*	18
Barbados	*	*	*		*	*		*	*	*		*	*	*	*		*	*	*	*	*	*	18
Belarus	*	*			*	*	*	*	*	*		*	*	*	*		*	*	*	*	*	*	17
Belgium	*	*	*	*	*	*	*	*	*	*	*	*	*	*	*	*	*	*	*	*	*	*	22
Belize		*			*	*		*	*	*	*	*	*	*	*		*	*	*	*	*	*	15
Benin	*	*	*		*	*	*		*	*	*	*	*	*	*		*	*	*	*	*	*	18
Bhutan					*									*	*		*	*					5
Bolivia	*	*	*		*	*	*	*	*	*	*	*	*	*	*		*	*	*	*	*	*	20
Bosnia & Herzegovina	*	*	*		*	*	*	*	*	*		*	*	*	*		*	*	*	*	*	*	18
Botswana		*			*	*		*	*	*	*	*	*	*	*		*	*	*	*	*	*	17
Brazil	*	*			*	*	*	*	*	*	*	*	*	*	*		*	*	*	*	*	*	19
Brunei						*								*	*		*	*		*	*	*	7
Bulgaria	*	*	*	*	*	*	*	*	*	*		*	*	*	*	*	*	*	*	*	*	*	22
Burkina Faso	*	*	*		*	*	*	*	*	*	*	*	*	*	*		*	*	*	*	*	*	20
Burundi	*	*			*	*	*	*	*	*		*	*	*	*		*	*	*	*	*	*	19
Cambodia	*	*			*	*	*	*		*		*	*	*	*		*	*	*	*	*	*	15
Cameroon	*	*	*		*	*	*	*	*	*		*	*	*	*		*	*	*	*	*	*	18
Canada	*	*	*		*	*	*	*	*	*	*	*	*	*	*	*	*	*	*	*	*	*	21
Cape Verde	*	*			*	*	*	*		*		*	*	*	*		*	*	*	*	*	*	15
Central African Republic	*	*	*		*	*		*	*	*			*	*	*		*	*	*	*	*	*	15
Chad	*	*	*		*	*	*	*	*	*		*	*	*	*		*	*	*	*	*	*	17
Chile	*	*			*	*	*	*	*	*	*	*	*	*	*		*	*	*	*	*	*	21
China & Tibet					*	*	*	*		*		*	*	*	*		*	*	*	*	*	*	15
Colombia	*	*	*		*	*	*	*	*	*	*	*	*	*	*		*	*	*	*	*	*	21
Comoros								*			*			*	*		*	*		*	*	*	10
Congo, Rep.	*	*	*		*	*		*	*	*			*	*	*		*	*	*	*	*	*	15
Congo, Dem. Rep.	*	*	*		*	*		*	*	*		*	*	*	*		*	*	*	*	*	*	15
Costa Rica	*	*	*		*	*	*	*	*	*	*	*	*	*	*		*	*	*	*	*	*	22
Côte d'Ivoire	*	*			*	*	*	*	*	*		*	*	*	*		*	*	*	*	*	*	20
Croatia	*	*	*		*	*	*	*	*	*	*	*	*	*	*	*	*	*	*	*	*	*	22

259

Country	ICESCR	ICCPR	CCPR-OP1	CCPR-OP2	CERD	CEDAW	CAT	Gen	ILO 87	CSR	ICC	CWC	BWC	BC	CBD	LMC	VCPOL	UNFCCC	KP	Geneva	Prot 1	Prot2	Total
Cuba					*	*	*	*	*			*	*	*	*		*	*	*	*	*	*	15
Cyprus	*	*	*	*	*	*	*	*	*	*	*	*	*	*	*	*	*	*	*	*	*	*	22
Czech Republic	*	*	*		*	*	*	*	*	*	*	*	*	*	*	*	*	*	*	*	*	*	21
Denmark	*	*	*	*	*	*	*	*	*	*	*	*	*	*	*		*	*	*	*	*	*	21
Djibouti						*		*	*	*					*	*	*	*		*	*	*	11
Dominican Republic	*	*	*			*		*	*	*		*	*	*	*		*	*		*	*	*	16
Ecuador	*	*	*	*	*	*	*	*	*	*	*	*	*	*	*	*	*	*	*	*	*	*	22
Egypt	*	*			*	*	*	*	*	*		*	*	*	*		*	*	*	*	*	*	18
El Salvador	*	*	*		*	*	*	*		*		*	*	*	*		*	*	*	*	*	*	18
Equatorial Guinea	*	*	*		*	*		*				*	*	*	*		*	*	*	*	*	*	16
Eritrea						*			*	*		*					*			*	*	*	8
Estonia	*	*	*		*	*	*	*	*	*	*	*	*	*	*		*	*		*	*		18
Ethiopia	*	*			*	*	*	*	*	*	*	*	*	*	*		*	*		*	*	*	18
Fiji					*	*		*		*	*	*	*	*	*		*	*	*	*	*	*	15
Finland	*	*	*	*	*	*	*	*	*	*	*	*	*	*	*		*	*	*	*	*	*	21
France	*	*	*	*	*	*	*	*	*	*	*	*	*	*	*		*	*	*	*	*	*	21
Gabon	*	*			*	*	*	*	*	*	*	*	*	*	*		*	*	*	*	*	*	19
Gambia	*	*	*		*	*	*	*	*	*	*	*	*	*	*		*	*		*	*	*	19
Georgia	*	*	*	*	*	*	*	*	*	*	*	*	*	*	*		*	*		*	*	*	20
Germany	*	*	*	*	*	*	*	*	*	*	*	*	*	*	*	*	*	*	*	*	*	*	22
Ghana	*	*	*		*	*	*	*	*	*	*	*	*	*	*		*	*		*	*	*	19
Greece	*	*	*	*	*	*	*	*	*	*	*	*	*	*	*	*	*	*	*	*	*	*	22
Guatemala	*	*	*		*	*	*	*	*	*	*	*	*	*	*		*	*	*	*	*	*	20
Guinea	*	*	*		*	*	*	*	*		*	*	*	*	*		*	*	*	*	*	*	19
Guinea-Bissau	*					*		*	*	*		*					*	*		*	*	*	11
Guyana	*	*	*		*	*		*		*		*	*	*	*		*	*	*	*	*	*	17
Haiti		*			*	*		*	*	*		*		*	*		*	*		*			13
Honduras	*	*				*	*	*	*	*		*	*	*	*	*	*	*	*	*	*	*	18
Hungary	*	*	*	*	*	*	*	*	*	*	*	*	*	*	*		*	*	*	*	*	*	21
Iceland	*	*	*	*	*	*	*	*	*	*		*	*	*	*		*	*	*	*	*	*	20
India	*	*			*	*		*				*	*	*	*		*	*		*			12
Indonesia & East Timor						*	*	*		*		*	*	*	*		*	*	*	*	*	*	14
Iran	*	*						*		*	*	*		*	*		*	*		*	*		12
Iraq	*	*			*	*		*					*							*			7
Ireland	*	*	*	*	*	*		*	*	*	*	*	*	*	*		*	*	*	*	*		19
Israel & Occupied Territiories	*	*			*	*	*	*		*		*	*	*	*		*	*		*	*	*	17
Italy	*	*	*	*	*	*	*	*	*	*	*	*	*	*	*	*	*	*	*	*	*	*	22
Jamaica	*	*	*		*	*		*	*	*	*	*	*	*	*		*	*	*	*	*	*	19
Japan	*	*			*	*		*		*		*	*	*	*		*	*	*	*	*		15
Jordan	*	*			*	*	*	*		*		*	*	*	*		*	*	*	*	*	*	17
Kazakhstan					*	*	*	*	*	*		*		*	*		*	*		*	*	*	13
Kenya	*	*				*		*	*	*	*	*	*	*	*		*	*	*	*	*	*	17
Korea, Dem. Rep.	*	*						*	*			*		*			*	*		*		*	10
Korea, Rep.	*	*	*		*	*	*	*	*			*	*	*	*		*	*		*	*	*	17
Kuwait	*	*			*	*	*	*	*	*		*	*	*	*		*	*		*	*	*	17
Kyrgyzstan	*	*	*		*	*	*	*		*		*		*	*		*	*		*	*	*	16
Laos					*	*		*				*	*	*			*	*		*	*	*	11
Latvia	*	*	*		*	*	*	*	*	*	*	*	*	*	*		*	*	*	*	*	*	20
Lebanon	*	*			*	*	*					*	*	*			*	*	*	*	*	*	15
Lesotho	*	*	*		*	*		*	*	*	*	*	*		*	*	*	*	*	*	*	*	19

Table R11 continued 2000 Country	ICESCR	ICCPR	CCPR-OP1	CCPR-OP2	CERD	CEDAW	CAT	Gen	ILO 87	CSR	ICC	CWC	BWC	BC	CBD	LMC	VCPOL	UNFCCC	KP	Geneva	Prot 1	Prot2	Total
Liberia					*	*		*	*	*	*		*		*	*	*			*	*	*	13
Libya	*	*	*		*	*	*	*	*	*			*		*	*	*	*		*	*	*	15
Lithuania	*	*	*	*	*	*	*	*	*	*	*	*		*	*	*	*	*	*	*	*	*	21
Luxembourg	*	*	*	*	*	*	*	*	*	*	*	*	*	*	*	*	*	*		*	*	*	22
Macedonia	*	*	*		*	*	*	*	*	*		*	*	*	*	*	*	*	*	*	*	*	19
Madagascar	*	*	*		*	*		*	*	*	*	*	*	*	*	*	*	*		*	*	*	18
Malawi	*	*	*		*	*	*	*	*	*	*	*	*	*	*	*	*	*		*	*	*	19
Malaysia						*		*				*	*		*	*		*	*	*		*	11
Maldives					*	*		*				*	*		*	*	*	*	*	*	*	*	14
Mali	*	*			*	*	*	*	*	*	*	*	*	*	*	*	*	*		*	*	*	20
Malta	*	*	*	*	*	*	*	*	*	*		*	*	*	*	*	*	*		*	*	*	21
Mauritius	*	*	*		*	*	*	*		*	*	*	*	*	*	*	*	*		*	*	*	19
Mexico	*	*			*	*	*	*		*		*	*	*	*	*	*	*		*	*	*	18
Micronesia, Fed.												*		*	*	*		*	*	*		*	8
Moldova	*	*			*	*	*	*		*		*	*	*	*	*	*	*		*	*	*	17
Mongolia	*	*	*		*	*	*	*		*		*	*	*	*	*	*	*		*	*	*	18
Morocco & Western Sahara	*	*			*	*	*		*	*		*	*	*	*	*	*	*		*	*	*	17
Mozambique		*		*	*	*	*	*	*	*		*	*	*	*	*	*	*		*	*	*	17
Myanmar						*		*	*	*	*		*		*	*	*	*		*			9
Namibia	*	*	*	*	*	*	*	*	*	*		*	*	*	*	*	*	*		*	*	*	20
Nepal	*	*	*		*	*	*	*		*			*		*	*	*	*		*			15
Netherlands	*	*	*	*	*	*	*	*	*	*	*	*	*	*	*	*	*	*		*	*	*	22
New Zealand	*	*	*	*	*	*	*	*	*	*		*	*	*	*	*	*	*		*	*	*	20
Nicaragua	*	*	*		*	*	*	*	*	*		*	*	*	*	*	*	*		*	*	*	19
Niger	*	*	*		*	*	*	*	*	*	*	*	*	*	*	*	*	*		*	*	*	20
Nigeria	*	*	*		*	*	*	*	*	*	*	*	*	*	*	*	*	*		*	*	*	19
Norway	*	*	*	*	*	*	*	*	*	*	*	*	*	*	*	*	*	*		*	*	*	22
Oman					*							*	*	*	*	*	*	*	*	*	*	*	11
Pakistan					*	*		*	*			*	*	*	*	*	*	*		*			11
Panama	*	*	*	*	*	*	*	*	*	*	*	*	*	*	*	*	*	*		*	*	*	22
Papua New Guinea					*	*			*	*		*	*		*	*	*	*		*			12
Paraguay	*	*	*		*	*	*	*	*	*	*	*	*	*	*	*	*	*		*	*	*	20
Peru	*	*	*		*	*	*	*	*	*	*	*	*	*	*	*	*	*		*	*	*	21
Philippines	*	*	*		*	*	*	*	*	*	*	*	*	*	*	*	*	*		*	*	*	21
Poland	*	*	*	*	*	*	*	*	*	*	*	*	*	*	*	*	*	*		*	*	*	21
Portugal	*	*	*	*	*	*	*	*	*	*	*	*	*	*	*	*	*	*		*	*	*	22
Qatar					*		*					*	*	*	*	*	*	*		*		*	12
Romania	*	*	*	*	*	*	*	*	*	*	*	*	*	*	*	*	*	*		*	*	*	22
Russian Federation	*	*	*		*	*	*	*	*	*		*	*	*	*	*	*	*		*	*	*	20
Rwanda	*	*			*	*	*	*		*			*		*	*	*	*		*	*	*	14
Samoa					*				*	*			*		*	*	*	*	*	*	*	*	11
Sao Tome & Principe					*	*			*	*			*		*	*	*	*		*	*	*	9
Saudi Arabia					*	*	*					*	*	*	*		*	*		*	*		11
Senegal	*	*	*		*	*	*	*	*	*	*	*	*	*	*	*	*	*		*	*	*	20
Sierra Leone	*	*	*		*	*		*	*	*			*		*		*	*		*	*	*	14
Singapore						*		*				*	*	*	*		*	*		*			9
Slovakia	*	*	*	*	*	*	*	*	*	*	*	*	*	*	*	*	*	*		*	*	*	22
Slovenia	*	*	*	*	*	*	*	*	*	*	*	*	*	*	*	*	*	*		*	*	*	22
Solomon Islands	*				*				*	*			*		*	*	*	*	*	*	*	*	13
Somalia	*	*	*			*	*		*				*							*			8
South Africa		*			*	*	*	*	*	*	*	*	*	*	*	*	*	*		*	*	*	18
Spain	*	*	*	*	*	*	*	*	*	*	*	*	*	*	*	*	*	*		*	*	*	22

Country	ICESCR	ICCPR	CCPR-OP1	CCPR-OP2	CERD	CEDAW	CAT	Gen	ILO 87	CSR	ICC	CWC	BWC	BC	CBD	LMC	VCPOL	UNFCCC	KP	Geneva	Prot 1	Prot2	Total
Sri Lanka	*	*	*		*	*	*	*	*	*		*	*	*	*		*	*		*			16
St. Lucia					*	*	*		*			*	*	*	*		*	*		*	*	*	14
St. Vincent & the Grenadines	*	*	*		*	*		*		*			*		*		*	*	*	*	*	*	15
Sudan	*	*			*	*			*	*			*		*		*	*		*			12
Suriname	*	*	*		*	*		*		*			*		*		*	*		*	*	*	16
Swaziland					*			*					*		*		*	*		*	*	*	11
Sweden	*	*	*	*	*	*	*	*	*	*		*	*	*	*	*	*	*	*	*	*	*	22
Switzerland	*	*		*	*	*	*	*	*	*		*	*	*	*	*	*	*	*	*	*	*	21
Syria	*	*			*			*	*			*		*	*		*	*		*	*		13
Tajikistan	*	*	*		*	*	*		*			*		*	*		*	*		*	*	*	16
Tanzania	*	*			*	*			*	*			*		*		*	*		*	*	*	16
Thailand	*	*				*				*			*		*		*	*		*			12
Togo	*	*	*		*	*	*		*			*		*	*		*	*		*	*	*	18
Trinidad & Tobago	*	*	*		*	*						*		*	*		*	*		*	*	*	15
Tunisia	*	*			*	*	*			*		*		*	*		*	*		*	*	*	18
Turkey					*	*	*			*		*		*	*		*	*		*			11
Turkmenistan	*	*	*	*	*	*	*		*			*		*	*		*	*		*	*	*	18
Uganda	*	*	*		*	*	*		*	*		*		*	*		*	*		*	*	*	18
Ukraine	*	*	*		*	*	*	*	*			*	*	*	*		*	*		*	*	*	20
United Arab Emirates					*			*				*		*	*		*	*		*	*	*	11
United Kingdom	*	*		*	*	*	*	*	*	*		*	*	*	*		*	*		*	*	*	21
United States		*			*		*	*		*		*	*	*			*	*		*			12
Uruguay	*	*	*	*	*	*	*	*		*		*	*	*	*		*	*		*	*	*	21
Uzbekistan	*	*	*		*	*	*					*		*	*		*	*		*	*		15
Vanuatu					*								*		*		*	*		*	*	*	9
Venezuela	*	*	*	*	*	*	*		*	*		*	*	*	*		*	*		*	*	*	20
Vietnam	*	*			*	*		*				*		*	*		*	*	*	*	*	*	15
Yemen	*	*			*	*	*		*	*		*		*	*		*	*		*	*	*	18
Yugoslavia	*	*			*	*	*	*	*	*			*		*		*	*		*	*		17
Zambia	*	*	*		*	*	*		*	*		*	*	*	*		*	*		*	*	*	19
Zimbabwe	*	*						*	*	*		*		*	*		*	*		*	*	*	12
Total State Parties	143	147	98	43	157	166	123	137	134	134	139	143	144	142	180	115	98	133	33	189	158	150	

ICESCR – International Covenant on Economic, Social and Cultural Rights
ICCPR – International Convenant on Civil and Political Rights
ICCPR-OP1 – Optional Protocol to the International Convenant on Civil and Political Rights
ICCPR-OP2 – Second Optional Protocol to the International Convenant on Civil and Political Rights
CERD – International Convention on the Elimination of all forms of Racial Discrimination
CEDAW – Convention on the Elimination of All Forms of Discrimination Against Women
CAT – Convention against Torture and Other Cruel, Inhuman or Degrading Treatment or Punishment
Gen – Convention on the Prevention and Punishment of the Crime of the Genocide
ILO 87 – Freedom of Association and Protection of the Right to Organise Convention
CSR – Convention relating to the Status of Refugees
ICC – Rome Statute on the International Criminal Court
CWC – Chemical Weapons Convention
BWC – Biological Weapons Convention

BC – Basel Convention on the Control of Transboundary Movements of Hazardous Wastes and Their Disposal
CBD – Convention on Biological Diversity
UNFCCC – United Nations Framework Convention on Climate Change
KP – Kyoto Protocol to United Nations Framework Convention on Climate Change
LMC – Convention on the Prohibition of the Use, Stockpiling, Production and Transfer of Anti-Personnel Mines and on their Destruction
VCPOL – Vienna Convention for the Protection of Ozone Layer
Geneva – Geneva Conventions
Prot 1 – First Additional Protocol to the Geneva Conventions
Prot 2 – Second Additional Protocol to the Geneva Conventions
Sources: Office of the UN High Commissioner for Human Rights, http://www.unhchr.ch/html/intlinst.htm; United Nations, http://www.un.org/law/icc/statute/status.htm;

Organisation for the Prohibition of Chemical Weapons, http://www.opcw.nl; Federation of American Scientists, http://www.fas.org/nuke/control/bwc/text/bwcsig.htm; Secretariat, Basel Convention on the Control of Transboundary Movements of Hazardous Wastes and Their Disposal, http://www.basel.int/ratif/ratif.html; Secretariat, United Nations Framework Convention on Climate Change, http://www.unfccc.de/resource/country/index.html; International Committee of the Red Cross, http://www.icrc.org/eng/party_gc and http://www.icrc.org/eng/party_cmines

Table R12 Human rights violations

This table displays information on human rights abuses by country, covering extrajudicial executions and disappearances, arbitrary detentions, torture, freedom of expression, and the situation of minorities, using three different sources: Human Rights Watch, Amnesty International, and the US State Department. The information offers an indication of whether certain basic human rights are violated, but it does not quantify the number of violations in each country. While Table R11 shows to what extent states have committed themselves to abide by international law, this table shows to what extent states actually respect international law in the field of human rights. Global civil society is instrumental in exposing human rights violations. At the same time, human rights violations form one of the main threats to the survival of local civil societies.

Country	Disappearances & extrajudicial executions			Arbitrary detentions			Torture			Discrimination against minorities			Freedom of expression & association		
	HRW	AI	SD	HRW	AI	SD	HRW	AI	SD	HRW	AI	SD	HRW	AI	SD
Afghanistan			yes	yes	yes	yes	yes	yes	yes	yes	yes	yes	no	no	no
Albania			yes			yes	yes		yes			yes	no		yes
Algeria	yes	yes	yes	yes	yes	yes	yes	yes	yes				no		no
Angola			yes	yes	yes	yes	yes		yes			no	no	no	no
Argentina	yes	yes	yes	yes		yes	yes	yes	yes			yes	no		
Armenia		yes	yes	yes	yes	yes		yes	yes		yes	no	no		partial
Australia		yes	yes		yes	no			yes		no	no			yes
Austria		yes	yes			no		yes	yes		no	yes			yes
Azerbaijan	yes	yes	yes	yes		yes	yes	yes	yes	yes	yes	yes	no		yes
Bahamas					yes	no			yes			no			yes
Bahrain				yes	yes	yes		yes	yes			no			no
Bangladesh			yes			yes		yes	yes						partial
Barbados									yes						yes
Belarus	yes	yes	yes	yes		yes	yes		yes			yes	no	no	restricted
Belgium		yes	yes		yes	no	yes	no			no	yes			yes
Belize		yes	yes					yes	yes						yes
Benin		yes	yes	yes					yes			yes			no
Bhutan						yes		yes	yes		yes	yes	no		restricted
Bolivia		yes	yes					yes	yes		yes	yes			partial
Bosnia & Herzegovina		yes	yes			yes	yes	yes	yes	yes	no	yes			partial
Botswana						no			yes						yes
Brazil	yes	yes	yes		yes	yes	yes	yes	yes			yes			yes
Brunei						yes	yes								yes
Bulgaria	yes	yes	yes	yes	yes		yes	yes	yes	yes	yes	yes	no		yes
Burkina Faso		yes	yes	yes	yes	yes	yes	yes	yes				no	no	no
Burundi		yes	yes	yes	yes		yes	yes	yes			yes	no		no
Cambodia	yes	yes	yes	yes	yes	yes	yes	yes	yes			yes	no	no	partial
Cameroon		yes	yes	yes	yes			yes	yes			yes		no	no
Canada		no				no			no			no			yes
Cape Verde		no				no			yes			no			yes
Central African Republic		yes				yes			yes			yes			yes
Chad		yes	yes		yes	yes		yes	yes			yes			limited
Chile		yes				yes		yes	yes			yes			partial
China & Tibet		yes	yes	yes	yes	yes		yes	yes			yes	no		no
Colombia		yes	yes			yes			yes		yes	yes			limited
Comoros		yes				yes			yes			yes			partial

263

Table R12 continued	Disappearances & extrajudicial executions			Arbitrary detentions			Torture			Discrimination against minorities			Freedom of expression & association		
Country	HRW	AI	SD	HRW	AI	SD	HRW	AI	SD	HRW	AI	SD	HRW	AI	SD
Congo, Dem Rep.		yes	yes	yes	yes	yes	yes	yes	yes			yes	no	no	no
Congo, Rep.		yes	yes		yes	yes			yes			yes		no	partial
Costa Rica						no			no			no			yes
Côte d'Ivoire			yes		yes	yes		yes	yes			yes			no
Croatia						yes		yes	yes	yes		yes		no	restricted
Cuba					yes	yes			yes			yes	no	no	no
Cyprus						no			yes			no			yes
Czech Republic						yes	yes	yes	yes	yes	yes	no			yes
Denmark						no			no			no			yes
Djibouti			yes			yes		yes	yes		yes	yes		no	no
Dominican Republic		yes	yes		yes	yes		yes	yes			yes			partial
Ecuador		yes	yes			yes		yes	yes			yes			yes
Egypt	yes	yes	yes	yes	yes	yes	yes	yes	yes			yes	no	no	partial
El Salvador		yes	yes			yes		yes	yes			no			yes
Equatorial Guinea			yes		yes	yes			yes			no			no
Eritrea		yes	yes		yes	yes			no			yes			no
Estonia						yes			yes			no			yes
Ethiopia			yes		yes	yes	yes	yes	yes	yes	yes	no	no	no	no
Fiji			?			no			yes			no			yes
Finland						no	yes		no			no			yes
France		yes	yes				yes		yes			no			yes
Gabon			yes						yes			no			partial
Gambia			yes		yes	yes		yes	yes			.		no	no
Georgia	yes	yes	yes			yes	yes	yes	yes	yes	yes	no			no
Germany		yes	yes			no	yes	yes				no			yes
Ghana		yes	yes		yes	yes			yes			no		no	partial
Greece			yes					yes	yes	yes	yes	yes	no		no
Guatemala		yes	yes			yes			yes	yes					yes
Guinea			yes		yes	yes		yes	yes			yes		no	no
Guinea-Bissau			yes			yes		yes	yes						partial
Guyana		yes	yes					yes	yes			yes			partial
Haiti	yes	yes	yes		yes	yes	yes	yes	yes			no	no		partial
Honduras		yes	yes			yes			yes		yes			no	partial
Hungary				yes	yes		yes	yes	yes	yes	yes	no			yes
Iceland						no			no						yes
India	yes	yes	yes	yes	yes	yes	yes	yes	yes	yes	yes	yes	yes	yes	yes
Indonesia & East Timor		yes	yes		yes	yes	yes	yes	yes	yes		yes	no		no
Iran	yes		yes	yes	yes	yes	yes	yes	yes	yes	yes	yes	no	no	no
Iraq	yes		yes	yes	yes	yes	yes	yes	yes	yes	yes	yes	no	no	no
Ireland									yes			no			yes
Israel & Occupied Territories		yes	yes	yes	yes	yes	yes		yes	yes		yes			yes
Italy						yes	yes	yes				no			yes
Jamaica		yes	yes			yes		yes	yes						yes
Japan					yes	no	yes	yes				no			yes
Jordan			yes		yes	yes		yes	yes			yes		no	no
Kazakhstan				yes		yes	yes		yes	yes		yes	no		no
Kenya		yes	yes			yes	yes	yes	yes	no		yes	yes	no	no
Korea, Dem. Rep.			yes			yes			yes						no

264

Table R12 continued	Disappearances & extrajudicial executions			Arbitrary detentions			Torture			Discrimination against minorities			Freedom of expression & association		
Country	HRW	AI	SD	HRW	AI	SD	HRW	AI	SD	HRW	AI	SD	HRW	AI	SD
Korea, Rep.					yes	yes		yes	yes			yes			yes
Kuwait						yes		yes	yes		yes	no		no	yes
Kyrgyzstan					yes	yes	yes	yes	yes	yes	yes	yes	no	no	no
Laos			yes		yes	yes		yes	yes		yes	no		no	no
Latvia			yes			yes			yes						yes
Lebanon		yes	yes		yes	yes		yes	yes			yes		no	no
Lesotho			yes			yes		yes	yes			no			yes
Liberia		yes	yes			yes	yes	yes	yes			yes	no	no	no
Libya						yes		yes	yes						no
Lithuania						no			yes						yes
Luxembourg						no			no			no			yes
Macedonia			yes				yes		yes	yes		no	no		yes
Madagascar						yes			yes			no			no
Malawi						yes			yes			no			yes
Malaysia			yes		yes	yes		yes	yes			yes		no	no
Maldives						yes		yes	yes						no
Mali									no			no			yes
Malta						no			no			no			yes
Mauritania			yes		yes	yes		yes	yes		yes	no		no	no
Mauritius		yes	yes					yes	yes						yes
Mexico	yes	yes	yes	yes	yes	yes	yes	yes	yes					yes	yes
Moldova					yes	yes		yes	yes			yes			yes
Mongolia			yes			yes			yes						yes
Morocco & Western Sahara		yes	yes			yes		yes	yes					no	no
Mozambique	yes	yes	yes			yes	yes	yes	yes			no		no	no
Myanmar		yes	yes	yes	yes	yes	yes	yes	yes			yes		no	no
Namibia			yes			yes		yes	yes			no			yes
Nepal		yes	yes		yes	yes		yes	yes		yes	yes		yes	yes
Netherlands						no			no			no			yes
New Zealand					yes	no			no			no			yes
Nicaragua		yes	yes			yes		yes	yes			no			yes
Niger			yes		yes	yes			yes			no			yes
Nigeria	yes	yes	yes			yes	yes	yes	yes	yes	yes		no	no	no
Norway						yes			no						yes
Oman									yes			yes			no
Pakistan	yes	yes	yes	yes	yes	yes	yes	yes	yes	yes	yes	yes	no	yes	yes
Panama									yes						no
Papua New Guinea		yes	yes			yes		yes	yes						yes
Paraguay		yes				yes		yes	yes						yes
Peru		yes	yes		yes	yes	yes	yes	yes			yes		no	yes
Philippines		yes	yes		yes	yes		yes	yes			yes			yes
Poland		yes			yes				yes			no			yes
Portugal						no		yes	yes			no			yes
Qatar					yes	yes			yes						no
Romania		yes	yes				yes	yes	yes	yes	yes	yes		no	yes
Russian Federation		yes	yes	yes	yes	yes	yes	yes	yes	yes	yes	yes		no	no
Rwanda	yes	yes	yes	yes	yes	yes	yes	yes	yes		yes	yes	no	no	no
Samoa															yes

Country	Disappearances & extrajudicial executions			Arbitrary detentions			Torture			Discrimination against minorities			Freedom of expression & association		
	HRW	AI	SD	HRW	AI	SD	HRW	AI	SD	HRW	AI	SD	HRW	AI	SD
Sao Tome & Principle						no			no			no			yes
Saudi Arabia	yes		yes	yes	yes	yes	yes	yes	yes		yes	yes	no	no	no
Senegal		yes	yes		yes	yes		yes	yes						yes
Sierra Leone	yes		yes			yes	yes	yes	yes			yes	no	no	no
Singapore					yes	yes			yes			no		no	yes
Slovakia		yes	yes	yes			yes		yes	yes	yes	no			yes
Slovenia						no			no						yes
Solomon Islands		yes	yes					yes	yes		yes	no			yes
Somalia			yes?			yes			yes			yes		no	no
South Africa	yes	yes	yes				yes	yes	yes	no		no	yes		yes
Spain					yes			yes	yes			no			yes
Sri Lanka		yes	yes	yes	yes		yes	yes	yes	yes	yes	yes	no	no	no
St. Lucia			yes						yes			no			yes
St. Vincent & the Grenadines			yes						yes			no			yes
Sudan	yes	yes	yes	yes			yes	yes	yes	yes		yes	no	no	no
Suriname			yes			yes			yes						yes
Swaziland						yes			yes						no
Sweden						no			no			no			yes
Switzerland		yes	yes		yes			yes	yes			no			yes
Syria	yes	yes		yes	yes	yes	yes	yes	yes	yes		yes	no	no	no
Tanzania			yes			yes			yes		yes	no			no
Tajikistan			yes			yes	yes	yes	yes			yes	no		no
Thailand			yes					yes	yes			no			yes
Togo		yes	yes		yes	yes		yes	yes			no		no	no
Trinidad & Tobago			no				yes		no			no		no	yes
Tunisia		yes	yes			yes	yes	yes	yes			no	no	no	no
Turkey	yes	yes	yes	yes		yes	yes	yes	yes	yes	yes	yes	no	no	yes
Turkmenistan	yes	yes	yes		yes	yes	yes	yes	yes	yes	yes	no	no		no
Uganda	yes	yes	yes			yes	yes	yes	yes			no		no	no
Ukraine		yes			yes	yes		yes	yes		yes				no
United Arab Emirates								yes	yes			yes			yes
United Kingdom		yes	yes				yes	yes	yes	no	no	no	yes	yes	yes
United States		yes					yes	yes				no	yes	yes	
Uruguay		yes	yes					yes	yes			yes			yes
Uzbekistan	yes	yes	yes	yes	yes		yes	yes	yes	yes	yes	no	no		no
Vanuatu						no			yes			no			yes
Venezuela	yes	yes	yes	yes	yes	yes	yes	yes	yes			no			yes
Vietnam			yes			yes	yes	yes	yes			yes	no	no	yes
Yemen			yes		yes	yes	yes	yes	yes			yes	no	no	no
Yugoslavia	yes	yes	yes	yes	yes	yes	yes	yes	yes	yes	yes	yes	no	no	no
Zambia	yes					yes	yes	yes	yes				no	no	yes
Zimbabwe			yes			yes		yes	yes		yes	yes	no		no

Data reflect number of categories violated and do not quantify the level of violation; an absence of data indicates that either no violations have been recorded or that no data are available In the first four categories, 'yes' denotes a violation, whereas in the final category, 'no' denotes a violation.

Sources: Human Rights Watch, *World Report 2000*; Amnesty International *Report 2000*; US State Department *Country Reports on Human Rights Practices for 1999* (2000).

Table R13 Corruption

This table presents three different kinds of indicators of corruption. The 2000 Corruption Perception Index combines assessments for the past three years to reduce larger annual fluctuations. As is the case for the transparency and bribery index, scores range between a score of 10, indicating high transparency and the absence of bribery and corruption, and 0, indicating lack of transparency and high levels of perceived corruption and bribery. Corruption does not only hinder economic development, it inhibits the formation of trust and social capital among people. It is therefore likely to be an obstacle to the growth of civil society, locally as well as globally.

Country	Transparency International — Corruption Perception Index, 2000	Institute for Management Development — Transparency of government Index, 1996	World Economic Forum — Bribery Index, 1997	Country	Transparency International — Corruption Perception Index, 2000	Institute for Management Development — Transparency of government Index, 1996	World Economic Forum — Bribery Index, 1997
Argentina	3.5	3.6	3.5	Lithuania	4.1		
Australia	8.3	5.7	6.0	Malaysia	4.8	6.1	
Austria	7.7	4.5	6.2	Mauritius	4.7		
Azerbaijan	1.5			Mexico	3.3	3.4	3.6
Belarus	4.1			Moldova	2.6		
Belgium	6.1	3.7	5.4	Morocco & Western Sahara	4.7		
Bolivia	2.7			Netherlands	8.9		
Botswana	6.0			New Zealand	9.4		
Brazil	3.9	5.8	3.8	Nigeria	1.2		
Bulgaria	3.5			Norway	9.1	7.1	6.6
Canada	9.2	6.5	6.3	Peru	4.4		4.6
Chile	7.4	4.2	5.7	Philippines	2.8	4.8	
China & Tibet	3.1			Poland	4.1	2.4	3.4
Colombia	3.2	2.3	2.9	Portugal	6.4	4.9	5.3
Costa Rica	5.4	3.7		Romania	2.9		
Croatia	3.7			Russian Federation	2.1	2.6	2.7
Czech Republic	4.3	4.3	4.7	Singapore	9.1	7.4	
Denmark	9.8	6.1	6.4	Slovakia	3.5		4.4
Ecuador	2.6			Slovenia	5.5		
Egypt	3.1			South Africa	5.0		
Estonia	5.7			Spain	7.0	5.4	5.2
Finland	10.0	7.0	6.7	Sweden	9.4	4.9	6.6
France	6.7	4.2	5.4	Switzerland	8.6	5.5	6.2
Germany	7.6	4.9	6.0	Tanzania	2.5		
Greece	4.9	3.9	3.0	Thailand	3.2	2.9	
Guatemala	2.6			Tunisia	5.2		
Honduras	2.6			Turkey	3.8		
Hungary	5.2	3.8	4.1	Uganda	2.3		
India	2.8			Ukraine	1.5	3.7	
Ireland	7.2	5.4	6.1	United Kingdom	8.7	4.5	6.5
Israel & Occupied Territories	6.6	4.4		United States	7.8	5.6	6.1
Italy	4.6	3.1	3.9	Uzbekistan	2.4		
Japan	6.4	2.7	5.8	Venezuela	2.7	2.7	2.8
Jordan	4.6			Zimbabwe	3.0		
Kazakhstan	3.0						
Korea, Rep.	4.0	3.1					
Latvia	3.4						

Sources: Transparency International, available at http://www.transparency.org/documents/cpi/2000/cpi2000.html#cpi; E. Friedman, S. Johnson, D. Kaufmann, and P. Zoido-Lobatón, 'Dodging the Grabbing Hand: The Determinants of Unofficial Activity in 69 Countries', *Journal of Public Economics*, 76 (2000): 459-93.

Table R14 Crime

The violent crime rate is an indicator of social ill in society at large. The table reports homicides, assaults, and total recorded crime per hundred thousand of population for 1986 and 1997. Like human rights violations, the incidence of violent crime undermines the 'health' of local civil societies.

| | Rate per hundred thousand of population | | | | | | % Change | | |
| | 1986 | | | 1997 | | | 1986–1997 | | |
Country	Homicides	Assaults	Total recorded crime	Homicides	Assaults	Total recorded crime	Homicides	Assaults	Total
Albania				77	10				
Argentina				9		2			
Australia	2		6,161	3	672		82		
Austria	2	402	5,274						
Azerbaijan				6	18	216			
Bahamas			6,493	25	1,697	6,688			3
Bahrain	0	607		1	523	3,011	232	-14	
Belarus			541	12	16	1,251			131
Belgium			2,570	5	530	8,035			213
Bulgaria	1		624	9	42	2,909	628		366
Chile		381		5	160	4,396		-58	
China & Tibet	2		51	2	6	131		232	158
Colombia				58	116	579			
Croatia				6	27	1,155			
Cyprus	2	120	1,939	1	16	523	-28	-87	-73
Czech Republic	1			3	225	3,917	124		
Denmark	6	118	11,091	5	165	10,051	-6	41	-9
Estonia				17	38	2,809			
Fiji			2,192	2	527	2,719			24
Finland	7	339	14,208	9	483	7,273	30	43	-49
Georgia				8	5	256			
Germany			5,618	4	129	8,025			43
Greece	2	60	2,933	3	267	3,591	103	344	22
Hungary	4	82	1,737	4	107	5,066	-2	31	192
India	3			7	24	179	104		
Ireland				1	16	2,482			
Israel & Occupied Territories	2	214		4	245	6,276	87	15	
Italy	4	28	2,479	4	44	4,243	2	54	71
Japan	1	26	1,302	1	21	1,507	-26	-20	16
Jordan	2	18	714	7	31	1,053	206	76	47

Country	Rate per hundred thousand of population						% Change		
	1986			1997			1986–1997		
	Homicides	Assaults	Total recorded crime	Homicides	Assaults	Total recorded crime	Homicides	Assaults	Total
Kazakhstan		3		16	18	1,028		618	
Korea, Rep.		359	1,948	2	11	3,041		-97	56
Kyrgyzstan				9	7	804			
Latvia	4	20		13	30	1,496	230	52	
Lesotho		204			303	1,078		49	
Lithuania	4	15		11		2,046	172	-100	
Malaysia		16	677	3	27	694		72	2
Maldives	2	223	3,976	4	169	2,725	91	-24	-31
Mauritius	3	11,731		3	1,157	32,928	5	-90	
Moldova	5	3		10	31	926	89	1083	
Netherlands	13	119	7,422	10	241	7,800	-21	103	5
New Zealand			13,368	3	791	12,591			-6
Norway	1	129	4,492	2	230	6,995	126	78	56
Peru		20	889	10	81	756		313	-15
Poland	1	42	1,356	3	87	2,577	106	108	90
Portugal	5	283	779	4	374	3,234	-17	32	315
Romania	3	6		6	7	1,601	95	19	
Singapore	3	29	2,134	1	20	1,833	-55	-31	-14
Slovenia	3	80		4	92	1,872	27	15	
South Africa				130	1,075	5,106			
Spain			2,284	2	154	1,764			-23
Sri Lanka	10	124	381	13	120	309	32	-3	-19
Sweden	6	391	13,087	10	623	13,516	49	59	3
Switzerland	2	50		3		4,769	28	-100	
Tanzania				8	2	1,688			
Thailand	12	18		15	26	464	24	44	
Turkey					76	520			
Uganda				11	33	221			
Ukraine			487	9	10	1,162			139
Zimbabwe			3,816	10	607	2,856			-25

Source: United Nations Crime Prevention and Criminal Justice Division, *Fifth United Nations Survey of Crime Trends and Operation of Criminal Justice Systems* (Vienna: United Nations Crime Prevention and Criminal Justice Division, 2000), http://www.uncjin.org.

Table R15 Refugee populations and flows

This table presents data on refugee population, both in total and per 1,000 inhabitants for 1990 and 1999. In addition, the table provides information on the inflow and outflow of refugees for 1999, and includes estimates of internally displaced persons (IDPs). This table has two functions: if a country generates many refugees or IDPs, it can be assumed that there is little respect for the rule of law in that country. On the other hand, countries that host a lot of refugees can be considered as extending international hospitality and bearing the associated financial burden.

Country	Refugee populations Total of population 1990	Refugee populations Total of population 1999	Refugee populations per thousand 1990	Refugee populations per thousand 1999	Refugee flows Inflow 1999	Refugee flows Outflow 1999	IDPs 1999
Afghanistan					60	104,330	258,600
Albania		3,930		1.3	435,000	860	
Algeria	169,110	165,250	5.4	5.3	0	1,140	
Angola	11,560	13,070	0.9	1.0	110	35,120	
Argentina	11,740	2,350	0.3	0.1	0	0	
Armenia		296,220		84.2	0	460	
Australia	97,920	59,730	5.2	3.2	1,440	0	
Austria	34,940	82,440	4.3	10.0	1,520	0	
Azerbaijan		221,640		28.7	0	830	569,600
Bahamas		100		0.3			
Bahrain	1,780		2.9				
Bangladesh	150	22,210		0.2	0	490	
Belarus		260			140	0	
Belgium	25,910	17,890	2.5	1.8	1,120	0	
Belize	30,660	2,890	127.4	12.0			
Benin	460	3,660	0.1	0.6	630	0	
Bolivia	200	350					
Bosnia & Herzegovina		65,650		16.5	72,300	1,700	809,500
Botswana	1,180	1,300	0.7	0.8	530	0	
Brazil	5,340	2,380			90	0	
Bulgaria		550		0.1	450	250	
Burkina Faso	350	680		0.1	0	0	
Burundi	268,400	22,110	40.1	3.3	1,330	65,100	50,000
Cambodia					0	480	
Cameroon	49,880	49,230	3.3	3.3	1,450	260	
Canada	154,760	107,220	5.0	3.4	11,780	0	
Central African Republic	4,280	49,310	1.2	13.6	18,320	0	
Chad		23,480		3.1	14,500	310	
Chile		320					
China & Tibet	287,280	293,300	0.2	0.2	0	2,790	
Colombia	460	230			0	950	
Congo, Dem. Rep.					65,040	143,300	
Congo, Rep.	2,990	39,870	1.0	13.5	12,310	62,090	
Costa Rica	276,210	22,900	68.7	5.7	170	0	
Côte d'Ivoire	272,280	138,430	18.4	9.4	9,000	0	
Croatia	28,370		6.3	2,880	16,720	52,400	
Cuba	3,990	970	0.4	0.1	0	670	
Cyprus	120		0.2				
Czech Republic	1,230		0.1	830	120		
Denmark	32,910	69,010	6.2	13.0	3,490	0	
Djibouti	77,610	23,270	121.7	36.5	0	150	
Dominican Republic	1,970	630	0.2	0.1			
Ecuador	510	310			60	0	
Egypt	1,990	6,550		0.1	2,690	380	

Country	Refugee populations				Refugee flows		
	Total		per thousand of population		Inflow	Outflow	IDPs
	1990	1999	1990	1999	1999	1999	1999
El Salvador	20,300		3.2		0	460	
Eritrea		2,970		0.8	930	220	
Ethiopia	773,760	257,690	12.4	4.1	13,040	2,950	
Finland	2,350	12,870	0.5	2.5	410	0	
France	193,000	129,720	3.3	2.2	4,080	0	
Gabon	420	15,070	0.3	12.3	11,940	0	
Gambia		17,220		13.2	8,370	0	
Georgia		5,180		1.0	5,160	170	278,500
Germany	816,000	975,500	9.9	11.9	11,980	0	
Ghana	8,120	13,260	0.4	0.7	890	0	
Greece	8,490	6,280	0.8	0.6	410	0	
Guatemala	223,380	730	19.6	0.1	0	570	
Guinea	325,000	501,540	43.7	67.5	23,100	220	
Guinea-Bissau	3,000	7,120	2.5	5.9	650	0	
Haiti					0	410	
Honduras	237,100		36.6		0	60	
Hungary	45,120	7,840	4.5	0.8	1,910	70	
Iceland	350		1.2				
India	212,740	180,030	0.2	0.2	5,290	1,010	
Indonesia & East Timor	3,280	162,510		0.8	0	1,220	
Iran	4,174,400	1,835,690	61.7	27.1	0	5,710	
Iraq	900	128,910		5.6	220	14,810	
Ireland		1,100		0.3	310	0	
Israel & Occupied Territories		130			410	0	
Italy	11,690	22,870	0.2	0.4	1,380	0	
Japan	6,820	4,240	0.1				
Jordan	640	1,010	0.1	0.2	1,070	0	
Kazakhstan		14,800		0.9	6,960	70	
Kenya	14,250	223,700	0.5	7.4	38,610	100	
Korea, Rep.	230						
Kuwait		4,330		2.2	80	70	
Kyrgyzstan		10,850		2.3	390	0	5,600
Laos					0	120	
Lebanon	2,550	4,170	0.8	1.3	440	110	
Lesotho	210		0.1				
Liberia		96,320		30.5	0	17,240	90,600
Libya		10,540		1.9	0	0	
Luxembourg	690	700	1.6	1.6			
Macedonia		21,200		10.5	355,000	0	
Malawi	926,730	1,700	84.8	0.2	920	0	
Malaysia	14,860	50,520	0.7	2.3	0	0	
Mali	13,410	8,300	1.2	0.7	90	0	
Malta		270		0.7			
Mauritania	60,000	220	22.5	0.1	100	410	
Mexico	356,400	24,510	3.6	0.2	0	370	
Moldova					0	0	8,100
Morocco & Western Sahara	310	900					
Mozambique	420	220			140	0	
Myanmar					0	1,680	
Namibia		7,350		4.3	4,170	180	
Nepal		127,940		5.3			
Netherlands	17,340	138,670	1.1	8.8	9,050	0	

Country	Refugee populations Total		per thousand of population		Refugee flows Inflow	Outflow	IDPs
	1990	1999	1990	1999	1999	1999	1999
New Zealand	4,670	4,800	1.2	1.2	230	0	
Nicaragua	16,000	470	3.2	0.1			
Niger	790	350	0.1		0	60	
Nigeria	3,570	6,940		0.1	510	300	
Norway	19,580	47,900	4.4	10.7	2,890	0	
Pakistan	3,255,980	1,202,020	20.8	7.7	93,190	1,520	
Panama	1,350	1,320	0.5	0.5	410	0	
Papua New Guinea	7,100		1.5				
Peru	720	700				650	
Philippines	19,860	170	0.3				
Poland		940					
Portugal	870	380	0.1				
Romania		1,240		0.1	520	210	
Russian Federation		80,060		0.5	230	13,010	498,400
Rwanda	23,600	34,370	3.1	4.4	120	6,170	
Saudi Arabia		5,560		0.3			
Senegal	58,110	21,540	6.1	2.3	50	2,560	
Sierra Leone	125,830	6,570	25.9	1.4	0	24,590	500,000
Singapore	150						
Slovakia		440		0.1			
Slovenia		4,380		2.2	500	0	
Solomon Islands							
Somalia	460,000	130	45.6		0	41,170	
South Africa	14,540		0.4	6,130	0		
Spain	8,300	6,430	0.2	0.2	350	0	
Sri Lanka				0	9,410	612,500	
Sudan	1,031,050	391,000	35.0	13.3	0	56,110	
Swaziland	42,070	620	41.7	0.6	0	0	
Sweden	109,660	159,510	12.3	17.9	4,260	0	
Switzerland	40,940	82,300	5.5	11.1	24,510	0	
Syria	4,130	6,470	0.3	0.4	1,410	660	
Tajikistan	4,540		0.7	1,060	500		
Tanzania	265,180	622,200	7.9	18.6	143,110	0	
Thailand	99,820	100,130	1.6	1.6	1,120	0	
Togo	3,480	12,110	0.8	2.6	300	290	
Tunisia	450			0	110		
Turkey	28,000	2,820	0.4		11,250	4,580	
Turkmenistan	18,460		4.1	380	0		
Uganda	145,720	218,190	6.7	10.0	14,460	80	
Ukraine		2,700		0.1	440	320	
United Arab Emirates		500		0.2			
United Kingdom	43,650	92,990	0.7	1.6	0	0	
United States	464,890	514,660	1.7	1.8	18,420	0	
Uruguay							
Uzbekistan		1,010			510	0	
Venezuela	1,750	190	0.1		0	60	
Vietnam	21,150	15,000	0.3	0.2	0	270	
Yemen	2,940	60,480	0.2	3.3	9,420	0	
Yugoslavia	920	500,690	0.1	47.1	6,000	895,470	234,900
Zambia	138,050	206,390	15.1	22.5	37,960	0	
Zimbabwe	190,950	2,070	16.4	0.2	350	0	

Empty cells indicates that the value is below 100, zero or not available. Inflows and Outflows based on primae facie arrivals. IDPs refer to internally displaced persons of concern to/assisted by UNHCR at end of 1999.

Source: United Nations High Commissioner for Refugees, *Refugees and Others of Concern to UNHCR - 1999 Statistical Overview*, http://www.unhcr.org.

Table R16 Peacekeeping and conflicts

This table reports the importance of peacekeeping forces relative to total military personnel for 1997. A country's preparedness to commit part of its armed forces to foreign conflicts can be seen as a commitment to international peace. **Figure R3** shows the number and regional distribution of major armed conflicts between 1990 and 1999.

Country	Total military personnel 1997	Peace-keeping forces 2000	Peacekeeping forces per thousand military personnel	Country	Total military personnel 1997	Peace-keeping forces 2000	Peacekeeping forces per thousand military personnel
Albania	52,000	1	0.0	Cuba	55,000		
Algeria	124,000	15	0.1	Cyprus	10,000		
Angola	95,000			Czech Republic	55,000	44	0.8
Argentina	65,000	522	8.0	Denmark	29,000	306	10.6
Armenia	60,000			Djibouti	8,000		
Australia	65,000	1629	25.1	Dominican Republic	22,000	15	0.7
Austria	48,000	731	15.2	Ecuador	58,000		
Azerbaijan	75,000			Egypt	430,000	189	0.4
Bahrain	9,000			El Salvador	15,000	3	0.2
Bangladesh	110,000	3258	29.6	Equatorial Guinea	1,000		
Barbados	0			Eritrea	55,000		
Belarus	65,000			Estonia	7,000	6	0.9
Belgium	46,000	17	0.4	Ethiopia	100,000		
Belize	1,000			Fiji	4,000	843	210.8
Benin	8,000	41	5.1	Finland	35,000	723	20.7
Bhutan	8,000			France	475,000	498	1.0
Bolivia	33,000	9	0.3	Gabon	10,000		
Bosnia & Herzegovina	40,000	12	0.3	Gambia	1,000	33	33.0
Botswana	8,000			Georgia	11,000		
Brazil	296,000	95	0.3	Germany	335,000	481	1.4
Brunei	5,000			Ghana	7,000	2002	286.0
Bulgaria	80,000	112	1.4	Greece	206,000	40	0.2
Burkina Faso	9,000	2	0.2	Guatemala	30,000		
Burundi	35,000			Guinea	12,000	793	66.1
Cambodia	60,000			Guinea-Bissau	7,000		
Cameroon	13,000	24	1.8	Guyana	2,000		
Canada	61,000	568	9.3	Haiti	0		
Cape Verde	1,000	2	2.0	Honduras	10,000	12	1.2
Central African Republic	5,000			Hungary	50,000	154	3.1
Chad	35,000			Iceland	0	5	
Chile	102,000	47	0.5	India	1,260,000	2738	2.2
China & Tibet	2,600,000	98	0.0	Indonesia & East Timor	280,000	49	0.2
Colombia	149,000	1	0.0	Iran	575,000		
Comoros				Iraq	400,000		
Congo, Dem. Rep.				Ireland	17,000	782	46.0
Congo, Rep.	10,000			Israel & Occupied Territories	185,000		
Costa Rica	10,000			Italy	419,000	276	0.7
Côte d'Ivoire	15,000	1	0.1	Jamaica	3,000		
Croatia	58,000	10	0.2	Japan	250,000	30	0.1

Country	Total military personnel 1997	Peace-keeping forces 2000	Peacekeeping forces per thousand military personnel	Country	Total military personnel 1997	Peace-keeping forces 2000	Peacekeeping forces per thousand military personnel
Jordan	102,000	1848	18.1	Portugal	72,000	990	13.8
Kazakhstan	34,000			Qatar	11,000		
Kenya	24,000	1241	51.7	Romania	200,000	109	0.5
Korea, Dem. Rep.	1,100,000			Russian Federation	1,300,000	290	0.2
Korea, Rep.	670,000	472	0.7	Rwanda	40,000		
Kuwait	28,000			Sao Tome & Principe	1,000		
Kyrgyzstan	14,000	6	0.4	Saudi Arabia	180,000		
Laos	50,000			Senegal	14,000	89	6.4
Latvia	5,000			Sierra Leone	5,000		
Lebanon	57,000			Singapore	55,000	104	1.9
Lesotho	2,000			Slovakia	44,000	161	3.7
Libya	70,000	3	0.0	Slovenia	10,000	47	4.7
Lithuania	12,000	9	0.8	South Africa	75,000	4	0.1
Luxembourg	1,000			Spain	107,000	195	1.8
Macedonia	15,000			Sri Lanka	110,000	29	0.3
Madagascar	21,000			Sudan	105,000		
Malawi	8,000	20	2.5	Suriname	2,000		
Malaysia	110,000	225	2.0	Swaziland	3,000		
Mali	10,000	9	0.9	Sweden	60,000	152	2.5
Malta	2,000			Switzerland	39,000	34	0.9
Mauritania	11,000			Syria	320,000		
Mauritius	1,000			Tajikistan	10,000		
Mexico	250,000			Tanzania	35,000	28	0.8
Moldova	11,000			Thailand	288,000	765	2.7
Mongolia	20,000			Togo	12,000		
Morocco & Western Sahara	195,000	4	0.0	Trinidad & Tobago	2,000		
Mozambique	14,000	15	1.1	Tunisia	35,000	18	0.5
Myanmar	322,000			Turkey	820,000	155	0.2
Namibia	8,000	10	1.3	Turkmenistan	21,000		
Nepal	35,000	1030	29.4	Uganda	50,000		
Netherlands	57,000	946	1.7	Ukraine	450,000	1400	3.1
New Zealand	10,000	723	72.3	United Arab Emirates	60,000		
Nicaragua	14,000			United Kingdom	218,000	594	2.7
Niger	5,000	8	1.6	United States	1,530,000	885	0.6
Nigeria	76,000	3525	4.6	Uruguay	25,000	62	2.5
Norway	33,000	75	2.3	Uzbekistan	65,000		
Oman	38,000			Vanuatu	..	34	
Pakistan	610,000	1219	2.0	Venezuela	75,000	3	0.0
Panama	12,000			Vietnam	650,000		
Papua New Guinea	5,000			Yemen	69,000		
Paraguay	16,000			Yugoslavia	115,000		
Peru	115,000	28	0.2	Zambia	21,000	862	41.0
Philippines	105,000	807	7.7	Zimbabwe	40,000	91	2.3
Poland	230,000	1192	5.2				

Figure R3: Major armed conflicts 1990–1999

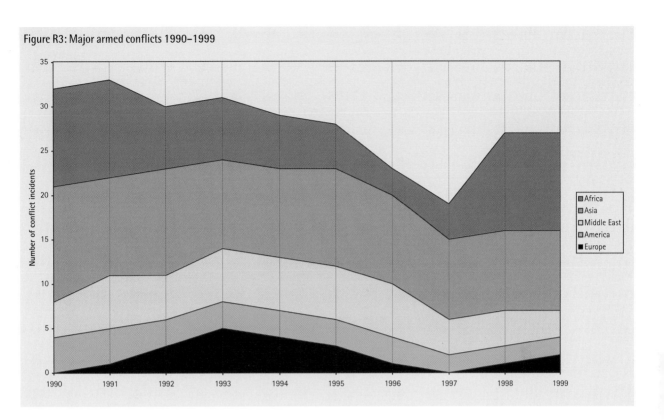

Table R17 Social justice

This table provides information on the level of social development and the extent of social justice. It shows the Human Development Index (HDI), where higher numbers suggest higher level of development. The HDI is a composite index of three separate indicators measuring GDP per capita, literacy and education, and life expectancy at birth. As further measures of social justice, we also show infant mortality, the extent of income inequality using the Gini coefficient, with higher numbers indicating greater inequality, and the percentage of women in tertiary education. The table thus shows indicators of poverty, inequality, and social exclusion. Growing inequality appears to be one of the characteristics of globalisation, as well as being one of the inhibitors of the emergence of global civil society.

Country	Human Development Index (HDI)		GDP per capita, PPP in current international $		Infant mortality rate per thousand live births		Life expectancy at birth (years)		Adult illiteracy (% adult population)		Income inequality (Gini Index)*	Women in tertiary education (% of pupils)	
	1990	1998	1990	1998	1990	1998	1990	1998	1990	1998	see note below	1990	1996
Afghanistan					164	149	43	46	73	65		31	
Albania	0.697	0.713	2,648	2,804	28	25	72	72	23	17		52	57
Algeria	0.642	0.683	4,546	4,792	46	35	67	71	46	35	35.3		
Angola		0.405	1,890	1,821	130	124	45	47					
Argentina	0.804	0.837	7,448	12,013	25	19	72	73	4	3			
Armenia	0.750	0.721	3,287	2,072	19	15	72	74	3	2			56
Australia	0.884	0.929	16,484	22,452	8	5	77	79			35.2	53	51
Austria	0.885	0.908	18,227	23,166	8	5	76	78			23.1	46	49
Azerbaijan		0.722	4,791	2,175	23	17	71	71				39	50
Bahamas		0.844	14,226	14,614	28	17	72	74	5	5			
Bahrain	0.797	0.820	10,800	13,111	23	9	71	73	18	14		56	
Bangladesh	0.412	0.461	953	1,361	91	73	55	59	65	60	33.6	16	
Barbados		0.858			12	14	75	76					
Belarus	0.804	0.781	6,714	6,319	12	11	71	68	1	1	21.7		55
Belgium	0.890	0.925	18,501	23,223	8	6	76	78			25.0	48	
Belize	0.748	0.777	3,792	4,566	34	28	73	75	11	7			
Benin	0.358	0.411	675	867	104	87	52	53	72	62		13	19
Bhutan		0.483	1,167	1,536	..	61	..	61					
Bolivia	0.595	0.643	1,751	2,269	80	60	58	62	22	16	42.0		
Bosnia & Herzegovina					15	13	71	73					
Botswana	0.651	0.593	4,773	6,103	55	62	57	46	32	24			47
Brazil	0.706	0.747	5,346	6,625	48	33	65	67	19	16	60.0	52	
Brunei	0.825	0.848	15,688	16,765	9	9	74	76	14	9			
Bulgaria	0.782	0.772	5,344	4,809	15	14	71	71	3	2	28.3	51	61
Burkina Faso	0.28	0.303	675	870	105	104	45	44	84	78	48.2	23	23
Burundi	0.339	0.321	711	570	119	118	44	42	62	54	33.3	27	
Cambodia		0.512	963	1,257	122	102	50	54	69	63	40.4		16
Cameroon	0.519	0.528	1,556	1,474	81	77	54	54	37	26			
Canada	0.925	0.935	19,672	23,582	7	5	77	79			31.5	54	
Cape Verde	0.611	0.688	2,382	3,233	65	55	65	68	36	27			
Central African Republic	0.372	0.371	1,059	1,118	102	98	48	44	67	56	61.3	13	
Chad	0.323	0.367	751	856	118	99	46	48	72	61			
Chile	0.780	0.826	4,813	8,787	16	10	74	75	6	5	56.5		45
China & Tibet	0.619	0.706	1,338	3,105	33	31	69	70	23	17	40.3		
Colombia	0.720	0.764	5,629	6,006	30	23	69	70	11	9	57.1		52
Comoros	0.496	0.510	1,596	1,398	84	63	56	60	46	42			
Congo, Dem. Rep.	0.450	0.430	1,421	822	96	90	52	51	52	41			
Congo, Rep.	0.503	0.507	1,007	995	88	90	49	48	33	22		18	

276

Country	Human Development Index (HDI) 1990	1998	GDP per capita, PPP in current international $ 1990	1998	Infant mortality rate per thousand live births 1990	1998	Life expectancy at birth (years) 1990	1998	Adult illiteracy (% adult population) 1990	1998	Income inequality (Gini Index)* see note below	Women in tertiary education (% of pupils) 1990	1996
Costa Rica	0.775	0.797	4,606	5,987	15	13	75	77	6	5	47.0		
Côte d'Ivoire	0.406	0.420	1,402	1,598	95	88	50	46	66	56	36.7		
Croatia	0.786	0.795	6,781	6,749	11	8	72	73	3	2	26.8		51
Cuba					11	7	75	76	5	4		57	60
Cyprus		0.886	12,605	17,482	11	8	77	78	6	3		52	56
Czech Republic	0.830	0.843	12,368	12,362	11	5	72	75			25.4	44	48
Denmark	0.883	0.911	17,942	24,218	8	5	75	76			24.7	52	
Djibouti		0.447			118	106	48	50	47	38			44
Dominican Republic	0.686	0.729	3,122	4,598	51	40	69	71	21	17	48.7		57
Ecuador	0.696	0.722	2,624	3,003	45	32	68	70	13	9	43.7		
Egypt	0.570	0.623	2,343	3,041	69	49	63	67	53	46	28.9	36	
El Salvador	0.642	0.696	2,886	4,036	46	31	66	69	28	22	52.3	33	50
Equatorial Guinea		0.555			121	106	47	50	27	19		13	
Eritrea		0.408		833	81	61	49	51	57	48			
Estonia	0.806	0.801	7,775	7,682	12	9	69	70			35.4	50	53
Ethiopia	0.287	0.309	468	574	124	107	45	43	72	64	40.0	18	20
Fiji	0.74	0.769	3,761	4,231	25	19	71	73	11	8			
Finland	0.892	0.917	17,172	20,847	6	4	75	77			25.6	52	53
France	0.892	0.917	17,278	21,175	7	5	77	78			32.7	53	55
Gabon		0.592	5,347	6,353	96	86	52	53					
Gambia	0.352	0.396	1,378	1,453	109	76	49	53	74	65	47.8		
Georgia		0.762	8,304	3,353	16	15	72	73				46	51
Germany		0.911		22,169	7	5	75	77			30.0		46
Ghana	0.510	0.556	1,394	1,735	77	65	57	60	42	31	32.7		
Greece	0.849	0.875	11,049	13,943	10	6	77	78	5	3	32.7		48
Guatemala	0.577	0.619	2,770	3,505	56	42	61	64	39	33	59.6		
Guinea		0.394	1,415	1,782	136	118	44	47			40.3	7	11
Guinea-Bissau	0.307	0.331	702	616	145	128	42	44	72	63	56.2		
Guyana	0.670	0.709	2,037	3,403	64	57	63	64	3	2	40.2		51
Haiti	0.436	0.440	1,603	1,383	85	71	53	54	60	52			
Honduras	0.624	0.653	2,057	2,433	50	36	67	69	32	27	53.7	43	
Hungary	0.798	0.817	9,009	10,232	15	10	69	71	1	1	30.8	50	
Iceland	0.906	0.927	20,112	25,110	6	3	78	79				57	58
India	0.51	0.563	1,382	2,077	80	70	60	63	51	44	37.8	33	36
Indonesia & East Timor	0.619	0.670	1,858	2,651	60	43	62	65	20	14	36.5		
Iran	0.653	0.709	3,798	5,121	47	26	66	71	36	25		27	36
Iraq		0.583			102	103	61	59	55	46			
Ireland	0.857	0.907	11,364	21,482	8	6	75	76			35.9	46	52
Israel & Occupied Territories	0.856	0.883	13,131	17,301	10	6	76	78	6	4	35.5	49	
Italy	0.875	0.903	16,997	20,585	8	5	77	78	2	2	27.3	48	54
Jamaica	0.72	0.735	3,167	3,389	25	21	73	75	18	14	36.4		
Japan	0.904	0.924	19,062	23,257	5	4	79	81			24.9		
Jordan		0.721	2,273	3,347	30	27	68	71	19	11	36.4	48	47
Kazakhstan	0.784	0.754	6,278	4,378	26	22	68	65			35.4		
Kenya	0.530	0.508	930	980	62	76	57	51	29	20	44.5		
Korea, Dem. Rep.					45	54	66	63					
Korea, Rep.	0.807	0.854	8,596	13,478	12	9	70	73	4	3	31.6	32	37
Kuwait		0.836			14	12	75	77	23	19			62
Kyrgyzstan		0.706	3,558	2,317	30	26	68	67			40.5		

Table R17 continued	Human Development Index (HDI)		GDP per capita, PPP in current international $		Infant mortality rate per thousand live births		Life expectancy at birth (years)		Adult illiteracy (% adult population)		Income inequality (Gini Index)*	Women in tertiary education (% of pupils)	
Country	1990	1998	1990	1998	1990	1998	1990	1998	1990	1998	see note below	1990	1996
Laos	0.415	0.484	1,141	1,734	108	96	50	54	64	54	30.4		30
Latvia	0.797	0.771	8,122	5,728	14	15	69	70	0	0	32.4	55	60
Lebanon	0.677	0.735	2,007	4,326	36	27	68	70	20	15			
Lesotho	0.561	0.569	1,097	1,626	102	93	58	55	22	18	56.0	58	54
Liberia					168	114	45	47	61	49			
Libya		0.760			33	23	68	70	32	22			
Lithuania	0.809	0.789		6,436	10	9	71	72	1	1	32.4		59
Luxembourg	0.870	0.908	22,756	33,505	7	4	75	77			26.9		35
Macedonia		0.763		4,254	32	16	72	73				52	54
Madagascar	0.461	0.483	784	756	103	92	55	58	42	35	46.0	45	45
Malawi	0.348	0.385	469	523	135	134	45	42	48	42		26	
Malaysia	0.725	0.772	5,328	8,137	16	8	71	72	19	14	48.5		
Maldives	0.677	0.725	2,676	4,083	60	31	62	67	6	4			
Mali	0.314	0.380	567	681	136	117	48	50	74	62	50.5	14	19
Malta	0.812	0.865	7,592	23,306	9	6	75	77	12	9		44	52
Mauritania	0.4	0.451	1,273	1,563	105	90	51	54	64	59	38.9	14	
Mauritius	0.718	0.761	5,422	8,312	20	19	70	71	20	16		37	
Mexico	0.757	0.784	6,225	7,704	36	30	70	72	12	9	53.7		48
Micronesia, Fed. Sts.		0.783			39	28	63	67					
Moldova	0.757	0.7		1,947	19	18	68	67	3	1	34.4		55
Mongolia		0.628	1,699	1,541	63	50	63	66	47	39	33.2	65	69
Morocco & Western Sahara	0.537	0.589	2,780	3,305	64	49	63	67	61	53	39.5	36	41
Mozambique	0.328	0.341	532	782	150	134	43	45	67	58	39.6		24
Myanmar		0.585			94	78	57	60	19	16			
Namibia	0.644	0.632	4,214	5,176	64	67	58	54	25	19			
Nepal	0.414	0.474	861	1,157	101	77	54	58	69	61	36.7	23	
Netherlands	0.897	0.925	16,848	22,176	7	5	77	78			32.6	44	48
New Zealand	0.871	0.903	14,088	17,288	8	5	75	77			43.9	52	56
Nicaragua	0.597	0.631	1,605	2,142	51	36	64	68	35	32	50.3	52	
Niger	0.273	0.293	719	739	150	118	45	46	89	85	50.5		
Nigeria	0.411	0.439	701	795	85	76	49	53	51	39	50.6		
Norway	0.895	0.934	18,389	26,342	7	4	77	78			25.8	53	56
Oman		0.730			22	18	69	73	45	31	..	45	46
Pakistan	0.462	0.522	1,313	1,715	111	91	59	62	64	56	31.2		
Panama	0.741	0.776	3,698	5,249	26	21	72	74	11	9	48.5		
Papua New Guinea	0.496	0.542	1,726	2,359	83	59	55	58	42	37	50.9		
Paraguay	0.713	0.736	3,876	4,288	31	24	68	70	10	7	59.1		55
Peru	0.698	0.737	2,814	4,282	54	40	66	69	14	11	46.2		
Philippines	0.713	0.744	3,083	3,555	37	32	65	69	8	5	46.2		
Poland	0.785	0.814	5,538	7,619	19	10	71	73	0	0	32.9	56	
Portugal	0.813	0.864	10,880	14,701	11	8	74	75	13	9	35.6	56	
Qatar		0.819			21	18	72	74	23	20		69	73
Romania	0.771	0.77	6,090	5,648	27	21	70	69	3	2	28.2	47	53
Russian Federation	0.812	0.771	9,875	6,460	17	17	69	67	1	1	48.7	55	
Rwanda		0.382			132	123	40	41	47	36	28.9		
Samoa		0.711	3,039	3,832	27	25	66	69	24	20			
Sao Tome & Principe		0.547	1,399	1,469	61	49	62	64					

Table R17 continued	Human Development Index (HDI)		GDP per capita, PPP in current international $		Infant mortality rate per thousand live births		Life expectancy at birth (years)		Adult illiteracy (% adult population)		Income inequality (Gini Index)*	Women in tertiary education (% of pupils)	
Country	1990	1998	1990	1998	1990	1998	1990	1998	1990	1998	see note below	1990	1996
Saudi Arabia	0.709	0.747	10,045	10,158	32	20	69	72	33	25		43	47
Senegal	0.376	0.416	1,145	1,307	74	69	50	52	72	65	41.3		
Sierra Leone		0.252	757	458	189	169	35	37			62.9		
Singapore	0.823	0.881	13,768	24,210	7	4	74	77	11	8		41	
Slovakia	0.812	0.825	8,646	9,699	12	9	71	73			19.5		50
Slovenia	0.840	0.861		14,293	8	5	73	75	0	0	26.8	56	56
Solomon Islands		0.614	1,797	1,940	29	22	69	71					
Somalia					152	121	42	48					
South Africa	0.705	0.697	7,934	8,488	55	51	62	63	19	15	59.3	44	
Spain	0.870	0.899	12,444	16,212	8	5	77	78	4	3	32.5	51	53
Sri Lanka	0.699	0.733	2,011	2,979	19	16	71	73	11	9	34.4		
St. Lucia		0.728	4,204	5,183	19	17	71	72			42.6		
St. Vincent & the Grenadines		0.738	3,440	4,692	21	22	70	73					
Sudan	0.406	0.477	900	1,394	85	69	51	55	54	44			
Suriname		0.766			34	28	69	70					
Swaziland	0.613	0.655	3,543	3,816	79	69	57	56	28	22	60.9	43	52
Sweden	0.889	0.926	17,537	20,659	6	4	78	79			25.0	54	56
Switzerland	0.901	0.915	23,257	25,512	7	4	77	79			33.1	35	
Syria	0.624	0.660	2,389	2,892	39	28	66	69	35	27		39	
Tajikistan	0.712	0.663	2,495	1,041	41	23	69	69	2	1		38	
Tanzania	0.406	0.415	437	480	99	85	50	47	36	26	38.2		18
Thailand	0.708	0.745	3,821	5,456	37	29	69	72	8	5	41.4		
Togo	0.456	0.471	1,377	1,372	81	78	50	49	54	45		14	17
Trinidad & Tobago	0.777	0.793	5,887	7,485	18	16	71	73	9	7	40.3	44	
Tunisia	0.642	0.703	3,840	5,404	42	28	68	72	41	31	40.2	39	45
Turkey	0.683	0.732	4,663	6,422	58	38	66	69	22	16	41.5	34	35
Turkmenistan		0.704	5,848		45	33	66	66			40.8		
Uganda	0.361	0.409	719	1,074	104	101	47	42	44	35	39.2	28	33
Ukraine	0.793	0.744	6,372	3,194	13	14	70	67	1	0	32.5		
United Arab Emirates	0.804	0.810	19,880	17,719	20	8	74	75	30	25		70	
United Kingdom	0.874	0.918	16,144	20,336	8	6	76	77			36.1	48	52
United States	0.909	0.929	22,537	29,605	9	7	75	77			40.8	54	
Uruguay	0.797	0.825	5,905	8,623	21	16	73	74	3	2	42.3		
Uzbekistan	0.690	0.686		2,053	35	22	69	69	17	12	33.3		
Vanuatu		0.623	3,162	3,120	56	36	61	65					
Venezuela	0.755	0.770	5,019	5,808	25	21	71	73	11	8	48.8		
Vietnam	0.602	0.671		1,689	40	34	67	68	10	7	36.1		
Yemen	0.399	0.448	664	719	110	82	52	56	67	56	39.5		13
Yugoslavia					23	13	72	72					54
Zambia	0.451	0.420	735	719	107	114	49	43	32	24	49.8		
Zimbabwe	0.599	0.555	2,385	2,669	52	73	56	51	19	13	56.8		36

* Survey year for Gini Index varies by country.

Sources: World Bank, World Development Indicators 2000 (CD-Rom); United Nations Development Programme, Human Development Report 2000 (New York: Oxford University Press).

Table R18 Energy consumption

This table measures energy consumption, efficiency of energy use, and changes over the previous ten-year period. Aspects of the environment and unsustainable energy use are close to the notion of a global commons, and the data suggest the extent to which countries and regions of the world benefit from and contribute to it. Neither of the two ways we measure efficiency of energy consumption is quite satisfactory, however. The TOE per capita measure discriminates against economically more developed countries, which will have higher energy consumption throughout. The TOE per GDP, on the other hand, discriminates against developing countries, where true economic output tends to be underestimated due to the general exclusion of informal sector activities.

Country	Energy Consumption Tons of oil equivalent (TOE), 1997	Energy Consumption in kilos of oil equivalent per capita, 1997	Efficiency measure thousand TOE/GDP 1997	Consumption change 1989-1997, in %	Efficiency change 1989-1997, in %
Albania	1,048	335	2.3	-63	49.6
Algeria	26,497	901	1.6	23	-15.6
Angola	6,848	585	0.9	37	-33.5
Argentina	61,710	1,730	4.8	36	1.9
Armenia	1,804	503	1.8	-77	
Austrailia	101,626	5,543	3.8	30	5.1
Austria	27,761	3,428	8.7	14	14.9
Azerbaijan	11,987	1,568	0.3	-63	-3.3
Bangladesh	24,237	198	1.7	28	26.4
Belarus	25,142	2,429	0.8	-40	20.8
Belgium	57,125	5,641	5.0	21	3.4
Benin	2,182	388	1.0	36	6.4
Bolivia	4,254	547	1.7	67	-18.1
Bosnia & Herzegovina	1,750	497		134	
Brazil	172,030	1,051	4.3	31	-8.8
Bulgaria	20,616	2,457	0.5	-33	4.4
Cameroon	5,756	413	1.5	24	-38.8
Canada	237,983	7,864	2.5	17	4.7
Chile	23,012	1,573	3.0	121	-5.4
China & Tibet	1,098,931	883	0.8	42	110.5
Colombia	30,481	761	3.2	29	17.5
Congo, Dem. Rep.	14,539	303	0.4	36	-76.6
Congo, Rep.	1,242	459	1.8	-12	24.3
Costa Rica	2,663	710	3.5	48	-1.7
Côte d'Ivoire	5,597	398	2.0	39	-12.3
Croatia	7,650	1,706	2.8	178	
Cuba	14,273	1,290		-5	
Czech Republic	40,576	3,939	1.3	-18	22.6
Denmark	21,107	4,016	9.1	4	19.7
Dominican Republic	5,453	673	2.5	25	18.7
Ecuador	8,513	713	2.2	44	-1.4
Egypt	39,581	611	1.7	41	11.9
El Salvador	4,095	693	2.5	49	5.3
Estonia*	5,556	3,839	1.0	-1713	1,689.9
Ethiopia	17,131	294	0.4	25	12.6
Finland	33,075	6,433	4.2	10	8.4
France	247,534	4,233	6.4	19	3.5
Gabon	1,635	1,438	3.3	10	51.9
Georgia	2,295	448	1.6	-63	-10.1
Germany	347,272	4,232	7.2	-5	

Country	Energy Consumption Tons of oil equivalent (TOE), 1997	in kilos of oil equivalent per capita, 1997	Efficiency measure thousand TOE/GDP 1997	Consumption change 1989–1997, in %	Efficiency change 1989–1997, in %
Ghana	6,896	370	1.0	44	10.2
Greece	25,556	2,418	4.8	36	-14.1
Guatemala	5,633	535	2.8	47	0.5
Haiti	1,779	227	1.5	16	-26.4
Honduras	3,182	532	1.4	44	-2.4
Hungary	25,311	2,492	1.9	-18	9.4
Iceland	2,330	8,516	3.3	22	-6.5
India	461,032	477	0.9	45	35.5
Indonesia & East Timor	138,779	682	1.6	71	37.1
Iran	108,289	1,676	0.7	83	-32.9
Iraq	27,091	1,279		33	
Ireland	12,491	3,415	6.3	31	63.7
Israel & Occupied Territories	17,591	3,002	5.2	70	-9.7
Italy	163,315	2,846	6.8	14	4.0
Jamaica	3,963	1,575	1.0	104	-86.9
Japan	514,898	4,085	10.6	37	-3.1
Jordan	4,795	783	1.4	52	-26.6
Kazakhstan	38,428	2,346	0.5	-65	23.5
Kenya	14,138	497	0.7	19	14.3
Korea, Dem. Rep.	23,323	1,015		-39	
Korea, Rep.	176,351	3,856	3.1	166	-57.8
Kuwait	16,165	9,332		29	
Kyrgyzstan	2,793	605	1.4	45	-74.1
Latvia*	4,460	1,812	1.2	505	-543.9
Lebanon	5,244	1,669	2.3	76	
Libya	15,090	2,896		33	
Lithuania	8,806	2,377	0.9	-40	22.1
Macedonia	2,841	1,430	0.9	184	
Malaysia	48,473	2,310	2.1	161	-30.3
Mexico	141,520	1,501	2.9	24	10.2
Moldova	4,436	1,014	0.7	-54	-5.9
Morocco & Western Sahara	9,275	345	3.9	61	-26.0
Mozambique	7,664	416	0.4	1	62.1
Myanmar	13,009	296		23	
Nepal	7,160	321	0.7	30	37.5
Netherlands	74,910	4,798	5.7	15	17.6
New Zealand	16,679	4,434	3.8	39	-17.6
Nicaragua	2,573	550	0.8	26	-24.2
Nigeria	88,652	853	0.3	36	19.7
Norway	24,226	5,511	6.6	12	22.4
Oman	6,775	2,939		265	
Pakistan	56,818	394	1.1	51	7.8
Panama	2,328	855	3.6	44	-10.5
Paraguay	4,191	824	2.2	49	-7.7
Peru	15,127	621	4.3	20	-6.0
Philippines	38,251	536	2.2	55	-10.2
Poland	105,155	2,718	1.4	-20	48.4
Portugal	20,400	2,068	5.5	58	-20.3
Romania	44,135	1,957	0.7	-36	13.0

Country	Energy Consumption Tons of oil equivalent (TOE), 1997	in kilos of oil equivalent per capita, 1997	Efficiency measure thousand TOE/GDP 1997	Consumption change 1989-1997, in %	Efficiency change 1989-1997, in %
Russian Federation	591,982	4,009	0.6	-52	13.6
Saudi Arabia	98,449	5,054	1.3	60	-22.2
Senegal	2,770	316	1.8	27	0.6
Singapore	26,878	7,843	3.6	202	-62.3
Slovakia	17,216	3,204	1.1	-23	21.1
Slovenia	6,380	3,197	3.2	19	
South Africa	107,220	2,766	1.5	15	3.2
Spain	107,328	2,709	5.5	43	-13.5
Sri Lanka	7,159	392	2.0	25	34.8
Sudan	11,480	414	0.7	21	52.9
Sweden	51,934	5,864	4.6	6	5.9
Switzerland	26,218	3,616	11.9	12	1.1
Syria	14,642	979	1.2	46	22.7
Tajikistan	3,384	571	0.6	61	-108.6
Tanzania	14,258	454	0.4	21	
Thailand	79,963	1,339	2.2	157	-35.0
Trinidad & Tobago	8,196	6,419	0.7	77	-66.2
Tunisia	6,805	739	3.0	43	7.1
Turkey	71,273	1,124	2.7	54	-3.6
Turkmenistan	12,181	2,878	0.2	-84	39.2
Ukraine	150,059	2,939	0.3	-24	-34.4
United Arab Emirates	30,874	13,381	1.6	62	-0.1
United Kingdom	227,977	3,894	5.1	9	12.5
United States	2,162,191	7,956	3.6	16	16.4
Uruguay	2,883	883	6.6	30	5.4
Uzbekistan	42,553	1,833	0.5	1	-4.4
Vanuatu					18.9
Venezuela	57,530	2,526	1.4	32	-3.0
Vietnam	39,306	515	0.6	68	40.1
Yemen	3,355	206	1.2	30	
Yugoslavia	15,842	1,491			
Zambia	5,987	697	0.6	13	1.2
Zimbabwe	9,926	885	0.8	17	24.1
World	9,521,506	1,635		16	
Asia (excl Middle east)	2,958,844	899		36	
Middle East & North Africa	525,927	1,388		58	
Sub-Saharan Africa		664			
Europe	2,553,858	3,507		-20	
North America	2,400,174	7,947		16	
Central America	198,317	1,202		26	
South America	379,732	1,148		35	
Oceania	118,305	4,038		31	
Developed	5,827,461	1,280,399		-4	
Developing	3,631,617	973,694		49	

*Data as found in source · "0" is either zero or less than one half the unit measure · TOE is Tons of oil equivalent · GDP at market prices (constant 1995 US$ mill)

Source: United Nations Development Programme, United Nations, Environment Programme, World Bank, World Resources Institute, World Resources 2000-2001; People and Ecosystems, The Fraying Web of Life (Oxford: Elsevier Science., 2000), http://www.wri.org/facts/data-tables-energy.html.

Table R19 Number of international non-governmental organisations (INGOs) and organisational density

This table gives the total number of international organisation secretariats of international non-governmental organisations (INGOs) in a given country for 1990 and 2000. These are the principal secretariats (headquarters, main office) of the organisation. Secondary (including regional) secretariats are not included. The table also indicates the expansion or contraction in the number of INGO secretariats by country over the time period, and the number of secretariats per 1 million population for both years.

Country	1990		2000		Absolute growth % 1990–2000	Density growth % 1990–2000
	Number of secretariats	Organisational density per million of population	Number of secretariats	Organisational density per million of population		
Afghanistan	0	0	0	0.0		
Albania	0	0	0	0.0		
Algeria	13	0.5	12	0.4	-7.7	-26.7
Angola	2	0.2	1	0.1	-50.0	-64.2
Argentina	79	2.4	95	2.6	20.3	5.7
Armenia			0	0.0		
Australia	100	5.9	213	11.3	113.0	92.3
Austria	144	18.6	202	24.6	40.3	32.2
Azerbaijan			0	0.0		
Bahamas	2	7.8	4	13.0	100.0	66.8
Bahrain	10	19.9	14	22.7	40.0	14.1
Bangladesh	8	0.1	15	0.1	87.5	60.2
Barbados	30	116.3	27	100.0	-10.0	-14.0
Belarus			5	0.5		
Belgium	1203	120.7	1666	163.3	38.5	35.3
Belize	1	5.3	3	15.0	200.0	183.5
Benin	12	2.5	15	2.5	25.0	-2.9
Bhutan	0	0	0	0.0		
Bolivia	4	0.6	12	1.4	200.0	137.6
Bosnia & Herzegovina			1	0.3		
Botswana	6	4.7	14	8.8	133.3	86.1
Brazil	49	0.3	72	0.4	46.9	27.8
Brunei	2	7.8	1	3.0	-50.0	-60.8
Bulgaria	21	2.4	19	2.3	-9.5	-3.8
Burkina Faso	28	3.2	31	2.6	10.7	-17.4
Burundi	2	0.4	4	0.6	100.0	62.9
Cambodia	0	0	3	0.3		
Cameroon	23	2.0	27	1.8	17.4	-10.8
Canada	160	5.8	261	8.4	63.1	45.8
Cape Verde	0	0	0	0.0		
Central African Republic	4	1.4	5	1.4	25.0	2.2
Chad	1	0.2	3	0.4	200.0	123.9
Chile	71	5.4	65	4.3	-8.5	-21.1
China & Tibet	8	0.0	63	0.0	687.5	599.7
Colombia	34	1.0	43	1.0	26.5	4.6
Comoros	0	0	0	0.0		
Congo, Dem. Rep.	16	0.4	4	0.1	-75.0	-81.9
Congo, Rep.	15	6.8	4	1.4	-73.3	-79.6
Costa Rica	53	17.7	62	15.5	17.0	-12.4
Côte d'Ivoire	39	3.4	44	3.0	12.8	-11.3
Croatia			6	1.3		
Cuba	12	1.1	16	1.4	33.3	26.5
Cyprus	3	4.4	16	20.4	433.3	362.1

Country	1990 Number of secretariats	1990 Organisational density per million of population	2000 Number of secretariats	2000 Organisational density per million of population	Absolute growth % 1990–2000	Density growth % 1990–2000
Czech Republic			31	3.0		
Denmark	242	47.1	247	46.6	2.1	-1.0
Djibouti	1	1.9	1	1.6	0.0	-19.0
Dominican Republic	5	0.7	4	0.5	-20.0	-33.1
Ecuador	26	2.5	36	2.9	38.5	12.8
Egypt	44	0.8	85	1.2	93.2	47.9
El Salvador	9	1.8	10	1.6	11.1	-9.9
Equatorial Guinea	0	0	0	0.0		
Eritrea			0	0.0		
Estonia	0	0	9	6.4		
Ethiopia	49	1.0	37	0.6	-24.5	-38.3
Fiji	21	28.5	34	41.6	61.9	45.9
Finland	120	24.1	128	24.6	6.7	2.3
France	1143	20.1	1188	20.1	3.9	-0.2
Gabon	11	11.5	6	5.0	-45.5	-56.4
Gambia	3	3.3	3	2.3	0.0	-29.5
Georgia			0	0.0		
Germany	492	6.2	610	7.4	24.0	19.8
Ghana	31	2.1	41	2.0	32.3	-2.6
Greece	20	2.0	51	4.8	155.0	144.4
Guatemala	23	2.6	22	1.9	-4.3	-26.6
Guinea	0	0	1	0.1		
Guinea-Bissau	0	0	0	0.0		
Guyana	17	21.4	16	18.6	-5.9	-13.1
Haiti	0	0.0	0	0.0		
Honduras	10	2.0	14	2.2	40.0	5.1
Hungary	36	3.5	45	4.5	25.0	29.6
Iceland	10	39.2	14	49.8	40.0	27.0
India	85	0.1	101	0.1	18.8	-0.4
Indonesia & East Timor	44	0.2	46	0.2	4.5	-12.5
Iran	3	0.1	9	0.1	200.0	141.1
Iraq	59	3.3	15	0.6	-74.6	-80.1
Ireland	23	6.6	42	11.4	82.6	73.0
Israel & the Occupied Territories	49	10.5	58	9.4	18.4	-11.0
Italy	310	5.5	418	7.3	34.8	33.5
Jamaica	22	9.2	16	6.2	-27.3	-32.8
Japan	108	0.9	136	1.1	25.9	22.8
Jordan	25	7.9	24	3.6	-4.0	-54.6
Kazakhstan			1	0.1		
Kenya	102	4.3	121	4.0	18.6	-7.2
Korea, Dem. Rep.	0	0	1	0.0		
Korea, Rep.	17	0.4	35	0.7	105.9	88.6
Kuwait	23	10.8	16	8.0	-30.4	-26.1
Kyrgyzstan			1	0.2		
Laos	0	0.0	1	0.2		
Latvia	0	0.0	7	2.9		
Lebanon	12	3.3	19	5.8	58.3	74.4
Lesotho	2	1.2	2	0.9	0.0	-21.7
Liberia	5	2.1	0	0.0	-100.0	-100.0
Libya	15	3.4	8	1.4	-46.7	-57.9
Lithuania	0	0.0	4	1.1		
Luxembourg	55	144.0	61	141.5	10.9	-1.7
Macedonia			1	0.5		
Madagascar	1	0.1	1	0.1	0.0	-26.8

Country	1990 Number of secretariats	1990 Organisational density per million of population	2000 Number of secretariats	2000 Organisational density per million of population	Absolute growth % 1990–2000	Density growth % 1990–2000
Malawi	4	0.5	4	0.4	0.0	-22.0
Malaysia	74	4.1	71	3.2	-4.1	-21.3
Maldives	0	0.0	0	0.0		
Mali	9	1.1	8	0.7	-11.1	-32.9
Malta	8	22.6	13	33.4	62.5	47.9
Mauritania	3	1.5	4	1.5	33.3	0.0
Mauritius	6	5.7	13	10.8	116.7	90.8
Mexico	77	0.9	93	0.9	20.8	1.6
Micronesia Fed. States	0	0.0	1	1.8		
Moldova			0	0.0		
Mongolia	2	0.9	2	0.7	0.0	-17.9
Morocco & Western Sahara	23	1.0	32	1.1	39.1	17.8
Mozambique	1	0.1	2	0.1	100.0	43.7
Myanmar	0	0.0	0	0.0		
Namibia	0	0.0	4	2.4		
Nepal	5	0.3	12	0.5	140.0	88.5
Netherlands	361	24.1	609	38.5	68.7	59.6
New Zealand	20	5.8	22	5.6	10.0	-3.1
Nicaragua	9	2.4	15	2.9	66.7	25.1
Niger	9	1.2	9	0.8	0.0	-27.7
Nigeria	56	0.6	42	0.4	-25.0	-35.3
Norway	123	29.0	135	30.0	9.8	3.5
Oman	0	0.0	1	0.4		
Pakistan	21	0.2	20	0.1	-4.8	-34.3
Panama	19	7.9	16	5.5	-15.8	-30.4
Papua New Guinea	3	0.8	1	0.2	-66.7	-73.3
Paraguay	3	0.7	7	1.3	133.3	79.0
Peru	52	2.4	53	2.1	1.9	-14.5
Philippines	86	1.4	88	1.2	2.3	-15.7
Poland	32	0.8	40	1.0	25.0	22.8
Portugal	11	1.1	35	3.5	218.2	218.1
Qatar	2	4.1	5	8.3	150.0	102.8
Romania	8	0.3	6	0.3	-25.0	-21.9
Russian Federation	52	0.4	54	0.4	3.8	4.8
Rwanda	7	1.0	2	0.3	-71.4	-74.2
Samoa	2	12.5	5	27.8	150.0	122.2
Sao Tome & Principe	0	0.0	0	0.0		
Saudi Arabia	53	3.4	52	2.4	-1.9	-28.2
Senegal	61	8.3	66	6.9	8.2	-16.6
Sierra Leone	5	1.3	5	1.0	0.0	-18.4
Singapore	39	14.4	72	20.0	84.6	38.7
Slovakia			7	1.3		
Slovenia			18	9.0		
Solomon Islands	1	3.1	2	4.5	100.0	44.6
Somalia	0	0.0	0	0.0		
South Africa	5	0.1	75	1.9	1400.0	1206.9
Spain	76	2.0	159	4.0	109.2	105.2
Sri Lanka	8	0.5	16	0.9	100.0	80.8
St. Lucia	7	52.2	7	44.9	0.0	-14.1
St. Vincent & the Grenadines	1	9.3	2	17.4	100.0	86.1
Sudan	12	0.5	12	0.4	0.0	-18.4
Suriname	0	0.0	0	0.0		
Swaziland	1	1.3	2	2.0	100.0	52.8
Sweden	247	28.9	255	28.7	3.2	-0.7

Country	1990 Number of secretariats	1990 Organisational density per million of population	2000 Number of secretariats	2000 Organisational density per million of population	Absolute growth % 1990–2000	Density growth % 1990–2000
Switzerland	650	96.8	630	85.1	-3.1	-12.1
Syria	24	2.0	18	1.1	-25.0	-43.6
Tajikistan			0	0.0		
Tanzania	17	0.7	23	0.7	35.3	2.9
Thailand	95	1.7	104	1.7	9.5	-0.9
Togo	15	4.3	22	4.8	46.7	12.0
Trinidad & Tobago	28	23.0	46	35.4	64.3	53.5
Tunisia	43	5.3	29	3.0	-32.6	-42.7
Turkey	13	0.2	38	0.6	192.3	146.3
Turkmenistan			0	0.0		
Uganda	5	0.3	13	0.6	160.0	94.8
Ukraine			8	0.2		
United Arab Emirates	7	3.8	8	3.3		-12.2
United Kingdom	949	16.5	1360	23.1	43.3	40.3
United States	1084	4.3	1624	5.8	49.8	34.2
Uruguay	36	11.6	57	17.3	58.3	49.0
Uzbekistan			4	0.2		
Vanuatu	0	0.0	1	5.0		
Venezuela	75	3.8	70	2.9	-6.7	-24.8
Vietnam	0	0.0	1	0.0		
Yemen	0	0.0	0	0.0		
Yugoslavia	37	3.5	3	0.3	-91.9	-91.9
Zambia	14	1.8	19	2.1	35.7	14.8
Zimbabwe	16	1.6	42	3.6	162.5	118.7
World	10140	8.0	13119	8.1	29.4	1.4
Low income	762	1.2	914	1.0	19.9	-21.5
Excl. China & India	669	1.3	750	1.0	12.1	-21.9
Middle income	1592	6.3	1928	6.2	21.1	-2.5
Lower middle income	836	3.5	967	3.8	15.7	8.9
Upper middle income	756	11.4	961	10.6	27.1	-7.2
Low & middle income	17791	8.2	23185	9.5	30.3	15.8
East Asia & Pacific	353	3.0	459	5.0	30.0	66.4
Europe & Central Asia	199	1.0	290	1.0	45.7	-0.5
Latin America & Carib.	752	10.9	879	10.9	16.9	0.4
Middle East & N. Africa	324	3.6	318	3.1	-1.9	-13.4
South Asia	127	0.1	164	0.2	29.1	53.7
Sub-Saharan Africa	599	1.8	732	1.7	22.2	-6.5
High income	7786	23.2	10277	26.5	32.0	14.4
Europe EU	6179	35.1	7810	39.7	26.4	13.0
U.S. & Canada	1244	5.1	1885	7.1	51.5	40.8
Australia & New Zealand	120	5.8	235	8.5	95.8	44.8
Japan	108	0.9	136	1.1	25.9	22.8

* 1990 figure is for the entire USSR

Source: © Union of International Associations, *Yearbook of International Organizations: Guide to Civil Society Networks*, 1990 and 2000 (presenting data collected in 1989 and 1999, respectively). Data have been restructured from more comprehensive country and organisation coverage in the Yearbook of International Organizations.

The sample of organisations used is 'international NGOs (non-profit)' corresponding to categories A to F of the *Yearbook of International Organizations*:

A. Federations of international organisations · B. Universal membership organisations · C. Intercontinental membership organisations · D. Regionally oriented membership organisations · E. Organisations emanating from places, persons or bodies (A-D above) · F. Organisations of special form, including foundations and funds

Table R20 Country participation in international non-governmental organisations (INGOs)

This table indicates the extent to which organisations and individuals in each country are members of INGOs, both for 1990 and 2000. Whether an INGO has a million members or a single member in a given country, this is counted as one membership. So a count of 100 for a country means that 100 INGOs have at least one member or member organisation in that country. The table also offers data on membership density for each country, expressed as the number of memberships in INGOs per 1 million population, for the same years, and presents the percentage growth during the decade.

| Country | 1990 | | 2000 | | Absolute growth | Density growth |
	Number of organisation memberships	Membership density (per million of population)	Number of organisation memberships	Membership density (per million of population)	%	%
Afghanistan	118	7	160	7	35.6	5.6
Albania	93	28	703	227	655.9	700.3
Algeria	700	28	1,044	33	49.1	18.4
Angola	259	28	460	36	77.6	27.1
Argentina	1,870	57	2,743	74	46.7	29.0
Armenia			451	129		
Australia	2,363	138	3,702	196	56.7	41.5
Austria	2,704	350	4,340	529	60.5	51.2
Azerbaijan			350	45		
Bahamas	375	1,465	515	1,678	37.3	14.5
Bahrain	281	559	453	734	61.2	31.4
Bangladesh	655	6	1,117	9	70.5	45.7
Barbados	446	1,729	642	2,378	43.9	37.5
Belarus			730	72		
Belgium	3,639	365	5,514	541	51.5	48.1
Belize	240	1,270	402	2,010	67.5	58.3
Benin	401	85	703	115	75.3	36.1
Bhutan	65	108	131	62	101.5	-42.4
Bolivia	764	116	1,168	141	52.9	21.1
Bosnia & Herzegovina			510	128		
Botswana	361	283	671	419	85.9	48.2
Brazil	2,072	14	3,068	18	48.1	28.8
Brunei	182	708	318	970	74.7	36.9
Bulgaria	970	111	2,004	244	106.6	119.6
Burkina Faso	398	45	692	58	73.9	29.7
Burundi	281	52	474	71	68.7	37.4
Cambodia	74	8	338	30	356.8	273.0
Cameroon	607	53	1,053	70	73.5	31.8
Canada	2,674	96	4,123	133	54.2	37.8
Cape Verde	105	308	239	558	127.6	81.4
Central African Republic	264	90	414	115	56.8	28.2
Chad	216	38	396	51	83.3	36.8
Chile	1,350	103	2,122	140	57.2	35.5
China & Tibet*	1,072	1	2,113	2	97.1	75.1
Colombia	1,258	36	1,920	45	52.6	26.2
Comoros	104	241	171	246	64.4	2.3
Congo, Dem. Rep.	653	17	898	17	37.5	-0.6
Congo, Rep	385	173	575	198	49.4	14.3
Costa Rica	899	300	1,390	348	54.6	15.7
Côte d'Ivoire	676	58	996	67	47.3	15.8
Croatia			1,756	390		
Cuba	579	54	995	89	71.8	63.0

Country	1990 Number of organisation memberships	1990 Membership density (per million of population)	2000 Number of organisation memberships	2000 Membership density (per million of population)	Absolute growth %	Density growth %
Cyprus	672	987	1,258	1,601	87.2	62.2
Czech Republic			2,982	292		
Denmark	3,362	654	4,844	914	44.1	39.7
Djibouti	137	265	232	364	69.3	37.2
Dominican Republic	647	91	904	106	39.7	16.9
Ecuador	866	84	1,270	101	46.7	19.5
Egypt	1,271	24	1,892	28	48.9	14.0
El Salvador	537	105	829	132	54.4	25.2
Equatorial Guinea	95	270	164	362	72.6	34.1
Eritrea			156	40		
Estonia			1,410	1,007		
Ethiopia	461	9	792	13	71.8	40.5
Fiji	396	538	651	797	64.4	48.1
Finland	2,692	540	4,310	829	60.1	53.5
France	4,537	80	6,945	118	53.1	46.9
Gabon	341	355	506	422	48.4	18.7
Gambia	330	359	502	385	52.1	7.2
Georgia			624	125		
Germany	5,203	66	6,144	75	18.1	14.1
Ghana	811	55	1,209	60	49.1	9.7
Greece	2,123	209	3,549	335	67.2	60.2
Guatemala	717	82	1,051	92	46.6	12.5
Guinea	249	43	495	67	98.8	54.6
Guinea-Bissau	121	124	256	213	111.6	71.5
Guyana	383	482	502	583	31.1	21.0
Haiti	419	65	609	74	45.3	14.7
Honduras	529	108	804	124	52.0	14.1
Hungary	1,585	153	3,294	329	107.8	115.4
Iceland	1,061	4,161	1,635	5,819	54.1	39.8
India	2,009	2	3,005	3	49.6	25.4
Indonesia & East Timor	1,129	6	1,827	9	61.8	36.0
Iran	632	12	932	14	47.5	18.5
Iraq	516	29	517	22	0.2	-21.6
Ireland	2,091	596	3,482	941	66.5	57.8
Israel	1,870	401	3,139	383	67.9	-4.6
Italy	3,719	66	5,638	98	51.6	50.1
Jamaica	689	287	903	347	31.1	21.2
Japan	2,347	19	3,569	28	52.1	48.3
Jordan	571	180	889	133	55.7	-26.3
Kazakhstan			429	26		
Kenya	1,024	43	1,614	54	57.6	23.3
Korea, Dem. Rep.	173	8	249	10	43.9	22.7
Korea, Rep.	1,187	28	2,099	45	76.8	62.0
Kuwait	538	253	738	369	37.2	45.7
Kyrgyzstan			226	48		
Laos	89	22	231	43	159.6	93.8
Latvia			1,197	499		
Lebanon	662	182	960	291	45.0	59.7
Lesotho	322	187	512	233	59.0	24.5
Liberia	415	170	449	140	8.2	-17.7
Libya	344	78	437	78	27.0	0.2
Lithuania			1,325	358		
Luxembourg	1,439	3,767	2,107	4,889	46.4	29.8

Table R20 continued	1990		2000		Absolute growth	Density growth
Country	Number of organisation memberships	Membership density (per million of population)	Number of organisation memberships	Membership density (per million of population)	%	%
Macedonia			600	300		
Madagascar	483	42	702	44	45.3	6.3
Malawi	396	47	647	59	63.4	27.5
Malaysia	1,148	63	1,851	83	61.2	32.2
Maldives	72	338	143	500	98.6	47.9
Mali	365	43	620	55	69.9	28.3
Malta	579	1,636	1,121	2,882	93.6	76.2
Mauritania	263	130	419	155	59.3	19.5
Mauritius	536	507	801	668	49.4	31.6
Mexico	1,786	21	2,716	27	52.1	28.0
Micronesia Fed. States	26	271	103	190	296.2	-30.0
Moldova			453	103		
Mongolia	122	55	377	140	209.0	153.6
Morocco & Western Sahara	895	37	1,339	47	49.6	26.7
Mozambique	284	20	620	31	118.3	56.8
Myanmar	258	6	398	9	54.3	37.1
Namibia	146	108	633	372	333.6	244.3
Nepal	376	20	781	33	107.7	63.1
Netherlands	4,058	271	6,188	392	52.5	44.3
New Zealand	1,679	489	2,680	687	59.6	40.6
Nicaragua	496	130	768	151	54.8	16.2
Niger	296	38	495	46	67.2	20.8
Nigeria	1,190	12	1,611	14	35.4	16.8
Norway	2,753	649	4,132	918	50.1	41.5
Oman	191	117	371	148	94.2	26.4
Pakistan	923	9	1,502	10	62.7	12.3
Panama	762	318	1,026	354	34.6	11.3
Papua New Guinea	463	121	714	149	54.2	23.3
Paraguay	606	144	939	171	55.0	18.9
Peru	1,179	55	1,702	66	44.4	21.2
Philippines	1,280	20	1,985	26	55.1	27.7
Poland	1,704	45	3,367	87	97.6	94.1
Portugal	2,316	234	3,858	390	66.6	66.5
Qatar	201	414	331	553	64.7	33.6
Romania	898	39	2,228	100	148.1	158.2
Russian Federation			2,864	19		
Rwanda	311	45	525	68	68.8	52.5
Samoa	176	1,100	298	1,656	69.3	50.5
Sao Tome & Principe	62	539	126	788	103.2	46.1
Saudi Arabia	612	39	1,039	48	69.8	24.2
Senegal	758	103	1,120	118	47.8	14.0
Sierra Leone	460	115	647	132	40.7	14.8
Singapore	1,033	382	1,716	477	66.1	24.8
Slovakia			1,936	359		
Slovenia			1,808	904		
Solomon Islands	153	477	280	631	83.0	32.3
Somalia	225	29	228	23	1.3	-22.0
South Africa	1,335	38	2,689	67	101.4	75.5
Spain	3,325	86	5,325	134	60.2	57.1
Sri Lanka	903	53	1,297	69	43.6	29.8
St. Lucia	227	1,694	348	2,231	53.3	31.7
St. Vincent & the Grenadines	179	1,673	273	2,374	52.5	41.9

Country	1990 Number of organisation memberships	1990 Membership density (per million of population)	2000 Number of organisation memberships	2000 Membership density (per million of population)	Absolute growth %	Density growth %
Sudan	565	23	733	25	29.7	5.8
Suriname	255	634	347	832	36.1	31.2
Swaziland	291	378	481	477	65.3	26.3
Sweden	3,171	370	4,972	559	56.8	50.8
Switzerland	3,216	479	4,980	673	54.9	40.5
Syria	438	36	572	36	30.6	-1.7
Tajikistan			176	28		
Tanzania	675	27	1,082	32	60.3	21.9
Thailand	1,112	20	1,795	29	61.4	46.2
Togo	435	124	672	146	54.5	17.9
Trinidad & Tobago	593	488	812	625	36.9	28.0
Tunisia	833	102	1,201	125	44.2	22.5
Turkey	1,214	22	2,222	33	83.0	54.2
Turkmenistan			145	32		
Uganda	541	33	990	45	83.0	37.1
Ukraine			1,433	28		
United Arab Emirates	353	191	707	295	100.3	53.9
United Kingdom	4,882	85	7,555	128	54.8	51.5
United States	3,859	15	6,134	22	59.0	42.4
Uruguay	1,019	328	1,484	450	45.6	37.1
Uzbekistan			343	14		
Vanuatu	144	980	273	1,365	89.6	39.3
Venezuela	1,330	68	1,828	76	37.4	10.8
Vietnam	253	4	811	10	220.6	165.9
Yemen	296	25	318	18	7.4	-29.5
Yugoslavia	1,580	150	1,477	139	-6.5	-7.1
Zambia	650	84	963	105	48.2	25.4
Zimbabwe	793	81	1,330	114	67.7	39.7
World	148,501	30	255,433	43	72.0	41.4
Low income	25,938	8	43,967	12	69.5	41.2
Excl. China & India	22,857	21	38,849	28	70.0	32.2
Middle income	47,547	45	94,089	62	97.9	39.8
Lower middle income	25,763	46	50,512	56	96.1	20.6
Upper middle income	21,784	43	43,577	73	100.0	69.1
Low & middle income	190,363	28	369,811	42	94.3	49.4
East Asia & Pacific	9,255	6	16,393	9	77.1	55.2
Europe & Central Asia	8,094	46	35,235	74	335.3	62.2
Latin America & Carib.	22,697	52	33,565	65	47.9	25.3
Middle East & N. Africa	8,242	35	11,964	39	45.2	12.6
South Asia	5,121	5	8,136	6	58.9	30.4
Sub-Saharan Africa	20,076	39	32,763	51	63.2	29.6
High income	75,016	93	117,377	135	56.5	46.3
Europe EMU	56,291	150	85,518	221	51.9	47.4
U.S. & Canada	6,533	24	10,257	33	57.0	40.6
Japan	2,347	19	3,569	28	52.1	48.3
Australia & New Zealand	4,042	197	6,382	280	57.9	42.0

Table R20 continued

* China and Tibet do not include Hong Kong and Macao.

Source: © Union of International Associations, *Yearbook of International Organizations: Guide to Civil Society Networks*, 1990 and 2000 (presenting data collected in 1989 and 1999, respectively). Data have been restructured from more comprehensive country and organisation coverage in the Yearbook of International Organizations.

The sample of organisations used is "international NGOs (non-profit)", see table R19.

Table R21 Links between international organisations

This table indicates different aspects of the inter-organisational network that links international non-governmental organisations (INGOs) to each other and to international governmental organisations (IGOs). It indicates the number of citations, or references, made by either INGOs or IGOs to any other international organisation (whether INGO or IGO). Examples of citations would be (1) '... founded under the auspices of "X"' .., (2) '... financed by annual subventions from "X", "Y" and "Z" .. ', (3) '... consultative relations with "X"'. The number of links is shown for 1990 and 2000, in addition to a percentage growth figure.

Citations from INGO to IGO and INGO; Citations from IGO to IGO and INGO

Paragraph	1990	2000	% change	
Founded				
INGOs	2,895	4,021	39	The citing organisation cites another organisation as having
IGOs	2,122	3,234	52	had some role in its founding or establishment.
Total	5,017	7,255	45	
Aims				
INGOs	8	13	62	The citing organisation cites another organisation as having
IGOs	5	2	-60	something to do with its principle objectives.
Total	13	15	15	
Structure				
INGOs	671	1,467	119	The citing organisation has a structural link with another
IGOs	1,035	1,840	78	organisation, for instance as sister organisations or parent
Total	1,706	3,307	98	and subsidiary organisation.
Staff				
INGOs	-	-	0	The citing organisation shares key staff with, or is provided
IGOs	64	116	81	with staff by, the other organisation it cites.
Total	64	116	81	
Finances				
INGOs	308	2,035	561	There is a financial link between the citing organisation and
IGOs	164	475	190	another organisation.
Total	472	2,510	431	
Activities				
INGOs	1,587	2,482	56	The citing organisation cites another organisation as having
IGOs	1,715	3,797	122	a role in its activities, for instance joint activities, or
Total	3,302	6,279	90	activities aimed at the cited organisation.
Publications				
INGOs	5	19	280	The citing organisation cites another organisation as having
IGOs	19	15	-21	a role in its publications, for instance joint publications, or
Total	24	34	42	publications about the cited organisation.
Members				
INGOs	4,412	11,187	154	There is a membership link between the citing organisation
IGOs	439	1,006	129	and another organisation, for instance because one of them
Total	4,851	12,193	151	is a federation of organisations, or coordinating body of which the other is a member.
Consultative status				
INGOs	3,151	3,031	-4	The citing organisation has consultative status with another
IGOs	4	4	0	organisation. This mainly concerns INGOs having such a
Total	3,155	3,035	-4	status with IGOs.

IGO relations

INGOs	5,064	12,007	137
IGOs	8,457	14,062	66
Total	13,521	26,069	93

The citing organisation has some other form of relation with an IGO.

INGO relations

INGOs	16,919	33,660	99
IGOs	8,567	11,832	38
Total	25,486	45,492	78

The citing organisation has some other form of relation with an INGO.

Total number of orgs. cited

INGOs	8,690	11,693	35
IGOs	1,769	1,732	-2
Total	10,459	13,425	28

Total number of citations

INGOs	35,020	69,922	100
IGOs	23,191	36,383	57
Total	58,211	106,305	83

Average number of citations per org.

INGOs	4	6	48
IGOs	13	21	60
Total	5.6	7.9	42

Source: © Union of International Associations, *Yearbook of International Organizations: Guide to Civil Society Networks*, 1990 and 2000 (presenting data collected in 1989 and 1999, respectively). Data have been restructured from more comprehensive country and organisation coverage in the Yearbook of International Organizations.

The sample of organisations used is 'international NGOs (non-profit)', see Table R19.

Table R22 Nationality and memberships of international organisation leaders

The first table (R22a) gives the country of citizenship of IGO and INGO executives for the years 1996 and 2000. These people occupy prominent positions, whether elected, voluntary, or salaried, in international 'non-profit' organisations of all types; they have titles such as 'Secretary-General', 'President', 'Director', 'Chief Executive Officer', 'Chairman', 'Secretary', 'Coordinator', 'General Manager', 'Commissioner', 'Head' etc. The table also shows the number of organisation memberships of IGO and INGO executives from different countries in 1996 and 2000, and its growth. The second table (R22b) shows the density of leadership and their networks, in different countries. These membership links are part of an emerging network among INGO and IGO professionals and activists. It exists, in overlapping fashion, next to the organisational networks indicated in Table R21.

R22a Number and percentage of leaders, number and percentage of memberships

Table R22a continued	1996				2000				1996–2000	
	Leaders		Organisation memberships		Leaders		Organisation memberships		Change in % of leaders*	Change in organisation memberships*, in %
Country	Number	%	Number	%	Number	%	Number	%		
Afghanistan	0	0.0	0	0.0	0	0.0	0	0.0		
Albania	0	0.0	0	0.0	1	0.0	1	0.0		
Algeria	8	0.2	16	0.3	7	0.3	17	0.4	30.7	51.6
Angola	1	0.0	1	0.0	0	0.0	0	0.0	-100.0	-100.0
Argentina	23	0.7	44	0.7	21	0.9	43	1.0	36.4	39.4
Armenia	0	0.0	0	0.0	0	0.0	0	0.0		
Australia	56	1.7	100	1.7	42	1.9	70	1.7	12.1	-0.1
Austria	32	1.0	46	0.8	29	1.3	43	1.0	35.4	33.4
Azerbaijan	0	0.0	0	0.0	1	0.0	1	0.0		
Bahamas	0	0.0	0	0.0	0	0.0	0	0.0		
Bahrain	0	0.0	0	0.0	0	0.0	0	0.0		
Bangladesh	7	0.2	14	0.2	4	0.2	8	0.2	-14.6	-18.5
Barbados	7	0.2	14	0.2	8	0.4	14	0.3	70.8	42.7
Belarus	1	0.0	1	0.0	1	0.0	1	0.0	49.4	42.7
Belgium	283	8.5	502	8.5	190	8.5	343	8.3	0.3	-2.5
Belize	0	0.0	0	0.0	2	0.1	5	0.1		
Benin	2	0.1	12	0.2	2	0.1	9	0.2	49.4	7.0
Bhutan	0	0.0	0	0.0	1	0.0	2	0.0		
Bolivia	3	0.1	5	0.1	2	0.1	2	0.0	-0.4	-42.9
Bosnia & Herzegovina	0	0.0	0	0.0	0	0.0	0	0.0		
Botswana	2	0.1	3	0.1	1	0.0	1	0.0	-25.3	-52.4
Brazil	16	0.5	29	0.5	20	0.9	34	0.8	86.8	67.3
Brunei	0	0.0	0	0.0	0	0.0	0	0.0		
Bulgaria	5	0.1	9	0.2	6	0.3	17	0.4	79.3	169.5
Burkina Faso	2	0.1	4	0.1	0	0.0	0	0.0	-100.0	-100.0
Burundi	0	0.0	0	0.0	0	0.0	0	0.0		
Cambodia	0	0.0	0	0.0	0	0.0	0	0.0		
Cameroon	7	0.2	14	0.2	4	0.2	4	0.1	-14.6	-59.2
Canada	100	3.0	185	3.1	72	3.2	142	3.4	7.6	9.5
Cape Verde	0	0.0	0	0.0	1	0.0	2	0.0		
Central African Republic	0	0.0	0	0.0	0	0.0	0	0.0		
Chad	0	0.0	0	0.0	0	0.0	0	0.0		
Chile	11	0.3	20	0.3	9	0.4	23	0.6	22.3	64.1
China & Tibet	12	0.4	24	0.4	7	0.3	9	0.2	-12.8	-46.5
Colombia	12	0.4	23	0.4	8	0.4	17	0.4	-0.4	5.5
Comoros	0	0.0	0	0.0	0	0.0	0	0.0		

| Table R22a continued | 1996 | | | | 2000 | | | | 1996-2000 | |
Country	Leaders Number	%	Organisation memberships Number	%	Leaders Number	%	Organisation memberships Number	%	Change in % of leaders*	Change in organisation memberships*, in %
Congo, Dem. Rep.	5	0.1	7	0.1	3	0.1	6	0.1	-10.3	22.3
Congo, Rep.	3	0.1	5	0.1	1	0.0	2	0.0	-50.2	-42.9
Costa Rica	7	0.2	11	0.2	4	0.2	8	0.2	-14.6	3.8
Côte d'Ivoire	7	0.2	10	0.2	6	0.3	9	0.2	28.1	28.4
Croatia	4	0.1	10	0.2	4	0.2	14	0.3	49.4	99.7
Cuba	5	0.1	6	0.1	4	0.2	6	0.1	19.5	42.7
Cyprus	4	0.1	5	0.1	2	0.1	4	0.1	-25.3	14.1
Czech Republic	9	0.3	21	0.4	7	0.3	12	0.3	16.2	-18.5
Denmark	61	1.8	94	1.6	45	2.0	85	2.0	10.2	29.0
Djibouti	0	0.0	0	0.0	0	0.0	0	0.0		
Dominican Republic	3	0.1	5	0.1	2	0.1	3	0.1	-0.4	-14.4
Ecuador	5	0.1	9	0.2	4	0.2	5	0.1	19.5	-20.7
Egypt	21	0.6	52	0.9	15	0.7	37	0.9	6.7	1.5
El Salvador	0	0.0	0	0.0	0	0.0	0	0.0		
Equatorial Guinea	0	0.0	0	0.0	0	0.0	0	0.0		
Eritrea	0	0.0	0	0.0	1	0.0	1	0.0		
Estonia	3	0.1	7	0.1	1	0.0	1	0.0	-50.2	-79.6
Ethiopia	7	0.2	16	0.3	3	0.1	8	0.2	-36.0	-28.7
Fiji3	0.1	5	0.1	3	0.1	9	0.2	49.4	156.8	
Finland	41	1.2	97	1.6	29	1.3	63	1.5	5.7	-7.3
France	321	9.6	517	8.7	208	9.3	356	8.6	-3.2	-1.8
Gabon	0	0.0	0	0.0	0	0.0	0	0.0		
Gambia	3	0.1	11	0.2	2	0.1	11	0.3	-0.4	42.7
Georgia	0	0.0	0	0.0	1	0.0	1	0.0		
Germany	214	6.4	345	5.8	135	6.0	244	5.9	-5.7	0.9
Ghana	15	0.4	27	0.5	7	0.3	13	0.3	-30.3	-31.3
Greece	17	0.5	39	0.7	16	0.7	34	0.8	40.6	24.4
Guatemala	4	0.1	6	0.1	1	0.0	2	0.0	-62.6	-52.4
Guinea	2	0.1	3	0.1	0	0.0	0	0.0	-100.0	-100.0
Guinea-Bissau	0	0.0	0	0.0	0	0.0	0	0.0		
Guyana	5	0.1	26	0.4	3	0.1	19	0.5	-10.3	4.3
Haiti	2	0.1	2	0.0	0	0.0	0	0.0	-100.0	-100.0
Honduras	1	0.0	1	0.0	0	0.0	0	0.0	-100.0	-100.0
Hungary	21	0.6	35	0.6	10	0.4	21	0.5	-28.8	-14.4
Iceland	7	0.2	15	0.3	4	0.2	12	0.3	-14.6	14.1
India	61	1.8	132	2.2	39	1.7	83	2.0	-4.5	-10.3
Indonesia & East Timor	10	0.3	20	0.3	5	0.2	8	0.2	-25.3	-42.9
Iran	5	0.1	11	0.2	2	0.1	3	0.1	-40.2	-61.1
Iraq	12	0.4	20	0.3	6	0.3	10	0.2	-25.3	-28.7
Ireland	23	0.7	41	0.7	13	0.6	17	0.4	-15.5	-40.8
Israel & Occupied Territories	14	0.4	23	0.4	9	0.4	19	0.5	-3.9	17.9
Italy	97	2.9	176	3.0	68	3.0	135	3.2	4.7	9.4
Jamaica	6	0.2	9	0.2	1	0.0	2	0.0	-75.1	-68.3
Japan	41	1.2	71	1.2	27	1.2	37	0.9	-1.6	-25.7
Jordan	10	0.3	23	0.4	4	0.2	7	0.2	-40.2	-56.6
Kazakhstan	0	0.0	0	0.0	0	0.0	0	0.0		
Kenya	12	0.4	23	0.4	8	0.4	16	0.4	-0.4	-0.8
Korea, Dem. Rep.	7	0.2	14	0.2	7	0.3	12	0.3	49.4	22.3
Korea, Rep.	0	0.0	0	0.0	0	0.0	0	0.0		
Kuwait	2	0.1	3	0.1	4	0.2	9	0.2	198.8	328.0
Kyrgyzstan	0	0.0	0	0.0	0	0.0	0	0.0		

Country	1996 Leaders Number	%	Organisation memberships Number	%	2000 Leaders Number	%	Organisation memberships Number	%	1996–2000 Change in % of leaders*	Change in organisation memberships*, in %
Laos	0	0.0	0	0.0	0	0.0	0	0.0		
Latvia	1	0.0	1	0.0	1	0.0	1	0.0	49.4	42.7
Lebanon	6	0.2	13	0.2	5	0.2	8	0.2	24.5	-12.2
Lesotho	1	0.0	8	0.1	1	0.0	7	0.2	49.4	24.8
Liberia	1	0.0	3	0.1	0	0.0	0	0.0	-100.0	-100.0
Libya	5	0.1	11	0.2	3	0.1	3	0.1	-10.3	-61.1
Lithuania	1	0.0	1	0.0	1	0.0	1	0.0	49.4	42.7
Luxembourg	18	0.5	23	0.4	8	0.4	12	0.3	-33.6	-25.6
Macedonia	0	0.0	0	0.0	1	0.0	1	0.0		
Madagascar	1	0.0	3	0.1	1	0.0	3	0.1	49.4	42.7
Malawi	1	0.0	6	0.1	0	0.0	0	0.0	-100.0	-100.0
Malaysia	17	0.5	33	0.6	14	0.6	25	0.6	23.1	8.1
Maldives	0	0.0	0	0.0	0	0.0	0	0.0		
Mali	4	0.1	5	0.1	2	0.1	6	0.1	-25.3	71.2
Malta	4	0.1	5	0.1	4	0.2	4	0.1	49.4	14.1
Mauritania	3	0.1	5	0.1	3	0.1	5	0.1	49.4	42.7
Mauritius	5	0.1	7	0.1	3	0.1	4	0.1	-10.3	-18.5
Mexico	20	0.6	29	0.5	9	0.4	14	0.3	-32.8	-31.1
Micronesia, Fed. States	1	0.0	1	0.0	1	0.0	1	0.0	49.4	42.7
Moldova	0	0.0	0	0.0	1	0.0	1	0.0		
Mongolia	1	0.0	1	0.0	1	0.0	1	0.0	49.4	42.7
Morocco & Western Sahara	3	0.1	4	0.1	3	0.1	3	0.1	49.4	7.0
Mozambique	0	0.0	0	0.0	1	0.0	2	0.0		
Myanmar	1	0.0	1	0.0	0	0.0	0	0.0	-100.0	-100.0
Namibia	0	0.0	0	0.0	1	0.0	1	0.0		
Nepal	4	0.1	8	0.1	2	0.1	4	0.1	-25.1	-28.7
Netherlands	151	4.5	254	4.3	110	4.9	177	4.3	8.8	-0.6
New Zealand	18	0.5	27	0.5	14	0.6	23	0.6	16.2	21.5
Nicaragua	1	0.0	2	0.0	1	0.0	1	0.0	49.8	-28.7
Niger	1	0.0	3	0.1	2	0.1	3	0.1	198.8	42.7
Nigeria	30	0.9	83	1.4	23	1.0	77	1.9	14.6	32.4
Norway	40	1.2	63	1.1	23	1.0	33	0.8	-13.9	-25.3
Oman	0	0.0	0	0.0	0	0.0	0	0.0	n/a	n/a
Pakistan	15	0.4	30	0.5	8	0.4	17	0.4	-20.3	-19.2
Panama	2	0.1	3	0.1	0	0.0	0	0.0	-100.0	-100.0
Papua New Guinea	0	0.0	0	0.0	1	0.0	4	0.1		
Paraguay	0	0.0	0	0.0	0	0.0	0	0.0		
Peru	9	0.3	14	0.2	3	0.1	5	0.1	-50.1	-49.0
Philippines	28	0.8	65	1.1	19	0.9	46	1.1	1.4	1.0
Poland	18	0.5	34	0.6	10	0.4	18	0.4	-17.0	-24.5
Portugal	8	0.2	9	0.2	8	0.4	10	0.2	49.8	58.5
Qatar	0	0.0	0	0.0	0	0.0	0	0.0		
Romania	4	0.1	10	0.2	2	0.1	3	0.1	-25.3	-57.2
Russian Federation	15	0.4	34	0.6	13	0.6	35	0.8	29.8	46.9
Rwanda	0	0.0	0	0.0	0	0.0	0	0.0		
Samoa	0	0.0	0	0.0	0	0.0	0	0.0		
Sao Tome & Principe	0	0.0	0	0.0	0	0.0	0	0.0		
Saudi Arabia	16	0.5	59	1.0	16	0.7	39	0.9	49.4	-5.7
Senegal	11	0.3	26	0.4	9	0.4	21	0.5	22.3	15.2
Sierra Leone	2	0.1	4	0.1	2	0.1	2	0.0	49.8	-28.7
Singapore	11	0.3	17	0.3	12	0.5	20	0.5	63.0	67.8

| Table R22a continued | 1996 | | | | 2000 | | | | 1996-2000 | |
| | Leaders | | Organisation memberships | | Leaders | | Organisation memberships | | Change in % of leaders* | Change in organisation memberships*, in % |
Country	Number	%	Number	%	Number	%	Number	%		
Slovakia	3	0.1	3	0.1	3	0.1	3	0.1	49.4	42.7
Slovenia	3	0.1	5	0.1	4	0.2	6	0.1	99.8	71.2
Solomon Islands	0	0.0	0	0.0	0	0.0	0	0.0		
Somalia	0	0.0	0	0.0	0	0.0	0	0.0		
South Africa	9	0.3	14	0.2	4	0.2	6	0.1	-33.4	-38.9
Spain	45	1.3	94	1.6	32	1.4	67	1.6	6.3	1.7
Sri Lanka	18	0.5	31	0.5	12	0.5	30	0.7	-0.4	38.1
St. Lucia	0	0.0	0	0.0	0	0.0	0	0.0		
St. Vincent & the Grenadines	0	0.0	0	0.0	0	0.0	0	0.0		
Sudan	8	0.2	20	0.3	6	0.3	19	0.5	12.1	35.5
Suriname	0	0.0	0	0.0	0	0.0	0	0.0		
Swaziland	0	0.0	0	0.0	1	0.0	6	0.1		
Sweden	72	2.2	122	2.1	45	2.0	80	1.9	-6.6	-6.4
Switzerland	93	2.8	160	2.7	68	3.0	120	2.9	9.5	7.0
Syria	2	0.1	3	0.1	2	0.1	6	0.1	49.4	185.3
Tajikistan	0	0.0	0	0.0	1	0.0	1	0.0		
Tanzania	7	0.2	8	0.1	5	0.2	7	0.2	7.0	24.8
Thailand	10	0.3	18	0.3	9	0.4	16	0.4	34.5	26.8
Togo	5	0.1	8	0.1	2	0.1	2	0.0	-40.2	-64.3
Trinidad & Tobago	1	0.0	2	0.0	1	0.0	2	0.0	49.8	42.7
Tunisia	11	0.3	21	0.4	10	0.4	18	0.4	35.8	22.3
Turkey	8	0.2	19	0.3	9	0.4	18	0.4	68.1	35.2
Turkmenistan	0	0.0	0	0.0	0	0.0	0	0.0		
Uganda	7	0.2	15	0.3	3	0.1	5	0.1	-36.0	-52.4
Ukraine	0	0.0	0	0.0	2	0.1	4	0.1		
United Arab Emirates	0	0.0	0	0.0	0	0.0	0	0.0		
United Kingdom	455	13.6	721	12.2	269	12.0	456	11.0	-11.7	-9.8
United States	378	11.3	667	11.3	227	10.2	440	10.6	-10.3	-5.9
Uruguay	12	0.4	30	0.5	8	0.4	20	0.5	-0.1	-4.9
Uzbekistan	0	0.0	0	0.0	0	0.0	0	0.0		
Vanuatu	0	0.0	0	0.0	0	0.0	0	0.0		
Venezuela	10	0.3	20	0.3	9	0.4	17	0.4	34.8	21.3
Vietnam	0	0.0	0	0.0	0	0.0	0	0.0		
Yemen	0	0.0	0	0.0	0	0.0	0	0.0		
Yugoslavia	1	0.0	1	0.0	0	0.0	0	0.0	-100.0	-100.0
Zambia	4	0.1	8	0.1	0	0.0	0	0.0	-100.0	-100.0
Zimbabwe	5	0.1	9	0.2	6	0.3	11	0.3	79.3	74.4
Stateless / UN Refugee	3	0.1	5	0.1	1	0.0	2	0.0	-50.1	-42.9
Total	3338	100.0	5928	100.0	2234	100.0	4155	100.0		

Sample sizes: *1996: 3,346 citizenships (= 3,275 individuals + 71 (individuals with dual nationality); 2000: 2,241 citizenships (= 2,218 individuals + 23 individuals with dual nationality); 1996: 5,942 organisations; 2000: 4,165 organisations.* * Adjusted for sample size

Sources: International organisation secretariats: © Union of International Associations, *Yearbook of International Organizations: Guide to Civil Society Networks,* 1990 and 2000 (presenting data collected in 1989 and 1999, respectively). Data have been restructured from more comprehensive country and organisation coverage in the *Yearbook of International Organizations.* International organisation leaders: © Union of International Associations, *Who's Who in International Organizations,* 1996 and 2000 (presenting data collected in 1995 and 1999, respectively. Data have been restructured from more comprehensive coverage in the *Who's Who.*

R22b Density of leaders, by country of citizenship, and their organisational memberships, by country of secretariat, 2000

Country	Leaders	Organisation membership	Country	Leaders	Organisation membership
	\(per million of population\)			\(per million of population\)	
Afghanistan	0	0	Ecuador	0.3	0.4
Albania	0.3	0.3	Egypt	0.2	0.5
Algeria	0.2	0.5	El Salvador	0.0	0.0
Angola	0.0	0.0	Equatorial Guinea	0.0	0.0
Argentina	0.6	1.2	Eritrea	0.3	0.3
Armenia	0.0	0.0	Estonia	0.7	0.7
Australia	2.2	3.7	Ethiopia	0.0	0.1
Austria	3.5	5.2	Fiji	3.7	11.0
Azerbaijan	0.1	0.1	Finland	5.6	12.1
Bahamas	0.0	0.0	France	3.5	6.0
Bahrain	0.0	0.0	Gabon	0.0	0.0
Bangladesh	0.0	0.1	Gambia	1.5	8.4
Barbados	29.6	51.9	Georgia	0.2	0.2
Belarus	0.1	0.1	Germany	1.6	3.0
Belgium	18.6	33.6	Ghana	0.3	0.6
Belize	10.0	25.0	Greece	1.5	3.2
Benin	0.3	1.5	Guatemala	0.1	0.2
Bhutan	0.5	1.0	Guinea	0.0	0.0
Bolivia	0.2	0.2	Guinea-Bissau	0.0	0.0
Bosnia &			Guyana	3.5	22.1
Herzegovina	0.0	0.0	Haiti	0.0	0.0
Botswana	0.6	0.6	Honduras	0.0	0.0
Brazil	0.1	0.2	Hungary	1.0	2.1
Brunei	0.0	0.0	Iceland	14.2	42.7
Bulgaria	0.7	2.1	India	0.0	0.1
Burkina Faso	0.0	0.0	Indonesia & East Timor	0.0	0.0
Burundi	0.0	0.0	Iran	0.0	0.0
Cambodia	0.0	0.0	Iraq	0.3	0.4
Cameroon	0.3	0.3	Ireland	3.5	4.6
Canada	2.3	4.6	Israel	1.3	2.9
Cape Verde	2.3	4.7	Italy	1.2	2.4
Central African Republic	0.0	0.0	Jamaica	0.4	0.8
Chad	0.0	0.0	Japan	0.2	0.3
Chile	0.6	1.5	Jordan	0.6	1.0
China & Tibet	0.0	0.0	Kazakhstan	0.0	0.0
Colombia	0.2	0.4	Kenya	0.3	0.5
Comoros	0.0	0.0	Korea, Dem Rep.	0.3	0.5
Congo, Dem. Rep.	0.1	0.1	Korea, Rep.	0.0	0.0
Congo, Rep.	0.3	0.7	Kuwait	2.0	4.5
Costa Rica	1.0	2.0	Kyrgyzstan	0.0	0.0
Côte d'Ivoire	0.4	0.6	Laos	0.0	0.0
Croatia	0.9	3.1	Latvia	0.4	0.4
Cuba	0.4	0.5	Lebanon	1.5	2.4
Cyprus	2.5	5.1	Lesotho	0.5	3.2
Czech Republic	0.7	1.2	Liberia	0.0	0.0
Denmark	8.5	16.0	Libya	0.5	0.5
Djibouti	0.0	0.0	Lithuania	0.3	0.3
Dominican Republic	0.2	0.4	Luxembourg	18.6	27.8

Table R22b continued	Leaders	Organisation membership	Country	Leaders	Organisation membership
Country	(per million of population)			(per million of population)	
Macedonia	0.5	0.3	Senegal	0.9	2.2
Madagascar	0.1	0.2	Sierra Leone	0.4	0.4
Malawi	0.0	0.0	Singapore	3.3	5.6
Malaysia	0.6	1.1	Slovakia	0.6	0.6
Maldives	0.0	0.0	Slovenia	2.0	0.0
Mali	0.2	0.5	Solomon Islands	0.0	0.0
Malta	10.3	10.3	Somalia	0.0	0.0
Mauritania	1.1	1.9	South Africa	0.1	0.1
Mauritius	2.5	3.3	Spain	0.8	1.7
Mexico	0.1	0.1	Sri Lanka	0.6	1.6
Micronesia Fed. States	1.8	1.8	St Lucia	0.2	0.0
Moldova		0.2 0.2	St Vincent & the Grenadines	0.0	0.0
Mongolia	0.4	0.4	Sudan	0.0	0.6
Morocco & Western Sahara	0.1	0.1	Suriname	0.0	0.0
Mozambique	0.1	0.1	Swaziland	1.0	6.0
Myanmar	0.0	0.0	Sweden	5.1	9.0
Namibia	0.6	0.6	Switzerland	9.2	16.2
Nepal	0.1	0.2	Syria	0.1	0.4
Netherlands	7.0	11.2	Tajikistan	0.2	0.2
New Zealand	3.6	5.9	Tanzania	0.1	0.2
Nicaragua	0.2	0.2	Thailand	0.1	0.3
Niger	0.2	0.3	Togo	0.4	0.4
Nigeria	0.2	0.7	Trinidad & Tobago	0.8	1.5
Norway	5.1	7.3	Tunisia	1.0	1.9
Oman	0.0	0.0	Turkey	0.1	0.3
Pakistan	0.1	0.1	Turkmenistan	0.0	0.0
Panama	0.0	0.0	Uganda	0.1	0.2
Papua New Guinea	0.2	0.8	Ukraine	0.0	0.1
Paraguay	0.0	0.0	United Arab Emirates	0.0	0.0
Peru	0.1	0.2	United Kingdom	4.6	7.8
Philippines	0.3	0.6	United States	0.8	1.6
Poland	0.3	0.5	Uruguay	2.4	6.1
Portugal	0.8	1.0	Uzbekistan	0.0	0.0
Qatar	0.0	0.0	Vanuatu	0.0	0.0
Romania	0.1	0.1	Venezuela	0.4	0.7
Russian Federation	0.1	0.2	Vietnam	0.0	0.0
Rwanda	0.0	0.0	Yemen	0.0	0.0
Samoa	0.0	0.0	Yugoslavia	0.0	0.0
Sao Tome & Principe	0.0	0.0	Zambia	0.0	0.0
Saudi Arabia	0.7	1.8	Zimbabwe	0.5	0.9

Sample sizes: 2,241 citizenships (= 2,218 individuals + 23 (individuals with dual nationality); 4,165 organisations

Sources: International organisation secretariats: © Union of International Associations, *Yearbook of International Organizations: Guide to Civil Society Networks*, 1990 and 2000 (presenting data collected in 1989 and 1999, respectively). Data have been restructured from more comprehensive country and organisation coverage in the *Yearbook of International Organizations*. International organisation leaders: © Union of International Associations, *Who's Who in International Organizations*, 1996 and 2000 (presenting data collected in 1995 and 1999, respectively. Data have been restructured from more comprehensive coverage in the *Who's Who*.

Table R23 Percentage and growth of international non-governmental organisations (INGOs) by purpose

Following the International Classification of Nonprofit Organisations, this table presents data on the purposes of INGO activities by the country in which the organisation secretariat is located, for the year 2000 (R23a). The classification is based on a content analysis by coding the title or statement of purpose of each INGO according to key words. It includes only countries with 100 or more coded references from the UIA database. The classification does not, therefore, report actual activities or expenditures but only statements of intent. Table R23b and **Figure R4** show the overall growth rate between 1990 and 2000 by purpose.

R23a

Country of secretariat	Culture and Recreation %	Education %	Research %	Health %	Social services %	Environment %	Economic Development, Infrastructure %	Law, policy, advocacy %	Religion %	Defence %	Politics %
Argentina	5.2	6.3	22.7	7.8	13.4	1.1	22.7	13.4	5.2	0.0	2.2
Australia	7.5	5.2	31.9	8.7	11.0	2.6	17.2	9.6	4.2	0.0	2.1
Austria	9.5	4.8	24.8	3.2	11.4	1.5	25.1	12.1	1.2	1.0	5.4
Belgium	4.3	4.6	18.5	4.7	11.4	3.2	37.2	9.9	2.4	0.5	3.4
Brazil	7.2	6.1	30.9	8.3	8.8	2.8	17.1	11.6	3.9	0.0	3.3
Canada	8.4	7.2	24.5	6.4	11.0	3.6	21.7	9.1	4.5	0.4	3.4
Chile	3.1	6.3	26.6	2.3	15.6	3.9	28.9	9.4	2.3	0.0	1.6
China (Hong Kong)	5.4	7.0	17.1	10.9	12.4	1.6	14.7	14.0	14.0	0.0	3.1
Colombia	3.6	9.8	22.3	6.3	9.8	2.7	23.2	9.8	11.6	0.0	0.9
Costa Rica	1.6	10.2	20.3	1.6	17.2	4.7	24.2	18.0	0.0	0.0	2.3
Côte d'Ivoire	13.9	9.6	17.4	3.5	7.8	4.3	27.0	8.7	5.2	0.0	2.6
Czech Republic	3.3	4.9	30.3	9.0	16.4	3.3	11.5	11.5	4.9	0.0	4.9
Denmark	6.7	6.0	27.8	10.2	11.0	3.6	22.2	7.2	1.9	0.2	3.1
Egypt	14.0	2.2	12.9	3.4	10.7	4.5	22.5	19.7	4.5	0.6	5.1
Finland	5.9	10.1	25.0	9.7	11.8	4.2	22.2	6.6	1.7	0.0	2.8
France	9.7	5.1	23.2	4.7	11.4	2.7	26.2	10.1	2.9	0.6	3.4
Germany	8.0	4.2	24.5	6.9	9.8	2.6	27.3	8.6	4.8	0.5	2.9
Ghana	4.7	10.3	11.2	2.8	11.2	1.9	19.6	12.1	20.6	0.0	5.6
Greece	10.6	6.5	25.9	10.6	7.1	4.1	10.6	12.4	5.9	2.4	4.1
Hungary	16.3	6.8	29.9	1.4	5.4	5.4	20.4	4.8	3.4	0.7	5.4
India	2.4	6.3	25.9	6.6	11.4	3.6	17.5	14.8	8.7	0.0	2.7
Ireland	6.7	8.7	23.1	8.7	16.3	1.9	25.0	6.7	0.0	0.0	2.9
Israel	8.5	1.7	18.1	1.1	6.2	1.1	13.6	20.3	24.3	1.1	4.0
Italy	6.7	3.7	29.3	5.5	9.3	2.2	20.5	9.8	10.5	0.7	1.8
Japan	7.5	4.3	29.8	5.0	11.1	2.4	23.6	8.7	1.7	1.0	5.0
Kenya	0.8	7.3	26.3	2.8	12.3	6.7	24.4	6.4	11.8	0.0	1.1
Luxembourg	12.6	0.9	12.6	4.5	17.1	2.7	31.5	9.0	5.4	0.9	2.7
Malaysia	4.5	1.9	21.3	8.4	12.9	5.8	28.4	9.7	5.8	0.0	1.3
Mexico	6.7	8.3	24.1	7.9	10.7	6.3	22.5	8.3	1.2	0.0	4.0
Netherlands	8.3	6.1	24.0	6.3	10.5	3.6	25.1	9.5	2.3	1.0	3.3
Nigeria	4.5	6.1	25.8	6.8	9.8	5.3	18.2	10.6	8.3	1.5	3.0
Norway	6.9	7.2	31.2	4.6	9.0	4.3	21.7	9.5	0.9	0.6	4.0
Peru	7.1	0.9	15.2	5.4	13.4	6.3	24.1	19.6	0.0	0.0	8.0
Philippines	2.2	6.9	16.8	5.8	12.4	6.9	28.1	11.7	5.8	0.0	3.3
Portugal	15.7	10.2	19.7	4.7	11.8	0.8	22.0	7.1	4.7	0.0	3.1

Table R23a continued

Country of secretariat	Culture and Recreation %	Education %	Research %	Health %	Social services %	Environment %	Economic Development, Infrastructure %	Law, policy, advocacy %	Religion %	Defence %	Politics %
Russian Federation	1.6	8.5	27.9	3.1	12.4	4.7	13.2	17.1	4.7	2.3	4.7
Senegal	6.9	3.1	18.2	0.6	13.8	3.1	37.1	13.2	1.3	0.0	2.5
Singapore	9.1	3.7	29.9	8.5	8.5	0.6	23.2	7.9	7.9	0.6	0.0
South Africa	7.2	3.6	24.4	6.4	9.2	7.2	20.4	6.4	13.6	0.0	1.6
Spain	7.0	5.0	27.6	6.3	9.3	4.0	25.7	9.8	1.2	0.8	3.5
Sweden	7.3	4.1	30.3	8.7	13.4	2.8	20.1	6.7	2.3	1.3	3.0
Switzerland	8.5	4.0	16.7	4.9	13.5	2.1	26.7	12.5	6.6	0.6	3.9
Thailand	0.9	5.2	27.4	6.1	13.7	8.5	17.0	16.0	2.8	0.0	2.4
United Kingdom	6.1	3.7	23.5	5.3	12.4	3.3	27.8	9.7	4.3	0.9	3.0
United States	6.4	4.0	26.9	6.0	11.6	2.9	21.1	10.9	6.0	0.5	3.5
Uruguay	4.7	3.9	28.9	5.5	13.3	6.3	18.8	15.6	1.6	0.0	1.6
Vatican	4.3	2.9	7.1	2.4	5.2	1.9	10.5	10.5	54.8	0.0	0.5
Venezuela	5.1	7.6	18.7	2.5	18.2	1.5	24.7	15.7	1.5	0.5	4.0
Zimbabwe	4.0	5.6	13.5	2.4	14.3	2.4	23.8	19.8	9.5	0.0	4.8

Source: © Union of International Associations, Y*earbook of International Organizations: Guide to Civil Society Networks*, 1990 and 2000 (presenting data collected in 1989 and 1999, respectively). Data have been restructured from more comprehensive country and organisation coverage in the Yearbook of International Organizations. *The sample of organisations used is 'international NGOs (non-profit)', see Table R19.*

R23b Overall growth rate of number of international non-governmental organisations (INGOs) by purpose

GCS Code	1990	2000	% Growth 1990-2000
Culture and recreation	2,169	2,733	26.0
Education	1,485	1,839	23.8
Research	7,675	8,467	10.3
Health	1,357	2,036	50.0
Social services	2,361	4,215	78.5
Environment	979	1,170	19.5
Economic development, infrastructure	9,582	9,614	0.3
Law, policy and advocacy	2,712	3,864	42.5
Religion	1,407	1,869	32.8
Defence	244	234	-4.1
Politics	1,275	1,240	-2.7
Totals	31,246	37,281	19.3

Figure R4: Growth of international non-governmental organisations by purpose

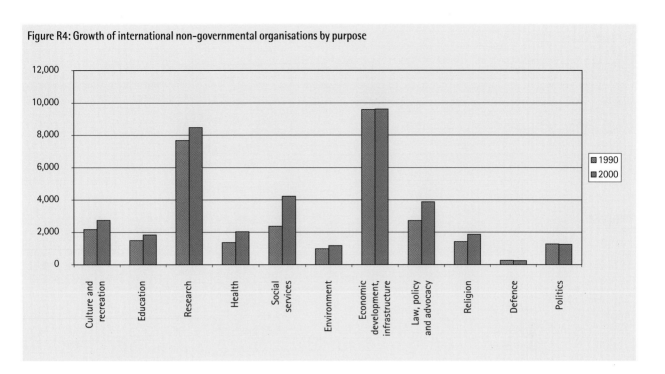

Table R24: Employment, volunteering and revenue of international non–governmental organisations (INGOs)

For a selected number of countries that participated in the Johns Hopkins Comparative Nonprofit Sector Project, these tables offer employment and volunteering figures (R24a), and revenue structure (R24b) for non-profit organisations operating primarily at the international level. This includes prominently international humanitarian and relief organisations as well as INGOs active in supporting development, but also associations promoting international understanding, exchange, and friendship. The first part of the revenue table shows the percentages in terms of pure cash flow, while the second accounts for the financial value of volunteer input.

R24a Employment and volunteering

1995/1996

Country	INGOs Paid FTE employment 1995	INGOs Number of FTE volunteers	Total non-profit sector Paid FTE employment 1995	Total non-profit sector Number of FTE volunteers	INGOs as % of total nonprofit sector In % of paid employment,	INGOs as % of total nonprofit sector In % of paid employment and volunteers, 1995
Argentina	5,201	7	395,315	26,4110	0.13	0.08
Australia	919	1,227	402,574	177,148	0.02	0.04
Austria	1,110		143,637	40,686	0.08	0.06
Belgium	594	1,018	357,802	99,099	0.02	0.04
Brazil	4,182		1,034,550	139,216	0.04	0.04
Colombia	181	22	286,861	90,756	0.01	0.01
Czech Republic	814	816	74,196	40,860	0.11	0.14
Finland	160	367	62,848	7,4751	0.03	0.04
France	17,403	30,986	959,821	1,021,655	0.18	0.24
Germany	9,750	28,510	1,440,850	97,8074	0.07	0.16
Hungary	342	226	44,938	9,878	0.08	0.10
Ireland	370	234	118,664	31,650	0.03	0.04
Israel	98		145,396	31,261	0.01	0.01
Japan	7,693	37,785	2,140,079	695,097	0.04	0.16
Mexico			93,809	47,215		0.00
Netherlands	3,860	8,644	652,829	390,101	0.06	0.12
Peru	3		133,557	26,883	0.00	0.00
Romania	485	2,828	37,353	46,508	0.13	0.04
Slovakia	138	68	16,196	6,851	0.09	0.09
Spain	9,380	9,794	475,179	253,599	0.20	0.26
United Kingdom	53,726	7,298	1,415,743	1,120,283	0.38	0.24
United States		45,026	8,554,900	4,994,162		0.03

Source: The Johns Hopkins Comparative Nonprofit Sector Project, 1999.

R24b Revenue structure

1995/1996 Country	Cash revenue only			Cash and volunteer input		
	Public sector payments %	Private giving %	Private fees and charges %	Public sector payments %	Private giving %	Private fees and charges %
Argentina	100	–	–	100	0	–
Australia	30	70	–	26	74	–
Austria	40	55	5	40	55	5
Belgium	33	58	9	28	64	8
Brazil	–	–	100	–	–	100
Colombia	–	99	1	–	99	1
Czech Republic	37	52	11	23	70	7
Finland	30	8	61	14	58	28
France	43	40	17	16	78	6
Germany	51	41	8	15	83	2
Hungary	66	14	20	64	17	19
Ireland	24	76	–	22	78	–
Israel	23	51	26	23	51	26
Japan	19	27	54	5	82	14
Netherlands	45	35	20	35	50	15
Peru	–	3	97	–	3	97
Romania	47	31	22	8	88	4
Slovakia	22	21	57	22	24	55
Spain	56	36	8	32	63	5
United Kingdom	40	33	27	38	36	26

Source: The Johns Hopkins Comparative Nonprofit Sector Project, 1999.

Table R25: Geographical identification

Based on population survey data provided by the European and World Values Survey, this table offers the responses to the following question: Which of these geographical groups would you say you 'belong to' first of all?

- Locality or town where you live?
- Region of country where you live?
- Your country as a whole
- Continent on which you life
- The world as a whole?

Country	in % of all respondents per country	1990–1993					2000				
		Locality or town	Region or county	Country	Continent	World	Town	Region	Country	Continent	World
Albania							62.0	15.2	21.3	1.4	0.1
Argentina		28.1	3.3	57.8	1.0	9.9	31.5	13.7	41.6	4.0	9.2
Armenia							33.1	10.0	45.5	1.5	10.0
Australia							32.7	12.8	43.8	0.8	10.0
Austria		34.5	31.5	27.3	3.5	3.2	35.0	33.9	24.0	4.2	2.9
Azerbaijan							20.6	16.2	45.1		18.0
Belarus							66.0	1.2	24.8	1.4	6.5
Belgium		49.0	14.0	20.1	7.8	9.1	32.1	20.3	27.9	9.3	10.4
Bosnia & Herzegovina							39.6	13.8	32.2	4.6	9.4
Brazil		36.9	11.2	30.6	1.8	19.6	30.9	11.6	28.5	2.2	26.8
Bulgaria		50.5	8.7	29.7	4.1	7.1	47.0	4.7	41.0	3.8	3.5
Canada		30.9	16.2	39.7	2.9	10.3					
Chile		32.5	14.5	39.6	5.1	8.3	32.4	13.9	39.7	6.1	7.9
China & Tibet		41.9	15.9	38.1	2.0	2.1	40.1	11.8	39.3	4.4	4.4
Colombia							34.5	8.8	25.1	5.4	20.7
Croatia							57.7	7.4	23.1	3.5	8.3
Czech Republic							42.9	13.7	35.5	2.7	5.3
Denmark		52.3	22.2	21.8	1.6	2.1	55.0	21.9	19.8	1.4	1.8
Dominican Republic							41.7	16.8	8.8	12.8	19.8
Estonia		31.2	55.7	8.4	1.4	3.3	61.4	12.2	21.4	1.4	3.6
Finland		32.5	11.9	41.3	5.4	8.8	48.6	12.2	31.0	3.2	4.3
France		40.5	13.8	27.9	7.9	9.9	43.8	12.6	29.0	4.1	10.5
Georgia							29.4	10.1	50.1	1.0	9.4
Germany*		38.0	33.2	15.7	5.9	7.3	55.2	29.6	10.1	2.9	2.2
Ghana							17.2	7.8	56.3	17.2	1.6
Greece							44.8	12.0	33.2	1.2	8.8
Hungary		58.0	5.8	27.4	5.9	2.8	67.3	6.3	20.1	2.0	4.3
Iceland		40.5	5.9	48.4	0.6	4.7	38.3	6.3	50.6	0.7	4.0
India		37.2	14.6	39.0	1.3	7.9	61.9	29.6	8.3	0.2	
Ireland		43.9	13.6	37.3	2.5	2.6	56.6	15.8	24.0	2.2	1.4
Italy		39.8	10.7	27.7	5.5	16.3	53.4	10.6	23.3	4.2	8.5
Japan		36.2	17.9	43.2	1.1	1.5	57.0	17.3	23.5	0.8	1.3
Korea, Rep.		18.1	23.7	58.3			41.5	21.2	33.7	0.5	3.2
Latvia		33.7	55.3	5.8	0.7	4.4	40.6	13.5	38.8	2.2	4.8
Lithuania		25.4	66.0	3.1	1.2	4.3	51.4	4.8	37.2	2.8	3.8
Luxembourg							43.1	11.0	24.4	13.4	8.0

Country	1990-1993 Locality or town	Region or county	Country	Continent	World	2000 Town	Region	Country	Continent	World
Macedonia						*48.8*	*6.9*	*34.7*	*2.6*	*7.0*
Mexico	38.2	15.5	28.4	8.2	9.7	33.4	10.3	35.4	3.7	17.1
Moldova						*34.8*	*9.6*	*31.4*	*1.8*	*22.4*
Netherlands	44.1	7.3	35.1	4.4	9.2	39.1	7.7	41.2	4.8	7.2
New Zealand						*28.9*	*7.9*	*53.3*	*1.7*	*8.2*
Nigeria	39.7	10.4	29.7	11.6	8.6	41.7	16.4	30.7	8.9	2.2
Norway	69.2	13.1	14.1	1.2	2.3	*56.3*	*17.8*	*20.2*	*3.2*	*2.6*
Peru						*38.0*	*21.2*	*29.2*	*4.4*	*7.2*
Philippines						*46.6*	*24.8*	*19.9*	*1.5*	*7.2*
Poland	29.0	12.1	52.3	4.2	2.4	62.7	15.0	19.1	2.3	0.9
Portugal	39.8	23.0	23.6	4.0	9.6	36.3	16.0	41.6	1.6	4.5
Romania	48.0	15.0	31.8	2.0	3.2	45.2	19.5	30.4	1.6	3.3
Russian Federation	39.8	28.7	12.6	1.1	17.9	50.6	7.9	25.2	0.4	15.8
Slovakia	36.9	30.7	23.0	4.5	4.9	54.0	10.5	26.7	4.6	4.2
Slovenia	45.6	8.5	41.7	2.0	2.3	52.8	8.7	32.1	2.4	3.9
South Africa	35.6	16.4	38.1	4.6	5.2	*32.7*	*13.3*	*44.9*	*3.7*	*5.4*
Spain	43.6	17.5	30.4	1.4	7.2	40.8	20.6	29.4	1.8	7.3
Sweden	56.3	12.6	24.7	3.2	3.3	58.7	9.5	22.4	4.2	5.3
Switzerland	51.2	20.2	16.6	3.6	8.4	*28.7*	*22.8*	*26.5*	*7.2*	*14.7*
Turkey	33.6	11.7	45.5	1.2	8.0	*25.0*	*7.2*	*51.3*	*0.6*	*15.9*
Ukraine						49.5	7.7	26.1	1.8	14.9
United Kingdom	41.9	19.5	28.2	2.3	8.1	48.9	13.7	28.4	1.9	7.2
United States	38.1	12.1	30.2	3.7	15.9	32.6	10.9	34.4	2.6	19.5
Uruguay						*23.0*	*7.7*	*52.0*	*6.9*	*10.4*
Venezuela						*26.4*	*18.8*	*42.1*	*3.8*	*9.0*
Yugoslavia						*55.1*	*11.3*	*25.8*	*2.6*	*5.3*
Average	40.1	19.0	30.6	3.5	7.2	43.2	13.5	31.7	3.5	8.1

*90-93 data West-Germany only

Values in italics indicate that 1995-1997 data have been used

Sources: © European Values Survey, WORC, Tilburg University, Netherlands, 1999-2000, by permission; © World Values Survey, Institute for Social Research, University of Michigan, by permission; R. Inglehart, M. Basañez, and A. Moreno, *Human Values and Beliefs: A Cross-Cultural Sourcebook: Political, Religious, Sexual, and Economic Norms in 43 Societies: Findings from the 1990–1993 World Values Survey* (Ann Arbor: The University of Michigan Press, 1998).

R26 Tolerance

Using two different questions from the European and World Values Survey, these tables present various aspects of tolerance in relationship to other values and as an attitudinal measure of discrimination against 'outsiders'. The first (R26a) shows responses to the following question: Here is a list of qualities which children can be encouraged to learn at home. Which, if any, do you consider to be especially important? (Multiple responses possible.)

- Tolerance and respect for other people
- Independence
- Responsibility
- Obedience
- Unselfishness

The second table (R26b) shows responses to the following question: On this list are various groups of people. Could you please tell me any that you would not, generally speaking, like to have as your neighbours?

- People of different races
- Immigrants / foreign workers

R26a Tolerance, responsibility, unselfishness, independence and obedience as qualities in children

Country	in % of all respondents per country	1990–1993					2000				
		Tolerance	Responsibility	Unselfishness	Independence	Obedience	Tolerance	Responsibility	Unselfishness	Independence	Obedience
Albania							85.5				
Argentina		77.6	80.3	4.8	43.2	32.0	70.2				
Armenia							48.5	68.6	30.6	32.0	18.0
Australia							80.7	66.1	39.7	52.9	29.2
Austria		65.7	84.5	7.3	63.2	25.3	71.4	86.1	5.4	70.5	16.7
Azerbaijan							59.1	65.5	16.6	59.7	24.8
Belarus		79.8	81.5	26.9	31.3	22.5	71.8	76.4	16.9	31.5	33.7
Belgium		69.2	72.3	27.4	35.5	37.3	83.5	80.0	35.3	41.0	41.9
Bosnia & Herzegovina							61.3	61.3	29.0	36.8	40.9
Brazil		65.5	71.8	28.3	26.5	41.3	59.4	64.6	32.4	19.9	59.0
Bulgaria		51.5	68.0	22.1	62.2	18.7	58.9	75.1	14.3	41.9	15.8
Canada		80.0	75.1	42.2	43.8	28.4					
Chile		79.0	88.3	7.9	30.5	52.2	76.0				
China & Tibet		62.1	67.5	29.3	85.8	9.4	43.0				
Colombia							68.5	77.0	37.4	27.1	43.1
Croatia							93.8	93.6	89.9	86.3	83.3
Czech Republic							62.9	65.6	36.8	68.9	17.2
Denmark		80.5	85.7	50.3	80.6	20.1	87.0	80.8	55.7	80.4	14.3
Dominican Republic							67.9	84.4	12.2	40.0	50.8
Estonia		70.2	76.1	24.9	42.6	18.8	70.9	78.3	16.4	21.7	28.4
Finland		78.9	82.7	20.7	56.6	25.2	82.5	86.0	20.7	57.5	30.1
France		78.0	71.5	39.8	26.7	52.8	84.4	73.1	40.1	28.9	36.3
Germany*		76.6	84.7	7.6	73.1	22.4	72.6	83.4	7.1	70.0	11.8
Greece							55.9	73.9	22.2	46.3	16.8

Country	1990–1993					2000				
	Tolerance	Responsibility	Unselfishness	Independence	Obedience	Tolerance	Responsibility	Unselfishness	Independence	Obedience
Hungary	61.6	65.7	25.7	69.7	44.6	64.7	72.4	21.1	70.0	32.9
Iceland	93.0	93.7	75.2	88.7	67.8	84.1	80.8	34.5	76.1	17.4
Ireland	76.7	61.1	52.8	43.3	35.0	75.0	53.2	49.3	50.6	47.4
Italy	66.9	83.4	39.8	33.8	32.0	74.7	81.2	41.3	41.0	27.7
Japan	59.5	84.3	44.0	64.5	10.1	71.2				
Korea, Rep.	55.4	90.8	10.6	54.4	18.1	*46.9*				
Latvia	69.7	75.2	15.8	72.5	15.3	69.5	74.1	11.5	50.8	20.4
Lithuania	56.7	72.3	33.2	80.8	24.5	56.5	75.0	28.0	75.4	19.4
Luxembourg						78.0	78.3	25.7	48.6	26.1
Macedonia						*70.6*	*73.8*	*60.5*	*61.9*	*18.4*
Malta						61.0	76.4	45.7	30.1	41.0
Mexico	64.3	76.6	11.0	47.3	45.1	71.8				
Moldova						*63.4*	*66.5*	*9.3*	*35.9*	*39.4*
Netherlands	87.3	85.4	21.8	50.7	32.4	90.4	86.0	26.7	52.4	26.8
Nigeria	75.1	35.9	17.3	16.3	70.7	59.1				
Norway	63.7	89.7	9.5	86.0	31.3	*65.9*				
Pakistan						*55.3*	*71.3*	*30.8*	*19.8*	*32.0*
Peru						*63.0*	*77.5*	*15.6*	*20.8*	*50.1*
Philippines						*47.6*	*57.9*	*30.6*	*51.1*	*44.3*
Poland	25.4	25.7	3.1	3.7	8.7	79.6	72.7	12.1	22.1	32.3
Portugal	68.8	76.7	28.2	23.8	45.0	65.3	60.0	40.0	22.4	38.7
Romania	56.0	56.1	19.7	23.8	19.5	55.6	59.2	6.5	28.4	18.0
Russian Federation**	70.0	68.6	25.0	27.7	28.5	66.9	75.6	20.5	30.8	33.6
Slovakia	62.7	67.0	27.7	22.1	38.0	57.0	66.8	18.6	61.3	26.4
Slovenia	74.5	71.3	33.1	32.6	39.8	70.1	76.0	37.6	70.3	25.1
South Africa	61.2	44.6	19.9	16.2	41.8	*67.9*				
Spain	72.7	77.2	8.4	36.2	42.8	82.1	84.6	3.4	33.6	48.4
Sweden	90.8	89.0	29.1	36.4	24.9	92.5	86.9	32.7	68.7	12.7
Switzerland	77.0	77.4	37.2	42.3	20.4	*78.6*				
Turkey	69.1	65.7	27.8	19.2	31.4	*61.3*				
Ukraine						65.0	74.5	15.3	31.6	35.1
United Kingdom***	79.2	47.6	57.4	42.9	39.4	83.0	56.1	59.7	52.9	48.8
United States	71.8	71.1	37.0	52.5	38.0	79.8	*69.0*	*36.0*	*45.2*	
Uruguay						*69.7*	*81.3*	*54.7*	*49.1*	*28.7*
Venezuela						*57.3*	*74.0*	*38.2*	*23.2*	*50.0*
Yugoslavia						*50.3*	*64.8*	*28.1*	*50.7*	*38.6*
World	69.8	72.9	26.9	45.9	32.1	68.9	73.7	29.6	46.6	32.4

*1990–1993 data West-Germany only.

** Russian Federation figures for 1990 are for USSR

***UK excluding Northern Ireland

Values in italics indicate that 1995–1997 data has been used

Sources: © European Values Survey, WORC, Tilburg University, Netherlands, 1999–2000, by permission; © World Values Survey, Institute for Social Research, University of Michigan, by permission; Inglehart, R., Basañez, M., and Moreno, A., *Human Values and Beliefs: A Cross-Cultural Sourcebook: Political, Religious, Sexual, and Economic Norms in 43 Societies: Findings from the 1990–993 World Values Survey*, (The University of Michigan Press, Ann Arbor, 1998).

R26b Unwillingness to have people of a different race, immigrants or foreign workers as a neighbour, 2000

in % of all respondents per country

Country	Immigrants & foreign workers Not mentioned	Mentioned	Different race Not mentioned	Mentioned
Albania	89.4	10.6	91.2	8.8
Argentina	94.3	5.7	95.4	4.6
Armenia	78.3	21.7	80.8	19.2
Australia	95.4	4.6	95.2	4.8
Austria	87.8	12.2	93.3	6.7
Azerbaijan	80.1	19.9	87.7	12.3
Bangladesh	70.5	29.5	82.7	17.3
Belarus	82.9	17.1	83.5	16.5
Belgium	83.9	16.1	85.7	14.3
Bosnia & Herzegovina	80.0	20.0	75.5	24.5
Brazil	96.5	3.5	97.2	2.8
Bulgaria	75.4	24.6	71.9	28.1
Chile	88.3	11.7	88.0	12.0
China & Tibet	78.7	21.3	76.1	23.9
Colombia	93.1	6.9	97.9	2.1
Croatia	80.7	19.3	82.7	17.3
Czech Republic	80.6	19.4	90.1	9.9
Denmark	89.4	10.6	92.6	7.4
Dominican Republic	82.4	17.6	81.5	18.5
Estonia	79.1	20.9	84.9	15.1
Finland	85.5	14.5	87.3	12.7
France	87.9	12.1	90.9	9.1
Georgia	89.2	10.8	90.7	9.3
Germany	91.4	8.6	95.2	4.8
Ghana	86.4	13.6	88.6	11.4
Greece	80.6	19.4	75.6	24.4
Hungary	38.0	62.0	48.0	52.0
Iceland	97.0	3.0	96.9	3.1
India	66.9	33.1	62.7	37.3
Ireland	87.7	12.3	87.9	12.1
Italy	83.5	16.5	84.5	15.6
Korea, Rep.	60.5	39.5		
Latvia	90.2	9.8	95.2	4.8
Lithuania	76.4	23.6	90.3	9.7
Luxembourg	91.6	8.4	93.7	6.3
Macedonia	76.3	23.7	73.6	26.4
Malta	84.3	15.7	81.0	19.0
Mexico	72.9	27.1	73.3	26.7
Moldova	86.8	13.2	92.2	7.8
Netherlands	94.7	5.3	94.5	5.5
Nigeria	72.6	27.4	75.5	24.5
Norway	88.8	11.2	90.8	9.2
Peru	89.7	10.3	88.4	11.6
Philippines	80.1	19.9	75.8	24.2
Poland	76.4	23.6	82.7	17.3
Portugal			92.4	7.6
Romania	78.9	21.1	75.8	24.2
Russian Federation	89.0	11.0	91.9	8.1
Slovakia	77.1	22.9	83.0	17.0
Slovenia	84.0	16.0	88.0	12.0
South Africa	78.7	21.3	88.8	11.2
Spain	90.7	9.3	89.7	10.3
Sweden	97.2	2.8	97.5	2.5
Switzerland	90.0	10.0	91.3	8.7
Turkey	63.6	36.4	67.8	32.2
Ukraine	85.1	14.9	89.5	10.5
United Kingdom*	84.5	15.5	91.4	8.6
United States	89.9	10.1	91.8	8.2
Uruguay	92.9	7.1	93.2	6.8
Venezuela	78.1	21.9	80.0	20.0
Yugoslavia	72.4	27.6	15.8	84.2
Average	82.9	17.1	84.6	15.4

*UK excluding Northern Ireland

Values in italics indicate that 1995–1997 data have been used

Sources: © European Values Survey, WORC, Tilburg University, Netherlands, 1999–2000, by permission; © World Values Survey, Institute for Social Research, University of Michigan, by permission.

Table R27: Willingness to help immigrants (Europe only)

Using the European Values Survey, this table shows to what extent people want to help immigrants, whether because they feel they have a moral duty to help, or because it is in the interest of society, or because they want to do something in return. The table shows the responses for all those reasons. Unfortunately, these data are available only for European countries.

Country	in % of all respondents per country		1999/2000		
	Very much	Much	To a certain extent	Not so much	Not at all
Austria	14.4	41.1	33.3	7.7	3.5
Belarus	34.1	55.6	11.6	7.7	0.0
Belgium	18.6	37.5	34.1	6.3	3.4
Bulgaria	13.1	28.5	42.1	12.0	4.5
Croatia	14.3	33.9	36.5	11.5	3.7
Czech Republic	14.3	33.2	43.0	8.9	1.5
Denmark	10.2	38.2	33.8	11.0	6.7
Estonia	13.2	25.9	46.1	11.5	3.3
France	22.9	34.8	29.5	9.1	3.7
Germany	13.1	47.8	28.9	6.8	3.4
Greece	16.3	33.1	36.8	11.5	2.3
Iceland	10.5	38.7	35.5	10.8	4.5
Italy	10.3	42.4	34.6	9.3	3.3
Latvia	11.9	34.5	43.6	6.3	3.8
Lithuania	6.9	48.9	33.5	10.8	0.0
Luxembourg	15.7	30.6	39.5	8.8	5.4
Netherlands	9.8	51.8	28.9	8.1	2.0
Poland	15.7	45.7	23.1	13.9	1.6
Portugal	30.7	31.9	29.0	7.2	1.2
Romania	33.3	33.4	19.6	7.9	5.8
Russian Federation	10.3	32.5	45.6	8.2	3.4
Slovakia	23.3	47.1	20.7	6.4	2.5
Slovenia	15.4	37.2	36.9	6.8	3.8
Spain	15.4	41.7	29.7	7.9	5.3
Ukraine	14.5	35.3	35.3	8.2	6.7
United Kingdom	19.3	29.9	28.8	12.1	9.9
Europe	16.4	38.1	33.1	9.1	3.7

Source: © European Values Survey, WORC, Tilburg University, Netherlands, 1999-2000, by permission.

Table R28: Concern about humankind (Europe only)

European and World Values Surveys provide information on the extent to which respondents are concerned about the conditions or humankind relative to their concerns about family, neighbours, or fellow countrymen. Unfortunately, these data are available only for European countries. The question asked was: to what extent do you feel concerned about the living conditions of...

- Your immediate family
- People in your neighbourhood
- The people of the region you live in
- Your fellow countrymen
- People on the continent where you live
- Humankind

Only responses to the final category (humankind) are shown.

Country	in % of all respondents per country Very much	Much	1999/2000 To a certain extent	Not so much	Not at all
Austria	4.2	13.0	33.1	31.9	17.9
Belarus	6.8	27.6	35.4	19.2	10.9
Belgium	6.8	15.8	38.1	26.0	13.3
Bulgaria	9.2	15.2	35.6	23.6	16.4
Croatia	14.2	22.6	32.5	22.3	8.4
Czech Republic	8.1	20.7	44.5	18.8	7.9
Denmark	12.7	23.5	36.2	15.4	12.3
Estonia	3.1	9.5	39.2	31.2	17.0
Finland	11.4	24.3	33.5	19.6	9.7
France	5.6	17.3	34.5	23.5	19.0
Germany	4.7	18.1	41.2	28.1	7.9
Greece	16.2	30.1	39.7	9.7	4.2
Hungary	6.1	16.5	29.6	28.5	19.4
Iceland	5.2	15.1	33.9	32.5	13.2
Ireland	15.7	19.3	41.0	18.4	5.7
Italy	6.0	22.7	44.1	21.7	5.5
Latvia	3.9	5.3	17.1	28.1	45.6
Lithuania	2.0	14.4	41.6	34.7	7.3
Luxembourg	5.8	23.3	40.5	20.1	10.4
Malta	7.4	28.8	40.1	17.3	6.3
Netherlands	7.9	25.7	41.0	19.2	6.2
Poland	2.2	11.6	29.3	38.5	18.4
Portugal	12.2	27.3	38.6	14.1	7.8
Romania	4.5	15.4	24.7	26.5	28.9
Russian Federation	6.0	12.7	37.8	24.4	19.1
Slovakia	6.4	13.5	43.1	24.0	13.0
Slovenia	8.3	16.3	45.6	21.2	8.6
Spain	8.1	27.0	44.7	16.2	4.1
Sweden	8.4	25.5	43.0	20.4	2.7
Ukraine	7.2	11.0	37.3	29.4	15.0
United Kingdom*	10.7	18.5	38.6	24.2	8.0
Europe	7.6	19.0	37.3	23.5	12.6

*UK excluding Northern Ireland

Source: © European Values Survey, WORC, Tilburg University, Netherlands, 1999-2000, by permission.

Table R29: Environmental concern

This table offers data on how people feel about the environment by looking at the extent to which they are willing to make sacrifices to prevent environmental pollution. Respondents were asked to respond to the following three statements:

'I would give up part of my income if I were certain that the money would be used to prevent environmental pollution.'

'I would agree to an increase in taxes if the extra money is used to prevent environmental pollution.'

'The government has to reduce environmental pollution but it should not cost me any money.'

in % of all respondents agreeing to reduce pollution	1990–93			2000		
Country	By giving up income	By paying higher taxes	At no cost	By giving up income	By paying higher taxes	At no cost
Argentina	62.0	50.0	72.0			
Austria	59.7	52.3	61.0	48.6	38.7	63.3
Belarus	80.0	67.0	72.0	57.7	46.4	75.3
Belgium	56.5	40.6	62.0	59.4	45.8	65.5
Brazil	72.0	71.0	65.0			
Bulgaria	82.8	70.4	74.0	57.5	44.6	82.7
Canada	73.6	63.7	52.0			
Chile	84.0	76.0	58.0			
China	78.0	82.0	46.0			
Croatia				82.4	67.5	77.9
Czech Republic				77.6	65.2	55.2
Denmark	84.3	69.5	29.0	78.8	65.1	30.0
Estonia	77.0	58.8	72.0	47.8	33.4	87.7
Finland	66.7	55.9	72.0	68.9	64.7	89.8
France	61.3	54.4	74.0	45.9	37.2	83.8
Germany*	52.5	49.2	57.0	33.3	29.0	67.6
Greece				76.4	61.8	79.0
Hungary	60.3	34.7	75.0	51.5	33.5	65.8
Iceland	77.9	60.1	28.0	63.5	57.2	32.4
India	81.0	66.0	52.0			
Ireland	69.5	50.6	60.0	54.6	38.8	69.5
Italy	67.5	53.7	80.0	64.8	43.6	81.1
Japan	68.0	51.0	56.0			
Korea, Rep.	84.0	76.0	50.0			
Latvia	77.5	63.9	71.0	70.5	45.3	76.9
Lithuania	74.6	65.4	69.0	26.5	20.0	88.8
Luxembourg				63.9	55.1	61.0
Malta				60.3	47.9	65.8
Mexico	81.0	67.0	40.0			
Netherlands	81.4	67.9	17.0	73.4	54.2	24.9
Nigeria	78.0	59.0	61.0			
Norway	79.9	73.3	44.0			
Poland	74.8	72.4		62.8	51.1	72.4
Portugal	84.3	65.4	92.0	57.0	42.7	75.2
Romania				52.2	46.4	
Russian Federation**	78.0	66.0	49.0	63.5	53.9	79.7
Slovakia	76.7	59.1		56.6	39.6	78.8

Country	1990–93			2000		
	By giving up income	By paying higher taxes	At no cost	By giving up income	By paying higher taxes	At no cost
Slovenia	88.7	69.4	56.0	82.1	61.5	63.2
Spain	64.9	54.7	76.0	57.8	47.7	85.1
Sweden	81.5	76.8	36.0	78.9	77.4	42.8
Turkey	87.0	72.0	56.0			
Ukraine				62.4	49.5	80.7
United Kingdom***	67.5	69.8		48.8	49.9	77.0
United States	74.2	63.9	53.0	69.1	60.1	57.8
Average	74.3	62.7	58.4	61.1	49.2	68.9

Notes: of respondents who 'agree' or 'strongly agree'; 1990 figures are rounded and sourced from World Values Survey.

*1990–993 data West–Germany only

** Russian Federation figures for 1990 are for USSR

***UK excluding Northern Ireland

Sources: © European Values Survey, WORC, Tilburg University, Netherlands, 1999–2000, by permission; © World Values Survey, Institute for Social Research, University of Michigan, by permission; R. Inglehart, M. Basañez, and A. Moreno, *Human Values and Beliefs: A Cross-Cultural Sourcebook: Political, Religious, Sexual, and Economic Norms in 43 Societies: Findings from the 1990–1993 World Values Survey* (Ann Arbor: The University of Michigan Press, 1998).

Table R30 Membership and volunteering

This table shows the extent to which respondents are members of community action groups, organisations concerned with development and human rights, and peace organisations. The table also offers data showing what proportion of respondents volunteers for these types of associations. The following question was asked: Look carefully at the following list of voluntary organisations and activities and say...

a) Which, if any, do you belong to?
b) Which, if any, are you currently doing unpaid work for?
- community action on issues like poverty, employment, housing, racial equality
- Third world development and human rights
- Environment, conservation, ecology
- Peace movement

% of respondents per country who are members of or volunteer in organisations, by type

	1990–1993								2000							
	Membership				Volunteering (unpaid)				Membership				Volunteering (unpaid)			
Country	Community action	Third world/human rights	Environment	Peace	Community action	Third world/human rights	Environment	Peace	Community action	Third world/human rights	Environment	Peace	Community action	Third world/human rights	Environment	Peace
Argentina	1.3	0.4	0.2	0.2	1.1	0.2	0.1	0.1	3.2	0.5	1.4		2.6	0.3	1.4	0.2
Austria	2.2	1.6	2.9	0.8	1.4	0.7	1.4	0.3	3.0	3.4	9.1	0.9	1.3	0.8	2.1	0.1
Belarus									0.1	0.5	0.9	0.1	0.9	0.7	2.2	0.6
Belgium	4.6	6.5	7.7	2.2	2.9	3.3	2.6	1.0	5.0	9.8	10.4	2.3	2.7	5.0	3.3	1.3
Brazil	7.9	1.3	2.8	2.2	4.4	0.7	1.4	1.2								
Bulgaria	2.0	1.5	3.8	1.1	1.7	1.4	3.4	0.9	1.1	0.4	1.3	0.7	0.8	0.2	1.2	0.4
Canada	5.1	4.6	7.5	2.0	4.0	2.7	3.5	1.6								
Chile	4.1	1.3	1.6	0.8	3.3	0.9	0.9	0.5	4.9	2.0	2.2	1.7	3.8	1.7	3.1	4.8
China & Tibet	0.5	0.2	0.8	0.3	3.9	0.1	1.5	0.5								
Croatia									1.3	0.5	3.0	1.0	0.7	0.4	2.1	0.8
Czech Republic									3.2	0.7	6.6	1.3	1.9	0.4	3.2	0.2
Denmark	5.2	2.8	12.5	2.1	1.9	0.9	0.9	0.2	6.2	4.1	13.2	0.8	3.1	1.2	2.3	0.4
Estonia	4.5	0.6	2.7	1.3	4.0	0.9	2.0	0.9	1.8	0.1	1.7	0.2	1.8	0.2	1.1	0.4
Finland	3.2	5.9	5.5	1.7	2.9	2.9	4.3	1.2		5.9	4.4	1.3		3.2	1.9	0.9
France	3.3	2.6	2.3	0.5	2.9	1.4	1.5	0.5	2.5	1.4	2.2	0.5	1.7	0.7	0.9	0.3
Germany*	1.7	2.1	4.5	2.0	1.0	0.8	1.4	1.0	0.7	0.6	2.7	0.2	0.3	0.2	1.0	0.0
Greece									4.3	1.8	5.8	2.9	6.7	3.2	5.4	4.7
Hungary	1.4	0.2	1.4	0.5	1.5	0.3	1.3	0.2	1.2	0.3	1.7	0.3	1.1	0.2	1.7	0.4
Iceland	2.0	3.4	4.8	1.4	0.6	0.4	2.0	0.3	2.5	7.5	4.6	1.1	0.7	1.3	1.3	0.1
Ireland	3.3	1.6	2.2	0.6	2.8	1.3	0.6	0.2	5.8	2.4	2.8	1.7	3.4	1.8	0.9	0.8
Italy	2.5	1.1	2.9	1.1	2.0	0.7	1.4	0.6	2.4	2.9	3.8	1.4	1.8	1.9	1.8	0.9
Japan	0.2	0.2	1.1	0.6	0.5	0.2	1.2	0.8	1.2	1.7	1.2	2.0	0.4	0.3	3.2	1.2
Korea, Rep.	12.5	2.4	2.0	2.0	3.4	1.8	2.4	2.1								
Latvia	5.4	1.3	4.3	1.2	8.4	4.0	4.9	0.9	0.7	0.6	0.7	0.2	1.7	0.3	0.5	0.1
Lithuania	2.1	1.0	2.1	0.6	1.5	0.9	1.8	0.8	0.7	0.2	0.7	0.2	0.7	0.1	0.4	0.1
Luxembourg									5.1	11.1	10.7	2.3	2.8	5.1	4.3	1.4
Malta									2.8	0.3	2.0	0.2	3.9	1.6	1.9	0.5
Mexico	4.3	0.9	2.8	1.4	2.7	0.6	2.4	0.7	5.0	2.5	3.4	2.8	4.2	1.4	4.7	3.3

Table R30 continued

Country	1990–1993 Membership				1990–1993 Volunteering (unpaid)				2000 Membership				2000 Volunteering (unpaid)			
	Community action	Third world/human rights	Environment	Peace	Community action	Third world/human rights	Environment	Peace	Community action	Third world/human rights	Environment	Peace	Community action	Third world/human rights	Environment	Peace
Netherlands	5.0	14.1	23.3	2.9	2.5	3.0	2.9	1.3	6.9	24.6	44.3	3.4		4.1	2.4	0.5
Poland		0.1	1.5	0.2		0.5	1.6	0.1	1.9	0.4	1.3	0.5	1.3	0.1	0.5	0.0
Portugal	1.7	0.6	1.5	0.5	0.8	0.6	0.7	0.2	1.5	0.8	0.5	0.6	1.1	0.6	0.4	0.1
Romania	1.1	0.2	1.0	0.2	0.6	0.1	0.9	0.1	0.9	0.6	1.0	0.1	0.6	0.4	0.6	0.0
Russian Federation**	2.5	0.3	1.6	1.1	1.7	0.3	1.3	0.8	0.9	0.1	0.7	0.1	0.6	0.0	0.4	0.0
Slovakia		0.4	5.8	1.6		0.2	3.0	0.1	8.3	0.2	2.6	0.3	6.8	0.2	2.0	0.2
Slovenia	5.8	0.1	1.7	0.1	2.7	0.5	1.4	0.3	9.2	0.8	3.3	0.8	5.8	0.4	2.9	0.6
Spain	1.2	1.0	1.4	0.7	0.4	0.8	1.0	0.5	2.2	2.4	1.2	1.6	1.9	1.3	1.0	0.7
Sweden	2.2	9.3	10.6	3.1	1.0	3.2	2.5	1.5	9.4	15.0	35.3	1.5	5.7	4.4	3.8	0.4
Switzerland	3.4		10.5													
Ukraine									1.9	0.7	0.6	0.1	1.0	0.2	0.2	0.0
United Kingdom***	3.5	2.3	5.9	1.3	1.0	1.1	1.8	0.6	3.5	2.6	1.5	0.6	1.7	4.3	7.8	4.2
United States	4.6	1.7	8.5	2.0	3.0	0.9	3.5	0.7	12.5	5.3	8.8	4.4	6.9	2.7	7.8	2.1
Average	3.4	2.2	4.5	1.2	2.3	1.2	1.9	0.7	3.5	3.2	5.5	1.1	2.4	1.4	2.3	0.9

*1990–1993 data West-Germany only

** Russian Federation figures for 1990 are for USSR

***UK excluding Northern Ireland

Sources: © European Values Survey, WORC, Tilburg University, Netherlands, 1999–2000, by permission; © World Values Survey, Institute for Social Research, University of Michigan, by permission; R. Inglehart, M. Basañez, and A. Moreno, *Human Values and Beliefs: A Cross-Cultural Sourcebook: Political, Religious, Sexual, and Economic Norms in 43 Societies: Findings from the 1990–1993 World Values Survey* (Ann Arbor: The University of Michigan Press, 1998).

Table R31: Willingness to participate in political events

People differ in the extent to which they are able or willing to take political action for or against a particular cause. As a general measure of political mobilisation, this table offers the results of the question, taken from the European and World Values Survey, whether respondents feel they might take any of these forms of political action.

in % of all respondents agreeing to reduce pollution / Country	1990–1993 Sign petition	Join boycott	Attend lawful demonstration	Join unofficial strike	Occupy building	2000 Sign petition	Join boycott	Attend lawful demonstration	Join unofficial strike	Occupy building
Argentina	22.4	3.4	15.0	7.3	2.7	30.4	1.4	16.7	5.9	3.1
Armenia						17.8	12.1	28.2	15.0	1.2
Australia						78.4	21.5	17.8	8.1	2.0
Austria	47.7	5.2	10.4	1.1	0.7	56.7	9.8	16.7	2.2	0.7
Azerbaijan						10.1	2.6	20.5	9.0	0.2
Belarus	27.0	4.6	18.1	2.3	0.8	8.8	4.1	16.3	1.1	0.6
Belgium	50.2	10.2	25.4	7.2	4.3	71.4	12.0	39.6	8.9	6.0
Bosnia & Herzegovina						22.0	8.8	9.0	5.8	0.7
Brazil	50.8	10.5	17.9	7.9	1.9	47.1	6.4	24.8	6.5	2.7
Bulgaria	21.6	3.4	14.5	3.2	1.5	11.2	3.6	14.8	4.9	3.1
Canada	76.8	22.3	20.8	7.0	3.0					
Chile	22.9	4.0	30.1	8.2	4.2	16.6	2.4	14.6	5.3	2.2
Colombia						18.9	7.7	11.5	4.9	1.3
Croatia						37.4	8.0	7.7	3.2	1.2
Czech Republic						58.7	9.2	27.8	10.2	1.0
Denmark	51.0	10.7	27.6	17.4	2.0	56.8	24.9	29.3	22.2	2.8
Dominican Republic						14.9	5.6	26.5	8.4	4.6
Estonia	39.0	3.3	25.9	4.2	0.8	20.7	2.9	11.1	1.3	0.1
Finland	40.7	13.5	14.2	8.1	1.6	52.4	19.9	19.8	9.6	6.8
France	53.7	12.5	32.7	10.1	7.9	68.0	13.0	39.4	12.7	9.3
Georgia						14.0	5.8	19.3	9.8	0.8
Germany*	56.5	10.0	20.5	2.3	1.1	50.6	10.2	27.0	1.9	0.7
Ghana						11.9	5.1	11.3	1.6	5.6
Greece						33.7	3.8	38.7	6.8	18.8
Hungary	18.0	2.2	4.4	2.9	0.1	14.7	2.8	4.5	0.8	0.5
Iceland	47.3	21.4	23.7	5.0	1.3	53.0	17.8	20.7	3.4	0.7
Ireland	42.1	7.4	16.4	3.5	1.7	59.5	9.0	20.9	6.3	2.3
Italy	48.1	10.9	36.0	6.1	7.6	54.6	10.3	34.8	5.4	8.0
Japan	61.5	3.8	13.2	3.0	0.4	56.1	8.1	11.1	2.9	
Korea, Rep.	42.0	11.3	19.8		10.7	39.8	16.0	14.5	3.9	2.3
Latvia	64.6	4.1	35.6	6.1	1.1	19.1	4.0	25.1	1.1	0.3
Lithuania	58.3	7.3	34.0	2.6	0.2	27.3	4.6	11.5	2.2	1.4
Luxembourg						53.2	8.9	28.3	6.5	1.6
Macedonia						15.4	8.0	10.8	2.5	0.5
Mexico	34.7	6.9	22.0	7.4	5.2	30.4	9.5	11.5	6.2	4.6
Moldova						10.4	1.0	8.3	1.9	0.3
Netherlands	50.8	7.8	25.3	1.9	3.0	61.3	23.4	34.1	4.6	5.5
New Zealand						90.6	19.1	21.4	5.2	1.2

Country	1990–1993					2000				
	Sign petition	Join boycott	Attend lawful demonstration	Join unofficial strike	Occupy building	Sign petition	Join boycott	Attend lawful demonstration	Join unofficial strike	Occupy building
Nigeria	7.2	13.1	20.2	5.5	2.3	6.7	10.2	16.9	5.2	5.5
Norway	61.1	12.0	19.5	24.4	1.0				5.1	1.8
Peru						20.6	2.8	12.2	4.1	2.9
Philippines						12.0	6.0	8.0	3.1	1.6
Poland	14.0	5.8	11.7	6.2	3.8	22.6	4.2	10.0	4.7	2.9
Portugal	29.1	4.7	24.8	3.6	1.4	22.6	4.6	14.9	3.0	1.2
Russian Federation**	27.1	4.2	34.5	2.4	0.7	11.6	2.6	23.3	1.6	0.7
Slovakia			20.2			59.3	4.3	14.3	2.3	0.9
Slovenia	27.6	8.0	10.1	1.5	0.8	32.4	8.2	9.8	3.6	1.6
South Africa	24.2	21.5	18.8	8.5	2.5			10.4	3.7	2.4
Spain	20.4	5.6	23.5	6.9	2.9	28.6	5.6	26.9	8.7	3.1
Sweden	71.7	16.5	22.6	3.1	0.2	87.4	33.0	35.2	4.6	2.6
Switzerland	62.9		15.4	2.1		63.6	12.2	16.9	1.9	1.1
Turkey	13.6	5.6	5.7	1.5	1.2	13.8	6.6	6.3	2.0	0.5
Ukraine						14.2	5.0	18.9	2.7	0.9
United Kingdom***	75.4	14.7	13.6	8.5	2.3	79.4	16.7	13.4	9.7	2.2
United States	70.9	17.9	15.5	4.4	2.0	81.1	24.7	20.0	5.4	3.8
Uruguay						35.5	4.0	5.0	10.2	7.6
Venezuela						22.7	2.4	9.7	2.4	2.6
Yugoslavia						19.4	6.7	7.5	4.6	1.2
Average	42.6	9.3	20.5	5.8	2.4	36.9	9.1	18.3	5.4	2.7

*West–Germany only

** Russian Federation figures for 1990 are for USSR

***UK excluding Northern Ireland

Values in italics indicate that 1995–1997 data have been used

Sources: © European Values Survey, WORC, Tilburg University, Netherlands, 1999–2000, by permission; © World Values Survey, Institute for Social Research, University of Michigan, by permission; R. Inglehart, M. Basañez, and A. Moreno, *Human Values and Beliefs: A Cross-Cultural Sourcebook: Political, Religious, Sexual, and Economic Norms in 43 Societies: Findings from the 1990–1993 World Values Survey* (Ann Arbor: The University of Michigan Press, 1998).

Table R32 Social characteristics of international organisation leaders

These tables provide basic information on executives of international non-governmental (INGO) and intergovernmental (IGO) organisations. Data are provided for the years 1996 and 2000 and are aggregated for all international organisation types. They give data about their age (**Figure R5**), gender (R32a), and level of education (R32b). Table R32c shows totals, percentages, and 1996–2000 changes for the combinations of the top ten languages they speak, and Table R32d shows their multilingual proficiency. Because of different sample sizes, the number of biographies for which this information is available varies by year and characteristic in question. INGO and IGO leaders tend to be highly educated middle-aged men, with a pronounced increase in their education and the share of women leaders since 1992.

A note of caution: The most serious flaw in the data, according to the editors of the *Who's Who in International Organizations*, is the limited amount of information included in most of the biographical entries. There are several reasons for this. (1) The structure of many organisations works against the collection and establishment of a list of its officers. Many organisations elect or appoint new officers annually or biannually, still others at irregular and sometimes unannounced intervals. (As of the 2000 edition, some people are also included who have held, but who no longer hold, a significant position in the organisation to which they are associated in the publication.) (2) Some organisations are publicly represented by individuals who do not hold the most significant positions in terms of the development and operation of the organisation. It was not always possible to gather information on anyone other than the known representative, usually the person with the 'most elevated' title.

R32a Gender

	1992		1996		2000	
	Number	Percentage	Number	Percentage	Number	Percentage
Male	4,096	87.5	4,100	82.8	3,343	71.3
Female	584	12.5	854	17.2	1,347	28.7
Total	4,680	100	4,954	100	4,690	100

Source: © Union of International Associations, *Who's Who in International Organizations*, 1992, 1996 and 2000 (presenting data collected in 1991, 1995 and 1999, respectively). Data have been restructured from more comprehensive coverage in the Who's Who.

R32b Education

	1996		2000		Change 1996–2000
	Number	%	Number	%	%
No tertiary (university/college) qualifications	1,962	51.1	806	34.9	–31.8
Bachelor, Candidate, Diploma or other basic degree	1,876	48.9	1,505	65.1	33.2
Postgraduate and higher degrees					
At least a Master (MS, MA equivalent)	1,462	38.1	1,135	49.1	28.9
At least a Master of Business Administration (MBA)	48	1.3	49	2.1	69.5
At least a Doctorate (PhD equivalent)	1,576	41.1	1,197	51.8	26.1
At least a Doctor of Medicine (MD equivalent)	202	5.3	140	6.1	15.1
Average number of degrees held per person	1.3		1.7		30.8
Total	3,838	100.0	2,311	100.0	

Note: More than one degree may be held by a person; totals are not additive.

Source: © Union of International Associations, *Who's Who in International Organizations*, 1996 and 2000 (presenting data collected in 1995 and 1999, respectively). Data have been restructured from more comprehensive coverage in the Who's Who.

R32c Combinations of languages spoken by international organisation leaders

Number of persons 1996

	Arabic	Dutch	English	French	German	Italian	Portuguese	Russian	Spanish
Dutch	–	Dutch							
English	98	338	English						
French	61	318	1,673	French					
German	15	270	993	809	German				
Italian	10	72	391	385	217	Italian			
Portuguese	4	22	139	124	56	57	Portuguese		
Russian	7	9	124	90	82	26	4	Russian	
Spanish	14	85	620	527	252	204	119	35	Spanish
Swedish	2	5	122	60	84	9	2	7	18

Percentage 1996

	Arabic	Dutch	English	French	German	Italian	Portuguese	Russian	Spanish
Dutch	0.0	Dutch							
English	3.8	13.1	English						
French	2.4	12.3	64.9	French					
German	0.6	10.5	38.5	31.4	German				
Italian	0.4	2.8	15.2	14.9	8.4	Italian			
Portuguese	0.2	0.9	5.4	4.8	2.2	2.2	Portuguese		
Russian	0.3	0.3	4.8	3.5	3.2	1.0	0.2	Russian	
Spanish	0.5	3.3	24.1	20.5	9.8	7.9	4.6	1.4	Spanish
Swedish	0.1	0.2	4.7	2.3	3.3	0.3	0.1	0.3	0.7

Number of persons 2000

	Arabic	Dutch	English	French	German	Italian	Portuguese	Russian	Spanish
Dutch	1	Dutch							
English	71	254	English						
French	45	239	1,041	French					
German	15	198	618	514	German				
Italian	12	57	259	250	148	Italian			
Portuguese	2	12	94	80	37	41	Portuguese		
Russian	5	10	84	62	58	24	4	Russian	
Spanish	11	63	418	354	168	143	85	27	Spanish
Swedish	2	5	74	44	53	10	4	8	20

Percentage 2000 *

	Arabic	Dutch	English	French	German	Italian	Portuguese	Russian	Spanish
Dutch	0.1	Dutch							
English	4.6	16.5	English						
French	2.9	15.5	67.4	French					
German	1.0	12.8	40.0	33.3	German				
Italian	0.8	3.7	16.8	16.2	9.6	Italian			
Portuguese	0.1	0.8	6.1	5.2	2.4	2.7	Portuguese		
Russian	0.3	0.6	5.4	4.0	3.8	1.6	0.3	Russian	
Spanish	0.7	4.1	27.1	22.9	10.9	9.3	5.5	1.7	Spanish
Swedish	0.1	0.3	4.8	2.8	3.4	0.6	0.3	0.5	1.3

Change 1996–2000 *

	Arabic	Dutch	English	French	German	Italian	Portuguese	Russian	Spanish
Dutch	100.0	Dutch							
English	20.9	25.4	English						
French	23.1	25.4	3.9	French					
German	66.9	22.4	3.9	6.0	German				
Italian	100.3	32.1	10.6	8.4	13.8	Italian			
Portuguese	-16.5	-9.0	12.9	7.7	10.3	20.1	Portuguese		
Russian	19.2	85.4	13.1	15.0	18.1	54.1	66.9	Russian	
Spanish	31.1	23.7	12.5	12.1	11.3	17.0	19.2	28.8	Spanish
Swedish	66.9	66.9	1.2	22.4	5.3	85.4	233.8	90.7	85.4

R32d Multilingual proficiency

					Number of languages					
	10	9	8	7	6	5	4	3	2	1	Totals
People	4	8	14	24	91	175	293	436	356	143	1,544
Percentage	0.3	0.5	0.9	1.6	5.9	11.3	19.0	28.2	23.1	9.3	100.0

Sample sizes: 1996: 2577 biographees whose language skills are known spoke a total of 104 languages; 2000: 1544 biographees whose language skills are known spoke a total of 79 languages; * adjusted according to sample size

Source: © Union of International Associations, *Who's Who in International Organizations*, 1992, 1996 and 2000 (presenting data collected in 1991, 1995 and 1999, respectively). Data have been restructured from more comprehensive coverage in the Who's Who.

Figure R5: Age structure of international organisation leadership

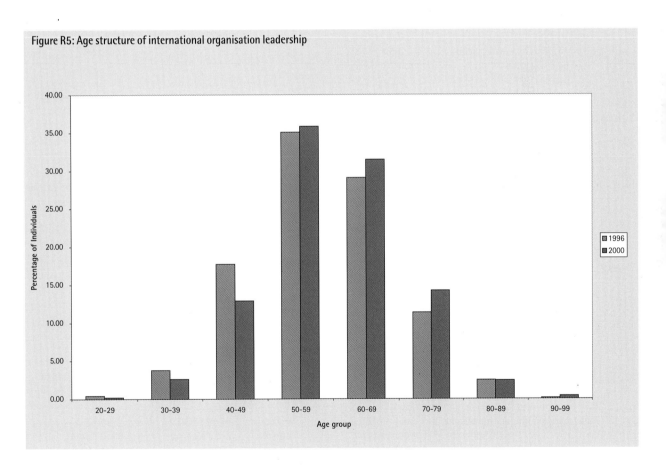

Glossary of Terms in Table Programme

Arbitrary detention. Deprivation of liberty imposed arbitrarily, that is, where no final decision has been taken by domestic courts in conformity with domestic law and with the relevant international standards set forth in the Universal Declaration of Human Rights and with the relevant international instruments accepted by the states concerned.

Bribery Index. The World Economic Forum's (WEF) index of governance and corruption contained within its *Global Competitiveness Survey*, produced in association with the Harvard Institute for International Development.

Corruption Perceptions Index (CPI) by Transparency International, measures corruption in the public sector and defines corruption as the abuse of public office for private gain. The CPI makes no effort to reflect private sector fraud. The index is based on surveys compiled by TI from other organisations which tend to ask questions in line with the misuse of public power for private benefits, with a focus, for example, on bribing of public officials, taking kickbacks in public procurement or embezzling public funds, etc. Surveys consulted: Economist Intelligence Unit (Country Risk Service and Country Forecasts); Gallup International (50th Anniversary Survey); Institute for Management Development (World Competitiveness Yearbook); Political & Economic Risk Consultancy (Asian Intelligence Issue); Political Risk Services (International Country Risk Guide); World Development Report (private sector survey by the World Bank); and World Economic Forum & Harvard Institute for International Development (Global Competitiveness Survey).

Daily newspapers. Newspapers published at least four times a week.

Discrimination. Any distinction, exclusion, restriction, or preference based on any ground such as race, colour, sex, language, religion, political or other opinion, national or social origin, property, birth, or other status which has the purpose or effect of nullifying or impairing the recognition, enjoyment, or exercise, on an equal footing, of human rights and fundamental freedoms in the political, economic, social, cultural, or any other field of public life.

Energy consumption. The amount of energy from all sources used by each country in the year specified. In addition to solid, liquid, and gaseous fuels and nuclear electricity, the total also includes hydropower, geothermal, solar, combustible renewables and waste, and indigenous heat production from heat pumps. Data are presented in a common unit of 1,000 metric tons of oil equivalent (toe), defined as 41.868 gigajoules.

Enforced disappearances. An enforced disappearance occurs when persons are arrested, detained, or abducted against their will or otherwise deprived of their liberty by officials of different branches or levels of government, or by organised groups or private individuals acting on behalf of, or with the support, direct or indirect, consent, or acquies-cence of the government, followed by a refusal to disclose the fate or whereabouts of the persons concerned or a refusal to acknowledge the deprivation of their liberty, which places such persons outside the protection of the law.

Engco model. Designed by the English Company (UK) Ltd as a means of examining the relative status of world languages and making forecasts of the numbers of speakers of different languages based on demographic, human development, and economic data. Further explanations of the model are available at http://www.english.co.uk

Ethnologue. Published by The Summer Institute of Linguistics, Ethnologue is a reference book of world languages. Information is available at htp://www.sil.org/ethnologue

Extrajudicial executions. Full expression 'extrajudicial, summary, or arbitrary executions': all acts and omissions of state representatives that constitute a violation of the general recognition of the right to life embodied in the Universal Declaration of Human Rights and the International Covenant on Civil and Political Rights.

Foreign direct investment. Investment to acquire a lasting management interest (10 per cent or more of voting stock) in an enterprise operating in an economy other than that of the investor. It is the sum of equity capital, reinvestment of earnings, other long-term capital, and short-term capital as shown in the balance of payments.

Foreign direct investment stock. Value of the share of capital and reserves (including retained profits) attributable to enterprises based outside the domestic economy, plus the net indebtedness of domestic affiliates to the parent enterprise. UNCTAD FDI stock data are frequently estimated by accumulating FDI *flows* over a period of time or adding flows to an FDI stock that has been obtained for a particular year.

Foreign labour. The number of foreign or foreign-born workers in a country's workforce.

Foreign population. The number of foreign or foreign-born residents in a country.

Freedom of association. The right to establish and, subject only to the rules of the organisation concerned, to join organisations of one's own choosing without prior authorisation.

Freedom of expression. Freedom to hold opinions without interference and to seek, receive, and impart information and ideas through any media and regardless of frontiers.

Full-time equivalent employment. This indicates total employment in terms of full-time jobs. Part-time employment is converted into full-time jobs and added to the number of full-time jobs.

GDP or gross domestic product. This is the total domestic expenditure, minus imports, and plus exports of goods and services.

GDP per capita, purchasing power parity (PPP). GDP PPP is gross domestic product converted to international dollars using purchasing power parity rates. An international dollar has the same purchasing power over GDP as the US dollar in the United States. Data are in current international dollars.

Gini index. Measures the extent to which the distribution of income (or, in some cases, consumption expenditures) among individuals or households within an economy deviates from a perfectly equal distribution. A Lorenz curve plots the cumulative percentages of total income received against the cumulative number of recipients, starting with the poorest individual or household. The Gini index measures the area between the Lorenz curve and a hypothetical line of absolute equality, expressed as a percentage of the maximum area under the line. Thus, a Gini index of zero represents perfect equality, while an index of 100 implies perfect inequality.

HDI. The Human Development Index is a composite index based on three indicators: longevity, as measured by life expectancy at birth; educational attainment, as measured by a combination of adult literacy (two-thirds weight) and the combined gross primary, secondary, and tertiary enrolment ratio (one-third weight); and standard of living, as measured by GDP per capita (PPP US$).

IDPs. Internally displaced persons are individuals or groups of people who have been forced to flee their homes to escape armed conflict, generalised violence, human rights abuses, or natural or man-made disasters, *and* have remained within the borders of their home country.

Illiteracy rate. Calculated as 100 minus the adult literacy rate, which refers to the people aged 15 and above who can, with understanding, both read and write a short, simple statement on their everyday life.

Imputed value for volunteers. This is calculated by converting the total volunteer hours into full-time equivalent employment, multiplied by the average wage for the group, industry, or the economy as a whole.

Infant mortality rate. The probability of dying between birth and exactly one year of age times 1,000.

Inflows of foreign population. The gross arrivals of immigrants in the country shown. The total does not include asylum seekers.

International organisations. Data included in these tables are, except where otherwise indicated, from conventional organisations, of genuinely international character (recognised according to criteria such as international governance, financing, membership, aims, etc.), their subsidiary organisations, and organisations of 'other types' which on available evidence but for exceptional characteristics would have been included in the preceding types. The latter include international banks, courts, training institutes, libraries, laboratories, etc., and organisations of exiles, common markets, and political parties. Notably excluded from these data tables are internationally-oriented national organisations, subsidiary and internal bodies, and nationally-oriented and special categories of organisations, such as religious orders and secular institutes.

Internet hosts. The number of computers with active Internet Protocol (IP) addresses connected to the Internet. All hosts without a country code identification are assumed to be located in the United States.

Major armed conflict. Defined by the Stockholm International Peace Research Institute (SIPRI) as the use of armed force between the military forces of two or more governments, or of one government and at least one organised armed group, resulting in the battle-related deaths of at least 1,000 people in any single year and in which the incompatibility concerns control of government and/or territory.

Merchandise trade. Includes all trade in goods. Trade in services is excluded.

Operating expenditures. The costs of the general operations of the organisation, including wage and salary disbursements, purchases of goods other than capital equipment, material and services, and fees and charges paid.

Other high-income economies include Cyprus, Hong Kong (China), Israel, Kuwait, Malta, Qatar, Singapore, Taiwan (China), and the United Arab Emirates. Some small high-income economies such as Aruba, the Bahamas, and Bermuda have been included in the Latin America and Caribbean group

Other industrial economies. These include Australia, Canada, Iceland, New Zealand, Norway, and Switzerland.

Overseas development assistance. Official development assistance and net official aid record the actual international transfer by the donor of financial resources or of goods or services valued at the cost to the donor, minus any repayments of loan principal during the same period. ODA data consist of disbursements of loans made on concessional terms (net of repayments of principal) and grants by official agencies of the members of DAC (Development Assistance Committee of the OECD), by multilateral institutions, and by certain Arab countries to promote economic development and welfare in recipient economies listed as 'developing' by DAC. Loans with a grant element of at least 25 per cent are included in ODA, as are technical cooperation and assistance.

Passengers carried. Air passengers carried include both domestic and international aircraft passengers.

Peacekeeping forces. Military personnel and civilian police serving in United Nations peace-keeping missions.

Public sector or Government. All branches of the government, including the executive, judicial, and administrative and regulatory activities of federal, state, local, or regional political entities; the terms 'government' and 'public sector' are used synonymously.

Public sector payments. These include: grants and contracts, i.e. direct contributions by the government to the organisation in support of specific activities and programmes; statutory transfers, i.e. contributions by the government, as mandated by law, to provide general support to an organisation in carrying out its public programmes, and third party payments, i.e. indirect government payments reimbursing an organisation for services rendered to individuals (e.g. health insurance, 'vouchers', or payments for day care).

Private giving. This includes: foundation giving, including grants from grant-making foundations, operating foundations, and community foundations; business or corporate donations, which includes giving directly by businesses or giving by business or corporate foundations; and individual giving, i.e. direct contributions by individuals and contributions through 'federated fundraising' campaigns.

Private fees and charges (programme fees). These essentially include four types of business or commercial income: fees for service, i.e. charges that clients of an agency pay for the services that the agency provides (e.g. fees for day care or health care); dues, i.e. charges levied on the members of an organisation as a condition of membership. They are not normally considered charges for particular services; proceeds from sales of products, which includes income from the sale of products or services and income from for-profit subsidiaries; and investment income, i.e. the income a nonprofit earns on its capital or its investments.

Refugee. As defined by the UN High Commissioner for Refugees, a person is a refugee if she/he qualifies under the Arrangements of 12 May 1926 and 30 June 1928 or under the Conventions of 28 October 1933 and 10 February 1938, the Protocol of 14 September 1939 or the Constitution of the International Refugee Organisation. See http://www.unhcr.ch for further information.

Revenues. Inflows of spendable resources received by the organisation during the year.

Telephone mainlines. Telephone lines connecting a customer's equipment to the public switched telephone network.

TNI. Transnationality Index is the average of three ratios: foreign assets to total assets, foreign sales to total sales, and foreign employment to total employment.

Torture. Any act by which severe pain or suffering, whether physical or mental, is intentionally inflicted on a person for such purposes as obtaining from him or a third person information or a confession, punishing him for an act he or a third person has committed or is suspected of having committed, or intimidating or coercing him or a third person, or for any reason based on discrimination of any kind, when such pain or suffering is inflicted by or at the instigation of or with the consent or acquiescence of a public official or other person acting in an official capacity. It does not include pain or suffering arising only from, inherent in, or incidental to lawful sanctions.

Total military personnel. Active duty military personnel, including paramilitary forces if those forces resemble regular units in their organisation, equipment, training, or mission.

Total trade. The sum of the market value of imports and exports of goods and services.

Tourists. Visitors who travel to a country other than that where they have their usual residence for a period not exceeding 12 months and whose main purpose in visiting is other than an activity remunerated from within the country visited.

Transparency of Government Index. This indicates the extent to which government does not communicate its policy intentions clearly. Included in the IMD's (International Institute for Management Development, Lausanne, Switzerland) *World Competitiveness Yearbook*.

CHRONOLOGIES

*Compiled by Marlies Glasius, with contributions from Andres Falconer,
Zafarullah Khan, Svitlana Kuts, Ahmad Lutfi, Alejandro Natal, Yahia
Said, Shameem Siddiqi, Sunna Trott, and Barbara Wisniewska.*

Note on Chronologies

Chronicles of the year, often published by newspapers, magazines, or in mass-produced books, are a familiar sight in news agencies and bookshops at the end of each year. They recapitulate the events of the past year that, so they tell us, are supposed to be worth remembering. In the last year, many lists of events and personalities of the century have also come out. These lists tend to concentrate on political leaders and celebrities, and if they are called 'world events' they often concentrate mainly on the North/West. In these pages, we try to focus on different events, giving centre stage to global civil society, showing globalisation from below, and giving more attention to the South and East. These chronologies can become a useful reference tool but they can also help us to build a global collective memory that looks beyond the handshakes of great power leaders.

This is a somewhat novel approach to world history and we are still in the process of learning how to do it. We have developed some criteria and we have begun to set up a network of correspondents. Their input is gratefully acknowledged, but we need many more. *Events of the Decade* and *Events of 2000* should not be seen as a definitive list of what happened in global civil society. On the contrary, we are hoping to improve our effort over the years, with your help.

If you have comments on the present effort, or if you are interested in becoming a correspondent for our next Yearbook, please let us know. We are looking for people who take an active interest in the activities of global civil society in their part of the world. We would like to have a mix of journalists, students and academics, and activists/practitioners, with men and women, young people and older people from all regions of the world represented. Correspondents should have a helicopter view of civil society activities in their region, embracing activism on more than one type of issue (for instance peace, human rights, the environment, consumer activism), and more than one country.

When is something important enough to be a 'global civil society event'? Our criterion was that, in our entirely subjective opinion, the event resonated, or had implications, beyond national boundaries. While this is a chronicle of global civil society events, government actions are occasionally included when they had significant impact on, or were a reaction to, global civil society. A little background on major 'governmental' events is given as context at the beginning of each year.

Elections are reported when they are the first democratic elections ever, or in a long time, in a country. This is based on the idea that there is a strong relationship between the development of civil society and democratisation. Referendums of historical importance have also been included.

Peace processes are also given much attention. Again, although there can be strong civil society resistance to war, in the long run civil society and peace are mutually dependent. In some peace processes (usually the more successful and lasting ones), civil society is given a role while in others it is not. We have decided to include both types.

Whether civil society can be violent or not is a hotly debated issue, but for the purposes of this chronology manifestations of non-state violence, from relatively benign ones to guerilla armies, assassins, and terrorists are included. Whether or not one thinks these are part of civil society, they certainly deeply affect civil society, and it would be strange to ignore them.

We have not systematically included natural disasters such as floods, earthquakes, and hurricanes, simply because we did not know where to begin. Nevertheless, their impact on civil society is clear and they tend to have consequences for both local and global civil society. This is one of the areas we hope to expand next year.

Global Civil Society
Events of the Decade

1989

This is the year in which the communist regimes of eastern Europe are toppled and the Iron Curtain is lifted. In China, on the other hand, the pro-democracy movement is crushed. Iran's Ayatollah Khomeini declares author Salman Rushdie's book The Satanic Verses offensive and issues a fatwa sentencing him to death. The Presidents of Costa Rica, El Salvador, Guatemala, Honduras, and Nicaragua meet in Honduras, taking some first steps towards an end to the civil wars and the return of democracy in the region. US troops invade Panama, seeking the capture of General Manuel Noriega.

6 February   Members of Poland's communist government hold Round Table talks with representatives of the hitherto illegal Solidarity trade union to negotiate changes in the system of government. The talks eventually lead to an agreement on partially free elections, to be held in June.

Mid-April   Chinese students and other supporters of freedom of speech and democratisation occupy Tiananmen Square in Beijing, China.

4 June   Soldiers of the Chinese army take control of Tiananmen Square by force, causing many casualties. Pro-democracy activists are arrested or flee abroad in the following days.

19 August   After a 'Pan-European picnic' near the Hungarian–Austrian border town Sopron, organised by the Hungarian Democratic Forum, hundreds of East Germans cross the recently opened border into Austria.

23 October   After many months of peaceful protest meetings at the Nicolai church in Leipzig, East Germany, every Monday evening, the protesting crowds swell to hundreds of thousands, chanting 'We are the people' and demanding political freedoms, freedom to travel, and the resignation of the communist regime.

7–11 November   In preparation for independence, the United Nations organises the first democratic parliamentary elections in Namibia, which have a 97% voter turn-out. The South West Africa People's Organisation (SWAPO) wins the elections.

9 November   Spontaneous celebrations are held on the Berlin Wall as citizens of the two German republics cross the border, popping champagne and beginning to demolish the Wall.

17 November   A student march in Prague, commemorating the killing of two students during the Nazi occupation, turns into a protest against the communist regime. Riot police respond with batons injuring scores of peaceful demonstrators.

25–29 November   A crowd of 700,000 Czechoslovaks turn out to protest against the violent suppression of the demonstration two weeks earlier, and demand the resignation of the communist government. In what has become known as the 'Velvet Revolution', the communist government of Czechoslovakia, the second in two weeks, steps down and hands over power to Civic Forum. Former dissident Vaclav Havel accepts the presidency.

14 December   The first democratic elections in 16 years are held in Chile. The elections follow a plebiscite held a year earlier, which was designed to keep General Pinochet in power for another eight years, but which was defeated by a No campaign, led by a broad coalition of centre and left-wing figures. Patricio Aylwin becomes the first democratically elected president of Chile since the overthrow of Salvador Allende in 1973. General Pinochet remains Senator for life and chief of staff of the armed forces, however.

17 December   Romanian troops and policemen attack protesters in Timisoara, causing many casualties. Unrest spreads to Bucharest and other parts of Romania.

25 December   In Romania, the people and the army wrest control from the Securitate, the secret service. Nicolae and Elena Ceausescu are captured and executed after a perfunctory trial.

1990

This year marks the official end of the Cold War. At the Paris Summit, the Conference on Security and Cooperation in Europe (CSCE) turns itself into a permanent organisation (OSCE) and adopts a declaration committing all CSCE states to free elections, multi-party systems, and the rule of law. NATO and the Warsaw Pact issue a joint declaration marking the end of the Cold War, and a US–Soviet summit reaches an accord on disarmament. The German Democratic Republic and the Federal Republic of Germany are reunited. In August, Iraqi troops invade and occupy Kuwait. The UN Security Council condemns the invasion, demands immediate withdrawal, and proclaims economic sanctions against Iraq.

11 February   After decades of anti-apartheid struggle inside and outside South Africa, ANC-leader Nelson Mandela is released from prison.

11 March   After an overwhelming victory by the nationalist Sajudis movement in the first multiparty elections in the Baltic republic, the newly elected Lithuanian parliament declares independence. Soviet President Gorbachev issues an ultimatum to withdraw the declaration. Two weeks later, Soviet army and KGB troops enter Vilnius and occupy Communist Party buildings, printing presses, and the Prosecutor's office. Estonia and Latvia also declare independence later this spring.

18 March   The first and last democratic elections of the German Democratic Republic take place. By electing the new Alliance for Germany, the East German electorate approves the move towards the unification of Germany.

6 April   More than 50 members of Nepal's People's Movement are killed by gunfire. Subsequently, however, the king of Nepal gives in to their demands, and Nepal is transformed from an absolute monarchy into a constitutional democracy.

7 April   300,000 people march for independence in Vilnius, Lithuania. A week later, Gorbachev issues a second ultimatum: the Lithuanian parliament should rescind independence or face an economic blockade. An oil and gas embargo is introduced.

27 May   While its leader Daw Aung San Suu Kyi is kept under house arrest, the National League for Democracy wins 82% of the vote in the first democratic elections in Burma in 30 years. The military regime refuses to cede power, however.

29–30 September   The World Summit for Children takes place in New York. 45 NGOs participate in the Summit.

16 December   Jean-Bertrand Aristide sweeps the polls in the first democratic presidential elections in Haiti.

1991

This is the year of the Gulf War. A coalition led by the United States and authorised by the UN Security Council conducts aerial bombardments of Iraq; Iraq fires Scud missiles at Israel in retaliation. Six weeks later, coalition forces invade Kuwait and Iraq. The UN Security Council sanctions, adopted before the war, remain in place to this day. A coup is committed against Soviet President Gorbachev; the failure of the coup spells the end of the USSR. This is also the year in which apartheid is repealed in South Africa.

11–13 January   After a final ultimatum by President Gorbachev, Soviet troops storm vital buildings, including the television tower, in Vilnius, Lithuania; the independent news agency Interfax is closed in Moscow. 14 people are killed.

17 January   Half a million people participate in the burial of the victims in Vilnius. The head of the Russian Orthodox Church participates in the Catholic mass and condemns the murder. Russian paratroopers heed calls by Russian President Yeltsin to refuse deployment in the Baltic Republics.

20 January   After more people are killed in Latvia, hundreds of thousands of people demonstrate across the Soviet Union to protest against the crackdown on the Baltic states and demand independence for the republics. In Moscow, 100,000 supporters of Russian President Boris Yeltsin turn out. In Baku, Azerbaijan, a million people participate, commemorating 130 victims killed by the Soviet army in a crackdown on pro-independence demonstrators a year earlier. Ten days later, Moscow announces the withdrawal of paratroopers from Lithuania, paving the way for independence.

27 February   After months of civil unrest, a caretaker government organises the first free and fair elections in Bangladesh in many years. They are won by Khaleda Zia's BNP, with the Awami League, also led by a woman, a close second.

Early March   After defeat in Kuwait, uprisings against Saddam Hussein take place both in northern and southern Iraq. An estimated 1.5 million people flee their homes as a result of the ensuing bloodshed.

17 March   A referendum on the preservation of the USSR is held. Armenia, Georgia, Moldova, and the Baltic states refuse to participate.

18 May   North-west Somalia declares unilateral independence as 'Somaliland'. No other states have recognised it to date, and development assistance is given only through voluntary aid agencies.

25 June   The parliaments of Croatia and Slovenia declare independence from Yugoslavia. Fighting breaks out between supporters of independence and the Yugoslav army. Within five days, an agreement is reached to withdraw federal troops from Slovenia.

7 July   The Helsinki Citizens' Assembly organises a meeting in Belgrade titled 'Disintegration of Yugoslavia–Integration of Europe', which attracts 150 activists, intellectuals, and politicians from eastern and western Europe. This meeting, the first since the beginning of the crisis, sets the stage for civic responses to the war in Yugoslavia.

19–21 August   While Soviet President Gorbachev is on vacation in the Black Sea resort of Sochi, KGB General Vladimir Kryuchkov, Vice-President Gennady Yanayev, and a group of co-conspirators announce that he is ill and declare a state of emergency. They send tanks into the streets of Moscow and ban all but Communist Party media as well as any demonstrations or gatherings. Russian President Boris Yeltsin reacts by barricading himself in the building of the Russian Parliament, where he is joined by thousands of civilians, a number of buses, and several armoured personnel carriers. A day later, the coup collapses, having failed to secure support from the army. Coup leaders are arrested. Gorbachev returns to Moscow significantly weakened.

Late September   400 anti-war activists from all over Europe, and thousands from Yugoslavia itself, take part in a peace caravan which travels through Trieste to Rijeka, Ljubljana, Zagreb, Subotica, Novi Sad, and Belgrade, culminating in Sarajevo. In Sarajevo, thousands form a human chain linking a mosque, a synagogue, an Orthodox church, and a Catholic church.

30 September General Raoul Cedras takes over power from Haiti's first democratically elected President, Jean-Bertrand Aristide. The military fires bullets at people in protest demonstrations, and randomly in the poor areas, where support for Aristide is strong. Hundreds are killed.

23 October The four parties in the Cambodia conflict and 19 other interested states sign the Paris Peace Accords, a comprehensive political settlement which is to include repatriation of over 360,000 refugees, arrival of UN peace-keeping troops, and free elections.

30 October A Peace Conference on the Middle East is opened in Madrid. Delegations from Israel, Lebanon, Syria, and a joint Jordanian-Palestinian delegation attend. The Conference is chaired by the United States and the USSR.

12 November Indonesian troops open fire on an unarmed demonstration in support of independence in Dili, East Timor, killing more than 100 people. The massacre galvanises solidarity groups in western and Lusophone countries and causes many new ones to spring up, leading to a sustained campaign to expose human rights violations and promote East Timorese independence.

26 December The Front Islamique du Salut wins 188 out of 430 seats in the first round of the first democratic general elections in Algeria since 1963, despite the fact that its leaders, Abbas Madani and Ali Belhadj, have been imprisoned. The army thereupon cancels the second round in elections and cracks down on the FIS. The country quickly descends into civil war.

1992

This year marks the birth of the European Union. The heads of state and government of the European Community sign the Maastricht Treaty, turning the organisation from a predominantly economic association into a political one. This is also the year in which the war in former Yugoslavia escalates. Failing to intervene in Bosnia, the international community intervenes in the conflict in Somalia. The Earth Summit in Rio with unprecedented participation from NGOs undertakes to address issues of climate change and bio-diversity.

16 January After a year and a half of negotiations, the government of El Salvador and the armed opposition movement FMLN sign a formal peace agreement and agree a ceasefire and disarmament programme, to be monitored by the UN Observer Mission in El Salvador (UNOSAL).

17 March In South Africa, a 'Whites only' referendum is held on whether to end the policy of apartheid. 68.7% of the voters vote 'Yes', while 31.3% vote 'No'.

29 April A US jury finds the four police officers not guilty of committing any crimes against Rodney King, despite the fact that George Holiday had captured the savage beating King received a year earlier on videotape from his apartment across the street. Riots break out in Los Angeles.

18 May 30,000 Thais defy a curfew, rallying against the military rule of general Suchinda and demanding that he step down. The army opens fire on the crowd, killing dozens and wounding hundreds. In response, rioters burn government buildings and vehicles. A week later Suchinda resigns, paving the way for democratic elections.

3 June The Australian High Court hands down a landmark decision in the struggle for Aborigine emancipation, known as Mabo 2. It recognises that before 1788 Australia was not *terra nullius* but belonged to the Aboriginal and Torres Strait Islander People.

3–14 June The United Nations Conference on Environment and Development (also known as the Earth Summit) takes place in Rio de Janeiro. It produces two conventions, the United Nations Framework Convention on Climate Change and the United Nations Convention on Biological Diversity, and three non-binding declarations. Some 2,400 representatives of NGOs attend the Conference; 17,000 people take part in the parallel NGO Forum.

19 July Two months after the murder of Italian mafia-prosecutor Giovanni Falcone, his wife and three escorts, his colleague Paolo Borsellino and five police escorts are killed by another massive bomb in Palermo, Sicily. The citizens of Palermo take to the streets in protest. Women hang bed sheets out of the windows with slogans like 'Enough!' and 'Thank you Falcone and Borsellino' written on them.

29 August Following months of growing political turmoil and street demonstrations, Brazilian President Collor is impeached by Congress on charges of corruption, and Vice-President Itamar Franco is sworn into office. Subsequent to this mass mobilisation, a Citizenship Action against Hunger and Misery and for Life is launched in Brazil by activist Herbert de Souza, known as 'Betinho'. The campaign leads to the creation of over 5,000 all-volunteer committees throughout the country to raise and distribute food donations for the poor. The success of the campaign following the impeachment crisis spurs interest in civil society and inspires numerous other civic initiatives.

29–30 September The first multiparty elections are held in Angola. MPLA-PT wins 54% of the vote, UNITA 34%. However, UNITA takes up arms again after losing the elections and plunges the country back into war.

4 October After nearly two years of negotiations, the government of Mozambique and the armed opposition movement RENAMO sign the final protocols of a General Peace Agreement. They invite the United Nations to participate in monitoring implementation of the agreement.

12 October Governments in Spain and the Americas celebrate the fact that Christopher Columbus first set foot in the Americas 500 years' ago. Indigenous people and sympathisers all over the continent stage manifestations mourning the near-obliteration of the native population and the environmental destruction that followed the 'discovery' of the Americas.

6 December Officials of the Hindu nationalist party BJP lead a march to the Babri Masjid mosque in Ayodhya, which is built over the remains of a Hindu temple. The crowd climbs the centuries-old mosque and demolishes it by hand and with explosives. Thousands of people lose their lives in the ensuing violence in India, Pakistan, Bangladesh, and the United Kingdom.

1993

In this year, the intervention in Somalia fails. The forces of Somali warlord Mohamed Farah Aideed attack and kill United Nations soldiers. Footage is shown of American bodies being dragged through the streets of Mogadishu, causing an about-face in the US's willingness to involve itself in the conflict. The United States and the Russian Federation sign the START II treaty, further limiting of the number of nuclear weapons they hold. China breaks the moratorium on nuclear testing. In the United States, eighty members of the Branch Davidian sect die by fire as the FBI raids their headquarters in Waco after a 50-day siege.

13 January After many years of exertions by NGOs and concerned scientists, the Convention on the Prohibition of the Development, Production, Stockpiling and Use of Chemical Weapons (Chemical Weapons Convention) is signed in Paris.

22 February At the instigation of human rights organisations, the UN Security Council adopts a resolution establishing an International Criminal Tribunal for former Yugoslavia (abbreviated as ICTY). The tribunal, based in The Hague, will prosecute persons who have been responsible for serious violations of international humanitarian law committed in former Yugoslavia since 1991.

24 May The first NGO International Conference on Landmines is held in London bringing together representatives of more than 50 NGOs to build a strategy for the International Campaign to Ban Landmines (ICBL).

23–28 May Over 4 million Cambodians cast their votes in elections supervised by the United Nations. The PDK, successor party to the Khmer Rouge, does not participate. The elections take place without major violent incidents. Observers declare them free and fair.

14–25 June The United Nations World Conference on Human Rights is held in Vienna, Austria. It recommends the establishment of the Office of High Commissioner for Human Rights and the study of the possibility of an International Criminal Court. More than 2,400 representatives of about 1,300 NGOs take part in the NGO Forum.

23 July A gang of hooded, off-duty military policemen opens fire on a group of 50 street children in downtown Rio de Janeiro; eight are killed in this 'Candelária Massacre'. Public outcry and international mobilisation eventually succeed in bringing nine men to court.

13 September After 14 months of secret negotiations, sponsored by Norway, Israel and the PLO sign the Oslo Agreement according to which Israel will withdraw from the Gaza Strip and from Jericho within five years, and a Palestine Authority will be established there. Israel and the PLO officially recognise each other.

21 September Russian President Boris Yeltsin dissolves the Russian Parliament and calls for early parliamentary elections. Vice-President Alexander Rutskoi and the Parliament declare this decision unconstitutional and claim the presidency. Two days later, the parliament holds a session in defiance of Yeltsin's decree. 2,000 protesters gather round the White House in support of the Parliament, but its call for strikes and civil disobedience fall on deaf ears. A day later, Yeltsin's troops encircle the Parliament and cut off water and electricity.

3 October 15,000 protesters break the siege of the Russian Parliament and join the rebellious parliamentarians. After receiving arms from the Parliament, the demonstrators move on to attack the mayor's office and the TV tower. The next day, troops storm the parliament building after a nine-hour battle. Tanks fire their canons at the building. 150 people are believed to have died in two days of fighting, and 1,500 people, including many parliamentarians, are arrested. Yeltsin purges opponents in Moscow and the regions, banning a number of groups and media outlets including the communist *Pravda*.

1994

This is the year of the genocide in Rwanda. The war in Bosnia continues and Sarajevo is under siege. The United States intervene in Haiti, pressuring the military junta to step down and go into exile. At the end of the year Russia attacks the secessionist republic of Chechnya. The World Trade Organization is established to replace the General Agreement on Tariffs and Trade.

1 January As a result of civil society pressure in Canada, Mexico and the United States, the North American Agreement on Environmental Cooperation (NAAEC) and North American Agreement on Labour Cooperation (NAALC) come into force along with the North American Free Trade Agreement (NAFTA).

1 January The Zapatista National Liberation Army (EZLN) takes seven towns in Chiapas, Mexico, and its leader, Subcomandante Marcos, issues the First Declaration of the Lacandon Jungle, declaring war on the Mexican government and army but also protesting against neo-liberal ideology, and in particular NAFTA. The Mexican army begins a bloody counter-offensive against the Zapatistas.

25 February An Israeli settler opens fire on a crowded mosque in Hebron on the West Bank, killing 48 Palestinians.

6 April The presidents of Rwanda and Burundi are killed in a mysterious air crash. Rwandan soldiers and Interahamwe begin a genocide in which between 500,000 and 1 million Tutsis and tolerant Hutus are slaughtered.

26–29 April Multiracial parliamentary and presidential elections are held in South Africa. The ANC wins 62.6% of the vote and Nelson Mandela wins the presidential election.

1 May Brazil's three-times Formula One champion Ayrton Senna dies tragically during a race in Italy. Thousands mourn publicly at his funeral at São Paulo and millions watch live TV coverage. Senna's sister soon establishes the Ayrton Senna Institute, which becomes one of Brazil's leading educational charities.

14 July More than 1 million Rwandans flood into the eastern Zaire town of Goma in four days. Cholera breaks out and as many as 50,000 people die within a matter of weeks. A huge international aid effort, costing 2 billion dollars in the first two weeks alone, is launched.

5–9 August Nearly 7,000 Mexican civil society activists attend the first 'Aguascalientes Forum' in the jungle of Chiapas, convoked by the Zapatistas, who call on civil society to 'defeat them' by achieving a peaceful transition to democracy.

5–13 September The UN Conference on Population and Development takes place in Cairo. It is attended by 1,254 accredited NGOs from 138 countries. More than 4,200 representatives of over 1,500 non-governmental organisations attend the parallel NGO Forum '94.

29 September At the 50th anniversary of the World Bank and International Monetary Fund, activists submit the Manibeli Declaration, signed by 326 groups from 44 countries, asking for a moratorium on World Bank funding for big dams. This date also marks the beginning of an international campaign against the activities of the Bank and Fund called 'Fifty Years is Enough'.

8 November The UN Security Council adopts a resolution establishing an International Criminal Tribunal for Rwanda, with its seat in Arusha, Tanzania, which will prosecute persons responsible for genocide and other serious crimes against humanitarian law committed in Rwanda during 1994.

11 December Russian President Yeltsin sends troops into Chechnya to put an end to three years of chaotic independence under the leadership of Jokhar Dudayev. According to a poll, 70% of Russians oppose the decision to send troops in. The opposition intensifies as the war drags on. Russian intellectuals, artists, and journalists widely proclaim their opposition to the war, and the

independent media provide damning information on army brutality and incompetence. The leading anti-war group, the Soldiers' Mothers, holds daily protest vigils outside military headquarters and the parliament and in Chechnya itself. It also provides advice to deserters and searches for missing soldiers and prisoners of war.

1995

This year marks the culmination and end of the war in Bosnia. The UN safe area Srebenica falls to the Bosnian Serb army. The Bosnian Serb army separates the men from the women and children and they are led away and killed. Richard Goldstone, the prosecutor of the Yugoslavia Tribunal, indicts Bosnian Serb political leader Karadzic and military leader Mladic on charges of genocide, war crimes, and crimes against humanity. NATO, with the backing of the United Nations, begins to launch air strikes against Bosnian Serb troops attacking Sarajevo. The Mexican economy is rescued by a $20-billion aid programme. Just before celebrating its 50th anniversary, the United Nations' financial crisis deepens, and it has to borrow from the Peacekeeping Fund.

17 January An earthquake strikes the region of Kobe and Osaka in south-central Japan, killing more than 5,000 people and causing hundreds of thousands to lose their homes. The relief effort by volunteers triggers a debate within Japan about the need to support non-profit organisations, which eventually leads to a new law.

6–12 March The World Summit on Social Development takes place in Copenhagen. The official Summit is attended by approximately 2,300 representatives from 800 accredited NGOs and over 2,800 journalists. About 12,000 NGO representatives attend a parallel NGO Forum which adopts an Alternative Copenhagen Declaration.

20 March A nerve gas attack by the Aum Shinrikyo sect in the Tokyo underground kills eight people and injures thousands.

10 July Burmese opposition leader Daw Aung San Suu Kyi is released from house arrest.

4–15 September The Fourth World Conference on Women takes place in Beijing. It adopts the Beijing Declaration and Platform for Action. Despite restrictions imposed by the Chinese government, representatives from 2,100 non-governmental organisations and 5,000 journalists attend the Conference. About 25,000 people participate in the independent NGO Forum '95, which the Chinese authorities have allocated to a location more than 50 km from the official conference site.

5 September France carries out the first of a series of underground nuclear explosions in French Polynesia. A consumer boycott strikes French wine and other products in response to the nuclear explosions, causing Bordeaux exports to drop by 5% almost immediately. Six months

later, French President Chirac announces the end of France's nuclear tests in the Pacific region.

19–22 October One week after the ceasefire in Bosnia, hundreds of people from the former Yugoslav republics and from other European countries gather for a general assembly of the Helsinki Citizen's Assembly in war-torn Tuzla to discuss the role the international community and civic initiatives from both Bosnia-Herzegovina and abroad can play in the solution of the conflict in Bosnia.

24 October The 50th anniversary of the United Nations is commemorated with the largest gathering of world leaders in history. Meanwhile, the first 'People's Assemblies' are held, one in San Francisco, and one in Perugia, Italy. This sparks a host of new initiatives; by 1997, ten People's Assemblies are held in cities including Tokyo, Wellington, Perugia, Sao Paulo, London, and Los Angeles.

4 November Israeli Prime Minister Yitzhak Rabin is assassinated by a religious nationalist after addressing a peace rally attended by tens of thousands of Israelis in Tel Aviv.

10 November Ogoni leader Ken Saro-Wiwa and eight other leaders of the Movement for the Survival of the Ogoni People (MOSOP) are executed by the Nigerian government after an unfair trial.

21 November The Dayton Agreement on peace in Bosnia–Herzegovina is initialled by Serbian President Milosevic, Croatian President Tudjman, and Bosnian President Izetbegovic. Bosnia–Herzegovina will have a new constitution, and the peace agreement will be implemented by the Implementation Force (IFOR) which will be under NATO command. The sanctions against Yugoslavia (Serbia and Montenegro) are conditionally suspended.

1996

Ethnic violence breaks out in Zairean refugee camps; a UN-backed relief mission for 1.2 million Hutu refugees starving in eastern Zaire allows hundreds of thousands to return to Rwanda. The United Kingdom is alarmed when scientists conclude that Creutzfeld–Jacob Disease can be caused by eating beef from cows who suffered from BSE or 'mad cow disease'. Russian President Boris Yeltsin is re-elected in a hotly contested campaign boosted by a controversial multi-billion rescue package from the IMF.

20 January PLO leader Yasser Arafat becomes the first-ever elected leader of the Palestinians following elections held in the West Bank, Gaza, and East Jerusalem.

12 February The Communist Party of Nepal-Maoist begins a 'people's war', seeking to destroy the constitutional monarchy and aiming to establish a Maoist people's democracy.

17 April Brazilian police troops open fire on demonstrators from the landless peasants movement (MST) who are blocking the road in the Brazilian state of Pará. 19 are killed and 51 injured. Commanders of the operation are later acquitted in a trial that mobilises international attention.

7 May In India, Phoolan Devi, the low-caste 'Bandit Queen' who was jailed for murdering the high-caste men who gang-raped her, is elected to Parliament. The Hindu nationalist party BJP emerges as the largest party nationally.

4–13 June The Second UN Conference on Human Settlement (Habitat II) takes place in Istanbul. More than 6,000 participants from 1,500 organisations take part in the NGO parallel forum.

10 July After Danish beer company Carlsberg drops its plans to establish a brewery in Burma because of the military regime's human rights record, its Dutch competitor Heineken also succumbs to public pressure and sells its interests in a Burmese brewery.

27 July Government-linked thugs attack and clear the party headquarters of Indonesian opposition leader Megawati Sukarnoputri, breaking up the free speech forum that had been established in the back garden. The attack sparks riots in Jakarta.

27 July–3 August The Zapatistas convoke the First Intercontinental Meeting for Humanity and Against Neo-liberalism in Chiapas, Mexico, attended by 3,000 people from 44 countries.

30 July Four women are cleared by a British jury of charges in the 'Ploughshares trial'. They had attacked and damaged a Hawk fighter plane due for export to Indonesia. The women argued that the plane would be used to reinforce repression in East Timor and that by smashing it they had averted a greater evil.

30 August The Russian government finally succumbs to pressure to end the unpopular war in Chechnya. Secretary of the Russian Security Council General Lebed and Chechen Chief of Staff Maskhadov sign a peace agreement. The treaty calls for the withdrawal of Russian forces from the republic and for elections at the end of the year. A decision on Chechnya's future political status is postponed until 31 December 2001.

10 September After many years of lobbying by anti-nuclear activists and NGOs, the United Nations finally adopts the Comprehensive Nuclear Test-Ban Treaty (CTBT).

14 September The first multiparty elections take place in Bosnia–Herzegovina and the Republika Srpska.

27 September The Afghan capital Kabul falls to the fundamentalist Islamist Taliban. They impose restrictions based on hard-line interpretations of Islam, including banning women from work and education and introducing punishments such as stoning to death and amputations.

13–17 November   The World Food Summit is held in Rome. The parallel NGO Forum is attended by 1,300 NGO representatives from 80 countries.

17 December   Members of the Movimento Revolucionario Tupac Amaru (MRTA) take guests hostage at a cocktail party at the Japanese embassy in Lima, Peru, demanding release of hundreds of MRTA prisoners. Hostages released in subsequent days sing their captors' praises. Four months later, Peruvian military forces storm and take over the embassy, killing all 14 MRTA revolutionaries.

29 December   A peace agreement is signed in Guatemala City between the President of Guatemala and various armed opposition groups.

1997

This is the year of the 'Asian crisis'. The Thai currency, baht, collapses, and other south-east Asian currencies follow. Conditions attached to IMF rescue packages spark mass protests in South Korea and other afflicted countries. In accordance with the 1842 Treaty of Nanking, the United Kingdom hands over authority over Hong Kong to the People's Republic of China. The 'one country, two systems' principle is supposed to guarantee democracy and civil rights in Hong Kong. After 32 years in power, President Mobutu of Zaire flees Kinshasa, surrendering power to the anti-Mobutu alliance led by Laurent Kabila, who renames the country Democratic Republic of Congo. The Khmer Rouge put their long-time leader Pol Pot on trial. In Britain, the sheep 'Dolly' is created by cloning.

Late January   The collapse of pyramid investment schemes leads to demonstrations and chaos in Albania as popular groups seize arms from the government's caches.

2–4 February   Over 2,900 people from 137 countries attend the Microcredit Summit in Washington DC, which launches a campaign to reach 100 million poor people with microcredit facilities by 2005.

5–6 February   In Ecuador, 2 million people go on strike and march against President Abdala Bucaram's corrupt government, prompting the Ecuadorian Congress to vote him out of office.

21 February   After three months of street protests, peaking at 500,000 demonstrators, Serbian President Slobodan Milosevic accepts the election results and opposition leader Zoran Djindjic is installed as mayor of Belgrade.

17 April   Thousands of landless Brazilians reach the capital Brasilia after a two-month march to pressure the government to implement land reform. The streets are lined with people to welcome them.

23 May   The people of Iran overwhelmingly elect moderate cleric Muhammad Khatami as President, marking the first serious challenge to the religious conservative establishment.

16–17 June   A European Council Meeting aimed at revising the Maastricht Treaty takes place in Amsterdam. Demonstrators from various EU states are arbitrarily detained in Amsterdam during the summit.

31 August   Diana, Princess of Wales, dies in a car crash in Paris. Millions mourn her death.

17 November   69 people are massacred by militant Islamists at the temple of Hatshepsut in Luxor, Upper Egypt, including 58 foreign tourists. This marks the culmination and the end of an eight-year insurgency by radical Islamists against the Egyptian regime.

3–4 December   121 states sign the Convention on the Prohibition of the use, stockpiling, production, and transfer of antipersonnel mines and on their destruction, known as the Mine Ban Treaty, in Ottawa, Canada. A People's Treaty endorsing the Mine Ban Treaty is signed by thousands of people around the world.

11 December   In Kyoto, Japan, the parties to the United Nations Framework Convention on Climate Change draw up the Kyoto Protocol, a treaty that would, after entering into force, require industrialised nations to reduce their emissions of greenhouse gases according to specific targets and timetables. The majority of the approximately 3,000 NGO representatives in attendance at Kyoto are of the opinion that massive restrictions on global energy use are critical and overdue.

18 December   South Korea elects Kim Dae Jung, a former democracy activist who has been imprisoned, kidnapped, and exiled by the former military dictatorship, to the presidency.

30 December   More than 400 Algerian villagers are murdered by the Groupe Islamique Armée (GIA) on the first evening of Ramadan. It is the biggest massacre in the Algerian civil war, which has already claimed tens of thousands of civilian lives.

1998

This is a year of renewed conflict in Africa and former Yugoslavia. Eritrea occupies an area in Ethiopia to which it claims to have title, and the two countries go to war. The armed opposition against President Kabila takes control of the eastern part of Congo. Despite international negotiations, the repression of Kosovar Albanians, and armed resistance to it, begins to escalate. Bombs explode at the US embassies in Kenya and Tanzania, killing more than 200 people. The US suspects that Osama bin Laden, a Saudi millionaire who lives in Afghanistan, is behind the bombing, and launches missiles against sites in Sudan and Afghanistan in retaliation. President Clinton narrowly survives an impeachment procedure. The aftershocks of the Asian crises sweep Russia and Brazil. The collapse of multi-billion dollar hedge fund LTCM threatens to spread to developed markets. The US Federal Reserve's rescue of LTCM and successive interest rates cuts prevent an all-out meltdown. Hurricane Mitch claims 10,000 lives in Central America.

11 January More than 10,000 Indians stage a sit-in to protest against the building of the Maheshwar Dam on the Narmada river, which would displace thousands of people.

1 March 300,000 rural Brits take part in a march on London to ask attention for the problems faced by people living in the British countryside, including fears for the future of hunting and other field sports, and concern at the problems facing livestock farmers.

10 April The Northern Ireland Peace Agreement (Good Friday Agreement) is signed in Belfast by representatives of eight political parties, including Sinn Féin and unionist parties, and by British Prime Minister Blair and Irish Prime Minister Ahern.

26 April Two days after presenting a comprehensive report on human rights violations in Guatemala during the civil war, bishop Juan Gerardi Conedara is battered to death.

12 May Four Indonesian students are shot dead by the army following a peaceful demonstration against the Soeharto regime. The shootings spark massive riots in six of the country's largest cities. Days later, hundreds of thousand students and members of the public pour into the streets, and thousands march to the parliament, which they occupy for several days. On 21 May, after 32 years in power, Indonesian President Soeharto is finally forced to resign, handing over power to his Vice-President, B. J. Habibie.

16 May 70,000 people form a human chain around the city centre of Birmingham, UK, where the leaders of the G8 are supposed to be meeting, in support of debt relief for developing countries. The G8 leaders have moved their summit to the countryside, however; only British Prime Minister Tony Blair comes to meet the demonstrators.

22 May In referendums in Northern Ireland and the Republic of Ireland, a great majority votes in support of the Good Friday agreement.

28 May Two weeks after India carries out a number of underground nuclear explosions, Pakistan explodes five nuclear devices. Both in India and Pakistan, peace groups emerge and create transnational links with each other and with other countries in an effort to oppose nuclear escalation.

1 June—Hundreds of children from over 50 countries reach the International Labour Organisation in Geneva at the end of a global march against child labour.

17 July A diplomatic conference in Rome adopts a Statute establishing the International Criminal Court, with its seat at The Hague. The NGO Coalition for an International Criminal Court now shifts its campaign towards achieving state ratifications.

23 July The Burmese police stops opposition leader Daw Aung San Suu Kyi from leaving Rangoon to meet other members of the National League for Democracy. She spends six days sitting in her car by the side of the road in protest. The authorities eventually seize her car and drive her back home against her will. These stand-offs are repeated a number of times over the next few years.

15 August The Real IRA detonates a bomb in the centre of Omagh, Northern Ireland, killing 28 people and wounding more than 200. The people of Northern Ireland are appalled, and public opinion in both communities turns further against sectarian violence.

20 September After leading a demonstration of 30,000 people against Prime Minister Mahathir, former Malaysian finance minister Anwar Ibrahim is arrested, sparking further demonstrations.

14 October France withdraws from the negotiations by the member states of the OECD on the Multilateral Agreement on Investment (MAI) which had met with widespread civil society resistance. The negotiations are subsequently halted.

16 October Former Chilean dictator Augusto Pinochet is arrested in London after an extradition request from Spain, where he is charged with having ordered torture, executions, and disappearances. The subsequent criminal process rekindles the idea that courts may have 'universal jurisdiction' for crimes against humanity, even when they are committed by heads of state.

15–17 November 38 national Jubilee 2000 Campaigns and 12 international organisations meet in Rome to decide on a common policy and strategy in their campaign for a one-off cancellation of the unpayable debts of the world's poorest countries by the year 2000.

3 December The Conference of Non-Governmental Organisations (CONGO), which consists of the NGOs accredited to the United Nations, celebrates its 50th anniversary.

9 December After years of lobbying by human rights organisations and resistance from certain governments, the UN General Assembly finally adopts the Universal Declaration for the Protection of Human Rights Defenders.

10 December The 50th anniversary of the Universal Declaration of Human Rights is celebrated, and victims of human rights violations are commemorated, all over the world.

1999

This is the year of the Kosovo war. Peace talks between the Serbian government and various Kosovar Albanian delegations at Rambouillet fail. NATO begins to bomb Serbia while Serbia steps up ethnic cleansing against Kosovar

Albanians. After two months, Milosevic accepts peace terms. NATO and Russian forces are deployed in Kosovo. Serbian President Slobodan Milosevic is indicted by the Yugoslavia Tribunal on charges of war crimes and crimes against humanity in Kosovo. After obtaining permission from Indonesian President Habibie, an Australian-led United Nations force lands in Dili, East Timor, which has been burnt to the ground by militias. In response to several explosions in Moscow, which are blamed on Chechen terrorists, Russia begins a second war against Chechnya.

15 February Kurdish rebel leader Abdullah Ocalan is captured and flown to Turkey in unexplained circumstances after turning up at the Greek embassy in Nairobi, Kenya. The arrest sparks passionate protests from Kurds all over Europe. He is subsequently sentenced to death in a trial behind closed doors.

24 March After the initial decision has been overruled because one of the Lords had links with Amnesty International, a party in the proceedings, the British House of Lords rules again in the case against Augusto Pinochet. It rules, with a four to three majority, that he can be extradited, but only on charges of torture committed after 1988. While Pinochet supporters are aghast, former victims, some of whom have been holding a vigil outside the House of Lords, see this as a moral victory. Human rights groups, however, criticise the judgment as too conservative in its interpretation of international law.

11–15 May The Hague Appeal for Peace conference, a conference only of civil society organisations, is held in the Hague, the Netherlands. It adopts the The Hague Agenda for Peace and Justice in the Twenty-first Century.

16 August A devastating earthquake hits the town of Izmit, near Istanbul, in Turkey. More than 15,000 people are killed, and more than 600,000 become homeless. While the government's response to the earthquake is sluggish and inadequate, citizens in many European countries set up a huge relief effort. The response from Greek citizens, in particular, initiates a softening in the historic fear and hostility between the Greek and the Turkish peoples.

30 August The people of East Timor vote in a UN-monitored referendum on independence. Despite months of intimidation and violence, 98.6% of those registered turn out to vote, and 78.5% support independence.

4 September On the day the UN announces the result of the vote in East Timor, militia violence, funded and organised by the Indonesian army, escalates, killing thousands and causing most of the population to flee.

14 September Nineteen Pakistani political parties form the Grand Democratic Alliance (GDA), which aims to dislodge Nawaz Sharif's government. The government responds by arresting more than 1,000 opposition activists in order to prevent a rally in Karachi. A month later, army chief General Parvez Musharraf stages a successful coup against Sharif.

16 September In a referendum, Algerians overwhelmingly vote in favour of approving President Abd al-Aziz Bouteflika's law on civil concord. According to this law, the result of long and largely secret negotiations with the armed wing of the FIS, the Islamic Salvation Army (AIS), thousands of AIS members and other armed groups are pardoned, provided they lay down arms.

8 November More than 1 million people march for a referendum on independence in Aceh, Indonesia.

30 November–3 December The World Trade Organisation holds a conference in Seattle. Governments fail to come to an agreement, and the talks collapse. Approximately 50,000 people, including trade unionists, environmentalists, farmers, development workers, and anti-capitalist campaigners, demonstrate, sometimes violently, in the streets. The police reacts by using teargas against the crowds.

Global Civil Society Events of 2000

January

1 January Communal violence in the Egyptian village of al-Kosheh leaves 21 people dead and 44 wounded. The incidents follow allegations of police brutality against Christian Copts related to a murder investigation. Reports on the incident result in increased state harassment of local NGOs that were involved in documenting the incident.

5 January 14-year old Urgyen Trinley Dorje, the 17th Karmapa Lama and third most important spiritual leader of Tibetan Buddhists, flees China, crossing the Himalayas to reach the Dalai Lama in India.

12 January An NGO called People's Solidarity for Participatory Democracy (PSPD), led by Park Won Soon, brings together 412 South Korean organisations in a campaign called Civil Action for the 2000 General Election (CAGE). It releases lists of politicians on the Internet whom they consider unsuitable to run in the upcoming elections because they are corrupt, have violated the election law, have been involved in a military coup or anti-human rights career, or are not diligently carrying out their parliamentary duties. In the end, 59 candidates out of 86 on the final list fail to win seats.

15–21 January Ecuadorian indigenous groups, oil workers, and students protest against President Jamil Mahuad's announcement that his country will exchange the plummeting national currency, the sucre, for the US dollar to fight the country's financial crisis. Aided by soldiers, indigenous groups occupy Congress. After a brief coup attempt, Mahuad agrees to step down in favour of Vice-President Noboa, who plans to continue the dollarisation plans.

18 January The Petrobrás refinery spills 1.3 million litres of oil into Rio de Janeiro's Guanabara bay, Brazil. A clean-up and animal rescue effort mobilises hundreds of volunteers.

24 January In an unprecedented event, Somali human rights activists, writers, aid workers, and other civil society figures meet in the port city of Bossasso, Puntland, to discuss the future role of civil society in reshaping Somalia. In contrast to twelve previous failed initiatives which aimed to secure peace among Somali warlords, this peace plan, supported by Djibouti President Guelleh, is based on Somalia's emerging civil society.

30 January A dam isolating a lagoon at a Romanian gold mine breaks. Around 100,000 square metres of toxic sludge contaminated with cyanides and heavy metals spill into nearby rivers, reaching the Hungarian border several days later. Virtually all aquatic life in Hungary's upper Tisza river is killed. 'Funerals' and mourning ceremonies for the river are held all along the banks.

February

3 February On the basis of a complaint filed by eight human rights organisations a week earlier, Senegal brings Hissene Habre, the former dictator of Chad, to trial on charges of torture.

4–9 February The citizens of Cochabamba, Bolivia, demonstrate and blockade roads in protest against the privatisation of water, which has more than doubled its price. The army and police use violence against the demonstrators, and the government declares martial law, but finally agrees to rescind the contract with US water company Bechtel.

8 February While refusing to recognise the National Women's Union headed by prominent feminist Nawal El-Saadawi, President Mubarak of Egypt establishes a National Women's Council, headed by his wife. He also plans to establish a similar state-sponsored National Human Rights Council later in the year.

15 February In a referendum, Zimbabweans vote against a proposal that would have given President Robert Mugabe even wider executive powers, as well as allowing the seizure of land from white farmers. It is the first victory for the new opposition party, Movement for Democratic Change, which evolved from the labour movement.

21 February This day is recognised by UNESCO as International Mother Language day, in remembrance of the Bangladeshis shot on 21 February 1952 when they demanded that Bengali be the official language of what was then East Pakistan.

21–28 February A demonstration by Christians in the northern Nigerian State Kaduna, protesting against the governor's intention to implement Islamic *sharia* law, sparks sectarian violence all over the country.

22 February After two weeks of heavy rain, cyclone Eline hits Mozambique. Despite an international rescue effort, at least 200 Mozambicans die and a million become homeless, some of them stranded in trees or on rooftops for many days.

27–29 February 20,000 miners in the north-eastern Chinese city Yangjiazhangzi clash with the police and army when they protest against being laid off with insufficient compensation. The riots do not come to the attention of the outside world until more than a month later.

28 February Backed by Robert Mugabe's government, Zimbabwean veterans, or supposed veterans, of the war of independence, begin to seize farms of white landowners. The violence and intimidation are also turned against the Movement for Democratic Change.

29 February Along with over 2,000 supporters, 90-year old Doris Haddock, known as Granny D., reaches Washington, DC after walking 2,800 kilometres from Los Angeles to show members of Congress her concern about campaign finance reform.

29 February In response to criticism from NGOs, De Beers, the world's largest diamond company, announces that its diamonds will henceforth carry a guarantee that they have not been bought from armed groups in conflict areas.

March

2 March British Home Secretary Jack Straw allows the former Chilean dictator Augusto Pinochet to fly home on the basis of his ill-health. This follows his arrest two years earlier and a legal decision in 1999 that, in principle, he can be extradited to Spain to face charges of torture. The announcement is followed by protests as well as demonstrations of support for the former dictator in England, Spain, and Chile.

2 March After a five-year international environmental campaign, President Zedillo of Mexico cancels plans to build one of the world's largest salt plants in Baja California, a joint venture between the Mexican government and Japan's Mitsubishi company. The campaign, supported by more than 50 Mexican and many US environmental groups, included a consumer and investor boycott, newspaper advertisements, billboards, and a letter-writing effort that sent more than 700,000 pieces of protest mail to Zedillo and Mitsubishi.

12 March Pope John Paul II asks God's forgiveness for the Catholic Church's past sins, including its treatment of Jews, heretics, women, and native peoples. Jewish and gay groups criticise the statement, however, for not explicitly mentioning the holocaust and not mentioning homosexuals at all.

17 March Hundreds of members of a cult called the Movement for the Restoration of the Ten Commandments are burnt to death in an act of mass murder in Uganda.

18 March Disenchanted with the corruption of the ruling party and undeterred by mainland China's threats, 76% of the Taiwanese electorate vote for the opposition. Democratic Progressive Party candidate Chen Shui-bian wins the presidency, ending 50 years of Kuomintang rule.

19 March Two weeks after a leaking sewer pumped contaminated waste into the Rodrigo de Freitas lagoon, killing more than 30 tons of fish, 10,000 residents of Rio de Janeiro, wearing white T-shirts, link hands around the lagoon to protest against the rising level of sewage in the sea.

23 March The government of Papua New Guinea and various groups in Bougainville sign the Loloata Understanding, which provides for Bougainvillean autonomy and opens the way for a referendum on autonomy in the long run.

April

15–17 April Tens of thousands of people blockade the streets surrounding the IMF and World Bank buildings in Washington, DC, where the annual board meetings are held, in protest against the policies of the financial institutions. Meetings are delayed by the blockade, and some delegates fail to make it through. Over 600 demonstrators are arrested.

22–30 April Cuban-Americans in Florida organise strikes and demonstrations in protest against the seizure and return to Cuba of six-year-old Elian Gonzalez.

22 April The governments of Brazil and Portugal celebrate the 500th anniversary of the 'discovery' of Brazil by the Portuguese explorer Pedro Alvares Cabral. Thousands of indigenous people attempt to stage a protest march near the site where Cabral set foot on land, in Porto Seguro, against the slavery, exploitation, and marginalisation of indigenous people that followed the 'discovery'. They are turned back by the police with teargas.

24 April–19 May The Review Conference of the Parties to the 1968 Treaty on the Non-Proliferation of Nuclear Weapons (NPT) takes place in New York. 141 NGOs, mainly peace and disarmament groups, monitor the conference.

26 April Thousands of Iranian students boycott classes and attend rallies in protest against the closure of 13 progressive newspapers and against the failure to proclaim the definitive results of the first round of parliamentary elections in February, in which reformists won a sweeping victory. The government closes three more newspapers the next day.

30 April The 25th anniversary of the fall of Saigon is commemorated, celebrated, or mourned, in the United States and Vietnam.

May

22–25 May The Millennium Forum, a 'civil society only' conference, takes place at UN headquarters in New York. The topics of discussion are peace, security and disarmament; poverty eradication; human rights; sustainable development and the environment; globalisation; and democratisation and strengthening of the United Nations and other global institutions.

27 May A quarter of a million people march across Sydney's Harbour Bridge in Australia on Corroboree 2000, a march for reconciliation between the aborigine population and other Australians.

31 May Hong Kong's last Vietnamese refugee camp is officially closed. Over 100 people refuse to leave, however, saying that they cannot afford housing in Hong Kong.

31 May While IMF officials are visiting the country, tens of thousands of Argentines, supported by trade unions and Catholic Church leaders, demonstrate against the 'financial dictatorship' of the IMF, calling for 'fiscal disobedience'.

June

5–9 June The UN General Assembly devotes a special session in New York to 'Women: 2000: Gender Equality, Development and Peace for the Twenty-First Century' (also known as Beijing +5). More than 1,000 NGOs are accredited as observers. They compile an NGO Alternative Global Report on gender issues.

13 June After a general strike and a series of riots in which at least 20 people die, Nigerian President Olusegun Obasanjo reaches an agreement with trade unions to reverse his decision, taken earlier that month, to double petrol prices.

26 June Two separate groups of researchers, a private US research team and a public-funded consortium of scientists from the United States, the United Kingdom, France, Germany, China, and Japan, both announce that they have completed rough drafts of the human genome. The discovery sparks hopes that advances will be made in human health but also concerns that the knowledge will be subject to private patenting, thus exacerbating the differences in treatment available to the rich and the poor. Indigenous peoples are particularly concerned that the information garnered from their genetic material will be turned into private profit rather than benefiting their communities. Further concerns are raised about the possibility of using the technology for eugenic purposes or human cloning.

26–30 June The UN General Assembly devotes a special session in Geneva to the 'World Summit for Social Development and Beyond: Achieving Social Development for All in a Globalizing World' (also known as Copenhagen +5). The summit features more than 150 parallel events, in which representatives of governments, NGOs, universities, and the business sector, as well as various UN agencies, take part.

30 June Tens of thousands of French farmers and other anti-globalisation protestors gather in Millau, France, where French farmer José Bové stands trial for attacking the local branch of McDonald's hamburger restaurant a year earlier.

July

1 July Egypt arrests one of the country's foremost activists, the academic Saad Eddin Ibrahim, Chair of Egypt's Ibn Khaldoun Center for Development Studies. His imprisonment followed the initiation of an ambitious plan for his Center to monitor the country's parliamentary elections in November.

2 July After 72 years of a single ruling party, the leader of the opposition Vicente Fox wins the presidential elections in Mexico. Civil society organisations played an important role in pressing the government for fair play, transparency, and respect for the elections results.

22 July The second oil spill this year causes public indignation against Petrobrás, Brazil's state-owned petroleum enterprise. Four million litres of oil leak into Iguaçú and other rivers in the Brazilian state of Paraná.

25–28 July The International Roma Union (IRU) holds its first Congress in ten years in Prague. More than 250

delegates from almost 40 countries meet to discuss such themes as the situation of the Roma in Kosovo, restitution for Romani victims of the Holocaust, and the standardisation of the Romani language, and to approve a new programme, statutes, and new leadership of the IRU.

28 July Tens of thousands of Peruvians, chanting 'the dictator will fall', are pitched against 40,000 riot police in Lima to mark the inauguration of President Alberto Fujimori's controversial third term. At least six people die and more than 80 are wounded in the subsequent riots.

August

8 August The Supreme Court of Chile confirms the decision of a lower court to strip Augusto Pinochet of his parliamentary immunity, opening the way for a domestic prosecution for a series of disappearances throughout the country, known as the Caravan of Death.

13 August Delegates selected from Somalia's main clans, who have formed a 'transnational assembly' in Djibouti, elect a new Somali President, Abdulkassim Salat Hassan. The proceedings are witnessed by members of the Somali diaspora and international observers. Warlord Mohamed Aideed and break-away regions Somaliland and Puntland do not recognise the new President.

14–16 August The so-called *Observatorio de las Americas* is launched in Morelia, Mexico. It brings together NGOs and academics in an effort to built a monitoring mechanism, based in civil society, to the process of integration of the Americas in a common free-trade area (FTAA). Participants include scholars and NGOs from the whole continent as well as leaders of international agencies such as WTO and WHO.

15 August As a result of South Korean president Kim Dae Jung's 'sunshine policy', 100 North Koreans and 100 South Koreans are allowed to visit their relatives in the other part of the country for a four-day reunion after nearly 50 years.

17–23 August 20,000 Chinese farmers engage in riots over rising taxes, looting government buildings and the houses of officials.

24 August Ricardo Miguel Cavallo, one of the torturers of the 'dirty war' in the 1970s in Argentina, is captured in Mexico, following strong pressure from Argentine, Spanish, and Mexican civil society organisations. The Mexican government decides to arrest Cavallo even though he has not committed any crime in Mexico and is not required by the Argentine government or Interpol. Both Spanish judge Baltasár Garzón and the French authorities request extradition.

28–29 August Over 1,000 representatives of all of the world's major religions, including the Bahá'í Faith, Buddhism, Christianity, Hinduism, Islam, Jainism, Judaism, Shintoism, Sikhism, and Zoroastrianism, as well as indigenous religions from nearly every continent attend the Millennium Summit of Religious Leaders in New York. Nearly all sign a declaration entitled 'Commitment to Global Peace', which states that 'there can be no real peace until all groups and communities acknowledge the cultural and religious diversity of the human family'.

September

2–7 September More than one million Brazilians vote in an unofficial referendum on debt repayment and the IMF. More than 90% answer 'no' to the question whether the Brazilian government should maintain its agreement with the IMF. On 7 September, Brazil's Independence Day, thousands of demonstrators back up this message with their 'Cry of the Excluded' manifestation in different cities.

6 September Only days after the people of East Timor have celebrated the first anniversary of their vote for independence, militias attack UNHCR staff in West Timor and kill three staff members. UNHCR and other human-itarian agencies withdraw from West Timor, where approximately 100,000 people are still detained in refugee camps.

6 September 16 Congolese environment experts and traditional chiefs who are meeting to discuss the protection of gorillas in their area are killed by a Hutu militia.

16 September Thousands of Peruvians celebrate outside the presidential palace in Lima when President Alberto Fujimori announces his resignation over a corruption scandal.

11–13 September The World Economic Forum, which normally meets in Davos, holds a regional meeting in Melbourne. Between 10,000 and 20,000 protestors, including people from church groups, trade unions, and NGOs, try to shut down the summit, expressing the opinion that the organisation is elitist and unaccountable.

23 September On the eve of the IMF–World Bank Meeting in Prague, Czech President Vaclav Havel hosts a debate between IMF and World Bank executives and their critics, moderated by UN Human Rights Commissioner Mary Robinson.

26–28 September Approximately 12,000 activists gather in Prague where the annual IMF–World Bank meeting is held. The meeting is disrupted, and demonstrators clash with the police, leading to many arrests.

28–29 September Hard-line Israeli politician Ariel Sharon makes a provocative visit to the Temple Mount in East Jerusalem, a sacred place to Jews and Muslims, sparking renewed violence between Palestinian protestors and Israeli police. A day later, six Palestinians are killed and nearly 200 wounded at the shrine, and the violence spreads.

October

Early October Palestinians and sympathisers demonstrate against Israeli violence in, among other countries, Egypt, Jordan, Libya, Syria, Denmark, and South Africa.

5 October Tens of thousands of people from all over Serbia come to Belgrade to demand that Yugoslav President Slobodan Milosevic step down in favour of the real winner of the presidential elections held two weeks earlier, Vojislav Kostunica. They storm the parliament and the television tower, and Milosevic eventually concedes power.

16–18 October At a peace conference in Costa Rica, Colombian and international peace, human rights, and humanitarian assistance groups voice opposition to 'Plan Colombia', the US aid package that proposes to combat coca-growing in Colombia mainly through military means.

23 October The G20, a group consisting of the G7 countries and the major developing countries as well as the IMF and the World Bank, meets in Montreal, Canada. Protestors throw balloons with paint at the hotel where the meeting is held. They are disbanded by police with teargas and pepper-spray.

23 October–3 November The Pacific Arts Festival takes place on the islands of New Caledonia, welcoming more than 2,000 guests from 24 Pacific states.

24 October Surrounded by people from the Narmada Valley and sympathisers, Medha Patkar, the leader of the Save the Narmada Movement, goes on a five-day fast in protest against the Indian Supreme Court ruling that the building of the dam is not harmful and construction can be resumed.

25 October Environmental groups in Russia collect 2.5 million signatures for a referendum that would prevent the country from importing nuclear waste as a source of income. The authorities declare more than 600,000 signatures invalid, however, so that the groups do not reach the required threshold for a referendum.

28 October Ibrahim Rugova's moderate party, the Democratic League of Kosovo, wins the first democratic local elections in Kosovo. Most members of the remaining Serb minority in Kosovo boycott the elections.

November

5 November 25 years after his death, Ethiopian emperor Haile Selassie is given a state funeral in Addis Ababa, attended by members of the Ethiopian Orthodox church and a few hundred Rastafarians from abroad. Most Rastafarians refuse to recognise the ceremony, however, because they believe the emperor/god is immortal.

8 November When it becomes clear, the day after the US elections, that George W. Bush has won Florida, and hence the elections, by the narrowest of margins, voters in Palm Beach, Florida, complain that the 'butterfly ballot' was too confusing, triggering the first of many court cases over the elections.

8 November South Africa reacts with horror to a video which shows an all-white police squad setting its dogs on three (probably immigrant) blacks in what they call a dog-training exercise. The South African Broadcasting Company receives 500 calls an hour about the video, and the newspapers and radio stations are flooded with outpourings of anger and horror for days to come. The policemen in question are immediately arrested.

18 November Thousands of activists build a dyke around the conference centre where the UN Conference on Climate Change is taking place in The Hague, in order to illustrate the dangers of climate change and rising sea levels. The US negotiator falls victim to the Dutch radical practice of 'taarting': a whipped cream pie is thrown into his face. Governments fail to come to an agreement in limiting CO_2 emissions at the conference.

December

5 December The International Year of the Volunteer is launched with events in 57 countries.

7 December An impeachment trial on charges of corruption begins against President Jose Estrada of the Philippines. In a protest styled 'People Power II', at least 30,000 of his opponents march around the Senate building to register disapproval of his corrupt and opulent lifestyle.

8–12 December More than 2,000 people from Spain and Italy spend four days in Saharawi refugee camps in Algeria as a sign of solidarity with their plight. The Polisario Front releases 200 Moroccan prisoners of war to move the drawn-out peace process forward.

13 December The US Supreme Court rules that recounts of the Florida ballot are invalid, bringing the five-week election confusion to an end and giving the presidency to George W. Bush. Many voters feel disenfranchised, however, and some continue to take legal action.

27 December The governments of Nepal and Bhutan come to an agreement to facilitate repatriation of 100,000 Nepali-speaking refugees who were forced to flee Bhutan ten years earlier. The refugees themselves are not represented in the negotiations, however.

RECOMMENDED READING

Advisory Council on International Affairs and Advisory Committee on Issues of Public International Law (2000). *Humanitarian Intervention: Legal and Political Aspects*. The Hague: AIV and CAVV.

Amnesty International (2000). *Report 2000*. London: Amnesty International.

Barker, Chris (1999). *Television, Globalisation and Cultural Identities*. Buckingham and Philadelphia: Open University Press.

Barnes, C, and Polzer, T. (2000). *Sierra Leone Peace Process: Learning from the Past to Address Current Challenges* (An Expert Seminar Report). London: Conciliation Resources, 27 September.

Beck, Ulrich (1992). *Risk Society: Towards a New Modernity*. London, Thousand Oaks, CA, New Delhi: Sage.

Bennett, John (1995). *Meeting Needs: NGO Coordination in Practice*. London: Earthscan.

Bennett, John (ed.) (1997). *NGOs and Governments: A Review of Current Practice for Southern and Eastern NGOs*. Oxford: INTRAC/ICVA.

Beynon, John and Dunlerley, David (eds) (2000). *The Globalization Reader*. London: Athlone Press.

Black, M. (1992). *A Cause for Our Time: Oxfam the First 50 Years*. Oxford: Oxfam and Oxford University Press.

Bozóki, András (ed.) (1999). *Intellectuals and Politics in Central Europe*. Budapest: CEU Press.

Buechler, Steven M. (2000). *Social Movements in Advanced Capitalism*. Oxford: Oxford University Press.

Castells, Manuel (1996). *The Rise of the Network Society*. Oxford: Blackwell.

CDD (Centre for Democracy and Development) (2000). 'Sierra Leone in Search of Peace'. Special Report in *Democracy and Development*, 2/4: 4–15.

CDD (Centre for Democracy and Development) (2000). *Engaging Sierra Leone* (Strategy Planning Series 4). London: CDD.

Central Intelligence Agency (CIA) (2000). *World Factbook 2000*. Available online at http://www.cia.gov/cia/publications/factbook/index.html

Chrispeels, Maarten (2000). 'Biotechnology and the Poor'. *Plant Physiology*, 124: 3–6.

Civicus (1999). *Civil Society at the Millennium*. West Hartford, CT: Kumarian Press in cooperation with Civicus.

Clapham, C. (1998). 'Rwanda: The Perils of Peacemaking'. *Journal of Peace Research*, 38/2: 193–210.

Clarke, W. and Herbst, J. (1996). 'Somalia and the Future of Humanitarian Intervention'. *Foreign Affairs*, March/April

Cohen, Robin and Kennedy, Paul (2000). *Global Sociology*. New York: Palgrave.

Cohen, Robin and Rai, Shirin M. (eds) (2000). *Global Social Movements*. London: Athlone Press.

Cooperrider, David L. and Dutton, Jane E. (eds) (1999). *Organizational Dimensions of Global Change*. Thousand Oaks, CA: Sage.

Cushing, C. (1995). 'Humanitarian Assistance and the Role of NGOs'. *Institutional Development*, II, No.2 .

Danish Institute of International Affairs (1999). *Humanitarian Intervention: Legal and Political Aspects*. Copenhagen: DIIA.

Dasgupta, P., and Serageldin, I. (2000). *Social Capital: A Multifaceted Perspective*. Washington, DC: World Bank.

Deacon, Bob, Hulse, Michelle, and Stubbs, Paul (1997). *Global Social Policy: International Organizations and the Future of Welfare*. London, Thousand Oaks, CA. and New Delhi: Sage.

Desai, M. (1994). *Measuring Political Freedom* (Discussion Paper 10). London: Centre for the Study of Global Governance, London School of Economics.

de Waal, A. (1994). 'Fine Feelings, Big Trouble; Relief Agencies Must Choose Between the Moral High Ground and the Battlefield'. *Independent*, 27 November.

de Waal, A. (1995). 'Compassion Fatigue: Famine Relief Agencies'. *New Statesman and Society*, 17 March.

DeMars, W. (2000). 'War and Mercy in Africa'. *World Policy Journal*, 17/2: 1–10.

Dumm, T. L. (1999). *A Politics of the Ordinary*. New York: New York University.

Dunne, Tim and Wheeler, Nicholas J. (eds) (1999). *Human Rights in Global Politics*. Cambridge: Cambridge University Press.

Economist (2000). 'A Survey of E-Management, "Inside the machine"'. 18 November.

Edwards, Michael and Hulme, David (eds) (1992). *Making a Difference: NGOs and Development in a Changing World*. London: Earthscan.

Edwards, Michael and Hulme, David (eds) (1996). *NGO Accountability in the Post-Cold War World.* Bloomfield, Conn.: Kumarian Press.

Ehrenberg, John (1999). *Civil Society: The Critical History of an Idea.* New York and London: New York University Press.

Elias, Norbert (1994). *The Civilising Process: Sociogenic and Psychogeneric Investigations.* Oxford: Blackwell.

Ero, C. (2000). *Sierra Leone's Security Complex* (The Conflict, Security and Development Group Working Papers). London: King's College, University of London (June).

Falk, R. (1999). *Predatory Globalisation: A Critique.* Cambridge: Polity Press.

Florini, Ann M. (ed.) (2000). *The Third Force: The Rise of Transnational Civil Society.* Washington, DC: Carnegie Endowment for International Peace.

Friedman, Thomas L. (2000). *The Lexus and Olive Tree.* New York: Farrar Straus Giroux.

Fukuyama, Francis (1996). *Trust: The Social Virtues and the Creation of Prosperity.* London: Penguin.

Furedi, Frank (1997). *Population and Development.* Cambridge: Polity Press.

Giddens, Anthony (1990). *The Consequences of Modernity.* Cambridge: Polity Press.

Giddens, Anthony (1999). *Runaway World: How Globalisation is Reshaping Our Lives.* London: Profile Books.

Goffman, Erving (1974). *Frame Analysis: An Essay on the Organization of Experience.* Cambridge, MA: Harvard University Press.

Grimwood-Jones, Diana and Simmons, Sylvia (eds) (1998). *Information Management in the Voluntary Sector.* London: Aslib.

Habermas, J. (1962). *Strukturwandel der Öffentlichkeit : Untersuchungen einer Kategorie der Bürgerlichen Gesellschaft.* Neuwied: Luchterhand.

Harriss, J. (ed.) (1995). *The Politics of Humanitarian Intervention.* London and New York: Pinter.

Harvey, Brian (1992). *Networking in Europe: A Guide to European Voluntary Organisations.* London: NCVO.

Harvey, Brian (1995). *Networking in Eastern and Central Europe: A Guide to Voluntary and Community Organisations.* London: Community Development Foundation and Directory of Social Change.

Held, David and McGrew, A. (1998). 'The End of the Old Order? Globalisation and the Prospects for World Order'. *Review of International Studies,* 24: 219–44.

Held, David, McGrew, Anthony, Goldblatt, David, and Perraton, Jonathan (1999). *Global Transformations.* Cambridge: Polity Press.

Human Rights. Foreign and Commonwealth Office and Department for International Development Annual Report for 1999 (1999). Report Presented to Parliament by the Secretary of State for Foreign and Commonwealth Affairs and the Secretary of State for International Development, London, FCO. July.

Human Rights Watch (2000). *World Report 2000.* New York: Human Rights Watch.

Ignatieff, M. (2000). *The Rights Revolution.* Toronto: Anansi Press.

Independent International Commission on Kosovo (2000). *Kosovo Report: Conflict, International Response, Lessons Learnt.* Oxford: Oxford University Press.

Inglehart, R., Basañez, M., and Moreno, A. (1998). *Human Values and Beliefs: A Cross-Cultural Sourcebook: Political, Religious, Sexual, and Economic Norms in 43 Societies: Findings from the 1990–1993 World Values Survey.* Ann Arbor: The University of Michigan Press.

International Telecommunications Union (ITU) (1999). *World Telecommunication Development Report 1999.*

Jordan, Tim and Lent, Adam (eds) (1999), *Storming the Millennium: The New Politics of Change.* London: Lawrence and Wishart.

Kaldor, Mary (2000) '"Civilising" Globalisation? The Implications of the "Battle in Seattle"', *Millennium,* 29/1: 105–14.

Kaldor, M. (ed.) (2000). *Global Insecurity.* London and New York: Pinter.

Kaldor, Mary (forthcoming). *Global Civil Society.* Cambridge: Polity Press.

Kaufmann, D., Kraay, A., and Zoido-Lobatón, P. (1999). *Governance Matters* (World Bank Policy Research Working Paper 2196). Washington DC: World Bank. http://www.worldbank.org/wbi/governance/pdf/ govmatrs.pdf

Kaufmann, D., Kraay, A., and Zoido-Lobatón, P. (1999). *Aggregating Governance Indicators* (World Bank Policy Research Working Paper 2195). Washington, DC: World Bank. http://www.worldbank.org/wbi/ governance/pdf/agg_ind.pdf.

Keck, Margaret E. and Sikkink, Kathryn (1998). *Activists Beyond Borders: Advocacy Networks in International Politics.* Ithaca, NY and London: Cornell University Press.

Korten, David C. (1990). *Getting to the 21st Century: Voluntary Action and the Global Agenda.* West Hartford, CT: Kumarian Press.

Lambsdorff, J. G. (1999). *Corruption in Empirical Research: A Review* (Transparency International Working Paper). Transparency International, http://www.transparency.de/ documents/work-papers/lambsdorff_eresearch.html

Lipschutz, Ronnie D. with Mayer, Judith (1996). *Global Civil Society and Global Environmental Governance: The Politics of Nature from Place to Planet.* New York: SUNY Press.

Lord, D. (ed.) (2000). 'Paying the Price: The Sierra Leone Peace Process'. *Accord*, Special Issue, No. 9. London: Conciliation Resources.

Lovell, David. W. (1999). 'Nationalism, Civil Society, and the Prospects for Freedom in Eastern Europe', *Australian Journal of Politics and History*, 45/1: 65–77.

Lynch, D. (2000). *Russian Peacekeeping Strategies in the CIS*. London: Macmillan.

Marden, Peter. (1997). 'Geographies of Dissent: Globalisation, Identity and the Nation', *Political Geography*, 16/1: 37–64.

Maynard, K.A. (1999). Healing Communities in Conflict: International Assistance in Complex Emergencies. New York: Columbia University Press.

Mercier, Michèle (1995). *Crimes Without Punishment: Humanitarian Action in Former Yugoslavia*. London, East Haven, CT: Pluto Press.

Misztal, Barbara A. (1996). *Trust in Modern Societies*. Cambridge: Polity Press.

Morris, Aldon D. and Mueller, McClurg (eds) (1992). *Frontiers in Social Movement Theory*. New Haven: Yale University Press.

Nelson, Paul J. (1995). *The World Bank and Non-Governmental Organizations: The Limits of Apolitical Development*. New York: St Martin's Press.

Oludipe, O. (ed.) (2000). *Sierra Leone: One Year After Lomé*. One-Day Analytical Conference on the Peace Process, London, 15 September (CDD Strategy Planning Series No. 5). London: CDD.

Overseas Development Administration (1995). *Developing Country NGOs and Donor Organisations*. London: ODA, January.

Parekh, B. (1997). 'Rethinking Humanitarian Intervention'. *International Political Science Review*, 18: 49–70.

Peizer, Jonathan (2000), 'Bridging the Digital Divide: First You Need the Bridge', www.mediachannel.org/views/oped/peizer.shtml. 21 June.

Peters, J. D. (1993) 'Distrust of Representation : Habermas on the Public Sphere'. *Media, Culture and Society*, 15: 541–72.

Pinter, Frances (2001). 'The Role of Foundations in the Transition Process in Central and Eastern Europe', in *Foundations in Europe*. Guetersloh: Bertelsmann Foundation.

Pugwash Study Group (2000). *Intervention, Sovereignty and International Security* (Occasional Papers 1). February.

Putnam, Robert D. (1993). *Making Democracy Work*. Princeton, NJ: Princeton University Press.

Putnam, Robert D. (2000*). Bowling Alone : the Collapse and Revival of American Community*. New York: Simon & Schuster.

Quigley, Kevin (1997). *For Democracy's Sake*. Washington, DC: Woodrow Wilson Center Press.

Reed, L. W., and Kaysen, C. (eds) (1993). *Emerging Norms of Justified Intervention*. Cambridge, MA: Committee on International Security Studies, American Academy of Arts and Sciences..

Renz, Lorenz (1997). *International Grantmaking: A Report on US Foundation Trends*. New York: The Foundation Center.

Salamon, Lester M. and Anheier, Helmut K. (1997). *Defining the Nonprofit Sector: A Cross-National Analysis*. Manchester: Manchester University Press.

Salamon, Lester M., Anheier, Helmut K., List, Regina, Toepler, Stefan, Sokolowski, S. Wojciech and Associates (1999). *Global Civil Society: Dimensions of the Nonprofit Sector*. Baltimore, MD: The Johns Hopkins Center for Civil Society Studies.

Saunders, Frances Stonor (1999). *Who Paid the Piper? The CIA and the Cultural Cold War*. London: Granta Books.

Shaw, Martin (1996). *Civil Society and Media in Global Crises: Representing Distant Violence*. London: Pinter.

Shawcross, W. (2000). *Deliver Us from Evil: Peacekeepers, Warlords and a World of Endless Conflict*. New York: Simon and Schuster.

SIPRI (Stockholm International Peace Research Institute) (2000*). SIPRI Yearbook 2000*: Armaments, Disarmament and *International Security*. Oxford: Oxford University Press.

Sklair, Leslie. (1995).*Sociology of the Global System*. Baltimore: Johns Hopkins University Press.

Smith, Jackie, Chatfield, Charles, and Pagnucco. Ron (ed.) (1997). *Transnational Social Movements and World Politics: Solidarity Beyond the State*. Syracuse, NY: Syracuse University Press.

Snow, David (1986). 'Frame Alignment Processes, Micromobilization and Movement Participation'. *American Sociological Review*, 51: 464–81.

Soros, George (2000). *Open Society: Reforming Global Capitalism*. London and New York: Little, Brown.

Stanley Foundation (2000). *Problems and Prospects for Humanitarian Intervention*. Muscatine, Iowa: Stanley Foundation.

Stapenhurst, Frederick (1992). *Political Risk Analysis around the North Atlantic*. New York: St Martin's Press.

Stiles, Kendall (ed.) (2000). *Global Institutions and Local Empowerment: Competing Theoretical Perspectives*. Houndsmills: Macmillan.

Strange, Susan (1998). *Retreat of the State*. Cambridge: Cambridge University Press.

Tariq, A. (ed.) (2000). *Masters of the Universe? NATO's Balkan Crusade*. London: Verso.

Tarrow, Sidney (1994). *Power in Movement: Social Movements, Collective Action and Politics*. Cambridge: Cambridge University Press.

Touraine, Alaine (2000). *Can We Live Together? Equality and Difference*. Cambridge: Polity Press.

Transparency International (TI) (1999–2000). The 2000 Corruption Perceptions Index (CPI). http://www.transparency.de/documents/cpi/2000/cpi2000.html#cpi

UNCTAD (2000). *World Investment Report, 2000: Cross-border Mergers and* Acquisitions and Development. Geneva: UNCTAD.

UNDP (2000). *Human Development Report 2000: Human Rights and Human Development*. New York: United Nations. http://www.undp.org/hdr2000/english/book/back1.pdf

UNDP, United Nations, Environment Programme, World Bank, World Resources Institute (2000). *World Resources 2000–2001; People and Ecosystems, The Fraying Web of Life*. Oxford: Elsevier Science.

UNESCO (2000). *World Culture Report: Culture, Diversity and Conflict*. Paris: UNESCO Publishing.

United Nations (1999). *Report on the Fall of Srebrenica* (UN Doc. A54/549). New York: United Nations (15 November).

United Nations (1999). *Report of the Independent Inquiry into Actions of the United Nations During the 1994 Genocide in Rwanda* (UN Doc. S/1999/1257). New York: United Nations,15 December.

United Nations (2000). *Report of the Panel on United Nations Peace Operations* (UN Doc. A/55/305-S/2000/809). New York: United Nations, 21 August.

United Nations High Commissioner for Refugees (UNHCR) (1999). *Statistical Overview 1999*. Available online at http://www.unhcr.ch/statist/99oview/toc.htm

United Nations Population Fund (UNFPA). Available online at: http://www.unfpa.org/swp/2000/english/indicators/indicators 2.html

United States State Department (2000). *Country Reports on Human Rights Practices for 1999*. February. Available online at: http://www.state.gov/g/drl/rls/hrrpt/2000

Van Tulder, R., van den Berghe, D., and Muller, A. (2001). *Erasmus (s)coreboard of Core Companies: The World's Largest Firms and Internationalization*. Rotterdam: Rotterdam School of Management.

Wapner, Paul (1996). *Environmental Activism and World Civic Politics*. New York: SUNY Press.

Waterman, Peter (1999). 'Activists Beyond Borders—and Theorists Within Them'. *Transnational Associations*, 51/1: 39–40.

Waters, Malcolm (1995). *Globalisation*. London and New York: Routledge.

Weisbrod, Burton A. (ed.) (1998). *To Profit or Not to Profit: The Commercial Transformation of the Nonprofit Sector*. Cambridge: Cambridge University Press.

Weiss, T. G. (2000). *Instrumental Humanitarianism and the Kosovo Report*. Human Rights Review (draft). 20 December.

Weiss, Thomas, Gordenker, Leon, and Watson, Thomas J. (eds). (1996). *NGOs, the UN, and Global Governance*. Boulder, CO and London: Lynne Rienner Publishers.

Wendt, A. (1999). *Social Theory of International Politics*. Cambridge: Cambridge University Press.

World Bank (2000) *Entering the 21st Century: World Development Report 1999/2000*. Oxford: Oxford University Press.